COLLECTOR'S GUIDE TO

SOUVENIR CHINA

KEEPSAKES OF A GOLDEN ERA
IDENTIFICATION AND VALUES

Laurence W. Williams

COLLECTOR BOOKS

A Division of Schroeder Publishing Co., Inc.

The current values in this book should be used only as a guide. They are not intended to set prices, which vary from one section of the country to another. Auction prices as well as dealer prices vary greatly and are affected by condition as well as demand. Neither the Author nor the Publisher assumes responsibility for any losses that might be incurred as a result of consulting this guide.

Searching for a Publisher?

We are always looking for knowledgeable people considered to be experts within their fields. If you feel that there is a real need for a book on your collectible subject and have a large comprehensive collection, contact Collector Books.

On the front cover:
Top left: Cobalt blue pin dish, depicting "Arrival of Steamer, Cottage City," *See page 120.*
Top center: Celery dish with novelty advertising of clam bake in Port Townsend, Wash. *See page 198.*
Center left: Folded corner dish with scene of "Gloucester Shore Fisherman." *See page 141.*
Bottom left: Cobalt blue dove figural dish with scene of "M.E. Church, Colebrook, N.H." *See page 132.*
Bottom right: Large chocolate pot with two scenes from Portland, Maine. *See page 97.*

On the back cover:
Center left: Fancy dish with scene from Tulsa, Indian Territories. *See page 69.*
Top left: Creamer with engraving of high school in No. Yakima, Wash. *See page 62.*
Bottom left: Colorful dish showing the center of Greenville, Ohio. *See page 172.*
Bottom right: Match box showing church and parsonage in Mankato, Kansas. *See page 156.*

Cover design: Beth Summers
Book design: Sherry Kraus

Additional copies of this book may be ordered from:

COLLECTOR BOOKS
P.O. Box 3009
Paducah, Kentucky 42002–3009

@ $19.95. Add $2.00 for postage and handling.

CONTENTS

Dedication/About the Author 4

Acknowledgments 4

Introduction 6

Chapter One – The Story of German Souvenir China 8

   Collecting Souvenir China in the U. S. 8

   The Source and Production of Souvenir China 11

   The Golden Era of Souvenir China 13

   The Pioneers – U. S. Importers 14

      Benjamin F. Hunt & Sons 14

      Wheelock China 18

      John H. Roth & Co. 26

      Other Importers 29

      Importers' Marks 33

   Identifying Souvenir China Producers 38

      Known Producers in Germany 38

      Known Producers in Austria 40

      Possible Producers and Unidentified Marks. 41

      Makers' Marks 42

Chapter Two – Souvenir China Items 45

   Shapes, Forms, and Styles 45

      White-based Items 46

      Color-glazed Items 119

Chapter Three – Souvenir China Views 140

Chapter Four – Provenance – Pathways to Our Past 207

Chapter Five – Related Items 214

   Historical Staffordshire 214

   Souvenir Plates .215

   German Made Stoneware 219

   American Ceramic Souvenirs 220

   Custard Glass Souvenirs 221

Appendix 222

Selected Bibliography 229

Index 230

DEDICATION

To Marie, my wife of 26 years, who has endured my obsession with souvenir china for most of those years, and whose assistance in preparing this book has been invaluable.

ABOUT THE AUTHOR

Laurence W. Williams was born in 1942 and has been an avid collector of souvenir china for more than 15 years. He holds a bachelor's degree in English composition from Syracuse University and a post-graduate degree in hotel administration from Cornell University. His career in the hospitality industry has included restaurant ownership and top management in a hotel company.

Currently, he is a hotel consultant and a part time dealer in antiques. He is married and has two grown children.

In the process of collecting souvenir china, Williams has organized a society of collectors and has written and lectured on the subject. He has recently written articles about souvenir china for *Cape Cod Life* magazine and *Down East* magazine. He lectures for historical societies, Quester groups, and others, and is the organizer of an annual show featuring souvenir china as its central focus.

ACKNOWLEDGMENTS

This book would never have been written without the constant encouragement and assistance of many avid collectors and dealers who specialize in this specific field of collecting. They share with me a passion for the history surrounding those little souvenirs brought home from journeys three and four generations ago, prior to the main thrust of the Industrial Revolution. Their assistance has contributed greatly to my knowledge of the scope of items, and their input has been essential in my presenting a thorough, objective overview of these collectibles.

Grateful acknowledgment is made to Clarence MacBride of Washington, Illinois, for providing inspiration and a wealth of historical information. "Mac," a true pioneer in this field, encouraged me to make this book a reality in order to share the wonders and artistry of German-made souvenir china.

Another personal friend and pioneer who has contributed immeasurably is Gary Leveille, publisher of *The Antique Souvenir Collector*, a journal which has focused on souvenir china continuously since its first issue in 1986. Gary is responsible for locating and presenting information on the subject of souvenir china; both he and his publication have been important resources for this book.

Ron Rainka is an antique collector/dealer, well known and respected among bottle collectors for many years. Over the past decade, he has become just as well recognized for his knowledge and enthusiasm relating to souvenir china. I am grateful to Ron for his friendship and assistance, and for making his collection available to be photographed.

Jan and Dick Vogel of Ocala, Florida, are recent authors of a book on Conta and Boehme (German-made porcelain) who operate frequent mail auctions of souvenir china. Their friendship and assistance have been important in this endeavor.

John H. Roth III is by both birth and occupation the man closest to the history of souvenir china. I am indebted to Jack for sharing his family's history with me, and allowing me to see all of the keepsakes related to John H. Roth & Co.

Frank Stefano, Jr. is a collector and author who wrote the first book ever to deal with this subject, *Pictorial Souvenirs & Commemoratives of North America* (Dutton: N.Y., 1976). I am ever grateful to Frank for allowing my text to ride the wave with him and draw from his knowledge.

Similarly, Arene W. Burgess, author of an early text titled *Souvenir Plates — A Collector's Guide*, has shared her information freely with me, and I am grateful.

I have also received valuable assistance from William Crowl of Parkersburg, West Virginia; David Ringering of Salem, Oregon; Daniel Manasselian of Fresno, California; Douglas Hendriksen of Merritt Island, Florida; Dr. Burton Spiller of Rochester, New York; Bernie and Sue Zwolinski of Greenland, New Hampshire; Ron Capers of Crownsville, Maryland; and, in small but important ways, countless other friends and fellow collectors.

Libraries, historical societies, and local historians have been particularly helpful in my research, especially the following:

New York City Public Library

Boston Public Library

Peoria Public Library (Jean Shrier)

Bradley University Library

Peoria Historical Society

Society for the Preservation of New England Antiquities, Boston, Massachusetts

Dawson Springs Branch Library, Dawson Springs, Kentucky

Colorado Historical Society

Chuck and Hetty Walker, Pembina, North Dakota

Lloyd House, Library of Virginia History and Genealogy, Alexandria, Virginia. (Sandra O'Keefe, Reference Librarian)

Georgetown County Historical Society, Georgetown South Carolina (Patricia D. Doyle, Publications Chairman)

Georgetown County Library, Georgetown South Carolina

Huntsville-Madison County Public Library, Huntsville, Alabama (Annewhite T. Fuller)

Pikes Peak Library District (Debbi Mikash, Photograph Librarian)

Deborah Harrison, Manitou Springs, Colorado.

INTRODUCTION

Within the scope of all antique pictorial souvenir china, three collectible genres have now clearly defined themselves. Historical Staffordshire dinnerware produced in the early part of the nineteenth century was well defined and valued as a genre by the time it had reached antique status of 100 years. The initial issue of *The Antique Collector* by Sam Laidacker in February, 1939, focused on those items and provided values. Countless articles and books have thoroughly covered the subject, and the consistently rising values of the items have been updated and published.

A second genre which has been defined is that of "souvenir plates." These are plates made subsequent to the historical wares, not for use in dinner services, but as commemoratives and souvenirs. A few have achieved the status of antique, but most were made during the first half of the twentieth century. Nonetheless, the genre has been established, and at least one comprehensive text focuses on souvenir plates.

This book concerns itself principally with a third genre, souvenir china, which is also occasionally referred to as view china, scenic china, or German view china. It is a collectible genre which is complex, yet clearly established by the growing number of collectors who concentrate on those items. Interest in this specific field of collecting has continued to grow, creating a demand for this text. The purpose of this book is to assist collectors, new or advanced, and to open a treasure trove of historical wonders for those who are interested in America in the pre-dawning and dawning years of the twentieth century.

The subject matter for this book was at the center of the burgeoning souvenir trade in the United States one hundred years before the first word of this text was ever written. Souvenir wares with pictures on them were being produced prolifically in Europe for sale in the United States. The range of items and the number of manufacturers were extensive, and the bulk of the trade involved a great diversity of porcelain items in the style of the so-called "thin china" made in Germany and Austria.

No comprehensive text and value guide has heretofore focused primarily on this subject. Several years ago, a book written by Frank Stefano, Jr. presented information on the subject as part of an overview of all pictorial souvenirs of North America *(Pictorial Souvenirs & Commemoratives of North America,* E. P. Dutton & Co., Inc., New York 1976). His book was an important work in the formulation of the body of knowledge relative to view china souvenirs. Stefano made the following prophetic statement in his book published 20 years ago: "The German wares provide the best source of a still completely overlooked aspect of collecting pictorial souvenirs: the shape and style of the ceramic ware itself. Granted the picture has interest and appeal, the surface on which it is found also reflects the culture and taste of the time." He could not have said it better; his statement from 1976 defines the genre and the reason for this book.

Although this book's main focus does not include Historical Staffordshire or the principal lines of souvenir plates, a chapter is devoted to an overview of those areas, providing selected details and values. References are presented to direct the reader toward additional information on those items.

The values assigned to items pictured in this book are estimates only, based on the experience of the author and the most active specialty dealers covering all parts of the country. Prices realized at recent auctions have also been used. It is a complex and non-scientific process of imparting estimates of values as a guide only, and should not be relied upon as the main criteria in purchasing and selling the items.

Each valuation assumes near mint condition, with no chips, cracks, or other damage unless specifically stated. Defects inflicted subsequent to manufacturing tend to diminish the value of an item significantly. It is important to note that defects which occurred "in the making" and "beauty marks" made on items in coal-fired kilns do not adversely effect their value. Price ranges are guidelines only and should not be relied upon for investment purposes. They are established on the date of publication and are subject to change with time and conditions of the market.

Although an effort has been made to cover the national scope of this subject, there is a built-in bias toward the Northeast. This is a natural result of the fact that the author has lived in and built a collection there. But, perhaps more importantly, it reflects the fact that trade in souvenir china favored that part of the country.

Undoubtedly, knowledge of relative facts will continue to evolve. The author welcomes calls, letters, and e-mail with questions or information: Laurence W. Williams, 741 Main Street, Chatham, MA 02633 1-800-255-7322, e-mail address: antiques@capecod.net

5" x 7" decorated dresser tray showing color scene of "Picking Cotton, Near Huntsville, Ala." $150.00+. (Courtesy Dr. Burton Spiller)

Backstamp shows that the item was made in or near Vienna, Austria, and imported by Wheelock for J.D. Humphrey & Son. The photo used for this scene has been attributed to Ira Collins, an early photographer in Huntsville. J.D. Humphrey was the owner of a drug store opened in 1888, which operated under that name until it merged with Twickenham Pharmacy in 1955. The item was likely sold in the late 1890s.

Close-up of scene on dresser tray.

CHAPTER ONE
THE STORY OF GERMAN SOUVENIR CHINA
COLLECTING SOUVENIR CHINA IN THE U.S.

The word "souvenir" literally means "to come to mind." It refers to any keepsake which serves as a reminder of a place, person or occasion. German-made scenic china is a very special form of souvenir which captivated a generation of Americans between 1890 and the mid 1930s. For simplicity, and because the political and geographic structures have changed significantly during the past 100 years, the "Germany" which was the source of German souvenir china is loosely defined as a region which included parts of Austria, Bohemia (now the Czech Republic and Slovakia), and Poland.

Early souvenir china produced after 1891 also enjoys an unusual and important provenance. The McKinley Tariff Act of that year required that the country of origin be shown on all imported items. Importers immediately turned that requirement into an attractive marketing feature by offering, free of charge, the opportunity for the merchants to have their names and towns incorporated into a backstamp on the items. Most items bore a phrase such as "Made in Germany for O. Snow & Son, Provincetown, Mass," often along with the importer's mark and occasionally the mark of the manufacturer as well. Although there are seldom any remaining vestiges of the merchants mentioned, their histories sometimes help to date an item.

Souvenir china with U.S scenes of a hundred years ago provides wonderful pathways to our past while it tells a story of a time when values in our society were quite different (see plate on page 7). It is not surprising that its devotees are history buffs, sentimentalists, and those who have an appreciation for art forms lost in the wake of progress.

A sense of the past, "that was the way it was," has been captured forever on each item. As these enduring souvenirs are understood and appreciated, they are being sought on an ever-increasing

A sense of the past has been captured on each item. This hand-painted 7" coupe plate or plaque shows the Birmingham, Alabama, terminal station and subway as it appeared in the early part of the century. $50.00 – 75.00.

The three marks on the bottom of the plate show that the plate was made in Bavaria, Germany, by the Tirschenreuth Porcelain Factory, and imported by Jonroth for Faulkner Novelty Shop.

The comparison between this personalized occupational shaving mug valued at $500 to $600 and a Wheelock "spade" creamer provides insight as to why collectors of view china souvenirs often come from other fields of collecting. Both items are made of excellent hard paste porcelain and have been decorated in the same manner. The porcelain mug was made in Limoges, France, and decorated in the U.S., while the creamer was made and decorated in Germany and imported by Wheelock. Note that both are frontal views with similar color tones. They are from the same era, and many of the same artists who decorated the shaving mugs in this country came from Germany, where they had gained their experience on items such as the creamer. $100.00 – 150.00.

scale by historical societies and collectors of Americana.

Most collectors of souvenir china arrive via other fields of collecting. Antique bottles and flasks, stoneware, postcards, old photographs, and occupational shaving mugs represent some of the items which are frequently collected in concert with souvenir china. In many cases the attractive factors of historical interest, nostalgia, and artistic representation are similar.

Most collectors are interested in a particular city, town or group of towns. Home town pride is undoubtedly the most common motivation but other interests motivate collectors to seek a wide variety of topics depicted on souvenir china. A seemingly endless list of topics attracts "crossover" collectors from other fields. Occupations of all kinds, early communications, mills, fire-related, sports-related, libraries, courthouses, railroad, and western topics are just some of those topics which are commonly being sought.

Still other collectors search for souvenir china in various shapes or forms, and there is an incredible variety of items available. Toothpick holders, match holders, creamers, jugs, bone dishes, pin trays, pen trays, shaving mugs, covered boxes, cups and saucers, salts and peppers, dishes and

Another common crossover topic involves railroad scenes. This 7¼" plate shows the M.K. & T. Station, Parsons, Kansas, in an unusual combination of lime tinting and a green engraving. The fineness of the engraving and the detail on the fancy cartouche framing the scene show the artistry of an era which distinguished these view china items. $50.00 – 75.00.

Figural animals, fish, and birds are highly prized by collectors. This cobalt blue dove is extremely rare and unusual. Appropriately, this symbol of peace and love depicts the M.E. Church, Colebrook, N.H. $150.00+.

Two cobalt blue touring cars represent a form which has become desirable and scarce; these cars are even rarer in other colors. Both of these have common scenes.
(L) Souvenir of Albany, N.Y. (State House) $75.00 – 125.00.
(R) Souvenir of Boston (Frog Pond). $75.00 – 125.00.

plates of all kinds, and countless other items can be found with scenes on them. A collector might concentrate on a certain type of "shell and bow" dish or toothpick holders or demitasse cups and saucers.

One of the hottest areas of collecting involves figural items, which are most commonly found in a rich cobalt blue. These include such items as wheelbarrows, cars, canoes, boats, fans, dice, watering cans, buckets, hats, submarines, and even tambourines! Highly prized among the figurals are forms of animals, fish, and birds, all of which are rare.

This Wheelock-Dresden mark is one which has become attractive to some niche collectors who like that particular pedigree.

There are advanced collectors who concentrate their efforts on finding coupe plates which feature large and exquisitely hand-painted scenes. (See example on page 8.) Those beautiful plates are the little understood and truly scarce ancestors of the limited edition collector plates which are turned out by the hundreds of thousands today.

There seems no end to niches available to collectors of souvenir china. Some even insist on finding certain marks on the items which go into their collections (i.e., Wheelock, Wheelock-Dresden, or Jonroth). No matter what their particular preference, virtually all serious collectors reach a fine appreciation for items which exemplify rare and unusual graphics, scenes with clarity and fine detail, complete and free of wear, which depict something especially interesting and unusual. Ultimately, the picture takes center stage.

This creamer represents an excellent example of rare and unusual graphics on souvenir china with a color scene, a Gold Dredger in Operation, La Grange, Cal. Note also the wonderful flowers which flank the scene. $150.00+. (Courtesy Daniel Manasselian; photo by John Walker)

Valuation is difficult in a field of collecting which is evolving as quickly as this. Since beauty is in the eye of the beholder and there is a finite supply of prime items available, it is necessary to use instinct along with trial and error to really learn the market. Collectors may often need to let passion rule while building good collections, and a few mistakes are inevitable along the way.

German souvenir china is becoming more appreciated as it becomes better understood. This book tells the story of European porcelain in a form highly reflective of the Victorian era. It shows how scenes of that important period in American history have been artistically captured to provide pleasure and reflection for future generations. Truly, we can thank our ancestors who lived in that time for these wonderful keepsakes of a golden era.

THE SOURCE AND PRODUCTION OF SOUVENIR CHINA

The genre of souvenir china includes primarily hard paste, white-based porcelain items produced in Germany or Austria (Bavaria and Bohemia being parts of each, respectively) upon which engraved scenes were depicted and which were most commonly sold as souvenirs. In addition to the availability of excellent kaolin, feldspar, and silica in that specific geographical region of the world, the genre involved a commonality of technical methods and artistic traditions. Political and economic conditions in Germany, Austria, and Bohemia were ripe to turn on the engines of production in this industry when American tastes and ability to pay came knocking on their door in the latter part of the nineteenth century.

Two folded edge dishes (approximately 5" square) attest to the fact that souvenir china made in Germany was sold in other parts of the world; this style of dish was popular in the late part of the nineteenth century.
(L) Industrial Exposition in Bergen 1898. $20.00 – 40.00.
(R) Exposition of Lyon 1894 (Germany is given as the source on the bottom). $20.00 – 40.00.

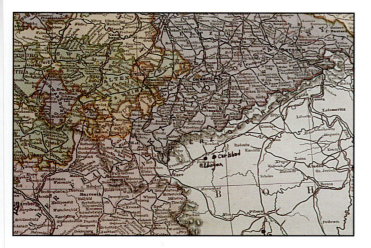

Map section showing the area of Germany and Austria where most souvenir china was produced.

The geographic area which produced virtually all German souvenir china has also produced the majority of all European porcelain. It consists of approximately 30,000 square miles extending from Bavaria in the west across Bohemia and Saxony into Silesia to the east. Nature endowed this land with rich deposits of kaolin, the excellent white clay required for the making of fine porcelain. The people of that region had a well-endowed work ethic to make the most of this resource. It is notable that Meissen, Dresden, Beyreuth, and Carlsbad, all well-known in connection with fine porcelain, are located in the center

of this area which spawned over 1,000 notable porcelain factories since European porcelain was invented there in 1708. KPM factories in and around Meissen were involved in the production of porcelain for royalty, elevating the art form to an incredible level for more than a century before a seemingly insatiable American appetite for fine porcelain in many forms, including souvenir china, began in earnest in the 1880s.

One significant difference between most of the porcelain produced in that part of the world and most other porcelain or ceramic products was the fact that it was true hard paste porcelain. This is one of the reasons many collectors have isolated this china from all the souvenir china that was produced, expressing a preference for its appearance, feel, and durability.

Certainly there were many beautiful and historically important souvenir items made in earthenware and ceramic compositions other than hard paste, many of which have been produced in England. However, souvenir china is distinguished by its hard paste structure which generally stands the test of time better than its many cousins. U.S. manufacturers (mostly based in Ohio) in the early part of the twentieth century worked principally with semi-porcelain, producing calendar plates and souvenirs which tended to craze, chip, and discolor easily in comparison to true hard paste porcelain. Virtually all of the hard paste souvenir china of the era was produced overseas, although a few excellent hard paste shops, such as Union Porcelain Works of Greensport, Long Island, had been established in the U.S.

A quick lesson on porcelain production helps to differentiate among ceramic wares. Fine white-based porcelain requires very pure, white kaolin from original deposits. Colored clays which are not so pure are used for porous fine ceramics such as pottery, terra cotta, majolica, and earthenware items. But, non-porous fine ceramics including stoneware, vitreous china, soft paste porcelain, and hard paste porcelain require varying degrees of higher purity in the clay. Both soft and hard paste porcelain use fine white kaolin. Most European porcelains from Limoges, France and those from Germany, Austria, and Bohemia are made of hard paste porcelain.

Although there is a difference in the composition of hard and soft paste porcelain, their principal difference results from the much higher temperature used for the second firing of hard paste porcelain. The hard paste formula is richer in kaolin and uses less feldspar and quartz than the soft paste formula. The bisque of each form is air dried and fired similarly at temperatures typically between 1500 and 1700 degrees Fahrenheit in the initial firing. After any desired heat resistant underglaze decoration has been applied, the glaze is applied. Soft paste is then fired at temperatures below 2500 degrees Fahrenheit, while hard paste is fired at higher temperatures. As temperature increases, kaolin changes to mullit and more of the quartz melts and fuses with that mullit and with molten feldspar. The resultant porcelain is white and very highly vitrified when it cools down.

As the adjective indicates, hard paste porcelain is much harder than soft paste china; in fact it is harder (though more brittle) than steel. It is far more resistant than soft paste to changing temperatures and impact with other objects. That is the reason discoloring and crazing are frequently seen on china from many sources, but are virtually non-

existent on German souvenir china. Only true porcelain is translucent, and both soft and hard paste porcelains have varying degrees of translucence. The harder and less porous the porcelain, the more resonant the tone will be when it is "rung." A highly resonant tone is generally a good indication of high quality porcelain.

The scenes or decorations on German souvenir china were usually transferred and/or painted on the porcelain after the second firing, and were affixed by a third, relatively low-temperature firing. This final firing endowed the decorations with an ability to stand the test of time well if the pieces did not receive unusually heavy use or abrasion.

An excellent example of the engraver's art is this school house scene, which was engraved on a steel or copper surface used for printing it onto transfer paper; check out the detail! The sharpness, fineness, and clarity of the scene are appropriately reflected in the value. The scene is featured on a small plate. $40.00 – 65.00.

The engravers' art flourished in nineteenth century Germany, and there were many accomplished engravers available to produce at extremely low cost the copper and steel engravings used to print the transfer decals for souvenir china. Engravers usually worked in natural light to produce very fine, detailed representations of the pictures submitted with orders. Sheets containing many different scenes were printed, cut, and sorted into groups of like images. The decals were then "rubbed" or burnished onto the selected pieces of undecorated porcelain. Approximately half of all souvenirs were decorated with the engraving alone, in one color, which was usually black. When color images were depicted, the scenes were sometimes hand-painted before being transferred onto items; sometimes they were hand-painted directly on the porcelain after the engravings had been transferred. All decorating was done, of course, prior to the final firing.

THE GOLDEN ERA OF SOUVENIR CHINA

As the country approached its twentieth century, many factors merged in the United States to create the great demand for souvenir china. Innovations in transportation, communication, and photography were rapidly opening new horizons. Americans had more leisure time and more wealth, and were able to travel and spend that time and money in new and grand hotels in countless vacation paradises throughout the country. They were creating special moments and sought tangible reminders of those times and places.

Also, there was a great deal of pride in what was being accomplished in the nation with its resources and resourcefulness. There was pride both in what was being produced and in civic accomplishments. Good citizens sought tangible items to display this pride, showing occupations, churches, and other public buildings.

At the same time, the Victorian era brought an insatiable taste for the finer things in life, many of which were attractive accouterments for the home. Fine china was universally a focus for that taste, and most of that china was being imported from Europe. Quality knick-knacks and novelties from the same sources were being displayed as decorations on plate rails and in china cabinets. Considering the factors, there would be no difficulty understanding the demand for quality souvenir china depicting meaningful scenes.

Photography had evolved to a point where pictures were readily available in convenient printed form to provide the basis for china engravings. Stereoscopic views had become extremely popular, and the evolution of private mailing cards and postcards was under way.

The Columbian Exposition of 1893 in Chicago occurred when all the elements were just right for launching a peak era of souvenir china which lasted for more than two decades. Although some

This color scene comes from a small plate and credits the photographer, H.H. Bennett. Early commercial photographers provided most of the source material for engravers of the scenes on souvenir china. $20.00 – 40.00.

souvenir china had been produced for the Centennial Exposition in 1876 and in the years leading to the Columbian Exposition, that was but a trickle in relation to the torrent that followed.

Only the import trade was able to meet the demand with acceptable price and quality. Germany and Austria had immense productive capacity in their porcelain industries as well as a plethora of engravers and artists. Importers in the U.S. enjoyed well-established relationships with manufacturers there. Thus the supply and demand were quickly and effectively matched by insightful entrepreneurs. Nearly all of the flood of souvenir china sold all over the United States in the 1890s and early part of the twentieth century came from Germany and Austria. For the most part, these were distinctive, high quality items.

As the new century dawned, England began

13

supplying a growing number of items, mostly in a well-established mode of blue and white china made by the Staffordshire potteries. Porcelain items from Germany continued to dominate the market until German blockades curtailed the supply in 1915.

Many wonderful souvenir china items were produced in Germany and Austria for the Louisiana Purchase Exposition of 1904 in St. Louis, Missouri. Undoubtedly, the Fair served to further advance the demand for such items. It is noteworthy that by the time of the 1904 World's Fair, advances in transportation made it possible for commercial travelers to cover the entire country as well as parts of Mexico, Alaska, and the Hawaiian Territory to solicit orders for souvenir china.

America's taste for souvenir china continued to be nearly insatiable up to the start of World War I, when the factors which fueled this marriage of supply and demand changed dramatically. Kodak "Brownie" cameras had entered the scene, and snapshots personally taken were becoming another souvenir option. Mass production techniques were dictating new economics which made low production volumes less feasible and lowered the price and quality of other competing items. Most importantly, the supply of items from Germany and Austria was completely halted for at least four years.

Between the world wars, a diminished supply of goods was reintroduced. Most were full-scene coupe plates and cylinder jug style creamers, sugar

Some people made notes regarding the source(s) of souvenir china items they received as gifts or inherited. Such a note was found in this sugar bowl from Fairfield, Me. This also shows that such German-made items were being sold between the two World Wars. $20.00 – 40.00.

bowls, and pitchers. Jonroth continued to offer these items to its customers well into the 1930s, and a nicely preserved catalogue from the late 1920s is still in the possession of John H. Roth III.

The trend toward cheaper, kitsch items was becoming well established as new sources of souvenirs were opened up in the Far East. Subsequent to World War II, items from sources in East Germany were not well received on the American market, and Bavarian sources in West Germany could not compete with the prices of Occupied Japan and other areas. For this variety of reasons, the era of German souvenir China closed with the onset of World War II.

THE PIONEERS – U.S. IMPORTERS

Although many companies imported German souvenir china, only a few individuals provided the driving force, recognizing the demand and doing what was necessary to satisfy it. Their stories amaze us today, especially when we consider the world in which they lived and worked. This section describes the known importers and provides insights into the individuals who were the leaders.

BENJAMIN F. HUNT & SONS

The firm of Benjamin F. Hunt and Sons was in business from 1893 to 1902, with wholesale and retail outlets in New York and Boston. Under the personal auspices of Hunt, it manufactured fine china in the Carlsbad area of Bohemia, Austria, focusing on its remarkable line of souvenir china which enjoyed sweeping popularity throughout the entire northeastern part of the U.S.

Portrait of a pioneer, Benjamin F. Hunt, Jr., taken from Boston: George W. Engelhardt, 1897. (Courtesy of Society for the Preservation of New England Antiquities)

Showroom of Benjamin F. Hunt & Sons, 95 Pearl Street, Boston, Mass. Note prominent display of souvenir china and sign, taken from Boston: George W. Engelhardt, 1897. (Courtesy of Society for the Preservation of New England Antiquities)

The porcelain souvenirs sold by this firm had a distinctive style and set a standard which was seldom equaled. The diversity of items with Victorian appeal included a fathomless range of shape, with most pieces artistically embossed and gilded, depicting a black engraving on the fine white china. Nearly all bore gold backstamps with superfluous information and promotion of the "BFHS" trademark.

Benjamin Franklin Hunt, Jr. was born in Rodman, New York, on March 15, 1844, the son of a successful retail merchant. In 1861, he moved to Boston and became associated with Horace Partridge, a toy merchant. He married Jenny Lind Partridge in 1868, and worked diligently in the firm of Horace Partridge Company, helping it to become the greatest toy business in the country and one of the first businesses to promote sporting goods ("Everything for Health & Sport"). He is given much of the credit for the successful development of the sporting goods business.

Hunt was treasurer of Horace Partridge Company in 1893 when he began using a part of one of their retail blocks at 53–55 Hanover Street to display and sell china items he was importing from Austria, where he had taken a financial position in a porcelain factory. He operated the new business under the name of Benjamin F. Hunt & Sons.

Hunt's twin sons, Horace P. and Homer F., were 21 in 1893 and Hunt was 49. Hunt was effectively retiring as a millionaire from a successful first career, and embarking on an adventure to establish a business with his sons. He apparently remained in a dual role for at least two years while he phased out of Horace Partridge Company. Even during that time, it appears that Hunt himself, spent much of his time in Haida and Elbogen, Austria, while his sons began to take charge of the new business in the U.S.

By 1897, Hunt had moved his Boston showrooms to 95 Pearl Street (see photo at left), and moved his principal selling offices to 31 Barclay Street in New York City. Curiously, that was the former address for the New York salesroom of the venerable Boston firm of Abram French Company, which had already been marketing souvenir china for several years (an advertisement from *Crockery and Glass Journal* attests to this).

An advertisement printed in an edition of Crockery and Glass Journal *in 1895 shows that Benjamin F. Hunt & Sons was earnestly engaged in the souvenir china business at that time. (New York City Public Library)*

Import lists from the ports of Boston and New York showed a significant volume of china goods being imported by BFHS from Germany throughout 1898. In 1899, the BFHS ads in the *Crockery and Glass Journal* showed two New York addresses (41 Barclay St. and 46 Park Place), as well as a new Chicago address at 320 American Express Building. By 1900, this firm was prosperous and growing, while its ads claimed the "Best of all Carlsbad China" and touted many wonderful items from their own factory in Austria.

An advertisement in Crockery and Glass Journal *at the end of 1902 signaled the end of their business. (New York City Public Library)*

What happened then is a mystery. Perhaps some irreconcilable family/business problem occurred, because an advertisement and press

release in December of 1902 announced that BFHS was going out of business; that Hunt would remain at the factory in Elbogen; that Horace and Homer would retire and pursue other lines. Perhaps another factor in the equation was Benjamin Hunt's relationship with Frank Winfield Woolworth.

Three items show some of the style of BFHS items made by their factory in Austria. Common features included innovative designs, embossing, and gilding on very thin fine porcelain. The great majority of BFHS items showed black engravings on white china. Items are occasionally found with color added to the engraving (center) or in full sepia tone as seen on the creamer at right.

Bottom marks are also pictured to show the differen[t] marks used by the firm.

Hunt was just eight years older than Wool[worth], and they were apparently well acquainted from their early years in upstate Rodman, New York. Undoubtedly, they remained in touch throughout their careers, as each became increas[ingly] successful. In an uncanny, almost planned way, their spheres began to intersect more and more. One strange piece of evidence shows Hun[t] with Woolworth in Germany on Woolworth's firs[t] buying trip to Europe in 1890! Was there a subtle but grand scheme between these two brillian[t] childhood friends? Hunt was a seasoned business man who moved decisively to become a highly traveled and well-connected cog in the important European production and supply of goods for the American market. Woolworth needed such a person, whom he could trust implicitly, to help him supply the goods he needed for his burgeoning chain of stores. Were they working together all this time?

In the early part of the century, the official

Although the great majority of BFHS items represent scenes in the northeastern part of the country, this plate from Seattle proves that the firm covered the country. $20.00 – 40.00.

Bottom marks on the Snoqualmie Falls plate.

connection was made. In 1906, at 62 years of age, Benjamin F. Hunt, Jr. became officially engaged in his third career as head of European buyers for F.W. Woolworth Company. The arrangement was a natural one, and Hunt's connections in Austria and Germany undoubtedly contributed to the incredible success of Woolworth during the following ten years. But, as World War I approached, Hunt remained too long in order to secure the many business interests of Woolworth in Germany, and he became a prisoner at Nuremburg for the duration of the war. After the war, Hunt remained in his position with Woolworth until retiring in January of 1925 at age 80.

Following his retirement, Hunt and his wife were on a Mediterranean trip, carrying a large amount of cash, when he was kidnapped and given up for lost in Rome in March of 1925. Somehow, Hunt survived, and he and his wife continued to travel in Europe until his death, four days before his 87th birthday, in 1931.

It is possible that Hunt's factory, with new owners, may have supplied souvenir china to other wholesalers such as Wheelock China after 1902; backstamps and style of many items originating in Austria were characteristic of those produced by Hunt's operation. Although Hunt had divested himself of ownership in the factory, it is likely that he continued to assist American wholesalers in purchasing souvenir china in Germany and Austria even after taking on his role with Woolworth.

Homer and Horace Hunt were winding down their business as 1903 dawned. Shortly thereafter, they were working as representatives for C.E. Wheelock & Co. from 1905 through 1907. Horace P. Hunt was listed as New York representative, while Homer F. Hunt was listed as Boston representative. By the end of 1907, the *Crockery and Glass Journal* reported that the Hunt twins were "on the road" and apparently disassociated from Wheelock. In 1908, they were associated with a firm called George F. Bassett & Co. Both apparently returned to Boston and to Pearl Street to form H.P. & H.F. Hunt Co. in 1913, where they acted as manufacturers' reps, dealing in giftwares, glass, and china. Their offices were later moved to a suite on Summer Street.

It is not known if their new firm was involved in the sale of souvenir china or if they enjoyed any business relationship with their father in Europe. Both of the men lived well into their eighties, remaining active in the business. Horace's daughter Eleanor and son-in-law, Edward B. Caines, ran the business until 1971, when it was listed for the last time in the Boston directory.

Longevity was a Hunt family asset along with success and wealth. Benjamin F. Hunt Sr. was married for the third time at the age of 87 to a childhood sweetheart who happened to be 90! The junior Hunt almost made it to 87, and the twins both lived into their mid-eighties.

One can make a logical assumption that any souvenir china marked "BFHS" was produced before 1903. The diversity and intricacy of items was amazing, including many items which were never produced by anyone else, such as watch holders, ring holders, and fancy boxes. There was an endless variety of condiment servers, pin and pen trays, fancy toothpick holders, fancy creamers and pitchers, etc. Highly stylized and without peer, the best of those items are considered extremely collectible.

Although geographic distribution under their own name was generally limited to an area which included all of New England and extended westward to Ohio, northward into the eastern Canadian Provinces, and southward into Virginia, BFHS marked items were made for merchants as far away as the west coast and Texas as well. Other items made in their style are commonly found featuring scenes from all parts of the country. Some have a Wheelock mark, some use the term "Carlsbad China," and others merely read "Made in Austria."

WHEELOCK CHINA

W. G. Wheelock & Son (Charles E. Wheelock) Crockery Store in South Bend, Ind., as photographed in 1882, likely showing Wadsworth G. Wheelock in the center with sons George H. on the left and Charles E. on the right. The South Bend operation later became G. H. Wheelock & Co. (Courtesy of Peoria Historical Society Collection, Bradley University Library)

The story of Wheelock China began in Janesville, Wisconsin, in 1855, when Wadsworth Grant Wheelock opened a store at 33 Main Street, selling crockery, china, glassware, and general goods for the home. Wheelock had been born 22 years earlier in Vermont and married a Boston girl, Martha Trott, when he was 18. The couple had moved to Janesville in 1854. The business thrived as the family grew with the gradual addition of four sons, all of whom eventually went into the business. An early printed invoice heading read "wholesale and retail dealer in crockery, china, earthenware, glassware, tea trays, looking glasses, table cutlery, kerosene fluid and oil lamps, lanterns, etc."

The oldest son, Charles E. Wheelock (born in Janesville September 21, 1858), after graduating from Janesville High School, helped his father open a branch store in South Bend, Indiana. Wadsworth purchased a store from James M. Pool in 1877, which had been in operation since 1852 at 113 W. Washington Street. In only a few years the store front was doubled and the interior space was greatly expanded. Charles was placed in charge of this store which carried the name of W. G. Wheelock and Son.

C.E. Wheelock Store (formerly Miller Brothers China Shop), 313 Main Street, Peoria, in the winter of 1890, l-r: John H. Roth, Clara Huverstuhl Todhunter, Fritz Reitz, and an unidentified man. (Courtesy of Peoria Historical Society Collection, Bradley University Library)

Colorful Wheelock trade card from the early years in Peoria. (Courtesy of Dr. Burton Spiller)

The next son, George Henry Wheelock (born in Janesville January 4, 1864) married Belle Ellsworth Cassaday on October 7, 1882, in Janesville, at the age of 18. The couple moved to South Bend immediately where George became a clerk in his older brother's store. Charles ran the store, while George was his apprentice. One year later, George took charge of another china store started by the brothers on South Michigan Street. In 1886, a financial arrangement initiated a transfer of ownership of the South Bend operations to George, and Charles moved on toward a grander scheme in Peoria. In 1888, the South Michigan Street branch was consolidated with the Washing-

ton Street store, when George concluded the purchase of Charles's interest in the business and put his own name on it.

October 17, 1908 photo of Wheelock's traveling men, known as The Bunch. R.W. Wheelock, son of C.E. Wheelock, is at top center. (Courtesy of Peoria Historical Society Collection, Bradley University Library)

Charles purchased the Miller Brothers China Shop on Main Street in Peoria in 1887, establishing a very successful retail business, as well as a wholesale business which already had the combined purchasing power of the three successful Wheelock stores. The business was immediately and vastly successful, and for many years was considered to be the primary Wheelock enterprise and leader in the wholesale trade. The corps of traveling salesmen which had been assembled in South Bend gradually came under the auspices of Charles and his right hand man, John H. Roth, in Peoria.

By 1889, the youngest brother, Arthur Washburn Wheelock, age 23, had been groomed, and was given the necessary support to establish "The City Crockery Store — A Wheelock China Store" in Rockford, Illinois. He went on to open stores in Des Moines, Iowa, and Milwaukee, Wisconsin. All six Wheelock stores were up and running by the turn of the century, and all of them advertised crockery, china, and glassware from around the world — both wholesale and retail. Arthur was also involved in domestic crockery manufacturing.

The youngest son, Frank, stayed with his

father in the original store in Janesville, where he continued to operate the store as its general manager after Wadsworth's death at age 62 in August, 1897. Ownership of the store remained with Wadsworth's widow Martha. Souvenir china items are known to bear the inscription "Wheelock China, Made in Austria for M. A. Wheelock, Janesville, Wisc." It is believed that the store was closed or sold in 1901 or 1902, but the exact date is not known. Martha A. Wheelock died June 22, 1919. Frank was still living in Janesville in 1919, but his occupation after the store closed is unknown. He died in Chicago in 1938.

In 1917, Arthur closed his Rockford store. He had previously closed the Milwaukee store in 1915 and sold the Des Moines store to his manager, Ed Austen, in 1916. These closings were attributed to the impact of factors leading up to World War I. Arthur bought a wholesale grocery business, which he operated for many years. He died in 1947 at the age of 81.

The subject of souvenir china brings the lens in on the C.E. Wheelock operation in Peoria because that is where its driving force was working in the person of John H. Roth.

John Herman Roth was born in St. Joseph's

Engraving of exterior view of C.E. Wheelock Store from Peoria Illustrated 1893, *published by* The Peoria Transcript *in that year.*

View of the building and street.

County, Indiana, on October 18, 1867. He joined C.E. Wheelock Company after completing his studies at Valparaiso College in 1888. In 1889, he was already minding the store while Wheelock was away on buying trips. Apparently, Roth and Charles Wheelock became interested in souvenir china around the time of the Columbian Exposition

Cabinet photo of John H. Roth, taken in Hamburg, Germany, in 1900 while on a buying trip for C.E. Wheelock. Roth was 32 at the time and vice president of the Wheelock firm. (Courtesy of John H. Roth III)

in Chicago (1892 – 93). Their overall business was thriving in Peoria, and, in 1893, C.E. Wheelock built a new six story building at 214–216 South Adams Street. Three more stories were later added making it one of the tallest buildings overlooking the Illinois River, complete with an observation deck on the roof for a view of the river.

Interior view of C.E. Wheelock's retail store at 214 – 216 S. Adams Street; photo taken in 1903. (Courtesy of Peoria Historical Society Collection, Bradley University Library)

C.E. Wheelock wholesale department with staff at work in February, 1903. (Courtesy of Peoria Historical Society Collection, Bradley University Library)

With such a solid base, these bright and like-minded businessmen saw an opportunity in souvenir china and seized it. Undoubtedly, Roth established or enhanced relationships for the production of souvenir china during his first trip to Europe in 1894, because Wheelock entered the market in a big way around that time.

Roth seemed particularly motivated by the marketability of these wares and took charge of developing the sales effort. Five salesmen were assigned to cover central Illinois, eastern Iowa, and eastern Missouri, and five more were soon added to expand the territory to include all of Illinois, Iowa, Missouri, Indiana, and Wisconsin. Within a short time, a well-trained sales force of 31 commercial travelers was covering the entire country, including parts of Mexico and Canada.

The story of Wheelock souvenir china is possibly the story of the earliest truly national sales force. The resourcefulness and drive of Charles Wheelock and John Roth built a remarkable distribution system in a century that did not even know the automobile. Wheelock souvenirs found their way to far outposts of the pioneer west. They turned up in Alaska, Hawaii, Mexican border towns, and Puerto Rico. The entire logistical operation was even more amazing considering the fact that those items were produced in Germany.

The synergistic relationship (and importance of German suppliers) was remarkably evident in the correspondence and many buying trips taken to that part of Europe during the era when souvenir china was so much in demand. Some advertisements even mentioned a Leipzig address for Wheelock.

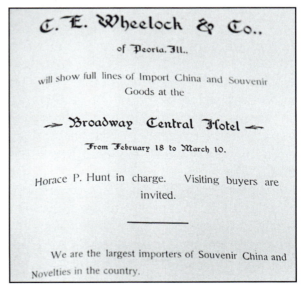

C. E. Wheelock & Co.,

of Peoria, Ill.,

will show full lines of Import China and Souvenir Goods at the

➤ Broadway Central Hotel ◄

From February 18 to March 10.

Horace P. Hunt in charge. Visiting buyers are invited.

We are the largest importers of Souvenir China and Novelties in the country.

Ad from 1907 Crockery and Glass Journal *implying a break between the operation of C.E. Wheelock and G.W. Wheelock and mentioning one of the Hunt twins (who were mentioned in Wheelock ads as early as 1905). (New York City Public Library)*

21

Selected German and Austrian manufacturers were given scenic photographs to be copied and printed on various pieces of china. Contrary to some reports of recent years, the items were not decorated the U.S.

The sales force received its directives from Peoria, and apparently, some form of regionalization was developed as well. At one point, The Fred J. Faulkner Co. of New York City was handling the New England and New York representatives, and, between 1905 and 1907, Horace and Homer Hunt were handling those territories. Salesmen in the northern Pacific Coast area worked through C.S. Walker in Washington State, while those in the southern Pacific area worked through M.F. Wynkoop in California.

John Roth was officially in charge of the overall operation when he became vice president and general manager in 1898. It is clear that period between 1898 and 1909 was marked by incredible growth in demand for souvenir china throughout the country. It is also clear that John H. Roth and his band of salesmen were responsible for fanning that demand into a business which saw Wheelock souvenir china items produced in Germany reach nearly every community in this country. A journal article of January 16, 1902 (*Crockery and Glass Journal*) mentioned that Roth had spent the holidays in Maine, and mentioned that "the souvenir business of his house is assuming large proportions, and dealers are ordering them freely." Another article, on June 30, 1902, said that C.E. Wheelock was in New York, and that "the souvenir business is increasing beyond their utmost expectations, They are placing the goods everywhere." The issue of January 15, 1903 mentions that Roth broke his thigh bone while stepping from a train in Cincinnati, Ohio.

Wheelock's standard of quality was high, and it was reflected in the quality of its souvenir china as well as in its promotion of it. A frequent ad in *Crockery and Glass Journal* offered a booklet entitled "Ask Mr. Dooley" explaining how retailers might promote Wheelock souvenir china. An important line in that ad read "it costs but little more than china decorated with commonplace decorations." It also mentioned "home-town pride" as an important marketing factor. Certainly,

"Ask Mr. Dooley" Wheelock souvenir china advertisement from a 1902 issue of Crockery and Glass Journal. *This ad ran many times from 1902 to 1904, but no copies of the pamphlet could be located currently despite exhaustive efforts by this author. (New York City Public Library)*

the new civic buildings and historical shrines around the country were ripe for depiction on Wheelock's quality porcelain wares.

Roth, who was a founder of the venerable Creve Coeur Club in Peoria, married Josephine Milliken of Saco, Maine, in 1902. He met Miss Milliken on one of his many Atlantic crossings. In 1903, John H. Roth, Jr. was born and a daughter Madeleine followed three years later.

Prior to 1907, the operations of George H. Wheelock in South Bend and Charles E. Wheelock in Peoria had always made a cooperative venture of the wholesale business and shared in its operation and profits. In that year, the Peoria firm took over the wholesale trade, which was heavily involved in the souvenir china business. It may have been the first signs of a falling out between Roth and the Wheelock family, undoubtedly precipitated by the gradually failing health of Charles and likelihood that Roth had ambitions about assuming that business.

In 1909, Charles Wheelock became increasingly ill with Brights disease. His two sons, Ralph W. and George R., were still in school, not ready to take over his business. A suitor was in the wings, however, in the person of John H. Roth, who was already secretary and treasurer of the C.E. Wheelock Corporation, and had managed to amass a sizeable stock holding in that corporation; he was already its de facto head. Wheelock's

Group of six ads run in Crockery and Glass Journal during the first five years of the century for the combined benefit of C.E. Wheelock & Co. of Peoria and G. H. Wheelock & Co. of South Bend while they were jointly operating the wholesale business. (New York City Public Library)

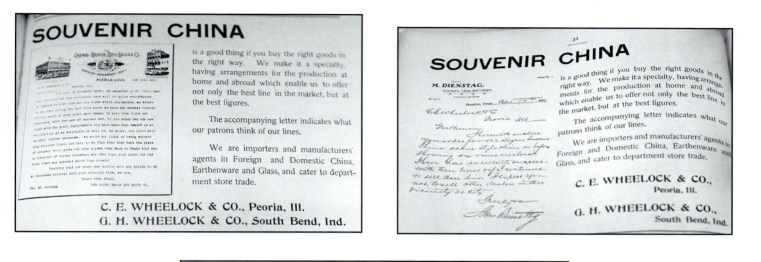

is all the rage. People cannot get enough of it. We make a specialty of this kind of ware and have some exclusive novelties in stock and are prepared to furnish specialties in any quantities. Making this a feature of our business we have unusual facilities for procuring and marketing Souvenirs. Write us for further information.

We are importers and manufacturers' agents in Foreign and Domestic China, Earthenware and Glass and cater to the department store trade.

C. E. WHEELOCK & CO., Peoria, Ill.
G. H. WHEELOCK & CO., South Bend, Ind.

DO YOU CARRY SOUVENIR CHINA?

If not, why not? Be up to date and send to us for information concerning the largest line of Souvenir Goods in America.

We are importers and manufacturers' agents in Foreign and Domestic China, Earthenware and Glass. Our specialties: Popular and moderate priced wares suitable for Department Stores.

Factory shipments and special import orders solicited.

C. E. WHEELOCK & CO., Peoria, Ill.
G. H. WHEELOCK & CO., South Bend, Ind.

HOLIDAY OR ANY DAY.

Souvenir China is always the proper thing. Having made the production of this class of wares a specialty for many years, and having connections abroad and at home which are unsurpassed, we offer to the trade attractive lines from stock or will design new patterns to suit any occasion or locality. Correspondence solicited.

C. E. WHEELOCK & CO.,
Peoria, Ill.

G. H. WHEELOCK & CO.,
South Bend, Ind.

Holiday Souvenirs.

Souvenirs always sell well, and particularly at this season of the year. Having made the production of Souvenirs a specialty, we are prepared to supply the trade with an attractive line at reasonable prices in foreign and domestic makes.

We are importers and manufacturers' agents and cater to the retail and department store trade.

C. E. WHEELOCK & CO.,
Peoria, Ill.

G. H. WHEELOCK & CO.,
South Bend, Ind.

brother George, who was running the successful South Bend store, had a strong interest in maintaining the integrity of the family business during its transition to Charles's sons.

As the sickness engulfed Charles, George realized the only way his two young nephews would ever really be able to gain control of the Peoria operation was to buy out Roth. In addition, it appears there was no love lost between George Wheelock and John Roth. Roth's price was high, but George paid it, making Roth a rich man virtually overnight. Roth left Wheelock China in 1909 with a bundle of cash; he had already laid the groundwork for his own company.

Early C.E. Wheelock & Co. letterhead with listing of officers and mentioning "View and Souvenir China" as a specialty.

George H. Wheelock became vice president of the corporation and one of Charles's sons, George R. was made secretary, while Ralph W. was made clerk. Charles became gravely ill and passed away on May 23, 1910. His obituary in a New York publication called his business "one of the largest concerns in the United States, doing an importing, wholesaling, and retail business of vast proportions." The company immediately reorganized with George H. as President, his nephew George R. as Secretary, and nephew Ralph W. as Treasurer. George H. divided his time between Peoria and South Bend until the end of 1911. In 1912, George H. turned the operation over to Ralph W. as president, and George R. as secretary and treasurer. The family integrity had been maintained.

Another important player at Wheelock was Fred Reitz. Reitz apparently worked with Wheelock and Roth from the early years in key manage-

ment roles. Letterhead from the mid 1890s showed Reitz as vice president and Roth as secretary/treasurer. In 1902, Reitz had apparently been bumped by Roth, who was listed as vice president, while Reitz was listed as treasurer. Reitz was listed as second vice president in 1909 when Roth left the firm.

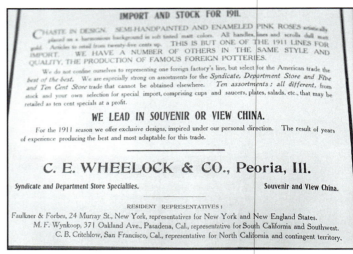

Two ads for C.E. Wheelock's wholesale business in 1909 and 1910 subsequent to the departure of John Roth. Wheelock was claiming the lead in souvenir china, while Roth was actually taking over much of Wheelock's market share. (New York City Public Library)

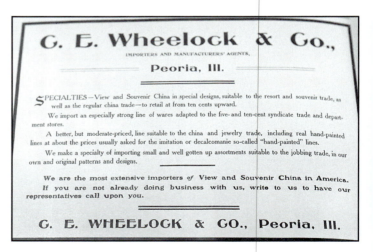

Reitz apparently took over the buying duties previously handled by Roth after his departure. Wheelock continued to pursue its well-established souvenir china business, but its zealot in that area had departed. It appears that the souvenir business continued to do well at Wheelock on its own inertia until around 1915 when supplies from Germany began to dry up. Although Wheelock continued to sell some Staffordshire souvenir items for a few years, it was apparently out of the souvenir business by 1922, according to the firm's last president, Fred Bodtke. Roth, on the other hand, decided to stake his future on a specialization in souvenir china.

George H. Wheelock's store in South Bend continued to be operated by his heirs until 1960. The heirs and successors of Charles Wheelock continued running the Peoria operation until 1975. Its last president was Frederic C. Bodtke. Both were apparently, at least in part, victims of large chain stores and their advantages.

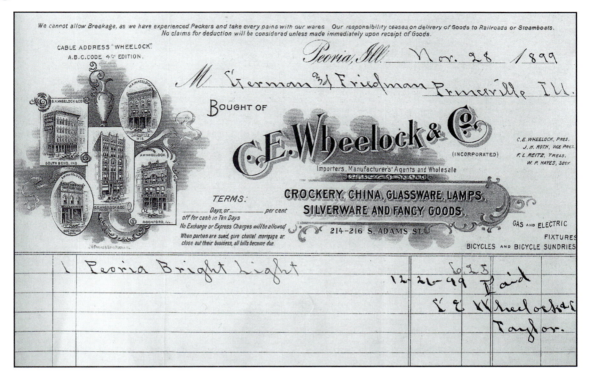

Rare 1899 billhead featuring an engraving of five Wheelock stores, along with a close-up of the engraving. (Collection of Chuck McDaniel)

JOHN H. ROTH & CO.

The illness of C.E. Wheelock precipitated the inevitable split between John Roth and the Wheelock consortium. Control was at stake, and the Wheelock family would not relinquish it to Roth,

One of only six hand-painted coupe plates or plaques made for John H. Roth personally, depicting his children, John H. Roth, Jr. and Madeleine Roth, in 1910 (shortly after the start of his own firm). Notice the fine details and gold border.

Reverse of plate, showing the Jonroth trade mark and describing the subjects.

who had gained one fifth of the C.E. Wheelock Co. stock. Apparently to head off future problems, George Wheelock purchased Roth's stock "at a splendid figure," as reported by the *Peoria Star* on March 3, 1909. The *Peoria Herald Transcript* of the same day reported that Roth had been a buyer for Wheelock for "15 years past" and that he had been bought out "for a small fortune."

After settling with the Wheelocks, John H. Roth had the resources ready to launch his new business in the middle of 1909. He opened the Peoria China Store at 102 South Washington Street, and positioned himself in direct competition with Wheelock. An article in the *Peoria Herald Transcript* on August 10, 1909, reported, "The new house will make a specialty of souvenir and view china — a branch in which Mr. Roth is thoroughly posted, having been largely instrumental in developing it to its present proportions." Roth soon changed the name of his firm to John H. Roth & Co. and moved his business to 228–230 S. Washington Street, where it was to remain for the next 24 years.

A typical ad placed during the first two years of operation (1910, 1911) by John H. Roth & Co. in the Crockery and Glass Journal. *The ads promoted only souvenir china.* (New York City Public Library)

Right from the start, John H. Roth & Co. made its mark in souvenir china in a grand way. Roth put a large band of salesmen under contract and immediately headed for Germany and Austria

This advertisement of 1912 extolled the features of "Placques (sic) in various sizes with large hand-painted views to retail at twenty-five cents each and upward." These items were a wonderful legacy for current and future collectors. (New York City Public Library)

Photo of a 7" coupe plate or plaque similar to the one featured in the ad. $30.00 – 50.00.

to solidify arrangements with suppliers. The Roth family is in possession of correspondence, including a letter of credit, between Roth and the firm of Reinhold Schlegelmilch in Suhl and Tilowitz, indicating that substantial business was done between the two firms. John H Roth & Co. souvenir china ads appeared in the *Crockery and Glass Journal* as early as January, 1910, and claimed a pre-eminent position in the industry.

John H. Roth & Co. corresponded frequently by telegram with its suppliers in Europe. Words on telegrams were costly, so the firm used the signature "Jonroth" as a logical contraction. This contraction soon became the trademark used on their items, while it also served as an a.k.a. trade name for the firm.

Apparently Roth's success was immediate, and he seemed especially interested in marketing a line of fully-painted coupe plates, which were the early ancestors of today's collector plates. The plates were available in several sizes and were often used as decorative wall plaques. Ads posted by Roth in 1910 touted those plates, and Roth had six copies of one such plate made for him in Germany, depicting his children, John Herman Roth Jr., age five and one-half, and Madeleine Roth, age two years (see plate on page 26). It is understandable that those plates are highly prized keepsakes in the family today, and that they are among the most important rare and unusual examples of German souvenir china which exist.

In the western U. S., Roth may have encountered competition in the marketing of his coupe plates, as H.H. Tammen, based in Denver, had established distribution of a similar line under the Lucky Buck trademark. It is believed that Roth made a deal with Tammen in 1909 resulting in the acquisition of Tammen's trademark and souvenir china business. The artist's palette which became an integral part of the J.H.R.& Co. logo for many years afterwards was apparently acquired from H. H. Tammen at that time, although Tammen items dated as late as 1912 continued to bear the palette mark also.

Jonroth competed head to head with Wheelock in the business of imported souvenir china right up to the advent of World War I when supplies of German-made items were cut off. Although Wheelock imported a few English-made plates, the firm soon discontinued its souvenir business. John H. Roth dug in his heels and made a transition toward a specialization in souvenir plates made in Staffordshire, England. Although Jonroth offered German-made items between the two world wars, the emphasis shifted to the Staffordshire plates being produced by William Adams & Co. (Tunstall) in the tradition of historical wares of a century earlier. The firm referred to its souvenir plates as "Old English Historical Ware."

John H. Roth left the day-to-day operation temporarily in the hands of his son, John H. Roth Jr. when he went on a lengthy world-wide journey in 1927, but he did not really relinquish control until 1945, when Roth Jr. took charge of the family business. John H. Roth Sr. died December 26, 1949. During his productive and well-traveled lifetime, he completed 102 crossings of the Atlantic by ship.

John H. Roth Jr. was born in 1903 and graduated from Bowdoin College in 1924. Following graduation, he went to work as a salesman for Northwestern Mutual Life Insurance Company. Although he left the life insurance business between 1927 and 1930 to run the family business while his father traveled, he later returned to it and earned his CLU designation. He continued selling life insurance until the end of World War II, when he went briefly to England to work with suppliers of souvenir china on behalf of John H. Roth & Co. He returned to again take charge of the family firm.

The years following World War II were big years for the firm under the guidance of John Roth Jr. who traveled extensively and was personally involved in generating sales. Only a trickle of Bavarian items (from West Germany) were imported during the cold war years. Most of the porce-lain suppliers had become eclipsed by the Iron Curtain. Americans would not buy items made in Russian Occupied Germany (which had to be marked on them). Both price and politics favored English suppliers.

In 1953, Roth made an attempt to revive trade in the German souvenir china lines, and engaged in communication with Rudolf Wachter in Bavaria, Western Zone. Wachter was able to find a file of engravings printed on transfer paper and lists of the U.S. locations for which designs had been formerly produced. The manufacturer who had them was Bauer & Lehmann in Thuringia. These were forwarded to Roth along with some

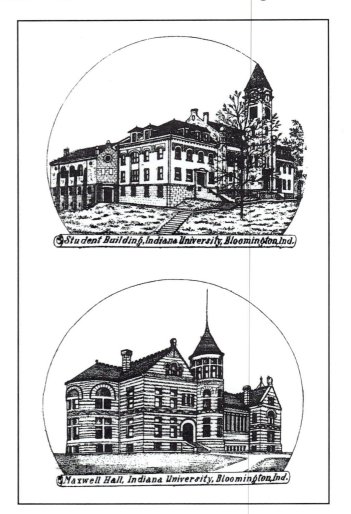

Two old engraved scenes of Indiana University which were depicted on the last two German souvenir china pieces known to have been produced. The items were sample butter chips produced by P. Seiler Porcelain Factory in Kahla in 1965 for John H. Roth & Co. (Courtesy of John H. Roth III)

Copy of one of the hundreds of old numbered engraved scenes printed on transfer paper which were received by the firm of John H. Roth & Co. from a Germany manufacturer in 1953. (Courtesy of John H. Roth III)

price quotes. Prices for various items purchased by the dozen ranged from 19 to 94 cents per item. Four dozen cups and saucers were quoted at $21.60 delivered. In another correspondence, samples were apparently sent utilizing a Eureka Springs, Arkansas, design from 1928. There was no evidence that any orders were ever placed.

The business concentrated on its niche of souvenir plates made in Staffordshire, England, working with various suppliers. In 1965, Roth received the last pieces of German souvenir china which utilized old engravings. The samples which came from P. Seiler at the Porcelain Factory in Kahla, depicted two scenes of Indiana University (Maxwell Hall and Student Building) on "9 cm Butter Chips." Roth's son was attending that university in Bloomington, Indiana, and the samples ended up in the possession of that school, where they are reportedly displayed in the Law School.

John H. Roth Jr. died at the age of 64 on September 14, 1967. His son, John H. Roth III assumed the helm of the business, which has continued the tradition of supplying quality souvenir plates made in Staffordshire. In 1970, he moved the offices from Peoria to Florida, and the business continues in the same manner today.

OTHER IMPORTERS

Plate by Clark, Adams & Clark from their series of White Mountain souvenir china. Since these were produced prior to 1891, the country of origin is not on the item. $40.00 – 65.00. (Collection of Woodrow Thompson)

Close-up of plate.

Clark, Adams & Clark of Boston was perhaps the earliest importer of excellent souvenir china to put its identity on the items it supplied. The only known examples depicted subjects in the White Mountains of New Hampshire apparently done in the 1880s. The mark found on the scene is "CAC Boston." According to early trade cards, this purveyor of china and glass was originally located at No. 1 Music Hall Place (off Winter Street) and moved to 65–67 Franklin Street. No evidence of this company doing business after 1890 could be found.

Abram French of Boston was importing porcelain items from Germany and France through his firm of French, Wells & Co. (#16–18 Federal Street) as early as 1862. By the early 1870s, Abram French and Co. was doing business from 151–153 Milk Street and had opened a store at 101–103 Wabash Avenue in Chicago.

During the 1880s, Abram French was touting the wonderful porcelain items made in Carlsbad, Bohemia. In 1892, it was focusing its advertising

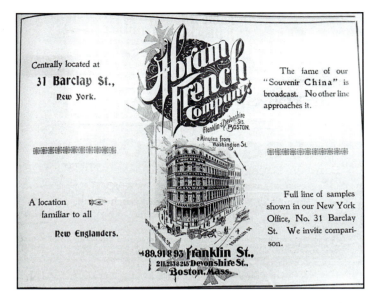

Abram French advertisement run several times in the mid 1890s in Crockery and Glass Journal *touting souvenir china. (New York City Public Library)*

Mark of Abram, French & Co. found in either red or black, primarily on folded edge dishes with White Mountain scenes; no country of origin listed indicates the item was probably produced before 1891.

on Vienna china, royal Vienna wares, and cobalt blue items. All of these items were in the same family as souvenir china. In 1898, the firm had grown tremendously and occupied 89–93 Franklin Street as well as 211–215 Devonshire Street in Boston and 31 Barclay Street in New York (note that was the same address being used by BFHS). Its full page ad in the Boston directory claimed "three generations in business." Most significantly, its advertising elsewhere prominently claimed, "The fame of our Souvenir China is broadcast. No other line approaches it."

It is highly probable that Abram French supplied its customers with souvenir china marked only with the merchant's name and the source. Only a few examples are found with the red or black Abram French mark, and those primarily constitute a series of folded edge dishes with White Mountain views done in full color.

Although listings appear for Abram French with a Summer Street address in 1901 and 1902, the firm appears to have been absorbed by

Portrait of Harry H. Tammen of Denver, Colo., souvenir wholesaler and retailer, newspaper publisher, and philanthropist. (Courtesy of Colorado Historical Society)

Mitchell Woodbury Co. during 1901. It was during that same period that Benjamin F. Hunt & Sons ceased doing business. Much of the wholesale distribution of view china souvenirs was left in the hands of the survivors, Wheelock and Mitchell Woodbury.

H.H. Tammen was a firm named after its founder Harry Heye Tammen, who was a pioneer in the truest sense of the word. Born in Baltimore in 1856, Tammen was the son of German attache of the Netherland's Consulate in Baltimore. When his father died at a relatively early age, Tammen left school to earn a living, and moved west, arriving in Denver in 1880. He established the H.H. Tammen Curio Company which was largely con-

Interior view of H.H. Tammen's Curio Shop in Denver.
(Courtesy of Colorado Historical Society)

cerned with mineral products. The brilliant and energetic Tammen became involved in the wholesale and retail souvenir business and at the same time established a journalistic venture, publishing *The Great Divide*, a monthly magazine featuring stories of the West with special emphasis on mining development.

Tammen's Curio Shop sold a broad array of Western items and souvenirs. Although many of the items were produced by native Americans, he also imported items such as souvenir china and postcards from Germany, which he apparently offered to the trade as well as to customers in his own shop. A line of full image souvenir china coupe plates was produced under the trade mark of "HHT Lucky Buck," printed on an artist's palette. Harry Tammen had already left his indelible mark on early souvenir china by the time his trade mark was obtained by John H. Roth & Co. at about the same time Roth commenced business in 1909.

Tammen teamed with noted photographer W.H. Jackson to produce a souvenir album depicting Western life for the Columbian Exposition in Chicago (1893). In 1895, he formed a partnership with Frederick G. Bonfils and became co-owner and co-editor of *The Denver Post*. Together they made the paper one of the largest in the entire country. Tammen reportedly showed great respect for his employees and for his fellow man. Over the years, his ventures and industrious habits were well rewarded with an accumulation of significant wealth.

Following the untimely death of his first wife, Elizabeth, in 1890, Tammen married Agnes Reid, and together they became important benefactors and stewards in their community. They were instrumental in funding the construction and maintenance of the Denver Children's Hospital. When he died in 1924, Harry Tammen left several million dollars to carry on his work of benevolence to those who were less fortunate.

Mitchell, Woodbury Co. advertisement prior to consolidation with Abram French Company in 1902.

Mitchell Woodbury Co., also based in Boston, was a significant importer of china. Transfers to the company via the ports of Hamburg and Boston showed enormous growth in the 1890s. In 1894, it had business locations at 56 Pearl Street and 215 Franklin Street. In 1896, it added a location at 25 Hartford Street. Its principals were Jacob Mitchell, C.H. Woodbury, and C.E. Austin.

Among the items it imported from Germany were novelties and high quality porcelain items bearing the MW Co. mark instead of (or along with) a maker's mark, such as Royal Beyreuth or a Schlegelmilch factory. In this regard, it did business much the same way as Wheelock China. Like Wheelock, Mitchell Woodbury was a major supplier of souvenir china. The firm also had offices in New York, Chicago, and San Francisco.

In 1899, Mitchell Woodbury Co. listed addresses as 80–86 Pearl Street (only one block away from Benjamin F. Hunt & Sons) and 25 Hartford Street. By 1902, it had expanded the main location to include 76–92 Pearl Street and changed its name to French, Mitchell Woodbury Co. An article in *Crockery and Glass Journal's* last issue of the year 1902 indicated that the company had a growing office in New York and was reaching the western trade. A manager named Henry Meyer was quoted saying, the "New England trade is immense." The company specialized in "French and fancy German china."

French, Mitchell, Woodbury Co. produced several blue and white souvenir plates made by William Adams and Co. in England. In 1906, the firm was once again doing business as **Mitchell Woodbury Co.** and by the end of 1909, their volume of imports from Germany was huge and

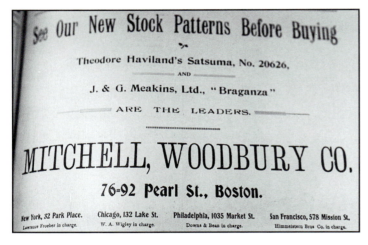

French, Mitchell, Woodbury ad run during the three years the firm was operated under that name (1902 – 1905). (New York City Public Library)

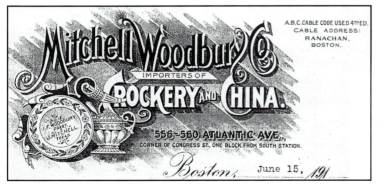

Copy of letterhead used after the firm moved to the largest building devoted exclusively to crockery and glassware in the world on the corner of Atlantic Avenue and Congress Street in Boston.

continuing to grow. The company moved to an enormous new building on Atlantic Avenue. According to *Crockery and Glass Journal,* the seven story building at the corner of Congress Street was "the largest building devoted exclusively to crockery and glassware in the world."

During the period of great growth, Charles H. Woodbury was apparently at the helm of the firm. In March of 1906, he was quoted announcing, "business is 20% in excess of last year." In the March 18, 1909, issue of *Crockery and Glass Journal,* there is a story about Woodbury's "flying visit" to New York for the day. It was apparently a milestone in commuting! He may have met with George H. and A. W. Wheelock who were, by another report, staying at the Belmont Hotel in New York.

For some reason, perhaps a desire to consolidate its operation in its new Boston headquarters, the New York City store operated by Mitchell Woodbury was for sale or lease in January of 1910. The firm continued to do business for several more years from its Boston address. Its demise undoubtedly coincided with the war and discontinuation of supply and demand. It is believed that all souvenir china items bearing the MW Co. mark were produced prior to 1917.

B. B. & F. is a mark commonly found on items sold in Southern states from Virginia to Texas, although some are found in other states. It appears to be the importer's mark on most items, but it is occasionally found in combination with a Wheelock mark. It has been suggested that it might have been a firm which "fronted" for Wheelock in the South, due to the feelings which lingered well after the close of the War between the States. The firm has not yet been identified.

Humes China apparently supplied stores in many Midwest and Western states with souvenir china in the late 1800s. No information on the company has been found, although the mark is relatively common on early items.

Jones, McDuffee & Stratton imported primarily Wedgwood souvenirs, but also imported some souvenir china from Germany. The firm is appropriately discussed in more detail in Chapter 4, Souvenir Plates.

A.C. Bosselman of New York imported primarily English-made items, although it did import some souvenir china items from Germany. Several items were imported by Bosselman for the Jamestown Exposition.

B.D. & C. is found only occasionally on souvenir china and may have been a mark used by the firm of Bawo & Dotter of New York, a major importer of German and Austrian china; which also owned a porcelain factory in Fischern, Austria.

Millar China is unidentified, and is not seen frequently. It is found most often on items from upstate New York and Pennsylvania.

P.C.C. is unidentified and seen infrequently, lettering only.

O.C. Co. probably stands for Oklahoma or Omaha Crockery (or China) Company, as most of the items bearing the mark are found on items representing either Oklahoma or Nebraska; the mark is not common, lettering only.

Burley and Tyrrell Co. of Chicago is seen only rarely as an importer's mark on souvenir china.

L.S. & S. stands for Lewis Straus and Son, New York City, and is relatively uncommon.

Bauscher Bros. of New York was the sales office for the producer of that name in Weiden, Germany, which principally supplied porcelain items to hotels and restaurants.

Knox China is a rare mark, used by an unknown importer in the Midwest; found on items undoubtedly produced by BHFS.

IMPORTERS' MARKS

Wheelock

Wheelock's Crown Mark, common on its Austrian wares.

Wheelock's Wheel and Lock mark #1, common on Austrian wares.

Wheelock's Wheel and Lock mark #2, used infrequently on Austrian wares

Wheelock's Imperial Eagle, used infrequently on Austrian wares.

Wheelock-Dresden mark, used frequently on German wares, usually found on cobalt blue and emerald green items.

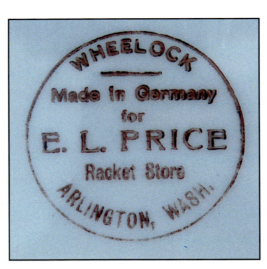

Two examples of Wheelock circle marks most frequently used on the bottom of creamers made in Germany.

Marks on bottom of plate made by Bauer, Rosenthal for C. E. Wheelock's Store in Peoria. This Wheelock mark is quite rare.

Wheelock custom mark incorporating the logo of the company for which the item was made and imported.

Group of marks showing that Wheelock used black, red, and gold lettering, and various presentations of information on the backs and bottoms of their items. The variations appear to be unlimited.

Benjamin F. Hunt & Sons

The marks on the bottom of a delicate souvenir shoe are typical of Benjamin F. Hunt & Sons.

A group of other marks typical of Benjamin F. Hunt & Sons.

H.H. Tammen Co.

H.H. Tammen Co. Lucky Buck palette mark, used up to 1909.

H.H. Tammen Lucky Buck palette mark, with blank center, used up to 1909.

H.H. Tammen mark used in 1903.

H.H. Tammen tepee mark, apparently used after Jonroth took over the palette mark in 1909.

John H. Roth Co.

Comparison of Tammen palette mark with rare John H. Roth & Co. palette mark, which includes the Lucky Buck trade mark and no mention of the Jonroth name per se.

Common Jonroth palette mark used with only minor variation in many colors and on many items from 1909 to 1939.

One example of a Jonroth mark without a definite logo. Like Wheelock, various colors and presentations were occasionally used without a logo; the palette mark is found on the great majority of Jonroth items.

John H. Roth Co. (continued)

One example of a Jonroth custom mark (in red ink and using a logo for the customer).

Jonroth monogram mark, which occasionally shows some minor variations from the one shown here.

B.B.&F.

Occasionally both Wheelock and B.B.& F. marks are seen on the same item such as on this one, although both usually stand alone as separate importers. It is unusual to find a B.B.&F. item outside the Southeast. This one from Pennsylvania is one of the exceptions.

B.B.& F. mark on souvenir china produced by Bauer, Rosenthal for a merchant in Macon, Ga. Note: that the presentation mimics one of the common layouts used by Wheelock.

Other Importers' Marks

Typical mark of Humes China, which did not mention the locality of the person or store as did the marks of other importers.

Typical mark of Millar China.

Typical mark of Mitchell, Woodbury Co. The intermingled M and W followed by Co. were used in many variations and colors.

Other Importers' Marks (continued)

Typical mark of Burley & Tyrrell of Chicago.

Most common of marks used by Lewis Straus & Sons of New York.

Mark on pin tray imported by Lewis Straus and Sons.

Mark of Three Crowns China; importer's mark not yet identified.

Mark used by Jones, McDuffee & Stratton on souvenir china items imported from Germany.

Mark of Jones, McDuffee & Stratton on souvenir china items imported from England.

Mark of unknown Midwestern importer of items apparently made by Benjamin F. Hunt & Sons.

Common Generic Marks

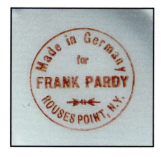

Circular generic mark.

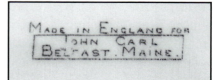

Most generic marks, such as these, involved a circle, millstone or a rectangle in a graphic presentation of where and for whom the item was made.

Six of the most common generic marks which give only the country of origin. Countless variations exist. Generic millstone or circle marks are especially common on color-glazed items.

IDENTIFYING SOUVENIR CHINA PRODUCERS

When a researcher ventures into mostly uncharted waters in an attempt to define the producers of souvenir china made in Germany and Austria, frustration is inevitable. There is no way to trace many of the producers, as the maker's mark was seldom used, firms and their records did not survive the two world wars, and the number of potential firms involved was enormous.

Perhaps the most meaningful statement which can be made is that most porcelain producers engaged in the export business supplied souvenir china to customers in the U.S. at one time or another. Manufacturers ran the gamut from those reputed for very high quality goods, such as the royally designated factory at Tettau, to many producers of utility wares who were ready and able to compete for the business.

It is believed that many of the items were manufactured at a porcelain factory and then decorated elsewhere. Most such decorating shops were located in Dresden, Germany, or Vienna, Austria, a fact which explains those specific designations on much souvenir china despite the knowledge that the manufacturer was located elsewhere. One such example is seen on items produced by Bauer, Rosenthal in Kronach and marked "Dresden." Another example is Merklin-made items which were marked "Vienna."

Firms known to have produced souvenir china are discussed independently of those whose involvement is only speculated. The known producers have been identified through their marks on items or from records made available by John H. Roth III.

KNOWN PRODUCERS IN GERMANY

Adolph Harrass, Grossbreitenbach, Thuringia, 1861 – 1898, and **Adolph Harrass Nachfolger** (successor), 1898 – 1930, produced decorative porcelain, souvenir and gift items, as well as pipe bowls and porcelain decorating. It is believed that this was a major source of souvenir china, for Wheelock and Jonroth. In 1930 the company continued as Grosebreittenbach Porcelain Factory which continued to supply some souvenir items to Jonroth in the 1930s.

Kahla Porcelain Factory (Porcellanfabrik Kahla), Kahla, Thuringia, 1844 – 1945, produced household, hotel, decorative, and technical porcelain. Apparently produced many of the full-scene coupe plates such as those sold by H. H. Tammen and Jonroth. The most common forms of creamer jugs and matching sugar bowls have also been traced to this factory.

C.A. Lehmann & Son, Kahla, Thuringia, 1895 – 1935, produced coffee and tea sets, household and decorative porcelain. Merged with **Franz Bauer Porcelain Manufactory** to form **Bauer & Lehmann**, 1935 – 1965, and joined with the decorating shop of **August Frank Porcelain Manufactory** in 1965 to form **Kahla Porcelain Manufactory**. In 1953, the Roth firm explored the possibility of reviving some of the business from German sources, and received a list of some 1400 engravings in the possession of **Bauer & Lehmann** which had been done for Jonroth between 1909 and 1939. Frank Stefano counted 115 towns and cities beginning with the letter "P" and presented that list in his book. It was an excellent example of the enormous scope of the business handled by just one producer or its predecessors for just one importer!

Julius Lange, Kahla, Thuringia, 1863 – circa 1940, produced decorative porcelain and gift articles. **Paul Seiler** assumed ownership around 1940.

Kahla China Corporation of New York City, was apparently a marketing consortium of producers in Kahla. Its "PK UNITY" mark has been found on a full-scene coupe plate made for Jonroth. The porcelain industry in Kahla was very involved in the production of souvenir china for the American market for a long period extending into the 1930s.

Tirschenreuth Porcelain Factory (Porcellanfabrik Tirschenreuth) was founded in 1838, and has produced a wide array of consumer goods for export. It was a major producer of souvenir china, and its mark is commonly found on full scene coupe plates alone or with the Jonroth palette mark. In 1927, it was acquired by **L. Hutschenreuther Porcelain Factory** (Porcellanfabrik L. Hutschenreuther), Selb, founded by Lorenz Hutschenreuther. The firm operated from 1857 to 1969 and acquired several porcelain factories after becoming a joint stock company in 1902. Made a wide variety of decorated household porcelain items, gift items, coffee/tea sets, and figurines. It

is believed this firm supplied some of the full scene coupe plates purveyed by Jonroth.

Approximately the same time it acquired the Tirschenreuth factory (1927), it also acquired another firm, **Bauscher Bros. Porcelain Factory** in Weiden, which had been founded in 1881 and produced hotel and technical porcelain. It also made a business of selling custom porcelain tip trays to hotels and restaurants, and apparently had a New York office which imported such specialty items.

Bauer, Rosenthal & Co., Kronach, Bavaria, circa 1897 – 1903, manufacturers of household and decorative porcelain, supplied registered patterns in many shapes, distinguished by embossed and painted flowers. Some of the finest souvenir china items bear their initials and crown logo. Although acquired earlier, in 1903 the company officially became part of **Philip Rosenthal & Co.** AG, based in Selb, Bavaria, which dated back to 1879, and which continues in business today as **Rosenthal Glass and Porcelain AG**. Manufacturers of table, household, hotel, and decorative porcelain and earthenware, figurines, gift and collector porcelains, and technical porcelain. It is a large, internationally known company which gradually absorbed many important producers, including the well-known and respected **Thomas Porcelain** operations, whose mark has been found rarely on full scene coupe plates.

Carl Schumann Porcelain Factory (Carl Schumann Porzellanfabrik), Arzberg, Bavaria, founded in 1881 by Heinrich Schumann. Producer of table and decorative porcelain, coffee and tea sets, and gift articles. Very active in the export business; a variety of pierced border "ribbon plates" and other view china items have been attributed to this factory.

Sontag & Son (Sontag & Sohn), Tettau, Bavaria, 1887 – 1902, continued in a tradition established by Schmidt & Greiner in 1794, assumed by Ferdinand Klaus, 1852 – 1866, and Sontag & Birkner, 1866 – 1887. The mark commonly found on souvenir china is the Sontag & Son mark or McCaslin #7 (Royal Bayreuth). The production of view china souvenirs was a natural extension of the business of this "Royal Bayreuth" factory, with its fine hard paste porcelain and staff of expert mold makers, engravers, and artists. It is surprising that so many of the items produced actually bore the maker's mark, as it was not the usual custom to put makers' mark on souvenir china. The firm became known as **Tettau Porcelain Factory** (Porzellanfabrik Tettau) in 1902, and the most recognized Royal Bayreuth blue mark was stamped on items made subsequently. The only known view china souvenirs bearing that mark relate to scenes in New Zealand.

Fasolt & Eichel, Blankenhain, Thuringia, 1856–circa 1918, acquired a factory started in 1790 by Christian Andreas Wilhelm Speck. Produced table porcelain, coffee and tea sets, washstand sets, and decorative porcelain. Established the trademark of a shield with the word "Weimar" slanted across it. It was succeeded in 1918 by **Blankenhain Porcelain Factory C. & E. Carstens**, 1918 – 1945. The most common form of souvenir china produced by these firms represented an early example of a photo transfer process, with the photo decals being printed in a sepia or brown tone and transferred to a variety of decorated porcelain pieces.

Roschutz (Roschützer) Porcelain Factory Unger & Schilde GMBH, Thuringia, 1881 – 1953, produced household, decorative and hotel items as well as figurines. This firm may have been the producer of items bearing the "Altenburg China" crown mark, as it is known to have used a mark with "Altenburg" and a crown on other items.

Schumann & Schreider Porcelain Factory, Schwarzenhammer, Bavaria, operated from 1905 as a producer of household and decorative porcelain, as well as various gift items.

Silesian Porcelain Factory P. Donath (Schlesische Porzellanfabrik P. Donath), Tiefenfurth, Silesia, operated approximately 1890 – 1916 as the successor to Louis Lovinsohn, a firm established in the decorative tradition of Meissen, producing coffee/tea sets and decorative items. Donath expanded production into other items as well, imitating Meissen porcelain.

New York and Rudolstadt Pottery, Rudolstadt, Thuringia, 1882 – 1918, made household, table, and decorative porcelain. The firm was owned by Lewis Straus & Sons of New York City, its sole importer in the U.S.

Lorenz Reichel Porcelain Factory, Schirnding, Bavaria, 1902 – 1909, manufacturer of household porcelain, was succeeded by **Schirnding Porcelain Factory AG**, which continued to produce similar items as well as additional commercial lines.

Rudolph Wachter Porcelain Factory (Rudolph Wachter Porzellanmanufaktur), Kirchenlamitz, Bavaria, was founded in 1893 and was primarily a decorating shop. Jonroth purchased samples from Wachter as late as 1953.

Oscar Schaller & Co., Schwarzenbach-Saale, Bavaria, 1882 – 1918, became **Oscar Schaller & Co**. Nachfolger, Kirchenlamitz, Bavaria, after 1918. Produced household, table, and decorative porcelain, as well as gift items.

Hermann Ohme Porcelain Factory (Porzellanmanufaktur Hermann Ohme), 1882 – circa 1930, made household, table, hotel, and decorative porcelain. Operated a branch factory in Waldenburg. Known for extensive production in "Old Ivory" pattern. Their mark is seen occasionally but is not common on souvenir china.

KNOWN PRODUCERS IN AUSTRIA

Karl Speck, Benj. F. Hunt & Sons, Elbogen, Bohemia, 1896 – 1902. This porcelain factory previously operated by Karl Speck was purchased by Benjamin F. Hunt, Jr. in 1896 and specialized in making souvenir china for the U.S. market during the following six years. In 1902, it was purchased by **Adolph Persch** (Hegewald) and operated as a branch until it was closed in 1937.

Another Bohemian producer of souvenir china

was **Marx & Gutherz** of Altrohlan. The firm operated from 1889, producing household and decorative porcelain. Items are known to have been produced by this firm for the Columbian Exposition (1893).

Bawo & Dotter, Fischern, Bohemia, 1883 – circa 1914, was owned by a firm of the same name with its main offices in New York City. This major importer undoubtedly participated in the generic souvenir china boom, as its facilities were producing decorative porcelain, coffee/tea sets, gift and collectors articles, and were heavily involved in the decorating end of the business.

Zettlitzer Kaolin Works Department Porcelain Factory, Merkelsgrun (Zettlitzer Kaolin-Werke Abteilung Porzellanfabrik Merkelsgrun), Merkelsgrun, Bohemia, produced household porcelain from 1912 – 1926, succeeded Bruder & Schwalb (1882 – 1912) and Becher & Stark (founded circa 1871), a firm known to have produced decorative porcelain. There is evidence that this firm produced some of the souvenir china commonly sold by Wheelock and bearing the "Vienna" designation.

Victoria Porcelain Factory, Schmidt & Co. (Porzellanfabrik "Victoria" Schmidt & Co.), Altrohlau, Bohemia, Austria, produced household, hotel, and decorative porcelain, was known for a distinctive style of black engraved transfers on white china, including multi-scene plates and tumblers. Made souvenir china items prolifically for the 1904 World's Fair in St. Louis.

POSSIBLE PRODUCERS AND UNIDENTIFIED MARKS

Perhaps the largest remaining mystery involves the Altenburg Crown mark. It is not even known whether this common mark is the maker's mark or an importer's mark. It is unrecorded in reference books, and has not been tied to any firm to date. The firm of Unger & Schilde (1881 – 1953) in Roschutz used the name Altenberg (in all capitals) along with a crown; however there are dissimilarities in the marks. Since the firm produced household, hotel, and decorative porcelain, it is possible that the mark was theirs.

Speculation that it may have been a mark used by a Schlegelmilch factory is based on the fact that items bearing the Altenberg mark were often decorated with shadow flowers similar to a Schlegelmilch decoration. Additional circumstantial support comes from the fact that an unresolved mark found on Schlegelmilch items is a crown mark with the words "SAXE ALTENBURG" printed in a similar red overglaze and in the same block caps letter style as the Altenburg China mark frequently found on souvenir china.

Another factor which tends to support a Schlegelmilch connection is a telegraphic correspondence between John H. Roth and the firm of Reinhold Schlegelmilch in September of 1909 (courtesy of John H. Roth III). The translation of the two telegraphs is printed below. The possible conclusion that some or all of the goods were souvenir china must rest on the fact that they were the main focus of Roth's new enterprise.

From:
Reinhold Schlegelmilch
Porcelain Factories
Suhl in Thuringia and Tillowitz in Silesia
Revolving Credit Account at the Reichsbank Suhl
Contract:
The following agreement has been made this day (1 September 1909) between Mr. John H. Roth and the firm of Reinhold Schlegelmilch, Suhl:
Mr. Roth obliges himself to the sum of 100,000 Marks over the next five years;
Mr. Roth agrees to accept porcelain goods from the factory at Suhl each year in the value of 20,000 Marks...this amount should be deposited in a German bank or credited to a transfer (forwarding) agent.
The firm of Reinhold Schlegelmilch accepts the responsibility to deliver the goods to Mr. Roth.
Agreed to and signed, Suhl, 1 September, 1909
(signature of Reinhold Schlegelmilch executed by his son Arnold, acting as general manager of the firm)
Answer:
25 September. 09
To: Reinhold Schlegelmilch, Suhl.
John H. Roth at Peoria has according to agreement deposited 20,000 Marks as the initial payment on the five year obligation as described in the agreement of September 1.
(signature of banker or transfer agent)

Wileman & Co., England. Although most collectible souvenir china was produced in Germany and Austria, it must be noted that the firm founded by Joseph Shelley and James Wileman in 1872 at Stokes-on-Trent also produced tea sets and miscellaneous souvenir china items for trade in the U. S. After 1925 this firm became known as **Shelley Potteries, Ltd.**

MAKERS' MARKS

UNITY was a mark representing a consortium of producers in Kahla. This mark was found on a full scene coupe plate made after 1922.

Mark of Tirschenreuth Porcelain Factory.

Marks of Hutschenreuth Porcelain Factory.

Mark of Roschützer Porcelain Factory.

Mark of Bauer, Rosenthal & Co.

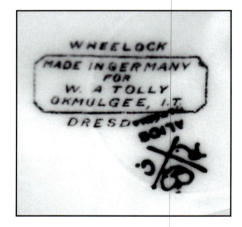

Mark of Philip Rosenthal & Co.

Mark of Carl Schumann Porcelain Factory.

Mark of Sontag & Son.

Mark of Fasolt & Eichel, later of Blankenhain Porcelain Factory C. & E. Carstens.

Mark of Schumann & Schreider Porcelain Factory Schwarzenhammer.

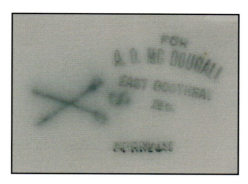

Mark of Silesian Porcelain Factory P. Donath.

Mark of New York and Rudolstadt Pottery.

Mark of Beyer & Bock Porcelain Factory, Rudolstadt Volkstedt.

Mark of Jaeger & Co., Marktredwitz.

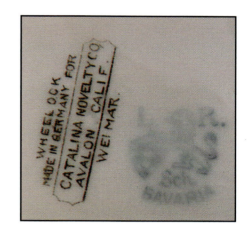

Mark of Lorenz Reichel Porcelain Factory.

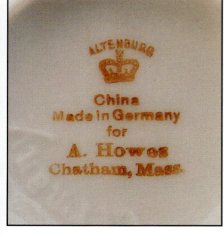

Common mark of Altenburg China. Manufacturer is unknown. Mark is found in several colors.

Mark of Thomas Porcelain

Mark of Rudolph Wachter.

Mark of Bauscher Bros., found in various colors and styles of type.

Mark of Hermann Ohme, also found with Silesia or Germany in place of Prussia.

Mark of Victoria Porcelain Factory found in many colors.

Another mark of Victoria Porcelain Factory also found frequently on souvenir china.

Clover mark of Zettlitzer Kaolin Works Department Porcelain Factory Merkelsgrun.

Elbogen, Austria mark.

Mark of Marx & Gutherz

Most common manufacturer's mark of Benjamin F. Hunt & Sons.

Mark of Foley China/Wileman & Co., Fenton, England.

Three unidentified Austrian marks found on souvenir china items.

CHAPTER TWO
SOUVENIR CHINA ITEMS
SHAPES, FORMS, AND STYLES

One of the most interesting features of souvenir china is the variety of items upon which the scenes are depicted. These include many distinctly different styles of porcelain, from simple utilitarian table ware to very ornate stylized items. Popular items distributed by the major wholesalers are seen repetitively. Interesting and unusual items, which are not seen frequently, such as a watch holder, an interestingly shaped covered box, or a figural animal dish, are now most appealing to collectors.

Since it would be impossible to cover the entire scope of items in existence in this text (or to even know the full extent of the scope), a reasonable representation of shapes, forms, and styles is presented. Perhaps the diversity will be more thoroughly covered in later editions, but for now it is left as an intriguing aspect of the hobby. The sampling presented is intended to provide insight into the scope of items available.

It was common for items made with the same mold to be decorated differently. For instance, one creamer style arbitrarily called Wheelock's "Signature Creamer" was decorated with many different combinations of color tints, gold accents and flowers. Some depicted single color engravings, while most showed color scenes. Various marks were found on the bottoms of different pieces. Page 56 shows some of the variations of the creamers, which were produced in three different sizes.

Underglaze or in-glaze tinting imparted beauty and character to an item. Rose was perhaps the most common tint used on areas of white-base items. Robin's egg blue, brown, canary, green, lime green, maroon, magenta, and even burnt orange were among the colors used. Items in this section have been selected to show many of those colors. There are also some examples of earth-to-sky toning, which was a relatively common technique. Other less common toning variations exist but are not specifically shown.

A distinction is made between white-based items and color-glazed items. Those which are partially tinted are white-based items, while those on which another color covers the key surfaces are color-glazed items. Distinctive lines of souvenir china were created by using color-glazed items. The most common color was cobalt blue, although emerald green, turquoise, brown, maroon, and even tan were also used. A copy of an advertisement (see page 119) from a 1903 publication in Rumford Falls, Maine, referred enthusiastically to the cobalt blue items as a distinct line of souvenir wares.

One distinctive style involving white-based porcelain is the Delft style, which presents the entire decoration in blue, often with artistic interpretation in the scene. On many such items, the back mark was embossed in either blue or green. Examples of common decorative features such as this are shown.

WHITE-BASED ITEMS

Porcelain Plates

Plates used as souvenir china typically cover a size range from 3" butter pats to 10" dinner plates or cake plates. Shown here are two such items featuring the same scene, Peabody Institute, Danvers, Mass.; both also have the same mark on their bases, Made in Germany for F.M. Spafford, Danvers, Mass. $20.00 – 40.00 (butter pat), $30.00 – 50.00 (cake plate).

Butter pats are typically between 3 – 4" in diameter; two of the many forms are shown:
(L) Memorial Hall, Lebanon, N.H.; back: Made in for Germany for N.C. Bridgman & Son, Lebanon, NH. Under $20.00.
(R) Head of New Found Lake; back: Made in Germany for Weymouth, Brown & Co., Bristol, N.H. Under $20.00.

Two typical small plates, approximately 6" diameter:
(L) plain white, rimmed plate with black engraving, Burros Loaded With Wood; back: red lettering Wheelock China, Made in Austria for The Jamieson House Furnishing Co., Trinadad, Colo. $40.00 – 65.00.
(R) rimmed plate with rose and lime green tints, embossing, gold filigree, and color scene, Sugar Factory, Loveland, Colo.; back: Wheelock Vienna, Made in Austria for Noah's Ark, Loveland, Colo. $40.00 – 65.00.

6" diameter rimless plate with blue tinting and black engraving, Standish House, Duxbury, Mass.; back: gold Wheelock Imperial Eagle, Wheelock Vienna, Made in Austria for N.M. Stetson, Druggist, Duxbury, Mass. $40.00 – 65.00.

6" diameter rimless plate with scalloped edge and distinctive embossing showing large color scene Sea Beach Hotel, Santa Cruz, Calif.; back: black letters, Wheelock Weimar, Made in Germany for C.J. Klein, Jeweler, Santa Cruz, Calif. This is one of the important Wheelock forms which is usually characterized by excellent graphics. $40.00 – 65.00.

5⅞" rimmed plate with rose tinting, gold filigree, and color scene, Court House, Canton, Ohio; back: black Wheelock Crown mark, Made in Austria for Wm. R. Zollinger & Co. $20.00 – 40.00.

Souvenir china items were popular Christmas gifts. This 8¼" diameter thin china plate was decorated appropriately for the season with holly boughs and berries. It features a picture of Mason's Building, Market & Fourth Streets, Williamsport, Pa.; bottom: Made in Austria for C.A. Reed, Williamsport, Pa. $30.00 – 50.00.

6" pierced rim plate with purple tinting and colo[r] scene, Washington's Headquarters, Newburgh N.Y.; back: BRC Moliere pattern, Wheelock Dres den, Made in Germany for J.H. Horton. $20.00 – 40.00.

A pair of 6¼" diameter luncheon, tea, or dessert plates are slightly tinted in a rose hue and accented with strong gold highlights around their borders. Both are marked on bottom, Wheelock Weimar, Made in Germany for Newell Bros. Jewelers, Chenoa, Ill.
(L) High School, Chenoa, Ill. $20.00 – 40.00.
(R) Presbyterian Church, Chenoa, Ill. $20.00 – 40.00.

Two small plates from Martha's Vineyard with pierced borders:
(L) 5¾" pierced rim plate with color scene, Gay Head Light and Cliffs, Cottage City, Mass.; back: Made in Germany for F.A. Marshall, Cottage City, Mass. $65.00 – 100.00.
(R) 6" pierced rim plate with color scene, Hotel Harbor View, Edgartown, Mass.; back: Made in Germany for Jurnigan & Huxford, Edgartown, Mass. $65.00 – 100.00.

Two medium-sized plates with different styles of pierced borders:
(L) 8¼" white with gold-accented leaves, decorated pierced rim, and black engraving, Str. Longfellow; back: Made in Germany for O. Snow & Son, Provincetown, Mass. $50.00 – 75.00.
(R) 7" pierced rim plate with color scene, Eldredge Public Library, Chatham, Mass.; back: Wheelock Weimar, Made in Germany for The Boston Store, Chatham, Mass. $40.00 – 65.00.

Small (6") and large (7¾") plates with solid color rims and black engravings, Hotel Mattaquason, Chatham, Mass.; back: Made in Germany for Eldredge Bros., Chatham, Mass. $40.00 – 65.00 each.

Two typical ribbon plates, which are found in many styles and sizes; generally considered one of the least desirable forms (although a desirable scene quickly overcomes any objection to the form!):

(L) 5½" ribbon plate, with gold border and color scene, Emma Willard School, Gift of Mrs. Russell Sage; back: black round mark, Made in Germany. $20.00 – 40.00.

(R) 7" ribbon plate with pierced and pointed edge, purple to green opalescent tinting, and color scene, Haymakers, Chebeague Island, Me.; back: red square mark, Made in Germany for H.G. Bowen, Chebeague Island, Me. $40.00 – 65.00.

Floral Enhancements

Floral enhancements were used in many ways on souvenir china plates and dishes. The examples here represent some of the wonderful floral embellishments which added to their appeal.

9¾" rimmed dinner plate in the rose shadow flower pattern depicts large hand-painted color scene, Fountain and Park, Savin Rock, Conn.; back: red script, Made in Germany. $30.00 – 50.00.

8" rimmed plate with a garland of roses around the rim and a central color scene, Iron Bridge over the North Platte River at Saratoga, Wyoming; back: gold mark of Hermann Ohme. $30.00 – 50.00.

(L) 8½" plate with floral groups on rose-tinted rim and large color scene, Santa Barbara, Calif. Mission; back: Wheelock Weimar, Made in Germany for A.A. Poole, Santa Barbara, Calif. $30.00 – 50.00.

(R) 7½" rimless plate decorated with carnations and large color scene, Silver Star, Bay Shore, L.I.; back: Wheelock Vienna Austria Crown mark, Made in Austria for E.S. Robinson, Bay Shore, L.I., N.Y. $30.00 – 50.00.

Two examples of embossed and painted floral plates produced by Bauer, Rosenthal for Wheelock (several different floral patterns were produced by that firm):

(L) 8⅜" plate with embossed purple flowers and tint on rim and center color scene, of M.E. Church, Fort Covington, N.Y.; back: Bauer, Rosenthal crown mark, Iris (pattern), Wheelock Dresden, Made in Germany for Mrs. G.A. Arquhar Cash Bazaar. $20.00 – 40.00.

(R) 8⅜" plate with pierced border and embossed, rose-colored flowers and color scene, Ogunquit Maine from Israel's Head; back: Wheelock Dresden, Made in Germany for C.S. Littlefield, Ogunquit, Maine. $40.00 – 65.00.

8⅜" rimless plate with green tinted border and decoration of roses with gold connections surrounding an oval color scene, Central School, Bisbee, Ariz.; back: Wheelock Vienna, Made in Austria for The Racket Store, Bisbee, Ariz. $65.00 – 100.00.

8¼" rimmed plate with extensive decoration including a beautifully hand-painted columbine, the State Flower of Colorado, and scene, Summit of Pikes Peak, 14,147 ft., Copyright 1903; back: BRC Fidelio (pattern). $40.00 – 65.00.

8¼" rimless plate in very thin china form and popular decorative style with robin's egg blue tint and pink flowers, with excellent color scene, Goose River Bridge, Rockport, Me.; back: wheel and lock logo #1, Wheelock Vienna Austria, Made in Austria for Spencer & Gould, Rockport, Me. $40.00 – 65.00.

This example of a very ornate and highly embossed 8" diameter plate depicts Coaching Day at Bethlehem, N.H.; back: Made in Germany for C.G. White & Son, Bethlehem, N.H. $40.00 – 65.00.

Decorations were extremely varied, as exemplified by the unusual colors on this 9½" diameter cake plate, and the enamel floral sprays flanking a scene, of The Right Place – H.E. Hitzemann, Palatine, Illinois; back: generic red circle mark, Made in Germany. $40.00 – 65.00.

Note the many subtle features that contribute to the beauty of this 7½" diameter plate featuring Ridgway High School, Ridgway, Pa. Scalloped border, floral sprays, rose-tinted accents and highlights, lime-tinted bowl, and gold filigree around the hand-painted scene. Back: Wheelock Vienna Austria wheel and lock logo #1, B.B. & F., Made in Austria expressly for Smith Bros. Co. Ltd., Ridgway, Pa. $30.00 – 50.00.

Special accents also contribute to the appeal of these two examples:
(L) 7½" diameter plate with rare oval lens styled scene, Pleasant Street, Brunswick, Me. on plate with interesting tinting and gilding; back: Wheelock Austria Crown and Circle mark, Made in Vienna Austria for H. W. Varney, Brunswick, Me. $40.00 – 65.00.
(R) 8¼" diameter plate with opalized yellow rim framing a large hand-painted scene, Beach Looking North, York Beach, Me.; back: Jonroth, Made in Germany for H. Gleekman, York Beach, Maine. $40.00 – 65.00.

7¼" diameter plate with embossed floral accents and sepia photographic transfer is typical of plates produced by Fasolt & Eichel; scene is Lisbon Public School, Lisbon, N.H.; bottom Wiemar in shield with Germany below, Made in Germany for N. G. English, Lisbon, N.H. $30.00 – 50.00.

Coupe Plates

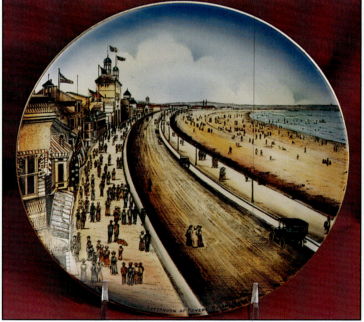

Full scene coupe plates or plaques were produced in many sizes, ranging from less than 4" to more than 10", but are most commonly found in sizes between 7" and 8½" in diameter. The example shown here is 8½" and depicts Condit's Dance Hall, Revere Beach, Mass.; back: red crown mark of Altenburg China, Made in Germany. $30.00 – 50.00.

Another full scene coupe plate (8" diameter) shows Sunday Afternoon at Revere Beach, Mass.; back: red script, Made in Germany. $30.00 – 50.00.

The smallest size of the full scene coupe plate is just over 3½". This one shows Fairbanks House, Dedham, Mass.; back: circular green mark, Three Crowns China, Germany. $20.00 – 40.00.

Variation of multi-scene coupe plate. Souvenir of Cheyenne, Wyoming. $50.00 – 75.00.

Variation of multi-scene coupe plate. Historical Fredericksburg, Virginia. $20.00 – 40.00.

Variation of multi-scene coupe plate. Souvenir of Elizabethtown, N.Y. $30.00 – 50.00.

Creamers

Souvenir china creamers were produced in an incredible range of shapes and sizes. The forms were often items of great beauty which represented well the tastes of the era. Many collectors have developed a definite preference for creamers, not only for their appearance, but for their practical aspects as well — they take up very little space and provide vertical presentations of the scenes.

The mold or shape of this creamer is found so frequently that it is arbitrarily referred to as Wheelock's signature creamer. It is a very desirable form, found with many variations in the decoration and in the bottom marks. Pictured here are five different decorations and three different sizes.
Left to right:
3⅜" h. with roses and black engraving, Patten Free Library, Bath, Me.; bottom: round red mark, Wheelock, Made in Germany for Jones 5 & 10 Cents Store, 57 Center Street, Bath, Me. $30.00 – 50.00.

3⅜" h. with bottom up rose tint and color scene, Kellogg Hubbard Library, Montpelier, Vt.; bottom: round red mark, Wheelock, Made in Germany for Boston Bargain Store, Montpelier, VT. $30.00 – 50.00.

4¼" h. with black engraving, High School, Bellows Falls, Vt.; bottom: round red mark, Wheelock, Made in Germany for W.E. Conway, Bellows Falls, Vt. $30.00 – 50.00.

3⅜" h. with bottom up dark green to lime tint and flowers depicting color scene, Williams Hall, University of Vermont, Burlington; bottom: round red mark, Wheelock, Made in Germany for Gardner Brewer, Burlington, Vt. $30.00 – 50.00.

3⅞" h. with top down robin's egg blue tint and color scene, Hitchcock Memorial Library, Westfield, Vt.; bottom: round red mark, H. B. Hitchcock, Westfield Vt. (no mention of Wheelock or Germany). $30.00 – 50.00.

The spade decoration at the rim gives these creamers their name. They were made in at least three sizes and featured some of the most outstanding graphics known to exist on souvenir china. Most bear the Wheelock name. Pictured here are:
(L) 3⅝" h. with gold spades, Hotel Potter, Santa Barbara, Cal.; bottom: blue letters MADE IN GERMANY. $40.00 – 65.00.
(C) 4½" h. with gold spades, Main Street, Looking West, Peshtigo, Wis.; bottom: black letters, Wheelock, Made in Germany for G. Nelson, Jeweler, Peshtigo, Wis. $40.00 – 65.00.
(R) 3⅝" h. with gold spades, Pilgrim Memorial Monument, Provincetown,

Mass.; bottom: black letters, Wheelock, Made in Germany for I.L. Rosenthal, Provincetown, Mass. $40.00 – 65.00. The form is also found in 3½" h. size.

This highly stylized concave form is seen in at least two sizes, generally bearing generic marks.

(L) 4½" h. with gold accents and green transfer, Soldier's Quarters, Winthrop, Mass.; bottom: green generic mark Made in Germany, Imported for A. Tewksbury, Winthrop, Mass. $40.00 – 65.00.

(R) 4¹⁄₁₆" h. with gold handle and black engraving, Paxinosa Inn, Easton, Pa.; bottom: black generic mark, Made in Germany for Wm. Laubach & Son, Easton, Pa. $40.00 – 65.00.

Many variations exist which are similar to popular common forms. Pictured here are examples of two more 4¹⁄₁₆" h creamers.

(L) Simple form with black engraving, Hotel Coburn; bottom: black generic mark, Made in Germany for Chas. A. Ross, Skowhegan, Maine. $20.00 – 40.00.

(R) Concave creamer with gilding and black engraving, The Home of the Pearl of Orr's Island; bottom: black generic mark, Made in Germany, Jennie Prince, Orr's Island, Me. An old sticker shows it was a gift in 1912. $40.00 – 65.00.

Three more variations:

(L) 3¼" h. similar in style to the Wheelock Signature form with top down rose tint and black engraving, Eastern Steamship Company Wharf, Eastport, Me; bottom marked in script Made in Germany $40.00 – 65.00.

(C) 3¼" h. wide-mouth creamer with roses and color scene, Logging on the Skagit, Burlington, Wash.; bottom: red circle mark Made in Germany. $30.00 – 50.00.

(R) 3⅜" h. simple form with color scene, Irrigation Ditch, Portales, N.M.; bottom: red monogram of JHR Co. in circle Made in Germany for Portales Drug Co., Portales, N.M. $40.00 – 65.00.

Souvenir China Items

Cylinder jugs were made in many shapes and sizes with gold borders around color scenes. These were produced in abundance from the early part of the century well into the 1930s.

(L) 2¾" h. creamer jug with color scene, The Battle of Lexington; bottom: Made in Germany for O.G. Seeley, Lexington, Mass. $30.00 – 50.00.

(C) 4⅛" h. jug with color scene, Cuckolds, Maine; bottom: Made in Germany for A.J. Kenniston, Boothbay Harbor, Me. $40.00 – 65.00.
(R) 3½" h. jug with color scene, Post Office, Pittsfield, Mass.; bottom: Made in Germany for The Wallace Co., Pittsfield, Mass. $20.00 – 40.00.

Common wide mouth creamer form with different decorations:
(L) 3" h. with top down lime tinting and color scene, Peanutine Team at Old Orchard, Me.; bottom: red script, Made in Germany. $50.00 – 75.00.
(C) 3" h. with bottom up magenta tint and color scene, Main Street, Springfield, Vt.; bottom: red block letters,

J.H.R.& Co., Made in Germany for O.E. Noyes, Springfield, Vt. $30.00 – 50.00.
(R) 3" h. with bottom up earth-to-sky toning and color scenes, Custom House and Post Office, Eastport, Me.; bottom: red block letters, Made in Germany for W. S. Milden, Eastport, Me. $30.00 – 50.00.

Examples of a creamer form in two sizes with similar decorations:
(L) 4¼" h. with magenta rim and color scene, Mount Washington House, Bretton Woods, NH; bottom: red letters enclosed in a square, Made in Germany for A.M. Allen, Fabyans, N.H. $40.00 – 65.00.
(C) 5" h. with magenta rim and color scene, of The Mt. Pleasant House, Bretton Woods, NH; bottom: purple lettering and Altenburg Crown logo, Made in Germany for A.M. Allen, Fabyans, N.H. $40.00 – 65.00.

(R) 4¼" h. with magenta rim and color scene, The Ovens, Chebeague Island, Me.; bottom: red lettering in a square, H.W. Bowen, Chebeague Island, Me. $30.00 – 50.00.

A Wheelock form found with different decorating schemes and varying degrees of thickness is 3¾" high.

(L) Bass Rocks, Gloucester, Mass.; bottom: Wheelock Austria Crown mark, Made in Vienna, Austria, for Frank P. Wonson, Gloucester, Mass. $30.00 – 50.00.

(R) Court House, Laconia, N.H.; bottom: Made in Vienna, Austria for Lougee-Robinson Co., Laconia, N.H. $30.00 – 50.00.

Fancy oval creamer forms with different decorations:

(L) 4⅜" h. with rose tint at top and yellow tint at bottom and black engraving, Melcher House, Groveton, N.H.; bottom: BFHS made in Austria for Hutchins & May, Groveton, N.H. $30.00 – 50.00.

(R) 4⅜" h. with robin's egg blue tint at top and yellow tint at bottom, and color scene, Steamer Martha's Vineyard, Onset, Mass.; bottom: BFHS Carlsbad China logo, Made in Austria for C.E. Macy, Onset, Mass. $50.00 – 75.00.

Creamer form with top down tinting, wide lip, high handle and large color scenes centered on the front:

(L) side view of 3⅝" h. creamer with scene, Cooper's Cave; bottom: red circle, Made in Germany for B.B. Fowler, Glens Falls, N.Y. $40.00 – 65.00.

(R) frontal view of 3⅝" h. creamer with scene, Court House in which John Brown was Sentenced, Charlestown, W.Va.; bottom: red circle, Charles W. Brown, Charlestown, W.Va. $40.00 – 65.00.

Two common forms of wide body creamers with top down rose tinting and large color pictures inside a gold arch.
(L) 3¼" h. with scene, Minot's Light, Cohasset, Mass.; bottom: red circle, Made in Germany for M.G. Sooveras, No. Scituate, Mass. $40.00 – 65.00.
(R) 4" h. with scene, Ferry Across Lake Champlain, Rouses Point, N.Y.; bottom: red circle, Made in Germany for Frank Pardy, Rouses Point, N.Y. $40.00 – 65.00.

A straight-sided design popular in hotels, restaurants, and dining cars is shown here in three sizes:
(L) 4⅜" h. version has black engravings on both sides: Corinthian Yacht Club House and the other side is depicted Making Lobster Traps; bottom: Made in Germany for W.F. Cloon, Marblehead, Mass. $50.00 – 75.00.
(C) 3" h. shows black engraving, Old Coffin House, Nantucket, Built 1686; bottom: Made in Germany for C.W. Hooper & Co., Nantucket, Mass. $75.00 – 100.00.

(R) 2⅜" h. shows green engraving, French Cable Co., Orleans, Mass.; bottom: Made in Germany for A.T. Newcomb, Orleans, Mass. $50.00 – 75.00.

Two more of the extremely popular small (2⅜" h.) creamers in the same form with well-detailed black engravings:
(L) Old Whalers, New Bedford, Mass.; bottom: Made in Germany for Bliss & Nye, New Bedford, Mass. $40.00 – 65.00.
(R) Wreck of the Pilot Boat Columbia at Sand Hills, Gale of November 27, 1898; bottom: Made in Germany for Chas. W. Frye, Scituate, Mass. $40.00 – 65.00.

Oval form found in several sizes and various decorations with a wide variety of bottom marks:
(L) 2" h. with black transfer, Post Office, Waldoboro, Me.; bottom: Wheelock, Vienna, Austria. $20.00 – 40.00.
(R) 2¼" h. with pea green tinting around rim and gilding around color scene, San Diego Mission (Founded 1769), California; bottom: Wheelock Vienna Austria for CHINA HALL, Kuert & Sons, 1034 5th Ave, San Diego, Calif. $20.00 – 40.00.

Popular creamer forms typically found with black engravings and generic marks (note left and center items are the same form repeated):
(L) 2⅞" h. showing Commonwealth Shoe and Leather Co., Gardiner, Me.; bottom: Made in Germany for Webber Bros., Gardiner, Me. $30.00 – 50.00.
(C) 2⅞" h. showing China Mills, Suncook, N.H.; bottom: Made in Germany for Simpson, Miller & Co., Suncook, N.H. $40.00 – 65.00.

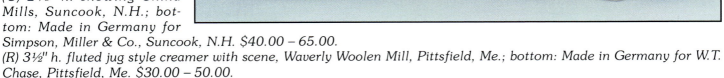

(R) 3½" h. fluted jug style creamer with scene, Waverly Woolen Mill, Pittsfield, Me.; bottom: Made in Germany for W.T. Chase, Pittsfield, Me. $30.00 – 50.00.

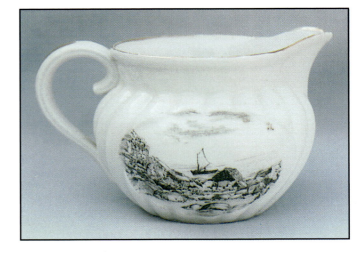

Left: 3¼" h. squatty, fluted creamer, often found in a set with open sugar bowl; pictures on both sides: (l) black engraving, Ogunquit River; (r) general view with sailboat; $30.00 – 50.00. Right: Made in Germany for W.F. Cousens, Ogunquit, Me.

Two more creamers (often found with matching open sugar bowls and black engravings):

(L) 3⅝" h. bulbous form with scene, a windmill in Orleans, Mass; bottom: Made in Germany for A.T. Newcomb, Orleans, Mass. $40.00 – 65.00.

(R) 2½" h. boat-shaped form with scene, Portland Head Light; bottom: Made in Germany for W.E. Whipple, Portland, Me. $30.00 – 50.00.

Bottom mark of pitcher made by Benjamin F. Hunt & Sons.

5" h. highly stylized creamer or milk pitcher with much embossing and fancy handle, showing black engraving, U.S. Life Saving Station, Orleans, Mass. $65.00 – 100.00.

Bottom mark of pitcher is also in the same style of gold lettering used by Benjamin F. Hunt & Sons, who apparently made the item for Wheelock.

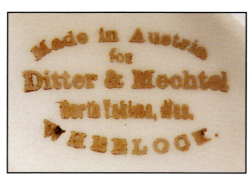

A 4¼" h. creamer made in the same mold style as the one shown to the left depicts High School, No. Yakima, Wash. $30.00 – 50.00.

Two small highly stylized oval creamers made by BFHS:
(L) 2⅝" h. showing Court House, Ellesworth, Me.; bottom: BFHS Carlsbad China logo, Made in Austria for J.P. Eldridge, Ellesworth, Me. $30.00 – 50.00.
(R) 3⅛" h. showing Wreck of The Glendon, Hampton Beach; bottom: BFHS Made in Austria for Obee, Emerson & Sons, Haverhill, Mass. $40.00 – 65.00.

This highly prized 3⅞" h. form bears the green mark of Sontag & Son, which was the mark used by the Royal Bayreuth factory prior to 1902. All aspects of this item, including the porcelain, gold cartouche, and graphics of the scene, are worthy of the pedigree. The large frontal color scene depicts Pioneer Mill, Pittsfield, Maine. $50.00 – 75.00.

This 4½" h. half gold creamer is in a category which loses favor among some collectors; the rapid coloring technique used on the scene breaks down its clarity, while the heavy gold tends to distract the eye from the scene. Pictured here is The Dorothy Q. House, Quincy, Mass.; bottom: Made in Germany for Quincy 5 & 10 Cent Stores, Quincy, Mass. Under $20.00.

Bottom mark on the Pioneer Mill, Pittsfield, Maine, creamer (shown above) is that of Sontag & Son, Made in Germany for G.I. Smith & Co.

Shown here are three more examples of the many variations in form used as souvenir china creamers.

(L) 2⅞" h. variation of the creamers shown at the top of page 61. This one features green tinting around the rim and a color scene, Temple, Onset, Mass.; bottom: black lettering, Made in Austria for C.H. Macy, Onset, Mass. $30.00 – 50.00.

(C) 4½" h. distinctively gilded form with black engraving, State Normal School, Hyannis, Mass.; bottom: Made in Germany for Myron G. Bradford, Hyannis, Mass. $40.00 – 65.00.

(R) 3¾" h. very wide mouth creamer with full pink or rose tint and black engraving inside gold circle, Hotel Fiske, Old Orchard, Maine; bottom: black generic mark, Made in Germany for W. E. Leavitt & Co., Old Orchard, Maine. $30.00 – 50.00.

3¼" creamer with top down rust colored tinting accented with enamel droplets, all surrounding a color scene, Quincy Mine Location, Hancock, Mich.; bottom: no mark. $30.00 – 50.00.

4½" h. creamer with very large frontal color view of First Parsonage, Stoneham, Mass.; bottom; mark of Roschützer Porcelain Factory. $30.00 – 50.00.

Two creamers made by and decorated in the style of the Victoria Porcelain Factory (many variations exist): (L) 2¼" h. individual oval creamer with gold rim and filigree, depicting black engraving, Palace of Manufactures, St. Louis Exposition, 1904; bottom: red Victoria Carlsbad Austria Eagle mark. $65.00 – 100.00. (R) 4¼" h. tall oval creamer with gold rim and filigree, depicting black engraving, School Building, Edna, Kans.; bottom: blue Victoria Carlsbad Austria Eagle mark. $30.00 – 50.00.

Variations of cylinder jug styles:
(L) 2¾" h. typical creamer with color scene, Public Library and Congregational Church, Leominster, Mass.; bottom: Made in Germany for W. H. Silverthorne, Leominster, Mass. $30.00 – 50.00.
(C) 3½" h. (base to top of finial) covered sugar bowl which shows minor variation in shape and top down opalized green-purple tint; scene, High School, Fairfield, Maine; bottom: green script, Made in Thuringia $20.00 – 40.00.
(R) 4¼" h. showing minor variation of style and top down rose tinted shadow flowers, Harbor Scene, Boothbay Harbor, Maine; bottom: MW Co. circle mark, Made in Germany for W.F. Dudley, Boothbay Harbor, Me. $40.00 – 65.00.

Large 8" high cylinder jug with tinting at the top depicts The Promenade, Nantasket Beach, Mass.; back: Made in Germany for A. Rosenbaum, Nantasket. $40.00 – 65.00.

65

Creamers are frequently found with matching sugar bowls or as parts of coffee or tea sets. This set features a 2½" h. creamer and a covered sugar bowl in the same style or pattern. The creamer has bottom down lime tinting, a gold handle, and a color scene, Old Mill Ruins, Rockport, Mass., while the sugar bowl features top down rose tinting, gold handles and top, and a color scene, Straightsmouth Life Sav-ing Station, Rockport, Mass. The bottom mark of both is a Bauer, Rosenthal Crown mark, Alice pattern, Souvenir – Made in Germany. $65.00 – 100.00.

The white or gilded handles of these items are the only key surfaces which have not been colored in the beige tone. The covered sugar and the cup and saucer came from the same set, while the creamer shows minor varia-tion in style and was added for the picture. It is practical-ly impossible to tell if it was a match or not.
(L) sugar bowl depicts black engraving, Street Scene, Tuc-son, Ariz.; bottom: Made in Germany for W.J. Corbett, Tucson, Ariz. $40.00 – 65.00. (C) cup shows a scene, San Xavier Mission 1796, Tucson, Ariz.; same bottom mark. $40.00 – 65.00. (R) creamer depicts hotel in Marblehead, Mass.; Made in Germany for W.F. Cloon. $40.00 – 65.00.

Dishes and Bowls

Undoubtedly, more than a thousand different variations fall into this category. Therefore, many forms exist beyond the scope of what is presented here. Any dish can be desirable with an attractive scene depicted on it; however certain character-istics of the form can add great appeal. Some highly desirable forms have become well established. Items presented here have been selected to show important styles and types of souvenir china dishes.

Folded corner dishes, also known as handker-chief dishes, were popular items at the turn of the century; they are approximately 4¾" square with color scenes. Among collectors, they are one of the more desirable forms. This one shows Point Hotel and Lookout, Battlefield, Lookout Mountain, Tenn.; back: unmarked. $20.00 – 40.00.

A group three highly decorated and colorful scenes from Gloucester, Mass. on folded corner dishes; back: Made in Germany for S.S. Hartwell, Gloucester, Mass. Shore Fisherman $75.00 – 125.00. Others $40.00 – 65.00.

Another folded corner napkin dish shows Horseshoe Falls, Niagara; back: unmarked. Even the most common subject (such as this one) has more appeal to collectors when excellent early graphics are found on this particular form. $20.00 – 40.00.

The 4¼" diameter Shell & Bow dish is a colorful and popular form in its most common color scheme as depicted on the three items shown here, all with bottom marks indicating they were made in Germany for local merchants:
(L) Poland Spring House, Poland, Me. $40.00 – 65.00.
(C) Echo Springs Near Idaho Springs, Colo. $40.00 – 65.00.
(R) Augustana College, Augustana, Ill. $30.00 – 50.00.

Embossed and painted floral cameo dishes are found in different molds and many color variations. Most of these are approximately 5" in diameter. Shown here is one with an uncommon scene followed by another with a common scene.
(L) Mold No. 265, Catholic Church and School, Howard, SD; back: overglaze blue block capitals, MADE IN GERMANY. $50.00 – 75.00.
(R) Mold No. 248, Gate-Way of The Garden of the Gods; back: Wheelock Weimar, Made in Germany for George Eastwood, Denver, Colo. $20.00 – 40.00.

(L) Another version of mold No. 248 depicting a Pikes Peak Railroad mule; back: Wheelock Dresden, Made in Germany for Frey & Collins, Canon City, Colo. $65.00 – 100.00.
(R) unnumbered cameo flower mold depicting Greenville, Ohio, Broadway Looking South; back: Wheelock Weimar, Made in Germany for Chas. P. Gibson, Bookseller & Stationer, Greenville, Ohio. $40.00 – 65.00.

Mold No. 242 is shown featuring a wonderful color picture, High School, Frankfort, Kansas; bottom: Wheelock Weimar, Made in Germany for Brown & Mason, Frankfort, Kansas. $40.00 – 65.00.

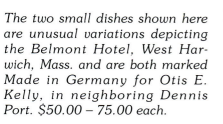

These two small rimmed dishes are 5⅜" in diameter and represent nice examples of robin's egg blue and canary yellow tinting. Both depict Exchange Building, Harwich, Mass., and are marked Made in Germany for Otis E. Kelley, Dennisport, Mass. $50.00 – 75.00 each.

The two small dishes shown here are unusual variations depicting the Belmont Hotel, West Harwich, Mass. and are both marked Made in Germany for Otis E. Kelly, in neighboring Dennis Port. $50.00 – 75.00 each.

This form is approximately 5½" square and typically presents large and colorful scenes from the 1890s, with embossed and painted floral accents on the porcelain. The result is a wonderful combination of Victoriana and Americana. Depicted here is the Public School Building, Tulsa, I.T. (Indian Territories); back: Wheelock Vienna, Made in Austria for G.W. Pittman, Jeweler, Tulsa, I.T. $100.00 – 150.00.

69

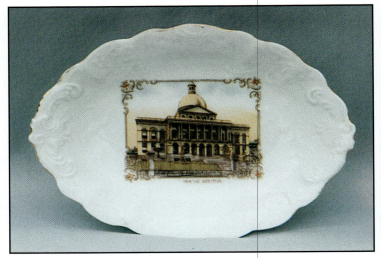

This 5¾" diameter fluted and rose-tinted dish features the Checkley House, Prout's Neck, Me., and is one example of the many souvenir dishes which are not found with any substantial repetition; back: Made in Austria for Fred M. Newcomb, Scarboro, Me. $40.00 – 65.00.

This 6" long oval dish features a scene, the State House, Boston (word missing) in a distinct style produced with the Elbogen, Austria mark shown on top of page 44. Under $20.00.

A small oval dish, 6⅝" long, shows a scene, Main Street, Ogunquit, Me.; bottom: Made in Germany for W.F. Cousens, Ogunquit, Me. $30.00 – 50.00.

An attractive little berry dish is 5½" in diameter and features a color scene, Public Library, Berlin, N.H.; back: red round mark, Wheelock, Made in Germany for Lemieux & Gilbert, Berlin, N.H. $30.00 – 50.00.

Fancy dish (or possibly a pin tray), approximately 6" long shows the Pine Tree Inn, Point Independence, (Onset, Mass.), produced with influences of Blue Delft and Flow Blue styles; no mark on back. $50.00 – 75.00.

Highly stylized 5¾" long dish with partially colored engraving, Harriet Beecher Stowe House, Hartford, Conn.; back: BFHS, Made in Austria for The Mellon & Howes Co., Hartford, Conn. $30.00 – 50.00. (Note: color is rare in scenes depicted on BFHS items.)

Pouring saucers are classified with dishes and bowls and stand well on their own alongside functional creamers or pitchers. This one is approximately 6" in diameter and features a scene from Brant Rock, Mass.; bottom: unknown. $20.00 – 40.00.

A more common pouring saucer is this 6¾" wide form featuring a prominent rose decoration. This one depicts Mattaquason Hotel, Chatham, Mass.; back: red Altenburg China crown mark, Made in Germany for A. Howes, Chatham, Mass. $50.00 – 75.00.

The scope of souvenir china dishes is practically endless. This one is approximately 9" long with handles on each end and a gilded opalescent finish with Statue of Liberty, New York Harbor depicted in an oval in the center of the bowl; bottom: green circle, Made in Germany, and black script in box, Siegel Cooper Co., New York. $30.00 – 50.00.

A 5" long oval sugar bowl with small decorative handle features a scene, Pebbly Beach, Sharon, Mass.; bottom: Made in Germany for Mrs. A.B. Elliott, Sharon, Mass. $20.00 – 40.00.

A rose-tinted shadow flower design on this beautiful 6⅛" (diameter) bowl frames a crisp color scene, Cahoon Hollow Life Saving Station, Wellfleet, Mass.; back: red Altenburg China crown mark, Made in Germany for Geo. P. Baker, Wellfleet, Mass. $100.00 – 150.00.

This 8" diameter bowl is stylized with pierced and tinted points, floral sprays, and gold filigree around a black engraving, State Street, Groveton, N.H.; bottom: Made in Germany for Hutchins & May, Groveton, N.H. $30.00 – 50.00.

Providing a stark contrast to highly decorated porcelain, this plain white cereal bowl has only a thin gold line around the edge and a black engraving, Stoughton Public Library in the center of the bowl; back: Made in Germany for Monk's Cash Store, Stoughton, Mass. $20.00 – 40.00.

Although sugar bowls stand well on their own, they are best when paired with a properly mated creamer. A perfect example is this wonderful set with two Block Island scenes in sepia by Benjamin F. Hunt and Sons. Bottom: red print, B.F.H.S., Made in Austria for John Rose & Co., Block Island, R.I. $150.00+ (set).

A 9" long celery dish features a color picture of Sparhawk Hall, Ogunquit, Maine; note the decoration is a distinctive pattern made by a recognized producer of fine porcelain dinnerware: back: BRC crown mark, Viola pattern, Wheelock Dresden, Made in Germany for C.S. Littlefield, Ogunquit, Me. $65.00 – 100.00.

This 5½" long English Shelly dish is well known without souvenir scenes in a wide variety of decorations, but it is unusual with a souvenir scene on it. This one shows a scene, Dixville Notch, N.H. Bottom: The Foley China Co. together with logo of Wileman & Co., Made in England for Chas. Colby, Colebrook, N.H. $30.00 – 50.00

Trays

There is an arbitrary and fine line to be drawn in defining the difference between a tray and a dish. For example, a folded corner dish also functions as a card tray or pin tray, and a card tray or a pin tray can also be a card dish or a pin dish. Some of the most common flat tea service trays, pin trays, dresser trays, and pen trays are shown here. As with all souvenir china, it is important to note that countless variations exist.

(TL) A 4½" long rectangular pin tray with scalloped border and gilding depicts black engraving, Lakeside Hotel; back: Made in Germany for G.W. Tarlson, The Weirs, N.H. $30.00 – 50.00.
(TR) 4⅜" long, rectangular pin tray with scene, Highland Life Saving Station, Cape Cod; back: Made in Germany for J. Morton Small, Highlands, No. Truro, Mass. $65.00 – 100.00.
(BL) 4¼" long, rectangular pin tray with scene, Hesperus Hotel, Magnolia, Mass.; back: Made in Germany for Frank P. Wonson, Magnolia, Mass. $40.00 – 65.00.
(BR) 3¾" square pin tray or dish with scene, Wellfleet Point Light; back: BFHS Carlsbad China logo, Made in Austria for P.W. Higgins, Wellfleet, Mass. $50.00 – 75.00.

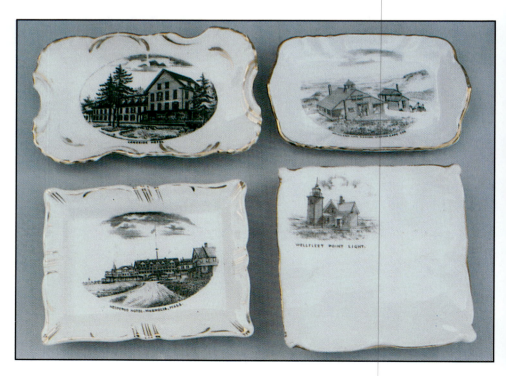

(L) 6¼" long, two-section pin tray with gilded border and center scene, Coffin House, Newbury; back: Made in Germany for Edward Osgood, Newburyport, Mass. $30.00 – 50.00.

(R) 5½" long, two-section pin tray with center scene, Norcross House; back: Made in Germany for P.H. Phinnay, Monument Beach, Mass. $40.00 – 65.00.

6½" high and 8¾" wide dresser tray with green engraving, High School, Fergus Falls, Minn.

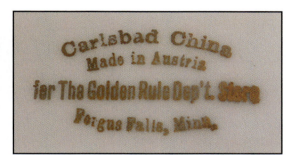

Back: as shown is suggestive of Benjamin F. Hunt & Sons as the manufacturer. $30.00 – 50.00.

6" long advertising/souvenir/hotel pin tray from the Hotel Astor. Back mark is Royal Rudolstadt and L. Strauss and Sons. $30.00 – 50.00.

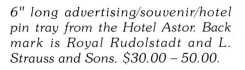

6½" long advertising/souvenir/hotel pin tray, The Palace Hotel, San Francisco, California; back: blue lettering, Patent Applied for, Especially made for Palace Hotel, San Francisco, by Bauscher Bros. New York & Weiden, Germany. $30.00 – 50.00.

Tea Tiles (a.k.a. Trivets or Hot Plates)

(L) 6⅜" diameter round hot plate with very faint purple tinted floral decoration and color scene, Main Street, Norway, Me., Showing Beal's Hotel; back: Altenburg China crown mark, Made in Germany for George W. Hobbs, Norway, Me. $30.00 – 50.00.

(C) 5" square hot plate with partially worn scene, Tower, Reading, Pa.; back: Made in Germany for C.K. Whitner & Son, Reading, Pa. Under $20.00. (Note: significant wear on the scene and the lettering results in reduction of value.)

(R) 6⅛" diameter round hot plate with color scene, Old Deerfield St.; back: Made in Germany for J.H. Briggs, Deerfield, Mass. $30.00 – 50.00.

(L) 5¼" diameter round hot plate with black engraving showing View on Commerce St., West Point, Miss. back: red letters (in the style of Benjamin F. Hunt & Sons), Made in Austria for R.C. Gibson, West Point, Miss. $40.00 – 65.00. (Note: slight wear on lettering has negligible impact on the value, but any more would definitely detract from the value.)

(R) 5¼" hot plate (same form as shown in center of preceding photo) features engraving, Scituate Light, Home of Rebecca and Abigail Bates, Heroines of the War of 1812; back: Made in Germany for Chas. W. Frye, Scituate, Mass. $40.00 – 65.00.

6¼" squarish tea tile with gold stippled border and central black engraving of Annisquam Yacht Club House; bottom: red lettering BFHS China, Made in Austria for the Boston Store, W. G. Brown & Co., Gloucester, Mass. $40.00 – 65.00.

Mugs and Cups and Saucers

Although souvenir china items were customarily purchased separately, tea and coffee sets were occasionally purchased complete or assembled over time. As with all forms, it is remarkable how many different sizes, types, and styles of souvenir china cups and saucers can be found. This is just as true of beverage mugs and shaving mugs. The items shown cover a large part of the scope, but necessarily leave many other forms to be discovered.

The most plain black and white cup and saucer set has its beauty in its simplicity. It is rare to find such a decoration without any gilding, embossing or ancillary decoration whatsoever. This one shows the Sanford Mill, Medway, Mass., and it has a purple scripted Made in Germany on the base of both the cup and saucer. $20.00 – 40.00.

Souvenir China Items

A few English-made items imitated the German-made items in some aspects, although the porcelain frequently became discolored over time. This simple cup and saucer show the Northport Hotel, Northport, Maine. This set has remained white; the cup's applied handle is an English design feature. Most German-made cups and saucers depicted two different scenes, while English-made sets typically used the same scene on both the cup and saucer. Back: unknown. $30.00 – 50.00.

Four cup and saucer sets produced by Benjamin F. Hunt & Sons include:

(TL) delicate demitasse in four-leaf clover shape with figural gold handle and an engraving, Bird Island Light on the cup and A Corner of Mr. Gilder's House on the saucer; back: gold letters, BFHS Carlsbad China, Made in Austria for Stephen Hadley, Marion, Mass. $50.00 – 75.00.

(TR) full-size cup and saucer with figural butterfly gold handle and an engraving of Steamer Mt. Washington, Alton Bay, N.H. on the cup and Steamboat Landing, Alton Bay, N.H. on the saucer; back: gold letters, BFHS Carlsbad China, Made in Austria for W.P. Emerson, Alton Bay, N.H. $40.00 – 65.00.

(BL) footed cup and saucer set with engraving, Elm House, Meredith, N.H. on both cup and saucer; back: BFHS Carlsbad China, Made in Austria for O.E. Osgood, Meredith, N.H. $30.00 – 50.00.

(BR) demitasse cup and saucer with engraving, Hotel Weirs, Weirs, N.H. on the cup and C&M Railroad Station, Weirs, N.H. on the saucer; back: BFHS Carlsbad China, Made in Austria for F.E. Nelson, Laconia, N.H. $40.00 – 65.00.

Examples of cup and saucer sets with mustache strainers on the cups (moustache cups):

(L) cup shows black engraving, of Broadway Church, Taunton, Mass., and saucer has the same scene; back: Made in Germany for W.N. & M.G. Smith, Taunton, Mass. $40.00 – 65.00.

(R) very heavy and nicely gilded set with cup depicting Carnegie Steel Works at Homestead, Pa., and saucer with an engraving, The Block House of Fort Pitt, 1764; back: BFHS China, Made in Austria for Joseph Horne & Co., Pittsburgh, Pa. $75.00 – 125.00.

This interesting mustache cup and saucer features dark green engravings of a railroad station and tracks entitled Callicoon on Delaware North Side, New York; back: Made in Germany for Chas. F. Starck, Callicoon, N.Y. $50.00 – 75.00.

Beige toned moustache cup features the Stmr. Katahdin at Wharf, Northport, Me.; bottom: Made in Germany for Mrs. John Carle, Belfast, Me. $75.00 – 125.00.

These forms are typical of the cups and saucers decorated with rose shadow flowers:
(L) full-size cup shows rare color scene, North Light, Block Island; back: red Altenburg China crown mark, Made in Germany for J.P. Malool & Bros., Block Island, R.I. $75.00 – 125.00.
(R) demitasse cup shows U.S. Life Saving Station, Cuttyhunk, Mass.; back: red script, Made in Germany. $75.00 – 125.00.

Other forms which were made with various tinted accents included these two which feature lime green tinting:

(L) demitasse featuring Nobscussett House, Dennis, Mass.; back: Made in Germany for E.C. Matthews & Co., Dennis, Mass. $65.00 – 100.00.

(R) full-size set features tinting in opposite areas from the one on left, features Malvern Hotel, Bar Harbor Me.; back: red circle mark, Wheelock, Made in Germany for F.E. Sherman, Bar Harbor, Maine. $30.00 – 50.00.

This small tea cup (L) and the child's cup (R) both show the nice visual effect of rose tinting with color scenes. The cup features A.C. Dougherty's Store, Henderson, Me.; back: red circle mark, A.C. Dougherty, Henderson, Me. $50.00 – 75.00.

The child's cup shows Islesboro Inn, Dark Harbor, Me.; back: same red circle mark, W.A. Ricker, Dark Harbor, Me. $40.00 – 65.00. (Note: neither mark mentions the country of origin.)

This low profile 2" h. mug is decorated in rose shadow flowers and features the Sanford Hall Block, Medway, Mass.; bottom: purple Altenburg China crown mark, Made in Germany for A.P Abbott. $30.00 – 50.00.

Two child's cups or mugs with black engravings are shown.
(L) Ferry Boat Passing Through Moline Lock; back: red print, Wheelock, Made in Germany for R.C. Leedy & Co., Moline, Ill. $30.00 – 50.00.
(R) The Oliver, South Bend, Ind.; back: purple script, Made in Germany. $30.00 – 50.00.

Full-size multi-scene mug with three scenes, New York City, circa 1907: Custom House, Statue of Liberty, and Brooklyn Bridge (not shown); bottom: Victoria Austria red crown mark. $30.00 – 50.00.

Mini mug which may have been used as a toothpick holder is just over 1¾" h. with color scene, Life Saving Station, Holly Beach, N. J.; bottom: Wheelock, Made in Germany for John N. Martin, Holly Beach, N. J. $40.00 – 65.00.

Four small mugs or child's cups show the diversity of forms.
(L) 2¾" h. with front-facing scene, Hoopston High School, Hoopston, Ill.; bottom: Wheelock Weimar, Made in Germany for Stine Bros., Hoopston, Ill. $30.00 – 50.00.
(CL) Dark Harbor, Me. cup also shown in center plate, page 80.

(CR) 2" h. cup with unusual handle features a scene, Old Man of the Mountain; bottom: Hand Painted, Made in Germany. $20.00 – 40.00.
(R) 2" h. cup with brown glaze featuring Home of Longfellow, Portland, Maine; bottom: illegible $20.00 – 40.00. **81**

Full-size mug (3" h.) with rose tinting and black engraving, Town Hall, Great Barrington, Mass.; bottom: red lettering inside square box, Made in Germany for Rorrison Bros., Great Barrington, Mass. $40.00 – 65.00. (Note: this same engraving can be found with full color applied.)

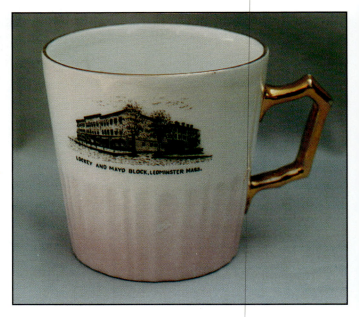

3¼" h. mug with rose tinted furls and gold handle, depicting Lockey and Mayo Block, Leominster, Mass.; bottom: gold letters, Made in Austria for R. B. Andrews, Leominster, Mass. $30.00 – 50.00.

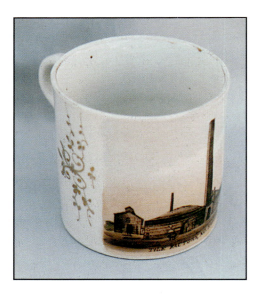

This 3" h. mug was probably a straight-sided shaving mug. The wonderfully executed manufacturing scene shows a Tile Factory, No. English, Iowa, flanked on each side by outstanding gold cartouche; bottom: Wheelock Weimar, Made in Germany for The Fair Store, No. English, Iowa $40.00 – 65.00.

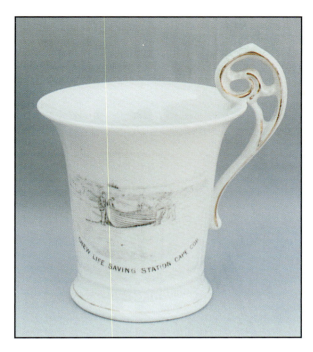

Tall mug or cup (4" h.) with ornate handle depicts Crew, Life Saving Station, Cape Cod; bottom: Made in Germany for D.S. Carlow & Co., Provincetown, Mass. $50.00 – 75.00.

Two examples of the Thimble and Scissors cup:
(L) Residence, Mt. Dora, Fla.; bottom: wheel and lock logo Wheelock, Vienna, Austria $50.00 – 75.00.
(R) Shohola Glen, Pa., Old Mill, Built 1790; bottom: red letters, Wheelock Vienna, Made in Austria for Edwin Higby, dealer in general merchandise, Shohola, Penna. $40.00 – 65.00.

Two open (barber shop style) shaving mugs:
(L) rose shadow flower decoration with modified trigger handle and color scene, Great Northern Hotel, Millinocket, Me.; back: MW Co. logo, Made in Germany for Fuller Furniture Co., Millinocket, Me. $40.00 – 65.00.
(R) common heavy weight barber shop form, decorated with flowers and a scene, Summit House Mt. Tom; bottom: J.C. Bavaria mark $50.00 – 75.00.

(L) Shaving mug with soap strainer and black engraving showing View of Shirley, Mass. (Note: the great advertising sign for Presidential Suspenders); bottom: Made in Germany for Brockelman Bros., Shirley, Mass. $40.00 – 65.00.

(R) Barber shop style open mug with large color scene, Old Orchard House; bottom: Wheelock Germany, Made for W.E. Leavitt & Co., Old Orchard Beach, Me. $40.00 – 65.00.

(L) Ornate shaving mug with color scene, Mount Washington House, Bretton Woods, N.H.; bottom: red lettering inside square, A.M. Allen, Fabyans, N.H. $75.00 – 125.00.

(R) fancy shaving mug with very light purple tinting and large black engraving, St. Barnabas Church, Falmouth, Mass.; bottom: BFHS Carlsbad China logo, Made in Austria for C.N. Thayer. $75.00 – 125.00.

4" h., rare full size scuttle style shaving mug with scene, Cradle Rock, Barre, Mass.; bottom: Made in Germany for W.R. Spooner, Barre, Mass. $75.00 – 125.00.

A sampling of toothpick holders includes:
(L) 2⅛" high, contoured holder with rose tinting near the top and sharp black engraving, Highland Light, Cape Cod, Mass.; bottom: Made in Germany for O. Snow & Son, Provincetown, Mass. $65.00 – 100.00.
(C) 2⅞" high, footed holder with scene, Orr's Island Bridge; bottom: Made in Germany for Jennie Prince, Orr's Island, Me. $40.00 – 65.00.
(R) 2½" high, tubular holder with embossed Take Your Pick on its side (not shown) and blue tinting at top, depicting Hotel Onset – Onset, Mass.; bottom: red letters, Carlsbad, Made in Austria for C.H. Macy, Onset, Mass. $40.00 – 65.00.

Three more toothpick holders, all approximately 2¼" h. with black engravings.
(L) A Pioneer residence, Puyallup, Wash.; bottom: round redmark, Wheelock, Made in Germany for G. P. Gray, Puyallup, Wash.; $40.00 – 65.00.
(C) Western Gypsum Mine, Blue Rapids, Kansas; bottom; Made in Germany for J. L. Barnes, Blue Rapids, Kansas. $50.00 – 75.00.
(R) Fort Comfort Pavilion, Belmar, N. J; bottom: red script, Made in Germany. $30.00 – 50.00.

These two toothpick holders with color scenes are also approximately 2¼" h.
(L) Hotel Fiske, Old Orchard Beach; bottom: Wheelock Germany, Made for W.E. Leavitt Co. $40.00 – 65.00.
(R) Bristol Harbor from Pappoosesquaw Road; bottom: Made in Germany for F. T. Remieres, Bristol, R. I. $40.00 – 65.00.

Another form of toothpick holder is this 2¼" high, blue tinted one which features a large and clear black engraving, Court House, Eatonton, Ga.; bottom: Made in Germany for R.H. Wooten, Milledgeville, Ga. $40.00 – 65.00. (Note: small town Georgia items are uncommon.)

Two variations of decorating a highly desirable thin china vase form are shown:
(L) The Red Man's Fact, Niagara Falls, N.Y.; bottom: Millar China Vienna, Made in Austria for Austin Bazaar, Niagara Falls, N.Y. $40.00 – 65.00. (Note: this scene is uncommon and desirable, while most views of Niagara Falls are common and undesirable).
(R) Bound for Oak Island Beach, Babylon, N.Y.; bottom: wheel and lock logo, Wheelock, Vienna, Austria. $50.00 – 75.00.

Nicely embossed, 6" h. watch holder/stand with sharp black engraving, Old Mill Chatham, Built 1797; bottom: BFHS Carlsbad China mark. $150.00+.

Outstanding rare form of a vase with burnt orange tint featuring Main Street, Vinalhaven, Me.; back: Made Expressly for Turner Fisheries, Vinalhaven, Me. $100.00 – 150.00.

5" h. vase with simulated graniteware finish and view of Confederate Monument, Savannah, Ga.; bottom: circle mark, Made in Germany. $30.00 – 50.00. (Note: Civil War items occasionally carry additional value among collectors with certain specialties). Although not marked as having been imported by Jonroth, this item is typical of souvenir china vases sold by Jonroth in the 1930s, featuring sleek, modern, contemporary styling which was quite a contrast to the earlier Victorian embellishments.

An unusual ornate vase with cobalt blue highlights, and scene, Willow Grove, Lake Keuka, N.Y.; bottom Made in Germany. $30.00 – 50.00.

Two 3½" h. tumblers:
(L) Grace Episcopal Church, Built prior to 1700, Yorktown, Va.; bottom: gold Jonroth palette mark, Made in Germany for J.S. DeNeufville, Lee Hall, Va. $30.00 – 50.00.
(R) Court House, Tripp Co., Winner, S.D.; bottom: block letters, MADE IN GERMANY. $20.00 – 40.00.

Multi-scene tumblers, 3¾" high, are found in color as well as black and white:

(L) highly colored example from San Antonio, Texas, with bottom mark J.H.R. & Co., Made in Germany; $30.00 – 50.00.

(R) black and white tumbler with scenes of New Orleans and blue crown Victoria Austria mark on bottom. $30.00 – 50.00.

A multi-scene tumbler from Buffalo showing typical colorful details; bottom is unmarked. $30.00 – 50.00.

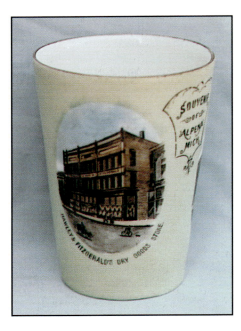

A lime green tumbler, representing another style of decoration, presents three scenes from Alpena, Mich.; bottom: red circle, Made in Germany. $40.00 – 65.00.

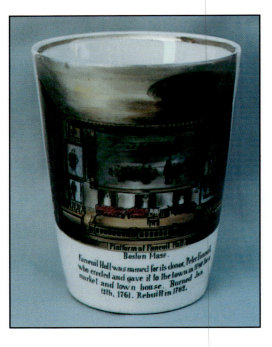

This early tumbler shows a rare interior view of The Platform at Faneuil Hall, Boston, Mass. along with important information on the historical landmark; bottom: unmarked. $50.00 – 75.00.

Condiment servers of various kinds and shapes were used as souvenir china. This 3¼" h. covered mustard pot has its original spoon and a detailed engraving, Rebecca Nourse House, Danvers, Mass. 1636; bottom: Made in Germany for F.M. Peabody, Danvers, Mass. $40.00 – 65.00.

This mustard pot is approximately 3½" high and shows a clear engraving of Falmouth Bell Made by Paul Revere 1796; bottom: BFHS Carlsbad China logo, Made in Austria for C.N. Thayer, Falmouth, Mass. $40.00 – 65.00.

A 4" h. ornate spooner with a scalloped rim makes a nice showpiece for Nickerson Place, Brewster, Mass., now part of an upscale resort hotel; bottom: Made in Germany for A.T. Newcomb, Orleans, Mass. $40.00 – 65.00.

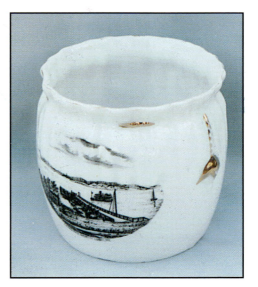

This 3½" h. spooner is made in the form of an open purse with drawstring handles. It features the scene (shown), Landing, North Lubec, Maine and on the other side (not shown), Toll Bridge, Eastport, Me.; bottom: Made in Germany for W.S. Mildon, Eastport, Me. $40.00 – 65.00.

Egg cups are found in several sizes, but this 2⅜" h. form is probably most common. This one depicts Condit's Dance Ball Room, Revere Beach, Mass; no mark on bottom. $20.00 – 40.00.

Individual or two-cup teapots are occasionally found in styles which match sugar bowls, creamers, and cups and saucers. This 4½" h. square form features a scene, Deane Winthrop House, Built about 1649 (which was also on the matching pieces); bottom: Made in Germany for St. John's Episcopal Church, Winthrop, Mass. $50.00 – 75.00.

Covered boxes are desirable forms of souvenir china. Benjamin F. Hunt and Sons made and imported some wonderful examples such as these:

(TL) 3¾" long, crescent-shaped box showing Provincetown Town House, Provincetown, Mass.; bottom: BFHS, Made in Austria for M. Chipman, Provincetown, Mass. $50.00 – 75.00.

(TR) 4½" triangular covered box with scene, Harwichport, Mass.; bottom: BFHS, Made in Austria for S.K Sears, Harwichport, Mass. $50.00 – 75.00.

(BL) 3" triangular box with scene, U.S. Life Saving Station, Orleans, Mass.; bottom: BFHS, Made in Austria for J.H. Cummings, Orleans, Mass. $85.00 – 120.00.

(BR) 2½" squarish box with scene, Steamer Martha's Vineyard, Onset, Mass.; bottom: BFHS, Made in Austria for C.H. Macy, Onset, Mass. $65.00 – 100.00.

This 3½" long, heart-shaped box features a nice rose tint and a scene from an old mining town (now a ghost town), Idaho Hotel, Silver City, Idaho; bottom: red circle, Made in Germany. $100.00 – 150.00.

This 3½" long heart-shaped box (same form as box at left) shows Stratton Falls, Roxbury, N.Y.; bottom: red circle, Made in Germany. $30.00 – 50.00.

A stylish little covered box, 3½" long, features a color scene, Lower Medomak Bridge, Waldoboro, Maine; marked under lid: Made in Germany for C.B. Stahl, Waldoboro, Me. $50.00 – 75.00.

Boxes in this shape were used as stamp boxes, match boxes or trinket boxes. Stamp compartments inside or a match striking surface on the inside of the lid will provide a clue to its intended use. This one (4¼" long) is a match box and the scene is National Bank of White River Junction, Vt.; bottom: Made in Germany for O.A. Randall, White River Junction, Vt. $40.00 – 65.00.

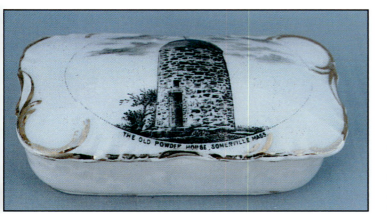

Another variation which might be a stamp box, a match box or a trinket box is this 3⅞" long form depicting The Old Powder House, Somerville, Mass.; bottom: Made in Germany for John F. Bacon, Somerville, Mass. $30.00 – 50.00.

The covered box on the left may have been a fairy lamp or a hair receiver. It shows a scene from Gardiner, Maine. $30.00 – 50.00.

The item on the right is a hair receiver showing Horseshoe Falls and Goat Island, Niagara Falls and is marked with a red Victoria Austria crown. Although the subject is common, the form is quite rare. $30.00 – 50.00.

Another form of covered box is a tea caddy (right); which is a very rare form of souvenir china. This one is 3¼" h. and features Pleasant View; bottom: Made in Germany for Continental American Tea Company, Concord, N.H. $50.00 – 75.00.

This powder jar (also a rare form) 6" h. with a scene, Old Stone Watering Trough, and showing and a scene on reverse, of Sugar River and Ascutney Mountain; bottom: Made in Germany for E.M. Spaulding, Claremont, N.H. $65.00 – 100.00. (Collection of Ron Rainka)

This attractive little wall pocket (approximately 3" wide) shows a nice color scene, Christ Episcopal Church, Salem and Hull Sts., Boston, where the lights for Paul Revere's ride were hung out; back: Made in Germany for J,McD, and S Co. $50.00 – 75.00. (Collection of Jan and Dick Vogel)

Many desk items were made into souvenir porcelain treasures, primarily by Benjamin F. Hunt & Sons.
(TL) 7" long, two compartment letter box with two scenes, Proctor Hill, Henniker, N. H., Birthplace of
Edna Dean Proctor; bottom: BFHS, Made in Austria for I.D. Huntoon, Henniker, N.H. $50.00 –
75.00.
(TC) 5" long ink blotter with scenes, Cave Mountain House, Bartlett, N.H. and Mt. Washington from
Maine Central R.R.; bottom: BFHS, Made in Austria for E.O. Garland, Bartlett, N.H. $75.00 –
125.00.
(TR) 4" long card holder with outstanding scene, Head Harbor Light; bottom: Made in Germany for
W.S. Mildon, Eastport, Me. $75.00 – 125.00.
(BC) pen tray as described in detail in Chapter 4 (pgs. 207 – 208). $40.00 – 65.00.

2⅜" x 3¾" paperweight with scene, Post Office Square,
Meredith, N.H.; bottom: BFHS, Made in Austria for O.E.
Osgood, Meredith, N.H. $40.00 – 65.00.

Another item used at the desk was an ink well such as
this 2½" h. example which has a metal hinged top and a
color scene, City Hospital, Belfast, Me.; bottom:
unmarked . $65.00 – 100.00. *(Collection of Ron Rainka)*

Ring holders such as this were typically found on Victorian dresser trays, although they are very rare among souvenir china. This one is 5" long and depicts an early view of the Tip Top House, Mount Tom, Holyoke, Mass.; bottom: BFHS Carlsbad China logo, Made in Austria for M.A. Allen & Son, Holyoke, Mass. $65.00 – 100.00.

Handsome 3¼" h. match safe/stand with strikers on both ends depicts Chatham Lights, Chatham, Mass.; bottom: BFHS, Made in Austria for A. Howes, Chatham, Mass. $75.00 – 150.00.

White porcelain chamberstick (5¾" diameter) with black engraving of Town Hall, Hanover, Mass.; bottom: Made in Germany for Thomas Drew & Co., So. Hanover, Mass. $40.00 – 65.00.

Chamberstick with color scene, Monadonock Mt. from Troy, N.H. $40.00 – 65.00. (Collection of C. McDaniel, photos also by McDaniel)

Bottom marks on chamberstick.

Chamberstick in the Delft style showing Old Mill, Nantucket 1746; bottom: Made in Germany for I. W. Westgate, Nantucket, Mass. $85.00 – 120.00.

Approximately 8" high candle stick holder showing black engraving, Kenilworth Inn, Asheville, N.C.; bottom: Made in Germany for Thad. W. Thrash & Bro., Asheville, N.C. $50.00 – 75.00. (Collection of Jan and Dick Vogel)

Pair of souvenir china hatpin holders:
(L) 4½" h. highly embossed pearl-like opalescent surface
with simple black engraving, Boston Church; no mark
on bottom. $75.00 – 125.00.
(R) 4¼" h. rose-tinted surface with color scene, Rosalind
Club, Orlando, Fla.; bottom: Made in Germany. $75.00
– 125.00.

Three different urns or loving cups:
(L) 4¾" h. with color scene, St. Joseph's Sanitarium, Mt.
Clemens, Mich. $40.00 – 65.00.
(C) 14" h. with color scene, Old Powder House, West
Somerville, Mass. $50.00 – 75.00.
(R) 8½" h. with color scene, Court House, Walworth County, Elkhorn, Wisc. $40.00 – 65.00. (All, collection of Ron Rainka)

3¼" h. salt shaker with
holes in the shape of an S
on the top and rose decals
flanking a scene, Mt. Vernon Mansion, Va.; bottom:
red script Made in Germany. Under $20.00. (Common subject.)

Rose tinted salt shaker, 3¼" h. with color
scene, Westfield River in the Berkshires
from the Jacob's Ladder Trail, Mass.; bottom: Made in Germany. Under $20.00.

Unusual 4" h. salt shaker with metal top and very clear color scene of Methodist Church, Minonk, Ill.; bottom: Wheelock China Dresden, Made in Germany for The Fair, J.S. Rose, Minonk, Ill. $40.00 – 65.00.

Large Serving Vessels

An array of large serving plates, dishes, bowls, pitchers, coffee and chocolate pots, and other large items can be found displaying souvenir scenes. Large English-made souvenir china items, including covered cracker jars and covered cheese servers, also exist, but tend to be discolored by age. A few large serving items are shown here.

A richly decorated covered chocolate pot, 9" h., with scenes on each side, Portland Observatory and Union Station, Built 1807. Bottom of chocolate pot: Made in Germany for Chas. W. Hadlock, 267 Congress St., Portland, Me. $150.00+.

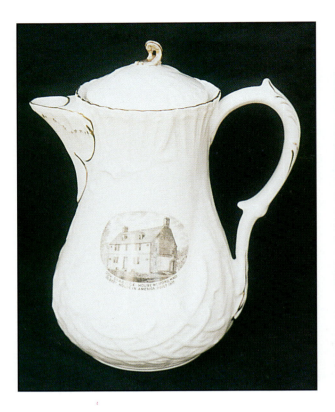

8" h. covered pitcher or chocolate pot features a black engraving, Gov. Craddock House, Medford, Mass., Oldest House in America, built 1634; bottom: Made in Germany for E.W. Mitchell, Medford, Mass. $100.00 – 150.00. *(Collection of Ron Rainka)*

This 10¾" wide shallow serving dish with handles features two scenes, Union Station and Soldier's Monument; bottom: Made in Germany for John M. Conway, 460 Congress St., Portland, Me. $20.00 – 40.00. *(Deduction in value for faded scenes)*

8¾" wide serving bowl with gilded edge and center engraving, Soldiers Monument and Christ Church, Fitchburg, Mass.; bottom: Made in Germany for L. Sprague & Co., Fitchburg, Mass. $40.00 – 65.00.

6" wide bowl with robin's egg blue tint and pierced sides would not be practical for serving many items other than bread or dinner rolls. It shows a color scene, Keene, N.H., and has no bottom mark. $40.00 – 65.00.

This 9¼" wide vegetable bowl has an interesting magenta and gold convoluted border and a nice scene in the bowl showing a view of Outer Harbor and Gloucester, Mass.; bottom: Wheelock Vienna Austria Crown mark, Made in Austria for Frank Wonson, Gloucester, Mass. $40.00 – 65.00.

This large (8" l., 5"h.) English-made covered cheese keeper is in remarkably good condition and features three excellent early scenes, Peabody, Mass.; bottom: Made for C. Pauley & Son. $40.00 – 65.00.

Bottom of cracker jar: Made in Germany for Kellogg Bros., Castile, N.Y. (Collection of Jan and Dick Vogel; photos by Jan Vogel)

7¼" h., 5¾" diameter, covered cracker jar with photographic sepia scene, Castile Sanitarium, Castile, N.Y. $65.00 – 100.00.

Porcelain souvenir steins are found in at least three sizes; some have lithophane scenes on their bases and others do not. This stein is just under 6½" high with a large color scene, Goodwin Park and Soldier's Monument, Portsmouth, N.H. It also features a lithophane hunting scene (not shown) on its base and is marked Jonroth, Made in Germany for Philbrick's Pharmacy, Portsmouth, N.H. $150.00+. (Note: most souvenir steins were ordered without the pewter tops.)

Lithophane scene on base of Bermuda skin. $150.00+. (Courtesy of Dr. Burton Spiller)

Another 6¼" h. porcelain stein depicting a wrap-around scene, The Royal Palms, Bermuda. Although not a U.S. scene, steins such as this can be found with U.S. scenes.

Steins

This 5¾" h. (³/₁₀ litre stein) has a large frontal color scene, Riverside Park, Jacksonville, FL, and a nice lithophane hunting scene on its base. Bottom: J.H.R. Co., Made in Germany for J. Osky, Druggist, Jacksonville, Fla. $150.00+.

A small 3¾" h. stein with frontal color scene of State Normal School, Cape Girardeau, Mo.; no lithophane on base; bottom: Wheelock Dresden, Made in Germany for E. Osterloh. $20.00 – 40.00.

Decorative Features

In addition to the most common color of black used to print engravings shown on white-based porcelain, other colors, including green, sepia, blue, and red, were also used. Green is much less common than black, but it is the second most common color. Sepia is not as common, blue is rare, and red is extremely rare.

(L) cup and saucer by Benjamin F. Hunt & Sons, showing two scenes, Bayville and Squirrel Island, Maine. Most blue engravings are found on BFHS items. $40.00 – 65.00. (R) 7" plate, green engraving of Orr's Island Bridge, Orr's Island, Maine. It bears a generic mark showing Made in Germany for Jennie Prince, Orr's Island, Me. $40.00 – 65.00.

Small ornate plate with sepia scene, Bass River Bridge in West Dennis, Mass. $40.00 – 65.00.

7½" plate with very rare red scene, M.E. Church, Thorn town, Ind. The plate was imported by Wheelock for a local merchant. Although church scenes are not generally among the most desirable scenes, this one has a special collectible feature in the color of its engraving. $40.00 – 65.00.

These three small dishes show some of the color tints used on porcelain souvenirs:
(L) Robin's egg blue.
(C) Rose.
(R) Canary.
All feature sharp and desirable black engravings. $50.00 – 75.00 each.

Earth-to-sky toning is the dominant decoration on these two items:
(L) cup and saucer with color scene, Burnt Island L.S.S., Port Clyde, Me. $100.00 – 150.00.
(R) creamer with large color scene, Main Street, Richmond, Me. $30.00 – 50.00.

Earth-to-sky or water-to-sky toning may also begin with just green at the bottom as on this creamer jug depicting New High School, Bangor, Me. $30.00 – 50.00.

Graduated coloring is a common decorative feature on souvenir china items. (L) Green tones deepen from bottom to top on this cup depicting Loon Island Light, Lake Sunapee, N. H. $40.00 – 65.00.
(R) Brown tones deepen from bottom to top on this creamer jug which also features shadow flowers in the design and a scene, Perry Transferring Flag, Put-in-Bay, Ohio. $50.00 – 75.00.

These items are representative of a large body of souvenir china which does not have the fineness highly prized by collectors. Such items are often heavily gilded (often only on one side) and feature scenes which were quickly colored in heavy brown tones and lack clarity. Common items and scenes have very little value while the more desirable scenes (such as those shown here) enjoy some favor, especially if the scenes are clear. Five items numbered from left to right:

(1) small urn or basket, Chief Keokuk, Keokuk, Iowa. $30.00 – 50.00.
(2) mug with heavy gold and scene, Atlantic House, Nantasket Beach, Mass. $20.00 – 40.00.
(3) large urn or basket with scene, Custom House & Post Office, Fall River, Mass. $20.00 – 40.00.
(4) vase with handles and scene, Independence Mine, Cripple Creek. Colo. $30.00 – 50.00. ·
(5) vase with heavy gold and handles depicting a sewing machine factory in Orange, Mass. $20.00 – 40.00.

Examples of embellished pink lustre souvenir china items which represented the Victorian appeal are shown on (R) mug with scene, Thunder Cave, Bailey's Island, Maine, $20.00 – 40.00; and a cup (with saucer), Lawrence High School, Falmouth, Mass. $40.00 – 65.00.

Some scenes were highlighted in gold which some find both attractive and distinctive; others believe it detracts from the realism of the scenes. This example is a view of Popham Light, Narragansett Bay. $40.00 – 65.00.

These three items show a common decoration of roses flanking the encircled engraving. The creamer on the left shows The Pier; Old Orchard Beach, Maine ; the open sugar bowl in the center features the Hotel Wentworth, Walpole, N. H. ; and the creamer on the right depicts Public Library, Derby, Conn. $40.00 – 65.00 each.

A simulated graniteware finish was used to decorate some souvenir china items, most of which bear a Jonroth mark. This dish is a good example; it features a scene from Long Point Light, Provincetown, Mass. $40.00 – 65.00.

Blue Delft style mug or cup with wrap-around scene, Highland Light, Cape Cod. The base of the particular cup features a lithophane scene, a girl holding a doll. $75.00 – 125.00.

German Delft style was used to decorate souvenir china, usually featuring an artistic rendering of the subject utilizing the same blue color throughout the decoration, as on this spoon dish featuring Eastern Point Light. $40.00 – 65.00.

Blue Delft style chamberstick depicting Old Mill, Nantucket 1746. $100.00 – 150.00.

Multi-scene decorating schemes such as these are found on plates, mugs, and tumblers in both color and black and white. The plate on the left shows scenes of St. Augustine, while the tumbler on the right shows scenes of Niagara Falls. $20.00 – 40.00 each.

This is the only known piece of Majolica souvenir china. The nicely decorated dish is approximately 3½" in diameter and features a scene, Public School, Westhope, N. D. $150.00+. *(Collection of Ron Rainka)*

Old Ivory souvenir china items are extremely rare. This 7¾" diameter plate was produced around the turn of the century in the style of Herman Ohme, by another producer. The scene is The Mount Washington, a hotel of renown in Bretton Woods, N.H.

Bottom mark on the Old Ivory plate may have belonged to K. Steinmann of Tiefenfurth. $75.00 – 125.00.

Figural Items

Shown here are three views of an extremely rare and life-like 6½" long fish with a color scene, Royal Palm Hotel, Miami, Florida; circle mark, Made in Germany. $150.00+.

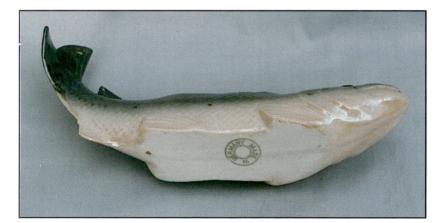

A wild boar may be the king of all piggy banks. This rare item is 4¾" long, tinted in life-like tones, and features a sharp black engraving, Knox County Court House, Rockland, Maine; bottom is unmarked. $75.00 – 125.00.

Two piggy banks show different decorating styles:
(L) simple black on white scene, Pier, Old Orchard Beach, Maine. $65.00 – 100.00.
(R) Pig with gold ears features color scene, Faneuil Hall, Boston. $65.00 – 100.00. (Collection of Ron Rainka)

Pigs and bears are found in figure groups in many situations. Pigs were considered good luck, while bears were especially popular during the time of Teddy Roosevelt (Teddy Bear). Teddy Bear figures are frequently mistaken for pigs. There is little doubt about this bear, which appears to be searching for honey in an inkwell tree stump. The scene is Grant's Old Home, Galena, Ill. $65.00 – 100.00.

This life-like bear is emerging from a small dish with a color scene, The Old Centre Church, Church Green, New Haven, Conn. $50.00 – 75.00. (Collection of Ron Rainka)

Souvenir china items can be found with either bears or pigs in cars, in hammocks, in boats, or in many other situations, alone or in pairs. These teddy twins are hanging out in front of a gazebo with a scene, Willows and Poplars, Lake Merritt, Oakland, Calif. $75.00 – 125.00. (Collection of Jan and Dick Vogel)

This is a pig smoking a pipe and feature a bird's-eye view of Beloit, Wis. $40.00 – 65.00.

Teddy bears smoked too! This cute white bear smokes a pipe as big as himself on a small dish with a scene, Portland, Me. $65.00 – 100.00. (Collection of Ron Rainka)

The following two pictures show the interchangeability
of bears and pigs on novelty souvenirs.

*Piggy bank shows front and back of the pig extend-
ing from the bank which features a scene, Stephenson County Court House, Freeport, Ill. $65.00 –
100.00.* (Collection of Ron Rainka)

*Teddy bank shows a front and back of a teddy
bear extending from a similar bank with a scene,
Opera House, Baker City, Ore. $65.00 – 100.00.*
(Collection of Ron Rainka)

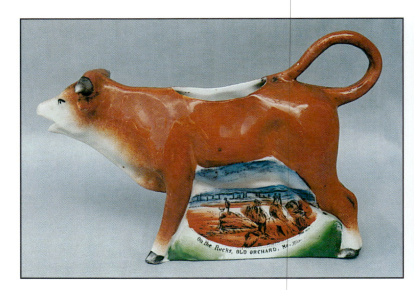

*Other animals are far less common on novelty
figure group souvenirs. This one features a
kangaroo peeking from a well with a scene,
Excursion Steamer Christopher Columbus.
$100.00 – 150.00.* (Collection of Ron Rainka)

*A rare large cow straddles a scene On the Rocks, Old Orchard,
Me. $150.00+.* (Collection of Ron Rainka)

A Dutch girl done in the style of Conta & Boehme shows off a scene, Hampton Beach, N.H. $150.00+. (Collection of Ron Rainka)
This is the only human figural souvenir china item known to the author.

A gold teddy bear listens to a Victorola on a small dish with a scene, New Armory, Adams, Mass. $75.00 – 125.00. (Collection of Ron Rainka)

Toothpick holders in the form of a hat were relatively common; shown here is the common form with nice coloration and a well-executed scene, The Old Mill and Mill Pond, Yarmouth, Me. $50.00 – 75.00.

Another hat found in both color and black and white is this chauffeur's cap (interior view) with a simulated patent leather brim and color scene, The Samoset, Bay Point, Rockland, Me. $50.00 – 75.00.

A pair of blue tinted watering cans: (L) miniature watering can with scene, Pilgrim House, Provincetown, Mass. $65.00 – 100.00.
(R) 2½" h. example with scene, The Grossmon House, Thousand Islands. $50.00 – 75.00.

Heavily gilded, open spout watering can with scene, Grammar School, South Bend, Ind. $30.00 – 50.00.

4½" h. ornate watering can with figural sea serpent spout, complex decoration, and scene, High School Building, Clay Center, Kans.; Humes China mark. $75.00 – 125.00. *(Collection of Jan and Dick Vogel)*

Open shoes were perhaps used to hold buttons, matches, etc.
These are two distinctive examples:

A delicate thin china baby's shoe or bootie with a sharp engraving, Court House, Ellesworth, Me. $50.00 – 75.00.

A small simulation of a Dutch wooden shoe depicts a color scene, The Flume in the White Mountains of New Hampshire. $40.00 – 65.00.

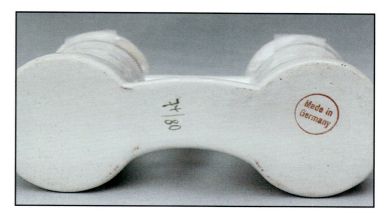

A pair of binoculars houses a set of salt and pepper shakers and shows two scenes, Home of Joseph C. Lincoln, Chatham, Mass. and Chatham Bars Inn, Chatham, Mass. $100.00 – 150.00.

The bottom mark is also shown.

Two rare figural still banks approximately 3" h. include:
(L) U.S. Mail Box with scene, Four Pines, Bellows Falls, Vt. $75.00 – 125.00.
(R) Whiskey or beer barrel with scene, State Normal School, Cortland, N.Y. $75.00 – 125.00. (Both items have Wheelock red circle logos with complete information on their bases.)

113

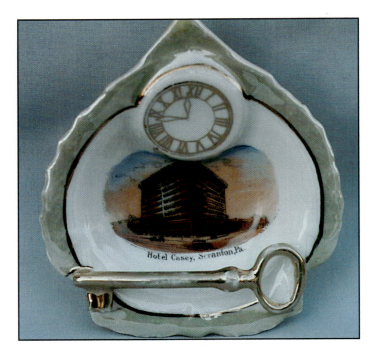

Pipe dishes and Clock & Key dishes are relatively common with quick-color scenes such as this Clock & Key dish with a view of Hotel Casey, Scranton, Pa. $20.00 – 40.00.

This horseshoe dish features a very early scene, horse-drawn trolleys on Broadway, New York. There is no bottom mark; this fact and the scene suggest that it was made before 1891. $40.00 – 65.00.

This interesting Good Luck vase has a horseshoe on its front and a four-leaf clover on its back (not shown). It features a wonderful color scene, P.E. Snyder Hardware Store, Blanchester, Ohio, showing a carriage in the window. Not surprisingly, the bottom indicates it was Made in Germany for P.E. Snyder. $50.00 – 75.00.

Bottom of the shell.

Shells were skillfully copied as porcelain souvenir china. This one, which is 5" wide, depicts Old Stone Mill, Newport, R.I. Notice that the feet are simulated snail shells. $30.00 – 50.00.

Bottom of the shell.

A smaller scallop shell, 4" wide, depicts Life Saving Station, Newport, R.I.; bottom: red round mark, Made in Germany and a logo, E.P. Allan, Newport, R.I. $50.00 – 75.00.

Very realistic and detailed 4" high conch shell vase with black engraving, Bay View Cottage, First at Onset; bottom: Carlsbad, C.H. Macy, Onset, Mass., Made in Austria. $100.00 – 150.00.

This salt shaker is an excellent simulation of a mushroom or toadstool; it depicts Longfellow's House, Portland, Me. $20.00 – 40.00.

This peculiar artist's tripod easel has an Oriental flair and a rear leg which also serves as a bud vase; some features of its design are not easily explained. The color scene is Gore Canyon, from Kremmling, Colo. $75.00 – 125.00.

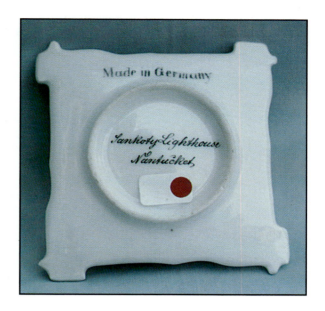

This rare and unusual form is a 3" square pin dish with four oars forming its border and an embossed rope forming the border of a hand-colored picture of a Sankoty Lighthouse named on its reverse in a form of calligraphy seldom found on souvenir china. $150.00+.

Bottom of dish.

6" long porcelain form of a dress shirt collar with black engraving, Opera House, Norway, Maine; manufactured in Austria for a local merchant. $40.00 – 65.00.

A very rare and ornate figural wheelbarrow depicts Palace of Liberal Arts, St. Louis Exposition 1906. The mark on the bottom is Victoria Austria. $150.00+. (Collection of Ron Rainka)

3" h. cow bell (with porcelain ringer), color scene, Congregational Church, Limerick, Maine. $40.00 – 65.00.

One of the most rare and unusual of known figural items is this wonderfully decorated purse (approximately 3" long) which features a view of Mt. Tom Summit House, Holyoke, Mass. $150.00+. (Collection of Ron Rainka)

Figural log, approximately 3¼" l. shows color scene, Mill Pond, McCloud, Calif. $50.00 – 75.00. (Collection of Ron Rainka)

Rare porcelain pipe with color scene, Lowell Textile School on the front and a poem on the subject of smoking along with the school seal on the reverse. This is shown along with figural items, but was probably intended for actual use. $150.00+.

Detail of pipe.

COLOR-GLAZED ITEMS

Cobalt Blue

Advertisement from The Rumford Falls Spray, *dated November 1903, testifies to the popularity of "Cobalt Blue German China" being sold in that year at 25 cents per piece.*

Some of the many common shapes and forms produced in cobalt blue. With average scenes, these items would be worth $20.00 – 40.00; on items such as these, the scene is the most important factor in determining value. The 2" high creamer in the center and the oval toothpick holder in front depict different views of the Southeast Light on Block Island and are valued at $50.00 – 75.00 because of the high demand for those scenes.

Salt and pepper shakers, cobalt blue, 3" h., (L) End of Cape Cod, Provincetown, Mass.; black circle mark, Made in Germany. $40.00 – 65.00; (R) Wood End Light, Provincetown, Mass., black circle mark, Made in Germany. $40.00 – 65.00.

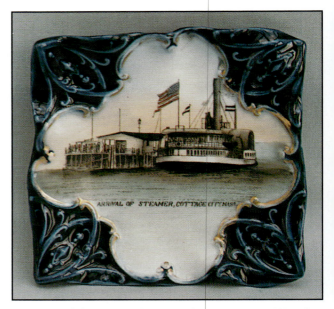

Arrival of Steamer, Cottage City, Mass. – Wonderfully detailed and toned color picture shows an early steamer arriving at a pier on Martha's Vineyard. The item is an unusual, highly embossed, square cobalt blue pin tray. $150.00+.

Group of basketweave dishes in cobalt blue: (TL) six-pointed star-shaped dish 3" diameter, Old Mill, Orleans, Mass., Wheelock, Dresden Germany for J.H. Cummings, $40.00 – 65.00; (CL) rectangular dish 2½" x 3" Oonuehkoi Bridge, Atlantic Highlands, NJ, Wheelock, Made in Germany for Roberts & White, $30.00 – 50.00; (BL) heart-shaped dish St. John's Church Portsmouth, N.H. Wheelock Dresden Germany, $30 – 50.00; (TR) round dish 4¾" diameter, Old Brick School House, Wolfboro, N.H. Made in Germany for G.H. Mason, $40.00 – 65.00; (BR) star-shaped dish 4" diameter, Bandstand, Ocean Park, Cottage City, Mass., Wheelock Dresden Germany, $65.00 – 100.00.

(L) Square covered box, cobalt blue, 2½" (square), Court House, Pittsfield, Mass., Made in Germany for England Bros., $40.00 – 65.00; (R) heart-shaped covered box, cobalt blue, 3" long, Memorial Hall, Laconia, N.H. Made in Germany, $40.00 – 65.00.

Three compartment condiment server with lid and spoon, cobalt blue, 3½" long, State House, Albany, NY, marked GERMANY. $40.00 – 65.00.

Large dinner plate, cobalt blue and gold rim, approx. 10" diameter, five scenes from picturesque Avalon, Catalina Island, Calif., marked Wheelock, Made in Germany. $40.00 – 65.00.

121

Chamberstick with snuffer, cobalt blue, 2" high and 5" diameter, Oldest House in Town, Chatham, Mass. Made in Germany for L. Sidney Atwood. $100.00 – 150.00.

Pair of candle holders, cobalt blue, 3¼" h. (L) Seal of Yale University; (R) Osborn Hall, Yale University, New Haven, Conn., Wheelock Made in Germany for Edward Malley Co. $30.00 – 50.00 each.

(L) Ink well with cover, cobalt blue, 4" long, Owl's Head Rock & Light, Owl's Head, Me., Made in Germany, $50.00 – 75.00;
(C) lady's spittoon, cobalt blue, 2¾" h., Maplewood Hotel, Bethlehem, N.H., black circle mark, Made in Germany, $40.00 – 65.00;
(R) inkwell with horseshoe front dish cobalt blue, 4" long, Wm. E. Auer's Steeplechase Camp, Ware Ave., Rockaway Beach L.I., marked GERMANY, $50.00 – 75.00.

(L) Open sugar bowl with handles, cobalt blue (with heavy gilding), 2¾" h. Heron Neck Light House, Vinal Haven, Me., Made in Germany for Bodwell Granite Co. $50.00 – 75.00;
(R) creamer, cobalt blue, 3½" h., Quoddy Hotel, Eastport, Me., Made in Germany for W. S. Mildon. $40.00 – 65.00.

(L) Creamer or individual tea pot, with two-finger handle, cobalt blue, 3¼" h., Union Station, Bangor, Me., Made in Germany. $30.00 – 50.00;
(C) creamer or small pitcher, cobalt blue, 4¼" h., Nubble Light and Ferry, York, Maine, Made in Germany, $30.00 – 50.00;
(R) round jug with round flanged top, cobalt blue, 4" h., State Bath House, Revere Beach, Mass., Made in Germany, $30 – 50.00.

(L) Creamer, cobalt blue, 4" h., Forster's Old Grist Mill, Manchester, Mass., Made in Germany for H. G. Nichols, $30.00 – 50.00; (R) creamer, cobalt blue, 4¾" h., Hotel Nantasket, Nantasket Beach, Mass., Made in Germany, $40.00 – 65.00.

(L) Creamer, cobalt blue, 3¾" h. Post Office, Manchester, N.H., Made in Germany for F. E. Nelson, $30.00 – 50.00.
(C) squat creamer or sauce pitcher (left-handed), cobalt blue, 2¾" h., East Main Street, Ayer, Mass., Made in Germany, $30.00 – 50.00.
(R) creamer, cobalt blue, 3¼" h., souvenir from Prince Edward Island (shape was used also for U. S. market), unmarked, $30.00 – 50.00.

(L) Eight-sided (paneled) creamer or pitcher, cobalt blue, 4" h. Land's End, Newport, R.I., marked GERMANY, $40.00 – 65.00;
(R) creamer, cobalt blue, 3½" h. Sankaty Light House, Nantucket, Mass., Built 1850, marked GERMANY, $75.00 – 125.00.

(L) Creamer or small rectangular pitcher, cobalt blue, 4½" h. Sperry Light, New Haven, Conn., marked GERMANY. $65.00 – 100.00; (R) creamer, cobalt blue, 3" h. Steamer Gay Head, Made in Germany, $50.00 – 75.00.

Shaving mug, barber shop style, cobalt blue, 3½" h. Surf Avenue, Coney Island, N.Y., Made in Germany for Henry Brumi & Co. $150.00+.

(L) Ink well (no top), cobalt blue, 2⅜" h. Col. Godfrey Mill, Built 1798, (Chatham, Mass.) Made in Germany for L. Sidney Atwood, $50.00 – 75.00; (R) toothpick holder, cobalt blue, 2½" h. Sandy Hook Light, Sandy Hook, N.J., Wheelock, Made in Germany for Roberts & White, $40.00 – 65.00.

(L) Creamer or ewer, cobalt blue, 3½" h. White Rocks, Hampton Beach, N.H., Made in Germany, $30 – 50.00;
(R) creamer or ewer, cobalt blue, 3½" h. High School, Fall River, Mass., Made in Germany, $30.00 – 50.00.

(L) Footed cup or mug, cobalt blue, 2½" h. Old Chapel Near Berryville, Va., Made in Germany for Coyner & Coiner, $20.00 – 40.00.
(C) highly embossed cup and saucer, cobalt blue, 3¾" h. Congregational Church Wellfleet, Mass., unmarked, $65.00 – 100.00.
(R) cup or mug, cobalt blue, 2¼" h. Court House, Brockton, Mass., Made in Germany, $20.00 – 40.00.

(L) *Individual tea pot, cobalt blue, Ericsson Pier and Steamer, Betterton, Md., Made in Germany. $50.00 – 75.00;*
(R) *tea pot, cobalt blue, State Capitol, Hartford, Conn., Made in Germany. $50.00 – 75.00.*

(L) *Tumbler or Beaker, cobalt blue, 3¾" h. The Tabernacle, Cottage City, Mass., Wheelock, Dresden, Germany. $65.00 – 100.00;*
(R) *flared top tumbler or beaker cobalt blue, 4" h. Gloucester Fishing Schooner, Gloucester, Mass., marked GERMANY. $50.00 – 75.00.*

Open sugar or urn, cobalt blue, 3½" h. Public Library, Littleton, N.H. Made in Germany for E. E. Eldridge & Co. $40.00 – 65.00.

(L) Ewer, cobalt blue, 4¾" h. Underground View of Little Boss Mine, Joplin, Mo., Wheelock Dresden, Made for Cooper Drug Co., rare form, rare and unusual scene, $150.00+;
(R) ewer, cobalt blue, 4¾" h. Yampah Springs and Bath House, Glenwood Springs, Colo., Wheelock, Dresden, Germany. $50.00 – 75.00.

Revere bowl, cobalt blue, 4" diameter, Paul Revere Bell, Wiscasset, Maine, Made in Germany for Sol. Holbrook. $40.00 – 65.00.

Covered dresser or pin box, cobalt blue, 3" diameter, Spectators' Boxes Luna Park, Coney Island, black circle mark, Made in Germany. $100.00 – 150.00.

Tall toothpick holder, cobalt blue, 3½" h. Oliver Typewriter Factory, Woodstock, Ill., red circle mark, Made in Germany. $40.00 – 65.00.

Three handle loving cup, cobalt blue, 3½" h. Meet Me on Cape Cod, black circle mark, Made in Germany. $50.00 – 75.00.

Egg cup, cobalt blue, 2½" h., Old Orchard Beach and Pier, Old Orchard Beach, Me., red circle mark, Made in Germany. $75.00 – 125.00.
(Collection of Dr. Burton Spiller)

Wall pocket match safe, cobalt blue, 5½" h. The Balsams, Dixville Notch, N.H., red circle mark, Made in Germany for A.F. Whittemore & Co., Colebrook, N.H. $75.00 – 125.00.

Hat pin holder and integral tray, mixed cobalt blue and white base china, 4¾" h. New Nautical Gardens, State Boulevard, Revere Beach, Mass. $75.00 – 125.00.
(Collection of Ron Rainka)

Mugs with lithophane bottoms:
(L) Cobalt blue with gilding, 2¾" h. Sankaty Light, Nantucket, Mass. $150.00+.
(R) Cobalt blue with gilding, 3" h. City Hall, Manchester, N.H. $75.00 – 125.00.

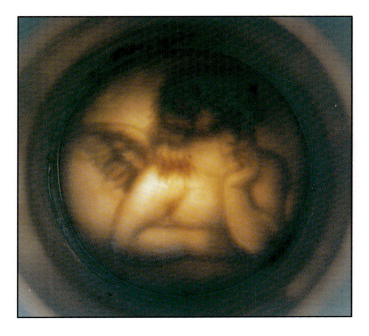

Lithophane bottom on mug at left in photo above. Cherubic angel.

Lithophane bottom on mug at right in photo above. Children embracing.

Emerald Green Souvenir Items

Creamer, 2¾" h. Stone Alley and Old South Tower Erected 1810 (Nantucket), marked GERMANY. $75.00 - 125.00.

Mini scuttle-style shaving mug, 2⅜" h. Boulevard, Revere Beach, Mass., Made in Germany for R.W. Austin, $65.00 – 100.00; mini ewer, 3" h. Marconi Wireless Station, Wellfleet, Mass., Wheelock Dresden Germany, $40.00 – 65.00; wall pocket (probably used for matches), 2½" h. Episcopal Church Hyannisport, Mass., Made in Germany for M.G. Bradford, $50.00 – 75.00.

Star-shaped basketweave dish , 3" across, Pluto Springs, French Lick, Ind., Wheelock Made in Germany for Smith & Glaxton General Merchants, French Lick, Ind., $65.00 – 100.00. (Collection of Dr. Burton Spiller)

Turquoise-Glazed Souvenir Items

Urn style vase with handles, dark turquoise, 3¼" high. The Cascade, Ogden Canyon, Utah, black circle mark Made in Germany. $40.00 – 65.00

Mini spittoon or vase with two handles, brown, 2' high. Hotel Nantasket, Nantasket Beach, Mass., black circle mark, Made in Germany, $40.00 – 65.00; match holder with striker and used match dish 1⅝" h. Boulevard, Revere Beach, Mass., Made in Germany Expressly for R.W. Austin. $40.00 – 65.00.

Lady's spittoon, brown, 2¾" h. The Beach, Revere Beach, Mass., Made in Germany Expressly for R. W. Austin. $40.00 – 65.00.

Maroon-Glazed Souvenir Items

Oval two-handled toothpick holder and mini mug, each approximately 2" h. Hotel Wendell, Pittsfield, Mass. $40.00 – 65.00 each.

Variety of Color-Glazed Figural Items

Fish toothpick holder, cobalt blue, 1¾" h. The Museum of Fine Arts, Boston, Mass., Made in Germany for H.G. Woolworth Boston, Mass. $75.00 – 125.00 (chip on bottom tail fin, would be $150.00+ if perfect).

Dove dish, cobalt blue, 4" long, M. E. Church, Colebrook, N.H., Made in Germany for Mrs. M. E. Stevens, very rare and unusual. $150.00+.

Figural fish with holder compartment behind fin, emerald green, 6¼" long, (also known to exist in cobalt blue), Universalist Church and Parsonage, Marion, Mass. Made in Germany for F. S. Cogeshall. $150.00+.

Flounder or sand dab dish, cobalt blue, 4" long, Sankaty Light, Nantucket, Mass., unmarked, $100.00 – 150.00.

(TL) Small right-facing swan toothpick holder, cobalt blue, 2¾" h. Old Stone Mill, Newport, R.I., $75.00 – 125.00;
(TR) small left-facing swan toothpick holder, cobalt blue, 2¾" h. Boothbay Harbor, Maine, $75.00 – 125.00;
(BL) large right-facing swan toothpick holder, cobalt blue, 4¼" h. Skating Rink & Post Office, Salisbury Beach, Mass. $75.00 –125.00;
(BR) large left-facing swan toothpick holder, cobalt blue, 4¼" h. Revere Beach & Boulevard from Nautical Gardens, $75.00 – 125.00 (Note: all have black circle marks, Made in Germany).

Musical lyre vase, cobalt blue, approx. 7" h. Rainbow Lake, Shenandoah Caverns, Va., $150.00+. (Collection of R. Rainka)

Dust pan, cobalt blue, 1", The Grand Ocean, Murray's Seaside, Rockaway Beach; Wainwright & Smith Co., marked GERMANY. $30.00 – 50.00. (Note: that small nick on lower right corner reduces value, which would be $65.00 – 100.00 if perfect).

Dust pan and sweeper, cobalt blue, 5" long and 4¾" h. Cold Spring House and Cottages, Averill, Vermont, Made in Germany for C.M. Quimby, West Stewartstown, N.H., $75.00 – 125.00. (Collection of R. Rainka)

133

Three forms of footwear (many shapes and sizes were produced):
(L) cobalt blue, 5½" long, 3¾" h. State Capitol, Albany, N.Y., marked GERMANY $40.00 – 65.00;
(C) cobalt blue, 4" h. Salisbury Beach Before the Fire, Made in Germany for A.F. Lewis, $40.00 – 65.00;
(R) cobalt blue, 4" long, Str. Kennebec Leaving Richmond, Maine, Made in Germany for Herbert Mansir, Richmond, Maine. $40.00 – 65.00.

Fancy slipper, cobalt blue, 6½" long, Public Library, Littleton, N.H., Made in Germany for E. E. Eldridge. $50.00 – 75.00.

High-top shoe, open laces, cobalt blue, 4" long, 3½" h. Far Rockaway Beach; unmarked. $50.00 – $75.00.

134

High-top shoe-shaped shallow dish, cobalt blue, 4½″ long, Soldier's and Sailor's Monument, Indianapolis, marked GERMANY. $30.00 – 50.00.

Dutch style shoe, cobalt blue, 4¼″ long, Spectators' Boxes Luna Park, Coney Island, Made in Germany. $65.00 – 100.00.

Dutch style shoe, cobalt blue, 4″ long, Birdseye View of Nantasket Beach, Mass., Made in Germany. $40.00 – 65.00.

Horseshoe dish, cobalt blue and gold, 4¾″ long, Box Canon, Rifle, Colo., Made in Germany for Peerless Jewelry Co. $40.00 – 65.00.

135

Submarine, cobalt blue, 4½" long. A Holiday Crowd at Revere Beach, Mass.; black circle mark, Made in Germany. $150.00+.

Open touring cars:
(L) cobalt blue, $100.00 – 150.00.
(C) brown, Statue of Liberty, $150.00+.
(R) turquoise. $150.00+. All have circle marks, Made in Germany. (Collection of R. Rainka)

(T) Wheelbarrow holder or dish cobalt blue, 1½" high x 4½" long, Museum of Fine Arts, Boston, Mass., Made in Germany for H.G. Woolworth, $75.00 – 125.00;
(BL) fan, cobalt blue, 5" long, Witch House, Salem, Mass., Made in Germany for Almy, Bigelow, and Washburn, Inc., $65.00 – 100.00;
(BR) tambourine, cobalt blue, 2¾" diameter, White Lake, N.Y., Millar China, Made in Germany for John Knight. $75.00 – 125.00.

(T) Row boat, cobalt blue, 4"
long, Chateaugay, N.Y., Made in
Germany for Geo. S. Franklin.
$150.00+;
(B) one-man scull, cobalt blue,
4¼" long, The Thriller, Rockaway
Beach, N.Y., marked GERMANY,
$100.00 – 150.00.

Ship's wheel dish, cobalt blue, 4" diameter, Summit
House, Mt. Tom, Holyoke, Mass., Jonroth, Made in
Germany for Holyoke Street Railway. $65.00 –
100.00.

Ornate watering can, one of the many different
watering cans produced, cobalt blue, 4¼" h.
The Tivoli, Oak Bluffs Mass., unmarked.
$75.00 – 125.00.

Dice dish, cobalt blue, 3" cube, View of Dreamland, Coney Island, N.Y., Made in Germany for Henry Broml & Co., Coney Island, N.Y. $100.00 – 150.00. *(Collection of Dr. Burton Spiller)*

Watering can with cover, cobalt blue, 4½" h. State Capitol, Albany, N.Y., Made in Germany for Abram De Blacy. $40.00 – 65.00.

(L) Canoe, cobalt blue, 4" long, Colonial Theater and Casino, Onset, Mass., black circle mark Made in Germany, $50.00 – 75.00;
(R) Canoe, brown, 5" long, Atlantic House and the Beach, Nantasket, Mass., black circle mark Made in Germany. $50.00 – 75.00.

(L) Open sugar bowl and (R) creamer with figural sea horse handle, cobalt blue, Whale's Back Light, Portsmouth, N.H., Wheelock, Dresden, Germany. Sugar $30.00 – 50.00, Creamer $50.00 – 75.00.

Seashell dish, cobalt blue, 4½" long, Seward Park, Auburn, N.Y., Jonroth, Made in Germany for Koon Bros. $40.00 – 65.00.

Cow bell with porcelain ringer, cobalt blue, 4" h. Stone Alley and Old South Tower, Erected 1810, unmarked. $125.00 – 175.00.

Top hat toothpick holder, Turquoise, 2" h. A Warm Day at Revere Beach, Mass. Made in Germany. $40.00 – 65.00.

Artist's easel and painted picture, cobalt blue, 6¼" h. bird's-eye view of Roscoe, N.Y., unmarked. $100.00 – 150.00.

Two of the more common examples of figural buckets: (L) Sap bucket, cobalt blue, 2½" high. Boothbay Harbor, Me., black circle mark, Made in Germany, $30.00 – 50.00;
(R) water bucket, cobalt blue, 2½" high. Union Station, Providence, R.I., black circle mark, Made in Germany. $30.00 – 50.00

139

CHAPTER THREE
SOUVENIR CHINA VIEWS

Merchants selected views to be depicted on souvenir china strictly according to market demand. A seemingly endless variety of features or points of interest in local communities appealed to both travelers and residents. In order to present the scope of those views in a meaningful way, they are categorized in this section. A few items which might fall into more than one of the categories have been assigned to the logically dominant classification. Most of the views selected are above average in quality. Scenes are valued by factors of supply and demand which become apparent over time; scarce scenes from desirable locations will undoubtedly continue to become increasingly valuable, In presenting the following items, no effort has been made to fully describe the items since the focus is on the elements and subject matter of the scenes.

OCCUPATIONAL AND INDUSTRIAL VIEWS

The era of German souvenir china coincided with an emergence of inventions and new industries in the United States, spawning abundant pride and fascination and captured in the medium of souvenir china. It is not surprising that many of the most unusual and desirable items present an aspect of that age, depicting a trade or factory now obsolete and relegated to history.

Milk Cart, New Orleans, La. – Outstanding picture of horse and two-wheel milk cart with milk man pouring milk and French Quarter architecture behind. Appealing graphics on Wheelock "spade" creamer. $150.00.

Making Lobster Traps, Marblehead, Mass. – Excellent black engraving of man and woman making net ends for lobster traps with shanties and rocky coast in background. On two-scene creamer or small pitcher. $65.00 – 100.00.

140

Gloucester Shore Fisherman – Large and colorful picture of a fisherman surrounded by typical gear of a shore fisherman. Appealing graphics on a folded edge dish. $75.00 – 125.00.

Sponge Diver, Tarpon Springs, Fla. – Color scene of man in early diving suit with sponges. On opalized yellow vase. $150.00+.

Hawaiian Fisherman – Color scene of native working in simplified fishing occupation. On rose tinted cake plate. $150.00+. *(Collection of D. Manesellian, photo by John Walker)*

Ice Industry on the Kennebec River, Gardiner, Me. – Excellent black engraving of large ice house with cutting and hauling crew in foreground along frozen river. On lunch plate. $50.00 – 75.00.

Souvenir Chaseburg Co-Operative Creamery – Color scene shows milk wagons outside creamery buildings in Chaseburg, Wisconsin. On fancy fan-shaped dish. $40.00 – 65.00.

Irrigation Ditch, Portales, N.M. – Color scene of two men working along an irrigation ditch. On creamer. $40.00 – 65.00.

Irrigating Canal, Bakersfield, Calif. – Color scene on cup and Bakersfield Oil Wells – Color scene on matching saucer. Set imported by Wheelock. $50.00 – 75.00.

Rice Harvesting, Beaumont, Texas – Wrap-around color scene (shown in two pictures) of several men, horses, and a machine in the process of harvesting and bagging rice. Appealing graphics on Wheelock "spade" creamer. $100.00 – 150.00.

Cape Cod Cranberry Picking – Sepia engraving of men and women working in a cranberry bog. On hot plate. $100.00 – 150.00.

Big Log, Arlington, Washington – Highly detailed black engraving of two loggers showing the enormous girth of a tree they have felled, as children in period dress stand nearby. On small plate. $50.00 – 75.00.

Sugar Factory, Garden City, Kansas – Full color scene of sugar beet factory with what appears to be freshly laid railroad track in foreground. On coupe plate. $65.00 – 100.00.

Oliver Typewriter Factory, Woodstock, Ill. – Color scene shows factory buildings with active smokestacks. On tall cobalt blue toothpick holder. $40.00 – 65.00.

Dolan & Darnal Coal Mine, North McAlester, Indian Territories – Color scene of elevated railway system and building with two functioning smokestacks. On toothpick holder. $75.00 – 125.00. (Collection of Bernie and Susan Zwolinski)

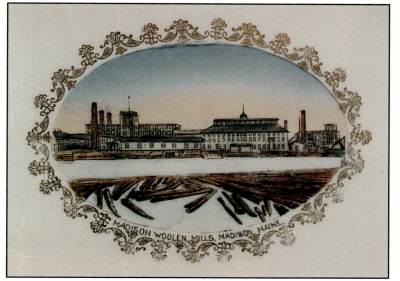

Madison Woolen Mills, Madison, Maine – Color scene of large woolen mill complex with logs in the river in foreground. On decorated plate. $50.00 – 75.00.

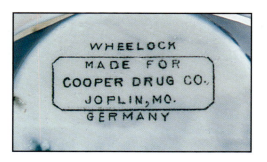

Mark on bottom of blue ewer.

Underground View, Little Boss Mine, Joplin, Mo. – Rare, unusual, and colorful scene of miners at work underground in lead or zinc mine. Appealing graphics on 4" high cobalt blue ewer; Wheelock, Germany, Made for Cooper Drug Co., Joplin, Mo. $150.00+.

Interior View Salt Works, Hutchinson, Kansas – Color view of men working on salt pile. On shell and bow dish; marked Wheelock, Made in Germany for The Fair Department Store. $75.00 – 125.00. (Collection of D. Manasellian, photo by John Walker)

Kennedy Mine, Jackson, Calif. – Color scene of mine buildings. On top hat toothpick holder. $100.00 – 150.00. (Collection of D. Manasellian, photo by John Walker)

Gold Mining Near Oroville, Calif. – Rare and unusual (somewhat faded) black engraving of man using a sluice to process gold pannings. On scalloped and embossed pin tray with Wheelock Imperial Austria Eagle mark, Made for Harry and Jacoby, Jeweler, Oroville, Calif. $150.00+. (Collection of D. Manesellian, photo by John Walker)

PUBLIC BUILDINGS AND CHURCHES

Civic pride was alive and well during the end of the nineteenth century and the beginning of the twentieth century. There was no big government, and people knew where the money came from to build public buildings — sacrifice and hard work or the benevolence of a successful citizen (as in the establishment of many free libraries which took on the names of their benefactors). The views on souvenir china depicted buildings of various types and with a variety of functions including schools, municipal buildings armories, custom houses, libraries, museums, churches, orphanages, and even prisons. Many of those buildings are gone now or have been adapted to other uses, but their images were captured for posterity on souvenir china. Pride and history continue to motivate collectors of these mementos.

State Capitol, Madison, Wis. – Color scene of State Capitol building, on pierced border plate. Wheelock produced a well-known set of postcards depicting State Capitol buildings for each of the states, and souvenir china featuring views of State Capitol buildings are relatively common. Under $20.00.

Perhaps the most common and certainly one of the most interesting of buildings shown on souvenir china was the local school building. The selection of that building indicates a sense of civic pride in an era when primary education was becoming increasingly important. Local school buildings are excellent expressions of the period's architecture, and this category provides good insight into the scope of souvenir china made for cities and towns across the country; therefore, several examples have been selected to show the variety of styles and features:

High School, Bellows Falls, Vt. – Black engraving of school building with two students sitting on wall in front of building. On Wheelock "Signature" creamer. $40.00 – 65.00.

School House & Pupils, Searsmont, Me. – Typical rural one-room school house with large contingent of students shown in sharp black engraving on small plate. $65.00 – 100.00.

High School, Franklin, Nebr. – Black engraving of prairie school building, ca. 1907. On small plate. $20.00 – 40.00.

High School, Frankfort, Kansas – Colorful and crisply executed picture of early school building. On attractively decorated dish featuring embossed flowers. $40.00 – 65.00.

High School, Wausau, Wisc. – Nicely detailed black engraving of an interesting school building with newly planted trees lining side walk, sharp engraving on shell-shaped dish. $20.00 – 40.00.

New School Building, Lansford, N.D. – Photo engraving transfer picture of two-story schoolhouse with children in front. On decorated pouring saucer, marked Burley & Tyrell, Chicago. $20.00 – 40.00.

Public School, Sheyenne, N.D. – Wonderfully toned picture of an early schoolhouse in a very small town graces a unique and attractively decorated creamer. The absence of a bottom mark suggests the item predates 1891. $65.00 – 100.00.

Public School, Latham, Ill. – Color picture, in nice tones, showing clapboard schoolhouse with American flag flying. Appealing graphics on small plate. $30.00 – 50.00.

High School, Pryor Creek, I.T. – Nicely toned color picture of simple school building in the Indian Territories. On dish with embossed floral decoration. $75.00 – 125.00.

149

Central School, Bisbee, Ariz. – Color scene of old school building. On highly decorated plate (a desirable town and state). $65.00 – 100.00.

Putnam High School, Newburyport, Mass. – Detailed engraving of school building and trees. On small plate with embossed and tinted border. $40.00 – 65.00.

High School, Marlboro, Mass. – Highly detailed black engraving shows a typical turn-of-the-century school building. This engraving is on an interesting pin tray. $40.00 – 65.00.

In addition to local schools, Town Halls were also frequently selected by merchants as scenes to be shown on souvenir china; two examples are shown below:

Town Hall, Great Barrington, Mass. – black engraving of Town Hall with cannon on lawn and large shade tree. On rose-tinted mug. $40.00 – 65.00.

Village Hall, Rio, Wisc. – Colorful scene shows a village hall which probably served as fire station and police station (note the bell tower and stalls) in a town of only 500 citizens; this butter chip was probably produced when the building was built in 1904 (as dated). $40.00 – 65.00.

Libraries were also a source of local pride and they were well represented on souvenir china. Exterior views are common, while interior views are rare.

Public Library, Perry, Okla. – Full color scene shows old library building with early sedan outside. On coupe plate. $40.00 – 65.00.

The Library, Warren, Mass. — Color scene on creamer shows typical small town library with Victorian features. $40.00 – 65.00.

Pillsbury Free Library — Highly detailed black engraving of elegant library interior in a small New Hampshire town, with gas light chandelier, work table and highback chairs. On two section pin tray. $50.00 – 75.00.

Another building frequently represented is the court house; the following examples show the scope covered in this category.

Reading Room, Town Library, Walpole, N.H. — Highly detailed color scene of a family using the Reading Room, showing many interesting details. Appealing graphics on folded edge dish. $100.00 – 150.00.

Court House, Ossipee, N.H. — Color scene, with beautiful color tones, showing a rural Court House. Appealing graphics on Wheelock's "signature" creamer with blue tinting at top. $75.00 – 100.00.

Bradford County Court House – Sepia photographic image of very typical county court house. On small plate. $30.00 – 50.00.

Decatur County Court House Tower, Greensburg, Ind. – Color picture of clock tower with famous trees growing on roof. On creamer. $40.00 – 65.00.

Other buildings covered a tremendous range of uses, including post offices, customs houses, hospitals, armories, prisons, orphanages, and even old people's homes.

Post Office & Custom House, Cairo, Ill. – Color picture of building complex on Wheelock "signature" creamer with tinting and gilding. $30.00 – 50.00.

Bottom mark of creamer on left.

153

Bottom mark of plate to left.

Washington County Hospital, Washington, Iowa – Color picture of four-story hospital building. On plate. $20.00 – 40.00.

Inside of the Prison Wall, Thomaston, Me. – Black engraving found in center of a plate with much embossing and gilding on rim. $30.00 – 50.00.

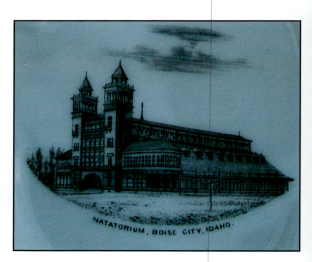

Iowa Hospital For The Insane, Independence, Iowa – Black engraving of large hospital complex. On small rectangular pin tray. $20.00 – 40.00.

Natatorium, Boise City, Idaho – Detailed black engraving shows impressive swimming pool building. On a fancy pin tray. $40.00 – 65.00.

154

Armory Co. I, Neenah, Wis. – Black engraving of Armory building with turrets. On small plate with scalloped, embossed blue-tinted border. $20.00 – 40.00.

The William Small Memorial Home for Aged Women, Leavenworth, Kansas – Color scene of interesting building with two wings, balconies and walkways. On nicely decorated plate. $30.00 – 50.00.

Corn Palace, Mitchell, S.D. – Color picture of famous landmark, dated 1900, with American flags flying from all eight sections. Building is made of corn, and the design was changed annually. On small plate. $30.00 – 50.00.

Y.M.C.A. Madison, N. J. – Color picture shows typical turn-of-the century brick recreational building. On a thin china pin dish. $20.00 – 40.00.

Churches were commonly depicted on souvenir china; some beautifully executed decorations have captured the way those buildings appeared.

Presbyterian Church & Parsonage, Mankato, Kansas, shown on covered match box with striker inside lid. $45.00 – 60.00.

Bottom mark of Morning Sun plate at right.

M.E. Church, Morning Sun, Iowa – Color scene in circle showing the church building and trees on decorated and tinted plate. $20.00 – 40.00.

Bottom mark of item at left.

Baptist Church, Friend, Nebr. – Color picture of church on decorated pin tray. $20.00 – 40.00.

HOTELS, RESORTS, SPAS, AND CAMPGROUNDS

As America grew and prospered, so did its hotels, resorts, and spas. It is far from surprising that a picture of "the place we stayed" would sell well. Thus, souvenir china was made with pictures of nearly every hotel and resort which was significant at or around the dawning of the twentieth century.

It was also an age when the mystical healing and preventative qualities of mineral springs were in vogue, and those spas were adequately represented, along with other fresh air resorts at the seashore and in the mountains. The railroads provided the transportation for rapidly escalating leisure travel, as well as for the host of commercial travelers who were hawking wares throughout the expanding country. Commercial hotels sprang up near the railroad stations in virtually every town and city. Many highly prized souvenir china items are emblazoned with images of hotels and resorts that clearly represent that era of growth and change in the United States.

Memphremagog House, Newport, Vt. – Exquisitely toned color scene of side-wheel steamer "Lady of the Lake" in front of the hotel. Appealing graphics on small tea cup with embossing and gilding. $75.00 – 125.00.

Lake View House, Bridgton, Me. A.L. Burnham, proprietor – Wonderful color scene of old stage coach drawn by a team of white horses, carrying people to or from the hotel. Appealing graphics on embossed small plate with scalloped border. $75.00 – 125.00.

Fountain Spring House, Waukesha, Wisc. – Nicely toned color picture of a period resort hotel which served guests at one of the many popular mineral springs approximately a century ago. Appealing graphics on wonderfully ornate soap dish. $65.00 – 100.00.

De Soto Hotel, Savannah, Ga. – Nearly full color scene of a brick hotel building with a horse-drawn wagon in front. On coupe plate with decorated border. $30.00 – 50.00.

Idaho Hotel, Silver City, Idaho – Color scene of old two-story "Western-style" hotel in early silver mining town (now a ghost town). On rose-tinted, heart-shaped, covered box marked Made in Germany. (Rare Western Frontier hotel item.) $100.00 – 150.00.

Old Mountain House, Catskill Mountains, N.Y. – Partially colored engraving of old hotel with large American flag flying in foreground. On rose-tinted creamer. $75.00 – 125.00.

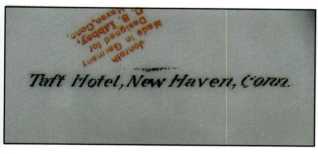

Bottom mark of item at right.

Taft Hotel, New Haven, Conn. – Color picture of city hotel building with title on reverse. On coupe plate with gold border. $20.00 – 40.00.

Monadnock House, Colebrook, N.H. – Nicely toned hand-colored picture of a very simple and typical old hotel building with veranda, shown in a stark setting. On small plate with Sontag mark. $65.00 – 100.00.

159

Bottom marks of plate on left.

Samoset Hotel, Rockland, Me. – Full face color scene showing a wonderful example of a large resort hotel. On coupe plate. $40.00 – 65.00.

Cold Spring House and Cottages, Leach Pond, Averill, Vt. – Colorful scene nicely presented on plate with pierced points along rim. $30.00 – 50.00.

Edgewood Cottages, McCloud, Calif. – Wonderful example of a decorated "shell and bow" dish, showing a row of gabled vacation "cottages" with fir trees and snow-covered Mt. Shasta in the background. $50.00 – 75.00.

Northport Campground Hotel, Souvenir of Belfast, Me. – Wonderful color scene of old hotel with many people in period dress on lawn. On stoneware mini-mug (rare). $40.00 – 65.00.

Second Advent Campground, Alton Bay, N.H. – Colorful scene showing the entrance to a Methodist Camp Ground, one of many such Camp Grounds which provided a combination of summer vacation and religious retreat. Appealing graphics on decorated Bauer Rosenthal plate (not shown). $50.00 – 75.00.

OCEAN, SHORE, LIGHTHOUSES, AND LIFESAVING

Seaside resorts and villages had a special appeal and offered a reprieve from hot cities. A great many of the largest cities were located on ocean ports, and the seashore was readily accessible. Anything representing the romance of the sea or its beaches became attractive subject matter when souvenir china hit its stride in the 1890s. Lighthouses, lifesaving stations, piers, beach attractions, and beach scenes were extremely popular subjects.

Although many of the great beach resorts near major cities do not have the same charm they once had, outlying seashore villages have remained attractive with the passing of time. A great variety of scenes from their early days were captured on souvenir china, and those items are frequently among those most desired by collectors today.

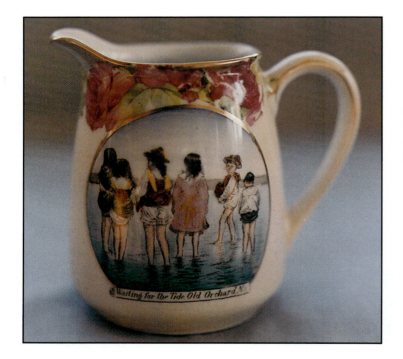

Waiting for the Tide, Old Orchard, Me. – Group of children in early bathing attire wading in shallow water at the seashore. On creamer decorated with roses. $150.00+.
(Zwolinski Collection)

Bathing Beach, Narragansett Pier, R.I. – Color scene of people in early bathing attire, lounging on popular Rhode Island beach. On Austrian-made creamer. $40.00 – 65.00.

Los Banos, (The Baths), San Diego, Calif. – Large color scene featuring a bath house at the beach in San Diego. On creamer. $50.00 – 75.00.

Patchogue Yacht Club, Patchogue, L.I. – Brightly colored scene of yacht club house from the boat dock with American flag flying. Appealing graphics on Wheelock "spade" creamer. $40.00 – 65.00.

Beach Scene, Galveston, Tex. – Color scene features well-dressed people strolling on the beach, a Sunday pastime of a century ago. Shown on small plate. $20.00 – 40.00.

Sevin Rock, Conn. – Colorful scene on cobalt blue creamer showing people in Sunday attire strolling on pier at famous Connecticut seashore resort. $65.00 – 100.00

The Beach Looking North, York Beach, Me. – Colorful scene of people on the beach (women with long dresses and parasols) and three large old resort hotels in the background. On Jonroth plate with yellow lustre rim. $30.00 – 50.00.

Bathing Scene, Provincetown, Mass. – Black engraving of bathers with pier in the background. On mustard pot without lid. $40.00 – 65.00

On the Rocks, Old Orchard Beach, Me. – Full-face color scene of people in period beach attire with rocks in the foreground and bathers in the water in the background. On coupe plate. $40.00 – 65.00.

Surf House Pavilion, Highlands Beach, N.J. – Large and colorful scene of pier and pavilion on the New Jersey shore. On decorated coupe plate with Jonroth mark. $50.00 – 75.00.

Torrey Pine, La Jolla, Calif. – A lone Torrey pine is shown standing against the elements high above the Pacific Ocean. On a full-scene coupe plate. $50.00 – 75.00. (Collection of C.S. MacBride)

South East Light, Block Island, R.I. – Spectacular brick light tower and keeper's house. On Altenburg China rose shadow flower creamer. $75.00 – 125.00.

Head Harbor Light, Eastport, Me. – Wonderfully complex engraving of a lighthouse on the rocky coast of Maine. On desirable card holder. $75.00 – 125.00.

Edgartown Light – Nicely toned lighthouse marking the entrance to Edgartown Harbor on Martha's Vineyard is shown on a tumbler. $50.00 – 75.00.

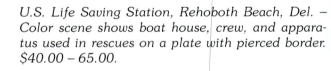

U.S. Life Saving Station, Rehoboth Beach, Del. – Color scene shows boat house, crew, and apparatus used in rescues on a plate with pierced border. $40.00 – 65.00.

Life Saving Station, Ottowa Point, East Tawas, Mich. – Color scene shown on decorated plate. $30.00 – 50.00.

MOUNTAINS, LAKES, AND RIVERS

America the beautiful was blessed with an abundance of majestic mountains, as well as sparkling clean rivers and lakes which provided attractive retreats from the growing industrial cities. As soon as railroad transportation became available, certain areas and attractions became well established as destinations.

Undoubtedly, Niagara Falls became the most popular attraction. The proliferation of souvenirs from Niagara Falls defies estimate, and that fact is certainly true of souvenir china depicting the falls. Even so, the very good early items made in Germany and Austria have become highly desirable to some collectors of Americana.

Souvenir china representing the White Mountains of New Hampshire was prolific and often wonderful. Some of the very earliest souvenir items imported by Clark Adams Clark and Abram French of Boston depicted scenes of the White Mountains and were outstanding works of art.

Throughout the country, tourist attractions in the mountains, lakes, and rivers were pictured on souvenir china pieces.

Horseshoe Falls, Niagara – Well-executed hand-painted scene with interesting background, on a folded corner dish. Although this is the most common of view china subjects, some early and not-so-common items, such as this one, manage to distinguish themselves. $20.00 – 40.00.

The Royal Gorge, Colorado – Hand-painted view of steaming train passing through the Royal Gorge. On full-scene coupe plate. $40.00 – 65.00.

Moonlight Scene on Mississippi River, Moline, Ill. — A steaming river boat on a shimmering river is well lighted by a full moon. On full-scene coupe plate. $65.00 – 100.00. *(Collection of C.S. MacBride)*

Cactus Forest, Tucson, Ariz. — Color scene of saguaro cacti on desert hillside is typical of Tucson surroundings. View china items from Arizona are not common. On gilded vase. $40.00 – 65.00.

Iron Bridge Over the North Platte River at Saratoga, Wyo. — "Modern" bridges such as this were a source of great pride and served a crucial commercial function, thus they became subjects on view china souvenirs. On a plate with floral rim. $30.00 – 50.00.

Echo Mountain House and Mount Lowe
Railway – Color scene of people riding the
incline railway at a famous California lookout attraction. On small plate. $40.00 –
65.00.

Winter, Lick Observatory, San Jose, Calif.
– Partially colored engraving shows snow
covered mountain with observatory buildings. On pin tray. $30.00 – 50.00.

Silver Cascade, Alton Bay, N.H. – Color scene
shows men fishing for trout in a mountain
stream. On folded corner dish. $30.00 –
50.00.

169

Pikes Peak, Colorado Springs – A well-detailed, hand-painted scene shows a trolley in the center of Colorado Springs with snow-covered Pikes Peak behind a landmark hotel. On a full-scene coupe plate. $75.00 – 125.00.

Fish Cone, Yellowstone Lake – Scene shows two people cooking freshly caught fish in the naturally boiling water of the "fish cone." On small cobalt blue dish. $40.00 – 65.00.

Coopers Cave – Large color scene shows the upstate New York cavern made famous in James Fenimore Cooper's "Last of the Mahicans," shown on the front of a creamer. (Note: several caves in various parts of the country were depicted on souvenir china.) $45.00 – 60.00.

VILLAGES, MAIN STREETS, AND SHOPS

Time has wrought major changes to the villages, main streets, and shops throughout the United States, but scenes on souvenir china show the way it was. Dirt roads, horses and buggies, early automobiles, and small local shops were common features in those scenes. Not surprisingly, the items bearing such scenes are becoming increasingly important artifacts of historical significance to collectors and historical societies in local communities.

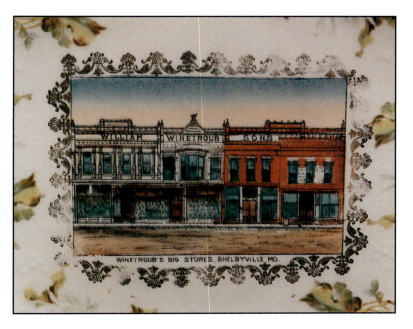

Mark on back of plate.

Winetroub's Big Stores, Shelbyville, Mo. – Panoramic color view of a block of stores owned by William Winetroub & Sons with a dirt street in front. On decorated thin china plate. $50.00 – 75.00.

Pleasant Street, Brunswick, Me. – Artistically presented dirt street and buildings. On highly decorated plate. $40.00 – 65.00.

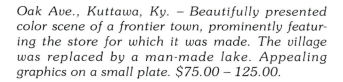

Mark on back of plate.

Greenville, Ohio, Broadway Looking South – Wonderfully detailed and colored scene with horses and a trolley on a dirt street with hitching posts and a row of awnings on the sunny side of the street. On an embossed cameo flower dish. $40.00 – 65.00.

Oak Ave., Kuttawa, Ky. – Beautifully presented color scene of a frontier town, prominently featuring the store for which it was made. The village was replaced by a man-made lake. Appealing graphics on a small plate. $75.00 – 125.00.

Main St. Looking West, McMinnville, Tenn. – Black engraving of an unpaved street lined with stores and churches. On a covered box. $65.00 – 100.00.

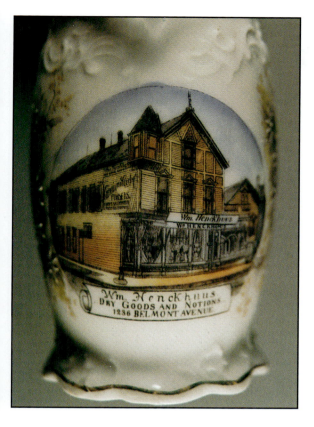

Festus Mercantile Co., Festus, Mo. – Outstanding scene of a brick store building with header sign and two state-of-the-art buggies in front. On small plate. $65.00 – 100.00.

Wm. Henckhuus Dry Goods and Notions, 1236 Belmont Avenue – Color scene of a store probably located in either Chicago or New York, although no indication is given, on front of highly embossed creamer. $75.00 – 125.00.
(Collection of D. Hendricksen)

Webb's Mills, Me. – Colorful rural village scene of a Maine town no longer known graces a nicely toned mug. $50.00 – 75.00.

South Side of Mechanic St., Canaan, N.H. – A rutted dirt street is shown in the foreground of this nice color scene of a village center. On a small dish. $40.00 – 65.00.

J. Gordino Jeweler Store, Salinas, Calif. – Black engraving of rare and highly detailed interior of a central California jewelry store. On a small plate. $100.00 – 150.00.

EARLY TRANSPORTATION

Various modes of early transportation are well chronicled on souvenir china. Stage coaches, early automobiles, trolleys, steamships, and railroad-related scenes are all found wonderfully portrayed on souvenir china.

Steamer Louise Nearing Tolchester Beach – Chesapeake Bay Steamer filled with people and flags flying in the breeze as it approaches the Eastern Shore. On creamer. $75.00 – 125.00. (Collection of D. Hendricksen)

174

*Steamers Nantucket and Gay Head –
Black engravings depict two island steam-
ers from the turn of the century, on a
BFHS pin tray. $75.00 – 125.00.*

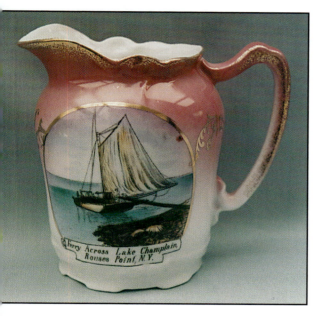

*Ferry Across Lake Champlain, Rouses Point, N.Y. –
color scene on rose-toned creamer shows early crude
sailing ferry boat (on Lake Champlain). $40.00 – 65.00.*

*Connecticut River Steamer Middletown – Black engrav-
ing depicts a typical river steamer circa 1907. On a
small plate. $40.00 – 65.00.*

*Lisbon Station, Lisbon, N.H. – Wonderful-
ly detailed color scene shows small town
railroad station with horse-drawn station
wagon, baggage carts and train approach-
ing. On small plate decorated with rose
shadow flowers. $75.00 – 100.00.*

175

B & M Station, West Ossipee, N.H. – Detailed black engraving surrounded by decorative cartouche depicts very small town railroad station. On plate. $50.00 – 75.00.

The North Union Station, Boston, Mass. Color scene of railroad station in major cit on cobalt blue vase. (Note that items fror large cities generally tend to be more com mon and have less demand than those fror small towns.) $20.00 – 40.00.

Casino Burgoyne, Daytona, Fla. – A full-face color scene shows early cars in Daytona, Florida, the era of souvenir china included the transition from horse-drawn vehicles to early automobiles such as this, shown here on a coupe plate. $40.00 – 65.00.

The Levee of New Orleans – An extremely detaile dark green engraving shows a long line of stear boats along the river front in New Orleans, the fore ground is bustling with the activity of handlin goods. On a small plate. $50.00 – 75.00.

176

FRONTIER PROSPECTORS AND COWBOYS

In the late 1800s, America's frontier had been opened by the transcontinental railroad. Western cities were exploding with growth built around farming and mining, as well as a new influx of tourism. Scenes which clearly relate to the frontier warrant a category of their own to stress the significance of the western expansion. This has also become a collectible category of Americana.

Deadwood, S.D. 1876 – Bustling color scene of a famous frontier town with many interesting details. On an early tea tile with no bottom mark. $150.00+.

1907 Orofino Trading Co. Ltd. – Well-detailed engraving, colored to achieve outstanding presentation. Shows a trading post, probably done from a picture taken at its opening in 1907. On an earth-to-sky toned plate. $75.00 – 125.00

San Juan Stage, Friday Harbor, Wash. – Color scene of two-horse open stage coach with people. On small oval bowl or dish. $65.00 – 100.00. (Collection of D. Manesellian, photo by John Walker)

Fortune Seekers, Idaho Springs, Colorado, 1857 – Beautifully toned scene of two prospectors with fully packed mules, on a very desirable creamer form probably made by Benjamin F. Hunt & Sons ca. 1894 using early photograph. $150.00+. (Collection of B. & S. Zwolinski)

The Prospector, in Cripple Creek in 1894 – Crisp black engraving of a prospector with all of his gear loaded on a burro, dated piece and desirable town, shown on small plate with rose-tinted border. $150.00+.

The Prospectus – Black engraving of burros loaded with the gear of prospectors (probably a misspelled title) in Aspen, Colorado, depicted on small plate with robin's egg blue tint on rim. $150.00+.

Let'er Buck – Full-face, hand-painted scene of rodeo rider in Miles City, Montana, shown on coupe plate. $75.00 – 125.00. (Collection of D. Manesellian, photo by John Walker)

Bronco Busting, Grabbing Leather – Outstanding full-face, hand-painted color scene shows a cowboy busting a "painted" pony. On coupe plate. $150.00+. (Collection of C.S. MacBride)

Close up of coupe plate at left.

COMMEMORATIVES — PEOPLE, PLACES, AND EVENTS

Occasionally a merchant deemed it prudent to produce a souvenir in honor of a popular local person or event. Poets were especially popular at that time, and many souvenir china items honored Longfellow, Whittier, and others in their hometowns. Presidents and politicians were honored as well. Battlefields such as Gettysburg and countless local monuments to soldiers and sailors also were depicted. National significance was not essential, and many events and people depicted on souvenir china related primarily to local histories.

The Burning of Tulares Irrigation Bonds, Oct. 17th, 1903 – Toned engraving on a cobalt blue cup shows a significant local event in Tulare, Calif. $65.00 – 100.00. (Collection of D. Manesellian, photo by John Walker)

Colonel George Croghan, Hero of Fort Stephenson, Aug. 2nd. 1813 – Color portrait of Colonel Croghan, native son of Fremont, Ohio, displayed on an oddly shaped pin tray. $30.00 – 50.00.

Henry Wadsworth Longfellow – Splendid and distinguished portrait of Longfellow with flowing white hair and beard, on a luncheon plate decorated with rose shadow flowers. $40.00 – 65.00.

Piers for Operating Tunnel, Pedro Miguel Lock, Panama Canal – Color scene commemorates construction of the Panama Canal, on cobalt blue bucket. $45.00 – 60.00.

Old Slave Huts at the Hermitage, Savannah, Ga. – Wonderfully executed hand-painted scene shows a row of historical buildings, on a full-scene coupe plate. $75.00 – 125.00.

Meriden in 1842, Showing First Steam Cars, Hotel, and Depot. – Black engraving shows a scene of a Connecticut town in 1842 on a creamer, likely produced for commemoration fifty years later, in 1892. $75.00 – 125.00.

Jackson Monument, Nashville – Sepia-toned engraving shows statue of Andrew Jackson (the first President from a frontier state) as a mounted colonel who led the defeat of the British in New Orleans in 1814. On a dinner plate. $20.00 – 40.00.

Residence of William L. Douglas – So famous was the high-profile Brockton, Mass., shoe magnate and politician, William L. Douglas, that he was not even named on the cup and saucer which colorfully depicts him and his residence. $40.00 – 65.00.

Close up of the residence of William L. Douglas as depicted on the cup and saucer above.

The Battle of Lexington – An important turning point in American history is depicted in color on a creamer jug. $30.00 – 50.00.

Postcard scene of the Battle of Lexington copied by the engraver for the scene on creamer jug above left.

Federal Warships in Harbor, 1865, New Bern, N.C. – Color scene of panoramic aerial view showing heavily occupied harbor at the end of the Civil War, on small cup and saucer with canary tint. $40.00 – 65.00.

General Banks – Engraving of Civil War General Banks of Waltham, Mass., was selected by a Waltham merchant to be shown on this cup and saucer. $40.00 – 65.00.

Two Wheelock "spade" creamers show scenes from Gettysburg:
(L) General Meade's Headquarters, Gettysburg, Pa., shows color scene of Meade's Headquarters with an inset image of General Meade, $40.00 – 65.00
(R) Jennie Wade and the House In Which She Was Killed July 3rd, 1863, Gettysburg, Pa. $40.00 – 65.00.

Fort Sewell, Marblehead, Mass. – Color view of historic fort, on rose shadow flower plate. $30.00 – 50.00.

DISASTERS

News and public interest have always been drawn to disasters of all types. Local disasters of significance are firmly impressed on the pages of history and in the folkways of generations yet unborn. The period of our history recorded on souvenir china saw many fires, shipwrecks, and train wrecks. The generation also experienced its share of natural disasters in the form of droughts, storms, earthquakes, and other phenomena. Many of these disasters were recorded on souvenir china.

Cyclone, Aug. 20, '04, Willow Lake, S.D. – A geometric wonder created by forces of nature is captured on a milk glass paper weight (rare variant), from the era when tornados were commonly called cyclones. $75.00 – 125.00.

Evans, Only Survivor Ship Jason – A sailor poses in his life jacket after surviving a ship wreck on Cape Cod in 1893. On a round hot plate. $75.00 – 125.00.

Wreck "Fortuna," Peaked Hill L.S.S. – Black engraving shows wreck of a coastal schooner on the coast of Cape Cod. On souvenir plate. $65.00 – 100.00.

A.T.& St. Fe R.R. Wreck, Chillicothe, Ill. – Outstanding color scene of two engines entwined, showing inspectors and train crew, on small, embossed plate. Appealing graphics. $100.00 – 150.00.

Burning Tank, 35,000 Barrels, Bradford, Pa. – Color scene shows billowing smoke from large oil fire, on small dish. $30.00 – 50.00.

Main Street, Johnstown, Pa. After the Flood, 1889 – Early photographic transfer shows devastation of the infamous Johnstown Flood. On fancy small plate. Very rare and historically important piece. $100.00 – 150.00.

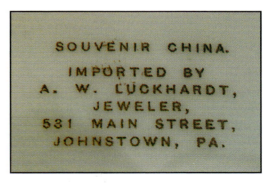

Bottom mark on Johnstown Flood plate.

Depot Square, Flood of March 2, 1896 – Wonderful black engraving shows flooded streets of Gardiner, Maine. (Note that several signs are readable.) On tea cup, $40.00 – 65.00. Value includes saucer.

Museum Golden Gate Park, San Francisco, Cal., Badly Damaged By Earthquake, April 18, 1906 – Color scene shows building which sustained earthquake damage in a major earthquake. On shell and bow dish. $40.00 – 65.00.

COLLEGES AND UNIVERSITIES

A great deal of pride has always been associated with America's colleges and universities. Most of the institutions of higher education which existed at the last turn of the century were represented on souvenir china items. Souvenirs and logo items from colleges and universities are a big business today, but early pictorial souvenirs of those schools have become quite scarce. The schools were much smaller then, and the scenes capture the sense of that earlier era.

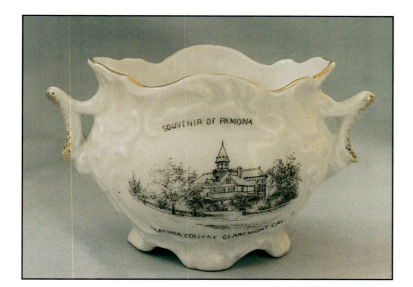

Pamona College, Claremont, Calif. – Black engraving on small Austrian-made sugar bowl imported by Wheelock; likely manufactured by Benjamin F. Hunt & Sons. $30.00 – 50.00.

Ladies Hall, University of Wisconsin – Black engraving of early University women's dormitory. On an interesting Austrian-made pin tray. $20.00 – 40.00.

The Ohio Northern University – Color scene showing university building, on a top hat with title on reverse. $30.00 – 50.00.

Florida State College for Women – Hand-painted, full scene coupe plate depicts a college building at Florida State in the 1920s. $40.00 – 65.00.

Old South College and Yale Fence – Nicely detailed and colored scene, on match holder with striker on base. $30.00 – 50.00.

Haskell Institute, Lawrence,
Kans. – Color scene showing
several school buildings. On
pierced-rim plate. $30.00 –
50.00.

*Knox College, Galesburg, Ill. – Color scene of early
college building, on small plate made by Royal
Beyreuth producer. $30.00 – 50.00.*

*St. Ansgar Seminary, St. Ansgar, Iowa – Excel-
lent color scene of small early school building.
On small mug. $30.00 – 50.00.*

*Mark on bottom of plate
shown above.*

*Mark on mug
shown above.*

State Normal School, Cape Girardeau, Mo. – Color picture of large college building, on the front of a small stein. $20.00 – 40.00.

Augustana College, Rock Island, Ill. – Clear color scene of college building, on shell and bow dish. $30.00 – 50.00.

University of Montana, Missoula, Mont. – Color scene (not clear) of university building and environs, on figural horseshoe pin dish. $20.00 – 40.00.

Pacific College, Newberg, Ore. – Nicely toned color picture shows early college building, on folded corner dish. $30.00 – 50.00.

AMUSEMENT PARKS AND RECREATION

Amusement parks and piers, pavilions, and casinos were the venues of many recreational activities, and the great era of souvenir china coincided perfectly with the early wonder years of places like Coney Island, Nantasket Beach, and Atlantic City. Amusement parks were well represented on souvenir china, and Revere Beach, north of Boston, appears to have established itself as the park most prolifically represented in terms of shapes, forms, and views.

It is surprising that sporting events, such as golf and the national pastime of baseball, were not better represented. Pictures relating to horse racing are also quite rare, although rodeo and bronco busting are found on Western items.

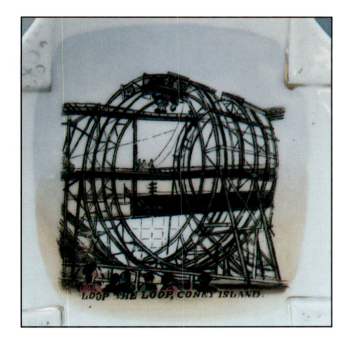

Loop the Loop, Coney Island – Hand-colored engraving with toned background shows close-up view of an early ride at Coney Island. On folded corner dish. Outstanding example of rare and unusual, highly appealing graphics. $150.00+.

(L) Surf Avenue, Coney Island, N.Y. – Color scene showing famous street in Coney Island's amusement park, on rare cobalt blue shaving mug. $150.00+.
(C) Spectator's Boxes, Luna Park, Coney Island – Color scene of amusement park, on small cobalt blue dutch style shoe. $65.00 – 100.00.
(R) Two Strings to Her Beaux; Color scene of woman with her arms around two men, all in early bathing attire, at Coney Island, on small urn or tooth-pick holder. $65.00 – 100.00.

191

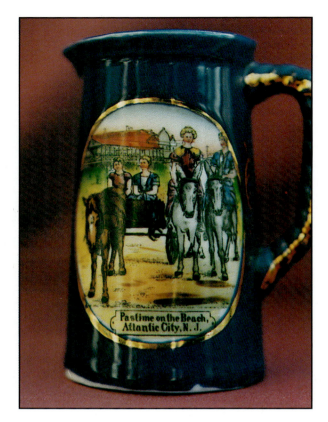

Pastime on Beach, Atlantic City, N.J. – Extremely colorful beach scene showing turn-of-the-century amusement and costumes, on a small cobalt blue creamer. $65.00 – 100.00.

Pavilion, Lord's Park, Elgin, Ill. – Clear color scene of lakeside recreational building, on pierced rim plate. $20.00 – 40.00.

Ready for the Big Canoe Race, July 4th, '07, Juneau, Alaska – Partially colored scene of large canoe racing teams preparing for race. On cup. $150.00+ (valuation includes saucer) (Collection of D. Manesellian, photo by John Walker)

Condit's Dance Hall, Revere Beach, Mass. – Colorful, full-face scene shows a typical casino or dance hall. Such facilities were available in many towns, but were an essential part of a resort community. On a coupe plate. $30.00 – 50.00.

Evidence of Native Americans on this continent dates back to before the last glacial period, approximately 8000 to 8500 B.C., at the Folsom site in New Mexico. Although their origins may have been elsewhere in the world, the term "native" can certainly be justified by the length of habitation. When white settlers arrived from across the Atlantic Ocean and gradually inhabited the entire United States, Native Americans had long been formed into countless tribes and sub-cultures, covering virtually the entire continent. Their displacement took approximately 200 years, a short and sad period in the evolution of their ancient culture.

Legendary tales and a growing fascination about Native Americans made the subject matter very marketable on souvenir china. Native cultures in the Alaskan and Hawaiian territories were also represented on early view china souvenirs

Seminole Indians at Miami, Fla. — Exquisite color scene of Seminole natives in motley attire. On nice early dish made in Austria. $150.00+.

Adrian Follow the Road — Magnificently hand-painted portrait of Mandan (North Dakota) Indian Chief in full ceremonial attire. On coupe plate. $150.00+.

Geronimo, Chief of Apache Tribe, Prisoner of U.S. Government at Fort Sill, Okla. – Colorful picture of famous chief proudly attired and carrying pistol in pose likely taken before he became a prisoner. On oval serving bowl. $100.00 – 150.00.

Bottom mark on serving bowl.

Souvenir of Muskogee, Ind. Ter. – Colorful portrait of unnamed chief. On small decorated plate. $100.00 – 150.00.

Navajo Blanket Weaver, Ancient Cliff Dwellings, Manitou, Colo. – Hand-painted, full scene coupe plate featuring weaver at work. $150.00+. *(Collection of C. MacBride)*

Umatilla Indians and Tepee, Pendleton, Oregon – Black engraving depicts brave (with famous Pendleton wool scarf) and squaw in front of traditional home. On small plate. $50.00 – 75.00.

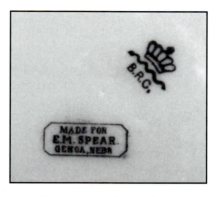

Bottom mark on plate.

Girls' Home – Indian School, Genoa, Nebr. – Color picture of frontier Indian school; on small plate. $50.00 – 75.00.

Lei Women, Hawaii – Color scene on front of tinted creamer shows native Hawaiian women and one bearded man making and hawking their wares. $150.00+. (Collection of Michele Rosewitz)

Native Grass House, Honolulu, H.I. – Sepia-tone view of native Hawaiian and traditional home. On small, lime tinted plate. $100.00 – 150.00.

Thunket Chief & Totem Pole, Ketchikan, Alaska – Color scene depicts native elements on early Alaskan souvenir creamer by Wheelock. $75.00 – 125.00.

Maricopa Olla Vender, Phoenix, Ariz. – Clear and colorful portrait of native woman displaying her wares on her head, depicted on cobalt blue creamer. $75.00 – 125.00.

Papago Squaw, Tucson, Ariz. – Color scene of squaw in her native environs with olla on her head. On cobalt blue creamer. $75.00 – 125.00. (Collection of Dr. Burton Spiller)

Smile of the Great Spirit, Lake Winnepesaukee, N.H. – Hand-painted, full scene coupe plate showing Indian maiden and canoe on the shore of the lake with an Indian name meaning "smile of the great spirit." $65.00 – 100.00.

Angeline, Daughter of Chief Seattle, Seattle, Wash. – Color portrait of Indian chief's daughter, on cobalt blue vase. $65.00 – 100.00. (Collection of R. Rainka)

Two creamers decorated with rose lustre shadow flowers and depicting native Americans; sold as souvenirs of the Mohawk Trail in Massachusetts. $20.00 – 40.00 each.

NOVELTY, MYTHICAL, ETHNIC, AND ADVERTISING

Occasionally, whimsy was used in producing souvenir china. In the South, that whimsy was often racially oriented. The items made a statement appropriate to the time in which they were made, but which has become outdated by political and social changes. As a result, the items have become a part of the vast field of "Black Collectibles." Any items which express whimsy, fantasy, or humor are considered part of the novelty category. Souvenir china items were occasionally used for advertising and some examples are presented in this category as well.

Cupid on the Warpath – A series of postcards and souvenir scenes copyrighted in 1902 by H.H. Tammen featured young Indian braves and a white rabbit in various situations such as the one shown here in color on a small cobalt blue plate. $40.00 – 65.00.

Bathing Beauty on a Shell was an Art Deco motif used in various ways along with script to name the souvenir.
(L) Color image on folded corner plate for Hotel Imperial. $30.00 – 50.00.
(R) Black and white image on decorated small plate sold as Souvenir of Wolfeboro, N.H. $30.00 – 50.00.

J.A. Kuhn Clam Bake, Port Townsend, Wash. – An outstanding rare and unusual color scene combines advertising, novelty and ethnic features in an extremely appealing graphic presentation on an oval dish. $150.00+. (Collection of Daniel Manesellian, Photo by John Walker)

Salem Witch, 1692, Salem, Mass. – Two cup and saucer sets depict the famous Salem Witch.
(L) Color scene shows the witch soaring over the village $75.00 – 125.00. *(Collection of Jan and Dick Vogel)*
(R) Black engraving on cup shows a different image. $65.00 – 100.00.

Bottom mark on above dish.

The Red Man's Fact, Niagara Falls, N.Y. – Color scene shows native American lore (as told in William Trumbull's poem "The White Canoe") of a Seneca chief's daughter (Wenolah) going over the falls in a canoe as a sacrifice; the chief (Kwasind) is in another canoe coming to join his only daughter in her journey to the Great Spirit. On a delicate vase. $40.00 – 65.00.

A Rexburg Baby – Color scene shows a baby on pillows in an ornate Victorian chair, depicted on a flesh-toned basketweave dish by Humes China. Presumedly, this piece represents family values and pride in the blood line being established in the Morman settlement of Rexburg, Idaho, during the 1890s. $75.00 – 125.00.

199

*Four Little Chinese Kids, Los Angeles, Calif. –
Full-face, hand-painted color scene shows four
boys in traditional garb, on small coupe plate.
$40.00 – 65.00.*

*The Early Bird Catches the Worm, Souvenir of Nor-
folk, Va. – A popular scene at the turn-of-the-century is
shown here in vivid color on a folded corner dish.
$50.00 – 75.00.*

*Southern Pines,
N.C. – Black
engraving shows
two young children
with baskets of
flowers at a popu-
lar golfing resort;
this tea cup and
saucer were made
in England and do
not have much of
the discoloration
frequently found on souvenir china items of tha
source. $40.00 – 65.00. (Collection of Ron Rainka)*

Bottom mark on saucer.

Souvenir of Florida — Color scene depicts black boy riding on the snout of an alligator, in bowl of cobalt blue basketweave dish. $75.00 – 125.00. (Collection of D. Manesellian, photo by John Walker)

Bottom mark on plate.

A Virginia Team — Color scene shows black woman in a cart pulled by an ox or steer, crossing what appears to be a park with several old cannons and stacks of cannon balls, on decorated plate with pierced border. $30.00 – 50.00.

Prince, a trick dog, undoubtedly well reputed in his home town of Sheboygen, Wisconsin, is shown exquisitely painted on a full scene coupe plate. $100.00 – 150.00. (Collection of C.S. MacBride)

Souvenir China Views

Abram French & Co. (Advertising) – The dish on the right was made as an advertising piece by Abram French & Co., utilizing a trade card image. $75.00 – 125.00. The dish on the left is a similar souvenir dish (also produced by Abram French) which depicts Schooner Head, Mt. Desert, Me. $40.00 – 65.00.

Globe Roller Mills (Advertising) – Emerald green dutch shoe form is used as an advertising piece for a salesman from Bangor, Pa. The "Wheelock-Dresden" bottom mark is also shown. $75.00 – 125.00.

Emery-Brown Company, Department Store, Waterville, Maine, H.L. Emery – Color scene on nicely decorated Victorian hatpin holder which was used by Mr. Emery for advertising purposes. $65.00 – 100.00.

Wiggenhorn Bros. (Cigar Manufactory), Watertown, Wisc. – Colorful full-face scene on small dish shows the building and the important bottom mark advertises its features and function, while it also states that the item was Made in Germany. $65.00 – 100.00.

WORLD'S FAIRS AND EXPOSITIONS

The enormous scope of souvenir china from World's Fairs hosted by U.S. cities from 1876 to World War I would undoubtedly be sufficiently complex to fill an additional book. It suffices here to list the Fairs and their host cities during the era of souvenir china. A few examples of the items produced are pictured, but no attempt is made to show a broad representation of items in this category or to provide extensive information on each fair. World's Fair references and price guides are available to provide more detailed information.

Souvenir china can be found commemorating the following World's Fairs:

Centennial Exposition, Philadelphia, 1876
World's Columbian Exposition, Chicago, 1893
California Mid-Winter International Exposition, San Francisco, 1894
Pan American Exposition Buffalo, 1901
Louisiana Purchase Exposition, St. Louis, 1904
Lewis and Clark Exposition, Portland, 1905
Jamestown Exposition, Norfolk, 1907
Alaska-Yukon-Pacific Exposition, Seattle, 1909
Panama-Pacific Exposition, San Francisco, 1915
Panama-California Exposition, San Diego, 1915

Centennial Exposition, Philadelphia, 1876

Centennial Exposition, Philadelphia 1876 – Color scene of main building is depicted on an open, barber shop style, shaving mug. $100.00 – 150.00.

Columbian Exposition, Chicago 1892 – 93

Machinery Hall is shown in an unusual blue decoration on a porcelain plate made in Austria by Marx and Gutherz. $65.00 – 100.00.

The Horticultural Building is shown in color on a cand *dish made in Austria. $65.00 – 100.00.*

Pan-American Exposition, Buffalo 1901

Two items which are typical of the items produced for the Pan-American Exposition of 1901 include:
(L) Stoneware advertising mini-stein which is actually a match holder with striker on its base. $75.00 – 125.00.
(R) Cobalt blue vase with color picture of a buffalo, which wa the common symbol adopted for souvenirs of the host city cobalt blue souvenirs of the 1901 Exposition were relatively common. $50.00 – 75.00.

Marketing of souvenir china throughout the United States was at fever pitch in 1904, and that trend was clearly reflected in the variety and number of items made for the St. Louis Fair. It may well be that its proximity to Peoria, Illinois, was also an important factor, as Peoria was the hometown of souvenir china importing.

Louisiana Purchase Exposition, St. Louis 1904

Administration Building shown in black engraving on footed rose bowl with two handles. $75.00 – 125.00.

United States Government Building shown in color on large egg cup. $75.00 – 125.00.

Palace of Electricity shown in color on decorated plate. $65.00 – 100.00.

Lewis and Clark Exposition, Portland 1905

Color scene of Lewis and Clark with Saca-
jawea at Pacific Ocean, on cobalt blue tea
pot. $100.00 – 150.00. *(Collection of Dr. Burton
Spiller)*

Rare piggy bank with scene of Lewis & Clark Centennial – Por
land, Oregon, 1905. $150.00+.

Jamestown Exposition, Norfolk 1907

Panama Pacific Exposition, California 1915

The Landing of John Smith 1607 shown in
color on decorated tumbler was a souvenir
of the Jamestown Exposition made for the
New York based importing firm of A.C.
Bosselman. $65.00 – 100.00.

California-Pan American Exposition logo and year are shown o
this souvenir creamer made in Germany just prior to the start o
World War I. $40.00 – 65.00.

CHAPTER FOUR

PROVENANCE

PATHWAYS TO OUR PAST

One very important aspect of souvenir china is that specific items can be examined in detail to provide interesting and important insights. The following examples have been carefully selected to show as many aspects as possible while providing fascinating insights into relevant events or places of historical significance. Few, if any, antiques can provide such a direct and well documented relationship to history.

THE MARSHALL HOUSE ALEXANDRIA, VIRGINIA

Pen tray with black engraving of The Marshall House by Benjamin F. Hunt & Sons, made for E.J. Miller & Co., Alexandria, Virginia, circa 1898. $40.00 – 65.00.

The gold mark on the back of the tray is a common mark used by Benjamin F. Hunt & Sons showing their designation as B.F.H.S. China. The

item was clearly made in their factory in Austria. Although New England was the main turf for the firm, which ceased business in 1902, items such as this one are found throughout the country. It is noteworthy that Benjamin F. Hunt & Sons was also the importer of this item.

The form is one of the countless variations of useful porcelain items typical of B.F.H.S. China. The high quality white base porcelain was molded into an ornate and delicate pen tray with embossing. Gold highlights and a transfer of the engraving were applied and affixed in a third firing. The graphics are highly detailed and the Marshall House sign on the hotel is distinctly legible.

The back mark also clearly states that the item was made for E. J. Miller & Co., Alexandria, Virginia. That venerable firm was established in 1822 by Robert H. Miller, a prominent Quaker businessman. It became a significant wholesale and retail importer and jobber in crockery and glassware, and even expanded to St. Louis in an effort to capture western clientele. Advertisements also appeared in Pennsylvania and western Maryland. Elisha Miller took over the reins of the company when his father retired in 1865.

In an 1897 advertisement in *The Alexandria Business Book,* the company billed itself as "The Oldest Crockery House in the South." Another advertisement in an 1899 business directory focused on its trade in souvenir china and stated, "We are the Oldest distributors of souvenirs on China of Photographs of Old Christ Church, where Washington worshiped; Marshall House, where first blood was spilled in our Civil War; Carlyle House, Braddock's Headquarters in the Revolutionary War." At that time, its president was Oscar F. Carter, a man reportedly raised to his business who had traded all over Virginia and the South, as well as in Washington. Succeeding gen-

erations of the Miller family (Ashby, followed by R. E. Miller) remained active in the business well into the new century. The business occupied various locations in the first three blocks of King Street.

> *The Marshall House was the site of a skirmish which purports to represent the first blood spilled in the Civil War. The event followed a near unanimous vote for secession by Virginia on May 23, 1861. On the day following the vote, Union troops were sent across the Potomac to occupy Arlington Heights and Alexandria, where the Confederate flag had been flying in sight of the Capitol. James W. Jackson, proprietor of the Marshall House, on the southeast corner of King and Pitt Streets, flew the Confederate flag at his hotel and had been known to advertise that "Virginia is determined, and will yet conquer under the command of Jeff Davis." The flag was the apparent provocation of the incident in which Col. E. Elmer Ellsworth of the New York Fire Zoaves was shot by Jackson upon removing the flag from its halyard on the third floor of the hotel. Jackson was in turn killed by Capt. Frank E. Brownell, who received the Medal of Honor for his part. Brownell wrote an important and interesting detailed report of the incident, which has provided historical researchers with an excellent perspective.*

RED RIVER CARTS
PEMBINA, NORTH DAKOTA

Celery dish decorated with embossed and painted flowers, depicting a color scene of Red River carts 1883, Pembina, North Dakota, made in Germany by Bauer Rosenthal & Co., imported by Wheelock for Charles Full Cheap Store, Pembina, N.D. $75.00 – 100.00.

The two backstamps on this attractive and useful item provide a wealth of information. The crown mark and initials indicate that it was made by the porcelain factory of Bauer, Rosenthal in Kronach, Germany, in 1897 using a pattern known as Viola (note the embossed and painted violets). The firm made both artistic and utility porcelain items and belonged to the venerable Rosenthal AG (established 1879), Selb, which is a noted producer of porcelain ranging from artistic luxury items to high quality commercial wares.

The second mark indicates Wheelock was the importer and that the product came from the Weimar region (Kronach is located in Bavaria very near S. Weimar and near Wheelock's office in Leipzig). Since Pembina was a small town in a remote area prior to the turn of the century, it is noteworthy that a Wheelock salesman handled the order, probably taking the order in person in 1896. Undoubtedly, the order went back to Peoria and was sent or carried to Germany where the item was made. It was shipped, probably through the port of Baltimore, to Peoria for distribution to Mr. Full in Pembina.

The mark also clearly states that it was made for Charles Full's Cheap Store in Pembina, a mercantile in the historically important settlement.

Pembina claims to be the oldest settlement in the Northwest. Located just south of the Canadian border, at the confluence of the Pembina and Red Rivers, two forts were constructed at that site in the first years of the nineteenth century, and a fur trading post was established there by the Hudson Bay Company prior to 1822. The first public school house in North Dakota was built there in 1876.

Charles Full was involved in the general retail trade and hotel business in Pembina beginning around 1880. By 1896, when this item was ordered by Charles Full, there were approximately 16 commercial buildings, all of which were in a row along the river on Cavalier Street. Charles Full's store was at the north end of the block, and the Winchester hotel, operated by the Full family from the 1880s until 1900, was just across Rosette Street on the next block north. The Great Fire of 1897 destroyed most of the 16 buildings, but Full's Store and the hotel survived.

The picture on the celery dish shows the "Red River Carts in 1883." Full apparently selected an earlier photograph, taken in the year 1883, which had captured a scene already historically significant in Pembina by the mid 1890s. It showed the carts, horses, and people in period dress with a building behind them which may have been Full's store from Rosette Street. The Red River carts were large-wheeled carts which had been developed locally for multiple uses, including the transport of furs. Furs from Pembina were transported through Winnepeg all the way to Hudson's Bay, and carts were pulled by both oxen and horses. They were apparently used in and around Pembina for work as well as for general transportation. Even today, one of these carts is depicted on the front page of the "Pembina Historical Tour brochure," an appropriate symbol of the settlement's past.

LUCAS OIL WELL
BEAUMONT, TEXAS

This is an example of a cobalt blue souvenir item, and it is simply marked with the required indices, "Made in Germany." There were literally hundreds of different cobalt blue items produced in German souvenir china, and many bore only a generic designation of origin such as seen on this

Cobalt blue chocolate cup and saucer with ornate handle and a picture of Lucas Oil Well, Beaumont, Texas. $30.00 – 50.00.

Made in Germany mark on bottom of cup.

one. However, approximately half of them did indicate the name of the importer and for whom they were made.

It is possible that this souvenir was rushed to market by Wheelock to satisfy a huge demand at the Beaumont Racket Store in 1902. A Wheelock ad in *Crockery and Glass Journal* (see page 210) utilized a copy of a letter from the Racket Store to C.E. Wheelock & Co. dated April 16, 1902, which clearly stated the urgency for such an item. That was only a little more than a year after the most spectacular and important oil well in American history was uncapped, along with a tale of legendary proportions.

On the morning of January 10, 1901, the drill of the Hamill brothers touched off the greatest oil

Advertisement from Crockery and Glass Journal *showing the enormous demand for these items. (New York City Public Library)*

boom in history when the Lucas Gusher spouted a heavy plume 200 feet into the air four miles south of the sleepy town of Beaumont, Texas. The well was the product of perseverance by a Beaumont native son named Patillo Higgins who had been on a 10-year quest for oil he was certain existed in that field, despite the fact that oil experts and fellow Beaumonters deemed him crazy.

After tapping three dry holes, he resorted to newspaper advertising with lofty promises of rich-

es, and was able to entice Captain Lucas, a former Austrian naval captain, to invest in the fourth attempt. Lucas, a naturalized American who had studied mining in Austria, had a theory which made him optimistic, but he needed to find additional investment for the project.

The original Standard Oil Co. turned him down, and their expert of considerable fame, Calvin Payne, visited the site and declared, "You will never find oil here." A top Standard Oil executive named John Archibold had previously declared that he would "drink every gallon of oil found west of the Mississippi River." Lucas finally found backing in Pittsburgh with a wildcatting team and the Mellon banking family. Lucas and his wife even hocked their furniture in their conviction that the well would pay off.

And pay off it did. In 1901 the Lucas Gusher could produce at least half of the total U.S. production of 58 million barrels a year. It could match the output of 37,000 eastern U.S. oil wells and double the yield of all wells in Pennsylvania, the top oil state at that time.

The Lucas well established the Spindletop Field as the largest oil field in the world. The development of that field and its super-abundant cheap oil fueled America's growth engine in industry and transportation, and the world was greatly changed almost overnight. In 1907, Gulf Oil Corporation was formed by the founders and developers of the field, and it quickly grew into a major international company.

The cobalt blue chocolate cup and saucer from 1902 provide an excellent pathway to a story of history which cannot be told in its entirety here. The trials and ingenuity of the Hamill brothers, the sudden growth of Beaumont from 9,000 people to 50,000 people, and the crazed rush for wealth are all interesting aspects which remain untold.

HAMBY'S SALTS, IRON AND LITHIA WELL DAWSON SPRINGS, KENTUCKY

This child's cup or small mug is only 2¼" high and 2¼" in diameter. The beautiful color picture

Child's cup or mug showing interior view of Hamby's Salts, Iron, and Lithia Well, Dawson Springs, Ky., in full color. $50.00 – 75.00.

John H. Roth & Co. mark on bottom of cup.

reputation of Dawson Springs water began at that time, the famous Hamby well came from another inexhaustible vein of mineral water discovered by Hamby in June of 1893 in front of an unpretentious hotel he was operating.

Hamby was proprietor of the Hamby Hotel, owner of Hamby's Salts, Iron & Lithia Well, president of the New Century Hotel Co., and president of the Dawson Salts & Water Co., sole bottlers and shippers of Dawson Springs Water. Although there were at least 19 renowned wells in its heyday, Hamby and the Hamby well were dominant in Dawson Springs.

This little mug captures the essence of an important mineral water spa in its prime. This health resort in Dawson Springs and others like it were an important part of life in America. This beautiful little porcelain souvenir captures important elements of that time and place.

WINYAH INN
GEORGETOWN, SOUTH CAROLINA

Ornate and colorful vase with view of only Colonial Bank building in U. S., now Winyah Inn. $50.00 – 75.00.

wraps around half of the mug, which is embossed and has an interesting applied handle. The mark on the bottom indicates that it was imported by Jonroth (John H. Roth & Co.) and made in Germany for Dawson Salts & Water Co. Incorporated. The picture was also seen on a postcard, which was probably copied by the engraver of the scene for this mug, produced between 1909 and 1915.

In the early years of the twentieth century, Dawson Springs, Kentucky, was one of the best known spas or health resorts in the South. There were some 40 hotels and boarding houses, in a thriving community with the most up-to-date facilities of all kinds. Curative claims of the mineral waters were profuse, and the water was shipped all around the world.

The original settler, discoverer, and most important promoter of Dawson Springs water was Captain W. I. Hamby, who struck "a strong vein of the finest chalybeate water" while digging a cistern on July 2, 1881. Although the health-enhancing

211

B.B.&F. mark on bottom of vase on bottom of page 211.

This colorfully decorated vase shows a very old colonial style building with a pair of horses pulling a wagon along the street in front. The mark on the bottom of the vase indicates that it was imported by B.B.& F. and made in Dresden, Germany. expressly for F. M. Brickman, Georgetown, South Carolina. The caption below the building claims that it is the "Only Colonial Bank Building in U.S., now Winyah Inn."

The firm of B.B.& F. has not been identified, although their mark shows up frequently on souvenir china, primarily in southern states. Occasionally it is seen along with the Wheelock mark, indicating that it was a regional wholesaler of china which used Wheelock to supply some or all of the souvenir china it distributed. Its wares were consistently compatible with those supplied by Wheelock. This vase did not bear a Wheelock mark, and the form is not a common one.

A bronze plaque on the building signed by the Georgetown Chapter, D.A.R states that the building was the "ONLY COLONIAL BANKING HOUSE IN AMERICA, BUILT 1735 WITH MATERIALS BROUGHT FROM ENGLAND."

According to a source at the Georgetown County Historical Society, "no one is able to substantiate that there was a colonial banking house there." However, there is no doubt that the building has a long history involving much alteration and many uses, and early records show that it was a banking house until 1870, when the Bank of Georgetown went into receivership. Apparently, the D.A.R. claim (same as the claim on the souvenir vase) is tied to an old safe found in the basement containing a seal of the British Crown and some English coins.

The property changed hands several times between 1870 and 1902 when Mrs. Jessie Theo Butler purchased the old stucco brick building, opened the Winyah Inn in 1902, and operated the inn until 1908. The souvenir vase was produced in Dresden during that period, with the engraver apparently using a wonderful old photograph now in the Georgetown Historical Society's Morgan Collection. Although several people and a goat cart were shown in the photograph, they were omitted by the engraver of this scene.

The building was purchased by the Georgetown Rifle Guards in 1908, who altered its appearance drastically to create The Armory. It has been a Masonic Lodge (Winyah Lodge, No. 40, A.F.M.) since 1914.

Fred M. Brickman, the man for whom the item was produced, was a prominent merchant who owned the Phoenix Furniture Company on Front Street. Apparently not many pieces were made, judging by their current rarity among collectors in the local community.

THE NARROWS
WILLIAMS CANON, COLORADO

Seven-inch coupe plate showing The Narrows, Williams Canon, Colorado, and mark on base "H.H.Tammen, Lucky Buck, Made in Germany." $40.00 – 65.00.

H.H.Tammen Co. mark on bottom of plate.

10056. The Narrows.
Almost at the entrance of the Canon is a spot where the trail takes a circuitous route, scarcely as wide as a carriage.

A postcard also produced by Tammen shows a copy of the same scene used to produce this plate.

This seven-inch hand-painted, full scene coupe plate is typical of a very popular style of souvenir china which was the predecessor of today's collector plates. It was produced for H.H. Tammen Co. in Germany, as indicated by the red trademark on the bottom of the plate.

Most of the plates done in this style were imported by Jonroth (John H. Roth & Co.) and dated from 1909 to approximately 1934, with an interruption between 1916 and 1922 for World War I. Some of the earliest plates in this style showing Colorado scenes were imported by H.H.

Tammen, who used an artist's palette as his logo along with the name "Lucky Buck Studios." Tammen was an important figure in the settling of the west and in Colorado history (see Chapter 1, The Pioneers). Jonroth somehow obtained the rights to the palette mark after 1909, although Tammen continued to use the mark on some items until at least 1912. Tammen was both a wholesaler and a retailer, and there is no way of knowing the store which sold this item or the manufacturer who produced it in Germany.

The scene is hand-painted and colorful, and the edge of the plate is gilded. The picture covers the entire bowl of the plate, and takes on a three-dimensional appearance due to its concavity. The view represents an early tourist attraction located west of Colorado Springs and north of Manitou Springs. Tourists would ride burros into the Williams Canyon (then spelled Canon), as they did to many of the other attractions in the Pikes Peak area. The Williams Canyon leads to the Cave of the Wind (which has become one of the premier attractions in the area), although, it has been closed as a route of access.

In the *Tourist Guide to the Pikes Peak Region*, published in August of 1912, the description of Williams Canon states, "Shortly after entering the canon, the way appears to be completely barred by the massive walls in front, but a turn in the road reveals a small opening between them, called the Narrows, a passageway hardly wide enough to clear the singletrees of the carriage...The bubbling brook runs over pebbles stamped with the language of the rocks and magnifies their tale." The picture on this plate captures the description perfectly, and proves that a picture is truly worth many words.

In its prime as a mineral springs resort (during the period when this plate was sold), Manitou Springs was a popular destination for people of means who stayed in its fashionable hotels. It was one of the earliest communities to feature electric lights. Visitors hired burros, such as the one shown on the plate, from local livery stables and ventured forth to see the natural wonders.

CHAPTER FIVE

RELATED ITEMS

Comprehensive coverage of related items is beyond the scope of this book. However, this chapter provides an overview of Historical Staffordshire, as well as the subject of more recently produced souvenir plates. Other souvenir china items produced for the U. S. market prior to World War II included pottery items made by Hampshire Pottery in Keene, New Hampshire, and some semi-vitreous souvenirs (other than plates) made in Ohio and New Jersey. They differ too significantly in composition and appearance to be an integral part of the collecting niche being covered by this book. Items produced in Japan are also generally outside of the genre of souvenir china as defined by this text.

Lists of manufacturers and importers of the Historical Staffordshire and souvenir plates were purposely eliminated from this chapter. They are editorially replaced with the statement that the information is readily available in texts dealing primarily with those items, but which do not include thorough coverage of souvenir china.

HISTORICAL STAFFORDSHIRE

This typical Historical Staffordshire plate with fruit and flower border depicts the Dam and Water Works, Philadelphia. It is 10" in diameter and was produced for the American market by Henshall, Williamson & Company, Longport, Staffordshire. $450.00 – 500.00.

Historical Staffordshire dinnerware was produced prolifically for the American market during the first half of the nineteenth century. The potteries surrounding Stokes-on-Trent, Staffordshire, England, had evolved the technology by the end of the War of 1812, and found an enormous demand fueled by patriotism and pride in the young country which had been their former enemy.

Most of the historical scenes were printed in cobalt blue ink which withstood the underglaze firing process well and caught the fancy of the market at the same time. Many of the early scenes involved pro-American battles scenes or war heroes. The British merchants effectively turned their past defeats into economic gains. Other scenes showed various aspects of the American way of life and its natural beauty. Buildings included churches, hotels and even an insane asylum in New York! The way scenes were selected was apparently not much different than for those depicted on the German souvenir china at the end of the century.

The subject of Historical Staffordshire is complex and has been well covered in comprehensive texts by several experts. The original issue of *The Antique Collector* (dated February 1939), by Sam Laidacker, depicted a group of six Historical Staffordshire cup plates on the cover with supporting descriptions on the inside. It also presented a feature article on "The Vine Leaf Border Series A33" and announced the publication of the book *American Historical Views on Staffordshire China* by Eloise Baker Larsen, which sold originally for $10.00 (a substantial price at that time). Considered by some to be the definitive book on the subject, it was well supplemented by publications of Laidacker.

The era of Historical Staffordshire began to close gradually around 1860, and a new generation of souvenir plates produced in Staffordshire entered the American marketplace toward the end of the century. These were not made of the same composition of earthenware/pearlware china as their predecessors, but were formed in a semi-vitreous china, more resistant to damage. They were no longer produced as service china, but strictly as commemoratives or souvenirs for the collector. The cobalt underglaze with its rich flow blue tone was modified in the newer transfer process.

This example of Wedgwood 9" souvenir plate with cabbage rose border features a scene of The Rock Mere in Marblehead, Mass. $50.00 – 75.00

Example of Pratt plate made for Centennial Exhibition in Philadelphia in 1976.

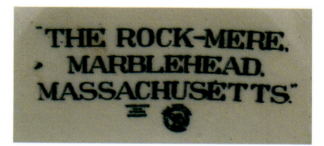

Bottom marks on Wedgwood plate include the Wedgwood mark, embossed production marks, and the mark of the importer Jones, McDuffee & Stratton.

Perhaps the most noteworthy chronological bridge between the Historic wares and the souvenir plates is represented by the brightly colored transfer ware made by Pratt of Fenton, England, during the mid-nineteenth century (not to be confused with the earlier cream colored, polychrome decorated wares made by Felix Pratt in Staffordshire). among the outstanding decorations on Pratt/Fenton plates and pot lids were excellent scenes of the Philadelphia environs during the Centennial Exhibition of 1876.

SOUVENIR PLATES

The earliest souvenir plates were produced at approximately the same time as the advent of German souvenir china, and the Centennial Exposition (1876) is commonly cited as the beginning of that era. A souvenir plate produced by Davenport in the early 1880s is shown as an early example in *Souvenir Plates – A Collector's Guide* by Arene W. Burgess. It was during the 1890s when the two most significant importers of souvenir plates began to import their plates from Staffordshire, England.

Perhaps the most distinguished and comprehensive series of blue plates involved 9" plates by Wedgwood with cabbage rose borders similar to a popular design previously used on Historical wares. These were imported by Jones, McDuffee & Stratton of Boston, which remained in business into the 1960s. That firm also imported a series of calendar tiles from 1881 to 1929 which feature a different scene for each of those years (see Glossary).

A popular and significant series of rolled edge plates was imported for some 40 years by Rowland & Marsellus, one of the chief competitors of Jones, McDuffee & Stratton. Both R & M and J, McD & S imported many other commemorative and souvenir items, however the significance of these two series deserves special mention and a listing of the scenes. A glossary presents those listings

An example of a Jones, McDuffee, & Stratton/Wedgwood calendar tile is this one from 1918 featuring Boston Light. $75.00 – 125.00.

This example of a Rowland & Marsellus Co. rolled edge plate features scenes from New Bedford, Mass. $50.00 – 75.00.

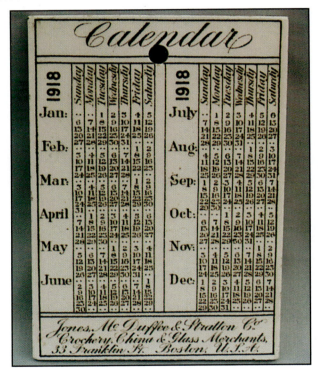

The calendar side of the tile.

Typical R & M bottom marks.

with the kind permission of the author/collectors who have compiled them.

Although the story of Jonroth has been previously related in detail, it is appropriate to mention the firm again in this section, as it is so closely associated with souvenir plates from Staffordshire, England. Jonroth has experienced outstanding longevity and has earned a reputation for quality in its continuing business of importing those plates. The Roth family has been in this trade for more than 80 years, and John H. Roth III continues to operate today in the same tradition. Jonroth plates have been made in many sizes and styles by William Adams & Co. and other fine Staffordshire producers for hundreds of locations here in the United States. Perhaps the most popular and well-known plate is 9¾" in diameter with a large center scene and four different scenes at the compass points, separated by sprays of roses.

This typical Jonroth 9¾" multi-scene plate showing scenes of Williamsburg, Virginia, was called Old English Staffordshire Ware, and was produced for Jonroth by Adams. $20.00 – 40.00.

Another significant style of souvenir blue plate was the 7½" coupe shaped, multi-scene shell plate. Various importers had these souvenirs made by a variety of producers made in England from the late 1890s to approximately 1928. There are minor variations in design, but an overall similarity prevails. The number of towns and cities for which these were produced appears to be infinite. Undoubtedly, these will be catalogued by some collector when their time comes. Although the great majority of these so-called shell plates were made in England, a few good copies were made in Germany. This one features views of Orleans, Mass., and was imported from England by Wheelock. $40.00 – 65.00.

This custom designed 7" plate exemplifies the variety of custom designs which can be found. This one features the Salem Witch; it was commissioned by Daniel Low, a well-known jewelry store in Salem, Mass., as shown on the bottom mark on right. $100.00 – 150.00.

English porcelain souvenir from an exhibition in 1857 shows the great capabilities of their porcelain industry at that time. Items such as this are not known to have been made for the American trade. $50.00 – 75.00.

English porcelain items began to compete with the dwindling supply of German items around 1915. They were generally more porous than the German items and many have become discolored with age. This one, depicting a statue of Nathan Hale, remains in excellent condition. Items such as this are closely related to the souvenir china of German and Austrian origin, which is generally considered the core of collectible souvenir china. In fact, some collectors may even prefer the items of English origin. Under $20.00.

Souvenir plates and trays from Limoges, France, fall into two categories. A few common scenes, such as Mt. Vernon with side pictures of George and Martha Washington, were actually decorated in France. Generally, these are common items with common scenes and do not command high prices. The other category involves items which were decorated by china painters here in the United States. Some such items, such as the one shown here, can be very desirable, depending on the subject and the quality of the art work. This scene of a lifesaving station was painted by a local artist in 1896. $100.00 – 150.00.

German Made Stoneware

German made stoneware souvenirs are closely related to souvenir china. The following examples were made during the same era by many of the producers of beer steins and beakers.

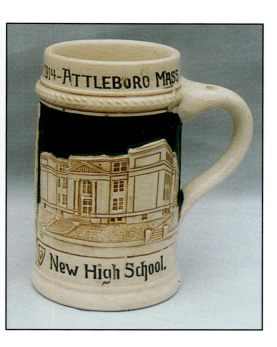

Three mini steins shown in relation to a toothpick, featuring excellent graphics of desirable locations; millstone bottom marks are shown below. These are becoming very collectible. $45.00 – 65.00 each.

A typical souvenir stein which was made in several sizes and features designs in relief, usually with a dark green background; seldom found with pewter tops, as the extra cost was generally prohibitive for the intended market. $30.00 – 50.00.

219

Stoneware beer mug which was a souvenir of a famous mineral spring resort. Many similar mugs were also made in the United States. $75.00 – 125.00.

AMERICAN CERAMIC SOUVENIRS

American ceramic firms produced souvenir china in various styles which did not include hard paste porcelain in the style of the continental wares. Two of the most notable firms which produced outstanding items on earthenware forms were Buffalo Pottery and Hampshire Pottery. Detailed references are available elsewhere on both of these firms.

Hampshire Pottery of Keene, New Hampshire, produced this beautiful heart-shaped dish with a tinted bow and a sepia scene of Windham Town Hall The bottom mark is shown below. $40.00 – 65.00.

Marked Metlach beaker features the very desirable Salem Witch. This form is well know, although American scenes are rare. $150.00+.

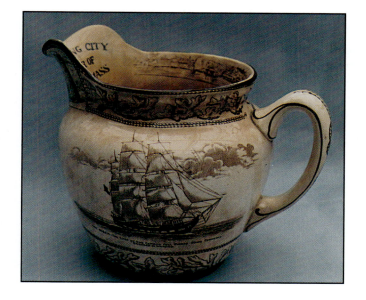

This magnificent pitcher was part of a series of similar items introduced by Buffalo Pottery between 1905 and 1908. The whaling subject matter pictured here makes this piece highly desirable. $350.00 – 450.00.

This creamer by Harker (probably in the 1930s) is made of semi-vitreous china and typical of the wares produced by American firms; most items were in the form of plates and many of those were made for churches. Under $20.00.

CUSTARD GLASS SOUVENIRS

Custard glass pictorial souvenirs are related to souvenir china through graphics, function, and the time period during which they were produced. Other glass ware was also used for pictorial souvenirs. Custard glass souvenir items were produced by Heisey and its competitors. Shown here are two creamers: (L) U.S.L.S.S. Lifeboat and Crew, near Aberdeen, Wash. $65.00 – 100.00; (R) Hotel Riverside, Cambridge Springs, Pa. $40.00 – 65.00.

APPENDIX
WEDGWOOD VIEWS OF THE UNITED STATES

(S) indicates series of plates exists, individual views not listed here; (1) indicates item produced for Daniel Low & Co., Salem, Mass.; (2) indicates item produced for A.S. Burbank, Pilgrim Book Store, Plymouth, Mass.; (3) indicates item produced for The Boston Store, Erie, Pa.

A:

Abbot Academy, Andover, Mass. 1829 – 1929
Acadia University 1838 – 1938 (S)
Agnes Scott College, Buttrick Hall
Agriculture & Mechanical College of Texas (S)
Aiken Homestead, Norwich, Conn.
Akron Woman's Club, Akron, Ohio
Alabama College (S)
Alabama State Capitol, Montgomery (Lebron Jewelry Co.)
Alamo (Newton, Weller & Wagner, San Antonio)
Albany, N.Y.: Capitol Building (John G. Myers)
       Old State Capitol 1806 – 1883 (John G. Myers)
Albion College (S)
Alden, Priscilla and John (1) (2) (3)
Alder, Jonathan Cabin, Jefferson, Ohio
Alexandria Bay, N.Y. (Cornwall Bros.)
Alexandria Bay, Heart Island (Cornwall Bros.)
Altoona, Pa.: Horsehoe Curve (Wm. F. Gable)
American Sailing Ships 1950 (S)
Amherst College (S)
Amsterdam, N.Y.: Fort Jackson (Montgomery County H.S.)
      Guy Park (Amsterdam DAR)
Antlers, Colorado Springs, Colo. (H. W. Wyman)
Arkansas Statehood, Commemorating the Centennial 1836 – 1936
Arlington, Home of Martha Custis
Augusta, Maine: World War Memorial (Augusta PTA)

B:

Baldwin, Mary College, Administration Building
Barton, Clara Birthplace
Bates College 1864 – 1939 (S)
Bath, Maine: The People's Church 1902 (D.T. Percy & Sons)
Battle of Lexington Common (1)
Baylor University (S)
Bennington Battle Monument (Oatman & Wood, A. J. Pendergast)
Benton Harbor, Michigan: City of (Young Peck & Co.)
Berry School, Mount Berry Chapel, Mount Berry, Ga.
Birth of the American Flag
Block Island, R.I.: South East Lighthouse (C.C. Ball)
Blue Mountain College, The Lowery, 75th Anniversary
Boston, City Hall
      Common & State House 1836
      Faneuil Hall
      Green Dragon Tavern
      Hotel Sheraton
      in 1768 (3)
      John Hancock House
      Kings Chapel
      Lamb Tavern 1746
      Old Boston Theatre
      Old Brick Church
      Old Corner Bookstore
      Old Feather Store (2)
      Old North Church (2) (3)
      Old South Church (1) (2)
      Old State House, East End
      Old State House Built 1717

      Old Sun Tavern
      Park Street Theatre
      Public Library
      State House
      State Street & State House in 1886
      Tea Party (1) (2)
      Town Hall
      University 1948 (S)
Bowdoin College 1931 (S)
Branford, Conn.: The Russell House
Brenau College (S)
Bridgeport, Conn.: Centennial of the City 1836 – 1936
Brown University (S)
Bryn Mawr (S)
Bunker Hill Monument (2)

C:

California Republic 1939 (S) (Barker Bros. L.A.)
Cambridge, Mass: Longfellow's House 1843 (1) (2)
      The Washington Elm (2)
Campus Martius, Marietta, Ohio (DAR Ohio)
Capitol, Washington, D.C. (1)
Carpenters' Hall, Philadelphia
Cedar Crest College, Administration Building
Chalfant House, Allegheny, Pa.
Champlain Memorial Monument, Plattsburg, N.Y. (Walker-Sherman Co.)
Charleston, S.C., (S) (James Allan & Co. Inc.)
Chatham, Va.: Chatham Hall
Chew House, Germantown, Pa.
Chicago, Ill.: Old First Congregational Church
      Union Park Congregational Church
Clark University 1837 – 1937
Clark, George Rogers Memorial 1931 (DAR Vincennes, Ind.)
Cleveland, Grover
Coker College (S)
Colby College, Waterville, Maine (S)
Colby Junior College (S)
College of the City of New York (S)
College of Holy Cross 1932 (S)
College of Notre Dame of Maryland 1895 – 1945
College of Our Lady of the Elms, Chicopee, Mass. (S)
Colorado State Capitol, Denver
Columbia College, Administration Building, Columbia, S.C.
Columbia University (S)
Concord, Mass.: First Parish Church 1636 – 1951
      Home of Ralph Waldo Emerson
      The Old North Bridge
Concord, N.H.: Pleasant View, Home of the Rev. Mary Baker Eddy
Converse College, Spartanburg, S.C.
Cornell University (S)
Custis Martha, Wife of George Washington
Cuyahoga County Solders & Sailors Monument, Cleveland, Ohio

D:

Davidson College 1837 – 1937
Denison University (S)
Dickinson College (S)
Duke University 1937 (S)

E:

Earlham College, Earlham Hall
East Boston Bethel Peoples Church
Easton, Md.: Old Third Haven Meeting House
Ellisworth (Oliver) Homestead, Windsor, Conn. (Conn. DAR 1929)
Elmira College (S)
Elmwood, Cambridge: Home of James Russell Lowell (3)
Emerson, Ralph Waldo; Home of, Concord, Mass. (2)
Erie Public Library (3)

F:

Fairbanks Family in America, Fairbanks, House, Dedham, Mass.
Fairleigh-Dickinson College, Rutherford, N.J. (S)
Faneuil Hall, Cradle of Liberty 1742
Fenimore Hall, N.Y.S.H.A., Cooperstown, N.Y.
Fifth Avenue Hotel, Madison Square, N.Y.
Fisher Junior College, Boston
Florida State University, Westcott Building
Fort Ticonderoga, N.Y. (S)
Foxcroft 1934 (S)
Fredericksburg, Va.: Kenmore
Fresno County Court House (Holland & Holland)
Friends University, Wichita, Kansas 1936 (S)
Frontenac Hotel, St. Lawrence River, N.Y. (C.A. Ellis, Clayton, N.Y.)
Furman University, Bell Tower

G:

Garden Club of America (S)
Gardner Mass.: Elisha Jackson House 1785 – 1935
Garfield Memorial, Cleveland, Ohio (Levy & Straus)
Gettysburg College Centennial 1832 – 1932 (S)
Glenwood Campanile & Chimes (F. Miller, Riverdale, Calif.)
Grant, General Ulysses S.
Grant's Tomb, Riverside Dr., N.Y.
Green Dragon Tavern, Boston
Greensboro College (S)
Greensboro Lodge 125th Anniversary 1946, Greensboro, N.C.
Greensboro Masonic & Eastern Star Home 1950, Greensboro, N.C.
Groton School 1935 (S)
Guildford College 1837 – 1937, Founders Hall

H:

"Half Moon" on the Hudson
Hamden, Conn.: The Old Red House (Hamden Historical Society)
John Hancock House, Boston
Harrisburg, Pa.: The New State Capitol (Edgar, Einstein & Co.)
Harrison, Home of Caroline Scott, Oxford, Ohio (Ohio DAR)
Harrison Mansion, Vincennes, Ind. (Ohio DAR)
Harrison, Wm. Henry Commemoratory Centennial 1841 – 1941
Hartford, Conn.: First Church
Harvard University (S)
Hawthorne, Nathaniel (1)
Heidelberg College 1850 – 1950 (S)
Hermitage, Home of Andrew Jackson
"Hetmere," Beverly, Mass.
High Rocks Springs (Charles A. Lee, Saratoga Springs, N.Y.)
Hill School 1936, Alumni Hall
Hingham, Mass.: Old Meeting House (2)
Hoboken, N.J.: Castle Point, Residence of E.A. Stevens, Esq.
   Trinity Church
Hollins College, Virginia (S)

Home of the United Woman's Efforts (Lynn's Women Clubhouse)
Hoosac Tunnel (Poor Bros. Jewelry, North Adams, Mass.)
Horseshoe Curve, Altoona, Pa. (Wm. F. Gable)
Howard College, Birmingham, Ala., Old Main
Huntington College, Flowers Hall, Centennial 1954

I:

In the Berkshires, Red Lion Inn, Stockbridge, Mass.
Independence Hall, Philadelphia (1) (3)
Indian Hinter Menotomy, Arlington, Mass.
Indiana, First State Capitol
Indiana University, Memorial Hall
Iroquois Sally Winter, Grand Champion Female, Nat'l. Dairy Show 1929

J:

Jones, McDuffee & Stratton 100th Anniversary plate
Jordan March Centennial Plates 1851 – 1951 (S)
Judson College

K:

Kansas Shawnee Mission Centennial (Kansas DAR 1937)
King's Chapel, Boston

L:

LaGrange College, Georgia; Smith Hall
Lake George, Monument Commemorating Battle of 1755
Lamb Tavern, 1746 Boston
Landing of the Pilgrims (1) (2)
Langdon House, Portsmouth, N.H. (Geo. B. French & Co.)
Lee Mansion (Marblehead Historical Society, Marblehead, Mass.)
Lexington Common, Battle on (1)
Library of Congress, 1897
Light House Point, Lake Superior (Geo. Conklin, Marquette, Mich.)
Limestone College 1945 Centennial (S)
Lincoln, Abraham
Lincoln House, Springfield, Ill. (John Bressner & Co.)
Lincoln Monument, Springfield, Ill. (John Bressner & Co.)
Livermore, Mary A.; Home of (W.A. Smith, Melrose, Mass.)
Lockport, N.Y. (Williams Bros.)
Long Island, Commemorating the Tercentenary 1636 – 1936 (A&S)
Longfellow, Birthplace of
Longfellow's Early Home, Portland, Maine (T.T. Foss & Sons)
Longfellow's House, Cambridge, Mass. 1842 (1) (2) (3)
Longfellow's House 1795 (W.W.M. Co., Portland)
Longfellow Series (S)
Longmeadow, Mass.: Town Settled 1644
Loretto, Pa.: St. Michael's Church (W.F. Sellers & Co., Altoona)
Louisiana Polytechnic Institute (S)
Lowell, Home of James Russell: Elmwood, Cambridge (3)

M:

Mabie, Jan House, Rotterdam, N.Y. (Montgomery County H.S.)
MacMurray College 1846 – 1946, Main Hall
Madison College, Harrisonburg, Va.: Woodrow Wilson Hall
Maine Capitol (Geo. W. Quimby, Augusta, Maine)
Manchester in the Mountains, Vermont (Oatman & Wood)
Maplewood Hotel 1900 (A. A. Mills, Pittsfield, Mass.)
Marietta College, Erwin Hall
Maryland College for Women 1935
Massachusetts Charitable Eye & Ear Infirmary 1850 – 1899

Massachusetts Institute of Technology 1930 (S)
"Mayflower" in Plymouth Harbor (1) (2) (3)
"Mayflower" in Provincetown Harbor (Hopkins, Town Crier Shop)
McKinley Home, Canton, Ohio
McKinley, Wm., In Memorial (Geo. Deeble, Canton, Ohio)
McKinley Monument, Buffalo, N.Y. (Walbridge & Co.)
Media Hotel & Mineral Baths (H.H. Lichtig Co., Mt. Clemens, Mich.)
Medical College of Virginia 1838 – 1938, Egyptian Building
Melrose Public Library, Melrose, Mass.
Memorial Continental Hall, D.C. (DAR'S)
Mendota, Minn.: The Sibley House (Wenonah DAR)
Mercersburg Academy (S)
Michigan College of Mines, Houghton, Mich. (Wm. B. Hoar)
Middlebury College (S)
Middlebury, Vt.: Congregational Church (Wm. H. Sheldon)
Milton, Mass.; 250th Anniversary
Minnehaha Falls, Minn. (Beard Art & Stationery Co.)
Monticello, Home of Thomas Jefferson (3) (Covington & Peyton)
Mormon Temple Block, Salt Lake City, Utah
Moorings, The, Hampton, Va. 1929
Mount Holyoke College (S)
Mount of the Holy Cross, Colorado
Mount Tom, Summit House (Mount Tom Railway)
Mount Vernon (1) (2)
Mount Washington from Intervale, N.H.

N:
Nantucket (H S Wyer)
Nantucket Island: Old Coffee House (H.S. Wyer)
          Old Windmill (H.S. Wyer)
          Sankoty Head Light (H.S. Wyer)
Nashville, Tenn.: Hermitage Mansion
Natchez on the Mississippi
Nebraska State Capitol, Lincoln, Neb. (Fitzgerald Dry Good Co.)
New Albany, Ind.: Scribner House
New American (A.A. Mills, Pittsfield, Mass.)
New Canaan, Conn.: Grace House in the Fields (L.M. Monroe)
New-Castle-on-the-Delaware, Read House 1801
New Harmony, Ind.: Old Faunlberry House
New Haven, Conn. 1931(S)
New Jersey Churches (S)
New London, Conn.: Old Town Mill (L. Lewis & Co.)
New York Fifth Avenue Hotel, Madison Square
York Series, Old New (S)
New York University (S)
Newark Art Club 1929 (S)
Newport, R.I. The Old Stone Mill (Walsh Bros)
Niagara Falls
Northeast Missouri State Teachers College, John R. Kirk
          Memorial

O:
Ohio University 1804 – 1954 (S)
Ohio Wesleyan University 1842 – 1942 (S)
Old Ironsides
Old Man of the Mountains (Flume Reservation, Franconia Notch, N.H.)
Old Nathan Hale School House, Built 1774 (L. Lewis & Co.)
Old Town Church, Oldest Bell Tower in America (Rhodes Bros., Tacoma)
Old Whale Ship, Gen. Williams (L. Lewis & Co., New London)
Oliver, Rebecca B. & David B. 1879 – 1936

Onota Lake (J.A. Maxin, Pittsfield, Mass.)
Ore Docks, Escanada, Mich. (The Fair Savings Bank)
Orrville, First Church in

P:
Paoli, Ind., Orange County Court House (DAR 1935)
Park Hotel & Baths (H.H. Lichtig & Co., Mt. Clemens, Mich.)
Parker, Captain John, Battle Green, Lexington
Parson, Cornet Joseph, Home of: Northampton, Mass.
Pasadena, Calif.: Hotel Green (Pasadena Grocery Co.)
          Hotel Raymond (Pasadena Grocery Co.)
          Maryland Hotel (Pasadena Grocery Co.)
Payne Memorial, John Howard "Home Sweet Home," East
          Hampton, N.Y.
Peabody Museum, Salem, Mass. 1799 – 1949 (S)
Pearl of Orr's Island," "The, H. Beecher Stowe's Story
Philadelphia, Pa. Carpenters' Hall
          Independence Hall (1) (3)
          Interior of Christ Church (Tyndale & Mitchell)
Pikes Peak from the Garden of the Gods, Colorado
Pilgrim's Exile (1) (2)
Pilgrim Memorial Monument (Provincetown Advocate & Town
          Crier Shop)
Pittsburgh, Pa.: Cloverly, Dallas Avenue 1886 – 1926
          "Holmhurst" 1922
Pittsfield, Mass. 1896, Old Elm Park
Plymouth, The Harbor 1622 (2)
Poe Lock, Sault Ste. Marie, Mich. (Ruddell Drug Co.)
Poland Springs
Pomona College (S)
Portland, Maine: The Birthplace of Longfellow
          Longfellow's Early Home, Built 1785
          State Street Church 1894
Prescott Colonel Wm., Homestead, Pepperell, Mass.
Princeton University (S)
Principia College 1898 – 1947, The Chapel
Priscilla and John Alden (1) (2) (3)

Q:
Quincy Homestead, Quincy, Mass.
Quincy, Mass.: Adjacent Lean-to-houses
          First Church 1639 – 1896 (G. Pettengell)

R:
Radcliffe College 1934 (S)
Randolph-Macon College, Ashland, Va., The Chapel
Randolph-Macon Woman's College (S)
Red Lion Inn, Stockbridge, Mass.
Regis College (S)
Return of the "Mayflower" (1) (2)
Paul Revere's Ride
Ripon, Wisc.: First Congregational Church
Riverdale, Calif.: Glenwood Campanile (Frank A. Milles)
Riverside County Court House, Calif. (Geo. F. Mott)
Rockland, Maine: Owl's Head (Fuller & Cobb)
Rockmere, Marblehead, Mass.
Rollins College
Roosevelt, Theodore
Rosedale, Miss. 1820 – 1940; Historic State Shrine DAR
Ruins of Old Spanish Mission, New Smyrna, Fla.
Russell Sage College 1916 – 1941, Gurley Hall
Rye Beach, N.H.: Farragut House

S:
Sailing Ships (S)
St. Ann's by the Sea (Geo. Bonser & Sons)
St. Augustine, Fla. (Greenleaf & Crosby Co.)
   Old City Gateway (W. H. DuBois)
   Watch Tower of Fort San Marco (W.H. DuBois)
St. Lawrence Hotel Columbian (James Morris, 1000 Islands)
St. Lawrence University (S)
St. Marks School (S)
St. Mary of the Woods College (S)
St. Mary's School & Junior College, Raleigh, N.C.
St. Paul's School 1928 (S)
St. Polycarps Church, Somerville, Mass. (S)
Salem Academy, Winston-Salem, N.C.
Salem, Mass.: First Church, Erected in 1634 (1)
   House of the Seven Gables (1)
   Pickering Dodge House
Salisbury, N.C.: St. Johns Lutheran Church 1953
San Carlos de Monterey or Carmel Mission (Show & Hunt, Santa
   Barbara)
San Fernando Rey Mission, San Fernando, Calif. (Hunt's China)
San Gabriel Archangel Mission (Show & Hunt)
San Luis Rey de Francia Mission (Hunt's China)
Santa Barbara, Calif.: Mission
   Picturesque (M. M. Potter, Hotel Potter)
Saratoga Springs, N.Y.: Battle Field, Period Block House
   (F.W. Beach)
   Battle Monument (F. W. Beach)
Saratoga Springs, N.Y.: Grand Union Hotel (Veronica Art Co.)
Sibley House, Centennial of (Minnesota Chapter DAR)
Sibley House, Mendota, Minn. (Winona DAR's)
Signing of the Declaration of Independence
Simmons College 1902 – 1952, Main Building
Skelton, Home of Doctor Henry; Southington, Conn.
Smith College 1932 (S)
Snow Camp, N.C.: Cave Creek Friends Church 1751 – 1951
Southern Methodist University, Dallas Hall
Spirit of '76, "Yankee Doodle" (1)
Springfield, Ill. Capitol Building 1900
Stanford University Memorial Chapel (H.W. Simkins, Palo Alto)
State Normal School, Mary Hall 1838 – 1939, Framingham,
   Mass.
State Teachers College, Bloomsburg, Pa.
State Teachers College, Fainville, Va. (S)
Stevens Institute of Technology, Hoboken, N.J.
Stockbridge, Mass.: Mission House 1739
Stratford Hall, Westmoreland County, Va.; Birthplace of Richard
   Henry Lee
Summit House, Mount Tom (Mount Tom Railway)
Sunderland, Mass.: The Old Hubbard Tavern
Sunnie Holme, Fairfield, Conn. 1927
Sunny Meadows Farm, near Melvin Village, N.H. 1932
Swarthmore College (S)
Sweet Briar College, Sweet Briar House

T:
Tamassee, S.C. DAR School (S)
Templeton, Mass.: John W. Stiles, Trader House 1810
Texas
Texas Christian University 1873 – 1948
Transylvania Club (S)
Trinity College, Washington, D.C. (S)

Tufts College 1932 (S)
Tulane University (S)

U:
Union College (S)
Union Station, Washington
United Commercial Travelers 14th Session Boston 1908
U.S. Frigate "Constitution"
U.S. Military Academy 1933 (S)
U.S. Naval Academy (S)
University of California (S)
University of Delaware (S)
University of Georgia (S)
University of Iowa (S)
University of Maine 1940 (S)
University of Michigan 1935 (S)
University of North Carolina, Main Entrance, Alumnae Hall
University of Oklahoma, Administration Building
University of Pennsylvania (S)
University of Richmond, The Tower, West Hampton College
University of Rochester (S)
University of Southern California 1933 (S)
University of Texas (S)
University of Toledo, Toledo Hall (S)
University of Virginia (S)
University of Washington, Seattle (S)
Upper Falls, Rumford Falls, Maine (G.A. Peabody & Co)
Upper Iowa University, College Hall 1940

V:
Van Alstyne House, Canajoharie, N.Y.
Van Corlandt House, Colonial Dames of New York
Vassar College (S)
Vincennes, The Capture of (DAR Chapter)
Virginia Female Institute, Old Main & Stuart Hall
Virginia Military Institute (S)

W:
Wadsworth-Longfellow House, Portland, Maine
Wake Forest College (S)
Warner House, Portsmouth, N.H. (Oren M. Snow)
Washington Bi-Centennial 1932 (S)
Washington Crossing the Delaware (3)
Washington Elm, Cambridge, Mass. (2)
Washington Headquarters, Newburgh, N.Y.
Washington, D.C.: The Capitol (1)
   First Congregational Church, 10th & G, NW
   National Gallery of Art
   Union Station
   Washington Monument
   The White House
Washington & Lee University (S)
Waterbury, Conn.: Rose Hill, Home of A. S. Chase
Waterville, Maine: City Hall, Built 1902
Wayside Inn, Sudbury, Mass. 1683
Webb House, Wethersfield, Conn. (Connecticut DAR)
Wells Commemorative Plate 1863 – 1943
Wells Fargo Coach, Wells Commemorative Plate 1868 – 1950
Wellesley College 1936 (S)
Wendell Hotel (A. A. Mills Co., Pittsfield, Mass.)
Wentworth Mansion, Portsmouth, N.H. (Oren M. Snow)
Wesleyan College, First Chartered College for Women 1836 (S)

Wesleyan University 1831 – 1931 (S)
Western College, Oxford, Ohio
Westtown School 1935 (S)
Wheaton College, Ill.
Wheaton College 1932 (S)
Whittier, Birthplace of (1) (2)
Emma Willard School, Troy, N.Y. (S)
Williams College (S)
Woodrow Wilson, Birthplace of: Staunton, Va.
Winchester, Va.: First Congregational Church 100th year 1940

Winona State Teachers College, Somsen Hall, Winona, Minn
Witch House, also known as Roger Williams House 1634 (1)
Worcester, Mass.: Union Congregational Church

Y:
Yale University (S)
Yale College and the Old Yale Fence (3)
"Yankee Doodle," Spirit of '76 (1)
Yarmouth, Mass.: Old Meeting House

CALENDAR TILES PRODUCED BY WEDGEWOOD FOR JONES, MCDUFFEE & STRATTON CO., BOSTON

1881	Washington Headquarters, Cambridge
1882	Washington Statue, Public Gardens
1883	Ribbon Badge
1884	(no view)
1885	Map of Boston, 1722
1886	Portland Vase
1887	AA "Britannia" & SS "Eturia"
1888	Josiah Wedgwood's Portrait
1889	Faneuil Hall
1890	Old State House
1891	Adams Lean-to-houses, Quincy
1892	Mount Vernon
1893	Independence Hall, Philadelphia
1894	Boston Public Library
1895	State House, Boston
1896	Trinity Church, Boston
1897	Old Federal Street Theatre
1898	King's Chapel
1899	Washington Elm
1900	John Hancock House
1901	Bunker Hill Monument
1902	Old North Church
1903	Elmwood, Home of James Russell Lowell
1904	United States Frigate "Constitution" in chase
1905	The Stephenson and Twentieth Century Locomotives

1906	Jones, McDuffee & Stratton Co. Store, Franklin Street
1907	Harvard Stadium
1908	Harvard Medical School
1909	Boston Art Museum
1910	"Mayflower" approaching land
1911	U.S. Frigate "Constitution" & Battleship "Florida"
1912	Cunard Line Dock (new) Boston
1913	Pier 46 Mystic Wharves
1914	Pier Head of Commonwealth Dock, Boston
1915	Boston Customs House
1916	M. I. T.
1917	U.S. Navy Yard, Boston
1918	Boston Light
1919	Memorial Hall, Harvard University
1920	"Mayflower" in Plymouth Harbor, 1620
1921	John Harvard, Founder of Harvard College (statue)
1922	Cathedral Church of St. Paul
1923	Minute Man, Concord
1924	The Appeal of the Great Spirit
1925	The Flying Cloud
1926	Coolidge Homestead
1927	Cathedral Church of St. Paul
1928	Plymouth Rock
1929	House of the Seven Gables

ROWLAND & MARSELLUS ROLLED EDGE PLATES

If a state's initials are shown in parentheses, state's name is not printed on the view; all plates have six border scenes, and plates imported by R&M unless otherwise stated; plates imported by R&M unless otherwise noted.

PLACE	CENTER SCENE	NOTES
Albany, (NY), Souvenir of	State Capitol	
Albany, (NY), Souvenir of	Fort Frederick, State Street in 1775	
Allentown, PA, Souvenir of	The Pike	
Altoona, PA, Souvenir of	Horseshoe Curve	
Arlington, VA		
Asbury, Park, NJ, Views of	Casino	Also in Multi-colors
Atlantic City, NJ, Souvenir of	Bathing Hour	Some with silver engraving. Also in multi-colors.
Baltimore, MD, Souvenir of	Court House	
Baltimore, Ind, Souvenir of	Court House	Identical to Baltimore, MD plate except for the Ind. misprint
Bangor, (ME), Souvenir of	River Front	
Battle Creek, MI, Souvenir of	B.C. Sanitarium	
Bermuda	Alias Somers Island, Islands of the Great Sound	
Bermuda	Alias Somers Island 1609 – 1909	Almost identical to above plate except for addition of dates.
Bermuda, Views of	Royal Palms, Hamilton, Bermuda	
Boston, Mass., Souvenir of	Tremont Street Mall	
Boston, (Mass.), Historical	Faneuil Hall	
Bridgeport, Conn., Souvenir of	Soldiers Monument at Seaside Park	
Brooklyn, NY, Souvenir of	New York and Brooklyn Bridge	
Buffalo, NY, Souvenir of	Buffalo Library and Soldiers Monument, Lafayette Square	
Butte, Montana, Souvenir of	Bronco Busting	
Carlisle, (PA), Souvenir of	New Denny Hall	

PLACE	CENTER SCENE	NOTES
Charleston, W.VA., Souvenir of	State Capitol	State buildings and churches around center scene. No importer mark.
Charleston, W.VA., Souvenir of	State Capitol – Inset State Seal	Churches around center scene. No importer mark.
Charlotte, (NC), Souvenir of	Independence Monument and County Court House	Also in green
Chicago, (IL), Souvenir of	State Street	Also in Royal Fenton
Chicago, (IL), Souvenir of	Old Fort Dearborn, Site of Chicago in 1804	
Cincinnati (OH), Souvenir of	City Hall	
Cleveland (OH), Souvenir of	The Garfield Memorial	
Columbus, OH, Views of	Ohio State Capital	
Cornell College, Souvenir of	Sage Walk	
Coven Hoven (Canada)	Sir Van Horne's Residence	
Dallas, Texas, Souvenir of	Confederate Monument	Bawo & Dotter
Daytona, Fla., Souvenir of	The Big Tree, Daytona, Fla.	
Decator, Ill., Souvenir of	An Illinois Cornfield	
Denver, Colo., Souvenir of	Capital Building	
Detroit, (MI), Souvenir of	Log Cabin at Palmer Park	Found with two different borders. One plate has Museum of Art as one of the outer scenes, the other has Woodware Avenue. Also in multi-colors.
Detroit, (MI), Souvenir of	City Hall	Four border scenes
East Hampton, NY	"Home Sweet Home"	
Fall River, Mass., Souvenir of	Public High School	Also Royal Fenton in purple
Fort Williams, Ontario, Souvenir of	Kakabeka Gorge	JonRoth, 1923 impressed in pottery. Five border scenes.
Gettysburg, Pa, Souvenir of	Pennsylvania State Monument	
Gettysburg, Pa, Souvenir of	Pennsylvania State Monument	Multi-color. Three border scenes.
Golden Rule Company	Golden Rule Company Store	No importer
Grand Rapids, MI, Souvenir of	City Hall	Acorn & oak leaf border.
Hamburg, Germany	Hamburg Harbor	
Hamilton, Canada, Souvenir of	Gore Park	Dated 1906
Harrisburg, (PA), Souvenir of	New Capital Building	Dated 1903
Hartford, Conn., Souvenir of	The State Capital	
Haverhill, (Mass.), Souvenir of	Merrimack Street	Also Royal Fenton in brown.
Hot Springs, VA, Souvenir of	The Homestead, Hot Springs, VA	Similar to Henrick Hudson plate, different captions.
Hudson River, Souvenir of	Landing of Henrick Hudson	Bosselman
Indianapolis, Ind., Souvenir of	Soldiers and Sailors Monument	
Indianapolis, Ind., Souvenir of	Soldiers and Sailors Monument	Also in multi-colors
Jackson, Miss.	New Capitol	
Jacksonville, Fla., Souvenir of	Government and Post Office Building	
Kalamazoo, MI, Souvenir of	Court House	
Kansas City, (MO), Souvenir of	Convention Hall	JonRoth, impressed 1913 in pottery.
Keokuk, Iowa	Longest Dam and Power Station in the World	
Lake Champlain, (NY), Souvenir of	Au Sable Chasm	
Lake George, (NY), Souvenir of	Paradise Bay	Eight border scenes
Lakewood, (NJ), Souvenir of	Cathedral Drive	
Leavenworth, Kansas, Souvenir of	Evening by Lake Jeannette, Soldiers Home	
Lenox, Mass., Souvenir of	Nathaniel Hawthorne Cottage. The Little Red House	Also in multi-colors
Lima, Ohio	Memorial Hall	
Lincoln, Nebr., Souvenir of	Nebraska State Capital	Not marked R & M
London, England	St. Paul's Cathedral	Also Royal Fenton in pink
Longfellow's Early Home	Longfellow's Early Home	
Lookout Mountain, Tenn., Souvenir of	Point Park Entrance	Bosselman/Ridgeway
Lookout Mountain, Tenn., Souvenir of	Moccasin Bend and Lookout. Battlefield from Point Park.	
Los Angeles, Cal., Souvenir of	Court House, Los Angeles	
Memphis, Tenn., Souvenir of	Skyscraper District	Bawo & Dotter
Miami, Fla., Souvenir of	Cape Florida Lighthouse	
Milwaukee, Wis., Souvenir of	City Hall	Bosselman/Ridgeway. 1923
Milwaukee, Wis., Souvenir of	City Hall	
Minneapolis, Minn., Souvenir of	Minnehaha Falls	No importer
Minneapolis, Minn., Souvenir of	Post Office	
Mobile, (Ala.), Souvenir of	Courthouse and Government Street	Also in pink
Montreal, (Canada), Souvenir of	Dominion Square	Found with two different borders; one plate has Nantucket Harbor
Nantucket, Mass.	Old Windmill Built 1746	Mass., as one of the outer scenes, the other has old fisherman "Why Worry."
Nashville, (Tenn.), Souvenir of	State Capitol	Found with two different borders. One plate has Hahne & Co. as one of the outer scenes. Another has Bamberger's store.
Newark, NJ, View of	City Hall	
Newport, RI, Souvenir of	Old Stone Mill	
New Bedford, Mass., Souvenir of	Whaling Monument	
New Bedford, Mass., Souvenir of	Wharf Scene in the Old Whaling Days	
New London, Conn., Souvenir of	The Market Place	Also in multi-colored.
New Orleans, (LA), Souvenir of	Canal Street	Bosselman/Ridgeway, 1913
New York, (NY), Souvenir of	Statue of Liberty	Eight border scenes.
New York City, (NY), Souvenir of	Statue of Liberty	Also Royal Fenton in brown and purple.
Niagara Falls, (NY), Souvenir of	General View of the Falls	
Norristown, Pa.	100th Anniversary of 1812 – 1912	
Omaha, (Nebr.), Souvenir of	The Omaha Auditorium	
Onset, Mass., View of	"Meet me on Cape Cod" (2 fishermen)	

Appendix

PLACE	CENTER SCENE	NOTES
Peoria, (IL), View of	Peoria County Courthouse	
Philadelphia, Pa., Souvenir of	City Hall	Also Royal Fenton in brown.
Philadelphia, Pa., Historical	Independence Hall 1776	Also in green.
Pittsburgh, (PA), Souvenir of	Allegheny County Court House	
Plymouth, Mass., Souvenir of	Landing of the Pilgrims	Bosselman/Ridgeway, 1918
Plymouth, (Mass.), Souvenir of	Return of the Mayflower	Design is similar to 10" flat plate dated 1907. Also in green.
Plymouth, (Mass.)	Plymouth Rock 1620	Also multi-colored & Royal Fenton in pink
Portland, ME, Souvenir of	City Hall	
Portland, (ME), Blue Plate	Longfellow's House 1785	Portland Blue Plate Co.
Portland, Ore., Souvenir of	Mount Hood	No Importer Mark. Two different center scenes, one with Mt. Hood with Lost Lake, the other Mt. Hood from wooded hillside.
Providence, (RI), Souvenir of	State House	
Provincetown, Mass., Souvenir of	Pilgrim Memorial Monument	Also in green & multi-colored.
Put-in-Bay, (OH), Souvenir of	Comm. Perry Transferring his Flag. Sept. 10, 1813	
Quincy, Ill., Souvenir of	Adams County Courthouse	
Richfield Springs, N.Y., Souvenir of	The Park	Also Royal Fenton in brown.
Richmond, VA, Souvenir of	City Hall	R & M or British Anchor on identical plates.
Richmond, VA, Souvenir of	New State Capital	No importer mark.
Sag Harbor, LI, NY	High School	Four border scenes.
Salem, Mass., Souvenir of	Witch House Built 1624	Found with two different borders; one plate has "Old Bakery" as one of the outer scenes, the other has "Old John Ward House, Built in 1684."
Salt Lake, (Utah), Souvenir of	Temple Square, Salt Lake City	
San Francisco, Cal., Views of	Golden Gate & Entrance to San Francisco Bay	Also in brown. Flowered border.
Saratoga, (NY), Souvenir of	Saratoga Lake	
Scranton, PA, Souvenir of	Court House	
Seattle, Wash., Souvenir of	Carnegie Library, Seattle, WA	
Sherbrooke, Que.	Head Office Eastern Townships Bank	
Spokane, Wash., Souvenir of	Lower Falls	
Standish Miles, Monument	Miles Standish Monument	1905; Also in green and Royal Fenton in pink and purple.
St. Augustine, Fla., Souvenir of	Old City Gates	
St. Joseph's, MO	Grand Council of MO June 5 & 6, 1907	No importer mark. Eight border scenes.
St. Louis, MO, Souvenir of	City Hall	
St. Patrick's Cathedral (Harrisburg, PA)	Dedicated 1906	Also Royal Fenton in brown.
St. Paul, MN, Souvenir of	Minnesota State Capital	
St. Pauls, Union Church	Trexlertown, PA Built in 1922	Dated 1924. Five border portraits
St. Peter's Reformed Church, New	Rittersburg, PA, 1914	
Syracuse, NY, Souvenir of	(Indian Portrait)	
Syracuse, NY, Souvenir of	Horse Racing at the State Fairgrounds, Syracuse, NY	
Tacoma, (Wash.), Souvenir of	Mount Tacoma 15,000 ft.	
Tampa, Florida	Tampa Bay Hotel	Found with 4 and 6 vignettes
Thousand Islands, NY, Views of	1000 Islands House Alexander Bay, NY	
Toledo, OH, Souvenir of	McKinley Monument	
Topeka, Kan., Souvenir of	Kansas City Capital, Topeka, Kansas	
Toronto (Canada), Souvenir of	City Hall	Also in multi-colored.
Troy, NY, Souvenir of	Emma Willard School	
Valley Forge, (PA), 1777 – 78	Washington's Headquarters	Summer scene dated Dec. 19, 1910
Valley Forge, (PA), 1777 – 78	Washington's Headquarters	Winter scene dated Dec. 19, 1910
Valley Forge, (PA), Souvenir of	Washington's Headquarters	Bosselman/Ridgeway, 1912
Vassar College, Souvenir of	General View	
Washington, (DC), Souvenir of	The Capital East Front	
Waterbury, Conn., Souvenir of	The Green	
West Point, Souvenir of	New Soldier's Monument	
White Mountains, NJ, Views of	The Old Man in the Mountain, Franconia Notch, NH	
Wilkes-Barre, PA, Souvenir of	The New Court House	
Williams College, Souvenir of	The Gymnasium	
Williamsport, PA, Souvenir of	City Hall	
(Winnegar's Store)	(Winnegar's Store in Grand Rapids, Mich.)	
Winnepeg, Manitoba, Souvenir of	The Canadian Buffalo	
Worcester, Mass., Souvenir of	City Hall	
Yale, Souvenir of	Old Brick Row	
Yarmouth, NS, Souvenir of	(Picture of sailing ship)	
Zanesville, Ohio, Souvenir of	New Y Bridge	Also multi-colored. Four border scenes.
Zion's Union Church, Souvenir of	Perry Township, Berks Co., Pa. 1908	

CREDITS: The lists of Wedgwood plates and calendar tiles were compiled by Frank Stefano, Jr. of San Diego, CA, and are presented with his kind permission.

The list of Rowland and Marsellus Co. rolled edge plates was compiled by David Ringering and is presented with his kind permission. Questions or comments can be addressed to: David Ringering
4063 Durbin Ave. SE
Salem, OR 97301
503-364-0464
(Pager) 503-588-3747

BIBLIOGRAPHY

Burgess, Arene W. *Souvenir Plates, A Collector's Guide*. Bethalto, Illinois, Arene Wiemers Burgess, 1978.

Capers, R. H. *Capers' Notes on the Marks of Prussia*. El Paso, Illinois: Alphabet Printing, Inc., 1996.

Dancket, Ludwig. *Directory of European Porcelain: Marks, Makers, and Factories* (English translation). N. A. G. Press Ltd., an imprint of Rogert Hale Limited, 1981.

Gaston, Mary Frank. *Collector's Encyclopedia of R. S. Prussia* (Fourth Series). Paducah, Kentucky: Collector Books, 1995.

Laidacker, Sam. *The Antique Collector* (Vol. 1, No. 1). Scranton, Pennsylvania: Sam Laidaker, Fed. 1939.

Mace, O. Henry. *Collector's Guide to Early Photographs*. Radnor, Pennsylvania: Wallace-Homestead Book Company, 1990.

McCaslin, Mary J. *Royal Bayreuth, A Collector's Guide*. Marietta, Ohio: Antique Publications, 1994.

Rainwater, Dorothy T. and Felger, Donna H. *American Spoons, Souvenir and Historical*. West Chester, Pennsylvania: Schiffer Publishing, Ltd., 1995.

Röntgen Robert I. *Marks on German, Bohemian and Austrian Porcelain, 1710 to the Present*. Exton, Pennsylvania: Schiffer Publishing, Ltd., 1981.

Snyder, Jeffrey B. *Historical Staffordshire, American Patriots & Views*. Atglen, Pennsylvania: Schiffer Publishing Ltd., 1995.

Staff. "Mister that's some gusher...." *Chevron World*. Summer 1996.

Stefano Jr., Frank. *Check-list of Wedgwood Old Historical Plates and Other Views of the United States Produced by Josiah Wedgwood & Sons Ltd. for the Sole Import of Jones, McDuffee & Stratton Co*. Brooklyn, New York: Frank Stefano, Jr., 1975.

Stefano Jr., Frank. *Pictorial Souvenirs & Commemoratives of North America*. New York: E. P. Dutton & Co., Inc., 1976.

INDEX

"Ask Mr. Dooley" .22
A.C. Bosselman 32, 206
Abram French 15, 29–31, 167, 202
Adolph Persch 40
Advertising 29, 30, 75, 76, 84, 198, 202, 204, 210
Alaska-Yukon-Pacific Exposition 203
Altenburg China . .40, 41, 43, 54, 71, 72, 76, 79, 80, 165
Altrohlan 40
Americana 9, 69, 167, 177
Amusement Parks 191
Arene W. Burgess 5, 215
Arzberg 39
B.B. & F. 32, 36, 53
B.D. & C. 33
B.F.H.S. . .15–18, 30, 59, 63, 71, 73, 74, 77, 78, 84, 86, 89, 90, 93, 94, 101, 175, 207
Bauer & Lehmann 28, 39
Bauer, Franz Porcelain Manufactory 39
Bauer, Rosenthal & Co. 34, 36, 39, 42
Bauscher Bros. 33, 39, 43, 76
Bavaria 8, 11, 39, 40, 83, 208
Bawo & Dotter 33, 40, 227
Bears 108–111, 212
Becher & Stark .41
Binoculars 113
Black Collectibles 198
Blankenhain Porcelain Factory 40, 42
Boats 10, 81, 109, 137, 163, 166, 168, 175, 176
Bodtke, Fred 25
Bohemia 8, 11, 12, 14, 29, 40
Bottles 9
Brown-Glazed Items 131
Bruder & Schwalb 41
Buffalo Pottery 220, 221
Butter Pats 46
C.A. Lehmann & Son 39
C.E. Wheelock 19–22, 26
C.E. Wheelock Corporation 22
CAC Boston 29
California Mid-Winter International Exposition . .203
Campgrounds 157, 161
Candle Stick Holders 95
Canoes 10, 138, 192, 197, 199
Card Holders 93, 166
Carlsbad 11, 14, 16, 18, 29, 59, 63, 65, 74, 78, 84–86, 89, 94, 116
Chambersticks 94, 95, 105, 122
Cheese Keepers 99
Child's Cups 80, 81, 210, 211
Chocolate Pots 97, 98
Churches 9, 13, 48, 51, 65, 68, 78, 84, 87, 90, 92, 96–98, 102, 109, 118, 121, 125, 130, 132, 147, 156, 172, 207, 214, 221–226, 228
Civil War 87, 183, 207, 208
Clark, Adams & Clark 29
Clock & Key Dishes 114
Cobalt Blue 9, 10, 30, 33, 45, 87, 119–129, 132–139, 144, 145, 163, 170, 176, 180, 181, 191, 192, 196–198, 201, 204, 206, 209, 210, 214
Colleges & Universities 20, 28, 67,

187–190, 222–228
Columbian Expositions 13, 20, 31, 40, 203, 204
Condiment Servers 18, 89, 121
Coupe Plates 8, 10, 14, 26, 27, 31, 39, 42, 54, 55, 144, 151, 158–160, 164, 165, 167, 168, 170, 176, 179, 181, 188, 192–194, 197, 200, 201, 212, 213
Cow Bells .118, 139
Cows 110
Cracker Jars .97, 100
Creamers 9, 10, 14, 16, 18, 34, 39, 45, 56–66, 71, 73, 90, 102–104, 120, 123–125, 130, 138, 140, 142, 143, 159, 162, 163, 165, 170, 173–175, 178, 181–183, 192, 195–197, 206, 221
Crockery and Glass Journal . .15–17, 21–23, 26, 27, 30, 32, 209, 210
Cups and Saucers 66, 77–79, 101, 102, 125, 182, 183, 199, 200, 209, 210
Custard Glass 221
Cylinder Jugs 14, 58, 65
Dice 10, 138
Disasters 184
Dresden 10, 11, 33, 38, 48, 51, 68, 73, 97, 101, 121, 126, 127, 130, 138, 202, 212
Earth-to-Sky 45, 58, 102, 103, 177
Earthenware 11, 12, 18, 39, 214, 220
Egg Cups 90, 128, 205
Elbogen 15, 16, 40, 44, 70
Emerald Green 33, 45, 130, 132, 202
England . . .5, 11, 13, 15, 18, 22, 27–29, 32, 37, 42, 44, 74, 121, 200, 207, 212, 214–217, 227
Engraver's Art 12
Engraving 9, 12, 13, 15, 16, 20, 25, 28, 29, 39, 45–47, 49, 56, 57, 59–62, 64–66, 71–79, 81, 82, 84–86, 89, 94–96, 98, 101, 102, 104, 108, 113, 116, 117, 140, 142, 144, 146–152, 154, 155, 159, 164, 166, 169, 172, 174–181, 183, 184, 186, 187, 191, 194, 199, 200, 205, 207, 226
Figural Items 10, 107–119, 132
Fischern 33, 40
Floral Cameo Dishes 68
Floral Enhancements 50–54
Fred J. Faulkner Co. 22
French, Mitchell, Woodbury Co. 32
Full-Scene 14, 38, 39, 165, 167, 168, 170, 181
Grossbreitenbach 38
H.H. Tammen 27, 30, 31, 35, 198, 213
Haida 15
Hampshire Pottery 214, 220
Harker 221
Hatpin Holders 96, 202
Hats 111, 188
Hegewald 40
Heisey 221
Historical Staffordshire 6, 214, 229
Horseshoe Dishes 114, 135
Hot Plates 76, 144, 184
Hotels 13, 32, 33, 38–41, 47, 49, 56, 57, 60, 64, 66, 69, 71, 74–76, 78, 80, 83,

85, 89, 91, 104, 106, 107, 114, 122, 123, 131, 157–161, 164, 170, 181, 198, 207–209, 211, 213, 214, 221–225, 228
Humes China 32, 36, 112, 199
Hunt, Benjamin F. Hunt & Sons . . .14–16, 30, 32, 35, 37, 62, 75, 76, 78, 93, 101, 178, 187, 207
Hunt, Homer F. 15–18, 22
Hunt, Horace P. 15–18, 22
Hutschenreuther, Lorenz 39
Indiana University 28, 29, 223
Ink Blotter 93
Ink Well 93, 122, 125
Jamestown Exposition 33, 203, 206
Jonroth . . .8, 10, 14, 26, 27, 35, 36, 38–40, 53, 87, 100, 105, 137, 139, 164, 165, 211, 213, 216, 217, 227
Julius Lange 39
Kahla 28, 29, 38, 39, 42
Kangaroos 110
Karl Speck, Benj. F. Hunt & Sons 40
Kirchenlamitz 40
Knox China 33
KPM 11
Kronach 38, 39, 208
L. Hutschenreuther Porcelain Factory 39
L.S. & S. 33
Lakes 46, 60, 87, 103, 109, 133, 136, 167, 170, 172, 184, 197, 223, 227
Letter Boxes 93
Lewis and Clark Exposition 203, 206
Lewis Straus & Sons 33, 37, 40
Lighthouses . .117, 123, 124, 162, 166, 222, 223, 227
Lithophane 100, 101, 105, 129
Lorenz Reichel Porcelain Factory 40, 43
Louisiana Purchase Exposition . .14, 203, 205
Loving Cups 96, 128
M.F. Wynkoop 22
Maroon-Glazed Items 45, 131
Marx & Gutherz 40, 44
Match Boxes 91
Match Safes 94, 128
Merkelsgrun 41, 44
Metlach 220
Millar China 33, 36, 86, 136
Misc. Color-glazed Items 132–139
Misc. White-based Items 86–97
Mitchell Woodbury Co. 30–32, 36
Mountains 29, 30, 66, 81, 92, 93, 113, 157, 159, 167, 169, 222–224, 227, 228
Mugs, Cups, Saucers 77–84
Multi-Scene 41, 55, 81, 88, 106, 217
Mustard Pot 89, 164
Native American 31, 193, 197, 199
New York and Rudolstadt Pottery 40, 43
O.C. Co. 33
Ocean 121, 133, 162, 165, 193, 206
Old English Historical Ware 28
Old Ivory 40, 106
Oscar Schaller & Co 40
Other Importers 29, 36, 37
P.C.C. 33
Pan American Exposition 203, 206
Panama Pacific Exposition 206

Paper Weights 184
Pen Trays 9, 18, 74, 93, 207
Piggy Banks 108, 110, 206
Pigs 108, 109
Pipe Dishes 114
PK Unity 39
Porcelain Plates 46–50
Post Cards 182
Powder Jars 92
Provenance 8, 207–213
Public Buildings 13, 147
Purses 89, 118
Reitz, Fred .24
Resorts 89, 157, 158, 160, 162–164,
    192, 200, 211, 213, 220
Ribbon Plates 39, 50
Ring Holders 18, 94
Rivers 21, 50, 52, 61, 91, 92, 96,
    102–103, 125, 142, 145, 167, 175, 176,
    208–210, 223, 226
Rose Shadow Flowers 50, 79, 80, 83,
    165, 175, 180, 183
Rosenthal Glass and Porcelain AG 39
Rosenthal, Philip & Co. 39, 42
Roth, John H. 19, 29, 36
Roth, John H. & Co. 5, 26–28, 31, 35,
    211, 213
Roth, John H. III 5, 14, 20, 28, 29, 38,
    41, 216
Roth, John H. Jr. 22, 26
Rowland and Marsellus . . .215, 216, 227, 228
Royal Bayreuth 39
Rudolph Wachter Porcelain Factory 10,
    17–25, 31, 33, 40, 46, 97, 202
Sage, Mrs. Russell 50
Sage, Russell 50, 224
Salt Shakers 96, 97, 116
Schirnding Porcelain Factory 40
Schlegelmilch, Reinhold 27, 31, 41
Schumann 39, 40, 42, 43
Schwarzenbach-Saale 40
Schwarzenhammer 40, 43

Sculls 137
Scuttle 84, 130
Seiler, Paul 28, 29, 39
Selb .39, 208
Semi-Porcelain 12
Sepia 16, 40, 54, 73, 100–102, 144,
    153, 181, 195, 220
Serving Bowls 98, 194
Shadow Flowers 41, 50, 65, 72, 79, 80,
    83, 103, 165, 175, 180, 183, 197
Shapes, Forms, and Styles 45
Shaving Mugs 9, 77, 82–84, 125, 130,
    191, 203
Shelley Potteries, Ltd 42
Shells 10, 67, 115, 116, 146, 148, 161,
    186, 190, 198, 217
Ship's Wheel 137
Shoes 35, 61, 113, 134, 182, 191, 202
Silesian Porcelain Factory P. Donath . . .40, 43
Sontag & Son 39, 42, 63
Souvenir Plates . . .5, 6, 27–29, 32, 215–219, 229
Spas 157, 211
Spittoons 122, 131
Spooner 84, 89
St. Louis Exposition 65, 118
Stamp Boxes 91
Steamers . . .59, 78, 90, 110, 120, 124, 126,
    157, 174, 175
Steins 100, 101, 190, 204, 219
Stoneware 9, 12, 161, 204, 219, 220
Subjects 26, 29, 162, 167, 168
Submarines 10, 136
Sugar Bowls 14, 39, 61, 62, 65, 66, 72,
    73, 90, 104, 123, 138, 187
Tambourines 10, 136
Tea Caddies 92
Tea Tiles 76, 77, 177
Teddy Bears 108–111
Tettau .38–40
Thimble and Scissors Cups 83
Thin China 6, 48, 52, 86, 113, 156, 171
Thomas Porcelain 39, 43

Thuringia 28, 38–41, 65
Tiefenfurth 40, 106
Tinting 9, 45, 47, 48, 50, 53, 58–61,
    64–66, 69, 80, 82, 84, 85, 152, 153
Tirschenreuth 8, 39, 42
Toothpick Holders . . .9, 10, 18, 81, 85, 111, 120,
    125, 127, 131–133, 139, 144–146, 191
Trays .74–76
Trinket Boxes 91
Trivets 76
Trott, Martha 18
Tumblers 41, 87, 88, 106, 126, 166, 206
Turquoise-Glazed 45, 130, 136, 139
Unger & Schilde 40, 41
Unidentified Marks 41
Vases 86, 87, 103, 114, 116, 130, 131,
    133, 141, 168, 176, 197, 199, 204, 211,
    212, 226
Victoria Porcelain Factory, Schmidt & Co. . . .41
Vienna 7, 9, 30, 38, 41, 46, 47, 51–53,
    59, 61, 69, 83, 86, 99
W.G. Wheelock 18
Waldenburg 40
Walker, C.S. 22
Wall Pockets 92, 128, 130
Watch Holders 18, 45, 86
Water-to-Sky 103
Watering Cans 10, 112, 137, 138
Wedgwood 32, 215, 216, 222, 226, 229
Weiden 33, 39, 76
Wheelbarrows 10, 118, 136
Wheelock, Arthur Washburn 19
Wileman & Co. 42, 44, 74
William Adams & Co. 27, 216
Woodbury, Charles H. 32
Woolworth 17, 132, 136
Woolworth, Frank Winfield 16
World's Fairs 14, 41, 203–206
Zettlitzer Kaolin Works Department Porcelain
    Factory 41, 44

INDEX BY LOCATION

Alabama
    Huntsville, 7
Alaska
    Ketchikan, 196
Arizona
    Bisbee, 52, 150; Phoenix, 196; Tucson, 66,
    168, 196
California
    Bakersfield, 143; Claremont, 187; Jackson,
    146; La Grange, 10; La Jolla, 165; Los
    Angeles, 200; McCloud, 118, 161; Mount
    Lowe, 169; Oakland, 109; Oroville, 146;
    Salinas, 174; San Diego, 61, 163; San Jose,
    169; Santa Barbara, 51; Santa Cruz, 47;
    Tulare, 180
Canada
    Prince Edward Island, 124
Colorado
    Canon City, 68; Denver, 30, 68, 227; Glen-
    wood Springs, 127; Kremmling, 116; Love-

land, 46; Pikes Peak, Manitou, 194; Manitou
Springs, 5, 52, 68, 170, 213; Rifle, 135;
Royal Gorge, 167; Trinadad, 46
Connecticut
    Hartford, 71, 126, 227; New Haven, 109,
    122, 124, 159; Savin Rock, 50
Florida
    Daytona, 176, 227; Jacksonville, 101, 227;
    Miami, 107, 193, 227; Mt. Dora, 83; Tar-
    pon Springs, 141
France
    Lyon, 11
Georgia
    Milledgeville, 85
    Savannah, 87, 158, 181
Germany
    Bergen, 11
Hawaii, 21, 141
Idaho
    Boise City, 155; Rexburg, 199; Silver City,

91, 158
Illinois
    Augustana, 67; Cairo, 153; Chenoa, 48;
    Chillicothe, 185; Freeport, 110; Galena,
    108; Hoopston, 81; Latham, 149; Minonk,
    97; Moline, 81, 168; Rock Island, 190;
    Woodstock, 127, 144
Indiana
    French Lick, 130; Greensburg, 153; Indi-
    anapolis, 135, 227; South Bend, 18, 81,
    112; Thorntown, 102
Indian Territories
    Muskogee, 194; North McAlester, 145; Pryor
    Creek, 149; Tulsa, 69
Iowa
    Independence, 154; Keokuk, 103, 227;
    Morning Sun, 156; No. English, 82; St. Ans-
    gar, 189; Washington, 154
Kansas
    Blue Rapids, 85; Edna, 65; Frankfort, 68,

148; Garden City, 144; Hutchinson, 146; Lawrence, 189; Leavenworth, 155, 227; Parsons, 9

Kentucky
Dawson Springs, 5, 210, 211

Louisiana
New Orleans, 139

Maine
Bailey's Island, 104; Bangor, 103, 123; Bath, 56; Belfast, 79, 93, 161; Boothbay Harbor, 58, 65, 139; Bridgton, 157; Eastport, 58, 89, 93, 123, 166; Ellesworth, 63, 113; Festus, 173; Gardiner, 61, 92, 142, 186; Limerick, 118; Madison, 145; Millinocket, 83; Mt. Desert, 202; Norway, 76, 117; Ogunquit, 51, 73; Old Orchard Beach, 64, 84, 104, 108, 128, 164; Orr's Island, 57, 85, 101; Owl's Head, 122; Pittsfield, 58, 121, 131; Poland, 67; Port Clyde, 102; Portland, 62, 97, 98, 109, 116; Richmond, 102; Rockland, 108, 111, 224, 160; Rockport, 52; Scarboro, 70; Searsmont, 147; Thomaston, 154; Vinalhaven, 86, 123; Waldoboro, 61, 91; Waterville, 202, 222, 225; Webb's Mills, 173; Wiscasset, 127; Yarmouth, 111; York Beach, 53, 164

Massachusetts
Adams, 111; Annisquam, 77; Ayer, 124; Barre, 84; Boston, 15, 88, 132, 136, 176, 226; Brant Rock, 71; Brockton, 125, 182; Cape Cod, 4, 74, 83, 85, 105, 120, 128, 144, 184, 227; Chatham, 49, 71, 94, 113, 122, 125; Cohasset, 60; Cottage City, 49, 120, 121, 126; Cuttyhunk, 79; Danvers, 46, 89; Dedham, 55; Dennis, 80, 102; Duxbury, 47; Eastern Point Light, 105; Edgartown, 49; Fall River, 103, 125, 227; Falmouth, 84, 89, 104; Gloucester, 59, 67, 77, 99, 126; Great Barrington, 82, 151; Hanover, 94; Harwich, 69; Haverhill, 63; Holyoke, 94, 118, 137; Hyannis, 64; Jacob's Ladder Trail, 96; Leominster, 65, 82; Lexington, 58; Magnolia, 74; Marblehead, 60, 140, 183, 215; Marlboro, 150; Marion, 78, 132; Martha's Vineyard, 49, 59, 90, 120, 166; Medford, 98; Medway, 77, 80; Middletown, 175; Mohawk Trail, 197; Monument Beach, 75; Nantasket, 138; Nantucket, 95, 124, 129, 132, 227; New Bedford, 60, 216, 227; Newburyport, 75, 150; Onset, 59, 64, 71, 85, 90, 116, 138, 227; Orange, 103; Orleans, 60, 62, 89, 90, 121, 217;

Peabody, 99; Provincetown, 49, 56, 83, 85, 90, 105, 112, 120, 164, 228; Quincy, 63; Revere Beach, 54, 123, 128, 130, 131, 136, 139, 192; Rockport, 66; Salem, 136, 199, 218, 228; Salisbury Beach, 133; Scituate, 60, 76; Sharon, 72; Shirley, 84; Somerville, 91, 96; Stoneham, 64; Stoughton, 73; Summit House, Mt. Tom, Holyoke, 137; Taunton, 78; Waltham, 183; Warren, 152; Wellfleet, 72, 74, 125, 130; West Dennis, 102; Winthrop, 57, 90

Michigan
Alpena, 88; East Tawas, 166; Hancock, 64; Mt. Clemens, 96

Minnesota
Fergus Falls, 75

Missouri
Joplin, 127, 145

Mississippi
West Point, 76

Montana
Miles City, 179

Nebraska
Franklin, 148; Friend, 156; Genoa, 195

New Hampshire
Alton Bay, 78, 161, 169; Auburn, 139; Bartlett, 93; Berlin, 70; Bethlehem, 52, 122; Bretton Woods, 84, 106; Bristol, 46; Canaan, 174; Claremont, 92; Colebrook, 9, 74, 128, 132, 159; Concord, 92, 222; Fabyans, 58, 84; Groveton, 59, 72; Hampton Beach, 111, 125; Henniker, 93; Keene, 99; Laconia, 59, 78, 121; Lake Winnepesaukee, 197; Lebanon, 46; Lisbon, 54, 175; Littleton, 126, 134; Manchester, 124, 129; Meredith, 78, 93; Old Man of the Mountain, Franconia Notch, 81, 224; Ossipee, 152, 176; Portsmouth, 100, 138, 223, 225; Roscoe, 139; Suncook, 61; The Weirs, 74; Troy, 95; Walpole, 152; West Ossipee, 176; West Stewartstown, 133

New Jersey
Atlantic City, 192; Highlands Beach, 165; Sandy Hook, 125

New Mexico
Portales, 57, 142;

New York
Albany, 10, 134, 138, 222; Babylon, 86; Bay Shore, L.I., 51; Brooklyn Bridge, 81, 226; Buffalo, 224; Callicoon, 79; Castile, 100; Catskill Mountains, 159; Chateaugay, 137; Coney Island, 125, 127, 135, 138,

191; Cortland, 113; Elizabethtown, 55; Fort Covington, 51; Keuka, 87; Rockaway Beach, 137; Rouses Point, 60, 175; Roxbury, 91; Statue of Liberty, 72, 81, 136, 227; Troy, 50, 226, 228; White Lake, 136

North Carolina
Southern Pines, 200

North Dakota
Lansford, 149; Pembina, 208; Sheyenne, 149

Ohio
Blanchester, 114; Fremont, 180; Greenville, 68, 172; Put-in-Bay, 103

Oklahoma
Fort Sill, 194; Perry, 151

Oregon
Baker City, 110; Newberg, 190

Pennsylvania
Bangor, 202; Bradford, 185; Gettysburg, 183; Johnstown, 185; Pittsburgh, 78; Reading, 76; Ridgeway, 53; Williamsport, 48

Rhode Island
Block Island, 73, 79, 165, 22; Narragansett Pier, 162; Newport, 115, 124, 133; Providence, 139

South Dakota
Deadwood, 177; Mitchell, 155; Willow Lake, 184

Tennessee
Lookout Mountain, 66, 227; McMinnville, 172

Texas
Beaumont, 143, 209, 210; Galveston, 163; San Antonio, 88

Utah
Ogden Canyon, 130

Virginia
Berryville, 125; Lee Hall, 87; Mt. Vernon Mansion, 96; Norfolk, 200; Shenandoah Caverns, 133

Washington
Arlington, 144; Friday Harbor, 178; No. Yakima, 62; Puyallup, 85; Seattle, 197

Wisconsin
Chaseburg, 142; Elkhorn, 96; Madison, 147; Neenah, 155; Rio, 151; Watertown, 202; Waukesha, 158

Wyoming
Cheyenne, 55; Saratoga, 50; Yellowstone, 170

STUDY GUIDE FOR

The Nature of Disease

PATHOLOGY FOR THE HEALTH PROFESSIONS

Vera A. Paulson, MD, PhD

Pathology Resident
Brigham and Women's Hospital,
Boston, MA

Mark A. Valasek, MD, PhD

Assistant Professor
University of California San Diego
Department of Pathology
Division of Anatomic/Surgical Pathology
La Jolla, CA

. Wolters Kluwer | Lippincott Williams & Wilkins
Health

Philadelphia · Baltimore · New York · London
Buenos Aires · Hong Kong · Sydney · Tokyo

Acquisitions Editor: David B. Troy
Development Editor: Laura Bonazolli
Marketing Manager: Leah Thomson
Product Development Editor: Eve Malakoff-Klein
Designer: Terry Mallon
Compositor: S4Carlisle Publishing Services
Printer: RRD

9 8 7 6 5 4 3 2 1

ISBN 978-1-60913-3-702

DISCLAIMER

Care has been taken to confirm the accuracy of the information presented and to describe generally accepted practices. However, the authors, editors, and publisher are not responsible for errors or omissions or for any consequences from application of the information in this book, and make no warranty, expressed or implied, with respect to the currency, completeness, or accuracy of the contents of the publication. Application of this information in a particular situation remains the professional responsibility of the practitioner; the clinical treatments described and recommended may not be considered absolute and universal recommendations.

To purchase additional copies of this book, call our customer service department at (800) 638-3030 or fax orders to (301) 223-2320. International customers should call (301) 223-2300.

Visit Lippincott Williams & Wilkins on the Internet: http://www.LWW.com. Lippincott Williams & Wilkins customer service representatives are available from 8:30 A.M. to 6:00 P.M., EST.

Preface

Welcome to the *Study Guide for The Nature of Disease: Pathology for the Health Professions*. The second edition of *The Nature of Disease* highlights both general and systems pathophysiology and seeks to integrate complex topics with a measure of holism. This companion *Study Guide* is designed to reinforce and consolidate complex concepts presented in the textbook, and to offer a study aid to help students attain content mastery.

The *Study Guide* offers a comprehensive set of self-study tools, including probing questions to enhance learning and to help frame and clarify complex topics presented in the textbook. For each **Learning Objective** in the main text, students are presented with a wide variety of custom designed exercises to help master that objective. Features include:

- **The Big Picture:** Briefly summarizes the fundamental background and overarching core concepts of the entire chapter.
- **Complete the Paragraph/Complete the Table:** Presents key terms in their context utilizing clarifying paragraphs and organized tables.
- **Pathology as a Second Language:** Presents vocabulary terms with their definitions in various formats including true/false and answer bank type questions.

- **Decision Tree:** Provides highly insightful algorithms for understanding the process of diagnostics and critical thinking for given topics in the health professions.
- **Mnemonics:** Provides important memory aids for pathophysiology and health professions-oriented material.
- **Remember This:** Highlights important test-worthy points worth remembering.
- **Test Yourself:** Provides a wide variety of questions including multiple choice, true/false, matching, and short answer. These are directed at specific Learning Objectives to promote a rigorous understanding of the topics.

Answers to the *Study Guide* exercises and questions can be found on thepoint.lww.com.

It is our hope that *this Study Guide* will greatly enhance understanding and provide confidence that comes from having mastery of the fundamental concepts of pathophysiology.

Vera Paulson
Mark Valasek

Contents

Preface, iii

PART 1
Mechanisms of Health and Disease

1 Health and Disease, 1

2 Cellular Pathology: Injury, Inflammation, and Repair, 9

3 Disorders of the Immune System, 22

4 Infectious Disease, 38

5 The Nature of Disease: Neoplasia, 57

6 Disorders of Fluid, Electrolyte and Acid–Base Balance, and Blood Flow, 70

PART 2
Disorders of the Organ Systems

7 Disorders of Blood Cells, 87

8 Disorders of Blood Vessels, 99

9 Disorders of the Heart, 108

10 Disorders of the Respiratory Tract, 124

11 Disorders of the Gastrointestinal Tract, 137

12 Disorders of the Liver and Biliary Tract, 157

13 Disorders of the Pancreas, 169

14 Disorders of the Endocrine Glands, 179

15 Disorders of the Urinary Tract, 193

16 Disorders of the Male Genitalia, 209

17 Disorders of the Female Genitalia and Breast, 218

18 Disorders of Bones, Joints, and Skeletal Muscle, 238

19 Disorders of the Nervous System, 260

20 Disorders of the Senses, 278

21 Disorders of the Skin, 294

PART 3
Disorders of the Stages and States of Life

22 Congenital and Childhood Disorders, 307

23 Disorders of Daily Life, 322

24 Aging, Stress, Exercise, and Pain, 337

Mechanisms of Health and Disease

CHAPTER

1

Health and Disease

The Big Picture

Disease, whether *functional* (physiology) or *structural* (anatomy), has many *etiologies* (causes), which range along the continuum of *nature* (innate qualities or genetic factors) and *nurture* (environmental factors), the combination of which is known as *multifactorial*. The study of these etiologies is the role of *epidemiology*; the rendered changes *pathology*; and the manner in which the disease is expressed, *pathophysiology*. Disease is expressed as, and thus often *diagnosed* as a result of, *symptoms* (subjective findings) and/or *signs* (objective findings). Signs include tests, the limits of which are described by *sensitivity* and *specificity* and which, when interpreted in the appropriate context, can aid in the diagnosis of a disease even if symptoms are not present.

Oh No! Not Another Learning Experience

LEARNING OBJECTIVE 1: Define *disease*, and compare and contrast acute and chronic disease.

EXERCISE 1-1

Complete the sentence below.

Disease is an unhealthy state caused by (1) _anatomical distortion or physiological dysfunction * injury_ ; it can be (2) _acute_ or chronic.

EXERCISE 1-2

Complete the table below.

	Acute Disease	Chronic Disease
Onset	(1) _arrises rapidly_	Slow
Symptoms	(2) _distinctive_	Nonspecific
Duration	Short lasting	(3) _long lasting/persistent_
Treatment	(4) _treatable often *_	Often cannot be prevented or cured

EXERCISE 1-3   PATHOLOGY AS A SECOND LANGUAGE

Test your vocabulary by writing the appropriate term in each blank from the list below.

Disease   Acute disease   Chronic disease

1. Disease that arises rapidly, accompanied by distinctive clinical manifestations, and lasts a short time.   _____acute_____

2. Disease that begins slowly and persists for a long time.   _____chronic_____

LEARNING OBJECTIVE 2: Describe the relationship between "structure" and "function."

EXERCISE 1-4

Complete the paragraph below.   *or functional disorder*

Structural disorder causes (1) ___dysfunction___ and vice versa. Structural and functional disorders are
inseparably locked together as one can cause the other. In many cases, the (2) ___structural___ disorder occurs
first, then the (3) ___functional___ impairment results (e.g., a broken arm after a fall leads to a loss of function
of that arm). In contrast, (4) ___functional___ disorders can lead to (5) ___structural___ changes (e.g., a change
in physiology like high blood pressure leads to increased size and thickness of the heart, i.e., hypertrophy).

EXERCISE 1-5   PATHOLOGY AS A SECOND LANGUAGE

Test your vocabulary by determining whether the following statements are true or false.

__T__ 1. A structural disorder is a defect in form (appearance or anatomy).

__T__ 2. A functional disorder is a defect in the ability to perform.

LEARNING OBJECTIVE 3: Discuss disease progression from latent period to complications/sequelae.

EXERCISE 1-6

Complete the paragraph below.

Although sometimes it is hard to decide the exact point in time, the beginning of a disease is its
(1) ___onset___. Prior to the onset, certain (2) ___predisposing factors___ are present. For example, lung cancer is
promoted by smoking. Initially, the disease may go undetected in a (3) ___latent period___ or subclinical state. In
the case of an infection, this period of feeling well, despite being infected with organisms that are multiplying, is
called an (4) ___incubation period___. In some diseases (especially infection), the initial mild symptoms are called the
(5) ___prodromal period___. Acute disease will usually be of quick onset and short duration, while chronic disease usually develops and recedes slowly. Diseases may quickly or slowly give rise to adverse consequences, which are
called (6) ___complications___ and (7) ___sequelae___, respectively. For example, untreated diabetes can lead to
poor circulation of the feet, ulcers, and infections (leading to the need for surgical amputation). When a disease
is quiet, it is in (8) ___remission___; when it reappears, it is a (9) ___recurrence___. After the main illness has
subsided, the patient enters a period of (10) ___recovery___ during which health improves.

EXERCISE 1-7   PATHOLOGY AS A SECOND LANGUAGE

See Exercise 1-6 for key terms covered in this section.

LEARNING OBJECTIVE 4: Compare and contrast the terms *etiology*, *pathogenesis*, and *pathophysiology*. Also compare and contrast the terms *idiopathic*, *iatrogenic*, and *nosocomial*.

EXERCISE 1-8

Complete the paragraph below.

(1) _Pathogy_ is the scientific study of changes in bodily structure and function that occur as a result of disease. Therefore, pathologists try to describe the (2) _lesion_ (the anatomic abnormality produced by the disease) or to explain the (3) _pathophysiology_ (the manner in which the incorrect function is expressed). The (4) _etiology_ is the cause of the disease, and (5) _pathogenesis_ is how the disease develops.

If the etiology is unknown, a disease is said to be (6) _idiopathic_. If the disease is a byproduct of medical diagnosis or treatment, it is (7) _iatrogenic_ (from Greek *iatros*, which means "physician"), or "The doctor did it!" (8) _nosocomal_ is similar and simply means "hospital acquired."

Mnemonic

When you see the term *idiopathic*, think "idioTpathic." We do not know or understand the cause of the disease or condition!

EXERCISE 1-9   PATHOLOGY AS A SECOND LANGUAGE

See Exercise 1-8 for key terms covered in this section.

LEARNING OBJECTIVE 5: Define *epidemiology*, *incidence*, and *prevalence*.

EXERCISE 1-10

Complete the paragraph below.

(1) _Epidemiology_ is a discipline of medicine that studies the broad behavior of disease in large populations. The (2) _incidence_ of a disease is the number of new cases of a particular disease each year, while the (3) _prevalence_ is the overall number of people with a certain disease in the population.

> **Remember This!** The prevalence of "disease X" is 2 million people in the United States and the incidence is 50,000 people per year. Is "disease X" an acute or chronic disease? It is most likely chronic because, at the rate of 50,000 per year, it will take 40 years to get 2 million people with the disease. If the disease lasted only a year, then the incidence and the prevalence would be equal!

EXERCISE 1-11   PATHOLOGY AS A SECOND LANGUAGE

Test your vocabulary by determining whether the following statements are true or false. If a statement is false, provide the correct word for the italicized term that will make the statement true.

_F_ 1. *Prevalence* is the number of people with an illness or complication of an illness.

morbidity

_T_ 2. *Mortality* is the number of people dying from a particular disease in a particular time frame.

_T_ 3. *Risk factors* are factors that may increase an individual's likelihood of developing a specific disease.

See Exercise 1-10 for additional key terms covered in this section.

LEARNING OBJECTIVE 6: Discuss the roles of environmental factors, genetic factors, and determinants of health in the disease process.

> **EXERCISE 1-12**

Complete the paragraph below.

(1) Injurious forces are _environmental_ (factors); that is, they arise from the world in which we live. They come in the form of physical trauma, radiation, chemical or metabolic toxins, and many others. These may damage the body on a large scale (e.g., amputation due to a car accident) or on a microscopic scale (e.g., radiation damage to DNA). (2) _Genetic defects_ are heritable defects that cause disease. They may arise in a single gene ([3] _monogenic_) or in multiple genes ([4] _polygenic_). Keep in mind, however, that *the majority of disease is* (5) _multifactorial_; that is, disease is usually a combination of genetic and environmental factors acting on each other. In addition to direct environmental and genetic causes, other psychosocial, economic, and cultural factors influence health indirectly; these are called (6) _determinants of health_

> **EXERCISE 1-13**   PATHOLOGY AS A SECOND LANGUAGE

See Exercise 1-12 for terms covered in this section.

LEARNING OBJECTIVE 7: Compare and contrast symptoms and signs.

> **EXERCISE 1-14**

Complete the paragraph below.

(1) _Symptoms_ are subjective and described by the patient (e.g., "I have pain right here."), or someone else on behalf of the patient during the medical history. (2) _Signs_ are objective and are revealed (prompted, elicited, or otherwise obtained) during the physical, lab, X-ray, or other examination (e.g., a fluid wave in a patient with ascites). Notice that both symptoms and signs are (3) _detectable_ manifestations of disease.

A person may have, for example, a liver tumor or other condition that produces no symptoms and is too small to be palpated or seen. As noted earlier, in such cases the disease is said to be (4) _latent_ (or subclinical). These signs and symptoms are used to make a (5) _diagnosis_; in other words, to identify the cause of the patient's problem(s).

> **EXERCISE 1-15**   PATHOLOGY AS A SECOND LANGUAGE

See Exercise 1-14 for key terms covered in this section.

LEARNING OBJECTIVE 8: List the types of tests used to study disease (consider anatomical and clinical pathology).

> **EXERCISE 1-16**

Complete the paragraph below.

In addition to the physical exam and radiologic imaging, pathologists use tissues and body fluids to perform tests to understand disease. (1) _Anatomic pathology_ is the study of anatomy and microanatomy of tissues to look for changes caused by disease. Often a (2) ___biopsy___ is taken to assess the tissue for cancer or other diseases; for example, a piece of colon tissue can be taken using an endoscope to determine whether a colon polyp is cancerous. (3) ___Clinical Pathology___ is the study of the functional aspects of disease by laboratory testing of tissue, blood, urine, or other body fluids; for example, blood glucose measurement to diagnose diabetes.

EXERCISE 1-17   PATHOLOGY AS A SECOND LANGUAGE

Test your vocabulary by writing the appropriate term in each blank from the list below.

Syndrome   Gross pathology   Biopsy
Microscopic pathology   Biopsy   Autopsy
Clinical pathology   Anatomic pathology

1. Assessment of a specimen conducted by eye   ___Gross pathology___

2. Assessment of a specimen conducted by microscope   ___microscopic Pathology___

3. Examination of a deceased person to determine the cause of death or
   the extent of disease   ___Autopsy___

4. Collection of signs and symptoms that occur together   ___syndrome___

5. Microscopic examination of a small tissue specimen removed
   from a living body   ___biopsy___

See Exercise 1-16 for additional key terms covered in this section.

LEARNING OBJECTIVE 9: Explain the meaning of the terms *mean, normal range,* and *standard deviation* as they relate to medical tests and the concepts of "normal" and "abnormal."

EXERCISE 1-18

Complete the paragraph below.

The (1) ___Normal range___ is established by testing a large group of healthy people to determine the spectrum within which a value usually falls. It is defined as the range between two standard deviations of the (2) ___mean___. The (3) ___mean___ is the average of the tested group, while the (4) ___standard deviation___ is a measure of the variability of the results. Five percent of people will fall outside two standard deviations, with the result that their tests are (5) "___abnormal___." Markedly abnormal results are more (6) ___significant___ than mildly abnormal results.

> **Remember This!** A normal test doesn't mean you *aren't* sick, and an abnormal test doesn't mean you *are* sick. Most tests are designed so that 5% of the population can have an "abnormal" test result and still be normal. This also means that if you are healthy and have 20 tests done, 1 will be abnormal!

EXERCISE 1-19   PATHOLOGY AS A SECOND LANGUAGE

Test your vocabulary by filling in the blanks in the following table. Each term may be used once, more than once, or not at all.

False negative   False positive   True positive
True negative   Sensitivity   Specificity
Predictive value

	Positive Test	**Negative Test**	**Equations**
Diseased	(1) _true positive_	(2) _true neg_	(3) _sensitivity_: TP/(TP+FN)
Healthy	(4) _false pos_	(5) _false = neg_	(6) _specificity_: TN/(TN+FP)

*(7) _____: Accuracy with which the test predicts who has (positive) and who does not have (negative) the disease. (Unless otherwise specified by your course instructor, the difference between the two will not be tested.)

LEARNING OBJECTIVE 10: List the factors that influence the use of diagnostic tests. How does disease prevalence and incidence affect a diagnostic test? How should these tests be administered, that is, why administer a sensitive test first?

EXERCISE 1-20

Complete the paragraph below.

Initial testing should be (1) _Sensitive_, while the follow-up test should be (2) _specific_ (see Decision Tree 1.1). Remember, the (3) _Sensitivity_ is how often the test is positive in the presence of disease (e.g., 99% sensitive if it is positive in 99 of 100 patients known to have the disease); (4) _specificity_ is how often the test is negative in the absence of the disease (e.g., 99% specific if it is negative in 99 of 100 persons known not to have the disease). In practice, then (although it seems counterintuitive), a sensitive test is more powerful when it is (5) _negative_ (rules out disease), and a specific test is more powerful when it is (6) _positive_ (rules in the disease).

In the case of (7) _prevalence_, a positive test is more likely to be truly positive (to have a high predictive value) if the prevalence of disease is high in the tested population.

Finally, a (8) _Sensitive test_ should be administered first in order to make sure the disease is not missed, and followed by a (9) _specific test_ to verify the diagnosis.

> **Remember This!** To find people with a disease, use the most sensitive test for the disease first. This will ensure that you have detected everyone with the disease. The problem with using sensitive tests is that some of the people who test positive may not have the disease, but may test positive simply because the test is so sensitive (false-positives). After a sensitive test is positive, a specific test can then verify that the individual does indeed have the disease (and is not false-positive).

Mnemonic

SP-IN SN-OUT
Specific rules in, and sensitive rules out.

EXERCISE 1-21   PATHOLOGY AS A SECOND LANGUAGE

See Exercises 1-20 and 1-21 for key terms covered in this section.

Decisions Decisions

DECISION TREE 1.1: TRY, TRY AGAIN

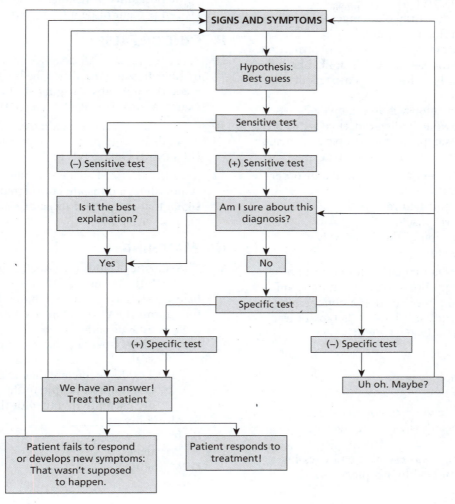

Test Yourself

I. MULTIPLE CHOICE

1. After having recently contracted mono (the "kissing disease"), your patient was told to maintain a healthy diet and get plenty of rest. Feeling better two weeks later, she decides to go for a run. That evening, her symptoms seem worse than ever, and she returns to your office the next day. You tell her that she is in what phase of her disease? [LEARNING OBJECTIVE 3]
   A. Onset
   B. Recovery
   C. Latent period
   D. Exacerbation

2. Which of the following is a sign? [LEARNING OBJECTIVE 7]
   A. Patient reporting a fever
   B. Blood pressure taken by a nurse
   C. Patient's mother telling you her child has been lethargic
   D. Patient reporting stomach cramps

3. Which of the following is a symptom? [LEARNING OBJECTIVE 7]
   A. Patient reporting that the throat hurts
   B. Nurse telling you that the patient's blood sugar is 105 mg/dl
   C. Hearing a heart murmur
   D. Doctor telling you the patient has jaundice

4. A 65-year-old Caucasian female was prescribed extrastrength ibuprofen (Motrin) for treatment of her rheumatoid arthritis. Several weeks later, she is back at the clinic, complaining of dark stools and shortness of breath. You immediately discontinue the Motrin prescription and advise the patient not to take any more as it has caused stomach ulcers and bleeding. The prescription of Motrin is said to be the _____ cause of your patient's symptoms. [LEARNING OBJECTIVE 4]
   A. Iatrogenic
   B. Idiopathic

C. Nosocomial

D. Subclinical

5. Which of the following statements is true?
[LEARNING OBJECTIVE 4]

A. Pathology is the study of changes in structure and function due to disease.

B. Anatomic pathology is the study of structural changes due to disease, while clinical pathology is the study of functional aspects of the disease.

C. Performing an autopsy is an example of gross examination, while finding cancer cells in a breast biopsy is an example of microscopic examination.

D. All of the above statements are true.

6. Which of the following is a functional disorder?
[LEARNING OBJECTIVE 2]

A. Congestive heart failure

B. Enlarged heart muscle

C. Bacterial infection of the mitral valve

D. Ulcers of the stomach

7. A 55-year-old Indian female is found to have a lump in her right breast. An operating room is scheduled and a piece of tissue obtained for an accurate diagnosis. What is this type of test called? [LEARNING OBJECTIVE 8]

A. Biopsy

B. Autopsy

C. Clinical Pathology

D. Epidemiology

8. Which of the following statements about disease versus health is true? [LEARNING OBJECTIVE 9]

A. A normal range was established by testing a small group of healthy people.

B. Normal is the range between one standard deviation above and below the mean.

C. A standard deviation is a measure of the degree of variability of results.

D. Ten percent of people are "abnormal."

II. TRUE OR FALSE

9. _____F_____ All diseases are characterized by objective abnormalities, be they observations made through labs, imaging studies, or physical examinations. [LEARNING OBJECTIVE 1]

10. _____T_____ The predictive value of a test depends in large part on the prevalence of disease. [LEARNING OBJECTIVE 10]

11. _____F_____ Lab values outside of two standard deviations are considered abnormal, and signal that the patient has a disease. [LEARNING OBJECTIVE 9]

III. MATCHING

12. The statistics below are associated with disease X. Match the terms (A–D) to the examples given below (i–iv). There may be more than one answer for a term. [LEARNING OBJECTIVE 5]

   i. 50% of patients die

   ii. 35% of patients have complication Y each year

   iii. 12,000 people are diagnosed each year

   iv. One million people in the United States are currently living with the disease

A. Morbidity ___ii___

B. Incidence ___ii___ ___iii___

C. Prevalence ___iv___

D. Mortality ___i___

IV. SHORT ANSWER

13. What are the factors that influence disease? [LEARNING OBJECTIVE 6]

_____

_____

_____

14. You are unable to find any physical explanation for your patient's symptoms. What should you tell the patient? [LEARNING OBJECTIVE 2]

_____

_____

_____

15. Using the Decision Tree algorithm, answer the following questions. What do you need to consider if you have a positive sensitive test but a negative specific one? What about a negative sensitive test despite a clinical picture consistent with the diagnosis? [LEARNING OBJECTIVE 9]

_____

_____

_____

Cellular Pathology: Injury, Inflammation, and Repair

The Big Picture

The human body seeks to maintain homeostasis, which stress or injury can imbalance. A mild injury may result merely in accumulations, repeated injury with adaptations, and severe injury with cell death via necrosis or apoptosis.

Inflammation is the body's first response to injury and serves a purpose: to kill organisms that may be causing infection, to limit the extent of the injury, and to repair the injury.

When tissue is injured due to disease, three outcomes are possible: regeneration, healing (fibrous repair), or a mixture of the two. The choice between these outcomes is dictated by the amount of damage, tissue/cell type, and host factors.

Oh No! Not Another Learning Experience

LEARNING OBJECTIVE 1: Name and describe the various types of stem cells.

EXERCISE 2-1

Complete the paragraph below.

Stem cells are undifferentiated cells that form the three initial tissue types: (1) _____, endoderm, and mesoderm; they are capable of differentiating into more than 200 specialized cell types in the body. Stem cells are classified based on their ability to differentiate into different cell types. (2) _____ stem cells are able to produce any cell type (think "total"), including a whole organism. (3) _____ stem cells can form cells for any organ system or tissue. (4) _____ stem cells are restricted to producing cell types in a particular organ system or tissue (think "multiple").

EXERCISE 2-2   PATHOLOGY AS A SECOND LANGUAGE

Test your vocabulary by writing the appropriate term in each blank from the list below.

Mitosis	Meiosis	Cell cycle
Asymmetric division	Stem cell	

1. Cell self-reproduction _____

2. Process that divides one cell into two identical cells _____

3. Unspecialized cell, can replicate itself or a specialized cell _____

4. Mitotic division that creates cells with two different fates (stem cells must do this!) _____

LEARNING OBJECTIVE 2: Explain the difference between labile, stable, and permanent cells.

EXERCISE 2-3

Complete the paragraph below.

(1) _____ tissues need to be constantly replenished due to constant damage; therefore, these tissues need to divide frequently, and include the epithelial lining of the GI tract and hematopoietic cells of the bone marrow. (2) _____ tissues have only a few cells in the cell cycle and do not divide frequently; however, they can ramp up cell division if needed, and include liver, pancreas, kidney, and smooth muscle cells, as well as fibroblasts and other connective tissue cells. (3) _____ (nondividing) tissues have very few or no cells in the cell cycle because they have very few or no stem cells, and include (4) _____, skeletal muscle, and cardiac muscle. They cannot generally grow new tissue in response to injury.

Mnemonic

Emotionally labile cells divide all over the place. Stable cells are solid, but occasionally fly off the handle and divide. Permanent cells are permanently stuck in place.

EXERCISE 2-4

Complete the table below.

Types	Labile	Stable	Permanent
Regenerate	Continuous, normal, rapid	Slowly, or upon (1) _____	No regeneration possible
Stem cells	Yes	Yes	(2) _____
Lifespan	(3) _____	Months to years	(4) _____
Examples	(5) _____, bone marrow	Kidney, liver	CNS, heart, skeletal muscle

LEARNING OBJECTIVE 3: Discuss the various mechanisms of cell injury.

EXERCISE 2-5

Complete the paragraph below.

Lack of sufficient oxygen (also known as "hypoxia" or "anoxia") is the (1) _____ cause of cell injury, and can be due to loss of blood supply termed (2) _____. Other factors include physical, thermal, or chemical agents; (3) _____ (which can form free radicals); toxins; microbes; inflammation and immune reactions; nutritional imbalance; genetic and metabolic defects; aging. Genetic defects can be specific diseases or the "permissive" soil on which persistent injury causes disease.

> **Remember This!** Hypoxia is the loss of oxygen, while ischemia is the deprivation of blood flow. While ischemia likewise results in oxygen loss, it also deprives the cells of nutrients and prevents waste removal making the injury worse.

EXERCISE 2-6 PATHOLOGY AS A SECOND LANGUAGE

Test your vocabulary by determining whether the following statements are true or false. If a statement is false, provide the correct word for the italicized term that will make the statement true.

_____ 1. The total lack of oxygen is termed *anoxia*.

_____

_____ 2. Ischemia causes *hypoxia*, decreased nutrient delivery, and accumulation of waste.

_____

_____ 3. *Hypoxia* is the partial loss of oxygen (or low O_2).

_____

_____ 4. Low temperatures may freeze the water in skin cells causing *hypothermia*.

_____

_____ 5. *Ionizing radiation* can break water into hydrogen and hydroxide radicals (causing cellular damage).

_____

LEARNING OBJECTIVE 4: Compare and contrast the response to reversible injury (i.e., accumulations and adaptations) with the response to irreversible cell injury (i.e., apoptosis and necrosis).

EXERCISE 2-7

Complete the paragraph below.

Reversible injury is mild injury that produces observable cellular changes but can return to normal when the cause of the injury stops. Reversible injury induces (1) _____ (vacuolar degeneration) or cellular swelling which is essentially due to loss of ATP and accumulation of sodium and calcium ions, or accumulation of other substances including: (2) _____ (steatosis), cholesterol, specific proteins, pigments (especially the "wear and tear" pigment (3) _____), and environmental particles (e.g., carbon in smoker's lungs). In addition, reversible injury can lead to adaptive changes including (4) _____ (smaller cells), (5) _____ (bigger cells), (6) _____ (more cells), or (7) _____ (change from one cell/ tissue type to another). These changes occur in response to a chronic injurious stimulus. At some point, the injury may begin to cause precancerous changes termed (8) _____ or abnormal or disordered growth. Dysplasia is a precursor to invasive cancer, but may be reversible early on. Irreversible cellular injury leads to cell death via (9) _____ (programmed cell suicide) or necrosis. Apoptosis can be nonpathologic; for example, in fetal development, the cells between the fingers undergo apoptosis to form individual separated digits. Although cells are irreversibly damaged by apoptosis or (10) _____, the tissue can still attempt to repair itself in other ways including scar formation.

Remember This! Think of injury and loss of homeostasis as a rubber band. Cells are capable of dealing with stress to a certain degree, making the changes necessary to compensate and restore balance to the body. They get larger (hypertrophy) or increase in number (hyperplasia) to generate more force. They may also change type in order to neutralize the stress of a particular irritant. For instance, chronic acid exposure of squamous esophageal cells results in the cells converting to a type designed to deal with acid—intestinal cells—hence the term intestinal metaplasia. Once the stress exceeds a certain limit, however, or if the injury is too severe for adaptation to succeed, the rubber band snaps—and the tissue can begin to fail—potentially resulting in death.

Mnemonic

Apoptosis versus necrosis

"LIFELESS" (since cells are dead): Differences are in:

Leaky membranes	Extent	Swell or shrink
Inflammatory response	Laddering	Stimulus
Fate	Energy dependent	

Mnemonic

Necrosis Types

Never Fear Life Can Conclude (NFLCC): Necrosis = fat, liquefactive, caseous, coagulative

EXERCISE 2-8

Complete the table below.

Adaptations	Alteration	Cause	Example
Atrophy	(1) _____	Decreased oxygen, reduced functional demand/hormone/neuron support, inflammation	Atherosclerosis of renal artery leading to dec. blood supply and kidney atrophy
(2) _____	Inc. size of cells	Hormonal stimulation or functional demand	Cardiac hypertrophy in response to high BP
Hyperplasia	(3) _____	Hormonal stimulation, functional demand, chronic stress	Endometrial hyperplasia due to inc. estrogen stimulation
Dysplasia	Abnormal cell growth	(4) _____	Cervical dysplasia
Metaplasia	Conversion of cell type from one type to another	Chronic injury/stress	(5) _____

EXERCISE 2-9

Complete the table below.

	(1) _____ (programmed cell death)	Necrosis
Type of death	Natural, programmed cell death	(2) _____ death due to injury
Histologic/pathologic changes	Cytoplasm & organelles condense.	Tissue architecture disrupted.
	Intense stain	Disruption of organelles
	Minimum disruption of tissue	Types of necrosis
	Apoptotic bodies; cytoplasm blebs	(3) _____
	Phagocytosis of apoptotic bodies	(4) _____
		(5) _____
		(6) _____
DNA changes	Chromatin condensation along nuclear membrane	Pyknosis, karyorrhexis, karyolysis: DNA smudge
	Laddering of DNA (200bp)	Eosinophilia (RNA loss)
+/− Inflammation	(7) _____	Inflammatory reaction

EXERCISE 2-10

Complete the table below.

(1) _____	Hypoxic death (infarct most common)	Structure preserved
		Pale necrosis, inflammation
	Heart, kidney & spleen	Pyknosis, karyolysis, karyorrhexis
(2) _____	Ischemic CNS.	Enzymes: lysis
	Bacteria/fungus (staph, strep, *E. coli*)	Architecture not preserved
		Cavity filled with liquid/empty
(3) _____	Bacterial or viral infections (most often TB, fungus)	Gross: Soft, grey–white, and cheesy Friable, semi-solid
		Cell boundaries completely lost
(4) _____	Injury to adipose tissue or organs with high fat (breast)	Enzymes digest triglycerides from fat
		Dystrophic calcification
	Enzymatic (acute pancreatitis)	

PATHOLOGY AS A SECOND LANGUAGE

Test your vocabulary by determining whether the following statements are true or false.

_____ 1. An abscess is a walled-off area containing pus.

_____ 2. An infarct is a region of necrotic tissue caused by ischemia.

See Exercises 2-8, 2-9, 2-10, 2-11, and 2-12 for additional key terms covered in this section.

LEARNING OBJECTIVE 5: Describe the cells and chemical mediators of the inflammatory process.

EXERCISE 2-12

Complete the paragraph below.

Inflammation is, in part, the body's cellular response to injury and is orchestrated by numerous chemical mediators. Cells involved in the inflammatory process are (1) _____ (white blood cells), including neutrophils, eosinophils, basophils, monocytes, and (2) _____ (T cells, B cells, [3] _____, which produce antibodies). (4) _____ are the primary cells in acute inflammation and are adept at phagocytosis. (5) _____ have bright red ("eosinophilic") granules and respond to parasites and also cause allergic reactions. (6) _____ have blue–purple granules, have histamine, and cause swelling and allergic reactions.

   Chemical mediators involved in the inflammatory process can be categorized into three groups: (7) _____ (chemicals that act on the cell of origin), (8) _____ (chemicals that act on nearby cells), or (9) _____ (chemicals that act at a distance, think "endocrine"). These mediators include histamine, serotonin, arachidonic acid, prostaglandins, and nitric oxide (NO). These compounds cause (10) _____ and a variety of other biologic effects. (11) _____ are also included, which attract cells (chemokines, chemoattractants) or change the "stickiness" of certain cells to allow them to move from the bloodstream into tissues.

   Three complex systems also participate in inflammatory responses. The (12) _____ promotes immune attack on targets; the kinin system causes vasodilation and promotes pain; and the clotting system prevents hemorrhage.

EXERCISE 2-13 PATHOLOGY AS A SECOND LANGUAGE

Test your vocabulary by writing the appropriate term in each blank from the list below.

Mast cell	Leukocytes	Granulocytes
Platelets	T lymphocyte	B lymphocyte
Chemokines	Chemotaxis	Clotting system

1. Similar to a basophil _____

2. WBCs including granulocytes, lymphocytes, and monocytes _____

3. Mature tissue monocytes, phagocytic _____

4. Fragments of megakaryocytes, important for clotting _____

5. WBCs that contain granules with digestive enzymes _____

6. Thymus-derived lymphocyte, responds to infections and malignancy _____

7. Bone marrow derived lymphocyte, produces humoral immunity, plasma cell precursor _____

8. Large WBCs with few granules _____

9. Secreted proteins that enhance immune reaction: vasodilation, attract WBCs, stimulate phagocytosis _____

10. Chemical attractants to lure WBCs toward the damage _____

11. Movement of WBCs up a chemokine gradient _____

12. Cascade causing blood clotting _____

See Exercise 2-14 for additional key terms covered in this section.

LEARNING OBJECTIVE 6: Compare and contrast acute and chronic inflammation.

EXERCISE 2-14

Complete the paragraph below.

(1) _____ follows a brief injury and lasts a few hours or days; it is characterized by vascular dilation and increased vascular permeability, with resulting accumulation of edema and infiltration of neutrophils. This leads to the classic clinical characteristics of inflammation: (2) _____ (literally "swelling"), (3) _____ ("redness"), (4) _____ ("heat"), and (5) _____ ("pain"). Types of inflammatory exudates are described in the table that follows. Acute inflammation may resolve quickly with complete resolution, or, if repeated or severe, lead to scarring. In some cases, (6) _____ may develop. In contrast to acute inflammation, (7) _____ is caused by continuous or at least long-term injuries such as persistent infections, autoimmune diseases, or chronic environmental exposure; it is characterized by (8) _____ and or macrophages/histiocytes. If the inflammatory cells forms small aggregates of macrophages/histiocytes surrounded by lymphocytes (granulomas), then the process is called (9) _____. This occurs in chronic fungal infections and tuberculosis. Chronic inflammation is usually accompanied by an ongoing healing (or partial healing) process with scarring of the tissue and loss of normal tissue architecture.

> **Remember This!** In some cases, chronic inflammation begins with acute inflammation, especially if the injury persists. In most cases, however, chronic injury appears without prior acute inflammation—as is seen in autoimmune diseases.

EXERCISE 2-15

Complete the table below.

	Acute Inflammation	**Chronic Inflammation**
Types of injury	Short-term injury	(1) _____
How long injury lasts	Lasts (2) _____	Lasts weeks/years
Pathogenesis	Vasodilation: edema and neutrophil infiltrate	Characterized by lymphocytes, monocytes/ macrophages, and plasma cells
Outcome	(3) _____, scar, abscess, chronic inflammation	(4) _____ or persistent chronic inflammation

EXERCISE 2-16

Complete the table below.

Types of Exudate (acute inflammation)	(1) _____	Fibrinous Inflammation	(2) _____
Characterized by	Effusion	(3) _____	Pus (neutrophils, necrotic cells, edema)
Permeability:	Inc. vascular permeability	Inc. vascular permeability	Inc. vascular permeability
Protein:	Dec. protein	Inc. protein	(4) _____
Inflammatory cells:	(5) _____	Inflammatory cells	Inflammatory cells
Example	Blister	Pericarditis after MI	Abscess, empyema

EXERCISE 2-17   PATHOLOGY AS A SECOND LANGUAGE

Test your vocabulary by determining whether the following statements are true or false. If a statement is false, provide the correct word for the italicized term that will make the statement true.

_____ 1. *Inflammation* is a body's cellular reaction to injury.

_____

_____ 2. *Edema* is the influx of blood into tissue.

_____

_____ 3. Accumulation of fluid in tissue is called *hyperemia*.

_____

_____ 4. *Giant cells* are multinucleated macrophage aggregate.

_____

See Exercises 2-16, 2-17, and 2-18 for additional key terms covered in this section.

LEARNING OBJECTIVE 7: Describe the systemic effects of inflammation.

EXERCISE 2-18

Complete the paragraph below.

Inflammation involves not just the local tissue environment, but it also has important systemic effects, including enlargement of lymph nodes (1) _____ which can be seen clinically; increased bloodstream inflammatory mediators such as C-reactive protein and (2) _____ (remember this leads to increased ESR); and others that cause fever, malaise, drowsiness, and poor (3) _____.

EXERCISE 2-19   PATHOLOGY AS A SECOND LANGUAGE

Test your vocabulary by writing the appropriate term in each blank from the list below.

Lymphangitis   Lymphadenitis   Lymphadenopathy
Reactive hyperplasia   Reactant proteins   C-reactive protein
Erythrocyte sedimentation rate

1. Coagulation protein; polymerizes into fibrin blood clot   _____

2. Enlarged lymph node reacting to an infection   _____

3. Inflammation of lymph vessels   _____

4. Reactant proteins   _____

5. Infection of lymph nodes   _____

6. Enlarged/tender lymph nodes   _____

7. Lab measurement of the time it takes for RBCs to settle in their plasma.   _____

See Exercise 2-20 for additional key terms covered in this section.

LEARNING OBJECTIVE 8: Distinguish between parenchymal and fibrous repair.

EXERCISE 2-20

Complete the paragraph below.

(1) _____ results in complete or near complete regeneration of the tissue (think "salamander tail"), which can occur to a limited extent in humans (e.g., liver) after a mild injury. Fibrous repair is (2) _____ formation. Fibrous repair occurs when injury destroys the normal architecture or framework of the tissue or if the damage is to tissue composed of (3) _____ (which cannot be replaced). Fibrous repair involves migration and proliferation of cells, especially inflammatory cells and fibroblasts, (4) _____ (growth of new blood vessels), and granulation tissue, then scar development. Most healing is a (5) _____ of regeneration and fibrous repair.

EXERCISE 2-21   PATHOLOGY AS A SECOND LANGUAGE

Test your vocabulary by determining whether the following statements are true or false. If a statement is false, provide the correct word for the italicized term that will make the statement true.

_____ 1. *Renovation* is the body's collective attempt to restore normal structure and function to the injured site, the wound.

_____

_____ 2. Short-term injury at a discrete site is called a *wound*.

_____

_____ 3. *Regeneration* is the complete, or nearly complete, restoration of normal anatomy and function, with little or no scarring.

_____

_____ 4. *Stroma* is normal-functioning cells.

_____

_____ 5. *Parenchyma* is supporting tissue.

_____

_____ 6. A scar is reshaped (*remodeled*) as mechanical forces pull it into a configuration that eases stress on the wound.

_____

See Exercise 2-22 for additional key terms covered in this section.

LEARNING OBJECTIVE 9: Compare and contrast healing by first and second intention.

EXERCISE 2-22

Complete the paragraph below.

Healing by (1) _____ is how narrow wounds with closely together edges, like surgical incisions, heal. With no complications, the tensile strength of the wound site is about 10% at one week, 75% at three months, and close to normal at one year. Healing by (2) _____ is how broad and irregular wounds with (3) _____ separated margins heal (e.g., deep skin burns or large intestinal ulcers). This mode of healing differs in that it requires a greater volume of tissue and a supporting framework consisting of a highly vascular mixture of capillaries, fibroblasts, residual edema, and small numbers of leukocytes termed (4) _____. This type of wound takes (5) _____ to heal, and the final scar may be as little as 10% of the size of the original defect.

EXERCISE 2-23

Complete the table below.

Type of Healing	First Intention	(1) _____
Edges	(2) _____ approximated edges	Widely separated margins
Example	(3) _____	Skin or intestinal ulcers
Healing	Inflammation->; Macrophage clean up->; neovascularize->; (4) _____	Same, but increased necrotic tissue Re-epithelization is a longer process.

LEARNING OBJECTIVE 10: List factors that cause abnormal wound healing.

EXERCISE 2-24

Complete the paragraph below.

Abnormal wound healing is a major cause of chronic disease. Factors that cause abnormal wound healing are numerous. Obvious factors are mechanical forces on the wound causing opening of the wound or (1) _____, retained foreign bodies, or (2) _____ of the wound site (most common cause). Other causes are poor nutrition (need vitamin C and macronutrients to produce collagen and other proteins), (3) _____ (decrease inflammatory cells and decrease production of collagen), and poor blood supply (e.g., in atherosclerosis or diabetes). Wounds can also heal in a pathologic fashion and form exuberant scars, called (4) _____, or vascular proliferations, called (5) _____.

EXERCISE 2-25   PATHOLOGY AS A SECOND LANGUAGE

See Exercise 2-24 for key terms covered in this section.

Decisions Decisions

DECISION TREE 2.1: RESPONSE TO INJURY

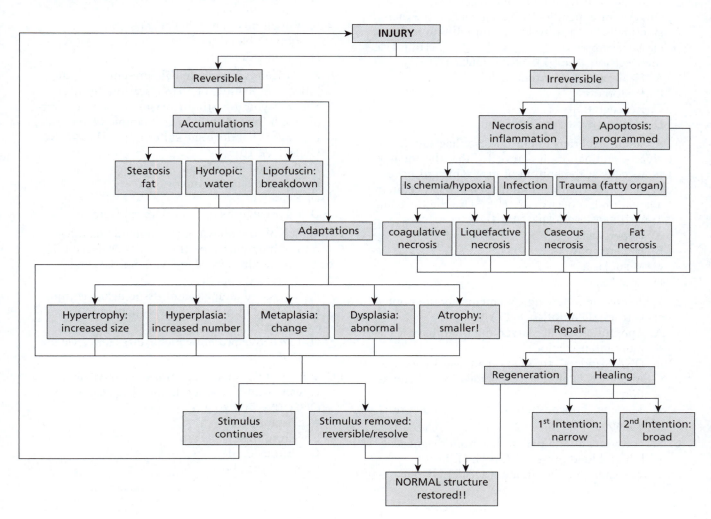

Test Yourself

I. MULTIPLE CHOICE

1. A patient presents to the ER with severe chest pain that he says started several hours ago. You diagnose him with a heart attack, and know that because of the amount of time that has passed, many of his heart cells will die. What type of death will these cells undergo? (Hint: Use the Decision Tree) [LEARNING OBJECTIVE 4]
   A. Caseous necrosis
   B. Liquefactive necrosis
   C. Coagulative necrosis
   D. Apoptosis

2. A biopsy shows cells that are disorderly in appearance, with enlarged, dark, irregular nuclei. What reversible cellular adaptation has occurred? (Hint: Use the Decision Tree) [LEARNING OBJECTIVE 4]
   A. Hyperplasia
   B. Metaplasia
   C. Dysplasia
   D. Atrophy

3. You visit your friend who has recently undergone surgery for appendicitis. He shows you the incision made by the physician. You tell him he is a classic example of _____. (Hint: Use the Decision Tree) [LEARNING OBJECTIVE 9]
   A. Healing by first intention
   B. Restoration
   C. Regeneration
   D. Healing by second intention

4. A patient experiences chronic esophageal reflux. Upon examination, it is revealed that the squamous cells at the bottom of his esophagus have been replaced with columnar cells. What cellular adaptation has occurred? (Hint: Use the Decision Tree) [LEARNING OBJECTIVE 4]
   A. Hyperplasia
   B. Hypertrophy
   C. Metaplasia
   D. Dysplasia

5. Which of the following statements about apoptosis is true? [LEARNING OBJECTIVE 4]
   A. Apoptotic cells are larger and often have a more intense color.
   B. DNA "ladders" are seen on an agarose gel.
   C. Apoptosis is often accompanied by inflammation.
   D. There is condensation of nuclear protein during apoptosis.

6. Several years after a patient has been diagnosed with high blood pressure, for which he was never treated, he dies in a car accident. Upon autopsy, you notice the increased size of his heart. A biopsy shows an increase in cell size. What cellular adaptation has taken place? (Hint: Use the Decision Tree) [LEARNING OBJECTIVE 4]
   A. Hyperplasia
   B. Atrophy
   C. Metaplasia
   D. Hypertrophy

7. A 20-year-old classmate sits down next to you during your exam. You notice a blister on her forehead. She tells you she was in a hurry and burned herself with a curling iron. You remind her that the type of inflammatory exudate she is experiencing is _____. [LEARNING OBJECTIVE 6]
   A. Supparative inflammatory exudate
   B. Serous inflammatory exudate
   C. Edema
   D. Fibrinous inflammatory exudate

8. Which of the following vascular responses happens first in acute inflammation? [LEARNING OBJECTIVE 6]
   A. Angioneogenesis
   B. Widening of endothelial gaps
   C. Smooth blood flow
   D. Vasodilation

9. An African American female presents to your office complaining of a large scar on her neck. She tells you it is still increasing in size. You recognize it immediately as an example of abnormal healing. What does she suffer from? [LEARNING OBJECTIVE 10]
   A. Pyogenic granuloma
   B. Injury of second intention
   C. Keloid
   D. Increased torsion / mechanical factors

10. Which of the following is a systemic manifestation of inflammation? [LEARNING OBJECTIVE 7]
    A. Chemokines causing fever, malaise, and decreased appetite
    B. Serous inflammation of tissue near the injury
    C. Clotting of plasma that has pooled in interstitial space
    D. C-reactive protein which causes an elevated ESR

11. Which of the following molecular mediators is responsible for vasodilation? [LEARNING OBJECTIVE 5]
    A. Histamine
    B. Serotonin
    C. Nitrous oxide
    D. All of the above

12. Which of the following layers differentiates into the bone, muscle, kidneys, and gonads? [LEARNING OBJECTIVE 1]
    A. Ectoderm
    B. Mesoderm
    C. Endoderm
    D. None of the above

II. TRUE OR FALSE

13. Hydropic changes may accumulate within reversibly injured cells. (Hint: Use the Decision Tree) [LEARNING OBJECTIVE 4]

14. Necrosis is an orderly, programmed cell death. [LEARNING OBJECTIVE 4]

15. Dystrophic calcification can occur with any type of necrosis. [LEARNING OBJECTIVE 4]

16. Meiosis is a process of organizing and dividing the nucleus into two daughter nuclei. [LEARNING OBJECTIVE 1]

17. Injury caused by hypoxia is more severe than ischemia. [LEARNING OBJECTIVE 3]

III. MATCHING

18. Match the following types of necrosis with their example (Hint: Use the Decision Tree): [LEARNING OBJECTIVE 4]
    i. Coagulative necrosis
    ii. Caseous necrosis
    iii. Liquefactive necrosis
    iv. Fat necrosis
    A. TB
    B. Acute pancreatitis
    C. Stroke in the CNS
    D. Hypoxia of the kidney

19. Match the following cells with their type: [LEARNING OBJECTIVE 2]
    i. Permanent cell
    ii. Labile cell
    iii. Stable cell
    A. Heart cell
    B. Kidney cell
    C. Epithelium
    D. Liver cell
    E. Nerve cell

20. Match the following causes of infection/inflammation with the appropriate inflammatory cells. [LEARNING OBJECTIVE 6]
    i. Lymphocytes
    ii. Neutrophils
    iii. Eosinophils
    A. Bacteria
    B. Allergens
    C. Syphilis
    D. Parasites
    E. Viruses

IV. SHORT ANSWER

21. How are stem cells classified? [LEARNING OBJECTIVE 1]

_____

_____

_____

22. What are the potential outcomes of acute inflammation? [LEARNING OBJECTIVE 8]

_____

_____

_____

23. Compare and contrast acute and chronic inflammation. [LEARNING OBJECTIVE 6]

_____

_____

_____

CHAPTER 3

Disorders of the Immune System

The Big Picture

The immune system is divided into **innate immunity** (*natural* or *native* immunity) and **adaptive immunity** (*acquired* or *specific* immunity). Innate immunity is a fast, nonspecific attack on *any* nonself substance or invader. In contrast, adaptive immunity is slower, but a *programmable* system that learns to target a *specific* invader, then remembers what it has learned for later attacks. The *"immune response"* refers solely to the *adaptive* immune system. Adaptive immunity is carried out by specific coordinated cells, antibodies, and other chemical mediators. Immunodeficiency states, including HIV/AIDS, predispose to diseases normally prevented by the immune system, including infectious diseases and malignancy.

Oh No! Not Another Learning Experience

LEARNING OBJECTIVE 1: Name the two principal nonimmune defense systems.

EXERCISE 3-1

Complete the paragraph below.

Physical and chemical barriers are the two principal nonimmune defense mechanisms. (1) _____ include intact skin surfaces and body (2) _____ (respiratory, gastrointestinal, and genitourinary). (3) _____ include (4) _____ pH (e.g., stomach), (5)_____ (in tears), digestive enzymes, mucus, and others.

Remember this! The nonimmune defense system is the first line of defense!

EXERCISE 3-2 PATHOLOGY AS A SECOND LANGUAGE

Test your vocabulary by writing the appropriate term in each blank from the list below.

Self	Nonself	Immunity
Nature	Nurture	Protection

1. A person's own normal DNA and its translated proteins   _____

2. Proteins of other living things   _____

3. A cellular and molecular defense mechanism against nonself threats   _____

See Exercise 3-1 for additional key terms covered in this section.

LEARNING OBJECTIVE 2: Describe the components of the lymphatic system and their function.

EXERCISE 3-3

Complete the paragraph below.

The lymphatic system is the necessary infrastructure for the immune system to function, producing and preparing the necessary cells of immunity and providing the thoroughfares for their transit. The (1) _____, which prepare lymphocytes for roles in immunity, are the (2) _____ and the (3) _____. The secondary lymphoid organs are the (4) _____ (MALT tissue that rings the throat), (5) _____ (abdominal organ which composes part of the immune system), (6) _____, and (7) _____ (specialized nodules of lymphoid tissue in the respiratory and gastrointestinal tracts). These organs are connected by lymphatic channels to other tissues and make up the (8) _____. It has three functions: to house and support immune cells; to filter lymph fluid from tissues; and to absorb dietary fat from the gut (in the form of chylomicrons).

EXERCISE 3-4   PATHOLOGY AS A SECOND LANGUAGE

Test your vocabulary by indicating whether the following statements are true or false.

_____ 1. Lymph vessels are composed of lymphatic capillaries; they absorb fluid from the intercellular space.

_____ 2. Lymph fluid, unlike interstitial fluid, lacks protein.

_____ 3. Lymph nodes are composed of immune system cells.

See Exercise 3-3 for additional key terms covered in this section.

LEARNING OBJECTIVE 3: Compare and contrast innate and adaptive immunity.

EXERCISE 3-5

Complete the paragraph below.

The similarity of the innate and adaptive immune systems is that they both defend the "self" against the (1) _____ invading pathogen. The differences are in the mechanism by which each system defends the self. (2) _____ is a fast (3) _____ attack on any nonself substance or invader. This system recognizes general categories of foreign organisms like bacterial or fungal lipids. In contrast, (4) _____ is slower, but (5) _____ system that learns to target a (6) _____ invader. Adaptive immunity is carried out by specific coordinated cells, (7) _____ (made by plasma cells), and other chemical mediators as outlined below.

Mnemonic
Innate versus Adaptive
I is for **I**nnate immunity: **I**nstant, **I**mmediate, **I**nitial response, **I**nduces, and **I**ntegrates with adaptive immunity
A is for **A**daptive immunity: **A**cquired, **A**wait days = no immediate response, **A**ccurate = specific, **A**utoregulation, **A**utoimmunity

EXERCISE 3-6

Complete the table below.

	Innate Immunity	Adaptive Immunity	
Speed	(1) _____	Slow	
Specificity	Nonspecific	(2) _____	
Memory	No	(3) _____	
Antibodies	(4) _____	Yes	

EXERCISE 3-7 PATHOLOGY AS A SECOND LANGUAGE

Test your vocabulary by writing the appropriate term in each blank from the list below.

Antigen   Hapten   Primary immune
Secondary immune   Nonimmune   Molecule

1. Any substance capable of inciting an adaptive immune response   _____

2. Combination of self and nonself that stimulates an immune reaction   _____

3. Initial reaction to antigen exposure   _____

4. Subsequent exposures   _____

LEARNING OBJECTIVE 4: List the cells of the immune system and describe their role in immunity.

EXERCISE 3-8

Complete the paragraph below.

Cells of the immune system include macrophages, dendritic cells, and lymphocytes. Macrophages are large tissue phagocytic cells derived from blood (1) _____, ingesting microbes and displaying their (2) _____. (3) _____ are tissue macrophages (evolved from monocytes or from lymphocytes) present and fixed in lymphoid organs and the (4) _____. They are termed (5) _____ because they capture antigens and prepare them for presentation to T lymphocytes. Lymphocytes are small white blood cells that are the (6) _____ of the immune system. They mature in the thymus into (7) _____, which are the (8) _____ (delayed adaptive) effectors, or the bone marrow into (9) _____, which mature into the adaptive antibody [(10) _____] producing factories called (11) _____ or form memory cells. A small third set of cells are the natural killer (NK) cells, which are considered part of the (12) _____ immune system.

EXERCISE 3-9 PATHOLOGY AS A SECOND LANGUAGE

Test your vocabulary by determining whether the following statement is true or false. If the statement is false, provide the correct word for the italicized term that will make the statement true.

_____ 1. *Compatibility markers* are present on cell membranes and may incite an immune reaction if transfused/implanted into another person.

_____

See Exercise 3-8 for additional key terms covered in this section.

LEARNING OBJECTIVE 5: Name the five types of antibodies and discuss the context in which they function.

EXERCISE 3-10

Complete the paragraph below.

Plasma cells secrete (1) _____, (antiantigen proteins that circulate in blood and other fluids), which normally constitute 20% of total plasma proteins. Because of this secretory nature, the B cell system is referred to as (2) _____. The antibodies may be produced by the person's own immune system (3) _____ or may be the result of the passive transfer of antibodies (4) _____ (which is temporary). Immunoglobulins are made up of two heavy (H) chains and two light (L) chains. The five classes f immunoglobulin are defined by the kind of heavy chain and are (5) _____, (6) _____, (7) _____, (8) _____, and (9) _____.

Complete the table below in Exercise 3-11 to reveal the properties, location, and function of each antibody.

Mnemonic
Order of Antibody Presentation

MADGE

Ig**M**   Ig**A**   Ig**D**   Ig**G**   Ig**E**

Mnemonic
Pay for **Passive**, **Active** for **Ages**:

Passive: **Pay** for a shot of antibodies for fast results following exposure to rabies, etc.

Active: Slow onset ("aging") and memory.

EXERCISE 3-11

Complete the table below.

CHIg	Ab properties	Location	Immunity
IgA	#1 Ab in GI/Respiratory mucosa	(1) _____, mucosal secretions (tears, mother's milk)	Offers (2) _____ immunity when passed from mother
IgD	—	Bound to (3) _____, not in blood	Promotes B cell activation
IgE	—	Attached to (4) _____, not in blood	(5) _____
IgG	(6) _____ (size), #1 Ab in blood; requires prior exposure	Found in blood, crosses the placenta	Persists, (7) _____ immunity
IgM	(8) _____ (size)	Found in blood/other fluids	Produced rapidly then (9) _____

> **EXERCISE 3-12**   PATHOLOGY AS A SECOND LANGUAGE

Test your vocabulary by writing the appropriate term in each blank from the list below.

Clonal expansion   Memory B cells   Compound

Helper cells   Replicate   Immune complex

1. Identical cells, derived from one cell   _____

2. Preprogrammed B cells that linger in the body and release a flood of
   antibodies the next time the antigen appears   _____

3. Combination of antigen and antibody   _____

See Exercises 3-10 and 3-11 for additional key terms covered in this section.

LEARNING OBJECTIVE 6: Explain the difference between MHC type I and type II display.

> **EXERCISE 3-13**

Complete the paragraph below.

There are two types of major histocompatibility complex (MHC): MHC type I and MHC type II. MHC I are pres-

ent on the surface of every cell in the body except (1) _____. They are (2) _____, which

sample the protein contents of cells, then display them as (3) _____ on the cell surface. Therefore, in

healthy cells, MHC I glycoproteins display normal self-antigens, whereas in infected cells, for example, they will

display (4) _____ proteins, including those made by the virus. MHC II complexes are similar, but are

present only on the surface of (5) _____, the macrophages and dendritic cells, whose job is to capture

and display foreign or nonself antigen. The immune system (6) _____ the cell with the MHC I dis-

playing nonself antigen, but just (7) _____ the MHC II display and goes looking for something else to

attack. MHC complexes on WBCs are called (8) _____.

Mnemonic

MHC I versus II: T cell interaction: The "= 8" equation:
$2 \times 4 = 8$ (MHC II goes with CD4) $1 \times 8 = 8$ (MHC I goes with CD8)

Mnemonic

T and B cells: types

When bacteria enter a body, T-cell says to B: "**H**elp **M**e **C**atch **S**ome!" B-cell replies: "**M**y **P**leasure!"
T-cell types: Helper, Memory, Cytotoxic, Suppressor
B-cell types: Memory cell and Plasma cells

> **EXERCISE 3-14**   PATHOLOGY AS A SECOND LANGUAGE

Test your vocabulary by determining whether the following statements are true of false. If a statement is false, provide the correct word for the italicized term that will make the statement true.

_____ 1. *Delayed (cellular) immunity* is T-cell–mediated immunity.

_____

_____ 2. *Cytotoxic effector T cells* target and destroy cells with alien antigens.

_____

_____ 3. Helper T cells facilitate the activities of *B cells only*.

_____

____   4. *Regulatory T cells* prevent development of autoimmune disease.

_____

____   5. Memory T cells mount a *slow* secondary response.

_____

See Exercise 3-13 for additional key terms covered in this section.

LEARNING OBJECTIVE 7: Discuss the pathogenesis of the four types of hypersensitivity and give examples of each type.

EXERCISE 3-15

Complete the paragraph below.

Hypersensitivity reactions are either B-cell mediated (types I, II, and III) or T-cell mediated, as in the case of (1) _____.

Type 1 is known as (2) _____ and is the result of (3) _____ (presumably from an earlier exposure). On subsequent exposure, the antigen combines with an IgE antibody already present on the surface of (4) _____ which triggers their activation and causes the release of preformed vasoactive substances, like (5) _____ and inflammatory mediators. This leads to a local response or systemic reaction.

(6) _____ (type II) reaction is caused by B cell production of antibodies (IgG and IgM) that react with antigens on the (7) _____ to form antigen-antibody complexes. These complexes mark the cells for killing by the complement system via (8) _____. This can happen in autoimmune disease or (9) _____ formation (when self looks like nonself because of drugs, toxins, etc.).

(10) _____ (type III) is an immune reaction of (11) _____ in which free/soluble antigen and antibody combine to form immune complex deposits in tissue, causing damage and inflammation. These can be local (Farmer's lung) or (12)_____, when the complexes circulate in the blood (serum sickness or post Streptococcal glomerulonephritis).

Finally, (13) _____ (type IV) reaction is the only hypersensitivity reaction mediated by T cells (no antibodies needed). Initially, antigen is captured by antigen-presenting cells for presentation to T cells. T cells react to produce clones of (14) _____ to attack the invader, but which attack normal self-antigen instead. Clones of *suppressor T cells*, *helper T cells*, and *memory T cells* are also produced. Examples are poison ivy and TB (granulomatous inflammation).

Mnemonic
Hypersensitivity reactions (I-IV): **ACID**
Anaphylactic type: type I
Cytotoxic type: type II
Immune complex disease: type III
Delayed hypersensitivity (cell mediated): type IV

Remember This! Type IV is the only T-mediated hypersensitivity; everything else is caused by errant B cells!

EXERCISE 3-16

Complete the table below.

Type	Etiology	Examples
Type I: Immediate Hypersensitivity	Preformed antibodies. Initial sensitizing exposure, causes reaction during (1) _____.	(2) _____ Hay fever
Type II: Cytotoxic Hypersensitivity	Antibody attaches directly to antigen. Causes (3) _____.	Immune hemolytic anemia, (4) _____
Type III: Immune Complex Hypersensitivity	Antigen and antibody form immune complex causing (5) _____.	Lupus Farmer's lung
Type IV: Delayed Hypersensitivity	T cell reaction independent of B cells (and Abs)	(6) _____

EXERCISE 3-17   PATHOLOGY AS A SECOND LANGUAGE

Test your vocabulary by writing the appropriate term in each blank from the list below.

Immediate hypersensitivity   Cytotoxic hypersensitivity
Immune complex hypersensitivity   Delayed hypersensitivity

TYPE 1 IMMUNE REACTION: (1) _____. Initial antigen exposure stimulates production of IgE antibodies, which attach to the surface of mast cells. On reexposure, the antigen combines with antibody on the mast cell surface to stimulate immediate release of histamine from mast cell cytoplasmic granules, which causes itching; bronchospasm, wheezing, and shortness of breath; and vasodilation and edema formation with low blood pressure, weakness, and tissue swelling.

TYPE 2 IMMUNE REACTION: (2) _____. Antibodies attach to target antigen, which is destroyed by inflammation (e.g., glomerular basement membrane) or phagocytosis (e.g., red blood cell).

TYPE 3 IMMUNE REACTION: (1) _____. Antigen and antibody bind together to create an immune complex.

TYPE 4 IMMUNE REACTION: (4) _____. Macrophages capture antigen and present it to T lymphocytes, thus programming (sensitizing) them. Some lymphocytes become cytotoxic T cells that attack the antigen wherever it is found; others become helper, suppressor, and memory T cells.

LEARNING OBJECTIVE 8: Using examples from the text, explain the pathogenesis of allergic reactions.

EXERCISE 3-18

Complete the paragraph below.

Allergy is an exaggerated immune response to a relatively innocuous foreign antigen, carried out primarily by mast cells and (1) _____. (2) _____ released from IgE-sensitized mast cells in skin, lungs, and gastrointestinal mucosa causes local vasodilation, edema, itching, (3) _____ muscle spasm in airways (wheezing) and gastrointestinal tract (increased motility, urgency), and increased salivary and bronchial gland secretion. These cause the symptoms of allergies and, if systemic and severe, can lead to

(4) _____, an acute life-threatening, IgE-mediated allergic reaction occurring in previously sensitized people when they are re-exposed to the sensitizing antigen.

EXERCISE 3-19   PATHOLOGY AS A SECOND LANGUAGE

Test your vocabulary by writing the appropriate term in each blank from the list below.

Allergen	Sensitivity	Atopy
Allergic rhinitis	Aversions	Food allergy

1. Any substance that induces an allergic reaction   _____

2. Allergy due to Type I hypersensitivity   _____

3. Itching, sneezing, rhinorrhea, nasal congestion, and conjunctivitis caused by exposure to pollens   _____

4. Exaggerated immune response to dietary proteins   _____

LEARNING OBJECTIVE 9: Briefly discuss the immune mechanisms and clinical findings in rheumatoid arthritis, Sjögren disease, systemic sclerosis, inflammatory myopathy, and systemic lupus erythematosus.

EXERCISE 3-20

Complete the paragraph below.

Rheumatoid arthritis is an autoimmune disease affecting the lining membrane (1) _____ of joints, and extra-articular tissue such as heart, lungs, skin, and blood vessels. Most patients have a characteristic immune complex (2) _____ in their blood.

(3) _____ is a chronic autoimmune inflammatory disease of the lacrimal and (4) _____ glands, which features dry eyes and mouth, and one-third have additional problems including pulmonary fibrosis, arthritis, or peripheral neuropathy. Most Sjögren patients have autoantibodies in their blood but will not have RA or other autoimmune disease. Diagnosis requires a (5) _____ biopsy to document inflammation of small accessory salivary glands.

(6) _____ (aka systemic sclerosis) is sometimes a severe disease causing (7)_____ of the skin, and may affect the GI tract, lungs, kidney, heart, skeletal muscle, and small blood vessels. It can cause disfigurement, trouble swallowing, and (8)_____ (spasm of small blood vessels that causes coldness, blanching, numbness, and pain in the fingers and toes).

The (9)_____ are a varied group of disorders characterized by autoimmune skeletal muscle injury. They feature widespread muscle weakness, soreness, fatigue, (10)_____ inflammatory cell infiltrates in affected muscle groups, and laboratory evidence of autoimmune disease.

Systemic lupus erythematosus is a multisystem autoimmune disease, usually occurring in women, caused by (11) _____ hypersensitivity. The facial butterfly, aka (12) _____ rash, is a classic finding, but many organ systems can be affected, especially the skin, serosal membranes, kidney, joints, and even the brain. SLE is associated in particular with the presence of (13) _____ targeting DNA or RNA. Clinical findings are diverse and include low blood counts, vasculitis, skin lesions, serous effusions, myocarditis, glomerulonephritis, arthritis, (14) _____ (inflammation of the anterior chamber of the eye), and brain involvement causing psychosis or dementia.

EXERCISE 3-21   PATHOLOGY AS A SECOND LANGUAGE

Test your vocabulary by determining whether the following statements are true or false.

_____ 1. Autoimmunity occurs when our own self-antigens become targets of the immune system.

_____ 2. The presence of the butterfly rash is characteristic of systemic lupus erythematosus.

_____ 3. Mixed connective tissue disease is a mix of two or more autoimmune diseases.

See Exercise 3-20 for additional key terms covered in this section.

LEARNING OBJECTIVE 10: Compare and contrast primary and secondary amyloidosis, and list the systemic effects of amyloidosis.

EXERCISE 3-22

Complete the paragraph below.

(1) _____ is a pathologic deposition of amyloid, a mixture of insoluble proteins, some of which may

be immunoglobulin fragments. It can be either primary (rare, hereditary such as [2] _____) or second-

ary due to aging, such as (3) _____, chronic inflammatory states (infection, autoimmune), or multiple

myeloma, which causes (4) _____. Symptoms are highly variable, and diagnosis requires a biopsy.

For example, renal deposits may cause (7) _____ or renal failure, while cardiac deposits may cause

(6) _____.

EXERCISE 3-23   PATHOLOGY AS A SECOND LANGUAGE

See Exercise 3-22 for key terms covered in this section.

LEARNING OBJECTIVE 11: Explain the factors taken into consideration with regards to tissue transplantation and blood transfusion and the consequences of a mismatch.

EXERCISE 3-24

Complete the paragraph below.

Transplants are matched to the recipient to reduce immune reactions ([1] called _____) against the

organ. Immunosuppressive drugs are also used to suppress or prevent rejection. There are three types of rejec-

tion that can occur. (2) _____ rejection is a reaction that occurs within minutes or hours when (3)

_____ antibodies in the recipient's blood react immediately with graft vasculature. The organ must

be removed. (4) _____ rejection usually occurs within a few weeks, owing to an immune vasculitis

mediated by (5) _____. (6) _____ rejection develops over a period of months to years and is

mainly the result of prolonged T-cell assault on donor cells. Even if well matched, the primary threat is chronic

rejection by T cells. (7) _____ is an especially severe complication of bone marrow transplantation in

which the donor cells attack the host, affecting the skin, GI tract, and other sites.

　　With blood transfusions, there are two major groups of antigens to consider, the (8) _____, which

consist of the autosomal dominant RBC antigens (A/B/O), and (9) the _____, which is an autosomal

dominant/recessive antigen (D, d). There are other blood groups that will not be discussed here. When these groups are not matched, mismatch reactions can arise, which range from the (10) _____, which manifests as fever, chills, back pain, hives, or rash in response to incompatible blood cells (not involving major blood group incompatibility) to the (11) _____, which is caused by natural antibodies in the recipient's plasma that agglutinate infused cells causing hemolysis.

> **Remember This!** Graft versus host most commonly attacks sites of epithelial cells—that is, the skin and GI tract.

EXERCISE 3-25

Complete the table below.

Rejection	Mediator	Time Frame	Pathogenesis
Hyperacute	Preformed Ab	(1) _____	React with (2) _____
Acute	B & T cell reaction	(3) _____ (longer w/ failed immunosuppressive therapy)	Immune vasculitis
Chronic	Prolonged T cell	(4) _____	-

EXERCISE 3-26   PATHOLOGY AS A SECOND LANGUAGE

Test your vocabulary by filling in the blank with the appropriate term from below. There may be more than one correct answer for each blank.

Autograft

Rh blood group

Major transfusion reaction

Minor crossmatch

Hemolytic disease of newborn

Minor transfusion reaction

Erythroblastosis fetalis

Major blood group antigens

Major crossmatch

Homograft

Xenograft

Blood typing

1. If the patient is both the donor and recipient   _____

2. A transplant between individuals   _____

3. Transplantation across species is a   _____

4. Severe or fatal hemolytic anemia, due to Rh mismatch   _____

5. Defining the ABO and Rh type of blood   _____

6. Mix of donor RBCs with potential recipient plasma   _____

7. Mix of donor plasma with potential recipient RBC   _____

See Exercise 3-25 for additional key terms covered in this section.

> **Remember This!** Fatal hemolytic disease of infants can be caused by Rh mismatch (negative mother, with positive fetus x 2. . .. 2 wrongs make it really wrong). However, it can happen in the first pregnancy too! Be careful when giving blood transfusions to match a negative female with negative blood. Also, it is appropriate in an obstetric history to ask about abortions/miscarriages, as these count towards the number of pregnancies! Remember, the health of the fetus depends on it!

LEARNING OBJECTIVE 12: Describe the deficiency of each of the following, and give examples of the organisms they are predisposed to: X-linked agammaglobulinemia, isolated immunoglobulin A (IgA) deficiency, thymic hypoplasia, and severe combined immunodeficiency.

EXERCISE 3-27

Complete the paragraph below.

(1) _____ (*Bruton disease*) is an X-linked recessive defect of B cells that leads to inability to produce normal immunoglobulin (no antibodies!). Patients present with a history of recurrent infections: bronchitis, pneumonia, sinusitis, pharyngitis, and ear and gastrointestinal infections. IgA deficiency is the most common immunodeficiency and is caused by an autosomal recessive defect that results in loss of IgA in the mucous membranes; therefore, recurrent infections of the (2) _____ sinus, and pulmonary tracts are common. Common variable immunodeficiency (CVID) causes very low antibodies, resulting in recurrent common infections, and its etiology is most often idiopathic. Thymic hypoplasia (3) _____ is the embryonic failure of the thymus to develop; therefore, no T cells (B cells are OK). Patients are susceptible to viral, fungal, and protozoan infections. Severe combined immunodeficiency (SCID) is a group of inherited disorders affecting both B- and T-cell function (hence "combined"). Patients are young and must be kept in strict isolation (think "bubble boy") as they can suffer a wide range of infections, many of them caused by *Pneumocystis*, *Candida*, and other opportunistic microbes.

Mnemonic

Bruton

boy, B cell

EXERCISE 3-28

Complete the table below.

Immunodeficiency	Cell Affected	Clinical
Bruton: X-linked agammaglobulinemia	No serum Igs, B cell development	X-linked recessive
Isolated immunoglobulin A (IgA) deficiency	(1) _____	(2) _____
Thymic hypoplasia (DiGeorge syndrome)	(3) _____	Embryonic failure of thymus to develop
Severe combined immunodeficiency	B and T cell function	(4) _____
Common variable deficiency	B cell malfunction, low levels of Ig	(5) _____

EXERCISE 3-29   PATHOLOGY AS A SECOND LANGUAGE

See Exercises 3-27 and 3-28 for key terms covered in this section.

LEARNING OBJECTIVE 13: Briefly discuss the phases of HIV/AIDS, and explain the role of infections, AIDS-defining neoplasms, and laboratory data in making the diagnosis.

EXERCISE 3-30

Complete the paragraph below.

HIV infection develops in three phases: (1) an _____; (2) a _____ in which most patients are asymptomatic; and (3) _____. After initial infection, most patients develop an acute flu-like syndrome which resolves over a few weeks. HIV is present in blood in high concentration and CD4+ (helper T cell) cell counts may fall markedly. Nevertheless, CD4+ T cells soon replenish, the number of virus particles in blood falls to low levels, and anti-HIV antibodies appear in blood as the HIV infection enters a latent phase, usually lasting from 2 to 10 years with few symptoms. Without treatment, a crisis phase appears as CD4+ T cell counts once again fall dramatically and HIV viral loads (4) _____ leading to AIDS. This near-complete breakdown of the immune system allows opportunistic infections to occur, especially in the lungs and gastrointestinal tract; neurologic symptoms and dementia to appear; and possibly secondary neoplasms to develop. Laboratory values of HIV status, CD4+ cell counts, and tests for infectious organisms are critical in diagnosing HIV and AIDS. AIDS-defining infections include (5) _____ pneumonia, Kaposi sarcoma, and others (see table below).

EXERCISE 3-31

Complete the table below.

AIDS Diagnosis	(1) _____	(2) _____	(3) _____
Labs: HIV Ag/Ab, CD4+ T cell: < 200/microliter, < 14% peripheral lymphs	Negative labs	Positive labs	Positive labs
CNS lymphoma	< 60 years old	Any age	
Kaposi sarcoma (due to virus)	< 60 year old	Any age	
Pneumocystis jiroveci pneumonia	X		
Nonlung crypto	X		
Myco avium (nonlung, skin, LN)	X		
PML	X		
Pulmonary TB		X	
Disseminated coccidioidomycosis		X	
Retinal CMV			X
Toxoplasmosis			X
Recurrent pneumonia			X

EXERCISE 3-32   PATHOLOGY AS A SECOND LANGUAGE

Complete the statements below.

1. _____ is a severe immunodeficiency caused by infection with HIV, which infects T cells and related macrophages.

2. _____ is a combination of antivirus drugs given in high concentrations to decrease HIV load.

Decisions Decisions

DECISION TREE 3.1: HYPERSENSITIVITY

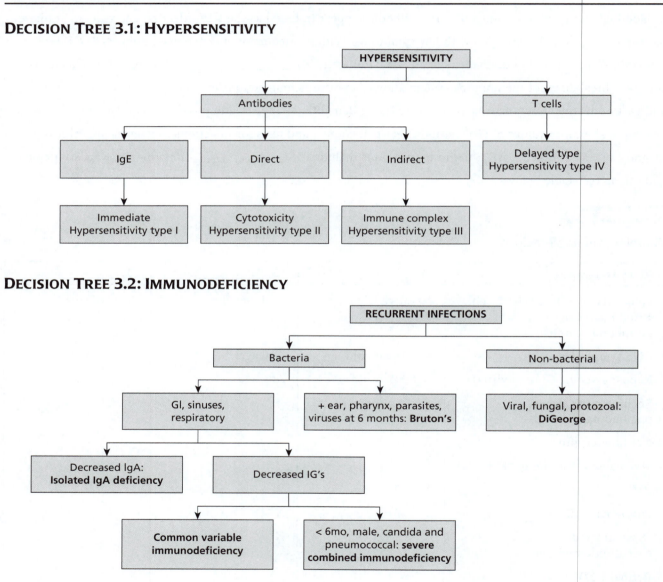

DECISION TREE 3.2: IMMUNODEFICIENCY

Test Yourself

I. Multiple Choice

1. An 8-year-old Hispanic female is brought to the free clinic by her mother. The child is covered with small fluid-filled pruritic vesicles. You suspect chicken pox, which you can verify by checking for the presence of which of the following antibodies? [Learning Objective 5]
   A. IgG
   B. IgM
   C. IgD
   D. IgA

2. Replacement of a patient's heart valve with a swine valve is an example of what type of graft? [Learning Objective 11]
   A. Xenograft
   B. Autograft
   C. Allograft
   D. Homograft

3. A 22-year-old medical student receives his yearly PPD to check for TB exposure. Forty-eight hours later, he returns to the clinic for the test to be read. He is anxious, as a large 1.2 cm, raised, indurated bump is evident at the injection site. This reaction is an example of what type of hypersensitivity? (Hint: Use Decision Tree 3.1) [Learning Objective 7]
   A. Immediate hypersensitivity
   B. Cytotoxic hypersensitivity
   C. Immune complex hypersensitivity
   D. Delayed type hypersensitivity

4. The survival of nontolerant B and T cells, in the bone marrow and thymus respectively, is caused by which of the following? [Learning Objective 9]
   A. Inaccessible self-antigens
   B. Infection and inflammation
   C. Imperfect fetal B- and T-cell programming
   D. Molecular mimicry

5. A 10-year-old African American male and his mother visit an infectious diseases specialist. His past medical history is significant for multiple viral, fungal, and protozoal infections. His physical exam is pertinent for an unusually small chin, a long face, and a high broad nasal bridge. What is his immune disorder? (Hint: Use Decision Tree 3.2) [Learning Objective 12]
   A. Bruton disease
   B. Severe combined immunodeficiency
   C. Isolated IgA immunodeficiency
   D. DiGeorge syndrome

6. Which rejection occurs following the failure of immunosuppressive therapy and involves both B and T cells? [Learning Objective 11]
   A. Hyperacute rejection
   B. Acute rejection
   C. Chronic rejection
   D. Latent rejection

7. 25-year-old African American female with a past medical history significant for a deep venous thrombosis and several spontaneous abortions receives counseling at a fertility clinic. Despite a history consistent with hypercoagulability, her labs are more consistent with a clotting deficiency. Which of the following autoimmune diseases explains the disparity between her symptoms and her test results? [Learning Objective 9]
   A. Rheumatoid arthritis
   B. Systemic lupus erythematosus
   C. Chronic discoid lupus erythematosus
   D. Sjögren syndrome

8. Which of the following is a nonimmune defense mechanism? [Learning Objective 1]
   A. Layering and shedding of the epithelial surface
   B. Acidic pH
   C. Cells composed of dense, indigestible protein
   D. All of the above

9. A 24-year-old Caucasian woman visits her physician's office complaining of blanching, numbness, and pain of her fingers and toes when she becomes cold. A review of systems is positive for dysphagia and shortness of breath, but is otherwise unremarkable, as is her physical exam. From what autoimmune disease does she suffer? [Learning Objective 9]
   A. Systemic lupus erythematosus
   B. Polyarteritis nodosa
   C. Inflammatory myopathy
   D. Systemic sclerosis

10. Translucent, smooth, glassy material deposited in the interstitial space of a patient with rheumatoid arthritis is likely caused by what type of amyloidosis? [Learning Objective 10]
    A. Hereditary amyloidosis
    B. Misfolded mutant proteins
    C. Reactive systemic amyloidosis
    D. Light chain amyloidosis

11. Within an hour of eating a peanut butter sandwich, a five-year-old boy's lips begin to swell, and an urticarial rash erupts across his skin. His breathing is also labored and accompanied by wheezing, and inspiratory stridor. What type of hypersensitivity reaction has occurred? [Learning Objective 7-8]
    A. Immediate hypersensitivity
    B. Cytotoxic hypersensitivity
    C. Immune complex hypersensitivity
    D. Delayed type hypersensitivity

12. A two-year-old male, who was recently admitted to the hospital for severe dehydration following a parasitic diarrheal disease, has a long history of recurrent infections, including pneumonia, ear, and gastrointestinal infections, which began when he was approximately six years old. What is the underlying cause of his multiple infections? (Hint: Use Decision Tree 3.2) [LEARNING OBJECTIVE 12]
    A. Severe combined immunodeficiency
    B. Common variable immunodeficiency
    C. Isolate IgA immunodeficiency
    D. Bruton disease

13. How does HIV infection affect B-cell function? [LEARNING OBJECTIVE 13]
    A. B cells are stimulated by HIV, CMV, EBV, and other infectious agents and produce large amounts of ineffectual antibodies.
    B. B-cell function is impaired as it requires helper T-cell support (and helper T cells are the prime targets of HIV).
    C. Both of the above are true.
    D. B-cell function is unaffected by HIV.

14. A 65-year-old Caucasian female presents to her doctor complaining of dry eyes and dry mouth. Her past medical history is negative and her physical exam is unremarkable. A lip biopsy reveals inflammation of small, accessory salivary glands. What is your diagnosis? [LEARNING OBJECTIVE 9]
    A. Sjögren syndrome
    B. Systemic sclerosis
    C. Systemic lupus erythematosus
    D. Inflammatory myopathy

15. Failure of what T-cell subtype causes autoimmune disease? [LEARNING OBJECTIVE 6]
    A. Cytotoxic T cells
    B. Helper T cells
    C. Regulatory T cells
    D. More than one of the above

II. TRUE OR FALSE

16. _____ The transplant of all organs requires strict matching of the MHC/HLA types. [LEARNING OBJECTIVE 11]

17. _____ Heterosexual contract is the predominant mode of HIV transmission in underdeveloped nations. [LEARNING OBJECTIVE 13]

18. _____ Tonsils and lymph nodes are secondary lymphoid organs. [LEARNING OBJECTIVE 1]

19. _____ An antigen incites an adaptive immune response. [LEARNING OBJECTIVE 3]

20. _____ The heart is most often involved in the amyloidosis of aging.

21. _____ Unlike the lymph nodes, the spleen and bone marrow do not capture or destroy nonself material. [LEARNING OBJECTIVE 2]

22. _____ Antibodies are produced only in response to freely circulating antigens from extracellular threats.

23. _____ Class MHC II cells, present only on the surface of every body cell except red blood cells, capture and display external nonself antigens. [LEARNING OBJECTIVE 6]

24. _____ Major transfusion reactions can result in severe hemolysis, systemic thrombosis of small blood vessels, disseminated intravascular coagulation, renal failure, and death. [LEARNING OBJECTIVE 11]

III. MATCHING

25. Match the following immune cells with their function; some functions may have more than one answer; some choices may be used more than once: [LEARNING OBJECTIVES 4, 5, AND 6]
    i. Macrophages
    ii. Microglia
    iii. Kupffer cells
    iv. Dendritic cells
    v. NK cells
    vi. Cytotoxic T cells
    vii. Memory B cells
    viii. Plasma cells
    A. Antibody-secreting cells
    B. Ingest and destroy microbes and other nonself antigens
    C. Capture antigens for presentation to T lymphocytes
    D. Attack and kill virus-infected cells and tumor cells
    E. Preprogrammed cells that quickly multiply and release a flood of antibodies the next time the antigen appears

26. Match the following diseases to their hypersensitivity type. [LEARNING OBJECTIVE 7]
    i. Direct hypersensitivity
    ii. Cytotoxic hypersensitivity
    iii. Immune complex hypersensitivity
    iv. Delayed type hypersensitivity
    A. Systemic lupus erythematosus
    B. Rheumatoid arthritis
    C. Immune thrombocytopenia
    D. Type 1 diabetes
    E. Poststreptococcal glomerulonephritis
    F. Farmer's lung

IV. SHORT ANSWER

27. What treatment options are available for patients with severe allergies (owing to histamine released from IgE-sensitized mast cells? [LEARNING OBJECTIVE 8]

_____

_____

_____

28. Why is blood group AB+ considered a universal recipient? [LEARNING OBJECTIVE 11]

_____

_____

_____

29. How is AIDS diagnosed? [LEARNING OBJECTIVE 13]

_____

_____

_____

CHAPTER 4

Infectious Disease

	The Big Picture

Infections, if taken as a group, are the most common cause of death worldwide, surpassing ischemic heart disease. Pneumonia is the most common type of infectious cause of death worldwide, ranking third in overall causes of death. Infections can be bacterial, viral, fungal, or parasitic, and can be differentiated based on the inflammatory reaction they incite within the body. Diagnosis depends largely on the clinical picture, special stains, and microbial cultures, though the advent of molecular techniques like PCR is making diagnosis faster and easier, especially in the case of viruses.

Oh No! Not Another Learning Experience:

LEARNING OBJECTIVE 1: List the most common worldwide causes of death resulting from infection.

EXERCISE 4-1

Complete the table below.

Rank	Condition	Deaths
1	(1) _____	7,200,000
2	Cerebrovascular disease	5,700,000
3	Pneumonia	4,200,000
4	Chronic obstructive pulmonary disease	3,000,000
5	(2) _____	2,200,000
6	(3) _____	2,000,000
7	Tuberculosis	1,500,000
8	(4) _____	1,300,000
9	(5) _____	1,300,000
10	Prematurity	1,200,000
11	Neonatal infections	1,100,000
12	Diabetes	1,100,000
13	Hypertension	1,000,000
14	(6) _____	900,000
	All infections above	11,900,000

Remember This! Infectious diseases altogether are the most common cause of death; otherwise it's cardiovascular disease!

EXERCISE 4-2   PATHOLOGY AS A SECOND LANGUAGE

Test your vocabulary by writing the appropriate term in each blank from the list below.

Infectious	Endemic rate	Epidemic rate
Hosts	Commensal	Coccobacilli
Aerobic	Molds	Parasites
Protozoa	Helminths	Prions
Ectoparasites	Microbes	Spirochetes
Anaerobic	Viruses	Bacteria
Bacilli	Fungi	Positive
Negative	Cocci	Yeast

1. An _____ disease occurs when **pathogens** (also called _____, due to their microscopic appearance) invade through physical barriers, overcoming the immune system to cause injury/disease.

2. _____ are organisms that live off of _____ (infected people, plants, or animals).

3. _____ are a corrupted form of normal brain protein.

4. _____ are packets of nucleic acid encased in a capsid.

5. _____ can come in two forms: long, branching, multicellular filaments (*hyphae*), which are referred to as _____, or multicellular clusters of budding round forms (*spores*) called _____.

6. _____ are unicellular organisms that cause disease.

7. The expected rate of infection in a population or geographic area is called an _____, while an above-normal rate of infection is called an _____.

8. _____ are parasitic worms.

9. The result of **gram stain** is either gram-_____ (where bacteria retain a deep purple coloring) or gram-_____ (where bacteria lose their purple coloring and are restained red).

10. Bacteria can come in several shapes: _____ (spheres), _____ (elongated rods), _____ (a combination of the two), and _____ (corkscrew shaped).

11. A _____ relationship is one in which the host is neither benefitted nor harmed.

12. Bacteria that require oxygen are _____; those that do not are _____.

13. _____ are motile, single-cell, nucleated organisms that reproduce within cells or extracellularly.

14. _____ are small, insect-like creatures that attach to or live in the skin.

LEARNING OBJECTIVE 2: Briefly describe how organisms spread in tissue.

EXERCISE 4-3

Complete the paragraph below.

Pathogenic organisms can spread between individuals and within tissues in a variety of ways. Perhaps the most obvious is by (1) _____ with the organism; for example, sexual intercourse transmits certain diseases such as syphilis (a bacterial disease) or herpes (a viral disease), which penetrate through breaks in skin or mucosa of the genital tract. Skin needle sticks, or injections, can also be categorized as direct contact and are a special hazard for people who use or abuse injected drugs and healthcare workers. (2) _____ of contaminated food is sometimes responsible, as in campylobacter or hepatitis A virus infection. If a contagious disease can be acquired through contaminated inanimate materials, termed (3) _____, then it is classified as (4) _____. Respiratory (5) _____ from coughing or sneezing are the mode of transmission for most upper respiratory infections ("colds"), influenza, pneumonia, mumps, and other diseases. Intermediate carriers such as mosquitoes, called (6) _____, often transmit malaria and other parasitic diseases.

EXERCISE 4-4   PATHOLOGY AS A SECOND LANGUAGE

Test your vocabulary by indicating if each statement below is true or false. If it is false, provide the correct word for the italicized term that will make the statement true.

_____ 1. *Epidemic* is the spread of infection from one person (host) to another.

_____

_____ 2. Infection acquired outside of a hospital is *community acquired*.

_____

_____ 3. Infection acquired in a hospital is *nosocomial*.

_____

_____ 4. A *reservoir* is a place where the pathogen exists and spreads to new hosts.

_____

_____ 5. A *vector* is a person or animal harboring the pathogen but with no obvious disease.

_____

_____ 6. A blood stream infection leading to severe symptoms such as hypotension is termed *septicemia*.

_____

See Exercise 4-3 for additional key terms covered in this section.

LEARNING OBJECTIVE 3: Name the three mechanisms that are responsible for causing damage to tissue.

EXERCISE 4-5

Complete the paragraph below.

Pathogenic organisms damage tissue thereby causing harm in a number of ways. They can (1) _____ tissues or directly contact cells. Organisms can release (2) _____ that cause local tissue damage, or circulate to cause cell death or damage at a distance. Perhaps the most important cause of damage by pathogenic organisms is the provocation of the (3) _____. Although initially directed at keeping the organisms at bay, the immune response itself can cause significant additional tissue damage.

Remember This! Host responses can be just as devastating as the actual infection itself!

EXERCISE 4-6   PATHOLOGY AS A SECOND LANGUAGE

Test your vocabulary by writing the appropriate term in each blank from the list below.

Virulence	Tropism	Endotoxin
Exotoxin	Host immunity	

1. _____ is the degree of harmfulness of a microbe.

2. A preference for infecting a particular type of cell is called _____.

3. A component of the cell membrane released as the organism dies is called _____.

4. A product synthesized and excreted by a pathogenic bacterium is called an _____.

5. Defense systems that help prevent infection by a pathogenic organism are called _____.

LEARNING OBJECTIVE 4: Describe the cellular inflammatory reaction to bacteria, viruses, mycobacteria, fungi, parasitic worms, and protozoa.

EXERCISE 4-7

Complete the paragraph below.

Viruses generally incite (1) _____ inflammation, which is characterized by accumulation of lymphocytes and macrophages. However, some viruses (e.g., *herpes*) cause cell death ([2] _____) and others (e.g., *human papillomavirus*) cause abnormal cell growth ([3] _____) or dysplasia. In contrast, bacteria usually incite suppurative (purulent) inflammation, usually called acute inflammation, which is characterized by (4) _____, edema at the site, and an increased number of neutrophils in blood (neutrophilia). Exceptions include two sexually transmitted diseases (STD) caused by bacteria, *Chlamydia trachomatis* and *Treponema pallidum*, (the agent of [5] _____) incite lymphocytic or plasmacytic inflammation. *Mycobacterium tuberculosis* and fungal infections can incite granulomatous inflammation. (6) _____ are a special variety of lymphocyte/macrophage inflammation, which form microscopic nodules.

See Exercise 4-8 for additional details regarding the inflammatory reaction in response to each of the above pathogens.

EXERCISE 4-8

Complete the table below.

Category	Immune Response	Examples
Bacteria	Neutrophils (suppurative, purulent, pyogenic)	(1) _____
Viruses	(2) _____	EBV, HCV, others
Mycobacteria	Granulomas	(3) _____
Fungi	(4) _____	Histoplasma, coccidioidies, etc.
Parasitic worms	(5) _____	Ascaris, tape worms, etc.
Protozoa	Variable	(6) _____

EXERCISE 4-9   PATHOLOGY AS A SECOND LANGUAGE

See Exercises 4-7 and 4-8 for key terms covered in this section.

LEARNING OBJECTIVE 5: List the clinical phases of infection that occur after an organism invades the body.

EXERCISE 4-10

Complete the paragraph below.

The natural clinical course of infection occurs in phases and begins with the invasion of the organism into the body. The time between invasion and appearance of signs or symptoms is the (1) _____. During this phase, the organism attempts to proliferate, and if unsuccessful, then no illness occurs. Next, a (2) _____ may occur in which the patient suffers from mild, nonspecific symptoms like headache, loss of appetite, and fatigue. During the (3) _____ of the illness, the typical and most severe clinical signs and symptoms of the infection are present. Then comes a period during which symptoms fade, called (4) _____. Finally, during the (5) _____, no symptoms are present, but the patient may feel fatigued. Real-life situations can be much more complex because of medical therapy, chronic disease, multiple concurrent infections, or other complications and death.

EXERCISE 4-11   PATHOLOGY AS A SECOND LANGUAGE

Please see Exercise 4-10 for the vocabulary terms for this section.

LEARNING OBJECTIVE 6: Discuss the signs, symptoms, and pathogenesis of the following virus infections: (a) rhinovirus, (b) adenovirus, (c) respiratory syncytial virus, (d) influenza, (e) rotavirus, (f) Norwalk virus, (g) coxsackie virus, (h) measles, (i) rubella, (j) mumps, (k) poliomyelitis, (l) herpes simplex virus, (m) herpes zoster virus, (n) cytomegalovirus, and (o) human papillomavirus.

EXERCISE 4-12

Complete the paragraph below.

Viral infections remain some of the most common and, on occasion, the most difficult human infections to treat (there's no cure for the common cold). Nevertheless, the body is usually adept at dealing with these infections without medical intervention and therefore these are "self-limited" diseases. (1) _____ cause the common cold. (2) _____ (RSV) causes lower respiratory tract infections in children and can cause severe respiratory compromise requiring hospitalization. (3) _____, or "the flu", is well known among the populace. (4) _____ is the number one cause of severe diarrhea among infants and young children; new vaccinations are highly effective. *Norwalk virus*, also known as (5) _____, is responsible for nonbacterial outbreaks of epidemic gastroenteritis around the world, and is notorious for causing outbreaks on cruise ships. (6) _____ type 1 is usually associated with oral cold sores; type 2 is associated with genital herpes, although each type can infect either site. (7) _____ is extremely common and persistent infection that leads to cervical dysplasia and cervical carcinoma; vaccinations are available and effective.

See Exercise 4-13 for details regarding additional viral infections.

EXERCISE 4-13

Complete the table below.

Viruses	Disease/Comment
Coxsackievirus	Type A – (1) _____ Type B – myocarditis, etc.
(2) _____	Rubeola, highly contagious
Rubella	Asymptomatic or may cause a brief, mild febrile illness featuring adenopathy, rash, and constitutional symptoms
Mumps	Acute, contagious infection caused by the *mumps virus*
Poliomyelitis	Acute, contagious infection caused by the *poliovirus*
(3) _____	Infects the upper respiratory tract causing tonsillitis, respiratory infections, and conjunctivitis
Herpes Zoster virus	Also known as (4) _____ and is closely related to HSV, causes chickenpox and shingles in older individuals
Cytomegalovirus	A type of herpesvirus infecting blood monocytes and many other cell types within various tissues
(5) _____	Acute viral hepatitis, an epidemic form of hepatitis transmitted by oral—fecal contamination
(6) _____	Causes chronic viral hepatitis, common worldwide prevalence, predisposes to hepatocellular carcinoma
(7) _____	Causes chronic viral hepatitis, leads to cirrhosis, and is the most common indication for liver transplant in the United States
HIV	The agent of (8) _____, infects T cells and causes immunosuppression
Kaposi sarcoma associated herpesvirus (KSHV)	Agent of *Kaposi sarcoma*, a malignant tumor KSHV is also known as (9) _____
EBV	The agent of infectious (10) _____

EXERCISE 4-14   PATHOLOGY AS A SECOND LANGUAGE

Test your vocabulary by writing the appropriate term in each blank from the list below.

Transformative infections   Productive infections   Latent virus infections

1. In _____, the virus persists in noninfectious form, but can periodically reactivate to cause recurrent disease and new infections.

2. In _____, there is persistent infectious virus that is replicating and causing chronic injury.

3. In _____, the virus persists in infectious form and can stimulate the transformation of normal tissue into a neoplasm (dysplasia).

See Exercises 4-12 and 4-13 for additional key terms covered in this section.

LEARNING OBJECTIVE 7: Categorize the following bacteria according to shape, oxygen require-ments, and staining characteristics, and describe the accompanying symptoms: (a) staphylo-coccus, (b) streptococcus, (c) diphtheria, (d) listeria, (e) Clostridium, (f) Neisseria, (g) Rickettsia, (h) Bordetella pertussis, (i) Pseudomonas, (j) campylobacter, (k) Borrelia burgdorferi, (l) mixed anaerobic infection, and (m) tuberculosis.

EXERCISE 4-15

Complete the paragraphs below.

Bacteria are prokaryotic organisms that inhabit almost every surface of our bodies, including the skin and (1) _____ tract. They are on every surface of the world we inhabit. Many bacteria are pathogenic. They can be broadly categorized by their shape and their (2) _____-staining qualities (positive or negative).

Of particular importance is (3) _____, because of its global impact as a major, chronic, progressive, communicable disease that is caused by *Mycobacterium tuberculosis*. This organism stains positively with (4) _____ stains. It incites chronic granulomatous inflammation in tissues with associated (5) _____ necrosis ("necrotizing granulomas"). Most infections are arrested in the lungs or bronchial lymph nodes by the immune system and become dormant without symptoms of disease; this is called (6) _____. If the initial infection cannot be controlled by the immune system and immediately progresses to active disease, it is known as (7) _____. Infection arising from dormant primary TB is called (8) _____ and causes chronic, debilitating disease. The initial lung lesion is called a (9) _____, and the combination of a lung lesion + mediastinal (hilar) lymph nodes is known as the (10) _____.

In contrast, (11) _____ is widespread bloodborne involvement of other organs. The purified protein derivative (PPD) skin test (aka [12] _____) helps to determine if TB has previously infected an individual. *See Exercise 4-16 for details regarding specific pathogenic bacteria.*

EXERCISE 4-16

Complete the table below.

Bacteria	Disease	Staining
Staphyloccocus	Acute, pyogenic infections	Gram-positive cocci
Streptococcus Groups A, B, D according to the character of the hemo-lysis they cause (alpha hemolytic and beta hemolytic).	**Group A** streptococci typically cause infection of superficial surfaces such as pharynx or skin. **Group B** streptococci are a major cause of neo-natal pneumonia, meningitis, and sepsis, and in adults are frequent culprits in urinary tract infec-tions. **Group D** streptococci (also called **entero-cocci**). *Enterococcus faecalis* and *Enterococcus faecium* are common commensal organisms in intestines.	(1) _____
(2) _____	Diptheria: Acute pharyngeal/skin anaerobic infec-tion passed through respiratory droplets or contact	Gram-positive bacilli
Listeria	(3) _____ features bacteremia, meningitis, encephalitis, and dermatitis.	Gram-positive bacilli
Clostridium	(4) _____ is caused by intestinal overgrowth of *C. difficile* which releases toxins causing a severe colitis.	Gram-positive anaerobic bacilli

Bacteria	Disease	Staining
(5) _____	**Gas gangrene** is caused by *C. perfringens.* **Tetanus** is caused by *C. tetani*, an acute poisoning from a neurotoxin. **Botulism** is caused by *C. botulinum*, a paralytic poisoning. **Meningococcal meningitis** is caused by *N. meningitides.* **Gonorrhea** is caused by *N. gonorrhoeae*, a sexually transmitted infection.	Gram-negative cocci
Rickettsia	(6) _____ is caused by *R. rickettsii.* **Epidemic typhus** is caused by *R. prowazeki.* **Scrub typhus** caused by *R. tsutsugamushi.*	Gram-negative variable shapes
Bordetella pertussis	(7) _____ *or* **pertussis**	Gram-negative, short, thick bacilli
Pseudomonas	Otitis externa and other infections	Gram-negative bacilli
Campylobacter	(8) _____	Gram-negative spiral-shaped
Borrelia burgdorferi	(9) _____	Spirochete
Mixed anaerobic infection	Aspiration pneumonia and other mixed anaerobic infections	Mixed bacterial types

---

EXERCISE 4-17   PATHOLOGY AS A SECOND LANGUAGE

Test your vocabulary by indicating if each statement below is true or false. If it is false, provide the correct word for the italicized term that will make the statement true.

_____ 1. *Bacillus anthracis* (the agent of anthrax) is a large, toxin-producing, encapsulated, aerobic or anaerobic *Gram-positive bacillus* that produces *spores.*

_____ 2. Nocardiosis is an acute or chronic, typically disseminated infection caused by various species of *Neisseria.*

_____ 3. *Syphilis* is an infection of the genital skin or mucous membranes caused by *Haemophilus ducreyi.*

_____ 4. *Leprosy* is caused by *Mycobacterium leprae* which has tropism for the low temperature found in peripheral nerves, skin, and oral-respiratory mucous membranes.

See Exercises 4-15 and 4-16 for additional key terms covered in this section.

LEARNING OBJECTIVE 8: Discuss how patient immune system functionality alters the types of fungal infections that patients acquire.

EXERCISE 4-18

Complete the paragraph below.

Immune system functionality alters how fungi interact with the human body. There are two distinctive forms of fungus: (1) _____ are composed of long, multicellular filaments (*hyphae*), and (2) _____ are composed of budding round forms singly or in clusters. For some important fungal pathogens, the form of growth is temperature dependent. In cool temperatures (e.g., on skin), they tend to grow as (3) _____, but at body temperatures, deep fungal infections occur in (4) _____ form. Immunocompromised patients are susceptible to many more infections. In fact, fungi that are normal residents of skin and intestines ([5] _____, *Aspergillus*) may cause disease in immunodeficient patients. Moreover, some infections, such as *Pneumocystis jiroveci* (6) _____, occur only in severely immunocompromised patients (e.g., those with AIDS). Fungi can often be seen on routine microscopic examination of tissue, scrapings, or fluid; however, special stains are sometimes necessary. Laboratory tests are available to test for the presence of antifungal antibodies in blood.

EXERCISE 4-19   PATHOLOGY AS A SECOND LANGUAGE

Test your vocabulary by writing the appropriate term in each blank from the list below.

Deep mycoses	Mycosis	Candidiasis/moniliasis
Coccidioidomycosis	Histoplasmosis	Blastomycosis

1. A fungal infection is a _____.

2. An infection by *C. albicans* is called _____.

3. _____ is an endemic fungal infection caused by *B. dermatidis*.

4. _____ is an endemic fungal infection of the San Joaquin Valley (southwest United States).

5. _____ is caused by a fungus found in bat droppings (guano).

6. Blastomycosis, coccidioidomycosis, cryptococcosis, histoplasmosis are all pathogenic as yeast forms and are examples of _____.

See Exercise 4-18 for additional key terms covered in this section.

LEARNING OBJECTIVE 9: Discuss the manifestations of the most common parasitic infections, including: protozoa (malaria, amebiasis, giardiasis); helminthes (intestinal nematodes, filariasis, schistosomiasis, tapeworms); and ectoparasites (lice, scabies).

EXERCISE 4-20

Complete the paragraph below.

Parasitic infections are a very common worldwide cause of disease. Such infections can induce eosinophilic inflammation in tissues. Please see Exercise 4-21 below for details on the manifestations of parasitic infections.

EXERCISE 4-21

Complete the table below.

Parasite	Infectious Agent	Diseases	Hallmarks
Protozoa	(1) _____	Malaria	Intermittent fevers, yellow discoloration
	Entamoeba histolytica	(2) _____	"Flask-shaped" GI ulcers
	Giardia lamblia	(3) _____	Diarrhea after drinking contaminated water
Helminthes	Small roundworms (nematodes)	Filariasis, elephantiasis	Transmitted by mosquitoes and found most commonly in Asia and Africa
	Large roundworms (nematodes)	(4) _____	Multiply in the intestine
	Schistosoma flukes	Schistosomiasis	Invade bladder, biliary tract
	Cestodes	Tapeworms, (5) _____	Segmented, ribbon-shaped worms
Ectoparasites	(6) _____	Pediculosis	Wingless, blood-sucking insects that infest hair
	Sarcoptes scabiei	Scabies	Very itchy skin mites

EXERCISE 4-22   PATHOLOGY AS A SECOND LANGUAGE

Test your vocabulary by writing the appropriate term in each blank from the list below.

Chagas	Protozoa	Ectoparasite
Echinococcus	Trichinosis	Cysticercosis
Leishmaniasis	Flatworms	Microsporidiosis
Pinworm	Trypanosomiasis	

1. _____ are unicellular, motile, microscopic pathogens with a nucleus.

2. _____ is a chronic inflammatory disease of skin, mucous membranes, and viscera caused by species of *Leishmania*, a microscopic, intracellular protozoan that infects white blood cells.

3. _____ (sleeping sickness) is caused by a microscopic protozoa that infect blood and are transmitted by tsetse fly.

4. _____ **disease** is a variety of trypanosomiasis, features periorbital edema, fever, hepatosplenomegaly, esophageal dysmotility, and, later, myocardial infection.

5. **Cryptosporidiosis** and _____ opportunistic intestinal pathogens in AIDS and other immunodeficiency states that cause diarrhea.

6. _____ infection is caused by *Enterobius vermicularis* and classically diagnosed by the "scotch tape" test.

7. _____ is infection by the *Trichina* roundworm from encysted larvae in certain meats.

8. _____ are *trematodes* (flukes) that infect blood vessels, gastrointestinal tract, lungs, or liver.

9. _____ involves the release of eggs into blood vessels which disseminate and deposit widely in many tissues (including the brain) as small cysts.

10. _____ (hydatid disease) is a tapeworm infection caused by larvae of several varieties of tapeworm passed back and forth between dogs and cows.

11. An _____ lives on the surface of the host.

See Exercises 4-20 and 4-21 for additional key terms covered in this section.

LEARNING OBJECTIVE 10: Using clinical presentations and pathological findings, distinguish amongst the most common sexually transmitted diseases.

EXERCISE 4-23

Complete the sentence below.

(1) A _____ (STI) is an infection communicated by sexual contact.

See Exercises 4-24 and 4-25 for details of sexually transmitted diseases.

EXERCISE 4-24

Complete the table below.

Agent/ Condition	Lesions	Conditions/ Complications	Therapy
Trichomonas vaginalis ([1] _____)	Males: urethritis, balanitis Females: vaginitis	None	Special antimicrobials
Human papillomavirus	Both : (2) _____	Males: none Females: dysplasia or cancer of the vulva, vagina, cervix	Excision or destruction
*Herpesvirus (**Genital herpes**)*	(3) _____	Adults: recurrent eruptions Neonates: fatal infection from mother	Antiviral drugs reduce frequency and duration of eruptions
Chlamydia trachomatis	Both: (4) _____ Males: proctitis, urethritis, prostatitis, epididymitis Females: cervicitis, salpingitis	Males: urethral stricture Females: tubal obstruction, ectopic pregnancy, infertility Neonates: conjunctivitis, pneumonia	Antibiotics
Neisseria gonorrhoeae	Both: urethritis, proctitis, pharyngitis Neonates: conjunctivitis Males: prostatitis, epididymitis Females: vulvovaginitis, cervicitis, salpingitis	Both: (5) _____ Males: urethral stricture Females: ectopic pregnancy, infertility	Antibiotics
Treponema pallidum (Syphilis)	*Primary:* (6) _____ *Tertiary:* dementia, aortic disease	(7) _____	

Agent/ Condition	Lesions	Conditions/ Complications	Therapy
HIV	*Secondary*: skin disease, condyloma lata, lymphadenopathy Both: initial skin rash	Both: opportunistic infections, neoplasms	Anti-HIV drugs suppress, not cure
Haemophilis ducreyi (8)	Either sex: painful genital ulcers	Important cofactor in spread of AIDs in Africa and SE Asia	Antibiotics
Molluscum contagiosum virus	Both: small white papules on genitalia (or other sites, not always due to sexual contact)	None	None

EXERCISE 4-25   PATHOLOGY AS A SECOND LANGUAGE

Test your vocabulary by writing the appropriate term in each blank from the list below. A term may be used more than once.

Trichomoniasis   Chancre   Syphilis
Tabes dorsalis   Chlamydiae   Congenital syphilis
Gonorrhea   Condyloma acuminatum   Condyloma lata
Tertiary syphilis   Secondary syphilis   Antitreponemal antibodies

1. _____ is an STI caused by the gram-negative coccus, *Neisseria gonorrhoeae.*

2. _____ is a vaginal/genital tract infection in which the organisms can be seen moving on a "wet mount" slide.

3. _____ are a group of gram-negative obligate intracellular bacteria.

4. _____ is a STI caused by *Treponema pallidum.*

5. _____ (*genital wart*) and *squamous carcinoma* occur in the vulva, vagina, or, most commonly, of the cervix.

6. The indurated (hard), moist, painless ulcer of primary syphilis is called a _____.

7. _____ presents clinically as lymphadenopathy and skin lesions on the palms of the hands and the soles of the feet.

8. Broad-based, cauliflower-like epidermal growths associated with syphilis are known as _____.

9. After a subclinical latency period of 5–20 years, _____ develops, affecting the cardiovascular system and the nervous system (neurosyphilis).

10. When the posterior (dorsal) nerve roots of the spinal cord are affected by syphilis, it is known as _____.

11. *T. pallidum* can cross the placenta to infect the fetus, causing _____.

12. Sensitive initial screening tests for syphilis are VDRL and RPR (called reagin antibodies), while specific follow-up tests to verify infection are called _____.

LEARNING OBJECTIVE 11: Know the "gold standard," as well as the newer diagnostic tests available, when it comes to identifying infectious organisms.

EXERCISE 4-26

Complete the paragraphs below.

Many laboratory tools and diagnostic tests are available to evaluate for pathogenic microorganisms. For bacteria, the simplest, quickest, and most widely available and reliable tool is the (1) _____, which helps to identify the shape (bacillus or coccus) and the Gram stain properties. However, (2) _____ is generally considered the "gold standard" for documenting an infectious organism.

Obtaining a specimen for culture may be as simple as swabbing pus from a wound or collecting a urine specimen, or may require an invasive technique such as a spinal tap to obtain (3) _____. Cultures are performed on specific nutrient media to support growth of the pathogenic bacteria and decrease background growth. In addition, (4) _____ testing is done by exposing the plated bacteria to discs soaked with various antibiotics, which may or may not kill or inhibit bacterial growth around the disc.

Most fungi are relatively easy to culture and identify using similar techniques. Viruses, *Chlamydia*, *Rickettsia*, and *Mycoplasma* are difficult to culture and require more elaborate techniques, expertise, and equipment.

Another way to detect infections is by measuring the immune response in the serum where (5) _____ (and microbial antigens) are measured to diagnose infection. This is especially true for viral infections such as hepatitis B. Direct detection of organisms in tissue, fluids, or smears may be accomplished by a variety of immune and genetic techniques or by direct microscopic examination (e.g., *Plasmodium* parasite of malaria can be seen in red blood cells). Finally, molecular techniques, such as (6) _____ (PCR), allow for very sensitive detection of DNA or RNA from any organism.

EXERCISE 4-27　PATHOLOGY AS A SECOND LANGUAGE

There are no vocabulary terms in this section.

Decisions Decisions

DECISION TREE 4.1: THE CLASSIFICATION OF INFECTIONS

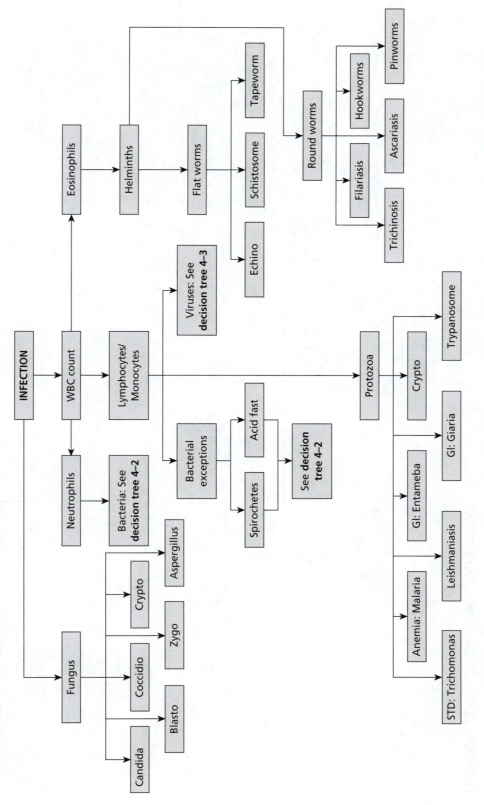

DECISION TREE 4.2: BACTERIAL INFECTIONS

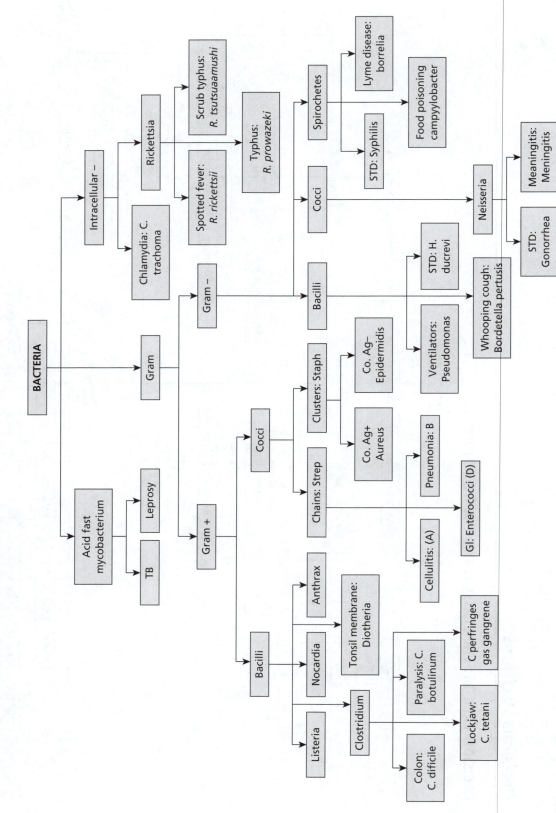

DECISION TREE 4.3: VIRAL INFECTIONS

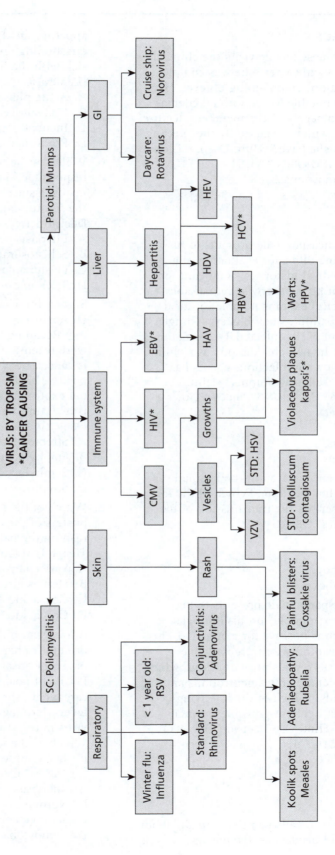

Test Yourself

I. MULTIPLE CHOICE

1. A 23-year-old Chinese female visits the clinic after her return from Brazil (where she was completing an away rotation) complaining of fever. Her physical exam is notable for periorbital edema and hepatosplenomegaly. You remember a lecture on her infection, which is caused by the "kissing bug." What does she have? (Hint: Use Decision Tree 4.1) [LEARNING OBJECTIVE 9]
   A. African Trypanosomiasis
   B. Leishmaniasis
   C. Amebiasis
   D. Chagas disease

2. A 65-year-old Caucasian male presents to his primary physician's office for evaluation of a rash. His past medical history is significant for hypertension, but he is otherwise remarkably healthy. His physical exam is notable for local outcroppings of painful, small blisters (shingles) in the distribution of the infected T4 dermatome. He confirms that he had chicken pox as a child. Which of the following infectious agents has reactivated to cause his symptoms? (Hint: Use Decision Tree 4.3) [LEARNING OBJECTIVE 6]
   A. Varicella zoster
   B. Herpes virus
   C. Cosackie virus
   D. Cytomegalovirus

3. A male acquired an infection in the hospital secondary to unwashed bedding. Which of the following terms describes the transmission of his disease? [LEARNING OBJECTIVE 2]
   A. Fomite
   B. Nosocomial
   C. Both of the above
   D. None of the above

4. A 22-year-old Hispanic male presents to his college clinic for a "pimple" on his buttocks. His physical exam is positive for a large (>1 cm) red abscess, but is otherwise unremarkable. Lancing the abscess reveals purulent fluid, which microscopically demonstrates neutrophils and gram-negative rods. Which of the following organisms is most likely responsible for inciting the abscess? (Hint: Use Decision Tree 4.1) [LEARNING OBJECTIVE 4]
   A. *Candida*
   B. Syphilis
   C. *E. coli*
   D. Herpes virus

5. Your youngest cousin calls you to complain about the recent onset of headaches, fatigue, and loss of appetite; she denies additional symptoms. Further questioning reveals that several of her friends are sick with the flu. What period of illness is she in? [LEARNING OBJECTIVE 5]
   A. Acute phase
   B. Convalescence
   C. Incubation phase
   D. Prodromal phase

6. Which of the following infectious organisms is responsible for infesting lymphatics and subcutaneous tissue and causing massive lymphedema of the scrotum and legs (elephantiasis)? (Hint: Use Decision Tree 4.1) [LEARNING OBJECTIVE 9]
   A. Filariasis
   B. Schistosomiasis
   C. Leishmaniasis
   D. Trichomoniasis

7. Several hours after a picnic, you begin to experience nausea, vomiting, and abdominal cramping. Recalling the infectious disease chapter you were recently reviewing, you believe your illness is caused by clusters of gram-positive coagulase positive cocci, which have secreted an intestinal exotoxin. What is the name of the organism? (Hint: Use Decision Tree 4.2) [LEARNING OBJECTIVE 7]
   A. Streptococcus pneumonia
   B. Staphylococcus aureus
   C. Staphylococcus epidermidis
   D. Streptococcus *pyogenes*

8. Which of the following infectious agents causes blisters of the oral mucosa (herpangina) and a rash on the palms and soles? (Hint: Use Decision Tree 4.3) [LEARNING OBJECTIVE 6]
   A. Varicella zoster
   B. Herpes virus
   C. Coxsackie A virus
   D. Coxsackie B virus

9. A four-year-old African American female is brought to her pediatrician's office for evaluation of recent onset of vomiting followed by diarrhea. Pertinent positives include being enrolled in daycare where she has sick contacts and a low-grade fever. Her diagnosis is confirmed by detection of virus in the stool through enzyme immunoassay. Which of the following etiologies is responsible for her symptoms? (Hint: Use Decision Tree 4.3) [LEARNING OBJECTIVE 6]
   A. Rotavirus
   B. Norovirus
   C. Staphylococcus aureus
   D. Campylobacter

10. Which of the following organisms is identified by finding nits on a fine-tooth comb after combing wet hair? [LEARNING OBJECTIVE 9]
    A. Scabies
    B. Lice
    C. Pinworm
    D. Roundworms

11. A 22-year-old coed presents to her campus clinic complaining of severe vaginal itching with a white discharge. Her past medical history is remarkable for a recent bacterial infection treated with antibiotics. Which of the following treatments would you prescribe? (Hint: Use Decision Tree 4.1) [LEARNING OBJECTIVE 8]
    A. Antibiotics
    B. Colposcopy
    C. Antimicrobials
    D. Antifungal drugs

12. A 12-year-old Caucasian male is brought to his pediatrician's office by his mother. She reports that he has a fever, cough, and congestion, but that she is most concerned by his rash. His physical exam is positive for conjunctivitis, a maculopapular rash, and Koplik spots on the buccal mucosa. What disease has he contracted, which could have been prevented by vaccination? (Hint: Use Decision Tree 4.3) [LEARNING OBJECTIVE 6]
    A. Poliomyelitis
    B. Measles
    C. Mumps
    D. Rubella

13. Which of the following descriptions characterizes impetigo? [LEARNING OBJECTIVE 7]
    A. Superficial, edematous, erythematous infection of skin, subcutaneous tissue, and lymphatics
    B. Massive bacterial infection of the blood stream
    C. Red, swollen, hot skin, that rapidly progresses to violet blisters and subsequent necrosis
    D. Transient small blisters that break form patches of red, "honey-crusted" lesions covered with dried exudate

14. A one-year-old Hispanic female is brought to the ER by EMS. Her frantic mother describes a recent respiratory infection that had become progressively worse with coughing and whistle when her daughter breathes in. The mother had made an appointment with the child's pediatrician for the following day, but called EMS when her daughter stopped breathing and expired. What infectious agent has caused this fatality? [LEARNING OBJECTIVE 7]
    A. *Bordetella pertussis*
    B. *Pseudomonas aeruginosa*
    C. *Legionella pneumophila*
    D. *Mycobacterium avium*

15. Which of the following worms enters through skin to infect the blood and results in intestinal bleeding and anemia? (Hint: Use Decision Tree 4.1) [LEARNING OBJECTIVE 9]
    A. Hookworms
    B. Ascaris
    C. Schistosomiasis
    D. Tapeworms

16. A 55-year-old male is evaluated for a proximal aortic aneurysm. A review of systems is positive for skin lesions on the palms of the hands and the soles of the feet five to six years ago, and a penile ulcer approximately one year before that. A test for the reagin antibodies is negative. What is your diagnosis? [LEARNING OBJECTIVE 10]
    A. Primary syphilis
    B. Secondary syphilis
    C. Tertiary syphilis
    D. None of the above (an agent other than syphilis)

17. A cattle farmer from east Texas visits the clinic for some worrisome itchy ulcerations on his forearms. His physical exam is remarkable for black eschars (scabs). Cultures of the sores are positive for a large encapsulated gram-positive bacillus with spores. What infectious agent is causing his symptoms? [LEARNING OBJECTIVE 6]
    A. *Nocardia*
    B. *Bacillus anthracis*
    C. *Listeria monocytogenes*
    D. *Tuberculosis*

II. TRUE OR FALSE

18. _____ Infectious disease is the number one cause of death. [LEARNING OBJECTIVE 1]

19. _____ Most infections require medical therapy to be completely cleared. [LEARNING OBJECTIVE 5]

20. _____ Latent infections are those in which the virus persists in infectious form and continues to replicate and cause chronic injury. [LEARNING OBJECTIVE 6]

21. _____ The most common cause of death by infectious disease is diarrheal. [LEARNING OBJECTIVE 1]

22. _____ Taenia solium is the fish tape-worm. [LEARNING OBJECTIVE 9]

23. _____ The virulence of a virus is a combination of its ability to kill the cell directly, to incite an immune reaction that kills the cell or damages adjacent tissue, or to transform normal cells into cancerous ones. [LEARNING OBJECTIVE 3]

24. _____ Viruses and other small nonbacterial pathogens are usually not visible by Gram-stain study and instead require PCR for diagnosis. [LEARNING OBJECTIVE 11]

IV. SHORT ANSWER

26. When is TB suspected, what are the risk factors, and how is it diagnosed? [LEARNING OBJECTIVE 7]

_____

_____

_____

27. What organism should you consider in a patient with episodic hemolysis, fever, and jaundice? How is the diagnosis made, and how is it treated? (Hint: Use Decision Tree 4.1) [LEARNING OBJECTIVE 9]

_____

_____

_____

28. What is the danger in not giving vaccines? [LEARNING OBJECTIVES 6 AND 7]

_____

_____

_____

29. How do STIs stand apart from other infections? Provide at least five characteristics that differentiate them. [LEARNING OBJECTIVE 10]

_____

_____

_____

III. MATCHING

25. Match the following *Clostridium* species with the disease they cause: [LEARNING OBJECTIVE 7]
    - i. Botulism
    - ii. Gas gangrene
    - iii. Lockjaw
    - iv. Pseudomembranous colitis
    A. *C. difficile*
    B. *C. perfringens*
    C. *C. tetani*
    D. *C. botulinum*

The Nature of Disease: Neoplasia

The Big Picture

Neoplasia (and a neoplasm) is an abnormal, uncontrolled "new growth" which may be either benign or malignant. Malignant neoplasms are what are commonly called "cancer."; They can invade, metastasize, and cause death. The most common type of malignant neoplasm ("cancer") is that of epithelial cells, called "carcinoma." Including all types, cancer is the second-leading cause of death after heart disease in the United States.

Oh No! Not Another Learning Experience

LEARNING OBJECTIVE 1: Explain how the name of a tumor provides insight into its composition and prognosis and whether there are any exceptions to this naming convention.

EXERCISE 5-1

Complete the paragraphs below.

Neoplasms are generally categorized as benign or malignant, and the terminology reflects this. Most benign neoplasms end with just "oma." In contrast, a malignant tumor of epithelium is a (1) _Carcinoma_ the type will precede this term (e.g., squamous cell [2] _Carcinoma_). A tumor of mesenchymal tissue (bone, cartilage, fat, muscle, etc.) is a (3) _Sarcoma_; again, the type will precede this term (e.g., leiomyo [4] _Sarcoma_). An understanding of Latin prefixes and suffixes can aid in understanding the composition of tumors (see Exercise 5-2).

Exceptions to this naming structure include (5) _melanoma_ (skin cancer) and lymphoma, which are indeed malignant.

EXERCISE 5-2

Complete the table below.

The Naming of Tumors		
Tissue of Origin	**Benign**	**Malignant**
Fibrous	(1) _fibroma_	Fibrosarcoma
Fat	(2) _lipoma_	Liposarcoma
Bone	Osteoma	Osteosarcoma
Cartilage	Chondroma	(3) _chondrosarcoma_
Blood vessels	Hemangioma	(4) _hemangiosarcoma_
Blood cells		
Granulocytes		Leukemia
Lymphocytes		Leukemia, if in blood
		(5) _lymphoma_ , if in lymph nodes or organs
Muscle		
Skeletal	(6) _rhabdomyoma_	Rhabdomyosarcoma
Smooth	Leiomyoma	Leiomyosarcoma
Epithelium		
Epidermis, Squamous	Squamous cell papilloma	(7) _squamous cell carcinoma_
Glands	Adenoma, papilloma	(8) _adenocarcinoma_
Melanocytes	(9) _nevus_	Malignant melanoma

EXERCISE 5-3   PATHOLOGY AS A SECOND LANGUAGE

Test your vocabulary by writing the appropriate term in each blank from the list below.

Malignant   Cancer   Benign
Oncology   Neoplasm

1. A ___benign___ growth is one that usually does not have the capacity to cause death.
2. A ___malignant___ growth is one that has the capacity to cause death.
3. A ___cancer___ is a malignant neoplasm.
4. A ___neoplasm___ is any abnormal uncontrolled growth of new cells.
5. ___Oncology___ is the study of neoplasms.

See Exercises 5-1 and 5-2 for additional key terms covered in this section.

LEARNING OBJECTIVE 2: List the seven hallmarks of cancer.

EXERCISE 5-4

Complete the paragraph below.

The body has a plethora of systems in place to *prevent* cancer. To become cancer, cancer cells must overcome these natural barriers by gaining certain **biologic capabilities**, called the "seven hallmarks of cancer."

1. Self-sufficiency of (1) ___growth___ ("go") signals
2. Evasion of growth suppression ("stop") signals
3. Divide indefinitely, that is, (2) ___unlimited reproduction___
4. Avoid (3) ___apoptosis___ (programmed cell death)
5. Recruit nutrients via growth of new blood supply, that is, (4) ___angiogenesis___
6. Invade nearby tissue and (5) ___metastasize___ (spread to distant tissue)
7. Evade immune surveillance, the cancer detection and elimination aspect of the body's immune system

EXERCISE 5-5   PATHOLOGY AS A SECOND LANGUAGE

See Exercise 5-4 above for key terms covered in this section.

LEARNING OBJECTIVE 3: Using examples from the text, explain the various etiologies responsible for carcinogenesis.

EXERCISE 5-6

Complete the paragraph below.

The primary etiologies responsible for carcinogenesis (the development of cancer) all tend to directly or indirectly damage DNA. These etiologies include (1) ___radiation___ (e.g., ultraviolet or nuclear), (2) ___viruses___ (HPV—cervical carcinoma, EBV—lymphoma), and a wide variety of chemical (3) ___carcinogens___. Carcinogens can be inhaled (such as [4] ___cigarettes___), ingested (smoked foods, molds), or absorbed by skin contact. These carcinogens cause (5) ___mutations___ or permanent damage to DNA. Mutations that lead to cancer are characterized as (6) ___carcinogenic___. In addition, it is now known that chronic inflammation may predispose to development of cancer.

EXERCISE 5-7   PATHOLOGY AS A SECOND LANGUAGE

See Exercise 5-6 for key terms covered in this section.

LEARNING OBJECTIVE 4: Name the four types of genes mutated in neoplasia.

EXERCISE 5-8

Complete the paragraph below.

An understanding of the four types of genes mutated in neoplasia (and cancer!!) reveals the biologic nature of this type of disease. Mutant genes that promote cancer fall into four categories: (1) ___oncogenes___ *proto-oncogenes*, tumor suppressors, genes that regulate apoptosis (or normal cell [2] ___death___), and (3) ___DNA repair___. Perhaps the most confusing is the tumor suppressors and the proto-oncogenes/oncogenes, because these genes are named based on their association with cancer. They are not necessarily named based on their normal biologic function! The normal "go" genes (which promote normal cell growth) can be considered (4) ___Proto-oncogenes___, but, when mutated, become (5) ___oncogenes___. So-called (6) ___tumor suppressor___ *genes* are the opposite of oncogenes—they are the normal "stop" switches that restrain cell growth by inhibiting cell division. When mutated, they no longer control cell growth.

See Exercise 5-9 for additional information.

EXERCISE 5-9

Complete the table below.

Type of Gene	Function	Examples
Tumor suppressors	(1) _stop growth_	Rb (retinoblastoma, a gene that when mutated causes retinal tumors)
Proto-oncogenes	Pro-growth, promote cancer	HER2 (A gene involved in a subpopulation of breast cancer)
(2) _Apoptosis_	Facilitate cell death	P53 (also considered a tumor suppressor), allows cancer cells to live when they should die
DNA repair	Repair (3) _damaged or_ DNA _misspelled_	Mismatch repair proteins (Lynch syndrome which causes colon cancer), Xeroderma pigmentosum (skin cancer)

EXERCISE 5-10 PATHOLOGY AS A SECOND LANGUAGE

Test your vocabulary by indicating if each statement below is true or false. If it is false, provide the correct word for the italicized term that will make the statement true.

_F_ 1. The HER2 gene is a *tumor suppressor* that produces *human epidermal growth factor 2*, a protein that promotes normal cell growth. The mutant, "amplified", or overexpressed (overactive) HER2 genes can be identified in breast cancer and promote uncontrolled growth.

proto-oncogene

_T_ 2. The p53 gene regulates *apoptosis*, and mutation of p53 is the most common genetic defect in human cancers.

_T_ 3. DNA is miscoded frequently, but the erroneous sequences (possible mutations) are quickly fixed by *DNA repair genes*, which can be conceived of as "spell checkers" for "misspelled" DNA.

_T_ 4. Because no single mutation in any of the gene types discussed above is sufficient to produce a malignant neoplasm, *carcinogenesis* is a multistep process.

_T_ 5. Germ cell defects that predispose to cancer and that can be passed on to the next generation are called *inheritable cancer syndromes*.

See Exercises 5-8 and 5-9 for additional key terms covered in this section.

LEARNING OBJECTIVE 5: Discuss the importance of heterogeneity, doubling time, growth fraction, angiogenesis, metastatic potential, and immunodeficiency in tumor prognosis.

EXERCISE 5-11

Complete the paragraph below.

All neoplasms are initially (1) _monoclonal_ as they arise from a single cell and grow as a clone of expanding generations of daughter cells. A (2) _clone_ is a set of identical cells descended from a single ancestor.

After a time, as a tumor grows, some cells acquire changes or mutations that make them different from the others; this causes (3) _tumor cell heterogeneity_, a tumor composed of multiple sets of differing cells. Some of these cells may gain (4) _metastatic potential_, the ability to metastasize, or may gain the ability to invade. (5) _Metastasis_ is the discontinuous spread of tumor from one site to another. (6) _Invasion_ is the direct extension of tumor into adjacent tissue. These abilities allow a neoplasm to become a malignant neoplasm ("cancer").

EXERCISE 5-12   PATHOLOGY AS A SECOND LANGUAGE

Test your vocabulary by writing the appropriate term in each blank from the list below.

Lymphatic spread	Seeding	Hematogenous spread
Carcinoma in situ	Premalignant changes	Angiogenesis
Doubling time	Growth fraction	Immune surveillance

1. Before becoming fully malignant, damaged DNA provokes in cells recognizable _pre malignant changes_

2. _Carcinoma in situ_ is a state that is cancer "in place" and is fully curable.

3. The amount of time it takes for the number of tumor cells to double is called the _doubling time_

4. _Angiogenesis_ is new vessel growth, used by a neoplasm to support its own growth.

5. The main determinant of growth rate is the _growth fraction_

6. _Seeding_ occurs as tumor cells float from point to point in a body fluid.

7. _Lymphatic spread_ occurs when tumor cells invade lymphatic vessels and are swept up the lymphatic chain by the flow of lymph fluid.

8. _Hematogenous spread_ occurs as tumor cells invade blood vessels and are disseminated by the circulation.

9. _Immune Surveillance_ is an antineoplastic function of the immune system. The immune system recognizes abnormal "nonself" proteins in the neoplasm (or cancer) and attack the cells. Therefore, **immunodeficiency** predisposes to cancer.

LEARNING OBJECTIVE 6: Describe the local and systemic (paraneoplastic) effects that might manifest secondary to tumor presence.

EXERCISE 5-13

Complete the paragraph below.

Cancers can "declare themselves" or present in a variety of ways due to their local effects in a tissue or to their systemic effects (also called [1] _paraneoplastic syndrome_ because the symptoms are not due to local or metastatic spread of tumor). (2) _Local effects_ can be mass effects of pressure of the expanding tumor mass on nearby tissue, infection, or bleeding from ulceration of surfaces, or infarction or rupture. Paraneoplastic effects include but are not limited to progressive loss of weight accompanied by weakness, lethargy, fatigue, and anemia (a generalized wasting called [3] _cachexia_), or production of hormones, such as (4) _Cortisol_, which causes Cushing.

Mnemonic

CAUTION

When asking assessment questions, remember the American Cancer Society's mnemonic device **CAUTION**:

C: Change in bowel or bladder habits

A: A sore that doesn't heal

U: Unusual bleeding or discharge

T: Thickening or lump
I: Indigestion or difficulty swallowing
O: Obvious changes in a wart or mole
N: Nagging cough or hoarseness

Mnemonic

ABCDE Rule

Use the **ABCDE** rule to assess a mole's malignant potential:
A: Asymmetry—Is the mole irregular in shape?
B: Border—Is the border irregular, notched, or poorly defined?
C: Color—Does the color vary?
D: Diameter—Is the diameter more than 6 mm?
E: Evolution—Is the mole changing?

EXERCISE 5-14   PATHOLOGY AS A SECOND LANGUAGE

See Exercise 5-13 for key terms covered in this section.

LEARNING OBJECTIVE 7: Discuss the available methods for diagnosing malignancy, as well as their benefits and caveats.

EXERCISE 5-15

Complete the paragraphs below.

Although many methods are available for diagnosing malignancy, the practice has become increasingly complex. This is partly because the treatment of cancer has become more tailored to the patient's exact type of cancer. In general, the assessment of neoplasms, especially malignant ones, is an exercise that involves obtaining a thorough clinical history, doing a complete physical examination, obtaining medical images and laboratory data, and often, undertaking microscopic study of tissues and cells. Important laboratory data include various (1) __markers__, which are substances produced by normal or neoplastic tissue and may appear *in blood* at increased levels in the presence of a neoplasm. These include (2) __Carcinoembryonic Antigen (CEA)__, a protein found in the blood of patients with colon cancer and some other malignancies (but also increased in liver disease); (3) __AFP__, which may be produced by neoplasms including testicular cancer; and (4) __PSA__, a protein made by the prostate and useful in evaluating prostate cancer.

Clinically discernible masses generally require obtaining tissue and performing a microscopic evaluation. In addition, ancillary studies such as (5) __immunochemistry__, which uses antibodies to detect specific proteins in tumors, are used to aid in the diagnosis. Additional methods for evaluating tissues are discussed below.

> **Remember This!** Tumor markers should never (or at least almost never) be used for screening! They can be used to monitor a disease or to detect its recurrence, but they should be used only rarely to make a diagnosis (as they lack sensitivity and specificity)!

EXERCISE 5-16 PATHOLOGY AS A SECOND LANGUAGE

Test your vocabulary by determining whether the following statements are true or false. If a statement is false, provide the correct word for the italicized term that will make the statement true.

___T___ 1. *Cytology* is the study of individual cells for evidence of cancer or other abnormality.

_____

___T___ 2. *Papanicolaou (Pap) smear* is a method for the cytologic evaluation of the female cervix.

_____

___F___ 3. *Flow cytometry* is a procedure in which a very thin needle is inserted into the lesion; clusters of cells and attendant fluid are aspirated then spread onto a slide for examination.

_____*needle biopsy*_____

___F___ 4. *Fine needle aspiration* is a method where many individual cells can be sorted according to certain physical characteristics and markers, including proteins expressed on the surface of the cells.

_____*flow cytometry*_____

___T___ 5. *Biopsy* is the obtaining of intact pieces of tissue by surgical excision or needle core for microscopic evaluation and diagnosis.

_____

See Exercise 5-15 for additional key terms covered in this section.

LEARNING OBJECTIVE 8: Compare and contrast the gross and microscopic appearances of benign versus malignant neoplasms, and explain the difference between histologic grading and clinical staging of a malignancy.

EXERCISE 5-17

Complete the paragraphs below.

The gross and microscopic appearances of a neoplasm are important diagnostic characteristics. (1) ___Benign___ neoplasms tend to have a rounded, smooth outline with a rim of compressed fibrous tissue at the edge (a fibrous capsule). (2) ___Malignant___ neoplasms, on the other hand, tend to be irregular, with fingers of tumor invading adjacent tissue; the cut surface has a varied appearance, with areas of necrosis, hemorrhage, calcification, or other.

The microscopic structure of a neoplasm correlates much better with tumor behavior than does its gross appearance. Normal cells are perfectly and fully differentiated to perform their several tasks, but neoplasms can have a loss of differentiation called (3) ___anaplasia___. Benign neoplasms are typically well differentiated and characteristic of their variety cell (e.g., fat cells in a lipoma). Malignant cells, however, lack normal differentiation and appear unlike normal cells (e.g., liposarcoma). The lack of differentiation is characterized by (4) ___pleomorphism___, great variety in the size and shape of cells and nuclei, and (5) ___hyperchromatism___ the darkening of the nuclei by extra genetic material. Mitotic figures are numerous and may have abnormal configurations.

(6) ___Grading___ is the assessment of the degree of cell differentiation (specialization), nuclear atypia, mitotic figures, and other gross and microscopic features of malignancy—the higher the grade the worse the tumor looks. (7) ___Staging___ is the evaluation of tumor behavior and is typically accomplished via the (8) ___TNM system___—size, regional nodes, and distant metastasis.

Remember This! If you think about it, it makes perfect sense. Cells that creep and crawl and infiltrate the surrounding tissue are more likely to be malignant than those that don't look normal (whether it be an absence of differentiation or a great deal of variation in size, shape, or color), or that are frequently dividing.

Remember This! The best indicator of future behavior is past behavior; hence, staging is better than grading when trying to determine diagnosis. If the tumor is already large in size or has spread to the lymph nodes or other distant sites, it is likely to behave more aggressively, regardless of what it looks like!

EXERCISE 5-18

Complete the table below.

Comparison of Clinical and Anatomic Characteristics of Benign and Malignant Neoplasms		
Clinical Behavior	**Benign**	**Malignant**
Growth	Slow	(1) _fast_
Invasive	No	Yes
Metastasis	(2) _no_	Yes
Gross Appearance		
Contour	Round, smooth	(3) _irregular branching_
Capsule	Present	Absent
Internal necrosis	Absent	Present
Internal hemorrhage	Absent	Present
Microscopic Appearance		
Organization	Resembles normal tissue	Poor resemblance, if any
Cells	(4) _resembles normal_	Poor resemblance, if any
Nuclei	Resemble normal	Abnormal size, shape
Mitoses	Few or none, normal shape, size	(5) _many / irregular shapes and sizes_

EXERCISE 5-19 PATHOLOGY AS A SECOND LANGUAGE

Test your vocabulary by writing the appropriate term in each blank from the list below.

Papilloma   Staging   Polyp
Grading   Metastasis

1. A _Polyp_ is a mass that protrudes from an epithelial surface.

2. A _papilloma_ grows in a fern- or finger-like pattern with prominent folds.

3. _grading_ is the assessment of the degree of cell differentiation, nuclear atypia, mitotic figures, and other gross and microscopic features of malignancy.

4. _Staging_ is an evaluation of tumor *behavior* that relies on the size of the primary tumor and its spread, either local or metastatic.

5. **TNM system**—T for the size of the *primary* tumor, N for the extent, if any, of *regional* lymph node involvement, and M for *distant* _metastasis_.

LEARNING OBJECTIVE 9: Discuss the types of treatment available to patients diagnosed with cancer.

EXERCISE 5-20

Complete the paragraph below.

Upon discovery of cancer, the initial hope is that it can be cured, although "cure" is hard to define. Many types of treatment are available and may be used in conjunction with each other. For example, following complete surgical resection, several courses of chemotherapy and/or radiation to nearby lymph nodes may be used in the hope that if micrometastases are present, they will be eliminated. (1) _Removal_ is typically the first choice of treatment for discrete tumors and often involves the removal of nearby lymph nodes, which may contain metastases. Related techniques that seek to destroy the tumor without removing it are (2) _radio frequency_ ablation, which heats the tumor tissue, and (3) _cryotherapy_, which freezes tumor tissue. (4) _Chemo_ is the treatment with drugs of malignant neoplasms; it can be administered orally or via injection. (5) _Ionizing radiation_ can be administered in several ways, usually as external radiation in the form of X-rays but also as gamma rays. New molecularly targeted therapies include (6) _hormonal manipulation_ (e.g., tamoxifen), (7) _growth factor supression_ (e.g., Herceptin), stimulating the immune destruction of tumor cells (via targeted antibodies), (8) _enzyme blockage_ (e.g., imatinib), and the blockage of vessel formation via (9) _non angiogenics_

EXERCISE 5-21 PATHOLOGY AS A SECOND LANGUAGE

Test your vocabulary by determining whether the following statements are true or false. If a statement is false, provide the correct word for the italicized term that will make the statement true.

__T__ 1. *Laser therapy* uses focused light to treat superficial cancers of skin or mucosa by burning the tumor away.

_____

__F__ 2. *Chemotherapy* is systemic drug treatment for malignant neoplasms, and the drug (chemical) has its greatest effect on ~~slowly~~ dividing cells.
     _____ rapidly dividing cells _____

__T__ 3. *Monoclonal antibody* drugs can be used as targeted drug therapies to identify specific proteins in tumors.

_____

LEARNING OBJECTIVE 10: Describe the screening guidelines for cervical, breast, prostate, and colon cancer.

EXERCISE 5-22

Complete the paragraphs below.

Screenings for cervical, breast, prostate, and colon cancers are among the most successful screening programs. Cervical cancer guidelines are constantly changing but current recommendations include: cervical cytology, or (1) __PAP-smear__, should begin approximately three years after the onset of vaginal intercourse, but no later than age 21, and should be done every one to two years until age 30, after which screening may continue every two to three years for those women who have had three consecutive negative results. Vaccination against the (2) __HPV__ types that cause approximately 70% of cervical cancers and 90% of genital warts is available and most efficacious when administered prior to initiation of sexual activity; current recommendations call for vaccination at age 11 or 12.

Breast cancer screening guidelines include clinical breast exam once every three years for women ages 20 to 40 and annually thereafter. Yearly mammograms should begin at age (3) __40__ and continue for as long as the woman is in good health.

Prostate cancer screening guidelines are controversial. A widely used screening tool is blood PSA measurement; however, it has low sensitivity and specificity. Elevated PSA > 4 ng/ml may warrant a prostate biopsy for tissue evaluation. Treatment for prostate cancer is also controversial, as most men do not die of the disease.

Because colonoscopy reduces the death rate from colorectal cancer more than 50%, the ACS recommends that beginning at age (4) __50__, adults at average risk should follow one of the following two regimens for colorectal cancer screening: have periodic testing that primarily detects cancer (such as a test for fecal occult [5] __blood__), or periodically have an annual test that detects polyps and cancer (such as a [6] __colonoscopy__).

Screening recommendations are available for other cancer types.

EXERCISE 5-23   PATHOLOGY AS A SECOND LANGUAGE

There are no key terms in this section.

Decisions Decisions

DECISION TREE 5.1: THE DIAGNOSIS AND TREATMENT OF CANCER

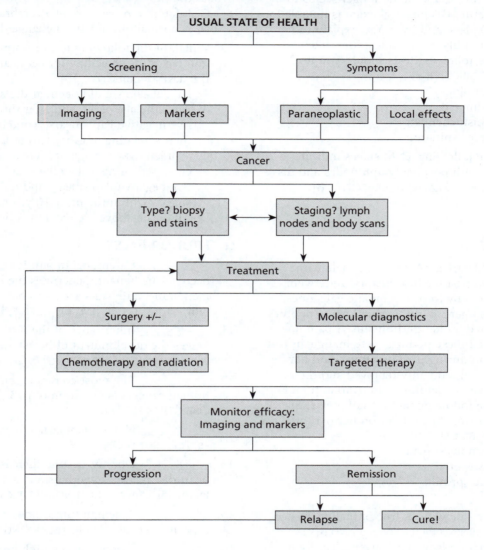

Test Yourself

I. MULTIPLE CHOICE

1. Which of the following tests are acceptable for colon cancer screening? [LEARNING OBJECTIVE 10]
   A. Occult blood in stool
   B. Flexible sigmoidoscopy or double-contrast barium enema
   C. Detection of cancer DNA in stool samples
   D. All of the above

2. A 54-year-old fair-skinned blonde Caucasian female comes to clinic for her first "all-over" skin check. Which of the following places should you pay particular attention to, as they are most susceptible to the carcinogenic effects of sunlight? [LEARNING OBJECTIVE 3]
   A. Her lower lip and forehead
   B. The back of her neck and the tops of her ears
   C. The back of her hands and the soles of her feet
   D. All of the above

3. Epidemiology can reveal subtle clues regarding the causes of cancer by evaluating which of the following factors? [Learning Objective 3]
   A. Geographic and environmental
   B. Personal habits
   C. Age and gender
   D. All of the above

direct result of an enlarging pituitary mass

4. An 11-year-old Hispanic male visits his pediatrician's office with his mother. She is concerned because he no longer plays outside, yet is often covered in bruises, and he no longer seems to have an appetite. His physical exam is notable for an enlarged spleen and liver. You explain to her that you would like to run a test for leukemia. Which of the following tests should you use? [LEARNING OBJECTIVE 7]
   A. Excisional biopsy
   B. Flow cytometry
   C. Immunohistochemistry
   D. Fine needle aspiration

5. Which of the following TNM stages indicates a small tumor with positive lymph nodes and distant metastases? [LEARNING OBJECTIVE 8]
   A. T4N1M2
   B. T3N0M1
   C. T1N3M1
   D. T1N0M0

6. A 73-year-old African American female with no significant past medical history underwent a cholecystectomy for symptomatic gallstones. During the surgery, multiple small white nodules were identified on her peritoneum. A pathologist confirmed these nodules were malignant (on frozen section during the operation), and her ovaries were subsequently removed and the primary malignancy identified (an ovarian tumor). Which of the following methods of metastasis/invasion explains the nodules on her peritoneum? [LEARNING OBJECTIVE 5]
   A. Hematogenous spread
   B. Direct invasion
   C. Lymphatic spread
   D. Seeding

7. Which of the following is true of malignant neoplasms? [LEARNING OBJECTIVES 5 AND 8]
   A. Their function is usually physiologically normal.
   B. They typically have a fibrous round capsule with a rounded smooth outline.
   C. They tend to have a variegated cut surface with necrosis, hemorrhage, and calcifications.
   D. They have multiple mitoses with an absence of pleomorphism

8. A 19-year-old college student visits the campus clinic complaining of double vision and a recent onset of headaches. During a review of systems, she sheepishly admits that she also appears to be lactating and her menstrual cycle has become irregular. Her nipples express a milky-white fluid during palpation on physical exam. Which of the following principles explains these findings? [LEARNING OBJECTIVE 6]

A. Local mass effects
B. Production of hormones or other molecules that affect distant organs (paraneoplastic syndrome)
C. Infarction or rupture of a cerebral blood vessel
D. A normal physiological change during puberty

9. Which of the following is a recommendation regarding screening for cervical cancer? [LEARNING OBJECTIVE 10]
   A. Pap smears should begin at the age of 18.
   B. After the age of 30, and after three consecutive negative Pap smears, women may decrease their screening to every two to three years.
   C. Women over the age of 50 may choose to cease screening if they have had three consecutive negative Pap smears and no abnormal Pap smears within the prior 10 years.
   D. All of the above are recommended.

II. TRUE OR FALSE

10. _____T_____ Carcinoma in-situ is neoplasia that becomes malignant, penetrates the basement membrane, and gains access to blood vessels and lymphatics. [LEARNING OBJECTIVE 5]

11. _____F_____ Inheritance of the BRCA gene guarantees the development of breast and ovarian cancer. [LEARNING OBJECTIVE 3]

12. _____T_____ The most common genetic defect in human cancers is mutation of p53. [LEARNING OBJECTIVE 4]

13. _____T_____ Not all neoplasms form tumor masses. [LEARNING OBJECTIVE 1]

14. _____F_____ Obesity, despite increasing the risk of heart disease and hypertension, is a negative risk factor for cancer. [LEARNING OBJECTIVE 3]

15. _____F_____ A benign tumor does not have the capacity to cause death. [LEARNING OBJECTIVE 1]

16. _____T_____ Tumors with a high growth fraction are usually affected by traditional chemotherapy. [LEARNING OBJECTIVE 5]

III. MATCHING

17. Match the following descriptions to the appropriate tumor; some choices may not be used: [LEARNING OBJECTIVE 1]
    i. Benign neoplasm consisting of adipose tissue
    ii. Malignant neoplasm consisting of adipose tissue
    iii. Cancer of granulocytes
    iv. Malignant neoplasm consisting of smooth muscle
    v. Benign neoplasms consisting of smooth muscle
    vi. Cancer of lymphocytes

vii. Benign neoplasm of skeletal muscle
viii. Malignant neoplasm of skeletal muscle
ix. Benign neoplasm of cartilage
x. Malignant neoplasm of cartilage

A. Lymphoma vi
B. Liposarcoma ii
C. Chondroma ix
D. Leiomyoma v
E. Rhabdomyoma vii

IV. SHORT ANSWER

18. Which of the hallmarks of cancer is the most important in carcinogenesis? [LEARNING OBJECTIVES 2, 3, AND 4]

_____
_____
_____

19. Explain the following statement: The immune system can both cause and prevent cancer. [LEARNING OBJECTIVES 2, 3, AND 5]

_____
_____
_____

20. Which two of the seven hallmarks of cancer function in the same pathway? [LEARNING OBJECTIVES 2 AND 4]

_____
_____
_____

21. Using examples from the chapter, discuss the future of cancer therapy. (Hint: Use the Decision Tree) [LEARNING OBJECTIVE 9]

_____
_____
_____

22. One of your friends tells you an interesting story about a man he knows who recently had not one DVT, but two! It seems that he has no significant medical history, although a recent chest X-ray demonstrated a new mass in the right upper lobe of his lung. Could the two be related? [LEARNING OBJECTIVE 6]

_____
_____
_____

Disorders of Fluid, Electrolyte and Acid–Base Balance, and Blood Flow

The Big Picture

Water is essential for life on Earth as we know it, in part because it is the major constituent of all cells and all body fluids, including the blood. Disorders of fluids involve abnormalities in fluid volume, fluid flow, and/or its components (i.e., electrolytes, acid–base balance). Therefore, understanding the behavior of fluids in the human body is essential for understanding health and disease.

Oh No! Not Another Learning Experience

LEARNING OBJECTIVE 1: Explain the difference between hydrodynamic pressure, hydrostatic pressure, and osmotic pressure.

EXERCISE 6-1

Complete the paragraphs below.

The flow of fluid is necessary for life, and flow requires pressure to move the fluid. (1) _Fluid pressure_ is defined as the physical/mechanical pressure exerted by one object on another. (2) _Hydrostatic_ pressure is caused by the weight of the fluid; (3) _Hydrodynamic_ pressure is created by resistance to the flow of fluid in a closed system such as the cardiovascular system.

(4) _Blood pressure_ is the hydrodynamic pressure of moving blood. In contrast, (5) _Osmotic pressure_ is a measure of the tendency of water to move by **osmosis** from an area of high water (low solute) concentration across a semipermeable membrane to an area of low water (high solute) concentration. Thus, the high solute (concentrated solution) "pulls" water across the membrane.

> **Remember This!** It all makes sense! Hydrodynamic pressure has to do with the dynamics of flow, while hydrostatic flow is the result of gravity—think stasis/constant/lacking movement—what could be more constant than gravity?

> **Remember This!** Osmosis is the movement of water, while diffusion is the movement of particles. Placing your head atop your textbook definitely won't have you learning the information by osmosis—though diffusion is also just as unlikely!

> **Remember This!** Osmotic pressure sucks water toward it, while hydrodynamic pressure pushes water away.

EXERCISE 6-2   PATHOLOGY AS A SECOND LANGUAGE

Test your vocabulary by indicating if each statement below is true or false. If it is false, provide the correct word for the italicized term that will make the statement true.

_F_   1. A solution is a mixture with the major component being the *solute*, and the minor component being the *solvent*.

_____ major component is solvent _____

_T_   2. The concentration of solute is expressed as *osmolarity*.

_____

_T_   3. *Albumin* is a small protein made by the liver.

_____

_F_   4. Cell membranes are examples of *permeable membranes*.

_____ Semi-permeable _____

LEARNING OBJECTIVE 2: Define cardiac output and what factors determine it.

EXERCISE 6-3

Complete the paragraph below.

Cardiac output is essential for maintaining blood pressure and perfusing the tissues. Blood pressure is equal to the cardiac output (flow into the circulatory tree) times the vascular resistance (resistance to outflow from the circulatory tree) (BP = CO × VR). (1) _Cardiac output_ is defined as the volume of blood pumped per minute and is calculated as the heart rate multiplied by the (2) _stroke volume_ (CO = HR × SV). Blood volume influences blood pressure by changing the cardiac output. In addition, blood pressure homeostasis is maintained by the renin-angiotensin-aldosterone system. In this system, the kidney responds to low blood pressure by secreting (3) _renin_, an enzyme that converts angiotensinogen (made by the liver) to angiotensin I. The angiotensin I is converted to angiotensin II by (4) _ACE_, an enzyme secreted by the lungs. Angiotensin II increases CO and VR and stimulates secretion of aldosterone, an endogenous steroid which causes salt and water retention to increase blood volume.

EXERCISE 6-4   PATHOLOGY AS A SECOND LANGUAGE

See Exercise 6-3 for key terms covered in this section.

LEARNING OBJECTIVE 3: Compare and contrast arteries, arterioles, capillaries, veins, and lymphatics.

EXERCISE 6-5

Complete the paragraph below.

Blood is carried by arteries, arterioles, (1) _Capillaries_, and veins. The arterial tree is high pressure and precedes the capillaries, where oxygen and nutrient exchange occur, while the venous system is low pressure and follows after the capillaries. Lymph is carried by a separate low-pressure system, the (2) _lymphatics_. The various types of vessels have differing structures because they have different functions.

See Exercises 6-6 and 6-7 for additional details.

EXERCISE 6-6

Complete the table below.

Blood Vessels	Structure	Function
Arteries	Thick, rubbery walls with multiple layers	Carry oxygenated blood under (1) _high pressure_ away from the heart
(2) _Arterioles_	Small with thin wrapping of smooth muscle cells	Regulate local flow to capillaries
Capillaries	Smallest vessels with thin endothelium	(3) _exchange_ of oxygen, nutrients, and waste
Venules	Small thin veins	Collect blood from capillary beds
(4) _veins_	Thin-walled, pliable, with valves	Carry blood under low pressure toward the heart (valves prevent backflow)

EXERCISE 6-7   PATHOLOGY AS A SECOND LANGUAGE

Test your vocabulary by writing the appropriate term in each blank from the list below.

Lymph nodes   Lymph fluid   Endothelium
Lymphatics

1. _Endothelium_ is the lining of all blood vessels and controls the exchange of substances between blood and tissue.

2. _Lymphatics_ are a low-pressure capillary-like system of vessels that collect interstitial fluid from between cells and eventually deliver it to the blood.

3. _Lymph fluid_ is protein-rich and also carries absorbed fat.

4. _Lymph nodes_ are small clusters of immune system cells that filter fluid and capture bacteria and other foreign matter.

LEARNING OBJECTIVE 4: Briefly discuss body water compartments, body water balance, and how salts regulate this balance.

EXERCISE 6-8

Complete the paragraphs below.

Water represents approximately 55–60% of the body. This total body water (100%) is divided into several compartments including (1) _intracellular_ (65%) and extracellular fluid (35%). Extracellular fluid is further divided into (2) _Interstitial_, blood (intravascular fluid), and a small amount of other fluids (<1%). Blood itself is about 45% cells (mainly red blood cells) and 55% (3) _plasma_ (90% water with solutes, 10% protein and small amounts of fat, etc.).

Water intake from food and drink must be balanced by that which is lost in stool, urine, perspiration, and respiratory air. Water intake is regulated by cells in the thirst center of the (4) _hypothalamus_ which senses high osmolarity. Water loss is regulated by three mechanisms:

- (5) _ADH_, secreted by the posterior pituitary in response to osmoreceptors, influences the kidneys to retain water in blood and concentrate urine.
- (6) _Aldosterone_, secreted by the adrenal cortex on command of renin secreted by the kidneys, influences the kidneys to retain sodium in blood.
- (7) _ANP_, secreted by the atrial cardiac muscle cells in response to increased blood volume, influences the kidney to release sodium and water, which lowers blood pressure by lowering blood volume.

EXERCISE 6-9   PATHOLOGY AS A SECOND LANGUAGE

Test your vocabulary by determining whether the following statements are true or false. If a statement is false, provide the correct word for the italicized term that will make the statement true.

_T_ 1. *Electrolytes* are salts dissolved in a solvent.

_____

_T_ 2. *Salts* are chemical compounds that separate into ions when dissolved in water.

_____

_T_ 3. An *ion* is an atom or molecule with a net positive or negative electric charge.

_____

_F_ 4. *Cations* (such as Cl^- or HCO_3^-) are negatively charged ions.

_____+ charge_____

_F_ 5. *Anions* (such as Na^+ or K^+) are positively charged ions.

_____⊖ charge_____

Remember This! Water follows solute.

Mnemonic

a**N**ion is **N**egative while a ca$^+$ ion is positive!

LEARNING OBJECTIVE 5: Discuss the types of edema and separate them into exudates and transudates.

EXERCISE 6-10

Complete the paragraph below.

(1) _Edema_ is an abnormal accumulation of fluid in a tissue or body cavity and is *always* the result of some underlying condition. Edema can have a high protein content (usually related to inflammation, which allows protein to leak through capillary walls); this is called an (2) _exudate_. Or, edema can have a low protein content caused by pressure imbalance; this is called a (3) _transudate_

See Exercise 6-11 for additional information.

EXERCISE 6-11

Complete the table below.

Edema	Protein	Exudate/Transudate	Pathology	Examples
Inflammatory edema	High	(1) _exudate_	Inflammatory cells present (injury)	Infection, sometimes cancer
(2) _Hydrostatic edema_	Low	Transudate	Usually in the legs because hydrostatic pressure is highest there	Congestive heart failure
Osmotic edema	Low	(3) _transudate_	Proteinuria causes hypoalbuminemia (low osmotic pressure). Water crosses into endothelial space.	Nephrotic syndrome, cirrhosis, malnutrition

EXERCISE 6-12   PATHOLOGY AS A SECOND LANGUAGE

Test your vocabulary by writing the appropriate term in each blank from the list below.

Anasarca   Ascites   Lymphedema

1. The common name for *hydroperitoneum* is _ascites_.

2. Severe, generalized edema is termed _Anasarca_.

3. Edema resulting from lymphatic obstruction due to many causes including iatrogenic surgical lymph node dissections for cancer is termed _Lymphedema_.

See Exercises 6-10 and 6-11 for additional key terms covered in this section.

LEARNING OBJECTIVE 6: Using examples from the chapter, discuss the difference between hypertonic, hypotonic, and normocytic dehydration.

EXERCISE 6-13

Complete the paragraph below.

(1) _Dehydration_ is a deficiency of body water, which may be due to insufficient water intake, excess water loss, or a combination of the two. The severity of dehydration is categorized by the relative amount of lost body weight. In general, (2) _2_ % loss is *mild* dehydration, (3) _5_ % is *moderate*, and (4) _8_ % is *severe*. (5) _Infants_, the elderly, or those with debilitating illness are most susceptible to dehydration, and it tends to be more severe.

See Exercises 6-14 and 6-15 for additional information.

EXERCISE 6-14

Complete the table below.

Type of Dehydration	Concentration of Lost Fluid	Examples
Hypertonic	High electrolyte fluid	(1) _diarrhea_
Hypotonic	Low electrolyte fluid	(2) _urine_
(3) _Normotonic_	Similar to plasma	Sweat

EXERCISE 6-15   PATHOLOGY AS A SECOND LANGUAGE

Test your vocabulary by indicating if each statement below is true or false. If it is false, provide the correct word for the italicized term that will make the statement true.

_T_   1. *Tissue turgor* is a distinctive sign in lost tissue elasticity, which can be observed by pinching skin into a fold and releasing it.

_____

_F_   2. *Dehydration* is a shift of fluid out of blood into another body space, which is associated with lost blood volume and low blood pressure.

_____Third spacing_____

LEARNING OBJECTIVE 7: Describe the signs and symptoms of electrolyte imbalances of sodium, potassium, calcium, phosphate, magnesium, and chloride.

EXERCISE 6-16

Complete the paragraph below.

Electrolytes are the ionic components of salts, which separate into their constituent positively charged ions ([1] _Cations_) and negatively charged ions ([2] _anions_) in water. Electrolytes have many physiologic roles, including maintaining the electric potential of the (3) _cell membrane_, propagating nerve signals, enabling muscle cell contraction, and influencing osmosis.

Mnemonic

Hypercalcemia = Bones, stones, groans, psychiatric overtones!

EXERCISE 6-17

Complete the table below.

Electrolytes	Imbalance	Causes/Symptoms
Sodium	Hypernatremia	Rare, weakness and agitation
	Hyponatremia	Vomiting and (1) _diarrhea_ ; swollen brain cells can cause marked increase of intracranial pressure with headaches, seizures, or death.
(2) _Potassium_	Hyperkalemia	Renal failure, acidosis, etc.; leads to weakness, paralysis, and sensory paresthesias. Usually asymptomatic until it interferes with cardiac function, slowing heart rate or, at very high levels, causes cardiac standstill and death.
	Hypokalemia	Diarrhea, diet, etc.; leads to cardiac *arrhythmias*, muscle fatigue and weakness, and tingling sensations (*paresthesias*).
Calcium	Hypercalcemia	(3) _hyperparathyroidism_, cancer, etc.; leads to weakness and fatigue, lethargy and depression, kidney stones, heart arrhythmias.
	Hypocalcemia	Many uncommon causes; leads to fasciculations, tetany, paresthesias and abdominal cramps are common; weak heart contractions and cardiac arrhythmias can occur.

EXERCISE 6-18 PATHOLOGY AS A SECOND LANGUAGE

Test your vocabulary by writing the appropriate term in each blank from the list below.

Vitamin D   Magnesium   Phosphate
Parathyroid hormone (PTH)   Chloride

1. _PTH_ regulates calcium balance.

2. _Vit D_ can be synthesized in the skin and regulates calcium absorption from the gut and movement of calcium from bone to blood.

3. _Phosphate_ is an integral part of bone and tooth mineralization and serves as an important acid/base buffering system in the control of blood pH; it can be elevated in renal failure.

4. _Mag_ aids in maintenance of other ions like potassium and is primarily stored in bone with slow turnover; low levels are caused by diet or drugs, while high levels are usually caused by renal failure.

5. _Chloride_ is the main extracellular anion.

LEARNING OBJECTIVE 8: Discuss the types of acid–base imbalance, and how compensation acts to restore homeostasis.

EXERCISE 6-19

Complete the paragraph below.

Acids and bases must be tightly balanced in the body as they influence every biochemical reaction. An (1) _acid_ is a compound that releases hydrogen ions when dissolved in water (pH <7), while a (2) _base_ is a compound that decreases the number of free H^+ ions, usually by releasing OH^- ions (pH >7). Therefore, an abnormally low blood pH is called (3) _acidosis_, while an abnormally high pH is called (4) _alkalosis_. To help stabilize pH, the body uses (5) _buffers_, which are any substance that quickly acts to restrain a change in pH following the addition of an acid or base. There are four types of acid–base imbalances: respiratory alkalosis, respiratory acidosis, metabolic alkalosis, and metabolic acidosis.

EXERCISE 6-20 PATHOLOGY AS A SECOND LANGUAGE

Test your vocabulary by indicating if each statement below is true or false. If it is false, provide the correct word for the italicized term that will make the statement true.

_T_ 1. Carbon dioxide is an example of a *volatile acid* because it can be exhaled.

_____

_F_ 2. Arterial carbon dioxide accumulates if the body fails to remove excess carbon dioxide resulting in a *metabolic acidosis*.

_____respiratory acidosis_____

_T_ 3. *Metabolic alkalosis* is much less common than metabolic acidosis and is caused by loss of acids (e.g., vomiting), or gain of bases (e.g., ingestion of large amounts of base).

_____

_F_ 4. Increased blood acidity resulting from fixed acids is called *respiratory acidosis*.

_____metabolic acidosis_____

___T___ 5. If respiration is greater than needed to remove excess carbon dioxide, then the pH may increase resulting in *respiratory alkalosis*.

_____

___T___ 6. Acids that cannot be exhaled are *fixed acids*.

_____

___F___ 7. The *chloride buffering system* is the most important buffer system and combines H$^+$ with bicarbonate (HCO3$^-$) to generate carbonic acid.

___bicarbonate buffering system_____

See Exercise 6-19 for additional key terms covered in this section.

LEARNING OBJECTIVE 9: Explain the difference between congestion and hyperemia.

EXERCISE 6-21

Complete the paragraph below.

(1) _Congestion_ is a passive process that causes increased blood volume in a tissue or region of the body and is caused by impaired venous outflow. In contrast, (2) _hyperemia_ is an active process that causes increased blood volume in a tissue or region of the body and is caused by inflammation, increased metabolic activity of the affected part, or other factors. These factors dilate arterioles filling the area with bright red, oxygenated blood, causing it to turn red, a condition called (3) _erythema_.

> **Remember This! When you think congestion—think traffic. A backup of the blood flow is similar to the clogged arteries (aka the highways and thoroughfares) into a city. Hyperemia is the opposite—the active recruitment of blood to an area.**

EXERCISE 6-22   PATHOLOGY AS A SECOND LANGUAGE

See Exercise 6-21 for key terms in this section.

LEARNING OBJECTIVE 10: Name the three elements of hemostasis that act to stop bleeding.

EXERCISE 6-23

Complete the paragraphs below.

(1) _Hemostasis_ involves coordination of three elements: the blood vessel endothelium, platelets, and plasma coagulation (clotting) factors. These must act in concert not only to stop bleeding but also to keep blood in a fluid, clot-free state.

Normal hemostasis is obvious in the case of injury. Injury causes immediate (2) _constriction/vasospasm_ and disrupts the vascular wall, exposing blood to tissue factors. This causes platelets to become "sticky" and to form an intravascular (3) _thrombotic plug_, while extravascular blood also forms a permanent plug or clot.

See Exercise 6-24 for additional details.

EXERCISE 6-24   PATHOLOGY AS A SECOND LANGUAGE

Test your vocabulary by writing the appropriate term in each blank from the list below.

Intrinsic coagulation pathway   Extrinsic coagulation pathway   Platelets

Endothelial cells   Coagulation factors   Coagulation

1. *Endo cells* lining blood vessels play a critical role in balancing pro- and anticlotting forces.

2. *Platelets* are tiny, non-nucleated fragments of cytoplasm shed into blood by bone marrow **megakaryocytes**.

3. *Coagulation* (*clotting*) cascade is a complex series of reactions involving several *Coagulation factors*.

4. The *extrinsic path* is initiated when *coagulation factor VII* comes into contact with *tissue factor* in extravascular tissue.

5. The *intrinsic path* is initiated when *coagulation factor XII* comes into contact with a foreign surface such as glass or plastic.

See Exercise 6-23 for additional key terms covered in this section.

LEARNING OBJECTIVE 11: Classify hemorrhages by size, and discuss their cause and manifestation.

EXERCISE 6-25

Complete the paragraph below.

(1) *Hemorrhage* is the escape of blood from a blood vessel. Hemorrhage confined to tissue is classified according to size (see Exercise 6-27 for details). In general, bleeding can occur from large vessels or from (2) *capillaries*. Bleeding from large vessels is usually caused by trauma or a (3) *coag factor deficiency* and leads to large hemorrhages, whereas capillary bleeding usually presents as skin or mucosal petechiae, nosebleed, or urinary bleeding.

> **Remember This!** Prothrombin time (PT) measures the extrinsic pathway, while partial thromboplastin time (PTT) measures the intrinsic pathway.

EXERCISE 6-26   PATHOLOGY AS A SECOND LANGUAGE

Test your vocabulary by indicating if each statement below is true or false. If it is false, provide the correct word for the italicized term that will make the statement true.

_T_   1. *Petechiae* are the smallest hemorrhages, about 1 mm.

_____

_F_   2. *Ecchymosis* is hemorrhage <1 cm.

           >

_F_   3. *Purpura* is hemorrhage >1 cm.

           <

_T_   4. *Hematoma* is a large, localized collection of blood.

_____

___T___ 5. *Hemorrhagic diathesis* is *excessive* bleeding beyond the expected amount for a certain injury, or bleeding without obvious injury.

___F___ 6. Low platelet count is *megakaryocytopenia*.

Thrombocytopenia

___T___ 7. *Immune thrombocytopenic purpura (ITP)* is a disorder in which the immune system destroys its own platelets.

___F___ 8. The thrombotic microangiopathies include *thrombotic thrombocytopenic purpura (TTP)* in which renal failure is the predominant symptom, and *hemolytic uremic syndrome (HUS)* in which neurological symptoms are common.

With TTP renal failure is less likely / HUS has few neurologic symptoms

___T___ 9. *von Willebrand disease* stems from a deficiency of von Willebrand factor (vWF), a coagulation factor made in endothelial cells and megakaryocytes.

___F___ 10. *Christmas disease* (~~hemophilia A or factor VIII deficiency~~) is the most common, serious, inherited coagulation disorder.

hemophilia B or factor IX deficiency / and is less common than classic Hemophilia

___T___ 11. Intracapsular joint hemorrhage is called *hemarthrosis*.

___F___ 12. *Classic hemophilia* (hemophilia B, factor IX deficiency) is clinically similar to hemophilia A, but is much less common.

hemophilia A, factor VIII and is the most common

___T___ 13. *Prothrombin time (PT)* is the time it takes for a sample of patient plasma to clot after the addition of *tissue factor* (extrinsic pathway).

___T___ 14. *Partial thromboplastin time (PTT)* is the time it takes for a sample of patient plasma to clot after addition of silica powder, an *artificial surface* (intrinsic pathway).

___T___ 15. Platelet count measures platelet *function* only.

and it does not account for platelets that do not function properly

___T___ 16. *Platelet function analysis* detects defective platelet function and can be performed by specialized analyzers in large laboratories.

___F___ 17. A *prothrombin time* can be performed to measure the length of time required for a patient to stop bleeding after skin prick with a standardized lancet.

bleeding time

See Exercise 6-26 for additional key terms covered in this section.

LEARNING OBJECTIVE 12: Compare and contrast clotting and thrombosis.

EXERCISE 6-27

Complete the paragraph below.

(1) _Thrombosis_ generally refers to a pathologic, intravascular (2) _thrombus_ composed of the cellular elements of blood (platelets, white blood cells, and red blood cells), in contrast to clotting, which forms clots to prevent further hemorrhage.

See Exercises 6-28 and 6-29 for additional information.

EXERCISE 6-28

Complete the table below.

(1) _Coagulation (book says clotting)_	**Thrombosis**
Designed to stop hemorrhages	(2) _Pathologic_ process
Structure: None	
clot = fibrin & platelets	(3) _Architecture_: Aggregation of platelets and white cells in layers
(4) _usually_ extravascular	Intravascular

EXERCISE 6-29   PATHOLOGY AS A SECOND LANGUAGE

Test your vocabulary by writing the appropriate term in each blank from the list below.

Thromboembolism	Thrombophlebitis	Embolism
Factor V Leiden	Lupus anticoagulant	

1. When venous thrombi occur the condition is usually called _Thrombophlebitis_ because the vein and adjacent tissue are inflamed and painful.

2. A thrombus can grow large, break loose, and embolize to another part of the body called _Embolism_.

3. _Lupus anticoagulant_ interferes with laboratory tests of blood coagulation, causing the tests to suggest that coagulation is deficient when, in fact, it promotes venous thrombosis in patients.

4. _Factor V Leiden_ is an abnormal form of coagulation factor V produced by a defective gene.

See Exercise 6-28 for additional key terms covered in this section.

LEARNING OBJECTIVE 13: List the causes of disseminated intravascular coagulation (DIC).

EXERCISE 6-30

Complete the paragraph below.

(1) _DIC_ is a condition in which clotting occurs abnormally inside the vascular space without exposure to tissue factor. It is always secondary and has many causes. These include obstetrical complications, infections like (2) _gram neg._ bacterial sepsis, neoplasms like various carcinomas and leukemia, massive tissue trauma like crush injuries or burns, and venomous snakebites. Regardless of the cause, this condition is usually characterized

by hemolytic anemia, thromboses, and hemorrhage. (3) ___Hemorrhage___ occurs because coagulation factors are con-

sumed by the clotting process and no longer exist in high enough concentration in blood to prevent abnormal

bleeding; thus the terminology (4) ___consumptive coagulopathy___

Remember This! DIC causes thrombosis *and* bleeding!!

EXERCISE 6-31   PATHOLOGY AS A SECOND LANGUAGE

See Exercise 6-30 for key terms covered in this section.

LEARNING OBJECTIVE 14: Discuss the different types of emboli.

EXERCISE 6-32

Complete the paragraph below.

An (1) ___embolus___ (plural = emboli) is an intravascular object that travels in the bloodstream from one place to

another. (2) ___Pulmonary embolus___ is a thrombus, usually formed in the deep veins of the legs, that dislodges and embo-

lizes to the lungs. It can be fatal and is a common hazard in patients hospitalized for pregnancy, surgery, or

malignancy. (3) ___Systemic thromboembolism___ refers to arterial thromboemboli that can end up in any organ, including the brain.

See Exercise 6-33 for additional details.

EXERCISE 6-33   PATHOLOGY AS A SECOND LANGUAGE

Test your vocabulary by indicating if each statement below is true or false. If it is false, provide the correct word for the italicized term that will make the statement true.

___F___   1. *Fat and marrow embolism* is common after long bone fracture and cardiopulmonary resuscitation, but usually does not cause clinical problems.

    ___does cause problems___

___F___   2. *Amniotic fluid embolism* is any introduction of gas into the vascular tree.

    ___introduction of amniotic fluid into the vasculature___

___F___   3. *Air embolism* is a fatal complication of pregnancy, caused by tears in the placenta.

    ___caused by intro of air (at least 100 ml)___

LEARNING OBJECTIVE 15: Explain why arterial occlusion is not always followed by infarction and why infarction may occur without arterial occlusion.

EXERCISE 6-34

Complete the paragraph below.

(1) ___Ischemia___ is the restriction of blood supply and the lack of oxygen supply to tissue caused by obstruction

of blood flow. An (2) ___Infarct___ is an area of ischemic necrosis of tissue. There are two types of infarcts.

(3) ___White___ form when arterial obstruction occurs in dense, solid tissue, such as the kidney, heart, or liver.

(4) ___Red___ (hemorrhagic infarcts) are bloody and are due to venous or arterial obstruction that occurs in

loose, spongy tissue or in the lungs or liver, which have dual blood supply. Infarction may occur without arterial

occlusion if there is simply not enough oxygen in the blood, or if the venous outflow is impaired.

| EXERCISE 6-35 | PATHOLOGY AS A SECOND LANGUAGE |

See Exercise 6-34 for key terms covered in this section.

LEARNING OBJECTIVE 16: Name the types and stages of shock.

| EXERCISE 6-36 |

Complete the paragraph below.

(1) _Shock_ or circulatory collapse is a state of systemic low blood flow (hypoperfusion) when cardiac output is reduced or effective blood volume is low. Circulatory collapse, if not immediate, may progress through three overlapping stages. The initial stage is the (2) _Non progressive_, characterized by reflex actions by the sympathetic nervous system to reestablish perfusion (increase HR, vasoconstriction) and stimulation of the renin-angiotensin system. The second stage, the (3) _Progressive stage_, is characterized by more severe hypoperfusion and hypoxia, with a resulting shift to anaerobic metabolism and lactic acidosis. This results in (4) _vasodilation_ and pooling of blood in the extremities, depriving the abdominal viscera of blood. Without effective intervention, a final (5) _irreversible stage_ occurs, with progressively severe hypotension, hypoperfusion and acidosis, decreased myocardial contractility, and leakage of inflammatory mediators and metabolites from dying cells, leading to greater vascular compromise and, finally, multiorgan failure and death.

| EXERCISE 6-37 | PATHOLOGY AS A SECOND LANGUAGE |

Test your vocabulary by writing the appropriate term in each blank from the list below.

Hypovolemic shock   Obstructive shock   Septic shock
Cardiogenic shock

1. _hypovolemic_ results from an underfilled vascular space, usually the result of hemorrhage.
2. _Cardiogenic_ (pump failure) often occurs with myocardial infarction or other myocardial disease.
3. _Obstructive_ is caused by mechanical interference with cardiac output.
4. _Systemic_ is associated with systemic microbial infection (*sepsis*).

Decisions Decisions

DECISION TREE 6.1: MAINTAINING CIRCULATION

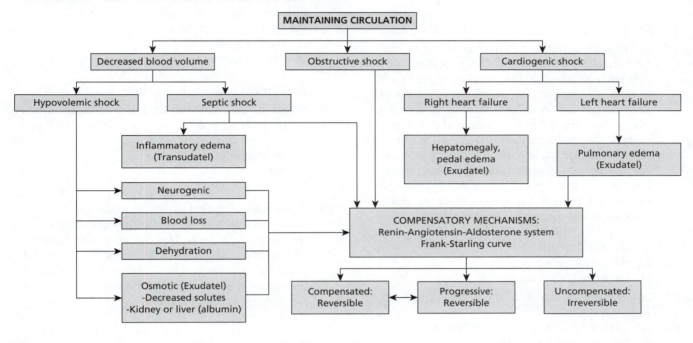

DECISION TREE 6.2: ACID-BASE FLOW CHART

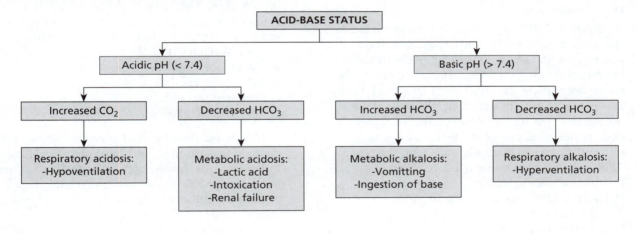

Test Yourself

I. MULTIPLE CHOICE

1. Infarcts in which of the following tissues will cause only a red infarct? [LEARNING OBJECTIVE 15]
   A. Kidney
   B. Heart
   C. Liver
   D. Lungs

2. A 22-year-old college student is found unresponsive at a fraternity house. His "brothers" report that, as part of his recruitment, he drank several gallons of water. They dismissed his complaints of headache and muscle cramps but quickly called 911 when his collapse was followed by convulsions. Water intoxication is responsible for causing which of the following electrolyte imbalances? [LEARNING OBJECTIVES 1 AND 7]
   A. Hyponatremia
   B. Hypernatremia
   C. Hypokalemia
   D. Hypochloremia

3. Which of the following is an anion? [LEARNING OBJECTIVE 4]
   A. Na
   B. K
   C. HCO₃
   D. Ca

4. A 54-year-old Hispanic female presents to her doctor's clinic for a regular checkup. You notice that she doesn't seem her usual happy self, and, in talking to her, she mentions that over the last year she has begun to feel weak, tired, and more than a "little blue." She attributes these changes to her "old-age" aches and pains, which she reports include constipation, kidney stones, and, six months ago, a broken hip. Checking her chart later, you notice her primary care physician has ordered a PTH test. What electrolyte imbalance does he likely suspect? [LEARNING OBJECTIVE 7]
   A. Hyperkalemia
   B. Hyperchloremia
   C. Hypercalcemia
   D. Hypermagnesemia

5. Solutes include which of the following? [LEARNING OBJECTIVE 1]
   A. Carbohydrates, proteins, vitamins
   B. Fats, vitamins, proteins
   C. Fats, salt, carbohydrates
   D. All of the above

6. A 73-year-old African American woman presses the panic button while in her nursing home bed and reports that she is experiencing shortness of breath and chest pain. When the nurse enters the room, she notices the rapid heart rate and low O₂ on the monitors. Unfortunately, the patient does not survive. During her autopsy, the local pathologist notices that one of the woman's legs is significantly larger in circumference than the other. Additional findings support his conclusion as to the cause of death, which is _____.
   [LEARNING OBJECTIVES 12 AND 14]
   A. a fat embolism
   B. a pulmonary embolism
   C. a clot
   D. a heart attack

7. Which of the following is characterized by tachycardia, increased vascular resistance, retained sodium and water, and an absence of anaerobic metabolism? (Hint: Use Decision Tree 6.1) [LEARNING OBJECTIVE 16]
   A. Nonprogressive shock
   B. Progressive shock
   C. Inevitable shock
   D. Irreversible shock

8. An eight-year-old Caucasian male is brought to his pediatrician's office for evaluation of an extremely swollen left knee (which occurred after he injured it in a fall). His mother's family history is notable for both a brother and an uncle with a clotting disorder. Which of the following tests is likely to confirm the cause of his hemarthrosis? [LEARNING OBJECTIVE 11]
   A. Bleeding time
   B. Prothrombin time
   C. Platelet count
   D. Partial thromboplastin time

9. Which of the following are buffers that counteract excess hydrogen ions? [LEARNING OBJECTIVE 8]
   A. Bicarbonate
   B. Hemoglobin
   C. Ammonia
   D. All of the above

10. A 34-year-old male is brought to the ER with burns over 30% of his body. Physical exam reveals pale cool skin (for the areas which are not burned), dry mucous membranes, low blood pressure, and a rapid pulse. What is the cause of his symptoms? [LEARNING OBJECTIVE 6]
    A. Third spacing of fluid
    B. Anasarca
    C. Inflammatory exudate (from an infection)
    D. Pain

11. Which of the following acid–base anomalies is the most likely to result from repeated episodes of vomiting? (Hint: Use Decision Tree 6.2) [LEARNING OBJECTIVE 8]
    A. Metabolic acidosis
    B. Metabolic alkalosis
    C. Respiratory acidosis
    D. Respiratory alkalosis

12. A 46-year-old breast cancer survivor, status post-bilateral mastectomy, complains about swelling in her left arm shortly after the surgeries. It does not pit on physical examination. What is the underlying etiology of her edema? [LEARNING OBJECTIVE 5]
    A. Lymphedema
    B. Progression of her disease
    C. Inflammatory exudate
    D. None of the above

13. Which of the following vessels is composed of endothelial cells and allows the circulation of O₂, CO₂, water, and other small molecules between blood and tissues (but not protein)? [LEARNING OBJECTIVE 3]
    A. Venules
    B. Arterioles
    C. Arteries
    D. Capillaries

14. A 16-year-old athlete is the victim of a car accident that results in spinal trauma. While on the scene, EMS notices that the boy's blood pressure continues to be low despite multiple transfusions. What is the underlying etiology of the boy's persistent low blood pressure? (Hint: Use Decision Tree 6.1) [LEARNING OBJECTIVE 16]
    A. Septic shock
    B. *(circled)* Hypovolemic shock
    C. Cardiogenic shock
    D. Obstructive shock

II. TRUE OR FALSE

15. ___F___ Sunburn is an example of congestion. [LEARNING OBJECTIVE 9] *Hyperemia (active process)*

16. ___F___ Myocardial cells and brain cells both die within 3 or 4 minutes of onset of hypoxia, while fibroblasts may tolerate up to 20 minutes. [LEARNING OBJECTIVE 15] *not myocardial cells, they have 20 minutes or so*

17. ___T___ The final step in the clotting cascade is the polymerization of fibrinogen into fibrin. [LEARNING OBJECTIVE 10] *p. 158*

18. ___T___ Blood pressure = cardiac output x vascular resistance. [LEARNING OBJECTIVE 2] *p. 143*

19. ___T___ A lengthy course of antibiotic therapy can result in deficiencies of factors VII, IX, X, and prothrombin. [LEARNING OBJECTIVE 11] *p 162 after the antibiotics*

20. ___F___ Water comprises a greater amount of body mass in women, as fat contains more water. [LEARNING OBJECTIVE 4] *fat has less H2O   men 60% H2O 40 solid   women 55   45*

21. ___T___ The formation of a thrombus does not depend initially on the coagulation process; thrombi begin and grow initially without clot formation. [LEARNING OBJECTIVE 12] *p. 164*

22. ___F___ Hydrodynamic pressure is higher in the legs than the arms. [LEARNING OBJECTIVE 1]

23. ___T___ *↑ of hydrostatic pressure* Hydrodynamic pressure and osmotic pressure combine to cause the flow of a small amount of fluid from blood into the interstitial space, where some of it enters the lymphatic system. [LEARNING OBJECTIVES 1 AND 3]

III. MATCHING

24. Match the following enzymes/hormones/proteins with their function: [LEARNING OBJECTIVES 1 AND 4]
    i. Antidiuretic hormone
    ii. Ángiotensinogen
    iii. Aldosterone
    iv. Atrial natriuretic peptide
    v. Renin
    A. A hormone secreted by the posterior pituitary, which causes the kidney to retain water in blood and concentrate urine *i*
    B. A hormone secreted by the adrenal cortex, which influences the kidneys to retain sodium in the blood *iii*
    C. An enzyme secreted by the kidney that initiates a cascade of events to maintain blood pressure *✓*
    D. A protein made by the liver *ii*
    E. A hormone secreted by the cardiac muscles to influence the kidney to release sodium and water *ANP iv*

25. Match the following types of dehydration with their descriptions and examples: [LEARNING OBJECTIVE 6]
    i. Normotonic dehydration
    ii. Hypertonic dehydration
    iii. Hypotonic dehydration
    A. Dehydration via excessive sweating *i*
    B. Loss of body fluid with low levels of electrolytes *ii*
    C. Dehydration via excessive urination *iii*
    D. Loss of body fluid equivalent to that of normal plasma *i*
    E. Loss of body fluid with high levels of electrolytes *iii*
    F. Dehydration via diarrhea *ii*

IV. SHORT ANSWER

26. What do the following diseases have in common: septicemia, acute promyelocytic leukemia, and toxemia? [LEARNING OBJECTIVE 13]
    All can result in DIC which is not primary but a complication. It may occur in many infections: sepsis, meningitis, malaria, OB complications (toxemia, abruptio placentae, amniotic fluid embolism, retained dead fetus,) and neoplasms

27. What happens to cardiac output when: blood volume decreases; vascular resistance increases; heart rate increases? [LEARNING OBJECTIVE 2]
    blood volume ↓ → CO ↓,   vascular resistance ↑ → CO ↓,   HR↑ → CO↑

28. What treatment option is the same for a child with easy bruisability, epistaxis, bleeding gums, and antiplatelet antibodies identified shortly after a viral illness and for a child with the same symptoms and renal failure following gastroenteritis (caused by an *E. coli* infection)? [LEARNING OBJECTIVE 11]

p. 162   ITP & HUS   both treated with steroids

29. What is meant by the following statement: "Endothelial cells are the balancing act of coagulation"? [LEARNING OBJECTIVE 10]

These cells balance pro and anti-clotting forces. On the one hand there is a natural tendency of platelets to adhere to endothelium. On the other hand it is antithrombolitic & anticoagulant activity that help prevent thrombosis and clotting unless injured

30. What tissues/fetal debris are responsible for causing amniotic fluid emboli? [LEARNING OBJECTIVE 14]

A torn placenta can cause amniotic fluid to get into the maternal circulation. Fetal skin, hair and mucin can embolize in the vasculature of the lungs

31. Compare and contrast the forward and backward effect of ventricular failure, and how it changes in a failing heart. [LEARNING OBJECTIVE 5]

forward → ↓CO, low BP, hypo-profusion to kidneys which ↑renin

Backward flow → pulmonary congestion/edema

systemic venous congestion and edema in belly, genitals and lower extremities

PART 2

Disorders of the Organ Systems

CHAPTER 7

Disorders of Blood Cells

The Big Picture

Blood is a vital mixture composed of cells (45% by volume) and fluid (55% by volume). The cellular component contains cells derived from the bone marrow including white blood cells and red blood cells. Abnormalities occur with deficiencies or overabundance (often neoplasms) of these cellular constituents with important clinical consequences.

Oh No! Not Another Learning Experience

LEARNING OBJECTIVE 1: List the three cell lines derived from hematopoietic stem cells.

EXERCISE 7-1

Complete the paragraph below.

The fluid part of blood is called (1) _plasma_; if the blood is clotted, the fluid is called (2) _serum_. The fluid part of blood contains 90% water with solutes and 10% protein (mainly albumin). Small but important volumes of lipid (cholesterol and triglyceride) and carbohydrate (glucose and other sugars) are also present in plasma. The (3) _formed elements_ of blood are **erythrocytes** (red blood cells, RBCs), **leukocytes** (white blood cells, WBCs), and thrombocytes, which are more commonly known as (4) _platelets_. The white blood cell count (**WBC count**) is the number of white cells per unit volume, while the (5) _white cell differential count_ is the percentage of white cells that are neutrophils, eosinophils, or basophils. The red blood cell count (RBC count) is the number of red cells per unit volume, while the hemoglobin is reported as the number of grams of hemoglobin per unit of volume. The (6) _hematocrit_ is the percentage of blood volume occupied by RBCs. Similarly, the **platelet count** is the number of platelets per unit volume.

Mnemonic

WBC Differential

"Never Let Mom Eat Beans" and "60, 30, 6, 3, 1"

- **N**eutrophils 60%
- **L**ymphocytes 30%
- **M**onocytes 6%
- **E**osinophils 3%
- **B**asophils 1%

EXERCISE 7-2   PATHOLOGY AS A SECOND LANGUAGE

Test your vocabulary by writing the appropriate term in each blank from the list below.

Complete blood count (CBC)	Erythropoietin	Myeloid progenitor cells
Hemoglobin	Megakaryocytes	Progenitor cells
Lymphoid progenitor cells	Bone marrow	Hematopoiesis
Extramedullary hematopoiesis		

1. Platelets are the fragments of the cytoplasm of ___Megakaryocytes___

2. ___Bone marrow___ can be either yellow (fatty) or red (hematopoietic).

3. Generation of blood cells from progenitors is called ___hematopoiesis___

4. ___Progenitor cells___ are specialized *multipotent* stem cells that can differentiate.

5. ___Lymphoid progenitor cells___ give rise to *lymphocytes*, a type of WBC.

6. ___Myeloid progenitor cells___ give rise to all other blood cells—*granulocytes, monocytes, erythrocytes,* and *megakaryocytes*.

7. ___Extramedullary hematopoiesis___ is a type of hematopoiesis that occurs outside medullary cavities that is either developmental or abnormal when in adults.

8. ___hemoglobin___ is the compound in RBCs to which oxygen attaches for transport from lungs to tissues.

9. ___Erythropoietin___ is a hormone made by the kidney, which stimulates blood formation.

10. The standard laboratory study of blood cells is the ___CBC___.

LEARNING OBJECTIVE 2: Explain what is meant by red cell indices, and how they are calculated.

EXERCISE 7-3

Complete the paragraph below.

The **red cell indices** are measurements of the size and hemoglobin content of the *average* RBC. They include the following: (1) ___MCV___ is the average size of an RBC, which can be normal sized (**normocytic**), too large (**macrocytic**), or too small (**microcytic**). (2) ___MCH___ is the average amount of hemoglobin in an average RBC, which can be normal (**normochromic**) or low (**hypochromic**). (3) ___MCHC___ is the average *concentration* of hemoglobin per unit of volume in an average RBC. (4) ___Reticulocytes___ are young RBCs that can skew these values, including the MCV and MCH.

Mnemonic

A little Latin can help!

Macro = big and micro = small.

EXERCISE 7-4 PATHOLOGY AS A SECOND LANGUAGE

See Exercise 7-3 above for key terms covered in this section.

LEARNING OBJECTIVE 3: Compare and contrast the major types and subtypes of anemia, including those caused by hemorrhage, production defects, and destruction.

EXERCISE 7-5

Complete the sentence.

Anemia is abnormally low (1) _hemoglobin_ in blood.

EXERCISE 7-6

Complete the table below.

Cause of Anemia	Subtype	Labs	Examples
Blood loss	(1) _acute_ (2) _chronic_	Normal CBC Increased reticulocytes, decreased MCV	Hemorrhage GI bleeding
Decreased production	Proliferative Maturation	Decreased reticulocytes Increased precursors	(3) _Myelophthisic_ (bone marrow replacement), kidney failure Vitamin or iron deficiency
(4) _Increased_ destruction (Hemolysis)	Immune, genetic, mechanical	Reticulocytosis Urobilinogen, inc. bilirubin Hemoglobinuria	Prosthetic cardiac valves, thalassemias, microangiopathic hemolytic anemia

EXERCISE 7-7 PATHOLOGY AS A SECOND LANGUAGE

Test your vocabulary by indicating if each statement below is true or false. If it is false, provide the correct word for the italicized term that will make the statement true.

_T_ 1. In *dilutional anemia*, the volume of lost red cells is initially replaced by water and albumin synthesis by the liver.

_F_ 2. Premature destruction of RBCs is called *hemorrhage*.

hemolysis

_T_ 3. *Hereditary spherocytosis* is a genetic disorder of a structural protein called "spectrin" in the red cell membrane.

_F_ 4. *Beta thalassemia* is an X-linked recessive genetic disorder that causes enzyme deficiency in red cells.

G6PD deficiency

_T_ 5. Hemoglobinopathies are autosomal recessive genetic disorders of hemoglobin synthesis and include hemoglobin S, the cause of *sickle cell disease*.

_T_ 6. Thalassemias are a group of inherited microcytic, hemolytic diseases that tend to occur most commonly in people of Mediterranean and Southeast Asian origin and include *beta thalassemia minor, beta thalassemia major, and alpha thalassemia*.

_F_ 7. Antibodies directed against antigens on the red cell membrane cause *microangiopathic hemolytic anemia*.

cause immune hemolytic anemia

_F_ 8. *Warm antibodies* (IgM) are most active at decreased body temperature, while *cold antibodies* (IgG) are most active at increased temperatures.

visa-versa

_T_ 9. *Mechanical hemolytic anemia* is caused by physical shredding of red cells as they pass through mechanical devices.

_F_ 10. *Progeria* is a parasitic disease that infects red cells.

Malaria

_F_ 11. *Ferroportin* is an iron-protein complex found in the bone marrow, liver, spleen, and skeletal muscle.

Ferritin

_T_ 12. Total transferrin is measured by testing the ability of transferrin to bind to iron and is expressed as *total iron-binding capacity (TIBC)*.

_T_ 13. *Iron deficiency anemia* develops as red cell production becomes impaired owing to lack of iron.

_F_ 14. Anemia associated with deficiency of either vitamin B_{12} or folic acid is characterized by *megaloblastic* or *microcytic anemias*.

macrocytic anemias

_____ T 15. B$_{12}$ absorption requires *intrinsic factor (IF)*, a protein secreted by the gastric mucosa.

_____ T 16. *Pernicious anemia (PA)* is an autoimmune disease featuring autoantibodies against the gastric mucosal cells (parietal cells) that produce IF, or against IF itself.

_____ T 17. Primary bone marrow failure is called *aplastic anemia*.

_____ T 18. *Pure red cell aplasia* is a variant of aplastic anemia affecting only RBCs and is usually caused by viral infection, especially in children.

_____ F 19. *Multiple myeloma* is the replacement of the marrow by malignancy or fibrosis.
Primary myelofibrosis   key says myelophthisis

LEARNING OBJECTIVE 4: Explain the difference between relative and absolute erythrocytosis.

EXERCISE 7-8

Complete the paragraph below.

(1) Polycythemia (also called **erythrocytosis**) is an excess number of red cells in blood.

(2) Relative Polycythemia is caused by a loss of plasma volume, which increases the red cell concentration.

In contrast, (3) absolute polycythemia is an actual increase in the total number of RBCs in the body. Primary

absolute polycythemia occurs with a bone marrow malignancy called (4) Polycythemia Vera, a proliferation

of primitive bone marrow red cell precursors that is related to certain leukemias and related neoplasms.

Secondary polycythemia can be caused by many factors, including neoplasms.

EXERCISE 7-9 PATHOLOGY AS A SECOND LANGUAGE

See Exercise 7-8 above for key terms covered in this section.

LEARNING OBJECTIVE 5: Distinguish between leukopenia, neutropenia, agranulocytosis, and leukemoid reaction, and explain the significance of a left shift.

EXERCISE 7-10

Complete the paragraph below.

A deficiency of WBCs (WBC count >4,000/µl) is termed (1) Leukopenia. If granulocytes are decreased,

especially neutrophils, the condition is called (2) Granulocytopenia or (3) Neutropenia; when neutropenia

is severe (>500/µl), it is called (4) agranulocytosis. Decreased lymphocytes in the blood is called

(5) Lymphopenia. Cellular elements of blood can also be increased.

EXERCISE 7-11   PATHOLOGY AS A SECOND LANGUAGE

Test your vocabulary by writing the appropriate term in each blank from the list below.

Lymphadenopathy   Granulocytosis   Lymphocytosis   Lymphadenitis
Leukemoid reaction   Neutrophilia   Band neutrophil   Leukocytosis

1. _Leukocytosis_ is an increase in WBCs.

2. _Granulocytosis_ is an increased number of granulocytes (neutrophils, eosinophils, basophils).

3. _Neutrophilia_ is an increased number of neutrophils.

4. A high reactive white count (e.g., as may occur during infection) that rises over 50,000/µl is termed a _Leukemoid reaction_

5. The least mature WBC found in the peripheral blood is the _band neutrophil_

6. _Lymphocytosis_ is an increase in the number of lymphocytes in blood.

7. _Lymphadenopathy_ is when lymph nodes involved in a disease process are enlarged.

8. _Lymphadenitis_ is inflammation and/or infection within lymph nodes.

> **Remember This!** Leukemoid reaction looks like leukemia, but it is not! It is due to infection or inflammation.

LEARNING OBJECTIVE 6: Distinguish between leukemia and lymphoma.

EXERCISE 7-12

Complete the paragraph below.

(1) _Leukemia_ is a malignancy of myeloid or lymphoid cells in which malignant cells are widespread in blood and bone marrow, while (2) _Lymphoma_ is a malignancy of lymphoid cells that grows as discrete masses in lymph nodes or organs. Sometimes, these malignancies overlap, and there is involvement of the marrow, blood, and lymph nodes.

EXERCISE 7-13   PATHOLOGY AS A SECOND LANGUAGE

Test your vocabulary by indicating if each statement below is true or false. If it is false, provide the correct word for the italicized term that will make the statement true.

_F_   1. *Lymphoid malignancies* are neoplasms arising from granulocytes, RBCs, and megakaryocytes precursors.
 myeloid malignancies
arise from lymphoid cells, B-lymphocytes (including plasma cells) and T. lymphocytes

_F_   2. *Myeloid malignancies* are neoplasms arising from B lymphocytes (including plasma cells), T lymphocytes, or natural killer (NK) lymphocytes.
Lymphoid malignancies

_T_   3. *Acute leukemia* is a lymphoid malignancy with abrupt onset which often presents as acute infection or hemorrhage, and the WBC counts can be extremely elevated (>100,000).

_T_   4. *Chronic leukemia* is an insidious lymphoid malignancy in which patients present with fatigue or pallor from anemia, night sweats, low-grade fever, secondary infection, or enlarged spleen or liver.

LEARNING OBJECTIVE 7: Compare and contrast acute myelogenous leukemia, myelodysplasia syndrome, and myeloproliferative diseases.

EXERCISE 7-14

Complete the paragraph below.

Myeloid malignancies are leukemias and related disorders that arise from myeloid progenitor cells; in normal hematopoiesis, these cells develop into normal bone marrow and blood cells. The myeloid malignancies are (1) __Leukemias__ *AML* (increased numbers of myeloblasts in the bone marrow and blood), (2) __CML__ (the chronic counterpart), the myelodysplastic syndromes, and the (3) _Chronic Myeloproliferative Syndromes_. The latter two groups of myeloid malignancies have distinctive characteristics and may evolve into leukemia or bone marrow fibrosis.

EXERCISE 7-15   PATHOLOGY AS A SECOND LANGUAGE

Test your vocabulary by writing the appropriate term in each blank from the list below.

Malignant thrombocythemia   **Myelodysplasia syndrome (MDS)**
Primary myelofibrosis   **Philadelphia chromosome**

1. The __Philadelphia Chromosome__ involves the translocation of genes between chromosomes 9 and 22.
2. __Myelodysplasia Syndrome__ is a group of hematopoietic progenitor cell disorders that features ineffective myeloid cell maturation, defective hematopoiesis, and increased risk for development of AML.
3. __Malignant Thrombocythemia__ is a rare myeloproliferative syndrome that occurs when malignant progenitor cells develop characteristics of megakaryocytes.
4. __Primary Myelofibrosis__ is a malignant disease of myeloid cells that stimulates nonmalignant obliteration of normal bone marrow by fibrous tissue (myelophthisis).

LEARNING OBJECTIVE 8: Compare and contrast lymphocytic leukemias and the lymphoma subtypes.

EXERCISE 7-16

Complete the paragraph below.

The term (1) "__Lymphoid Leukemia__" is used for neoplasms that present with widespread involvement of the bone marrow and peripheral blood; they usually also present with symptoms of bone marrow suppression: anemia, infection, or bleeding. In contrast, (2) "__Lymphoma__" is used for neoplasms that arise as discrete masses in lymph nodes, organs, or tissues. Overall, about 90% are (3) __B-cell origin__. Histologic evaluation is required for diagnosis. Flow cytometry and molecular advances are enabling better categorization of these neoplasms.

EXERCISE 7-17   PATHOLOGY AS A SECOND LANGUAGE

Test your vocabulary by indicating if each statement below is true or false. If it is false, provide the correct word for the italicized term that will make the statement true.

_T_   1. *Acute lymphoid (lymphoblastic) leukemia (ALL)* is a malignant proliferation of immature lymphocyte precursors, usually B cells.

and is the most common malignancy of children

_F_   2. Chronic lymphoid (lymphocytic) leukemia (CLL) and *diffuse large B-cell lymphoma* are different manifestations of the same disease with few neoplastic lymphocytes in SLL.

CLL and small-cell lymphocyte lymphoma (SLL)

_F_   3. *Non-Hodgkin lymphoma* is a group of lymphomas distinct from all the others because it has a distinctive microscopic appearance and is curable in most instances.

The above is true for HL

_T_   4. *Reed-Sternberg (RS) cell* is a neoplastic cell in classical Hodgkin lymphoma that is of B-cell lineage and has a distinctive appearance.

_T_   5. *Nodular sclerosing Hodgkin (NSHL)* is the variety that accounts for about 70% of cases and is the least aggressive form of HL.

_F_   6. *Hodgkin lymphomas (HL)* represent the majority of malignant lymphoid tumors.

NHL

_F_   7. Lymphomas with a follicular microscopic appearance are called follicular lymphoma, and those lacking follicles are called *afollicular lymphoma*.

those lacking follicles are called diffuse lymphoma

Remember This! Hodgkin lymphoma is a specific group of highly treatable lymphomas; everything else is Non-Hodgkin lymphoma!

LEARNING OBJECTIVE 9: Discuss plasma cell proliferations and explain why patients have abnormal blood proteins.

EXERCISE 7-18

Complete the paragraph below.

(1) *Plasma Cell proliferations* are overgrowths of a single clone of plasma cells, with most being malignant. They are often referred to as plasma cell dyscrasias. The normal function of plasma cells is to produce immunoglobulin protein; therefore, **plasma cell neoplasms** often secrete greatly increased amounts of plasma protein. Because these proteins are the product of a single clone of plasma cells, they are referred to as (2) *monoclonal proteins* (or **M-proteins**). When these proteins are run on a gel (called [3] *protein electrophoresis*), they appear as a dense band or as a tall peak (called a [4] *monoclonal spike*) if displayed as a graph. Any plasma cell proliferation that produces monoclonal protein in blood or urine is called a **monoclonal gammopathy**.

EXERCISE 7-19   PATHOLOGY AS A SECOND LANGUAGE

Test your vocabulary by writing the appropriate term in each blank from the list below.

1. Free light chains pass out of the renal glomerulus into the renal tubule and urine, where they are known as _Bence-Jones protein_

2. The most common plasma cell proliferation is _MGUS_. Monoclonal gammopathy of undetermined significance

3. _Multiple Myeloma_ is a malignant neoplasm of plasma cells that features multiple lytic bone lesions.

4. A _Solitary myeloma_ (or *plasmacytoma*) may precede multiple myeloma.

5. _Lymphoplasmacytic Lymphoma_ is a B-cell neoplasm of older adults that is related to chronic lymphocytic leukemia and small cell lymphocytic lymphoma.

6. If malignant plasma cells secrete IgM, the result is *hyperviscosity syndrome*, also called _Waldenstrom Macroglobulinemia_.

LEARNING OBJECTIVE 10: Define hypersplenism.

EXERCISE 7-20

Complete the paragraph below.

The (1) _spleen_ is the largest organ of the immune system and home to the largest collection of macrophages in the body. These macrophages help to remove damaged RBCs and other cells from the blood. The spleen can become enlarged (called [2] _Splenomegaly_) due to various causes. (3) _Congestive splenomegaly_ is when the spleen enlarges as it congests with venous blood. An enlarged spleen may become overactive and remove more than the normal number of red cells, white cells, and platelets, a condition called (4) _hypersplenism_.

EXERCISE 7-21   PATHOLOGY AS A SECOND LANGUAGE

Test your vocabulary by indicating if each statement below is true or false. If it is false, provide the correct word for the italicized term that will make the statement true.

_F_ 1. The *thyroid* is an organ critical for T-cell development.
     The Thymus not the Thyroid

_F_ 2. *Thymoma* is a term applied to increased thymic lymphocytes.
     Thymic hyperplasia is the term. Thymoma is a tumor of thymic epithelial cells

_T_ 3. *Myasthenia gravis* is a rare, acquired autoimmune disease in which antibodies block transmission of nerve signals across the neuromuscular synapse.

_F_ 4. *Thymic hyperplasia* is a tumor of thymic epithelial cells.
     Thymoma

Decisions Decisions

DECISION TREE 7.1: ANEMIA

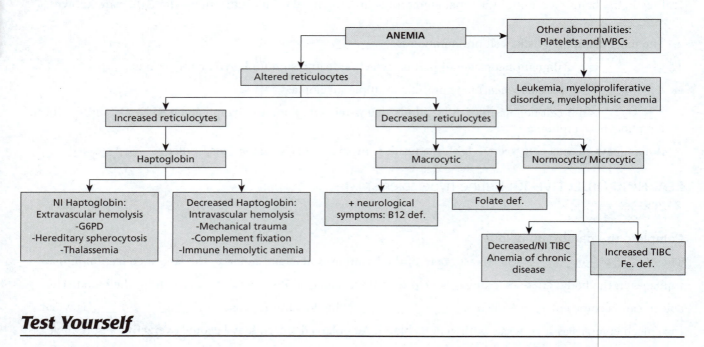

Test Yourself

I. MULTIPLE CHOICE

1. A 12-year-old Hispanic male is brought to the pediatrician's office by his father for evaluation of a long-standing fever, night sweats, and weight loss. His physical exam is notable for enlarged cervical lymph nodes. A biopsy of one of these lymph nodes demonstrates Reed Sternberg cells. Which of the following viruses may be responsible for his disease? [LEARNING OBJECTIVE 8]
   a. Epstein-Barr virus
   b. Cytomegalovirus
   c. Human papillomavirus
   d. Parvovirus

2. Which of the following diseases is precipitated by exposure to cold air, drinking cold fluid, and hand washing with cold water? [LEARNING OBJECTIVE 3]
   a. Cold antibody anemia
   b. Warm antibody anemia
   c. Raynaud phenomenon
   d. Polycythemia vera

3. A 43-year-old African American woman with a past medical history significant for morbid obesity, now status post a partial gastrectomy, complains of fatigue, shortness of breath, and a vibratory sensation in her extremities accompanied by weakness. Her CBC reveals macrocytic anemia, without an increase in reticulocytes, as well as a low platelet and WBC count. Which of the following is the underlying etiology of her symptoms? (Hint: Use the Decision Tree) [LEARNING OBJECTIVE 3]
   a. Folate deficiency anemia
   b. Anemia of chronic disease
   c. Iron deficiency anemia
   d. B_{12} deficiency anemia

4. Which of the following stimuli can increase erythropoietin production? [LEARNING OBJECTIVE 1]
   a. High altitude
   b. Chronic lung disease
   c. Chronic hypoxia
   d. All of the above

5. A 63-year-old Caucasian male presents to the ER with dizziness, headache, and vision changes. Chemistries are drawn and demonstrate a markedly elevated protein level; further testing reveals a monoclonal gammopathy (of IgM). The patient's X-rays are clean, and there appear to be no bony lesions. What is the most likely explanation of the patient's symptoms? [LEARNING OBJECTIVE 9]
   a. Multiple myeloma
   b. Waldenström macroglobulinemia
   c. Plasmacytoma
   d. Polycythemia vera

6. A 45-year-old Japanese sushi chef presents to the hospital complaining of numbness and tingling in his left ring finger. His past medical history is

significant for hypertension and similar events affecting different areas of his body. His physical exam is notable for a markedly plethoric face, and his CBC demonstrates an extremely high hematocrit (≥60%). What disease do you suspect (and which would be confirmed by a low erythropoietin)? [LEARNING OBJECTIVES 4 AND 7]
a. Relative erythrocytosis
b. Plasmacytoma
c. Polycythemia vera
d. Essential thrombocytosis

7. Which of the following presentations is most consistent with chronic leukemia? [LEARNING OBJECTIVE 6]
a. Abrupt onset, which often presents as acute infection or hemorrhage
b. Severe anemia, thrombocytopenia, with leukopenia
c. Insidious onset with fatigue, pallor, night sweats, low-grade fever, and infections.
d. Severe anemia with chronic hemolysis

8. A 52-year-old Hispanic male, with a past medical history significant for hypertension, visits his primary care physician complaining of fatigue and shortness of breath. His physical exam is notable for an enlarged spleen and liver as well as axillary lymphadenopathy. His WBC count is greater than 100,000 and a bone marrow aspirate has greater than 20% blasts. What is his diagnosis? [LEARNING OBJECTIVE 7]
a. Chronic lymphocytic leukemia
b. Hodgkin lymphoma
c. Chronic myelogenous leukemia
d. Acute myelogenous leukemia

9. A 22-year-old African American male Army enlistee is sent to the clinic by his commanding officer, who noted that the private was having a hard time keeping up with his company. His physical exam is notable for pallor of the oral mucosa as well as the beds of his fingernails, jaundice of the conjunctiva, and an enlarged spleen. A review of symptoms is positive for recent onset of dark urine. Reviewing his chart, you notice that he was recently started on antimalarial drugs in preparation for his trip overseas. What is the likely cause of his anemia? (Hint: Use the Decision Tree) [LEARNING OBJECTIVE 3]
a. Glucose-6-phosphate dehydrogenase deficiency
b. Hereditary spherocytosis
c. Sickle cell anemia
d. Beta thalassemia

10. Which of the following statements is true regarding diffuse lymphoma?
a. It typically occurs in teenagers and is associated with AIDS.
b. Its growth is insidious and presents quickly; lethal unless treated.
c. On pathology, it has a uniform microscopic pattern without follicles.
d. All of the above are true.

II. TRUE OR FALSE

11. ___F___ Lymphadenopathy is painful enlargement of lymph nodes usually caused by prolonged antigenic exposure. [LEARNING OBJECTIVE 5] *usually painless*

12. ___T___ The largest component of plasma is water. [LEARNING OBJECTIVE 1]

13. ___F___ Lymphoplasmacytic lymphoma is the only cause of IgM hyperviscosity. [LEARNING OBJECTIVE 9]

14. ___F___ Most cases of agranulocytosis are caused by overwhelming bacterial or fungal infection. [LEARNING OBJECTIVE 5]

15. ___F___ Half of lymphoid neoplasms are T cells, while the other half are B cells. [LEARNING OBJECTIVE 8] *90% are B-cell*

16. ___T___ Patients with sickle cell disease are especially susceptible to pneumococcus, *Salmonella*, and parvovirus. [LEARNING OBJECTIVE 3]

17. ___T___ Fetal and embryonic blood is produced primarily in the liver and spleen, but by the time of birth, has gradually shifted to the red marrow. [LEARNING OBJECTIVE 1]

III. MATCHING

18. Match the following red cell indices to their description or their example: [LEARNING OBJECTIVE 2]
   i. MCV
   ii. MCH
   iii. MCHC
A. Macrocytic
B. The average size of an RBC
C. Hyperchromic
D. The average amount of hemoglobin in an average RBC
E. The average concentration of hemoglobin per unit of volume in an average RBC
F. Hypochromic
G. Normocytic
H. Microcytic

IV. SHORT ANSWER

19. How does the presentation of acute lymphoid leukemia differ from that of chronic lymphoid leukemia? [LEARNING OBJECTIVE 8]

_____

_____

_____

20. A new resident attempted to obtain a bone marrow aspirate on a patient with anemia, leukopenia, and thrombocytopenia, but after three tries has only achieved "dry taps" (in other words, very few cells have been obtained). Which myeloproliferative disorder could cause this complication? [LEARNING OBJECTIVE 7]

_____

_____

_____

21. What functions does the spleen carry out? [LEARNING OBJECTIVE 10]

_____

_____

_____

22. What are the clinical features of Non Hodgkin lymphoma? [LEARNING OBJECTIVE 8]

_____

_____

_____

Disorders of Blood Vessels

The Big Picture

Blood vessels are essential for circulation to oxygenate and nourish the body's tissues, including the pump itself, the heart. A disorder of coronary blood vessels, namely coronary atherosclerosis, leads to the majority of deaths. Hypertension (high blood pressure) is also very common and contributes to the development of atherosclerosis. Less common diseases include inflammation of vessels (vasculitis) and vascular neoplasms.

Oh No! Not Another Learning Experience

LEARNING OBJECTIVE 1: Discuss how vessel structure varies with its function.

EXERCISE 8-1

Complete the paragraphs below.

Blood vessel (1) _____ varies with its function. For example, blood vessels have different diameters; decreasing the diameter in half increases (2) _____ to flow 16-fold (inverse of ½ is 2; $2^4 = 16$). Indeed, the diameter can be dynamically changed with sympathetic tone, thereby changing resistance and changing blood pressure. Blood flow to the kidneys plays a major role in control of blood pressure. As discussed previously, (3) _____ carry high-pressure, pulsating blood away from the heart. (4) _____ carry low-pressure, nonpulsating blood toward the heart. (5) _____, the smallest vessels, lie in tissues and join the arterial network to the venous network.

Blood vessels are composed of three layers. The (6) _____ is the outermost layer composed of supporting fibrous tissue. The (7) _____ is the middle layer composed mainly of smooth muscle. The (8) _____ in most vessels is composed of a single layer of endothelial cells that rest on a basement membrane. In the muscular arteries and arterioles, regional flow and pressure are regulated by the change in lumen size as smooth muscle cells of the media contract to narrow the lumen (called [9] _____) and decrease blood flow, or relax to enlarge it (called [10] _____) and increase blood flow. This process is controlled by the autonomic nervous system, hormones, and local metabolic factors.

Mnemonic

Intima = **In**ner layer.

EXERCISE 8-2

Complete the table below.

Vessel	Description
(1) _____ arteries	Large, include the aorta and its initial branches, the main pulmonary arteries
	Smooth muscle of their media is rich with elastic fibers.
(2) _____ arteries	Middle-sized, include the renal and coronary arteries.
	Media is composed of encircling smooth muscle cells.
	Regulate regional blood flow.
(3) _____	Tiny precapillary arteries less than 0.1 mm, which are wrapped by a thin layer of smooth muscle.
	Regulate local blood flow.
Small arteries	Less than about 2 mm in diameter, and include the retinal arteries.
(4) _____	Approximately the diameter of a red blood cell (7–8 μm).
	Composed only of endothelial cells resting on a basement membrane, promotes free exchange of gases and fluids.
Venules and veins	Blood from capillaries flows into and then sequentially through small, medium, and large veins.
	Large veins have one-way valves to prevent backflow.

EXERCISE 8-3   PATHOLOGY AS A SECOND LANGUAGE

Test your vocabulary by indicating if each statement below is true or false. If it is false, provide the correct word for the italicized term that will make the statement true.

_____ 1. *Sphygmomanometer* is the name for a blood pressure cuff.

_____

_____ 2. *Contractility* is the volume of blood per unit of time (L/min) ejected by the left ventricle into the aorta.

_____

_____ 3. *Cardiac output* is the resistance to flow that must be overcome for blood to flow through the circulatory system.

_____

LEARNING OBJECTIVE 2: Classify the plasma lipids.

EXERCISE 8-4

Complete the paragraph below.

A (1) _____ is a slick, greasy organic substance not soluble in water. Lipids can be divided into those

that are solid at room temperature (called [2] _____), and those that are not solid at room temperature

(called [3] _____). To be soluble in plasma, lipids must be attached to specialized plasma proteins

(called [4] _____). The combination of an apoprotein and a lipid is a **lipoprotein** (or **apolipoprotein**).

Mnemonic

Lousy cholesterol = LDL
Helpful cholesterol = HDL

EXERCISE 8-5

Complete the table below.

Apolipoprotein	Abbreviation	Composition
High-density lipoproteins	HDL	Half protein and half lipid, most of which is phospholipid and cholesterol.
Low-density lipoproteins	LDL	22% protein, and most of their lipid is (1) _____, with smaller amounts of phospholipid and triglycerides.
(2) _____	VLDL	10% protein, and most of their lipid is triglycerides, with smaller amounts of phospholipid and cholesterol.
(3) _____	Cm	Exceedingly small lipid droplets that pass from bowel mucosa into intestinal lymphatics, then the bloodstream.

EXERCISE 8-6   PATHOLOGY AS A SECOND LANGUAGE

See Exercise 8-5 for key terms covered in this section.

LEARNING OBJECTIVE 3: Discuss the risk factors, clinical manifestations, and pathological findings associated with hypertension.

EXERCISE 8-7

Complete the paragraph below.

High-blood pressure is very common. Risk factors include diet, genetics, stress, obesity, smoking, and lack of exercise. In most cases, no specific underlying disease or condition is present; such patients are classified as having (1) _____ (95%). The remaining incidence of hypertension is due to a specific underlying disease (mostly renal disease); this is called (2) _____ (5%). Severe hypertension may cause retinal hemorrhages and exudates, called (3) _____, but hypertension also causes damage throughout the body. In any tissue, hypertension can cause narrowing of the arteriolar lumen and waxy (hyaline) degenerative changes of the arteriolar wall, called (4) _____. (5) _____ occurs in severe hypertension—it is seen as concentric layers of hyperplastic cells in the thickening arteriolar wall ("onionskinning").

EXERCISE 8-8   PATHOLOGY AS A SECOND LANGUAGE

See Exercise 8-7 for key terms covered in this section.

LEARNING OBJECTIVE 4: List the predisposing factors, indicators of risk, pathologic processes, clinical complications, and treatment of atherosclerosis.

EXERCISE 8-9

Complete the paragraph below.

(1) _____ is probably the single most important disease process in the industrialized world. Atherosclerosis begins in infancy and progresses throughout life. The primary risk factors are age,

(2) _____, obesity, smoking, high cholesterol, male gender or postmenopausal women, diabetes, genetics, and vascular inflammation.

EXERCISE 8-10   PATHOLOGY AS A SECOND LANGUAGE

Test your vocabulary by writing the appropriate term in each blank from the list below.

Stenosis	Atheroma	Trans fats
Statin drugs	Arteriosclerosis	Atherosclerosis
Saturated fats	C-reactive protein (CRP)	

1. _____ literally means "hardening of the arteries."

2. _____ is a lifestyle disease associated with an unhealthy diet, obesity, smoking, and lack of exercise. It is characterized by fatty deposits in the arterial wall.

3. An _____ is a fatty deposit in the arterial wall.

4. A valuable marker of systemic inflammation that may be linked to atherosclerosis is _____.

5. _____ are completely reduced triglycerides that can be broken down by the body to make cholesterol.

6. _____ are artificially transformed unsaturated plant oils into more animal-like fats.

7. _____ is another term for narrowing and is usually used in reference to arteries.

8. _____ decrease cholesterol by blocking a liver enzyme important in cholesterol synthesis. They have proven very effective in lowering levels of LDL-C, total cholesterol, and the incidence of atherosclerotic vascular disease and death.

LEARNING OBJECTIVE 5: Name the most common causes of aneurysms and dissections.

EXERCISE 8-11

Complete the paragraph below.

Aneurysms and dissections are usually caused by (1) _____ and (2) _____. Rarely, an aneurysm may be the result of local infection (mycotic aneurysm), late stage syphilis, congenital defect, or trauma. In younger men, a dissection may be due to a hereditary connective tissue defect such as (3) _____ or Ehlers-Danlos syndrome. Dissections produce severe, tearing chest and back pain or cause partial or complete occlusion of one of the great vessels, which may cause neurological symptoms or a difference in blood pressure between the right and left arms. Rupture in aneurysms and dissections can cause immediate death.

EXERCISE 8-12   PATHOLOGY AS A SECOND LANGUAGE

Test your vocabulary by indicating if each statement below is true or false. If it is false, provide the correct word for the italicized term that will make the statement true.

_____ 1. *Vascular dissection* is the term for a localized dilation of an artery or heart chamber, usually owing to a weakness of the wall.

_____

_____ 2. *Aneurysm* is the term for a longitudinal tearing within the wall of an artery caused by blood that enters the wall through a defect, usually a tear in an atheroma.

_____

LEARNING OBJECTIVE 6: Describe the pathological findings associated with the affected vessel and the clinical manifestations of the following vasculitides: (a) Temporal arteritis, (b) Takayasu arteritis, (c) Polyarteritis nodosa, (d) Kawasaki disease, (e) Microscopic polyangiitis, (f) Wegener granulomatosis, and (g) Thromboangiitis obliterans.

EXERCISE 8-13

Complete the paragraph below.

(1) _____ (plural [2] _____) is a general term that applies to a group of rare diseases (despite how often it occurred on the television show "House"!) that feature inflammation of blood vessels. When small vessels are involved, it may be called (3) _____; when large arteries are involved, it may be called (4) _____. Most vasculitides are autoimmune; however, rarely they can be infectious.

EXERCISE 8-14

Complete the table below.

Vasculitis	Vessel types affected	Additional features
(1) _____	Large and medium-size arteries	Chronic granulomatous inflammation, also called "giant cell arteritis"
(2) _____	Aorta and its main branches	Granulomatous inflammation, also called "pulseless disease," often seen in Asian women
Thromboangiitis obliterans	Small and medium-size vessels	Affects in the hands and feet, also called "Buerger disease"
Polyarteritis nodosa	Small and medium-size muscular arteries	Generalized autoimmune disease, tends to affect the kidneys and abdominal viscera
(3) _____	Coronary arteries	Affects children and causes acquired heart disease
Microscopic polyangiitis	Arterioles, capillaries, and venules	Can affect any tissue, especially kidney (glomerulonephritis) and pulmonary capillaries, also called "hypersensitivity vasculitis"
(4) _____	Small to medium-size arteries	Affects the nose, throat, sinuses, lungs, and kidneys of middle-aged men

EXERCISE 8-15   PATHOLOGY AS A SECOND LANGUAGE

See Exercise 8-14 for key terms covered in this section.

LEARNING OBJECTIVE 7: Compare and contrast primary and secondary Raynaud syndrome.

EXERCISE 8-16

Complete the paragraph below.

(1) _____ is a common condition that results from exaggerated vasomotor reactivity in the small arteries and arterioles in the hands and fingers. The trigger is usually cold or emotional stress. Typically one or more fingers whiten at the tip when exposed to cold, after which the fingers may then turn blue (cyanotic), then become red and flushed with blood (hyperemic) on rewarming. When no underlying disease can be found, the condition is called (2) _____ (most patients). When an underlying cause is found, the condition is (3) _____, mostly occurring with autoimmune diseases like systemic sclerosis and systemic lupus erythematosus (SLE).

Mnemonic

Raynaud is a patriotic disease—look for the red, white, and blue sign.

EXERCISE 8-17   PATHOLOGY AS A SECOND LANGUAGE

See Exercise 8-16 for key terms covered in this section.

LEARNING OBJECTIVE 8: Describe the pathogenesis of varicose veins and thrombophlebitis.

EXERCISE 8-18

Complete the following sentence.

Varicose veins and (1) _____ are both diseases of the veins.

EXERCISE 8-19   PATHOLOGY AS A SECOND LANGUAGE

Test your vocabulary by indicating if each statement below is true or false. If it is false, provide the correct word for the italicized term that will make the statement true.

_____ 1. Varicose veins are abnormally dilated veins due to *high blood pressure* because of age-related relaxation of supporting tissues.

_____

_____ 2. Thrombophlebitis is the formation of venous thrombi with associated *inflammation* and pain.

_____

LEARNING OBJECTIVE 9: Know whether the following are benign or malignant: hemangioma, lymphangioma, vascular ectasia, Kaposi sarcoma, and angiosarcoma.

EXERCISE 8-20

Complete the paragraph below.

Tumors of blood vessels and (1) _____ may be either benign such as hemangiomas or lymphangiomas, or malignant, such as angiosarcoma. (2) _____ can result from chemical or radiation exposure, while Kaposi sarcoma can result from human herpesvirus-8 (HHV-8, also termed KS-associated herpesvirus, KSHV) infection in AIDS patients.

Mnemonic
Plain -omas are GOOD; sarc -omas are BAD.

EXERCISE 8-21   PATHOLOGY AS A SECOND LANGUAGE

Test your vocabulary by writing the appropriate term in each blank from the list below.

Kaposi sarcoma (KS)	Hemangioma	Lymphangioma
Angiosarcoma		

1. _____ is common and usually is found in skin as small, red, blood-filled lesions composed of capillary-size blood vessels.

2. _____ is a lesion composed of benign collections of lymphatic capillaries.

3. _____ is an intermediate-grade malignant vascular tumor that is most often seen in patients with AIDS.

4. _____ is a rare malignant tumor of vascular endothelial cells that occurs most frequently in skin, breast tissue, soft tissue, and liver.

Decisions Decisions

DECISION TREE 8.1: VASCULITIDES

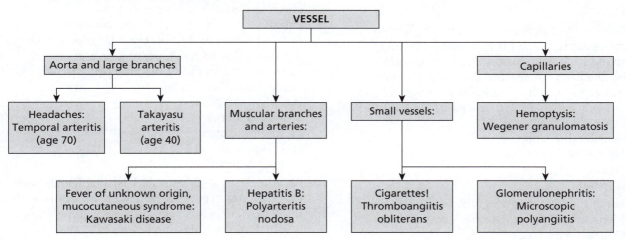

Test Yourself

I. MULTIPLE CHOICE

1. A 54-year-old African American male is seen for his yearly checkup. His past medical history is significant for hypertension and elevated cholesterol. Despite changing his medications repeatedly (and increasing the doses to maximum), he continues to have elevated blood pressure. His test results are notable for elevated renin levels, but normal levels of cortisol, epinephrine, and norepinephrine. Which of the following secondary causes of hypertension could explain his failure to respond to medication? [LEARNING OBJECTIVE 3]
   a. Renal artery stenosis
   b. Cushing disease
   c. Pheochromocytoma (adrenal medullary tumor)
   d. None of the above

2. To be soluble in plasma, lipids must be attached to a specialized plasma protein called _____. [LEARNING OBJECTIVE 2]
   a. Lipoprotein
   b. Solvency factor
   c. Triglycerides
   d. Apoprotein

3. Which of the following conditions is associated with deep venous thrombi? [LEARNING OBJECTIVE 8]
   a. Pregnancy and prolonged immobilization
   b. Heart failure
   c. Obesity and paraneoplastic syndrome
   d. All of the above

4. A 35-year-old Caucasian male with Marfan syndrome presents to the ER with severe, tearing chest and back pain. Suspecting a complication of the disease, you measure the blood pressure in both arms, which is markedly different. What is the likely explanation of his pain? [LEARNING OBJECTIVE 5]
   a. Vascular dissection
   b. Abdominal aneurysm
   c. Angina
   d. Vasculitis

5. Which of the following vasculitides are associated with hepatitis B? (Hint: Use the Decision Tree) [LEARNING OBJECTIVE 6]
   a. Takayasu arteritis
   b. Temporal arteritis
   c. Polyarteritis nodosa
   d. Microscopic polyangiitis

6. A 6-month-old infant is evaluated for a flat, pink lesion on the back of his neck. The "birthmark" is a small, blood-filled lesion. You explain to the infant's parents that the lesion will likely go away on its own. The birthmark is a type of _____. [LEARNING OBJECTIVE 9]
   a. Lymphangioma
   b. Hemangioma
   c. Pyogenic granuloma
   d. Angiosarcoma

7. What is the earliest stage for which drug treatment of hypertension should be initiated immediately? [LEARNING OBJECTIVE 3]
   a. Stage 1 hypertension
   b. Stage 2 hypertension
   c. Stage 3 hypertension
   d. Stage 4 hypertension

8. A 6-year-old Caucasian female presents to her pediatrician's office with a week of unexplained fever. On physical exam, bilateral lymphadenopathy, conjunctivitis, oral ulcers, and desquamation of the palms and soles of her feet are noted. What treatment should she receive? (Hint: Use the Decision Tree) [LEARNING OBJECTIVE 6]
   a. Aspirin
   b. Intravenous immunoglobulin
   c. High-dose aspirin and intravenous immunoglobulin
   d. Steroids

9. A 43-year-old African American male with HIV presents to his local physician for a viral titer check and a refill of his prescriptions. Upon entering the patient's room, you notice small, purple plaques on his forehead. He reports that these nodules started appearing several months ago when he ran out of his prescriptions. Which of the following neoplasms do you suspect? [LEARNING OBJECTIVE 9]
   a. Hemangioma
   b. Angiosarcoma
   c. Lymphangioma
   d. Kaposi sarcoma

10. An autopsy of a 68-year-old Hispanic female with longstanding hypertension demonstrates nephrosclerosis, which is caused by an accumulation of which of the following lesions? [LEARNING OBJECTIVE 3]
    a. Hyperplastic arteriolosclerosis
    b. Hyaline arteriolosclerosis
    c. Diabetic nephropathy
    d. Glomerulonephritis

II. TRUE OR FALSE

11. _____ Chylomicrons, which are approximately 25% triglycerides, are cleared by the liver, which processes them into HDL, LDL, and VLDL. [LEARNING OBJECTIVE 2]

12. _____ 80% of patients with systemic sclerosis and 20% with SLE have primary Raynaud phenomenon. [LEARNING OBJECTIVE 7]

13. _____ As total cross-sectional area increases, the speed of blood flow falls; therefore, the speed of blood flow in capillaries is significantly lower than that of the aorta. [LEARNING OBJECTIVE 1]

14. _____ Prior to the development of transient ischemic attacks, angina, or intermittent claudication, approximately 70% stenosis must occur. [LEARNING OBJECTIVE 4]

15. _____ At any given moment, about two-thirds of all blood is in veins. [LEARNING OBJECTIVE 1]

16. _____ The vast majority of sodium passes from glomerular filtrate back to plasma, as the renal tubules reabsorb it. [LEARNING OBJECTIVE 3]

17. _____ Thoracic aortic aneurysms are caused solely by late-stage syphilis. [LEARNING OBJECTIVE 4]

18. _____ Hemorrhoids and esophageal varices are examples of varicose veins. [LEARNING OBJECTIVE 7]

III. MATCHING

19. Classify the following arteries; answers may be used more than once, or not at all: [LEARNING OBJECTIVE 1]
    - i. Elastic arteries
    - ii. Muscular arteries
    - iii. Arterioles
    - iv. Small arteries

    A. Aorta
    B. Coronary arteries
    C. Main pulmonary arteries
    D. Retinal arteries
    E. Carotid
    F. Renal arteries

IV. SHORT ANSWER

20. While on a camping trip, you hear someone calling for a medical professional. A 52-year-old Caucasian male is complaining of pain in his left arm and jaw, as well as nausea, sweating, and dizziness. He tells you that he has a history of angina, and forgot his medication at home. What over-the-counter medication should he take while you drive him to the hospital? [LEARNING OBJECTIVE 4]

_____

_____

_____

21. Why is temporal arteritis considered a medical emergency? [LEARNING OBJECTIVE 6]

_____

_____

_____

22. Hypertensive vascular disease begins with injury to the endothelium. Using examples in the text, cite the various possible causes of endothelial injury, and the consequences of the injury. [LEARNING OBJECTIVE 3]

_____

_____

_____

23. What are the risk factors of coronary artery disease, and why is it so important to minimize as many of them as possible? [LEARNING OBJECTIVE 4]

_____

_____

_____

CHAPTER 9

Disorders of the Heart

The Big Picture

The heart is a unique and critical organ with an intricate, perfectly timed electrical system and an indefatigable myocardium. Normally, these work together to provide the flawless, quiet pumping of about 6,000 liters of blood each day for a lifetime. Nevertheless, in the United States, heart disease alone accounted for nearly one out of four deaths in 2010—more than all types of cancer combined. It follows, therefore, that heart disease is a major and often severe problem.

Oh No! Not Another Learning Experience

LEARNING OBJECTIVE 1: The anatomy of the heart is a reflection of its function; describe its manifestation in muscle contraction, one-way valves, blood supply, and conduction.

EXERCISE 9-1

Complete the paragraph below.

The anatomy of the heart includes the atria, ventricles, great vessels, valves and the electrical (1) _conduction system_. Deoxygenated blood flows from the periphery into the superior or inferior vena cava into the right atrium, then through the right AV (2) _tricuspid_ valve into the right ventricle, then through the (3) _pulmonary_ valve and pulmonary arteries to the lungs. The blood is oxygenated in the lungs and then enters the pulmonary veins into the left atrium, then through the (4) _bicuspid_ [mitral or] valve into the left ventricle. The left ventricle pumps oxygenated blood to the systemic circulation through the (5) _aortic_ valve into the aorta. The aortic valve prevents backflow of blood into the lumen of the left ventricle, and the adjacent coronary ostia allow for blood flow into the (6) ~~ventricle~~ _coronary arteries_ during relaxation of the left ventricle.

EXERCISE 9-2   PATHOLOGY AS A SECOND LANGUAGE

Test your vocabulary by indicating if each statement below is true or false. If it is false, provide the correct word for the italicized term that will make the statement true.

_F_   1. The heart muscle is called the *epicardium* composed of specialized muscle cells or cardiac myocytes.

　　　 myocardium

_F_   2. Contraction of the ventricles with ejection of blood occurs during *diastole* while relaxation of the ventricles occurs during *systole*.

　　　 the other way around

_T_   3. *Atrial natriuretic peptide* is present within atrial myocytes and acts to produce a number of systemic effects, including vasodilation and increased sodium and water excretion by the kidney.

_T_   4. Valves with failure to open (stenosis) or to close fully (incompetence, or *regurgitation*) is a feature of some cardiac disease.

_F_   5. The free ends of the tricuspid and mitral valve leaflets are tethered by thin ligaments to papillary muscles called *tendon sheaths*.

Chordae tendineae

_T_   6. *Papillary muscles* project from the interior of the heart wall and help to ensure the leaflets do not invert.

LEARNING OBJECTIVE 2: List the three waves of an EKG and give their source.

EXERCISE 9-3

Complete the paragraph below.

An (1) _electrocardiagram_ (or ECG, EKG) is a graphical tracing of the electrical voltage changes during each heartbeat. Although complex, there are three basic "waves." The first wave is the (2) _P_, which is small and represents atrial depolarization. Then comes the (3) _QRS_, which is really a rapid series of three waves that represent ventricular depolarization. Finally comes the (4) _T_, which is a mid-size wave that represents ventricular repolarization.

EXERCISE 9-4   PATHOLOGY AS A SECOND LANGUAGE

Test your vocabulary by writing the appropriate term in each blank from the list below.

Atrioventricular node   Sinoatrial (SA) node   **Bundle of His**
Right and left bundle branches   Cardiac conduction system

1. The _SA_ initiates each normal heartbeat by a self-excited, automatic discharge of an electrical signal making the natural pacemaker.
2. This signal is carried throughout the heart as a wave of electrical stimulation by the _electrical conduction system_, composed of specialized myocardial muscle fibers.
3. After the electrical signal leaves the SA node, it sweeps over the atria and passes into a second node located at the superior aspect of the interventricular septum, called the _AV node_.
4. Beneath the AV node, the signal passes through a thick bundle of conductive fibers called the _bundle of his_.
5. The bundle of His branches into two main bundles of conducting fibers called the _L + R bundles_

purkinje fibers are the specialized muscle cells that conduct the current

LEARNING OBJECTIVE 3: Name the five principles of healthy cardiac function.

EXERCISE 9-5

Complete the paragraph below.

The principles of healthy cardiac function include proper contraction, proper blood flow (unobstructed, forward, unshunted), and proper electrical function. Cardiac dysfunction is highlighted by a failure of one or more of these principles. Weak contraction of the heart muscle (or [1] _HF pump failure_), which can be due to infarcted, diseased, or stiff muscle, results in poor cardiac output. Obstructed flow of blood either to the heart or through the heart can occur, that is, atherosclerosis may impair coronary blood flow to heart muscle, or any of the four valves may become (2) _Stenosed / stenotic_ (stiff or fused), causing the heart to work harder to force blood past the obstruction. (3) _Regurgitant_ (or backward) blood flow across a valve decreases efficiency and requires extra cardiac effort. (4) _Shunting_ also decreases efficiency because blood is abnormally diverted, usually by congenital defect. Abnormal conduction or conduction defects result in ill-timed, premature or late, mechanically (5) _inefficient_ beats resulting in low cardiac output.

EXERCISE 9-6   PATHOLOGY AS A SECOND LANGUAGE

No vocabulary terms are covered in this section.

LEARNING OBJECTIVE 4: Compare and contrast the different types of heart failure, discussing their etiology, clinical signs/symptoms, and the lifestyle changes and medications indicated for treatment.

EXERCISE 9-7

Complete the paragraphs below.

(1) _HF_ is a syndrome of ventricular dysfunction in which the heart cannot pump blood at a rate sufficient to meet metabolic demand. Prior to failing, the heart compensates first by (2) _Sympathetic_ nervous stimulation (i.e., release of epinephrine) to increase the heart rate and the force of contraction, then long term by cardiac muscle (3) _hypertrophy._ If these adaptations are unable to maintain cardiac output, then congestive failure occurs.

There are several categorizations of heart failure. Perhaps the most important are the following: (4) _Systolic failure_ , in which the ventricle contracts poorly and empties incompletely and the fraction of total ventricular volume ejected with each stroke, called the (5) _EF_ , is abnormally low; and (6) _diastolic failure_ , in which ventricular relaxation and filling are impaired, leading to decreased cardiac output.

EXERCISE 9-8

Complete the table below.

Left (Forward) Heart Failure	Right (Backward) Heart Failure
Causes low cardiac output, causing congestion in the (1) _lungs_	Produces (2) _peripheral_ venous congestion and edema _generalized_
Pulmonary congestion & edema: Rales, (3) ~~positional dyspnea~~ _orthopnea_ (shortness of breath lying down), fatigue, tachycardia, enlarged heart.	Systemic congestion: dependent edema in feet, legs, genitals, ascites, pleural effusion, hepatosplenomegaly.
	Complications: deep venous thrombi, and pulmonary thromboemboli _Left HF_
Low cardiac output -> low blood pressure and low blood flow to kidney. Releases renin -> aldosterone secretion from cortex-> acts on kidney to retain (4) _sodium / H₂O_ Increases vascular volume and vicious cycle	(5) ____ can cause right-heart failure (the most common cause!) (6)_cor pulmonale_: pulmonary hypertension from lung or pulmonary vascular disease.

EXERCISE 9-9   PATHOLOGY AS A SECOND LANGUAGE

Test your vocabulary by indicating if each statement below is true or false. If it is false, provide the correct word for the italicized term that will make the statement true.

_F_   1. The relationship between ventricular dilation and cardiac performance as indicated by *vascular resistance* is described by the Frank-Starling Law.
_____ stroke volume

_T_   2. Dilation of the ventricular wall to maintain cardiac output is known as *compensated heart failure*.

_T_   3. Excessive dilation of the ventricles leading to weakening of the heart and decreased cardiac output is termed *uncompensated heart failure*.

_T_   4. *Left-heart failure* causes increased pulmonary venous pressure and forces fluid into the alveoli where it accumulates as pulmonary edema.

_T_   5. Pulmonary hypertension resulting from lung or pulmonary vascular diseases is a combination known as *cor pulmonale*.

_F_   6. General breathlessness is called *orthopnea*, whereas breathlessness when lying down is called *dyspnea*.
_____ other way around

_T_   7. Severe heart failure may be associated with low-blood oxygen, called hypoxia, and blue–gray skin color *cyanosis*.

Remember This! The most common cause of right-heart failure is left-heart failure (LHF -> RHF).

LEARNING OBJECTIVE 5: Discuss the etiology of coronary artery disease, distinguishing angina pectoris from a true myocardial infarct, and identify the signs/symptoms, diagnosis, treatment, and complications of each.

EXERCISE 9-10

Complete the paragraph below.

Coronary artery disease is essentially (1) _atherosclerosis_ of the coronary arteries, which are preferentially affected by this process. Atherosclerotic lesions (atheromas) can cause (2) _stenosis_ (narrowing) of vessels limiting blood flow to the heart, or may rupture and cause thrombi at the site and completely block blood flow beyond that point (occlusion). The process of formation of such an occluding thrombus is called (3) _coronary thrombosis_ Limited or blocked blood flow to the heart can cause ischemia and necrosis of the myocardium, called (4) _MI_.

EXERCISE 9-11

Complete the table below.

Myocardial Infarct (MI)	Angina Pectoris	Sudden Cardiac Death	Chronic Ischemic Heart Disease
Infarcts evolve, with the (1) _subendocardial_ muscle dying first. Restore blood = stop necrosis.	Stable: precipitated by exertion/stress Unstable: angina at rest (platelets on plaque) Unremitting: MI	Usually due to (2) _electrical malfunction_ (asystole) or (3) _disorganisation_ (ventricular fib)	Caused by repeated infarcts/accumulated effects of repeated anginal attacks, and chronic (4) _ischemia_
(4) _____ substernal pain radiating to left arm/jaw. Sweat, dyspnea, nausea vomiting. Increased CK-MB and cardiac troponin Sudden death, cardiac rupture, congestive heart failure, mitral regurgitation, mural thrombus, arrhythmia, thromboembolism, cardiogenic shock	Ischemia Substernal pain radiating to left arm/jaw that remits with rest/medication No change in CK-MB/cardiac troponin	Death within (5) _60_ minutes of symptom onset.	Dilated, thin-walled, flabby ventricles May lead to (6) _CHF_

Mnemonic

Myocardial Infarction (MI) Signs and Symptoms = PULSE

Persistent chest pain, **U**pset stomach, **L**ightheaded, **S**hortness of breath, **E**xcessive sweating

EXERCISE 9-12 PATHOLOGY AS A SECOND LANGUAGE

Test your vocabulary by writing the appropriate term in each blank from the list below.

Angina pectoris   Unremitting angina   Unstable angina

Stable angina   Ischemic cardiomyopathy

1. _Angina pectoris_ is a distinctive sensation caused by myocardial ischemia with or without infarction.

2. _stable angina_ rises and falls smoothly over a period of a few minutes and is relieved by rest or medication.

3. _unstable angina_ is caused by aggregates of platelets accumulating on an atherosclerotic plaque.

4. _Unremitting angina_ is angina that does not fluctuate and cannot be relieved by therapy; it is caused by myocardial infarction.

5. _Ischemic Cardiomyopathy_ is a condition in which heart failure develops as the muscle deteriorates because of accumulated ischemic damage due to numerous small and large infarcts over time.

LEARNING OBJECTIVE 6: Discuss the etiology, signs/symptoms, diagnosis, treatment, and complications of valvular degeneration, rheumatic heart disease, and endocarditis.

EXERCISE 9-13

Complete the paragraph below.

As mentioned earlier, (1) _Valvular stenosis_ is failure of the valve to open fully; it is usually due to stiff or fused valve leaflets caused by chronic inflammation and scarring. In contrast, (2) _valvular insufficiency_ (regurgitation, backflow, incompetence) is failure of the valve to close fully. Various diseases, including valvular degeneration, rheumatic heart disease, and endocarditis, can cause these mechanical problems with the cardiac valves.

EXERCISE 9-14 PATHOLOGY AS A SECOND LANGUAGE

Test your vocabulary by indicating if each statement below is true or false. If it is false, provide the correct word for the italicized term that will make the statement true.

F 1. *Medial calcific arteriosclerosis* is when the valves are stiff and laden with lumps of rock-hard calcific nodules.

Calcific Aortic Stenosis

T 2. *Congenital bicuspid aortic valve* can lead to valvular stenosis in older age.

T 3. Calcific deposits that can develop in the ring of fibrous tissue that supports the mitral valve are simply called *annular calcification*.

F 4. *Bacterial endocarditis* is the most common valvular disease.

Mitral valve prolapse

T 5. *Acute rheumatic fever* is an acute autoimmune disease that occurs in children about two to six weeks after group A strep pharyngitis.

T 6. Recurrent or chronic streptococcal infection can lead to *chronic rheumatic valvulitis*.

F 7. Noninfective thrombotic endocarditis is characterized by 1–5 mm valvular vegetations composed of *collagen* and fibrinous material.

Platelets

F 8. Infective endocarditis is usually a bacterial infection (bacterial endocarditis) of the endocardium, usually the *pulmonic or tricuspid* valves, which appear as ragged masses or vegetations.

Aortic or mitral

LEARNING OBJECTIVE 7: List the causes of myocarditis, and describe disease presentation and diagnosis.

EXERCISE 9-15

Complete the paragraph below.

(1) Myocarditis _____ is any inflammatory disease of the myocardium, in contrast to cardiomyopathies, which are generally noninflammatory. The disease presents as heart failure or arrhythmia in an otherwise healthy person with no cardiovascular risk factors. It is most often caused by (2) Coxsackie viruses _____, but can also be autoimmune, or due to many other etiologies.

EXERCISE 9-16 PATHOLOGY AS A SECOND LANGUAGE

See Exercise 9-15 for key terms covered in this section.

LEARNING OBJECTIVE 8: Compare and contrast dilated, hypertrophic, and restrictive cardiomyopathy.

EXERCISE 9-17

Complete the paragraph below.

Cardiomyopathies can be categorized in several ways. (1) _Primary_ _Cardiomyopathy_ refers to intrinsic disease of cardiac muscle, usually thought to be due to genetic defects. In contrast, (2) _Secondary_ _Cardiomyopathy_ is a result of other disease processes such as ischemic heart disease, hypertension or valve disease, infections, acquired metabolic disturbance, congenital heart abnormalities, nutritional deficiency, or immune dysfunction.

EXERCISE 9-18

Complete the table below.

Types	Dilated Cardiomyopathy	Hypertrophic Cardiomyopathy	Restrictive Cardiomyopathy
Causes	Intrinsic diseases caused by inflammation, metabolic disorders, autoimmune diseases, muscular dystrophy, genetic causes, or for unknown reasons.		
	(1) _alcohol, chemo, viral, peri/postpartum_	About half caused by (2) _genetic_ mutation	(3) _Amyloidosis, radiation, hemochromatosis_
Findings	Hypertrophy, dilations, (4) _low EF_; flabby weak heart	Hypertrophic (5) _football_ shaped heart, dyspnea, fainting, or irregular heart beat	(6) _stiff_ noncompliant ventricle
Symptoms	Weak systolic contractions	(7) _Powerful ineffective systolic_ contraction, incomplete diastolic filling, dead athlete	Systole not forceful

EXERCISE 9-19 PATHOLOGY AS A SECOND LANGUAGE

Test your vocabulary by matching each term to its definition.

Hypertrophic cardiomyopathy   Dilated cardiomyopathy   Restrictive cardiomyopathy

1. _Dialated_ is characterized by progressive heart failure with cardiac hypertrophy, dilation, and low ejection fraction.
2. _Hypertrophic_ can be marked by myocardial hypertrophy, which can be congenital or acquired, with half of occurrences resulting from an autosomal dominant gene defect.
3. _Restrictive_ is the rarest cardiomyopathy and is characterized by a stiff, noncompliant ventricle that fills incompletely in diastole.

LEARNING OBJECTIVE 9: Discuss the etiology, presentation, diagnosis, and treatment of pericardial effusions and pericarditis.

EXERCISE 9-20

Complete the paragraph below.

Fluid can accumulate abnormally in almost any body space. A (1) _pericardial effusions_ is an increased amount of fluid within the pericardial sac. If the fluid is undiluted blood, the accumulation is called a (2) _hemopericardium_

EXERCISE 9-21   PATHOLOGY AS A SECOND LANGUAGE

Test your vocabulary by indicating if each statement below is true or false. If it is false, provide the correct word for the italicized term that will make the statement true.

_T_   1. *Pericarditis* is inflammation of the pericardium.

_____

_F_   2. *Obstructive pericarditis* is rare, usually due to viral infection or autoimmune process, and occurs when the pericardium becomes stiff enough to impair cardiac filling making it difficult to distinguish from cardiomyopathy.

_____ This is restrictive pericarditis _____

LEARNING OBJECTIVE 10: Compare and contrast acyanotic, cyanotic, and obstructive heart disease, and give examples of each.

EXERCISE 9-22

Complete the paragraphs below.

Congenital heart malformations occur in about 1% of live births, can be genetic or environmental, and can be categorized anatomically or clinically. There are three types of anatomic defects: (1) _malrotation_ defects, which result in misplacement of a vessel (e.g., transposition of the great vessels); expansion defects, which result in hypoplastic chambers or vessels (e.g., coarctation of the aorta); and (2) _septal_ defects, which result in direct connections between atria or ventricles, or a combination of these. Clinically, congenital heart disease falls into two major categories: shunts (cyanotic and acyanotic) and obstructions.

A (3) _cardiac shunt_ is a defect that diverts blood abnormally from one side of the heart or great vessels to the opposite side (e.g., from aorta to pulmonary artery). Blood always flows from high pressure to low pressure. (4) _R to L shunts_ are less common than left-to-right and result from malrotation of the embryonic chambers. This creates a defect that allows deoxygenated venous (right side) blood to flow into the oxygenated left side of the circulation and mix, resulting in poor oxygenation of arterial blood, leading to blue skin discoloration or (5) _cyanosis_. (6) _L to R_ are those in which blood bypasses tissues and high-pressure, oxygenated blood flows from the arterial (left) side of the heart or one of the great vessels directly into the low-pressure, unoxygenated venous (right) side of the circulation. Timely correction of left-to-right shunts is critical. In some left-to-right shunts, right-side pressure can rise high enough to exceed left-side pressure, causing a (7) _reversal_ of shunt flow and late cyanosis as the shunt conveys unoxygenated blood into the systemic circulation.

Mnemonic
Cyanotic Congenital Heart Diseases = 5 Ts

Truncus arteriosus, **T**ransposition of the great arteries, **T**etralogy of Fallot, **T**ricuspid atresia, **T**otal anomalous pulmonary venous return

Remember This! Uncorrected left-to-right shunts lead to shunt reversal (i.e., to a right-to-left shunt) with late cyanosis.

Remember This! Tetra = 4; Tetralogy of Fallot = 4 abnormalities (VSD, pulmonary stenosis, misplaced aorta, and RVH)

EXERCISE 9-23 PATHOLOGY AS A SECOND LANGUAGE

Test your vocabulary by appropriately labeling each of the images and matching the following terms to their correct definition.

Patent ductus arteriosus   Tetralogy of fallot (TOF)   Patent foramen ovale

Coarctation of the aorta   Ventricular septal defect   Persistent truncus arteriosus

Atrial septal defect   Transposition of the great arteries

1. The most common right-to-left shunt is ___TOF___ in which there are four anatomical abnormalities.
2. _Transposition of the great arteries_ is the second most common cause of early cyanotic heart disease and requires an additional defect, an L-R shunt (ASD or VSD) to be compatible with life.
3. _persistent truncus arteriosus_ is a condition in which the roots of the pulmonary artery and aorta are fused into a single vessel that receives blood from both ventricles.
4. _AS defect_ is an incomplete closure of the embryonic atrial septum.
5. _Patent foramen ovale_ is a condition in which the foramen ovale, which usually closes in the first year of life, remains at least partially patent.
6. _VSD_ is incomplete closure of the embryonic ventricular septum.
7. _Patent ductus arteriosus_ is an isolated defect in about 90% of cases and causes a continuous, "machinery-like" heart murmur.
8. _Coarctation of the aorta_ consists of a ring-like fibrous narrowing of the aorta and can cause different blood pressures in regions of the body.

LEARNING OBJECTIVE 11: List the tumors that can arise in the heart.

EXERCISE 9-24

Complete the paragraph below.

The most common tumors of the heart are (1) _metastatic_, with primary heart tumors being quite rare. About 90% of primary cardiac tumors are benign. Diagnosis is by echocardiography, with surgical excision being curative. The most common primary tumor is a (2) _myxoma_, which usually arises in the atria. (3) _Papillary Fibroelastomas_ are benign papillary growths with hairlike appendages located most commonly on the aortic valve. (4) _Lipomas_ are benign, fatty tumors in the myocardium, but can occur anywhere in the body. (5) _Rhabdomyomas_ are benign tumors of cardiac muscle that usually come to attention in children because they obstruct blood flow.

EXERCISE 9-25 PATHOLOGY AS A SECOND LANGUAGE

See Exercise 9-24 for key terms covered in this section.

LEARNING OBJECTIVE 12: Explain the causes of arrhythmia, the locations from which they can arise, and their diagnostic findings on ECG.

EXERCISE 9-26

Complete the paragraph below.

A (1) _heartbeat_ is defined as a ventricular contraction and its timing is critical for heart function. A heart beating at a smooth, normal rate in response to normally initiated sino-atrial (SA) node signals is said to have a (2) _NSR_. When this timing is not correct and there are abnormalities in the rhythm, it is called an (3) _arrhythmia_. If the heart (i.e., ventricles) is beating too fast, the condition is called (4) _techycardia_; when it is too slow, it is called (5) _brady_. In either case, arrhythmias are mechanically inefficient because they cause the ventricles to be underfilled or overfilled with blood as systole begins. Minor arrhythmias, like a single premature beat, are fairly common. More severe arrhythmias can lead to death.

EXERCISE 9-27   PATHOLOGY AS A SECOND LANGUAGE

Test your vocabulary by indicating if each statement below is true or false. If it is false, provide the correct word for the italicized term that will make the statement true.

_T_ 1. Rhythms not initiated by the SA node are called *escape rhythms*.
_____

_T_ 2. Any beat that originates at a site other than the SA node is said to be an *ectopic beat*.
_____

_F_ 3. *Sinus tachycardia* is an otherwise normal sinus rhythm in which the ventricle is beating slower than the normal resting rate.
_____Sinus brady_____

_F_ 4. *Sinus bradycardia* is an otherwise normal sinus rhythm in which the ventricle is beating faster than the normal resting rate.
_____Sinus tach_____

_T_ 5. *Sinus arrhythmia* is a condition in which the heart sometimes beats slow or fast in response to otherwise normal signals from the SA node.
_____

_F_ 6. *Heart attack* is an imprecise term that is widely used to describe sudden cardiovascular collapse and unconsciousness.
_____Cardiac arrest_____

_T_ 7. *Sinus arrest* is absence of electrical discharge from the SA node.
_____

_T_ 8. Ectopic beats originating in the atria are called *premature atrial beats*.
_____

___F___ 9. *Atrial fibrillation* is an unusually rapid, but *regular*, evenly spaced beating of the atrium (and ventricle) at rates from 120 to 350 beats/minute.

A-fib B Irregularly irregular   A. Flutter

___T___ 10. *Atrial flutter* is an unusually rapid and *irregular*, unevenly spaced beating of the atria, commonly referred to as "irregularly irregular."

___T___ 11. *Junctional arrhythmia* occurs when the ectopic beats originate near the atrioventricular (AV) node.

___T___ 12. *Premature ventricular contractions* (PVC) arise in the ventricles and cause an early ventricular beat, but the signal does not travel retrograde into the atria, so the SA node continues to discharge regularly.

___T___ 13. *Ventricular tachycardia* is defined as three or more consecutive ectopic ventricular beats at a rate that exceeds 120 beats/minute.

___T___ 14. *Ventricular fibrillation* is the uncoordinated contraction of myocardium—the ventricles more or less quiver ineffectively, and cardiac output is essentially zero.

___T___ 15. Slowing or complete obstruction of a sinus impulse in its course through the conduction system is called *atrioventricular block*.

___F___ 16. Some people have congenital abnormalities of the conduction system, called *progressive pathways*, that provide an alternate route for the sinus signal.

accessory pathways

___T___ 17. Either bundle branches can be blocked as a *right bundle branch block* or *left bundle branch block*.

___T___ 18. In *electroconversion*, also known as "defibrillation," a strong electrical current is passed through the heart to terminate the irregular pattern and allow a sinus rhythm to begin again.

___T___ 19. Implanted device to treat some arrhythmias are called *pacemakers*.

Decisions Decisions

DECISION TREE 9.1: SHORTNESS OF BREATH

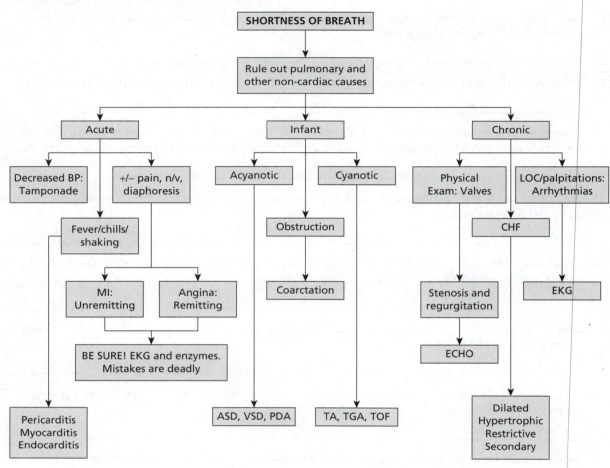

DECISION TREE 9.2: READING AN EKG

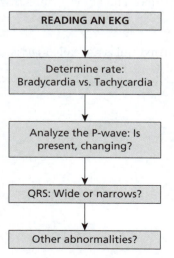

Test Yourself

I. MULTIPLE CHOICE

1. An autopsy is requested for a 56-year-old Caucasian female with a past medical history of widely metastatic cancer, to document the extent of her disease. Her mitral valve is notable for multiple millimeter tan/white valvular vegetations. What are they most likely composed of? [LEARNING OBJECTIVE 6]
   A. Bacteria
   B. Platelets and fibrinous material
   C. Lipids and macrophages
   D. Collagen

2. Which type of heart failure is characterized by poor ventricular contraction with decreased ejection fraction and is caused by ischemia, infarction, or inflammation? [LEARNING OBJECTIVE 4]
   A. Systolic failure
   B. Diastolic failure
   C. Right heart failure
   D. Left heart failure

3. A 35-year-old male with a past medical history of diabetes and arthritis arrives in the ER complaining of difficulty breathing and chest pain. Tests reveal increased end diastolic and pulmonary venous pressure due to poor ventricular compliance as well as thickening of the right and left ventricle. A biopsy of his heart is notable for iron deposition. What is your diagnosis? [LEARNING OBJECTIVE 8]
   A. Dilated cardiomyopathy
   B. Restrictive cardiomyopathy
   C. Hypertrophic cardiomyopathy
   D. Ischemic cardiomyopathy

4. Which of the failures of proper cardiac function is represented by the fusion of the valve leaflets? [LEARNING OBJECTIVE 3]
   A. Pump failure
   B. Obstructed flow
   C. Regurgitant flow
   D. Shunted flow

5. A 67-year-old African American man returns to his family physician for his yearly checkup. While there, he describes repeated episodes of smothering pressure beneath his sternum radiating to his left jaw and shoulder. The episodes appear to be brought on by climbing more than three flights of stairs and are relieved with rest. What is the most likely explanation of his symptoms? [LEARNING OBJECTIVE 5]
   A. Stable angina pectoris
   B. Unstable angina pectoris
   C. Myocardial infract
   D. Pericarditis

6. A five-year-old Hispanic male is brought to the clinic for evaluation of a rash. His mother also notes that he has stopped standing and walking, preferring to crawl on the floor. In addition to his rash, a physical exam is notable for subcutaneous nodules and a new onset mitral regurgitation murmur. Further review of the patient's history is likely to reveal what recent infection? [LEARNING OBJECTIVE 6]
   A. Staph aureus pharyngitis
   B. Group D strep pharyngitis
   C. Group A strep cellulitis
   D. Group A strep pharyngitis

7. Which of the following agents is capable of causing myocarditis? [LEARNING OBJECTIVE 7]
   A. Coxsackie A/B virus
   B. Autoimmune disease
   C. Infectious agents, drugs, and pregnancy
   D. All of the above

8. Which of the following findings would you expect to find in a patient with a systolic crescendo-decrescendo murmur? [LEARNING OBJECTIVES 5 AND 6]
   A. Ballooning collagenous degeneration
   B. Valvular vegetations composed of platelets and fibrinous material
   C. Calcific nodules on a bicuspid valve
   D. Infective endocarditis

9. A 53-year-old Caucasian male with a past medical history of alcoholism is hospitalized for chest pain and dyspnea requiring oxygen therapy. His EKG was abnormal; however, his troponins were within normal limits and his coronary angiogram demonstrated minimal stenosis. What is the most likely explanation of his symptoms? [LEARNING OBJECTIVE 8]
   A. Restrictive cardiomyopathy
   B. Hypertrophic cardiomyopathy
   C. Ischemic cardiomyopathy
   D. Dilated cardiomyopathy

10. A 25-year-old African American female involved in a car accident (with a deployed air bag) is seated in the ambulance when she begins to complain of shortness of breath. Her vitals are notable for a markedly decreased blood pressure as well as tachycardia. You note her distant heart sounds on exam and diagnose her with cardiac tamponade, which requires that you administer what treatment immediately? [LEARNING OBJECTIVE 9]
    A. Needle drainage of her pericardial effusion
    B. The administration of diuretics
    C. Saline bolus and pressors
    D. CPR and oxygen

11. Which of the following set of symptoms is caused by the backward component of uncompensated right ventricular heart failure? [LEARNING OBJECTIVE 4]
    A. Distended neck veins
    B. Enlargement of the liver and spleen
    C. Edema in the feet and pleural effusions
    D. All of the above

12. A 16-year-old female with a past medical history of Turner syndrome is noted to be markedly hypertensive during a physical exam; you also note a machinery-like murmur during her cardiac exam. On a hunch, you measure the blood pressure in her legs, which is decreased. Which of the following test results supports your diagnosis of coarctation of the aorta? [LEARNING OBJECTIVE 10]
    A. Decreased aldosterone and renin
    B. Elevated aldosterone and renin
    C. Elevated aldosterone and decreased renin
    D. Decreased aldosterone and elevated renin

13. Annular calcification of the mitral valve can cause which of the following complications? [LEARNING OBJECTIVE 5]
    A. Regurgitation, arrhythmia
    B. Stenosis, thrombus formation
    C. Infective endocarditis
    D. All of the above

14. A 19-year-old Hispanic youth presents to the ER with high fevers and shaking chills. A physical exam is notable for oral, conjunctival, and subungual petechiae. He admits to IV drug use. What is your diagnosis? [LEARNING OBJECTIVE 6]
    A. Subacute bacterial endocarditis
    B. Acute bacterial endocarditis
    C. Noninfective endocarditis
    D. Myocarditis

II. TRUE OR FALSE

15. _____ The conduction pathway of the heart is a looped system in which every part of the conduction network is capable of self-stimulation. [LEARNING OBJECTIVE 1]

16. _____ An atrial septal defect occurs when there is incomplete closure of the foramen ovale. [LEARNING OBJECTIVE 10]

17. _____ Ventricular contraction begins at the apex of the heart. [LEARNING OBJECTIVE 2]

18. _____ Cardiac myocytes contract together in an "all or nothing" manner. [LEARNING OBJECTIVE 1]

19. _____ Infectious pericarditis is most often caused by viral infection, which may also cause an associated myocarditis. [LEARNING OBJECTIVE 9]

20. _____ The first muscle supplied, secondary to its proximity to the interventricular surface, is the subendocardial muscle; it is therefore resistant to ischemia. [LEARNING OBJECTIVE 5]

21. _____ The distance each muscle bundle shortens during contraction determines the amount of force generated. [LEARNING OBJECTIVE 1]

22. _____ Congenital heart malformations occur in about 1% of live births, and the majority of these are secondary to specific genetic defects. [LEARNING OBJECTIVE 10]

23. _____ Temporary papillary muscle dysfunction with mitral regurgitation occurs in about one-third of MI patients in the first few days. [LEARNING OBJECTIVE 5]

III. MATCHING

24. Match the following arrhythmias with their signs and/or symptoms: [LEARNING OBJECTIVES 6 AND 12]
    i. Sinus arrhythmia
    ii. First-degree block
    iii. Second-degree block
    iv. Third-degree block
    v. Atrial fibrillation
    vi. Ventricular fibrillation
    vii. Wolf-Parkinson white
    A. Normal slight increase of rate with inspiration and a corresponding lower rate with expiration
    B. Normal P, QRS, and T waves are absent and replaced by irregular wiggles along the baseline
    C. Prolonged P-QRS interval
    D. Complete obstruction of the sinus signal
    E. QRS with a slurred stroke in the initial movement (delta wave)
    F. Prolonged P-QRS interval, with occasional missing QRS complexes
    G. Rapid and *irregular*, unevenly spaced beating of the atria

25. Match the following tumors with their description: [LEARNING OBJECTIVE 11]
    i. Myxoma
    ii. Rhabdomyomas
    iii. Lipomas
    iv. Papillary fibroelastomas
    A. Tumors caused by a genetic defect that can fragment and cause embolic phenomena
    B. Benign papillary growths, commonly occurring on the aortic valve
    C. Benign tumors of cardiac muscle
    D. Benign fatty tumors in the myocardium

IV. SHORT ANSWER

26. A 15-year-old athlete with a family history of sudden cardiac death is evaluated prior to playing sports. He is found to have increased end diastolic and pulmonary venous pressure with lung congestion and dyspnea. An ECHO demonstrates a forceful systolic ejection that is ineffective, and his upper ventricular septum is thickened. What treatments are available to him? [Learning Objective 8]

_____

_____

_____

27. Discuss the changes that may accompany a myocardial infarct and aid in its diagnosis. [LEARNING OBJECTIVE 5]

_____

_____

_____

28. What are the four major voltage changes with each heartbeat? [LEARNING OBJECTIVE 2]

_____

_____

_____

29. What are the three types of pathological processes that affect valves? [LEARNING OBJECTIVE 1]

_____

_____

_____

30. Discuss the treatment of various treatment options of CHF. [LEARNING OBJECTIVE 4]

_____

_____

_____

31. What are the etiologies of sinus tachycardia? [LEARNING OBJECTIVE 12]

_____

_____

_____

32. What heart arrhythmia results in two nonconnected circuits? [LEARNING OBJECTIVE 10]

_____

_____

_____

CHAPTER 10

Disorders of the Respiratory Tract

The Big Picture

The respiratory tract serves the important function of respiration, which includes ventilation (breathing), gas exchange, and oxygen utilization. Because the lungs, like the skin and GI tract, are open to the environment, they are exposed to toxins and pathogenic organisms. Lung cancer is the single greatest cause of respiratory-related death in the United States, followed by chronic lower respiratory disease and respiratory infections (e.g., pneumonia). The main risk factor for respiratory disease-related mortality is smoking, a completely modifiable risk factor.

Oh No! Not Another Learning Experience

LEARNING OBJECTIVE 1: Discuss the organization of the respiratory tract, and explain how its varying morphology reflects its function.

EXERCISE 10-1

Complete the paragraph below.

The respiratory tract is divided into the upper respiratory tract and the lower respiratory tract. The

(1) _____ consists of the nose, sinuses, pharynx, epiglottis, and larynx. The nose and sinuses are lined by

mucin-secreting, ciliated pseudo-stratified columnar epithelium, called (2) _____. The (3) _____

consists of the trachea, bronchi, lungs, and pleurae.

EXERCISE 10-2 PATHOLOGY AS A SECOND LANGUAGE

Test your vocabulary by indicating if each statement below is true or false. If it is false, provide the correct word for the italicized term that will make the statement true.

_____ 1. Air enters through the *bronchi*, which divides into right and left main *trachea*, one for each lung.

_____

_____ 2. The lobar bronchi continue to divide into progressively smaller communicating airways, the smallest bronchial division of which is the *alveolus*.

_____

_____ 3. Distal to the bronchioles are the *alveoli*, the blind-end sacs of the lung and smallest division of the airway, where gas exchange occurs.

_____

____ 4. Alveoli are lined by a specialized epithelium composed of *Type I and Type II pneumocytes*.

_____

____ 5. The gas exchange surface of the alveoli is sometimes called the *pulmonary membrane*.

_____

____ 6. The capacity of the pulmonary membrane to allow oxygen and carbon dioxide exchange between air and blood is called the *forced expiratory volume*.

_____

LEARNING OBJECTIVE 2: Using spirometry patterns, distinguish between obstructive and restrictive airway disease.

EXERCISE 10-3

Complete the paragraph below.

(1) _____ is a diagnostic procedure that measures lung volumes and the flow rate (liters per second) of air going into and out of the lungs. This procedure also allows for calculation of (2) _____, the sum of volumes. Using this data, respiratory disease can be classified into two categories. Obstructive disease is characterized by limitation of airflow and restrictive disease is characterized by limitation of lung expansion. Both obstructive and restrictive disease limit gas exchange

Remember This! Obstructive = can't get air OUT; Restrictive = can't get air IN.

EXERCISE 10-4

Complete the table below.

Lung Disease	FEV1	FVC	Ratio (FEV1:FVC)
(1) _____	Decreased	Normal or increased	Low
(2) _____	Decreased	Decreased	Normal

EXERCISE 10-5 PATHOLOGY AS A SECOND LANGUAGE

Test your vocabulary by writing the appropriate term in each blank from the list below.

Dyspnea   FEV1/FVC ratio   Forced vital capacity (FVC)
Hypoxia   Forced expiratory volume (FEV1)

1. _____ is the *volume* of air expelled from maximum inspiration to maximum expiration.

2. _____ is a *rate*, the amount of air expelled from maximum inspiration in the first second of effort.

3. The _____ is critical in separating obstructive and restrictive lung disease.

4. Classic signs and symptoms associated with impaired ventilation include wheezing, _____ or low arterial blood oxygen, _____ or shortness of breath, and cyanosis.

LEARNING OBJECTIVE 3: List the diseases affecting the upper respiratory tract and describe their etiology.

EXERCISE 10-6

Complete the paragraph below.

The upper respiratory tract is susceptible to pathology, including infections and neoplasia. Among the most common of respiratory ailments are _____, most of which occur in children.

EXERCISE 10-7   PATHOLOGY AS A SECOND LANGUAGE

Test your vocabulary by indicating if each statement below is true or false. If it is false, provide the correct word for the italicized term that will make the statement true.

_____ 1. *Allergic rhinitis* is essentially synonymous with "common cold" or upper respiratory infection (URI).

_____

_____ 2. *Infectious rhinitis* (also called "hay fever") is very common and represents an exaggerated immune reaction to plant pollens, fungi, animal dander, or dust mites.

_____

_____ 3. *Nasal polyps* are exaggerated folds of edematous mucosa with inflammation and epithelial hyperplasia.

_____

_____ 4. An accumulation of sinus mucus is called a *mucocele.*

_____

_____ 5. *Chronic sinusitis* is generally bacterial and causes pain, nasal drainage, congestion, fullness, and fever; it is treated with a two-week course of antibiotics.

_____

_____ 6. *Acute sinusitis* is due to chronic poor drainage and persistent infection of the sinuses; cases due to fungus can be especially severe.

_____

_____ 7. *Sinonasal papillomas* are benign neoplasms and are caused by HPV.

_____

_____ 8. Pharyngitis and *sinusitis* are inflammations of the throat secondary to infection; they are viral or caused by Group A streptococcus (acute streptococcal pharyngitis = "strep throat").

_____

_____ 9. *Laryngitis* is inflammation of the larynx and usually occurs as a part of a URI or upper airway irritation.

_____

_____ 10. *Vocal cord nodules* are small, benign, smooth fibrous nodules or polyps caused by smoking or chronic vocal stress.

_____

____ 11. *Laryngeal papillomas* are small, benign, raspberry-like squamous growths that may cause hoarseness or bleeding.

_____

____ 12. Carcinoma of the larynx, like other invasive head and neck carcinomas is usually *basal-cell carcinoma*.

_____

LEARNING OBJECTIVE 4: Identify the three types of atelectasis and their respective causes.

EXERCISE 10-8

Complete the paragraph below.

(1) _____ is collapse of a part of the lung that keeps that portion from exchanging gas properly. There are three types of atelectasis: resorption atelectasis, compression atelectasis, and contraction atelectasis.

EXERCISE 10-9

Complete the table below.

Type of Atelectasis	Cause	Examples
(1) _____	Bronchial obstruction	Mucus plugs, foreign object, mass
(2) _____	External pressure	Pleural effusion, pneumothorax, surgery
(3) _____	Scarring	TB, chronic inflammation

EXERCISE 10-10 PATHOLOGY AS A SECOND LANGUAGE

See Exercises 10-8 and 10-9 for key terms covered in this section.

LEARNING OBJECTIVE 5: Discuss the pathophysiology, signs and symptoms, and treatment of pulmonary edema.

EXERCISE 10-11

Complete the paragraph below.

(1) _____ is an abnormal accumulation of fluid in the alveoli, which normally have only a thin film of surfactant to decrease surface tension and promote gas exchange. Patients will generally have shortness of breath. There are two types of pulmonary edema. (2) _____ edema accumulates when there is increased hemodynamic pressure (blood pressure) in the lung vascular bed, most often as a result of left-heart failure. (3) _____ edema occurs when capillaries in the alveolar walls are injured and leak protein-rich inflammatory fluid into the alveolar space because of toxins, drugs, sepsis, or many other conditions. Treatment is targeted at the cause and at removing fluid from the body (e.g., diuresis).

EXERCISE 10-12 PATHOLOGY AS A SECOND LANGUAGE

See Exercise 10-11 for key terms covered in this section.

LEARNING OBJECTIVE 6: Describe the etiology, clinical presentation and findings, prognosis, and treatment of acute respiratory distress syndrome.

EXERCISE 10-13

Complete the paragraph below.

(1) _____ is a medical emergency associated with alveolar or pulmonary capillary injury. It is essentially the adult version of so-called (2) _____. The condition can be caused by just about anything so long as there is injury to the (3) _____ and/or alveoli. This injury leads to membranes that thicken and dry, impeding gas exchange. Over time, fibrosis replaces these membranes. The fatality rate is about 40%. Treatment is mechanical ventilation with oxygen supplementation, steroids, and elimination of the underlying cause. Some patients survive the acute phase and regain normal pulmonary function; however, others have permanent lung damage.

EXERCISE 10-14   PATHOLOGY AS A SECOND LANGUAGE

See Exercise 10-13 for key terms covered in this section.

LEARNING OBJECTIVE 7: Compare and contrast the symptoms and associated pathological findings of obstructive apnea, asthma, bronchiectasis, and chronic obstructive pulmonary disease.

EXERCISE 10-15

Complete the paragraph below.

In (1) _____, there is some general barrier to the smooth flow of air, usually at the level of the small branches of the bronchial tree. Inhalation is usually unimpaired; however, exhalation is difficult and slow and may be accompanied by audible expiratory wheezes. This is reflected in the spirometry findings of decreased (2) _____, and normal or slightly expanded functional vital capacity (FVC).

> **Remember This!** Acute asthma can be fatal; STATUS ASTHMATICUS -> DEATH.

EXERCISE 10-16

Complete the table below.

Obstructive Lung Diseases	Features
(1) _____	Sleep-related episodes of partial or complete closing of the upper airway that lead to breathing cessation (a breathless period of >10 seconds)
(2) _____	Chronic inflammatory disease of bronchioles that is characterized by recurring episodes of wheezing, bronchospasm and excessive production of mucus
(3) _____	Composed of two main types: emphysema and chronic bronchitis, "pink puffers" and "blue bloaters," due to smoking or rarely alpha-1-antitrypsin deficiency (emphysema)

EXERCISE 10-17   PATHOLOGY AS A SECOND LANGUAGE

Test your vocabulary by writing the appropriate term in each blank from the list below.

Bronchiectasis   Chronic asthmatic bronchitis

Emphysema   Chronic bronchitis

1. _____ is characterized by irreversible destruction of alveolar walls and merging of alveoli to form large air spaces.

2. _____ is a clinical diagnosis that can be made in any patient who has had a chronic cough that produces sputum for three consecutive months two years in a row.

3. Some patients with chronic bronchitis have sudden episodes of asthma-like wheezing and are said to have _____.

4. _____ is dilation of the bronchi caused by chronic, necrotizing bronchial infection.

LEARNING OBJECTIVE 8: Discuss the clinical presentation and diagnostic findings of restrictive lung disease.

EXERCISE 10-18

Complete the paragraph below.

(1) _____ is a disease of stiff lungs, which limits the volume of lung expansion and the rate of expansion and contraction. Consequently, the spirometry findings include a decreased FEV1 as well as a decreased FVC, leading to an essentially normal FEV1/FVC ratio.

EXERCISE 10-19   PATHOLOGY AS A SECOND LANGUAGE

Test your vocabulary by indicating if each statement below is true or false. If it is false, provide the correct word for the italicized term that will make the statement true.

_____ 1. *Idiopathic pulmonary fibrosis* is fibrotic disease of the lung that originates from unknown causes.

_____

_____ 2. *Pneumoconiosis* is lung disease caused by inhaled dusts and fumes.

_____

_____ 3. *Sarcoidosis* is a chronic interstitial lung disease caused by inhalation of tiny silicate fibers. These fibers were formerly used in industry, especially for fireproofing and insulation. Inhalation of these fibers is thought to increase the risk of mesothelioma.

_____

_____ 4. *Asbestosis* is a systemic granulomatous disease of unknown cause that affects many tissues.

_____

_____ 5. *Viral pneumonitis* is a T-cell mediated, delayed hypersensitivity immune reaction.

_____

LEARNING OBJECTIVE 9: Summarize the etiology, presentation, findings, and potential complications of pulmonary thromboemboli, including pulmonary hypertension; and explain alternative causes of pulmonary hypertension.

EXERCISE 10-20

Complete the paragraphs below.

The pulmonary arterial tree is fed by venous blood returning to the heart through the great veins. If deep vein thrombi develop in the venous network, they can dislodge and migrate (embolize) to the lungs and block (occlude) pulmonary vasculature (arteries); these are called (1) _____.

   Chronic thromboembolic disease can occlude many of the vessels, increasing the pulmonary vascular resistance and lead to (2) _____, or increased pulmonary pressure. Pulmonary hypertension is defined as abnormally high blood pressure (mean pressure ≥25 mm Hg at rest) in the pulmonary vascular tree. The increased pulmonary pressure can itself damage the pulmonary vascular bed, making the problem even worse.

EXERCISE 10-21   PATHOLOGY AS A SECOND LANGUAGE

See Exercise 10-20 for key terms covered in this section.

LEARNING OBJECTIVE 10: Characterize, where applicable, the etiologies of pneumonia as: lobar or interstitial, and/or nosocomial, community acquired, aspiration, chronic, or occurring in an immunodeficient host.

EXERCISE 10-22

Complete the paragraph below.

The respiratory tract is infected more often than any other organ system, with pneumonia being the biggest killer. Successful infection must overcome barriers such as the "mucociliary escalator" and (1) _____ immune defense. Risk factors include age, tobacco/drugs/toxins, immunosuppression, loss of cough reflex, and excessive mucus or pulmonary fluid. Pneumonia is inflammation of the lungs. It can be classified into (2) _____ according to the setting in which it occurs, or it can be anatomically classified. The syndromes include community-acquired pneumonia, hospital-acquired (nosocomial) pneumonia, (3) _____, chronic pneumonia, or pneumonia in the immunodeficient host.

EXERCISE 10-23

Complete the table below.

Anatomic Pneumonia	Features
(1) _____	Acute inflammation that completely fills alveoli with neutrophils
(2) _____	Patchy, noncontiguous inflammation, usually involving the alveoli of more than one lobe; is most likely to occur in the inferior (basilar) parts of the lower lobes
(3) _____	Intense, consolidated acute inflammation of the alveoli in an entire lobe; more likely to occur in patients with congestive heart failure, COPD, diabetes, or alcoholism
(4) _____	Inflammation confined to the alveolar septa, rather than within alveolar spaces; generally diffuse and bilateral; often caused by viral infection

EXERCISE 10-24 PATHOLOGY AS A SECOND LANGUAGE

Test your vocabulary by writing the appropriate term in each blank from the list below.

Community-acquired pneumonia (CAP)   Lung abscess

Histoplasmosis   Coccidioidomycosis

Candidiasis   Cryptococcosis

Primary atypical pneumonia (PAP)   Aspiration pneumonia

1. _____ is acute pneumonia not acquired in a special circumstance, such as within a hospital.

2. _____ is generally a mild pneumonia with interstitial rather than alveolar inflammation. It can be due to atypical organisms such as *Mycoplasma*, *Chlamydia*, or *Rickettsia*.

3. _____ is caused by aspiration of gastric contents in inebriated or debilitated patients.

4. _____ is a collection of suppurative inflammation that can occur in the setting of postobstructive pneumonia and a mass.

5. _____ is a fungal infection caused by *C. albicans*.

6. _____ is a disseminated or pulmonary infection acquired by inhalation of soil contaminated with the yeast *Cryptococcus neoformans*.

7. _____ is caused by inhalation of bird droppings containing *H. capsulatum*. It is one of the most common endemic fungal infections in the general region of the Ohio River, the central Mississippi River, and along the Appalachian Mountains.

8. _____ , also known as "valley fever," is caused by *C. immitis*, a fungus endemic in the southwestern United States, particularly the San Joaquin Valley.

LEARNING OBJECTIVE 11: Compare and contrast small-cell and nonsmall-cell carcinomas of the lung.

EXERCISE 10-25

Complete the paragraph below.

Lung cancer is the most common fatal cancer, and its most important risk factor is smoking. Lung cancers are sometimes called (1) _____ because they are malignancies of the bronchial epithelium. The major division for categorization of these carcinomas is into (2) _____ and (3) _____. This distinction is clinically crucial because these categories of carcinomas behave differently and are treated with different regimes (e.g., with chemotherapy for the very aggressive small-cell carcinoma and surgical excision for the relatively less aggressive, nonsmall-cell carcinomas). Small-cell carcinoma is most lethal, resists therapy, and is composed of distinctive small, dark cells that, although epithelial in nature, look much like large lymphocytes. Nonsmall-cell carcinomas have a variable appearance and can therefore be further subcategorized.

EXERCISE 10-26

Complete the table below.

Nonsmall Cell-Cancer Types	Location	Differentiation	Other Features
(1) _____	Peripheral	Most well differentiated	Formed into glandular structures
(2) _____	Central	Relatively well differentiated	Starts as squamous metaplasia then dysplasia; differentiates toward squamous epithelium similar to skin, mouth, esophagus, and vagina
(3) _____	Central	Lacks differentiation	Composed of large, fleshy, rounded or elongated cells
(4) _____	Most are central	Well-differentiated neuroendocrine cells	Not carcinoma; rarely, secrete vasoactive amines that cause systemic flushing, tachycardia, diarrhea, and cyanosis, or other hormones (paraneoplastic syndrome)

EXERCISE 10-27   PATHOLOGY AS A SECOND LANGUAGE

See Exercises 10-25 and 10-26 for key terms covered in this section.

LEARNING OBJECTIVE 12: Identify the potential substances that might be found in the pleural space, and the consequences of their accumulation.

EXERCISE 10-28

Complete the paragraph below.

The pleural space is a potential space between the parietal pleura of the chest wall and the visceral pleura covering the lung into which various substances can enter. When air enters the pleural space it is called a (1) _____. This may occur spontaneously in young adult smokers, but it more often occurs in patients with emphysema who have pleural "blebs." A (2) _____ is a potentially life-threatening condition. The accumulation of fluid in the pleural space is called a (3) _____.

EXERCISE 10-29 PATHOLOGY AS A SECOND LANGUAGE

Test your vocabulary by indicating if each statement below is true or false. If it is false, provide the correct word for the italicized term that will make the statement true.

_____ 1. Pleural inflammation causes sharp pain on breathing and is called *pleuritis*.

_____

_____ 2. *Inflammatory exudates* have a high protein and cellular content.

_____

_____ 3. Thin, noninflammatory pleural effusion can also be called *suppurative effusions*.

_____

_____ 4. *Hemothorax* is when whole blood expands the pleural space.

_____

_____ 5. *Mesenchymal hamartoma* is a rare malignancy of the pleura that is a late complication of inhalation of asbestos fibers.

_____

Decisions Decisions

DECISION TREE 10.1: PULMONARY DISEASE

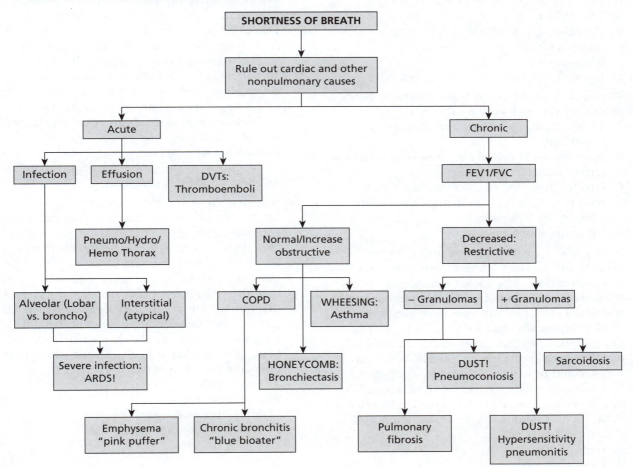

Test Yourself

I. MULTIPLE CHOICE

1. A 19-year-old college student presents to the free clinic complaining of congestion with clear watery nasal discharge and fever of three days duration. He denies yellow, purulent mucous, ear and sinus pain, itchy watery eyes, and sneezing. What is your diagnosis? [LEARNING OBJECTIVE 3]
   A. Antibiotics
   B. Acute sinusitis
   C. Allergic rhinitis
   D. Infectious rhinitis

2. Bronchioles are composed of which of the following? [LEARNING OBJECTIVE 1]
   A. Smooth muscle, epithelium, and mucous glands
   B. Smooth muscle and epithelium
   C. Cartilage, mucous glands, and smooth muscle
   D. Epithelium only

3. A 63-year-old Caucasian male presents to the ER complaining of bloody sputum. His past medical history is notable for two recent bouts of pneumonia over the last three months. A review of systems is remarkable for a 20 lb weight loss, flushing, and diarrhea. What do you expect to find on biopsy? [LEARNING OBJECTIVE 11]
   A. Glandular acini
   B. Dysplastic flat squamous epithelium
   C. Small, dark cells that look like large lymphocytes
   D. Large, fleshy, rounded or elongated cells

4. Which of the following is true concerning lung abscesses? [LEARNING OBJECTIVE 10]
   A. They are a complication of aspiration pneumonia.
   B. Approximately half of lung abscesses contain anaerobic bacteria.
   C. Greater than 90% of abscesses found in the mouth contain bacteria that do not usually infect other body sites.
   D. All of the above are true.

5. A 16-year-old Hispanic female arrives in the ER via ambulance. The EMS team tells you she was in a car accident, where a second vehicle struck the driver's side. On the scene, she was minimally responsive, but intermittently complaining of chest pain; she also had a decreased O_2 saturation. A quick physical exam reveals diminished breath sounds in the left lung fields. While an X-ray would be diagnostic, you are confident that a broken rib has caused her findings and quickly insert a needle beneath the left fourth rib. What life-threatening diagnosis did you make? [LEARNING OBJECTIVE 12]
   A. Hydrothorax
   B. Pneumothorax
   C. Hemothorax
   D. Pleuritis

6. What type of atelectasis is the patient described in question number 5 at risk for had a needle not been inserted? [LEARNING OBJECTIVE 4]
   A. Contraction atelectasis
   B. Compression atelectasis
   C. Resorption atelectasis
   D. Obstructive atelectasis

7. A 75-year-old African American female is brought to the physician's office by her grandson, who is concerned by his grandmother's high fever, shaking chills, and cough productive of copious yellow sputum. Her physical exam is notable for diminished breath sounds and crackles in the left lower lobe. A chest X-ray demonstrates a solidified, airless, left lower lobe. Which of the following types of pneumonia is the most likely diagnosis? [LEARNING OBJECTIVE 10]
   A. Lobar pneumonia
   B. Interstitial pneumonia
   C. Bronchopneumonia
   D. Aspiration pneumonia

8. Which of the following statements regarding carcinoma of the larynx is true? [LEARNING OBJECTIVE 3]
   A. Laryngeal carcinoma develops through progressive stages of hyperplasia, dysplasia, carcinoma in situ, and invasive carcinoma.
   B. Alcohol, smoking, and HPV infection are the leading causes of laryngeal carcinoma.
   C. Most laryngeal cancers are widely metastatic at the time of diagnosis.
   D. Patients with laryngeal carcinoma have a poor prognosis, as the tumor does not respond to chemotherapy or radiation.

9. A 19-year-old Caucasian male working as a ranch hand at a local farm visits your practice complaining of another flu-like illness (malaise, chest tightness, cough, and fever), his third in the month since beginning his internship. When questioned about exacerbating factors, he notes that his symptoms seem worse after working in the drafty hay barn. A chest X-ray demonstrates ground-glass density in the lower and middle lung zones. You prescribe abstinence from the barn, as moldy hay is likely causing which of the following illnesses? [LEARNING OBJECTIVE 8]
   A. Sarcoidosis
   B. Pneumoconiosis
   C. Idiopathic pulmonary fibrosis
   D. Hypersensitivity pneumonitis

10. Which of the following causes hemodynamic edema? [LEARNING OBJECTIVE 5]
    A. Left-heart failure
    B. Septicemia
    C. Intravenous drug abuse
    D. Toxic inhalation injury

11. A 43-year-old morbidly obese African American male presents for evaluation of his chronic fatigue. He reports that in addition to his fatigue, he has had increasing difficulty staying awake at work. Incidentally, his wife has requested that something also be done about his snoring. After a normal spirometry test, you recommend a sleep study to confirm which of the following diagnoses? [LEARNING OBJECTIVE 7]
    A. Emphysema
    B. Chronic bronchitis
    C. Obstructive sleep apnea
    D. Asthma

12. Which of the types of lung cancer is the most common in nonsmokers? [LEARNING OBJECTIVE 11]
    A. Adenocarcinoma
    B. Small-cell carcinoma
    C. Squamous cell carcinoma
    D. Large-cell carcinoma

13. Your daughter and her friend are playing with your new kitten on the living room floor when you notice that her friend starts coughing and wheezing. Despite their protests, you immediately remove the kitten and place it in another room. When her mother comes to pick her up, you recommend that her daughter be tested for what type of asthma? [LEARNING OBJECTIVE 7]
    A. Nonatopic asthma
    B. Atopic asthma
    C. Reactive asthma
    D. Occupational asthma

14. Which of the following statements concerning Coccidioidomycosis is true? [LEARNING OBJECTIVE 10]
    A. Infection with Coccidioidomycosis is known as "valley fever."
    B. Many people are infected but few become diseased.
    C. Coccidioidomycosis is an endemic fungus in the western United States.
    D. All of the above are true.

15. A 17-year-old high-school student visits the nurse's office complaining of a bloody nose (right) and a history of unilateral nasal obstruction on the same side. Examination of the right nostril reveals an exophytic, cauliflower-like growth. You recommend that the lesion be removed as it may transform into squamous cell carcinoma.

What lesion has caused his nasal obstruction? [LEARNING OBJECTIVE 3]
    A. Mucocele
    B. Cartilage nodules
    C. Sinonasal papilloma
    D. Nasal polyps

16. Which of these is critical in separating obstructive versus restrictive disease? [LEARNING OBJECTIVE 2]
    A. FVC
    B. FEV1
    C. FVC/FEV1
    D. VEF1/FVC

II. TRUE OR FALSE

17. _____ The single main function of the lower respiratory tract is to oxygenate blood. [LEARNING OBJECTIVE 1]

18. _____ The cause of approximately 15% of idiopathic pulmonary fibrosis is due to a genetic defect in the maintenance of telomeres. [LEARNING OBJECTIVE 8]

19. _____ Both obstructive and restrictive disease limit CO_2 and O_2 exchange. [LEARNING OBJECTIVE 2]

20. _____ Pneumonia caused by one microbe renders the lungs vulnerable to superinfection by another microbe. [LEARNING OBJECTIVE 10]

21. _____ Lung volume is not affected in obstructive lung disease. [LEARNING OBJECTIVE 7]

22. _____ Anthracosis, caused by the inhalation of rock or stone dust, is the most common chronic occupational disease in the world. [LEARNING OBJECTIVE 8]

23. _____ A hemothorax is caused by trauma and should be treated by immediate drainage of the fluid (no analysis required). [LEARNING OBJECTIVE 12]

III. MATCHING

24. Match the following infectious organisms to the type of pneumonia they cause. Answers may be used more than once.
    i. Community-acquired pneumonia
    ii. Nosocomial pneumonia
    iii. Aspiration pneumonia
    iv. Chronic pneumonia
    v. Pneumonia in the immunodeficient host
    vi. Interstitial pneumonia

    A. Anaerobic oral flora
    B. *Staphylococci, streptococci, H. influenza*
    C. *E. coli, Pseudomonas, Methicillin-resistant Staphylococcus aureus, vancomycin-resistant Enterococcus*
    D. *Pneumocystis,* cytomegalovirus
    E. *Chlamydia, mycoplasma*
    F. Histoplasma, *Blastomyces,* or *Coccidioides, Candida,* and *Cryptococcus*

IV. SHORT ANSWER

25. A 65-year-old African American male without a significant past medical history presents to your office complaining of shortness of breath. He is notably hunched forward while in a seated position, with his hands on his knees and his elbows spread out. He is barrel chested with neck muscles that bulge with each breath through pursed lips. He admits to a 75 pack-year smoking history. Discuss the pathogenesis of his disease, and your recommendations for his treatment. [LEARNING OBJECTIVE 7]

_____

_____

_____

26. What defense systems does the respiratory system employ to protect itself from the environment? [LEARNING OBJECTIVE 1]

_____

_____

_____

27. What factors predispose a patient to thromboemboli and what are the prophylactic measures that can be employed in their prevention? [LEARNING OBJECTIVE 9]

_____

_____

_____

28. What are the possible causes of heavy, dark, airless, wet lungs filled with edema on autopsy and seen as "white lungs" on chest X-ray? [LEARNING OBJECTIVE 6]

_____

_____

_____

29. Bronchiectasis, a secondary condition owing to both infection and obstruction, can be the result of what underlying disorders? [LEARNING OBJECTIVE 7]

_____

_____

_____

Disorders of the Gastrointestinal Tract

The Big Picture

The digestive system consists of the gastrointestinal tract (the "tubular gut"), the liver, and the pancreas. The gastrointestinal tract has critical functions that include absorbing nutrients and acting as a barrier to the outside world (with immune protection as well). Diseases occur with the breakdown of these critical functions (e.g., diarrhea and/or infection). In addition, the gastrointestinal tract is contiguous with the outside world and thus exposed to metabolic/environmental toxins and prone to neoplasia, including esophageal, stomach, and colon cancer.

Oh No! Not Another Learning Experience

LEARNING OBJECTIVE 1: Explain how the organs of the gastrointestinal system perform its six functions.

EXERCISE 11-1

Complete the paragraphs below.

The first of the GI system's six functions is (1) _____ (the intake of food into the oral cavity, which incidentally requires hunger). Food that is taken in must be broken down into smaller pieces by digestion, of which there are two types. (2) _____ digestion is the tearing, mashing, cutting, and churning of food by teeth and GI muscles (especially the mouth and stomach), while (3) _____ digestion is the cleaving of large food molecules into smaller ones by the selective release of fluids—mainly water, acids, buffers, and enzymes from the salivary glands, liver, gallbladder, and pancreas (the role of each of the enzymes is addressed in additional detail in the table that follows). Thus, (4) _____, the selective release of fluids, is another function of the GI system. Notably, some of these fluids also serve to lubricate the GI tract, aid in absorption, and protect the wall of the digestive tract.

Following the breakdown of foodstuff by digestion, the small nutrient molecules are taken up from the lumen of the GI tract through gut epithelium and transferred to the blood or lymph by (5) _____, while the remnants of compacted indigestible food material, bacteria, and shed epithelial cells are removed by the body via (6) _____. From the beginning of the GI tract to end, the foodstuffs, nutrients, and waste products are propelled by muscular contractions, which is the final function of the GI tract, (7) _____.

It is important to note that the organization of the GI tract influences its ability to perform various functions. Digestion and absorption are both dependent on the properties particular to that area of the GI system. Cells of the GI tract mucosa may be (8) _____ in nature, allowing the easy passage of food, or (9) _____, conducive to digestion or absorption, which is further aided by the organization of lower GI tissue into smaller and smaller infoldings: plica → villi → (10) _____ (the smallest infoldings). Enzymes are localized and under neuronal (enteric plexus) and/or hormonal control (see the table that follows). Further, an interesting balance is struck between preventing infection ([11] _____ tissue paints the GI tract with (12) _____ antibodies), and symbiosis with bacteria, which produce significant amounts of vitamin (13) _____ and folic acid.

EXERCISE 11-2

Complete the following table.

Enzyme	Important Locations	Function
Amylase	Saliva, pancreas	Breaks down (1) _____
Bile	Liver, gallbladder, absorbed in ileum (bile salts)	(2) _____
Gastric Acid	(3) _____	Activates digestive enzymes (composed of hydrochloric acid)
Lipase	Saliva, stomach, pancreas, liver	Breaks down triglycerides into (4) _____ and (5) _____
Protease	(6) _____	Breaks down proteins
Pepsin	(7) _____	Breaks down proteins
Saccharidases (e.g., Lactase)	Small Intestine	Breaks down (8) _____

EXERCISE 11-3

Complete the following table.

Table 11.1 Chemical and Neural Signals Involved in Digestion

Hormone signal	Origin	Stimulus	Action
(1) _____	G cells	Proteins/peptides in stomach	Stimulates secretion of hydrochloric acid
Gastric inhibitory peptide	K cells	(2) _____ in small intestine	Stimulates release of insulin; inhibits secretion of hydrochloric acid
Insulin	Beta-cells	Increased blood glucose	Stimulates uptake of glucose in muscle and adipose
Pepsinogen	(3) _____	Hydrochloric acid	Converted to pepsin, which digests protein
Cholecystokinin	I cells	Fat and protein in duodenum	Slows gastric motility; stimulates release of (4) _____ (from gallbladder) and pancreatic enzymes
(5) _____	S cells	Acidic (6) _____ in duodenum	Stimulates release of bicarbonate

Neural signal	Route	Stimulus	Action
Parasympathetic	(7) _____	Sight, smell, taste, or thought of food	Stimulates secretions and peristalsis
Sympathetic	Multiple routes	Stress	(8) _____ secretions and peristalsis
(9) _____	Local, within bowel wall	Multiple	Modulates secretions and peristalsis

EXERCISE 11-4   PATHOLOGY AS A SECOND LANGUAGE

Test your vocabulary by writing the appropriate term in each blank from the list below.

GI tract	Abdominal cavity	Enterogastric Reflex
Enteric Nervous System	Peritoneum	Hydrolysis
Chyme	Mesentery	Parietal peritoneum
Visceral peritoneum	Peritoneal fluid	Triglyceride
Chylomicron	Cholesterol	Peritoneal space

1. Consists of the mouth, teeth, and tongue; the pharynx; the esophagus; the stomach; and the small and large bowel; digests and absorbs food _____

2. Myenteric and submucosal nerve plexus _____

3. Mixed food and secretions _____

4. Translucent membrane composed of flat (squamous) epithelial cells _____

5. Portion of peritoneum that folds over the abdominal organs _____

6. Portion of peritoneum that lines the interior abdominal wall _____

7. Fluid filling the peritoneal space _____

8. Space between the parietal and visceral peritoneum _____

9. Space bound by parietal peritoneum, contains organs and peritoneal space _____

10. Two layers of peritoneum that envelop vessels, nerves, and adipose tissue _____

11. Space behind the peritoneum in the abdominal cavity _____

12. Molecules broken down by their interaction with water _____

13. A molecule of glycerol attached to three long-chain fatty acids _____

14. Protein and phospholipid coated spheres containing triglyceride _____

15. Lipid absorbed by the intestinal epithelium _____

16. Parasympathetic reflex activated by chyme entering the duodenum _____

LEARNING OBJECTIVE 2: Describe the various signs and symptoms of GI disease including: anorexia, nausea, emesis, diarrhea, dysentery, steatorrhea, belching, flatulence, constipation, bleeding, and obstruction.

EXERCISE 11-5

Complete the paragraphs below.

Gastrointestinal disease can have very complex symptoms, in part because it may involve almost any anatomic location within the tubular gut or the accessory organs (i.e., the liver and the pancreas). Conversely, anything that causes belly pain could be erroneously construed as being a symptom from the GI tract.

(1) _____ is lack of appetite and a frequent sign of gastric or intestinal disease causing inflammation or irritation, including infections or neoplasia. (2) _____ is difficulty swallowing and is the most common sign of esophageal or neuromuscular disease (see Decision Tree 11.1 later in this chapter for more information). (3) _____ is an unpleasant sensation with an urge to vomit (emesis, a refluxive forceful ejection of contents from the stomach caused by many, many things). Vomitus characteristics are important: undigested stomach contents indicate gastric origin; yellow or green vomitus indicates the presence of duodenal (4) _____; dark brown vomitus suggests origin from below the duodenum (think feces); coffee grounds or red vomitus indicate (5) _____.

(6) _____ and (7) _____ is air/gas, either direction. (8) _____ is very hard to define but is basically too much, too loose, or too many feces. (9) _____ is bloody diarrhea, while (10) _____ is fatty diarrhea (it floats) (see Decision Tree 11.2 for more information about diarrhea).

(11) _____, the opposite of diarrhea, is difficulty passing stool and is usually associated with compacted, dry, hard fecal matter, which can become (12) _____, requiring intervention to facilitate its passage. If (13) _____ occurs, that is no gas in addition to no feces, one should think paralytic ileus (with air-fluid levels in the bowels), which can be caused by surgery, intra-abdominal inflammation, ischemia, or hypokalemia (see Decision Tree 11.3 for more information on constipation and obstipation).

EXERCISE 11-6   PATHOLOGY AS A SECOND LANGUAGE

Test your vocabulary by completing the following using the terms in the list below.

Upper GI	Lower GI	Melena
Hematemesis	Hematochezia	

(1) _____ bleeding is bleeding from the esophagus, stomach, or first few centimeters of the duodenum

Bloody vomitus is a type of bleeding termed (2) _____.

(3) _____ bleeding is bleeding occurring past the first few centimeters of the duodenum

Dark tarry stool is a type of bleeding termed (4) _____.

Red blood in the stool is a type of bleeding termed (5) _____.

EXERCISE 11-7   PATHOLOGY AS A SECOND LANGUAGE

Test your vocabulary by indicating if each statement below is true or false. If it is false, provide the correct word for the italicized term that will make the statement true.

____ 1. *Occult bleeding* is bleeding not visible to naked eye.

_____

____ 2. *Asphyxiated her*nia is an ischemic or infarcted hernia.

_____

_____ 3. *Ileus* is intestinal paralysis (lack of peristalsis).

_____

_____ 4. *Material obstruction* is caused by physical obstruction of bowels.

_____

_____ 5. *Adhesions* are bands of fibrous tissue caused by abdominal surgery, infection, or other inflammatory conditions, which can cause loops of bowel to become entangled, trapped, and obstructed.

_____

_____ 6. *Volvulus* is the telescoping of bowel, in which the distal (downstream) segment swallows the proximal one.

_____

_____ 7. *Intussusception* is the twisting of a segment of bowel on its pedicle.

_____

_____ 8. A hernia that is entrapped is called an *incarcerated hernia*.

_____

_____ 9. A *hernia* is a protrusion of anatomy through a dilated space.

_____

Mnemonic

When you see VOLVulus, think reVOLVe. It revolves around the pedicle.

LEARNING OBJECTIVE 3: Name and describe the lesions that can affect the oral cavity, including malformations, tooth loss, ulcers, autoimmune disease, and cancer.

EXERCISE 11-8

Complete the paragraphs below.

(1) _____ and (2) _____ are related congenital malformations that cause a gap near the midline in the lip and/or palate respectively, and make feeding difficult.

Bacteria, which cause (3) _____ (cavities), (4) _____ (inflammation of the gums), (5) _____ (deeper inflammation and infection of soft tissues around the tooth root), and (6) _____, can accumulate on teeth as a (7) _____ that calcifies as (8) _____.

(9) _____ (small, painful, shallow ulcers) in the mouth are common and have many etiologies, but can indicate more serious disease, such as Crohn disease. However, one should be careful not to confuse them with (10) _____ ,an infectious cause of multiple shallow ulcers.

(11) _____ of the mouth (also called *thrush*) is a fungal infection (*Candida albicans*) that can indicate that the patient is immunosuppressed.

(12) _____ is an autoimmune disorder that attacks the salivary glands and lacrimal glands, causing dry eyes and mouth. It is but one cause of (13) _____ (inflammation of salivary glands).

(14) _____ is a clinical term that refers to a small white patch of oral mucosa, and may indicate a precancerous lesion, that, if left untreated could lead to (15) _____ (an epithelial cell malignancy). These can occur anywhere in the mouth or on the lips (usually lower) and are typically associated with poor oral hygiene, alcohol abuse, and tobacco use.

Finally, (16) _____, a predominately benign neoplasm, may occur in the salivary glands.

EXERCISE 11-9   PATHOLOGY AS A SECOND LANGUAGE

See Exercise 11-8 for key terms covered in this section.

LEARNING OBJECTIVE 4: Compare and contrast esophageal adenocarcinoma with squamous cell carcinoma.

EXERCISE 11-10

Complete the paragraph below.

(1) _____ accounts for about 4% of malignant neoplasms in the United States. Approximately

(2) _____ % are *squamous cell carcinomas* of the mid or upper esophagus, and (3) _____ % are *adeno-*

carcinomas that arise near the gastroesophageal junction and are strongly associated with chronic (4) _____

(chronic reflux is responsible for the rapidly increasing incidence of esophageal adenocarcinoma). Prognosis is based

on (5) _____, however, esophageal adenocarcinomas are often discovered at (6) _____ and have a poor

prognosis. Key features of each are covered in the table that follows (see Decision Tree 11.1 for additional insights).

> **Remember This!** The best indicator of future behavior is past behavior.
> If a tumor is already large, has invaded the lymph nodes, or can be found elsewhere
> in the body, it does not bode well for the future of the patient!

EXERCISE 11-11

Complete the table below.

	Squamous Cell Carcinoma	**Esophageal Adenocarcinoma**
Risk factors	Male, heavy (1) _____ use, African American, (2) _____	(3) _____, obesity, Caucasian, male
Trends	Steady or decreasing incidence	Rapidly (4) _____ incidence
Precursor lesions	Squamous dysplasia	(5) _____ (intestinal metaplasia), glandular dysplasia
Location	(6) _____ esophagus	(7) _____ esophagus (GE junction)
Treatment	Radiation and surgical intervention	Ablate Barrett esophagus to prevent progression; surgically resect adenocarcinoma

Mnemonic
bARRett

A= adenocarcinoma, RR= results from reflux.

EXERCISE 11-12   PATHOLOGY AS A SECOND LANGUAGE

Test your vocabulary by writing the appropriate term in each blank from the list below.

Esophageal varices	Esophagitis	Mallory Weiss Syndrome
Achalasia	Atresia	Hiatal hernia GERD

1. Protrusion of part of the stomach superiorly into the chest through the esophageal hiatus, which can lead to reflux. _____

2. Spasm of lower esophageal sphincter due to lack of autonomic ganglion cells. _____

3. Absence/narrowing of a passage, +/− obstruction (in the esophagus, may connect to the trachea, i.e. tracheoesophageal fistula). _____

4. Esophageal (or gastric) laceration, which may be caused by severe and frequent retching or vomiting, as in bulimia. _____

5. Dilated esophageal veins, full of blood. Usually secondary to cirrhosis. May rupture and cause life-threatening bleeding. _____

6. Inflammation of the esophagus. _____

LEARNING OBJECTIVE 5: Discuss the manifestations and treatment options for the following stomach (gastric) diseases: pyloric stenosis, bleeding gastric erosions, autoimmune gastritis, chronic peptic ulceration, Helicobacter pylori infection, and stomach cancer including lymphoma.

EXERCISE 11-13

Complete the paragraphs below.

(1) _____ is obstruction of the stomach outlet due to hypertrophy of the sphincter muscle, causing

(2) _____ vomiting (nonbilious) shortly after eating. The diagnosis is confirmed on ultrasound, and surgery to incise the hypertrophic muscle is the treatment.

(3) Complaints of _____ (gastric discomfort/pain) should prompt a history and physical to determine whether the patient may have gastritis or ulcers. (4) _____ is a transient inflammation of the gastric mucosa without ulceration, and can be due to drugs, alcohol, or other chemicals. (5) _____ is more severe with erosions (superficial) and ulcers (deep). Ulcers due to stress (e.g., burns or trauma) are called (6) _____, while those due to brain trauma or tumor are called (7) _____.

In contrast, **chronic gastritis** is usually caused by (8) _____ (over 90% of cases) or by (9) _____ (aka *pernicious anemia*). H. Pylori is also known to cause (10) _____ (a usually solitary deep defect of gastric, duodenal, or esophageal mucosa). *H. pylori* infection is confirmed by blood tests, (11) _____ tests (to detect urease), or a biopsy showing the bacteria; it is treated with a multiple antibiotic regimen. In auto-immune gastritis, autoantibodies attack the (12) _____ of the gastric epithelium, thereby reducing pro-duction of hydrochloric acid and (13) _____, which is important for the eventual absorption of vitamin B_{12} in the small intestine. B_{12} deficiency leads to anemia. Patients whose ulcers are resistant to treatment should be tested to rule out (14) _____ (a pancreatic islet tumor that secretes gastrin, thereby increasing gastric acid).

Gastric cancer includes (15) _____ and (16) _____ (usually so-called MALT lymphomas, Mucosa Associated Lymphoid Tissue). Amazingly, both of these cancers are associated with chronic *H. pylori* infection. Treatment of gastric adenocarcinoma includes chemotherapy and resection; whereas, treatment of MALT lymphoma associated with *H. pylori* may just require eradication of the organism.

EXERCISE 11-14 PATHOLOGY AS A SECOND LANGUAGE

See Exercise 11-13 for key terms covered in this section.

LEARNING OBJECTIVE 6: Define the following congenital anomalies of the small and large intestines: Meckel diverticulum, omphalocele, gastroschisis, Hirschsprung megacolon.

EXERCISE 11-15

Complete the paragraphs below.

(1) _____ is a small, blind pouch opening into the distal ileum, present in about 2% of the population.

(2) _____ is a midline congenital defect in which herniated viscera are covered by a thin peritoneal membrane, whereas (3) _____ is a related, larger defect in which the intestines and other viscera protrude through the abdominal wall with no membrane covering.

The most common defect is (4) _____ due to the absence of the (5) _____ neurons in the smooth muscle of the colon wall, usually near the rectum, impeding passage of bowel contents.

Mnemonic

Gastroschisis: usual location Gas**TR**osc**HI**sis usually occurs on the **RIGHT** side of the umbilicus. (while omphalocele is midline)

Mnemonic

Cele = chamber, Omphalocele is contained in a chamber (surrounded by a sac)!

EXERCISE 11-16 PATHOLOGY AS A SECOND LANGUAGE

Test your vocabulary by determining whether the following statements are true or false.

_____ 1. Partial obstruction is referred to as stenosis.

_____ 2. Atresia is the absence or narrowing of a passage, with/without obstruction.

_____ 3. An umbilical hernia is a finger-sized opening in the abdominal wall at the umbilicus.

LEARNING OBJECTIVE 7: Define ischemic vascular disease and hemorrhoids.

EXERCISE 11-17

Complete the paragraph below.

(1) _____ includes chronic ischemia, which produces few symptoms, or acute ischemia, caused by blockade of (2) _____ due to thrombosis, embolism, or vasculitis, or by the twisting of bowel loops ([3] _____) or incarceration and strangulation in a hernia sac, or intussusception (in localized areas).

(4) _____ are dilated anal veins (*varices*) and can be located within the anal canal (*internal hemorrhoids*) *or* outside the anal canal (*external hemorrhoids*). Sometimes these become very painful or bloody and require surgical removal.

EXERCISE 11-18 PATHOLOGY AS A SECOND LANGUAGE

Test your vocabulary by determining whether the following statement is true or false.

_____ 1. Angiodysplasia is a tortuous collection of small blood vessels in the mucosa or submucosa of the ascending colon or cecum.

LEARNING OBJECTIVE 8: Discuss the pathogenesis and manifestations of the viruses, bacteria, and protozoa responsible for causing infections of the bowel.

EXERCISE 11-19

Complete the paragraphs below.

GI infections are extraordinarily common. Most GI infections involve the small and large bowel, and not the stomach, with the result that the term *enterocolitis* is probably better than the term *gastroenteritis*, although both are used. (1) _____ refers to inflammation of stomach lining, as well as the lining of the small and large intestines.

Viruses and bacteria, which cause most cases in the developed world, tend to produce (2) _____ illness; parasites and protozoa, which cause most cases in developing nations, are often associated with (3) _____ or recurrent disease.

(4) _____ (common in daycare) and (5) _____ (common on cruise ships) are the main causes of acute viral gastroenteritis in the United States. Though less common than viral gastroenteritis, (6) _____ (inflammation owing to bacteria, see the table that follows for additional information) is frequently more severe and protracted, often causing bloody diarrhea. Bacteria cause gastroenteritis by several mechanisms including:

- Ingested (7) _____ from contaminated food (e.g., unrefrigerated potato salad)directly damages the intestinal epithelium. Exotoxins generally cause acute nausea, vomiting, and diarrhea within a few hours of ingestion.

- (8) _____ produced within the GI tract (e.g., *Vibrio cholera*, the agent of *cholera*, which adheres to the intestinal mucosa and produces enterotoxins that impair intestinal absorption and cause secretion of electrolytes and water leading to potentially lethal watery diarrhea). (9) _____ the agent of *pseudomembranous colitis* (discussed shortly) produces a similar toxin.

- Other bacteria (e.g., *Shigella*, *Salmonella*, *Campylobacter*, and some species of *E. coli*) cause diarrhea by actually invading the mucosa of the small intestine or colon, and cause ulceration, bleeding, and secretion of electrolytes and water.

  These bacteria are the most common in the United States.

  The gold standard for diagnosis of bacterial infection is (10) _____;, however, immunologic tests of stool for toxins and PCR for pathogen DNA (or RNA) are widely used as well. These newer tests are much faster, but are testing for something different than live organisms. Supportive care with or without antibiotic therapy is usually effective.

Important protozoa include the following three organisms. *E. histolytica*, the cause of (11) _____, burrows deeply into the colonic wall, and in about half of cases spreads up the portal vein to the liver to produce hepatic amebic abscesses. (12) _____, a noninvasive protozoan, mainly affects the duodenum and small bowel and may produce an acute diarrhea or a chronic malabsorption. *Cryptosporidium*, can cause gastroenteritis in any population group, but both *Cryptosporidium* and *Giardia* are common causes of (13) _____ in immunodeficient patients (e.g., those with HIV/AIDS).

Mnemonic

Exo = outside, the toxins were formed outside the body and ingested. Endo = inner, the toxins were formed inside the body.

EXERCISE 11-20

Complete the table below.

Table 11-4

	Agent	Name of disease caused/ characteristics
Rotavirus	Virus	#1 young children; fecal contamination
Norwalk virus	Virus	Older children, adults, common on (1) _____; 1–3 days nausea, vomiting, diarrhea; Supportive therapy
Staphylococci	Bacteria	Enterotoxin formed (2) _____ body
E. coli	Bacteria	Enterotoxin formed in the body, normal inhabitant, but some pathogenic strains; (3) _____ **diarrhea** (*Enterotoxigenic E. coli*): watery **Enterohemorrhagic** (O157:H7): bloody diarrhea
Vibrio cholerae	Bacteria	**Cholera**: Enterotoxin formed in the body
Salmonella	Bacteria	Transmitted by contaminated food/drink; **Salmonellosis**: sudden fever, chills, nausea, vomiting, diarrhea, dx by stool culture (caused by (4) _____) **Typhoid fever**: slow onset, fever, headache, sore throat, splenomegaly, bloating, constipation (caused by (5) _____); **Chronic infection, bacteremia, infection of bones, joints, heart, pericardium, or lungs** Antibiotics, vaccine available
Shigella	Bacteria	**Shigellosis** (*Bacillary dysentery*)
Campylobacter jejuni	Bacteria	(6) _____: bloody diarrhea
C. difficile	Bacteria	**Pseudomembranous colitis**: Caused by (7) _____, which alters intestinal flora. Enterotoxin damages mucosa resulting in inflammatory exudate forming membrane, pus, and dead tissue.
Necrotizing enterocolitis	Bacteria	Affects immature or low birthweight infants; acute necrotizing (dead cells) inflammation of small bowel and colon; The cause is (8) _____.
Entamoeba histolytica	Protozoa	(9) _____: Spread by fecal/oral (food and water); burrows into wall and spreads up portal vein to liver; amebic abscesses
Giardia lamblia	Protozoa	(10) _____: Spread by food and water; noninvasive affecting duodenum and small bowel; acute diarrhea or chronic malabsorption
Cryptosporidium	Protozoa	Common in immunodeficient patients

EXERCISE 11-21   PATHOLOGY AS A SECOND LANGUAGE

See Exercises 11-19 and 11-20 for key terms covered in this section.

LEARNING OBJECTIVE 9: Among patients with malabsorption syndrome, distinguish between luminal and intestinal malabsorption.

EXERCISE 11-22

Complete the paragraphs below.

(1) _____ is the poor digestion or absorption of dietary substances with excess fecal excretion of nutrients. Signs and symptoms include diarrhea (possibly chronic), steatorrhea, bloating, gas, weight loss, dehydration, and mineral or vitamin deficiencies. Diagnosis may require fecal fat output, administration of (2) _____ (test in which low blood and urine levels suggest impaired mucosal function), or endoscopy +/− biopsy.

(3) _____ includes problems with the breakdown of fats, carbohydrates, and proteins within the lumen of the intestines. Examples include pancreatic disease such as the lack of lipase or (4) _____ (thickened pancreatic secretions block enzyme flow), liver or biliary disease (impaired fat emulsification), and alteration of gut bacteria (bacterial overgrowth). Abnormal anatomy, altered motility, or change of pH, or anything capable of promoting intestinal stasis, causes (5) _____, which leads to increased consumption of nutrient and bile salts, impairing fat absorption. Diagnosis is with endoscopic culture or a positive (6) _____ breath test.

(7) _____ can be caused by absence of enzymes within the epithelial cells (such as lactose intolerance, which is a (8) _____ intolerance), mucosal inflammation (such as Crohn and ulcerative colitis), immune reaction to dietary content (celiac sprue) or the transport of the molecules once absorbed (blocked lymphatic ducts by scar, tumor, or congenital defect). (9) _____ presents with excess gas and watery diarrhea after milk consumption, and is diagnosed by hydrogen breath test. Crohn and ulcerative colitis are discussed extensively below, but can also present with diarrhea and malabsorption. (10) _____ is a T-cell mediated mucosal inflammatory reaction to gluten, which produces villus atrophy resulting in bulky, soft, tan, malodorous stools. Additional findings such as *dermatitis herpetiformis* or an iron deficiency anemia may also point towards such a diagnosis, which is made following a small-bowel biopsy with demonstration of villus atrophy or the presence of antigluten antibodies (presence of this antibody rules out (11) _____, which has similar findings but is likely caused by infection).

(12) _____ causes malabsorption simply because there isn't enough intestine to absorb the meal!

Some diseases responsible for malabsorption fall under the heading of (13) _____ and include inflammatory bowel disease (as discussed above), chronic ischemia, amyloid deposits, radiation enteritis, etc.

Mnemonic
Celiac sprue gluten sensitive enteropathy: gluten-containing grains

Barley
Rye
Oats
Wheat

- Flattened intestinal villi of celiac sprue are smooth, like an eye**BROW**.

EXERCISE 11-23   PATHOLOGY AS A SECOND LANGUAGE

See Exercise 11-22 for key terms covered in this section.

LEARNING OBJECTIVE 10: Compare and contrast ulcerative colitis and Crohn disease, including the extraintestinal manifestations.

EXERCISE 11-24

Complete the following sentence.

Crohn disease and ulcerative colitis are both forms of (1) _____ (chronic colitis); however, they differ in their patterns. See the table that follows for additional information.

EXERCISE 11-25

Complete the table below.

Table 11-5

	Crohn Disease	**Ulcerative Colitis**
Affected areas	(1) _____ in GI tract, most often in terminal ileum	Left-sided or entire colon.
Pattern	"Skip areas" present between diseased segments ("patchy" enteritis/colitis).	(2) _____ involvement of the colon, beginning from rectum ("diffuse" colitis).
Histology	Inflammation involves full thickness of bowel wall ([3] _____).	Inflammation is usually confined to mucosa.
	Fissuring ulcers.	Pseudopolyps and ulcers.
	Granulomas relatively common.	No granulomas.
Fistulas	Yes	(4) _____
Fat/vitamin malabsorption	Yes	(5) _____
Malignant potential	Yes	Yes
Response to surgery	(6) _____	Good
Associated disease	Less risk (than UC) of PSC, colon cancer	Greater risk of PSC, colon cancer
Antibodies	Most pANCA negative	Most pANCA (7) _____

Mnemonic

CHRISTMAS Crohn

Cobblestones
High temperature
Reduced lumen
Intestinal fistulae
Skip lesions
Transmural (all layers, may ulcerate)
Malabsorption
Abdominal pain
Submucosal fibrosis

EXERCISE 11-26   PATHOLOGY AS A SECOND LANGUAGE

Test your vocabulary by writing the appropriate term in each blank from the list below.

Ulcerative colitis   Inflammatory bowel disease
Crohn disease   Inflammatory bowel syndrome

1. Cell-mediate immune response that causes a chronic inflammation of mucosa at various sites in the GI tract. _____

2. Autoimmune inflammatory bowel disease that can affect any part of the bowel. _____

3. Autoimmune inflammatory bowel disease beginning in the rectum and moving proximally. _____

4. Combination of diarrhea and constipation that has no objective findings. _____

LEARNING OBJECTIVE 11: Explain the importance of non-neoplastic polyps of the colon, and their relationship to colonic carcinoma.

EXERCISE 11-27

Complete the paragraphs below.

Nonneoplastic polyps do not lead to colon cancer. These include very common (1) _____ which are heaped-up nonneoplastic accumulations of colon epithelium (hyperplasia) found in the colonic mucosa of elderly adults, and rare (2) _____ which are polypoid accumulations of disorganized, but otherwise normal, glands and stromal tissue normally present. (3) _____ can be a part of several familial syndromes (e.g., *Peutz-Jeghers syndrome)* that include a variety of other defects: skin, epithelial, neural and bone lesions; tumors in other organs; increased risk of cancer; and other features.

   In contrast, (4) _____ (or colonic adenomas) are neoplastic, precancerous growths of the colonic epithelium. They are more common in older patients and those on a high-fat, low fiber (read "Western") diet. These lesions lead to cancer if left untreated. They can be categorized as (5) _____ (abnormal crypt structures), (6) _____ (finger-like projections), or (7) _____ (both patterns). The larger the adenoma, the greater the chance of finding carcinoma.

EXERCISE 11-28   PATHOLOGY AS A SECOND LANGUAGE

Test your vocabulary by writing the appropriate term in each blank from the list below.

Polyp   Tubular Adenoma   Tubulovillous Adenoma

Villous Adenoma   Adenomatous Polyp

1. _____ is any polyp that has dysplasia and is a precursor to carcinoma.

2. _____ is a polyp made of dysplastic (precancerous) epithelium arranged in tubules.

3. _____ is any protrusion of the colonic mucosa that is identifiable by endoscopic examination and may or may not lead to cancer if untreated.

4. _____ is a polyp with hair-like or fingerlike projections and is usually large in size.

5. _____ is a polyp with a combination of tubules and hair-like projections.

EXERCISE 11-29   PATHOLOGY AS A SECOND LANGUAGE

Test your vocabulary by indicating if each statement below is true or false. If it is false, provide the correct word for the italicized term that will make the statement true.

_____ 1. *Hereditary Non-Polyposis Colorectal Carcinoma Syndrome* is an autosomal dominant genetic disorder characterized by colon cancer and cancer in multiple other organs.

_____

_____ 2. *Carcinoid* tumors of the GI tract derived from mesenchymal precursor cells in the intestinal wall.

_____

_____ 3. *Familial Adenomatous Polyposis Syndrome* is an autosomal dominant disorder with hundreds of polyps caused by defective APC gene.

_____

_____ 4. *Colon adenocarcinoma* is a gland-forming malignant neoplasm of colon epithelia.

_____

_____ 5. *Gastrointestinal stromal* tumors arise from neuroendocrine cells.

_____

LEARNING OBJECTIVE 12: Define diverticulosis, anal fissure, anorectal abscess, and anal fistula.

EXERCISE 11-30

Complete the paragraph below.

(1) _____ is characterized by multiple small outward protrusions (blind pouches, diverticula) of colonic mucosa through the muscular wall that arise at weak points where small (2) _____ penetrate from the external surface. When they become inflamed and infected with bacteria (and sometimes microperforate), the result is called (3) _____, which is characterized by fever and low, left-side abdominal pain. It should be treated with antibiotics; however, if there are repeated episodes, the affected section of colon may need to be resected. An (4) _____ is a longitudinal tear in the anal mucosa, whereas an (5) _____ is a collection of neutrophils (pus) that forms in an *anal crypt*. An (6) _____ is a tubular tract from the anus to some other surface, usually perianal skin, and may indicate an underlying condition such as Crohn disease.

EXERCISE 11-31 PATHOLOGY AS A SECOND LANGUAGE

Test your vocabulary by writing the appropriate term in each blank from the list below.

Proctitis	Rectitis	Pilonidal cyst
Rectal cyst	Analitis	Anal cyst

1. Blind pouch in the midline skin behind the anus near the coccyx. _____

2. Inflammation of the anal mucosa. _____

See Exercise 11-30 for additional key terms covered in this section.

LEARNING OBJECTIVE 13: Discuss the pathogenesis and manifestations of appendicitis.

EXERCISE 11-32

Complete the paragraph below.

(1) _____ is acute inflammation of the appendix caused by obstruction of the lumen by hyperplasia of lymphoid (MALT) patches in the mucosa, impacted feces ([2] _____, literally 'stone'), a foreign body, or intestinal parasitic worms. After obstruction, pressure increases behind the obstruction, decreasing blood flow into the appendix and causing edema, ischemia, necrosis, and bacterial overgrowth of the strangulated tissue. The inflammation cause acute abdominal pain in the (3) _____ (from generalized epigastric pain), fever, and leukocytosis. Treatment is an appendectomy.

> **Remember This!** Better safe than sorry. If you suspect appendicitis, even if you cannot prove it, that patient has likely just won a trip to the operating room.

EXERCISE 11-33 PATHOLOGY AS A SECOND LANGUAGE

Test your vocabulary by determining whether the following statements are true or false.

_____ 1. Peritoneal carcinomatosis is the widespread seeding of carcinomas of the abdominal or pelvic viscera on the surface of the peritoneum to cause a secondary form of cancer.

_____ 2. Inflammation of the peritoneum is called peritonitis.

Decisions Decisions

DECISION TREE 11.1: DYSPHAGIA

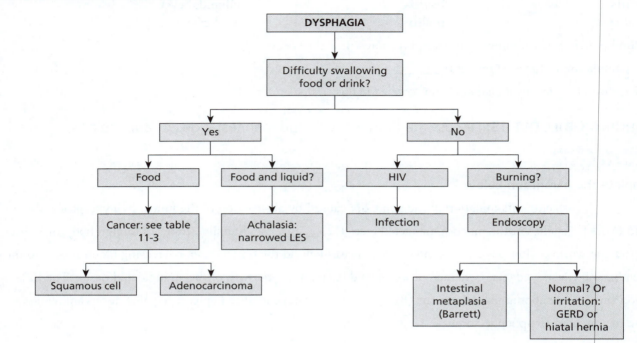

DECISION TREE 11.2: DIARRHEA

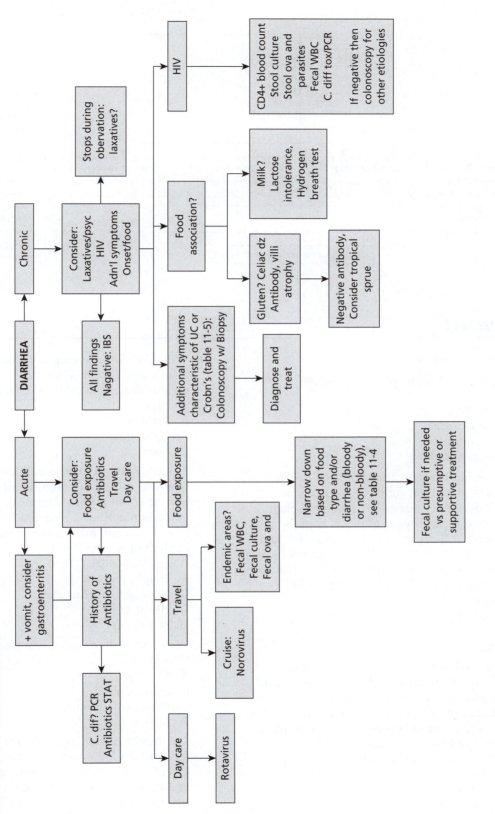

DECISION TREE 11.3: CONSTIPATION AND OBSTIPATION

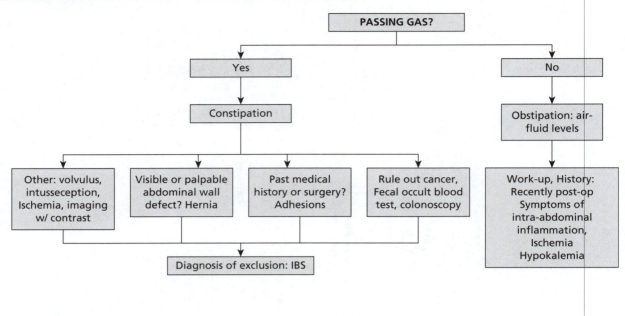

Test Yourself

I. MULTIPLE CHOICE

1. Where does the digestive process begin? [LEARNING OBJECTIVE 1]
   A. With saliva
   B. In the stomach
   C. In the intestine
   D. None of the above

2. A 32-year-old Hispanic male, post-op day 2, complains of nausea, vomiting, and lack of bowel movements and gas. His physical exam is notable for the absence of bowel sounds, and an abdominal X-ray reveals horizontal air-fluid interfaces within the bowel loops. From which of the following does your patient suffer? (Hint: Use Decision tree 11.3) [LEARNING OBJECTIVE 2]
   A. Volvulus
   B. Adhesion
   C. Ileus
   D. Hernia

3. A 60-year-old morbidly obese Caucasian male with a past medical history significant for chronic constipation (secondary to a low fiber diet) arrives in the ER complaining of left-sided abdominal pain. He also complains of a low-grade fever for the last 24 hours. A barium enema confirms your presumptive diagnosis of _____. [LEARNING OBJECTIVE 13]
   A. Diverticulosis
   B. Anal fistula
   C. Anorectal abscess
   D. Diverticulitis

4. Which of the following is a pancreatic enzyme responsible for breaking down fat, protein, or carbohydrates? [LEARNING OBJECTIVE 1]
   A. Lactase
   B. Amylase
   C. Bicarbonate
   D. Bile

5. A four-week-old male is brought to the ER for repeated episodes of vomiting. His mother reports that he vomits after every meal, and that the vomit is nonbilious, nonbloody. She denies fussiness, fever, and other complaints. An ultrasound confirms the diagnosis of _____. [LEARNING OBJECTIVE 4]
   A. Esophageal atresia
   B. Hirschsprung disease
   C. Hiatal hernia
   D. Pyloric stenosis

6. Which layer of the gastrointestinal tract contains the basement membrane? [LEARNING OBJECTIVE 1]
   A. Mucosa
   B. Submucosa
   C. Muscularis propria
   D. Serosa

7. Two hundred passengers aboard a cruise ship were quarantined following an outbreak of acute gastroenteritis characterized by vomiting and diarrhea of 3 days duration. Which of the following agents is likely responsible for this epidemic? (Hint: Use Decision Tree 11.2) [LEARNING OBJECTIVE 8]
   A. Campylobacter
   B. Rotavirus

C. Noroviris

D. Enterotoxigenic E. Coli

8. Which hormone is responsible for stimulating the secretion of hydrochloric acid? [LEARNING OBJECTIVE 1]

A. Gastrin

B. Gastric Inhibitory Peptide

C. Cholecystokinin

D. Secretin

9. A 63-year-old African American male with a past medical history significant for abdominal surgery presents with complaints of abdominal pain, vomiting, and constipation. He denies obstipation (he is passing gas). His physical exam is significant for hyperactive bowel sounds and the absence of an abdominal protrusion with increased abdominal pressure. What is the likely cause of his constipation? (Hint: Use Decision Tree 11.3) [LEARNING OBJECTIVE 2]

A. Volvulus

B. Ileus

C. Hernia

D. Adhesions

10. The patient reports dark tarry stools. You report to the doctor she has _____. [LEARNING OBJECTIVE 2]

A. Hematemesis

B. Hematochezia

C. Melena

D. Occult bleeding

11. A routine prenatal ultrasound reveals an abdominal defect of the fetus. She is delivered by C-section (due to fetal distress), and a large defect, with protrusion of the abdominal contents to the right of midline is observed. No membrane covers the protruding viscera. What is her diagnosis? [LEARNING OBJECTIVE 6]

A. Hirschsprung disease

B. Gastroschisis

C. Omphalocele

D. Hernia

12. A 35-year-old female presents to the clinic with a history of progressive dysphagia and esophageal pain. She reports that it is now causing difficulty swallowing food, and a sensation that food and now liquids are stuck. A barium swallow is done revealing a narrowing of the lower esophageal sphincter. What is your diagnosis? (Hint: Use Decision Tree 11.1) [LEARNING OBJECTIVE 4]

A. Gastroesophageal reflux disease

B. Hiatal hernia

C. Achalasia

D. Atresia

II. TRUE OR FALSE

13. _____ Plaque and tartar are both irritants, and their accumulation promotes dental caries, gingivitis, and ultimately periodontitis. [LEARNING OBJECTIVE 3]

14. _____ Appendicitis typically presents with the classic features of epigastric or periumbilical pain followed by nausea, vomiting, and anorexia. [LEARNING OBJECTIVE 11]

15. _____ Sialadenitis is always a result of the autoimmune disease Sjögren syndrome. [LEARNING OBJECTIVE 3]

16. _____ Autoimmune gastritis occurs when autoantibodies attack the parietal cells of the gastric epithelium and results in a B_6 deficiency anemia. [LEARNING OBJECTIVE 5]

17. _____ Angiodysplasia is a small, tortuous collection of small blood vessels found in the mucosa or submucosa of the ascending colon or cecum. [LEARNING OBJECTIVE 7]

18. _____ Lactose intolerance is diagnosed with a hydrogen breath test following a standardized dose of lactose. [LEARNING OBJECTIVE 9]

19. _____ Hereditary nonpolyposis colon cancer is due to a mutation in the APC gene. [LEARNING OBJECTIVE 12]

III. MATCHING

20. Match the following causes to their respective ulcers. [LEARNING OBJECTIVE 5]

    i. Aphthous ulcers

    ii. Herpesvirus

    iii. Curling ulcers

    iv. Cushing ulcers

    v. Peptic ulcers

A. Defects due to stress such as burns or other trauma

B. Deep defect of gastric, duodenal, or esophageal mucosa, usually solitary

C. A cluster of small vesicles that soon rupture, leaving a small painful ulcer

D. Defects owing to brain trauma or tumor

E. Small, painful, shallow ulcers of the oral cavity

21. Determine whether each of the following relates to one of the Crohn, Ulcerative colitis, or IBS. There may be more than one answer. [LEARNING OBJECTIVE 10]

    i. Crohn

    ii. Ulcerative colitis

    iii. IBS

A. Characterized by skip lesions

B. Transmural

C. Superficial

D. Fistulas are common

E. Bowel wall affected uniformly

F. No objective findings

G. Absence of granulomas

H. Diarrhea is a common symptom

I. Ankylosing spondylitis

IV. SHORT ANSWER

22. Beyond the cosmetic, what problems arise in children with a cleft lip or palate? [LEARNING OBJECTIVE 3]

_____

_____

_____

23. What serious complication may arise from infection with *enterohemorrhagic E. coli*, particularly the O157:H7 subtype? [LEARNING OBJECTIVE 8]

_____

_____

_____

24. Hematemesis in alcoholics can be caused by Mallory-Weiss syndrome or esophageal varices. How can you tell the two apart? [LEARNING OBJECTIVE 4]

_____

_____

_____

25. Despite medical treatment, as well as diet and lifestyle modifications, your patient's peptic ulcers persist. What disease should you consider, and how is it diagnosed? [LEARNING OBJECTIVE 5]

_____

_____

_____

Disorders of the Liver and Biliary Tract

CHAPTER
12

The Big Picture

The liver is critical for metabolism, detoxification, and synthesis of proteins, while the biliary tract is critical for handling bile acids, which are needed for absorption of dietary lipids. Chronic liver disease is caused by viruses, alcohol, autoimmunity, genetics, and other factors, which all can eventually lead to cirrhosis, or severe fibrosis of the liver. Cirrhosis predisposes to the most common primary liver malignancy, hepatocellular carcinoma.

Oh No! Not Another Learning Experience

LEARNING OBJECTIVE 1: Explain the function and structure of the liver circulatory systems.

EXERCISE 12-1

Complete the paragraph below.

The anatomy of the liver can be difficult to visualize. The functional anatomy of the liver has been described in terms of plates of hepatic cells arranged around the central vein called (1) _____, or as concentric zones surrounding the portal triads, called acini. The (2) _____ are composed of a branch of the hepatic artery bringing blood from the aorta, a portal vein carrying blood from the GI tract, and a small bile duct. Oxygenated blood flows from the aorta through the hepatic artery to the portal triads of the liver; blood also flows from the intestine to the liver via the portal vein whose terminal branches enter the portal triads. The blood entering the liver, therefore, begins at the portal triad, then flows through the (3) _____, large fenestrated capillaries between cords of hepatocytes, and toward the (4) _____, which connects to the inferior vena cava in order to return blood to the heart. Bile flows in the opposite direction, essentially starting from tiny (5) _____, which coalesce into small (6) _____ at the periphery of the lobule in the portal triads.

Mnemonic

Liver functions

PUSHDoG: Protein Synthesis, Urea Production, Storage, Hormone synthesis, Detoxification, Glucose and fat metabolism.

Mnemonic

The most common causes for increased bilirubin = **HOT Liver**: **H**emolysis, **O**bstruction, **T**umors, and **L**iver disease.

EXERCISE 12-2   PATHOLOGY AS A SECOND LANGUAGE

Test your vocabulary by filling in the terms that correspond to their appropriate structure in the image, and their corresponding definition below. Terms may be used once, more than once, or not at all.

Kupffer cells	Portal venous system	Common bile duct
Gallbladder	Jaundice	Icterus
Bilirubin	Bile	Bile acids

1. The _____ refers to a system where blood arises from one capillary bed (the intestine) and flows to a second capillary bed (the liver).

2. _____ is a mixture of metabolic waste and bile acids.

3. The _____ connects to the intestine at the ampulla of Vater in the duodenum.

4. The _____ stores bile until it is ready for release into the intestine.

5. _____ is an intensely yellow pigment, produced in the spleen from the hemoglobin of old red blood cells the spleen has removed from the circulation.

6. _____ is yellow discoloration of skin, while yellow discoloration of the sclera is called _____.

7. _____ emulsify fat, like soap does grease, blending it with water for absorption in the intestine.

8. Venous sinusoid walls contain fixed macrophages known as _____.

LEARNING OBJECTIVE 2: Discuss the complications associated with liver injury.

EXERCISE 12-3

Complete the paragraph below.

Most liver disease is chronic and disease is often advanced when it appears clinically. The most important liver diseases are viral hepatitis, alcoholic liver injury, (1) _____, and malignancy. Acute liver failure can also occur and is usually due to toxins (e.g., acetaminophen toxicity). The great variety of diseases that may affect the liver usually emerge clinically as one of just four clinical syndromes of liver disease: jaundice and cholestasis, cirrhosis, portal hypertension, or hepatic failure. (2) _____ is widespread severe fibrosis or scarring of the liver, which can cause (3) _____ (increased blood pressure in the portal venous system). (4) _____ is obstruction in the excretion of bile, which can lead to increased bilirubin in the skin causing the discoloration called (5) _____. (6) _____ is defined as a loss of hepatic metabolic function severe enough to cause impaired brain function, or "hepatic encephalopathy."

Mnemonic

The causes of **HEPATIC** *Cirrhosis:* **H**emochromatosis, **E**nzyme deficiency (alpha-1-anti-trypsin), **P**harmaceuticals (drugs), **A**lcohol, **T**umor, **I**nfection, **C**holestatic, **C**opper

Mnemonic

The **ABCDEs** *of portal hypertension*

Ascites, **B**leeding (hematemesis, piles), **C**aput medusae, **D**iminished liver, **E**nlarged spleen

EXERCISE 12-4 PATHOLOGY AS A SECOND LANGUAGE

Test your vocabulary by indicating if each statement below is true or false. If it is false, provide the correct word for the italicized term that will make the statement true.

_____ 1. *Crigler-Najjar syndrome* is a mild deficiency of the enzyme glucuronyl transferase (UGT1A1), causing unconjugated hyperbilirubinemia.

_____

_____ 2. *Gilbert syndrome* is an unconjugated hyperbilirubinemia which also owes to genetic defect or mutation of UGT1A1.

_____

_____ 3. *Dubin-Johnson syndrome* is a hereditary conjugated hyperbilirubinemia.

_____

_____ 4. *Rotor syndrome* is an autosomal recessive disease in which the hepatocellular secretory apparatus appears to be defective.

_____

_____ 5. *Biliary cirrhosis* occurs when scar tissue disrupts the lobular anatomy; the pattern of scarring does not follow the anatomic outlines of the lobules.

_____

_____ 6. *Portal cirrhosis* is caused by chronic disease of the biliary tree; the pattern of scarring follows the outline of the hepatic lobules.

_____

_____ 7. *Portosystemic shunts* are diversions of blood around the liver through alternate channels into the systemic venous circulation.

_____

_____ 8. Brain dysfunction owing to accumulated toxins/ammonia is termed *splenic encephalopathy*.

_____

_____ 9. *Hepatopulmonary syndrome* is development of kidney failure in a patient with severe chronic liver disease.

_____

_____ 10. *Hepatorenal syndrome* is a syndrome of respiratory failure in patients with liver failure.

_____

LEARNING OBJECTIVE 3: Compare and contrast the transmission route, incubation time, clinicopathologic syndromes associated with, and diagnostic findings of HAV, HBV, and HCV, and briefly comment on the clinical significance of infection with HDV and HEV.

EXERCISE 12-5

Complete the paragraph below.

(1) _____ is infection by one of the several viruses that preferentially infect the liver (hepatotropic viruses) and includes hepatitis viruses A, B, C, D, and E. Many patients are asymptomatic, but harbor the virus and are capable of infecting others; this is called a (2) _____. (3) _____ is defined as viral hepatitis proven by liver biopsy, with six months or more of laboratory or clinical evidence of disease activity. Hepatitis viruses can cause acute and/or chronic infections depending on the virus.

EXERCISE 12-6

Complete the table below.

Hepatitis	Contraction	Acute Marker	Carrier?	Chronic?	Complications/Comments
(1) _____	Oral-fecal	IgM	No	No	Self-limiting, IgG indicates immunity
HBV	(2) _____	HBsAg, anti-HBc Ab	Yes	Yes	Small % fulminant failure, vertical transmission, can cause HCC
HCV	(3) _____	HCV-RNA (from initial infection and persists)	Yes	Yes	No acute hepatitis, can cause HCC
HDV	IV/Sex	HDV Antibody or RNA	Yes	Yes	Requires (4) _____ infection
HEV	(5) _____	IgM	No	No	Pregnant-fulminant failure

EXERCISE 12-7   PATHOLOGY AS A SECOND LANGUAGE

Test your vocabulary by writing the appropriate term in each blank from the list below.

HAV   HBV   HCV   HDV   HEV

Hepatitis B surface antigen (HBsAg)

Antibody to hepatitis B core antigen (anti-HBc)

Antibody to hepatitis B surface antigen (anti-HBs)

1. _____ is the cause of epidemic hepatitis and is the most common form of clinically recognized hepatitis.

2. _____ and _____ indicate infection.

3. The appearance of _____ marks the beginning of recovery and development of immunity.

4. _____ is transmitted by food and water, causing periodic epidemics in Asia and Africa. It is particularly dangerous in pregnant women.

5. _____ causes only chronic liver disease (i.e., chronic hepatitis with subsequent cirrhosis, and sometimes hepatocellular carcinoma).

6. _____ is peculiar because it requires coinfection (simultaneous) or superinfection (previous infection) with HBV.

7. _____ is a worldwide cause of acute hepatitis and chronic liver disease. It can be passed by vertical transmission (mother to child), sexually, or intravenously.

LEARNING OBJECTIVE 4: Name the nonviral causes of inflammatory liver disease.

EXERCISE 12-8

Complete the paragraph below.

Although inflammation can be the result of alcoholic fatty liver disease or (1) _____ (discussed

in Learning Objectives 6 and 7), additional nonviral causes of liver inflammation include bacterial or fungal infections, which generally present as (2) _____. Protozoa and parasites can also infect the liver including (3) _____ and (4) _____, respectively. In addition, (5) _____ is a syndrome of chronic, progressive hepatitis not associated with infection (microscopic features may be indistinguishable from viral hepatitis), but rather with autoantibodies.

EXERCISE 12-9   PATHOLOGY AS A SECOND LANGUAGE

See Exercise 12-8 for key terms covered in this section.

LEARNING OBJECTIVE 5: Using examples from the text, compare and contrast dose- and nondose-related liver reaction; briefly discuss Reye syndrome.

EXERCISE 12-10

Complete the paragraph below.

Liver damage is a common side-effect of drugs or effect of toxins. Some of these effects are well understood, and liver damage is certain if enough concentration of the drug or toxin is present. This is known as (1) _____. A good example is acetaminophen toxicity, wherein the larger the dose, the greater the damage to the liver (hepatic necrosis). Other reactions are well known to occur, but are "idiosyncratic"—which patient will have the reaction is unpredictable and the reaction can occur regardless of the amount of drug or toxin taken—these are termed (2) _____ injury where the damage is often out of proportion to the dose. (3) _____ is a well-known toxic effect due to aspirin given to children for an acute viral illness. It usually develops in a few days with a combination of fatty liver and encephalopathy (brain dysfunction).

EXERCISE 12-11   PATHOLOGY AS A SECOND LANGUAGE

See Exercise 12-10 for key terms covered in this section.

LEARNING OBJECTIVE 6: Describe the acute and chronic changes induced in the liver by alcohol abuse.

EXERCISE 12-12

Complete the paragraph below.

Alcohol abuse leads to the clinical symptoms of (1) _____, which are also seen in other causes of cirrhosis, with acute and chronic changes within the liver. Alcohol is a known toxin of the liver and alcoholic fatty liver disease begins with fatty accumulation within hepatocytes known as (2) _____. This can progress to (3) _____, which includes inflammation and/or overt damage to the liver. The pathologic findings are called (4) _____, which is characterized by steatosis, inflammation, hepatocyte damage (necrosis or "ballooning degeneration"), and early fibrosis. Alcoholic steatohepatitis is considered a progressive disorder that leads to more and more severe fibrosis, ending in (5) _____, the final and irreversible stage of alcoholic liver disease.

EXERCISE 12-13 PATHOLOGY AS A SECOND LANGUAGE

See Exercise 12-12 for key terms covered in this section.

LEARNING OBJECTIVE 7: Discuss the etiology of metabolic liver disease, distinguishing nonalcoholic fatty liver disease, hemochromatosis, Wilson disease, and Alpha-1 antitrypsin deficiency from one another, and identify the signs/symptoms, diagnosis, treatment, and complications of each as applicable.

EXERCISE 12-14

Complete the paragraph below.

Because one of the core functions of the liver is metabolism of various compounds, each with complex biochemical pathways, metabolic liver disease is a group of diverse diseases. Perhaps the most important metabolic disease to recognize, which is closely associated with (1) _____ and diabetes, is (2) _____. This is a spectrum of related conditions featuring fatty liver in patients who consume very little or no alcohol. Much like alcohol-related disease, NAFLD can progress from simple steatosis to fatty liver with inflammation and liver injury, called (3) _____. This can progress to cirrhosis with its clinical symptoms and complications. Selected additional metabolic pathways are discussed below in Exercise 12-16.

> **Remember This!** Hemochromatosis = bronze diabetes

EXERCISE 12-15

Complete the table below.

Disease	Pathway	Signs/Symptoms Diagnosis	Treatment	Complications Notes
(1) _____	Iron—Excess iron storage in tissues, including liver, heart, pancreas	Genetic, 10% people are carriers in some populations, discoloration of skin, diabetes	Phlebotomy	Cirrhosis, heart failure, diabetes, arthritis, Secondary (acquired) hemochromatosis = hemosiderosis
(2) _____	Copper—Excess copper in liver	Autosomal recessive, Kayser-Fleischer rings, increases copper on liver biopsy	Copper chelators (e.g., penicillamine)	Psychosis, cirrhosis, liver failure
(3) _____	Protein processing—Alpha1AT inhibits digestion of tissue by trypsin and other proteases	PAS-positive, Alpha1AT globules in liver, can cause neonatal hepatitis	Enzyme replacement, stop smoking, lung transplant	Causes emphysema of the lungs, cirrhosis

EXERCISE 12-16 PATHOLOGY AS A SECOND LANGUAGE

See Exercise 12-15 for key terms covered in this section.

LEARNING OBJECTIVE 8: Compare and contrast secondary biliary cirrhosis with primary biliary cirrhosis and sclerosing cholangitis.

EXERCISE 12-17

Complete the paragraph below.

Although (1) _____ can be caused by different etiologies that lead to chronic obstruction of the biliary tree, including gallstones and (2) _____, primary biliary disease is generally due to autoantibodies and includes primary biliary cirrhosis and (3) _____. These diseases can also be seen in conjunction with another autoimmune disease that affects the liver, (4) _____. Any obstruction of the biliary tree may allow bacteria to ascend the common duct to infect the biliary tree and liver; this is called (5) _____.

EXERCISE 12-18

Complete the table below.

Disorder	(1) **Primary biliary** _____	(2) **Secondary** _____	(3) **Primary** _____
Definition	Autoimmune disease that evolves from inflammatory destruction of intrahepatic bile ducts	Acquired chronic cholestasis leading to fibrosis and cirrhosis of the liver	Chronic cholestatic liver disease caused by inflammation and fibrosis of intra- and extrahepatic bile ducts
Diagnosis	Autoantibodies, liver biopsy	Liver biopsy, evidence of obstruction, gallstone disease, etc.	Imaging of the biliary tree "beads on a string" (ERCP), strongly assoc. with UC (70%)

EXERCISE 12-19 PATHOLOGY AS A SECOND LANGUAGE

See Exercise 12-18 for key terms covered in this section.

LEARNING OBJECTIVE 9: Name the causes of prehepatic, intrahepatic, and posthepatic obstruction of blood flow.

EXERCISE 12-20

Complete the paragraph below.

Blood flow may be obstructed in the portal vein as it flows into the liver, as it flows through the liver, or in the hepatic vein as it flows out of the liver; however, obstruction of arterial flow through the hepatic artery is uncommon and usually due to atherosclerosis. Extrahepatic portal vein blockage is caused generally by (1) _____ and leads to portal hypertension. More commonly, the cause of portal hypertension is blockage of intrahepatic blood flow by (2) _____. This can also be caused by (3) _____ with chronic passive congestion of the liver ("back up" of blood into the liver). Obstruction of blood flow *out* of the liver is caused by obstruction of one or more hepatic vein tributaries or the main hepatic vein. Occlusion of the main hepatic vein is called (4) _____.

EXERCISE 12-21   PATHOLOGY AS A SECOND LANGUAGE

There are no vocabulary terms in this section.

LEARNING OBJECTIVE 10: List the tumors that can arise in the liver.

EXERCISE 12-22

Complete the paragraph below.

The most common malignant tumors of the liver are metastatic tumors from other sites, primarily the
(1) _____. Benign and malignant primary tumors of the liver are derived from the hepatocytes or from
the biliary tree. Benign lesions of the liver include: (2) _____, which is a neoplasm of hepatocytes
encountered most often in young women taking oral contraceptives; focal nodular hyperplasia, which is a proliferation of hepatocytes that has a scar-like central area; and biliary adenomas (hamartomas), which can cause
tumors. Perhaps the most common benign liver neoplasm is (3) _____. Primary malignant tumors are
discussed below in Exercise 12-24.

EXERCISE 12-23   PATHOLOGY AS A SECOND LANGUAGE

**Test your vocabulary by indicating if each statement below is true or false. If it is false, provide the cor-
rect word for the italicized term that will make the statement true.**

_____ 1. *Hepatocellular carcinoma (HCC)* is a malignant tumor of hepatocytes that occurs in children.

        _____

_____ 2. *Hepatoblastoma* is a malignant neoplasm of hepatocytes that is usually related to chronic HBV and
        HCV infections.

        _____

_____ 3. *Cholangiocarcinoma* is a malignancy of bile duct epithelium.

        _____

LEARNING OBJECTIVE 11: Describe the etiologies, risk factors, symptoms, and complications of extrahepatic bile duct obstruction.

EXERCISE 12-24

Complete the paragraph below.

Nearly all diseases of the extrahepatic biliary ducts are related to gallstone disease. Gallstones can lead to inflammation (e.g., [1] _____) and obstruction. Chronic obstruction of the biliary tree leads to scarring, or
(2)_____ of the liver. Gallstone disease often causes right upper quadrant pain, and obstruction can lead
to jaundice, change in stool color, and steatorrhea. Risk factors for gallstone disease include (3) _____
gender, ethnicity, obesity, and drugs, including oral contraceptives.

> **Remember This!** Patients most at risk for cholesterol gallstones = fat, female, forty, fertile.

EXERCISE 12-25   PATHOLOGY AS A SECOND LANGUAGE

Test your vocabulary by filling in the terms that correspond to their appropriate structure in the image, and their corresponding definition below. Terms may be used once, more than once, or not at all.

Extrahepatic biliary atresia   Cholesterol gallstones
Choledocholithiasis   Cholelithiasis
Pigment gallstones   Cholecystitis

1. Stones in the gallbladder or biliary tree are referred to as _____.

2. Stones in the bile ducts are referred to as _____.

3. _____ are generally semi-translucent, yellowish, and egg shaped.

4. _____ account for 20% of gallstones and are dark brown or black, have multiple flat surfaces (facets), and are composed of bilirubin and bile.

5. _____ is acute or chronic inflammation of the gallbladder.

6. _____ is an obstruction of extrahepatic bile ducts, occurring in children.

Decisions Decisions

DECISION TREE 12.1: CAUSES OF JAUNDICE

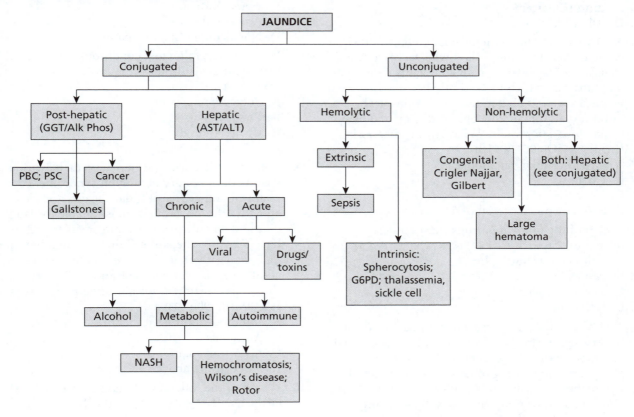

Test Yourself

I. MULTIPLE CHOICE

1. A three-day-old infant is brought to the emergency room by his mother for evaluation of a recent change in skin color. After a careful physical exam reveals a mild case of jaundice, you diagnose the infant with physiologic jaundice of the newborn. What treatment do you recommend? [LEARNING OBJECTIVE 2]
   A. Exchange transfusion
   B. Plasmapheresis
   C. Antivirals
   D. No treatment is necessary

2. Which of the following statements is true concerning extrahepatic biliary atresia? [LEARNING OBJECTIVE 11]
   A. Caused by the failure of bile duct development
   B. On histology the ducts appear scarred and obstructed
   C. It is the result of TORCH infections during the third trimester
   D. All of the above

3. A 55-year-old Chinese female is brought to the clinic by her daughter-in-law, who serves as her translator. The elder woman complains of abdominal bloating, which has recently become much worse, as well as abdominal pain. A physical exam reveals a markedly enlarged liver, and elevated alpha-fetoprotein. What is your diagnosis? [LEARNING OBJECTIVE 10]
   A. Hepatocellular carcinoma
   B. Cirrhosis
   C. Hepatitis
   D. Spontaneous bacterial peritonitis

4. Which of the following drugs causes a dose-related liver toxicity? [LEARNING OBJECTIVE 5]
   A. Sulfonamide antibiotics
   B. Isoniazid
   C. Acetaminophen
   D. Halothane

5. A 36-year-old Caucasian male with past medical history significant for ulcerative colitis, diagnosed 10 years previously, presents to his primary care physician complaining of fatigue, jaundice, and steatorrhea. His labs are significant for elevated bilirubin and liver enzymes as well as the presence of antismooth muscle antibodies. A liver biopsy demonstrates onionskin fibrosis encircling his bile ducts. What is the underlying etiology of his symptoms? [LEARNING OBJECTIVE 8]
   A. Hepatitis
   B. Primary biliary cirrhosis
   C. Cholangiocarcinoma
   D. Sclerosing cholangitis

6. Which of the following is the most common cause of chronic liver disease and the most common indication for liver transplant? [LEARNING OBJECTIVE 3]
   A. Alcohol abuse
   B. HCV infection
   C. Nonalcoholic steatohepatitis
   D. Acetaminophen overdose

7. A 40-year-old male, with a past medical history of diabetes and arthritis, visits the fertility clinic, concerned that he and his wife are having trouble conceiving. The man's appearance is remarkable for a tan in the middle of winter, and his labs are notable for increased levels of blood ferritin. Which of the following diseases explains this constellation of symptoms? [LEARNING OBJECTIVE 7]
   A. Wilson disease
   B. Hemochromatosis
   C. Addison disease
   D. Nonalcoholic steatohepatitis

8. Which of the following conditions can cause Budd-Chiari syndrome? [LEARNING OBJECTIVE 8]
   A. Polycythemia vera
   B. Pregnancy
   C. Coagulation disorders
   D. All of the above

9. A 43-year-old African American female, with a past medical history of Sjögren syndrome, complains of fatigue, nausea, dark urine, and loss of appetite. Her physical exam is notable for jaundice and an enlarged liver, and she is found to have a positive hepatitis C titer (though her viral PCR is negative), and antinuclear antibodies, in addition to an elevated AST and ALT. What is the proper treatment for her underlying disease? [LEARNING OBJECTIVE 4]
   A. Immunosuppressive therapy
   B. Antivirals
   C. Liver transplant
   D. None of the above

10. Which of the following diseases causes biliary cirrhosis? [LEARNING OBJECTIVE 2]
    A. Alcohol
    B. Viral hepatitis
    C. Gallstones
    D. All of the above

11. A father brings his six-year-old daughter to the emergency room, concerned by her lethargy. He reports that several days ago she had a cold and fever, which he treated with over-the-counter medication, and that yesterday she became irritable and began to vomit prior to becoming lethargic. What over-the-counter medication did he administer to reduce her fever? [LEARNING OBJECTIVE 5]
    A. Acetaminophen
    B. Naproxen
    C. Aspirin
    D. Ibuprofen

12. A 25-year-old college student visits the clinic complaining of pain in the upper right abdomen. When questioned as to whether she might be pregnant, she replies that she is taking oral contraceptives. Imaging demonstrates a large 7 cm mass in the liver. What treatment do you recommend? [LEARNING OBJECTIVE 10]
    A. Excision
    B. Chemotherapy
    C. Discontinuation of oral contraceptives
    D. Higher doses of progesterone

13. A 23-year-old college student returns from his spring-break trip to Mexico with jaundice, dark urine, and vomiting. Which of the following antibodies or antigens would confirm a recent infection with a hepatitis virus? [LEARNING OBJECTIVE 3]
    A. IgM Anti-HBs
    B. IgG Anti- HAV
    C. HBsAg
    D. HCsAg

14. Which of the following is true concerning fatty liver? [LEARNING OBJECTIVE 6]
    A. Two-thirds of all alcoholics develop fatty livers.
    B. Steatosis is the first sign of alcoholic injury.
    C. Mallory bodies are dying hepatocytes.
    D. All of the above are true.

15. A 55-year-old female, with a past medical history of lupus, presents with fatigue and pruritus. Her physical exam is notable for hepatomegaly, jaundice, and xanthelasmas on both eyelids. Her labs are notable for an antimitochondrial antibody in addition to elevated alkaline phosphatase, and a hepatic biopsy demonstrates an accumulation of lymphocytes surrounding bile ducts. What is your diagnosis? [LEARNING OBJECTIVE 8]
    A. Primary biliary cirrhosis
    B. Primary sclerosing cholangitis
    C. Viral hepatitis
    D. Alcoholic cirrhosis

16. Which of the following is an autosomal recessive condition in which the patient has conjugated hyperbilirubinemia and a deeply pigmented liver? [LEARNING OBJECTIVE 2]
    A. Gilbert Syndrome
    B. Crigler-Najjar Syndrome
    B. Dubin-Johnson Syndrome
    D. Rotor Syndrome

17. A 46-year old Caucasian male with a history of sickle-cell anemia presents to the Emergency Department with right upper quadrant pain, nausea, and vomiting. He denies fever and chills. On ultrasound imaging, he has evidence of numerous stones within the gallbladder consistent with cholelithiasis. Which of the following best describes the attributes of his gallstones? [Learning Objective 11]
    A. Yellow, friable stones
    B. Dark brown to black stones with multiple flat surfaces
    C. Blue rounded stones
    D. Translucent radio-opaque stones

18. Which of the following statements concerning cholangiocarcinoma is true? [LEARNING OBJECTIVE 10]
    A. It may occur in the intrahepatic or extrahepatic bile ducts or in the gallbladder.
    B. Cholangiocarcinoma of the liver tends to be more aggressive than hepatocellular carcinoma, with only 15% surviving two years.
    C. Risk factors include sclerosing cholangitis, HCV infection, and chronic liver schistosomiasis.
    D. All of the above are true.

II. TRUE OR FALSE

19. _____ All nutrients absorbed by the intestine enter the portal venous system directly. [LEARNING OBJECTIVE 1]

20. _____ Unlike patients with HBV, approximately half of HCV infected patients become jaundiced. [LEARNING OBJECTIVE 3]

21. _____ Approximately two-thirds of obese persons have some degree of nonalcoholic fatty liver disease, making it the most common liver disease in the United States. [LEARNING OBJECTIVE 7]

22. _____ Right-heart failure and restrictive pericarditis are among the most common causes of posthepatic flow restriction. [LEARNING OBJECTIVE 2]

23. _____ Approximately 200 gm of alcohol or two bottles of wine consumed regularly for 10 to 16 years are necessary to produce cirrhosis. [LEARNING OBJECTIVE 6]

24. _____ Albumin levels can serve as an indicator of the severity of liver injury. [LEARNING OBJECTIVE 2]

25. _____ Cholangiocarcinomas of the gallbladder or liver have a better prognosis than extrahepatic bile duct cholangiocarcinomas. [LEARNING OBJECTIVE 11]

26. _____ Bilirubinuria can be caused by either excess conjugated or unconjugated bilirubin. [LEARNING OBJECTIVE 1]

III. MATCHING

27. Match the following descriptions with their disease; answers may be used more than once. [LEARNING OBJECTIVE 11]
    - i. Cholelithiasis
    - ii. Choledocholithiasis
    - iii. Cholangitis
    - iv. Acute Cholecystitis
    - v. Chronic Cholecystitis
    - vi. Empyema
    - A. Gallbladder filled with pus
    - B. Stones in the gallbladder
    - C. Most common complication of gallstones
    - D. Characterized by episodes of mild to moderate right upper quadrant pain with nausea, vomiting, and intolerance for fatty foods
    - E. Stones in the bile ducts
    - F. Enlarged, tense, inflamed gallbladder
    - G. Bacterial infection of the biliary tree

IV. SHORT ANSWER

28. How does the liver contribute to glucose homeostasis? [LEARNING OBJECTIVE 1]

_____

_____

_____

29. What are the causes of portal vein obstruction? [LEARNING OBJECTIVE 9]

_____

_____

_____

30. What are the mechanisms responsible for causing jaundice? [LEARNING OBJECTIVE 2]

_____

_____

_____

31. Name the methods of diverting blood around a cirrhotic liver. [LEARNING OBJECTIVE 2]

_____

_____

_____

32. Name the most common underlying etiologies of liver infection as dependent on location. [LEARNING OBJECTIVE 4]

_____

_____

_____

Disorders of the Pancreas

The Big Picture

The pancreas is divided into endocrine and exocrine portions that serve different functions. The endocrine pancreas is responsible for glucose homeostasis, primarily via insulin. The exocrine pancreas is responsible for producing and transporting digestive juices to the gastrointestinal tract. Diabetes is the major disease of the endocrine pancreas affecting millions in the United States, while pancreatic adenocarcinoma (of the exocrine pancreas) is one of the most feared cancers, as it is quickly lethal.

Oh No! Not Another Learning Experience

LEARNING OBJECTIVE 1: Discuss the anatomy of the pancreas, and make a clear distinction between the digestive and the hormonal pancreas.

EXERCISE 13-1

Complete the paragraph below.

The (1) _____ is a tadpole-shaped organ about 5 to 6 inches in length, located adjacent to the stomach. Its head is wrapped around the duodenum and its tail extends to the spleen. It is composed of two anatomic and functional portions. The (2) _____ is made up of glands composed of acini that empty their contents into pancreatic ducts. This (3) _____ is a cocktail of about 20 digestive agents, water, bicarbonate, and mucus, and is a necessary aid in digesting food. In contrast, the (4) _____ is composed of hundreds of thousands of tiny (5) _____ scattered throughout the gland. These islets secrete various hormones, including insulin for the regulation of blood glucose.

EXERCISE 13-2 PATHOLOGY AS A SECOND LANGUAGE

Test your vocabulary by indicating if each statement below is true or false. If it is false, provide the correct word for the italicized term that will make the statement true.

_____ 1. Protein-digesting enzymes called proteases are stored in their inactive forms, called *zymogens*.

_____

_____ 2. The enzyme secreted by the pancreas that digests triglyceride is called *bile acid*.

_____

_____ 3. *Amylase* is also present in saliva and digests carbohydrate.

_____

LEARNING OBJECTIVE 2: Explain the relationship of insulin, glucagon, somatostatin, and glucose to one another and to stored glycogen.

EXERCISE 13-3

Complete the paragraph below.

Insulin, glucagon, and (1) _____ act in concert to regulate blood glucose levels. Insulin promotes glucose utilization and glucose storage as glycogen, thereby (2) _____ blood glucose levels. This is important for the treatment of diabetics, as (3) _____ is the standard treatment for reducing elevated blood glucose levels present in the disease. In contrast, glucagon converts stored liver (4) _____ to glucose and promotes conversion of amino acids to glucose to maintain blood glucose. Somatostatin essentially inhibits both insulin and (5) _____ and slows peristalsis of food to slow absorption of food and decrease metabolism of glucose.

EXERCISE 13-4   PATHOLOGY AS A SECOND LANGUAGE

Test your vocabulary by writing the appropriate term in each blank from the list below.

Amylase   PP cells   Inactive protease (zymogen)
Alpha cells   Beta cells   Delta cells
Lipase

1. _____ secrete glucagon, a hormone that stimulates the liver's output of glucose by converting glycogen to glucose and forming glucose from amino acids; may stimulate the breakdown of fat for energy.

2. _____ secrete pancreatic polypeptide, acts on the stomach to stimulate the secretion of gastric enzymes and on the small intestine to inhibit motility.

3. _____ secrete somatostatin, a hormone that inhibits glucagon and insulin secretion and slows peristalsis in the gastrointestinal and biliary systems.

4. _____ secrete insulin, a hormone that stimulates cell uptake of glucose from blood, thereby lowering blood glucose levels.

5. _____ is an inactive form of an enzyme so that it can be stored within the cell prior to utilization.

6. _____ is a pancreatic enzyme and a sensitive, but less specific marker for pancreatitis.

7. _____ is a pancreatic enzyme and a more specific marker for pancreatitis.

LEARNING OBJECTIVE 3: Compare and contrast the etiology, clinical presentation, and complications of acute and chronic pancreatitis.

EXERCISE 13-5

Complete the sentence below.

Pancreatitis is a major cause of morbidity and mortality by itself; however, it can also sometimes form cysts or mass lesions, mimicking (1) _____.

Please see Exercises 13-6 and 13-7 for additional information regarding this learning objective.

EXERCISE 13-6

Complete the table below.

Condition	(1) _____	(2) _____
Cause	Gallstones, alcohol	Recurrent acute pancreatitis Autoimmune
Symptoms	Sudden painful, medical emergency	Less dramatic
Labs	Increased amylase (rise and fall quickly) Increased lipase (rise slowly, stays elevated)	Nonspecific, may have characteristic imaging findings
Complications	Pancreatic pseudocyst, hypovolemic shock, hypocalcemia, hemorrhage	Pancreatic fibrosis/calcification, migratory thrombophlebitis, malabsorption, diabetes

EXERCISE 13-7   PATHOLOGY AS A SECOND LANGUAGE

Test your vocabulary by indicating if each statement below is true or false. If it is false, provide the correct word for the italicized term that will make the statement true.

_____ 1. Acute reversible inflammation of the pancreas that can be very dangerous, with a high mortality rate, is called *chronic pancreatitis*.

_____

_____ 2. Fibrous "walling off" of inflammatory fluid and edema in pancreatitis that can sometimes be mistaken for cancer is called *pancreatic intraepithelial neoplasia*.

_____

_____ 3. *Acute pancreatitis* is repeated episodes of symptomatic or subclinical acute pancreatitis that cause irreversible destruction and scarring.

_____

Mnemonic

Causes of Pancreatitis = **GET SMASHED**
Gallstones, **E**thanol, **T**rauma
Steroids, **M**umps, **A**utoimmune, **S**corpion stings, **H**yperlipidemia/Hypercalcemia, **E**RCP, **D**rugs

LEARNING OBJECTIVE 4: Compare and contrast the underlying etiology of type 1 and type 2 diabetes, paying special attention to its most important contributing factors where applicable.

EXERCISE 13-8

Complete the paragraph below.

Diabetes is a major growing problem in the United States. Although all diabetic patients share (1) _____ as a defining feature, there are two types of diabetes and the vast majority of patients are the second type.

(2) _____ is an autoimmune disorder featuring destruction of (3) _____ and an absolute lack of insulin. This category represents about 10% of cases and is usually diagnosed in patients younger than age 20. (4) _____ is a multifactorial disease that features peripheral cell resistance to the effects of insulin and an inadequate secretory response or a (5) _____ lack of insulin. The great majority of cases are this type. Although almost all of them occur in overweight adults, the current epidemic of childhood (6) _____ is causing an increase of type 2 diabetes in children. The clinical aspects and complications of diabetes are addressed below.

EXERCISE 13-9   PATHOLOGY AS A SECOND LANGUAGE

Test your vocabulary by writing the appropriate term in each blank from the list below.

Euglycemia   Glucose intolerant   Hyperglycemia
Hypoglycemia   Diabetes mellitus

1. _____ is a disorder of insulin action and/or secretion that results in high blood glucose.

2. High blood glucose is called _____.

3. Abnormally low blood glucose is called _____.

4. Having normal blood glucose levels with no evidence of diabetes or prediabetes is called _____.

5. Patients who do not meet the criteria for diabetes but still have problems "clearing" glucose from the blood (i.e., prediabetic) are called _____.

LEARNING OBJECTIVE 5: List the accompanying signs and symptoms of diabetes, in addition to its diagnostic criteria.

EXERCISE 13-10

Complete the paragraph below.

Although obesity increases the chances of developing (1) _____, diabetes in general is a "wasting" disease wherein the body is unable to properly utilize and clear glucose from the blood. Diabetes causes various symptoms related to (2) _____. These include increased urination ([3] _____), increased thirst ([4] _____), and increased appetite ([5] _____). The urine contains abnormal amounts of glucose, too much to be reabsorbed; therefore, the urine is actually sweet like honey ("mellitus"). Diabetes can also present clinically with one of the complications listed in Learning Objective 6. Additional tests can be performed to assess diabetic patients.

EXERCISE 13-11   PATHOLOGY AS A SECOND LANGUAGE

Test your vocabulary by indicating if each statement below is true or false. If it is false, provide the correct word for the italicized term that will make the statement true.

_____ 1. An *oral glucose tolerance test (OGTT)* measures blood glucose two hours after a standard carbohydrate load (an oral dose of 75 gm of glucose).

_____

_____ 2. Diabetics have urine with abnormally increased amounts of glucose called *polyuria*.

_____

_____ 3. *Glycohemoglobin (Hgb A1C)* is formed by the attachment of glucose to globin, the protein part of hemoglobin, and approximates average glucose levels.

_____

LEARNING OBJECTIVE 6: Describe the complications of diabetes, noting the leading cause of mortality.

EXERCISE 13-12

Complete the paragraph below.

Complications of diabetes are very common and lead to significant morbidity and mortality in patients with the disease, with enormous resulting healthcare costs. Complications can occur early or late in the course of the disease, but the most important cause is (1) _____. Both high extracellular glucose and high intracellular glucose are contributing factors. Excess glucose binds to extracellular proteins, in a process called (2) _____, to form abnormal (3) _____ that have multiple adverse effects on vascular endothelium. Diabetes accelerates atherosclerotic disease as well as hyperlipidemia and hypertension. Intracellular glucose increases (4) _____, resulting in new, abnormal, blood vessel growth and damage to the kidneys. Specific complications are discussed in the sections that follow.

Mnemonic

KetONE bodies are seen in type 1 diabetes.

EXERCISE 13-13   PATHOLOGY AS A SECOND LANGUAGE

Test your vocabulary by writing the appropriate term in each blank from the list below.

Myocardial Infarct	Coronary atherosclerosis	Infections
Diabetic nephropathy	Diabetic neuropathy	Diabetic retinopathy
Diabetic microangiopathy	Diabetic ketoacidosis	
Microalbuminuria	Hyperosmolar coma	

1. _____ is thickening of the basement membrane of small blood vessels causing end organ damage.

2. _____ is chronic kidney damage accelerated by diabetes consisting of vascular damage and nodular glomerulosclerosis.

3. _____ is often the clinical presentation of type 1 diabetes and consists of life-threatening metabolic catastrophe, including hyperosmolarity, acidosis, ketosis, potassium depletion, and rapid, deep breathing to help expel acid in the form of ketones and carbon dioxide.

4. The combination of loss of solvent and increased glucose (solute) produces very high blood osmolarity, leading to altered mental state and _____.

5. Protein in the urine signals damage to the kidney, beginning with low amounts of albumin in urine called _____.

6. _____ is a mixture of exudates, hemorrhages, edema, new blood vessel growth, small aneurysms, and scarring of the retina leading to vision loss.

7. _____ is damage to peripheral nerves leading to pain, sensory loss, and other complications, including joint problems.

Mnemonic

Diabetes Complications = SHAKE

Stroke, **H**eart attack, **A**mputations, **K**idney disease, **E**ye damage (retinopathy)

LEARNING OBJECTIVE 7: Discuss potential lifestyle modifications and available therapeutics in the treatment of diabetes.

EXERCISE 13-14

Complete the paragraphs below.

Obviously, the main thrust of treatment is careful control of (1) _____. All diabetic patients must clearly understand that their diet and exercise influence their blood glucose levels. The (2) _____ is a ranking of foods according to their ability to be converted quickly into glucose, thus raising blood glucose. Also important are the types of daily activities and exercises that can burn glucose (calories).

For (3) _____, insulin replacement is of prime importance. For (4) _____, various drugs can be used to regulate insulin resistance and glucose levels. (5) _____ can be given to increase insulin secretion, insulin itself can be given, or a combination can be used. Even a moderate amount of (6) _____ can markedly decrease the need for these drugs and improve insulin sensitivity in (7) _____. For diabetes, the daytime goal for blood glucose is 80 to 120 mg/dL, while the bedtime goal is 100 to 140 mg/dL. The glycohemoglobin goal is < 7%.

EXERCISE 13-15 PATHOLOGY AS A SECOND LANGUAGE

See Exercise 13-14 above for key terms covered in this section.

LEARNING OBJECTIVE 8: Explain the clinical presentation and complications of adenocarcinoma of the pancreas, and give a reasonable estimate of the five-year survival rate.

EXERCISE 13-16

Complete the paragraph below.

Pancreatic adenocarcinoma is one of the most lethal of cancers; about half of patients die within three months of diagnosis and only about (1) _____% survive five years. It is usually insidious, causing few symptoms until it has progressed too far. Symptoms usually start with back pain or sometimes (2) _____. Unexplained weight loss should always suggest a hidden malignancy. Trousseau sign (or (3) _____) is a classic sign resulting from the formation of intravenous thrombi. Unfortunately, to date there is no good screening test for pancreatic cancer.

Remember This! Pancreatic cancer is among the most lethal of malignancies.

EXERCISE 13-17 PATHOLOGY AS A SECOND LANGUAGE

There are no vocabulary terms in this section.

LEARNING OBJECTIVE 9: Aside from adenocarcinoma of the pancreas, name the other pancreatic tumors and describe their diagnostic findings.

EXERCISE 13-18

Complete the paragraph below.

In addition to pancreatic adenocarcinoma, there are several other pancreatic tumors. Some of these are cystic, including (1) _____, mucinous cystic neoplasm, and (2) _____. Others are derived from the (3) _____ (pancreatic endocrine tumors like insulinomas). The most well-known occurrence of pancreatic endocrine tumor was the case of Apple Computers guru Steve Jobs, who died of the disease in 2011.

EXERCISE 13-19   PATHOLOGY AS A SECOND LANGUAGE

Test your vocabulary by indicating if each statement below is true or false. If it is false, provide the correct word for the italicized term that will make the statement true.

_____ 1. *Mucinous cystic neoplasms* are benign, filled with thin, clear, watery fluid, and lined by epithelium derived from pancreatic duct epithelium.

_____

_____ 2. *Serous cystadenomas* are filled with stringy, thick mucus and lined by columnar, mucus-producing cells derived from ductal epithelium with an ovarian stroma.

_____

_____ 3. *Intraductal papillary mucinous neoplasms* are rare tumors that may sometimes be associated with invasive carcinoma (malignant).

_____

_____ 4. *Gastrinomas* are beta cell (endocrine) tumors that are usually benign and occur as a single, small, tumor mass; they can secrete enough insulin to produce hypoglycemia.

_____

_____ 5. *Zollinger-Ellison syndrome* is a constellation of clinical findings resulting from gastrin-producing tumors.

_____

_____ 6. *Insulinomas* are endocrine tumors that secrete gastrin.

_____

Decisions Decisions

DECISION TREE 13.1: PANCREATIC DISEASE

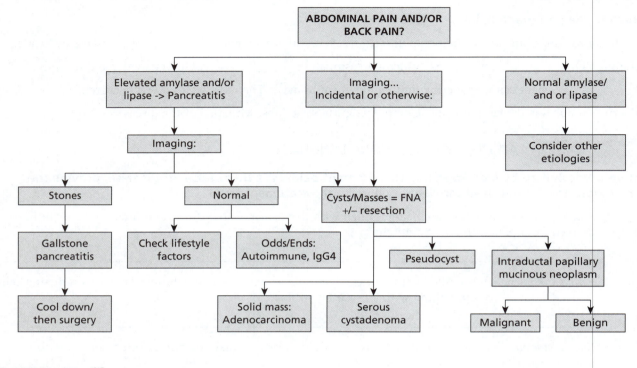

Test Yourself

I. MULTIPLE CHOICE

1. While walking home from school, you notice that your friend has become quiet. She is pale, sweating profusely, and trembling, and when you place your hand against her forehead, it is cool and clammy. You remember that she skipped lunch, and usually doesn't eat breakfast. The enzyme needed to combat these symptoms is secreted by which pancreatic endocrine cell? [LEARNING OBJECTIVE 2]
   A. Alpha cell
   B. Beta cell
   C. Delta cell
   D. PP cells

2. Which of the following would also cause symptoms like those described in the question above? [LEARNING OBJECTIVES 2 AND 9]
   A. Beta cell tumors
   B. Munchausen
   C. Recent ingestion of alcohol (after not eating)
   D. All of the above

3. A 43-year-old male, recently diagnosed with type 1 diabetes, is brought to the ER comatose. He is accompanied by his wife, who reports that they have both had gastroenteritis for the last two days, but while she improved her husband continued to be symptomatic. His physical exam is notable for decreased skin turgor, tachycardia, and rapid deep breathing. A Foley drains dark brown urine, which is positive for glucose and ketones. What is your diagnosis? [LEARNING OBJECTIVE 6]
   A. Hyperosmolar coma
   B. Diabetic ketoacidosis
   C. Hypoglycemia
   D. Hyperketosis coma

4. A 65-year-old Caucasian female complaining of pelvic pain undergoes a CT scan which identifies a large pancreatic mass. Concerned that it might represent a malignancy, the patient undergoes an ultrasound-guided FNA, which is read by the pathologist as suspicious for malignancy. Shortly thereafter, the patient undergoes a Whipple procedure (in which her pancreas is removed). Histology demonstrates a cystic structure, surrounded by ovarian-like supporting stromal cells, containing thick mucus and lined by columnar, mucus-producing cells. What is your diagnosis based on the histology described? (Hint: Use the Decision Tree) [LEARNING OBJECTIVES 3 AND 9]
   A. Serous cystadenoma
   B. Mucinous cystic neoplasm
   C. Intraductal papillary mucinous neoplasms
   D. Pseudocyst

5. Diabetic neuropathy can lead to postural hypotension and/or fainting due to its effects on which of the following types of nerves? [LEARNING OBJECTIVE 6]
   A. Motor nerves
   B. Sensory nerves
   C. Autonomic nerves
   D. All of the above

6. A patient recently diagnosed with type 2 diabetes returns to your office three months after his diagnosis 30 pounds lighter, thanks to dieting and exercise. His Hgba1c, which was measured earlier that morning, is 6.5%. What is your advice to him regarding his disease and treatment options? [LEARNING OBJECTIVE 7]
   A. Continue the good work; I'd like to see you in another three months.
   B. Congratulations, you are doing very well, but we should supplement your routine with oral hypoglycemic agents.
   C. You should continue to diet and exercise as well as starting insulin replacement.
   D. All of the above

7. While watching your cousins play volleyball outside, you notice your youngest cousin (a slender 14-year-old teenager) pull up a chair alongside the net to watch her sisters play. Your aunt comments on the fact that she is usually very active, but lately tires easily in addition to having lost a great deal of weight despite a ravenous appetite. Which of the following results would be characteristic of your cousin's disease? [LEARNING OBJECTIVES 4 AND 5]
   A. Deposition of amyloid in pancreatic vasculature
   B. A slight accumulation of lymphocytes in the islets
   C. Destruction of beta cells
   D. Scarring and fibrosis with dystrophic calcifications

8. Which of the following statements is true about diabetic nephropathy? [LEARNING OBJECTIVE 6]
   A. Nephrosclerosis is diagnostic of diabetes.
   B. While deposits of hyaline material are often seen in diabetic nephropathy, they are not diagnostic.
   C. The earliest manifestation of diabetic nephropathy is diabetic microalbuminuria.
   D. All of the above are true.

9. A 55-year-old African American male presents to the clinic complaining of abdominal pain, nausea, and vomiting that is different from his previous bouts of pancreatitis. On physical exam, a palpable mass is felt in the upper mid-abdomen. CT imaging demonstrates a large cystic structure in the body of the pancreas, and a subsequent fine needle aspiration, guided by ultrasound, reveals bloody fluid and necrotic debris without lining epithelium. What type of cyst does the patient have? (Hint: Use the Decision Tree) [LEARNING OBJECTIVE 3]
   A. Serous cystadenoma
   B. Mucinous cystic neoplasm
   C. Intraductal papillary mucinous neoplasms
   D. Pseudocyst

II. TRUE OR FALSE

10. _____ Hyperosmolar coma is usually seen in elderly or debilitated patients with type 2 diabetes who are unable to medicate themselves properly or to drink enough water. [LEARNING OBJECTIVE 6]

11. _____ Recurrent peptic ulcers should prompt consideration of Zollinger-Ellison syndrome, a constellation of clinical findings resulting from somatostatinomas. [LEARNING OBJECTIVE 9]

12. _____ Along with urinary water loss, the urine wastes electrolytes resulting in a decrease of H^+, Na^+, and K^+. [LEARNING OBJECTIVE 6]

13. _____ Intraductal papillary mucinous neoplasms may be benign or malignant. (Hint: Use the Decision Tree) [LEARNING OBJECTIVE 9]

III. MATCHING

14. Match the pancreatic functions with the below traits: [LEARNING OBJECTIVE 1]
    i. Endocrine
    ii. Exocrine
    iii. Both
    A. Produce enzymes
    B. Control sugar and fat absorption
    C. Produce hormones
    D. Are composed of islets
    E. Empty contents into the blood
    F. Empty contents into acini, ducts, and ultimately small intestines
    G. Compose 80–85% of pancreatic tissue

IV. SHORT ANSWER

15. An obese 35-year-old woman, with a fasting blood glucose of 120 mg/dL, is seen at her OB/GYN's office for prepregnancy counseling. What should she know about her condition prior to becoming pregnant? [LEARNING OBJECTIVES 4 AND 5]

_____

_____

_____

16. Why are tumors arising in the tail of the pancreas more advanced than those arising in the head of the pancreas? [LEARNING OBJECTIVE 8]

_____

_____

_____

17. A 22-year-old Caucasian female presents to the ER with nausea, vomiting, weight loss, and nagging upper midgastric/epigastric abdominal pain radiating to the back. Physical exam demonstrates a well-developed, slender female with moderate abdominal tenderness and scleral icterus (yellowing of the eyes). Her labs are notable for an increase in lipase, while amylase is normal and abdominal imaging fails to identify choleliths. What is your next step? [LEARNING OBJECTIVE 3]

_____

_____

_____

Disorders of the Endocrine Glands

The Big Picture

The endocrine system is key for maintaining homeostasis through the action of hormones, which are bioactive substances secreted into the bloodstream. Because hormones powerfully impact body function, they require tight regulation. Any imbalance (too little or too much hormone) causes disease if not properly compensated for (see table below). Tight regulation is accomplished by negative feedback loops, where a downstream product inhibits the pathway that produces it. The hypothalamic-pituitary axis is central to this regulation.

Organ	Increased Function	Decreased Function
Pituitary	Adenoma, prolactinoma, corticotroph adenoma, growth hormone adenoma	Sheehan, radiation, apoplexy, Rathke cleft cyst, empty sella syndrome
Thyroid	Thyrotoxicosis,	Congenital, Iodine deficiency
	Thyroiditis (infection, Hashimoto disease, subacute granulomatosis, subacute lymphocytic, fibrous), Graves, goiter	
Parathyroid	Adenoma, hyperplasia, carcinoma	Renal failure, vitamin D deficiency
Adrenal	Cushing syndrome, hyperaldosteronism, congenital adrenal hyperplasia, cortical tumors (adenoma/carcinoma), medullary tumor (pheochromocytoma)	Addison disease, chronic steroid use

Remember This! Homeostatic negative feedback loops are extremely important in endocrine disease.

Oh No! Not Another Learning Experience

LEARNING OBJECTIVE 1: Using examples from the text, explain homeostatic negative feedback loops.

EXERCISE 14-1

Complete the paragraph below.

(1) _____ are molecules that are used by the (2) _____, which includes the pituitary and its target organs (the thyroid gland, parathyroid glands, adrenal glands, testes, and ovaries). (3) _____ are released from neurons in the hypothalamus to act on the anterior pituitary to control the secretion of its hormones, which in turn act on the target organs.

EXERCISE 14-2

Complete the table below.

Cells	Hormone	Effects
Anterior pituitary, (1) _____	Growth hormone	Body growth
Anterior pituitary, (2) _____	Prolactin	Milk production
Anterior pituitary, (3) _____	Proopiomelanocortin	Makes ACTH and MSH, stimulates release of corticosteroids
Anterior pituitary, (4) _____	Thyroid stimulating hormone	Stimulates thyroid hormone release
Anterior pituitary, (5) _____	Follicle stimulating hormone (FSH) and luteinizing hormone (LH)	Ovarian and endometrial cycles, sex steroid release and effects
Posterior pituitary	(6) _____	Acts on renal tubules to reabsorb water
Posterior pituitary	(7) _____	Acts on smooth muscle in breast ducts to eject milk in lactating women; acts in the uterus to cause contractions during childbirth.
Parafollicular cells (C cells)	(8) _____	Promotes absorption of calcium by bones and prohibits bone resorption by osteoclasts
Adrenal cortex, (9) _____	Mineralocorticoids (aldosterone)	Act on the kidney to retain sodium and water and excrete potassium
Adrenal cortex, (10) _____	Glucocorticoids (cortisol)	Acts glucose utilization, stress response
Adrenal cortex, (11) _____	Sex steroids (*estrogens* and *androgens*),	Has effects on bone, muscle, brain, and genitalia
(12) _____	Catecholamines Epinephrine, Norepinephrine	Connected by nerve fibers to the autonomic nervous system Regulates blood pressure, etc
Parathyroid glands	(13) _____	Regulates calcium homeostasis in a negative feedback loop with free calcium
(14) _____	thyroxine (tetraiodothyronine, or T4, L-thyroxine), triiodothyronine (liothyronine, or T3)	Regulates metabolism

Mnemonic

*Layers of the Adrenal Cortex = **GFR** (Glomerular Filtration Rate, adrenal is next to the kidney!)*

Zona **G**lomerulosa, Zona **F**asciculata, Zona **R**eticularis

produces. . .

Salt (mineralocorticoids), **Sugar** (glucocorticoids), **Sex** hormones

EXERCISE 14-3 PATHOLOGY AS A SECOND LANGUAGE

Please review The Nature of Disease Figure 14.2 then test your vocabulary by writing the appropriate term in each blank from the list below.

Thyroglobulin	Euthyroid	Colloid
Thyroid gland	Follicles	Hyperthyroid
Adrenal glands	Hypercalcemia	Adrenal cortex
Hypothyroid	Chromaffin cells	Thyroxine-binding globulin (TBG)

1. The _____ sits just under the skin in the anterior neck, above the breastbone (sternum), below the larynx, and in front of the trachea.

2. Thyroid _____ are tiny units formed by thyroid epithelial cells that synthesize thyroid hormones.

3. The thyroid contains follicles filled with a gelatinous fluid called _____.

4. _____ is a specialized protein that binds thyroid hormones (T_3 and T_4) for storage until they are released into the blood.

5. Normal thyroid function is called _____.

6. High blood levels of thyroid hormone are hypermetabolic and are called _____.

7. Low blood levels of thyroid hormone are hypometabolic and are called _____.

8. T_3 and T_4 are transported to peripheral tissues bound to a specialized blood protein known as _____.

9. _____ are neuroendocrine cells derived from the embryologic neural crest; they form the adrenal medulla.

10. _____ are important endocrine organs located adjacent to the kidneys.

11. The _____ has three distinct layers: a thin outer *zona glomerulosa*; a broad middle layer, the *zona fasciculata*; and a thin inner layer, the *zona reticularis*.

12. Elevated blood calcium is termed _____.

See Exercises 14-1 and 14-29 for additional key terms covered in this section.

> **Remember This!** There is a difference between thyrotoxicosis and hyperthyroidism—
> hyperthyroidism is but one cause of thyrotoxicosis.

Mnemonic

Symptoms of hyperthyroidism = **STING**

Sweating

Tremor **or T**achycardia

Intolerance **to** heat, **I**rregular menstruation, **and I**rritability

Nervousness

Goiter and **G**astrointestinal (loose stools/diarrhea)

LEARNING OBJECTIVE 2: Classify the types of functioning pituitary adenomas according to cell of origin, hormone produced, and clinical findings; include a description of mass and stalk effect.

EXERCISE 14-4

Complete the paragraph below.

(1) _____ are neoplasms of the pituitary that can have deleterious effects on a patient, either because of endocrine disturbance or because of growth of the mass. (2) _____ is excretion of excess trophic hormones and can be caused by hyperplasia, adenoma, or carcinoma of any of the cell types of the anterior pituitary. (3) _____ is deficiency of trophic hormone excretion and is usually due to a local destructive process, such as infarction, surgery, radiation, inflammation, and nonfunctional pituitary adenomas. Pituitary adenomas, or other masses, can sometimes exert a mass effect called (4) _____, a term applied to the effect when tumor mass blocks the inhibitory effect of the hypothalamus on prolactin secretion.

EXERCISE 14-5

Complete the table below.

Adenoma	Effects
Prolactinoma	(1) _____ , milk secretions from the breast
(2) _____	do not secrete hormones
(3) _____	excessive secretion of cortisol and related hormones from the adrenal cortex
Growth hormone adenomas	(4) _____
(5) _____	secrete LH and FSH

EXERCISE 14-6   PATHOLOGY AS A SECOND LANGUAGE

Test your vocabulary by indicating if each statement below is true or false. If it is false, provide the correct word for the italicized term that will make the statement true.

_____ 1. *Acromegaly* is a syndrome that occurs when abnormal secretion of growth hormone occurs in adults after bone growth plates disappear.

_____

_____ 2. *Gigantism* is a general increase in body size, with especially long arms and legs. It occurs when a child or teenager develops an adenoma that secretes growth hormone before growth plates close at the ends of long bones.

_____

LEARNING OBJECTIVE 3: Describe the presentation of hypopituitarism and catalog the potential underlying etiologies.

EXERCISE 14-7

Complete the paragraph below.

(1) _____ is decreased secretion of pituitary hormones and is usually due to a local destructive process, such as infarction, surgery, radiation, inflammation, or masses, including nonfunctional (2) _____ or a (3) _____ (or craniopharyngioma), a benign neoplasm. These suprasellar masses make themselves known by mass effect. Disease usually presents as deficiency of hormones excreted by the target organs, including adrenal cortex, thyroid gland, testes, and ovary, which undergo (4) _____. Patients typically become easily fatigued, lose weight, and are mildly anemic. Often there is sexual dysfunction; however, the diagnosis can be difficult to make because the symptoms are (5) _____.

EXERCISE 14-8 PATHOLOGY AS A SECOND LANGUAGE

See Exercise 14-7 for key terms covered in this section.

LEARNING OBJECTIVE 4: Compare and contrast diabetes insipidus and syndrome of inappropriate ADH secretion.

EXERCISE 14-9

Complete the paragraph below.

(1) _____ and syndrome of inappropriate ADH section (SIADH) are both due to abnormal levels of ADH, either too low or too high, respectively. **Diabetes insipidus** (DI) is a syndrome of ADH deficiency and features (2) _____ production of dilute urine. In contrast, (3) _____ is associated with excessive ADH production, usually from an ectopic source (i.e., not from the [4] _____ , but rather, e.g., from small cell carcinoma of the lung). However, it may occur in a wide variety of other conditions, including brain, pulmonary, and endocrine disorders. Symptoms are essentially due to water intoxication and include (5) _____ and cerebral edema, with associated neurologic problems.

EXERCISE 14-10 PATHOLOGY AS A SECOND LANGUAGE

See Exercise14-9 for key terms covered in this section.

LEARNING OBJECTIVE 5: Categorize the diseases of the thyroid—goiter, euthyroid sick syndrome, thyrotoxicosis, Grave disease, cretinism, myxedema, Hashimoto thyroiditis, and subacute granulomatous thyroiditis—as hyperthyroid, euthyroid, or hypothyroid, and give their characteristic features and diagnostic findings.

EXERCISE 14-11

Complete the sentence below.

Diseases of the thyroid are related to iodine deficiency, (1) _____, infections, and the downstream effects of too much or too little thyroid hormone.

EXERCISE 14-12

Complete the table below.

Disease	Hormone Imbalance	Labs	Effects
(1) _____	Variable or normal	Variable or normal	Enlarged nodular gland, results from chronic nontoxic goiters; can be related to iodine deficiency
(2) _____	Low thyroid hormones	Low T_3/T_4, high TSH, autoimmune antibodies (antithyroglobulin, etc.)	Most common type of thyroiditis; myxedema
(3) _____	High thyroid hormones	High T_3/T_4, low TSH, autoimmune antibodies (thyroid-stimulating immunoglobulin, i.e., anti-TSH receptor)	Exophthalmos
(4) _____ (*de Quervain thyroiditis*)	No specific hormone imbalance	No specific labs	Due to infection, self-limited; causes fever, malaise, and weakness

EXERCISE 14-13   PATHOLOGY AS A SECOND LANGUAGE

Test your vocabulary by writing the appropriate term in each blank from the list below.

(RAI) uptake	Exophthalmos	Thyrotoxicosis
Myxedema	Thyroiditis	Nontoxic goiters
Colloid goiters	Diffuse nontoxic goiters	RAI scan
Hyperthyroidism	T_3-toxicosis Radioactive iodine	Goiter
Toxic adenoma	Euthyroid sick syndrome	Cretinism

1. A _____ is an enlarged thyroid gland.

2. A severe nonthyroidal illness that may have abnormally low thyroid function tests, but patients are clinically euthyroid and appear to have normal function, is called _____.

3. _____ is a hypermetabolic clinical state caused by increased levels of blood T_3 and/or T_4.

4. _____ is overproduction of T_3 and/or T_4 by the thyroid gland.

5. Selective hypersecretion of T_3 is simply called _____.

6. _____ examination can be used to assess thyroid function relative to normal, which is uptake of about 10–30% of the injected dose as it synthesizes hormone. This uptake can be scanned by a camera to create an image called an RAI scan.

7. A functioning thyroid adenoma is also called a _____.

8. An accumulation of material in the orbit behind the globe can push it forward causing the condition _____.

9. Hypothyroidism in infants or children has been termed _____.

10. _____ is hypothyroidism that develops in an older child or an adult, and refers to swelling of connective tissues, as in the pretibial area of the leg.

11. _____ is inflammation of the thyroid gland.

12. Goiters that are the result of impaired synthesis of thyroid hormone are called _____.

13. The largest early nontoxic goiters are often referred to as _____ or _____.

LEARNING OBJECTIVE 6: List the types of thyroid cancer and describe their associated morphology and clinical course.

EXERCISE 14-14

Complete the paragraph below.

Thyroid cancers are associated with various risk factors including (1) _____, preexisting thyroid disease, iodine deficiency, and genetic syndromes. Treatment most often involves (2) _____ of part or all of the thyroid gland. Exercise 14-16 provides information on specific thyroid cancers.

EXERCISE 14-15

Complete the table below.

Neoplasm	Cell of Origin	Gross/Histologic Features	Epidemiology/Outcome
(1) _____	Thyroid follicular epithelial cells	Well-circumscribed and encapsulated nodule of follicular cells	Benign
(2) _____	Thyroid follicular cells	Follicular mass with capsular or vascular invasion	10% to 15% of thyroid cancers; mortality variable based on extent of invasiveness
(3) _____	Thyroid follicular cells	Characteristic "coffee bean" nuclei, papillary structures	Most common thyroid cancer (80%); most occur between 25 and 50 years old, F > M; excellent prognosis (90% survival)
(4) _____	C-cells (parafollicular)	Neuroendocrine cells with amyloid (calcitonin)	Genetic predisposition (MEN2A/B, familial); most sporadic; 5% of thyroid cancers
(5) _____	? Unknown/Stem Cells	Grossly invasive, anaplastic and pleomorphic cells	Highly malignant; mortality > 90%; less than 5% of thyroid cancers

EXERCISE 14-16 PATHOLOGY AS A SECOND LANGUAGE

See Exercise 14-15 for key terms covered in this section.

LEARNING OBJECTIVE 7: Discuss the etiology, clinical presentation, and diagnostic findings of Cushing syndrome, primary hyperaldosteronism, congenital adrenal hyperplasia, and causes of adrenocortical failure including Addison disease.

EXERCISE 14-17

Please review The Nature of Disease Figure 14.4 then complete the paragraph below.

Lesions at various levels of the hypothalamic-pituitary axis can cause imbalance of adrenal hormones. Moreover, the type of hormone can differ depending on whether the adrenal cortex or adrenal medulla is involved. For example, (1) _____ is autonomous, chronic excessive aldosterone secretion by the adrenal cortex. In general, (2) _____ features excess cortical hormone from any source. (3) _____ results in concurrent deficiency of all three corticosteroids, of which cortisol and aldosterone deficiency are clinically most important.

EXERCISE 14-18

Complete the table below.

	Cortisol	Cause	Signs and Symptoms
(1) _____	Increased	Any, including drugs or diseases that increase cortisol	Cushingoid appearance, "moon face," "buffalo hump," striae, etc.
(2) _____	Increased	Pituitary adenoma secreting ACTH	Visual disturbances (field of vision loss), other cortisol symptoms

Remember This! Most of the signs and symptoms of Cushing syndrome are due to excess cortisol.

EXERCISE 14-19   PATHOLOGY AS A SECOND LANGUAGE

Test your vocabulary by indicating if each statement below is true or false. If it is false, provide the correct word for the italicized term that will make the statement true.

_____ 1. *Dexamethasone suppression test* is used to determine the level at which hypercortisolism is occurring (i.e., primary, secondary, or tertiary).

_____

_____ 2. *Congenital adrenal hypoplasia* is a congenital disorder of sexual differentiation that arises from one of several varieties of autosomal recessive genetic defects that cause cortical enzyme deficiency, androgen excess, and adrenal hyperplasia.

_____

_____ 3. *21 ß-hydroxylase deficiency* is a congenital enzyme deficiency that leads to increased androgens and decreased cortisol.

_____

_____ 4. Urinary loss of sodium is termed *salt wasting*.

_____

_____ 5. *Addison disease* is the most common cause of *primary chronic* cortical failure called *autoimmune adrenalitis*.

_____

Remember This! Most of the danger of Addison disease is due to lack of cortisol.

LEARNING OBJECTIVE 8: Explain why patients with pheochromocytoma have high blood pressure.

EXERCISE 14-20

Complete the paragraph below.

(1) _____ are rare yet also the most common neoplasm of the adrenal medulla. Because the tumor secretes large amounts of (2) _____, including epinephrine and norepinephrine, the blood pressure increases by way of increasing (3) _____ and sometimes increased vascular resistance. Other similar neurogenic tumors may arise at various sites outside the adrenal medulla and are known as (4) _____.

EXERCISE 14-21   PATHOLOGY AS A SECOND LANGUAGE

See Exercise 14-20 for key terms covered in this section.

LEARNING OBJECTIVE 9: Distinguish hypo- from hyperparathyroidism using signs and symptoms, and offer a brief profile of the possible laboratory abnormalities.

EXERCISE 14-22

Complete the paragraph below.

(1) _____ is defined as oversecretion of PTH by the parathyroid glands, thereby causing hypercalcemia. The finding that usually first raises the possibility of parathyroid disease is (2) _____. (3) _____ is caused by overproduction of PTH and is usually due to parathyroid hyperplasia, or a benign neoplasm of the parathyroid, called (4) _____. (5) _____ is a situation in which low blood calcium (hypocalcemia) is caused by a nonparathyroid condition that stimulates compensatory parathyroid hyperplasia and secretion of excess PTH. (6) _____ is usually due to chronic kidney disease and features a loss of sensitivity to serum calcium levels.

EXERCISE 14-23

Complete the table below.

	PTH	Calcium	Phosphate
Primary hyperparathyroidism	High	High	(1) _____
Secondary hyperparathyroidism	High	(2) _____	High (vitamin D deficiency or chronic renal failure)
Tertiary hyperparathyroidism	(3) _____	High	High (also has history of chronic renal failure)

Remember This! The parathyroids are not regulated by the pituitary!

EXERCISE 14-24   PATHOLOGY AS A SECOND LANGUAGE

See Exercise 14-22 for key terms covered in this section.

LEARNING OBJECTIVE 10: Compare and contrast the MEN syndromes.

EXERCISE 14-25

Complete the paragraph below.

The (1) _____ are a group of heritable disorders due to gene defects that cause endocrine cell growth—hyperplasia, adenoma, or carcinoma—in various endocrine organs. Therefore, these syndromes can be grouped with other (2) _____ that have genetic predispositions for cancer. Indeed, overall in MEN2 patients, there is a greater than 90% chance of getting (3) _____.

EXERCISE 14-26

Complete the table below.

Syndrome	Inheritance	Gene	Clinical Associations
MEN 1 (Wermer)	Autosomal dominant	(1) _____	Abnormalities of parathyroid, pancreas, pituitary, and gastrin-secreting cells of the duodenum
(2) _____	Autosomal dominant	RET	Medullary thyroid carcinoma, pheochromocytoma, parathyroid hyperplasia
(3) _____	Autosomal dominant	RET	Medullary thyroid carcinoma, pheochromocytoma, diffuse ganglioneuromas of the GI tract

EXERCISE 14-27   PATHOLOGY AS A SECOND LANGUAGE

See Exercises 14-26 and 14-27 for key terms covered in this section.

Decisions Decisions

DECISION TREE 14.1: HYPOTHALAMIC AXIS DISEASE

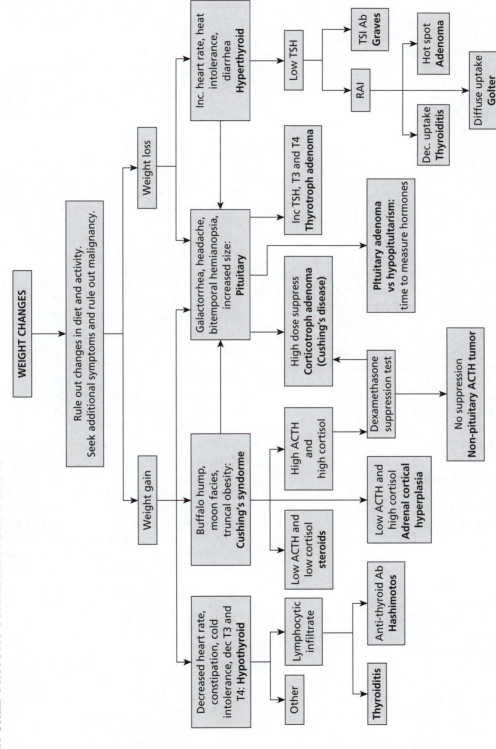

WEIGHT CHANGES

Rule out changes in diet and activity. Seek additional symptoms and rule out malignancy.

Weight gain

Decreased heart rate, constipation, cold intolerance, dec T3 and T4: **Hypothyroid**

- Other
- Lymphocytic infiltrate
  - Anti-thyroid Ab **Hashimotos**
  - **Thyroiditis**

Buffalo hump, moon facies, truncal obesity: **Cushing's syndorme**

- Low ACTH and low cortisol **steroids**
- Low ACTH and high cortisol **Adrenal cortical hyperplasia**
- High ACTH and high cortisol
  - Dexamethasone suppression test
    - No suppression **Non-pituitary ACTH tumor**
    - High dose suppress Corticotroph adenoma (**Cushing's disease**)

Galactorrhea, headache, bitemporal hemianopsia, increased size: **Pituitary**

- Inc TSH, T3 and T4 **Thyrotroph adenoma**
- **Pituitary adenoma vs hypopituitarism:** time to measure hormones

Weight loss

Inc. heart rate, heat intolerance, diarrhea **Hyperthyroid**

- Low TSH
  - TSI Ab **Graves**
  - RAI
    - Dec. uptake **Thyroiditis**
    - Hot spot **Adenoma**
    - Diffuse uptake **Golter**

189

Test Yourself

I. MULTIPLE CHOICE

1. A 42-year-old Caucasian female, with a past medical history of Cushing syndrome, status post bilateral adrenalectomy, presents with marked darkening of the skin and new onset bitemporal hemianopsia. Her labs are notable for increased POMC. What is your diagnosis? [LEARNING OBJECTIVE 2]
   A. Recurrent Cushing syndrome
   B. Nelson syndrome
   C. Sheehan syndrome
   D. Addison disease

2. Which of the following tissues are neuroendocrine tissues? [LEARNING OBJECTIVE 1]
   A. Breast and uterus
   B. Bone and muscle
   C. All of the above
   D. None of the above

3. A 35-year-old African American female presents to the clinic complaining of insomnia, fatigue, diarrhea, and weight loss. Her physical exam is further notable for tachycardia, flushed skin, and fine tremor in addition to lid-lag and exaggerated reflexes. As expected, labs demonstrate both elevated T_3 and T_4 and decreased TSH, and a radio iodide scan shows a single hot-spot. What is the underlying etiology of her symptoms? (Hint: Use the Decision Tree) [LEARNING OBJECTIVE 5]
   A. Grave disease
   B. Thyroid adenoma
   C. Thyrotroph adenoma
   D. De Quervain thyroiditis

4. The constellation of pheochromocytoma, medullary thyroid carcinoma, and parathyroid hyperplasia is seen in which of the following syndromes? [LEARNING OBJECTIVE 10]
   A. MEN-1A
   B. MEN-2A
   C. MEN-2B
   D. MEN-1B

5. A 42-year-old Hispanic female with a past medical history significant to hypertension and diabetes presents with a constellation of signs and symptoms characteristic of Cushing syndrome, including thin atrophic limbs, truncal obesity, a buffalo hump, thin friable skin with purple striae, menstrual irregularities, and recurrent infections. Her labs are notable for elevated cortisol in the setting of decreased ACTH. What is the underlying cause of her disease? (Hint: Use the Decision Tree) [LEARNING OBJECTIVE 7]
   A. Pituitary corticotroph adenoma
   B. Exogenous steroids

C. Small cell lung carcinoma
D. Adrenocortical adenoma

6. Which of the following statements concerning chromaffin cells are true? [LEARNING OBJECTIVE 1]
   A. They secrete catecholamines such as epinephrine and mineralocorticoids.
   B. They are located in the zona glomerulosa.
   C. Their effects include increased heart rate, dilated bronchioles, and increased metabolic rate.
   D. All of the above are true.

7. A 15-year-old Caucasian female is admitted to the hospital for severe dehydration. Despite being dehydrated, with labs notable for elevated blood sodium and osmolality, she continues to excrete large quantities of dilute urine, with a specific gravity of 1.001. What is your diagnosis? [LEARNING OBJECTIVE 4]
   A. Diabetes insipidus
   B. Syndrome of inappropriate ADH secretion
   C. Hyperaldosteronism
   D. Deficiencies of 21 ß-hydroxylase

8. Decreased PTH, elevated calcium, and elevated phosphorus are characteristic of which of the following? [LEARNING OBJECTIVE 9]
   A. Primary hyperparathyroidism
   B. Secondary hyperparathyroidism
   C. Tertiary hyperparathyroidism
   D. Hypoparathyroidism

9. A 23-year-old female with a recent diagnosis of depression presents to the college clinic complaining of fatigue, weight gain, cold intolerance, and constipation. Her labs are notable for low T_3 and T_4, increased TSH, and an absence of antithyroid antibodies. A biopsy of the thyroid is negative for lymphocytic infiltrate. Which of the following is the most likely explanation for her symptoms? (Hint: Use the Decision Tree) [LEARNING OBJECTIVE 5]
   A. Lithium toxicity
   B. Hashimoto disease
   C. De Quervain thyroidits
   D. Cretinism

10. The hormone responsible for retaining sodium and excreting potassium is synthesized in which of the following locations? [LEARNING OBJECTIVE 1]
    A. Zona glomerulosa
    B. Zona fasciculata
    C. Zona reticularis
    D. Medulla

11. A 55-year-old African American male presents to the clinic for his yearly checkup. He notes

that his glove and shoe size have drastically increased over the previous year. His exam is further notable for enlargement of the skull and jaw with prominent brown and gapped teeth. Which of the following diseases is most likely to have caused these physical manifestations? [LEARNING OBJECTIVE 2]

A. Gigantism
B. Acromegaly
C. Conn syndrome
D. Waterhouse-Friderichsen syndrome

12. Thyroid follicular adenomas are characterized by which of the following pathologic findings? [LEARNING OBJECTIVE 6]

A. Solitary, round, and discrete nodules composed of thyroid epithelium formed into follicles
B. Cauliflower-like microscopic growth pattern composed of cells with abnormal grooved nuclei that resemble coffee beans
C. Round, polygonal or spindle cells with granular cytoplasm and round/oval nuclei in nests, cords or follicles, defined by sharply outlined fibrous bands
D. Large, pleomorphic giant cells resembling osteoclasts with cellular connective tissue separated by fibrous bands

II. TRUE OR FALSE

13. _____ Releasing hormones delivered to the posterior pituitary by a network of small veins stimulate target organs through the secretion of hormones. [LEARNING OBJECTIVE 1]

14. _____ Waterhouse-Friderichsen syndrome can be caused by meningococcal septicemia associated with meningococcal meningitis. [LEARNING OBJECTIVE 7]

15. _____ Parathormone secretion is controlled by the level of total blood calcium. [LEARNING OBJECTIVE 1]

16. _____ Carcinoma is the most common cause of hyperpituitarism. [LEARNING OBJECTIVE 2]

17. _____ Papillary carcinomas, despite their preferential spread to lymph nodes, are actually less aggressive than follicular carcinomas. [LEARNING OBJECTIVE 6]

18. _____ The adrenal functions as two organs in one: the outer cortex, which comprises 90% of the gland, under control of the autonomic nervous system; and the inner medulla, under control of the pituitary gland. [LEARNING OBJECTIVE 1]

III. MATCHING

19. Match the following diseases with their cause or effect; answers may be used more than once: [LEARNING OBJECTIVES 2, 5, 7, 8, AND 9]

    i. Pheochromocytoma
   ii. Addison disease
  iii. Cushing syndrome
   iv. Gigantism
    v. Hashimoto
   vi. Acromegaly
  vii. Parathyroid adenoma

A. Increased epinephrine
B. Increased growth hormone
C. Steroid use
D. Deficiency of cortisol
E. Thyroiditis
F. Decreased parathormone

IV. SHORT ANSWER

20. A 29-year-old Caucasian male is back in the ER four hours after you sent him home with the same complaint of chest pain and abdominal pain, nausea, and palpitations. His EKG and CKs are still negative; however, his blood pressure is dangerously elevated, despite medication given earlier in the day to treat it. What test should you run? [LEARNING OBJECTIVE 7]

_____

_____

_____

21. If the patient described in question number 20 had presented with chronic hypertension despite medication and without exacerbations, what other tests might you consider running? [LEARNING OBJECTIVE 8]

_____

_____

_____

22. A 36-year-old female with a history of uncontrolled Grave disease visits your clinic two weeks after her thyroidectomy complaining of intermittent muscular aches and spasms (tetany) as well as a tingling sensation

of the face, lips, and tongue. Her reflexes are hyperactive on exam. What complication of Grave disease does she suffer from? [LEARNING OBJECTIVE9]

_____

_____

_____

23. What types of treatments might someone suffering from anterior pituitary hypofunction require? [LEARNING OBJECTIVE 3]

_____

_____

_____

24. What important implications must be immediately addressed in a female infant born with ambiguous genitalia? [LEARNING OBJECTIVE 7]

_____

_____

_____

Disorders of the Urinary Tract

The Big Picture

The upper urinary tract (i.e., kidney, renal pelvis) and lower urinary tract (i.e., ureter, bladder, urethra) have different sets of nonneoplastic and neoplastic diseases. Nonneoplastic disorders of the kidney can impair filtration of the blood or other critical functions. Disorders of the lower tract can impair the proper storage and passage of urine. For neoplasms, the kidney most commonly develops renal cell carcinoma; whereas any surface covered by urothelial mucosa, including the renal pelvis and lower urinary tract, may develop urothelial (transitional cell) carcinoma.

Oh No! Not Another Learning Experience

LEARNING OBJECTIVE 1: Discuss the relationship between the anatomy of the kidney and its five functions, including the transformation of glomerular filtrate to urine.

EXERCISE 15-1

Complete the paragraph below.

The functions of the kidney are, 1) excretion of metabolic waste, 2) adjustment of blood pH by excretion of more or less acid, 3) adjustment of plasma salt concentration (plasma osmolality) by excretion of more or less salt and water, 4) adjustment of blood volume and blood pressure by secretion of renin, and 5) stimulation of red blood cell production by secretion of erythropoietin.

The kidney has specific anatomic structures to accommodate these functions and convert glomerular filtrate into (1) _____, the fluid ultimately excreted by the kidneys. (2) The _____ consists of the kidneys, renal pelvises, ureters, urinary bladder, and urethra. The kidneys and renal pelvises form the (3) _____, while the ureters, bladder, and urethra form the (4) _____. Blood is filtered in the kidney by the (5) _____ and enters Bowman space as (6) _____. After leaving Bowman space, the fluid, known as (7) _____, moves down the tubule, being modified as water, electrolytes, acid, and other substances are exchanged. After exiting the tubule, the remaining fluid is (8) _____.

Remember This! Normal urinary tract health depends on smooth, brisk, unobstructed flow of urine.

EXERCISE 15-2   PATHOLOGY AS A SECOND LANGUAGE

Please review The Nature of Disease Figures 15.1–3 then test your vocabulary by writing the appropriate term in each blank from the list below.

Glomerular membrane	Glomerular filtration rate	Tubular epithelial cells
Collecting system	Ureters	Juxtaglomerular apparatus
Urinary bladder	Urethra	Urothelial cells
Parietal epithelial cells	Barrier effect	Bowman space
Internal sphincter	Nephron unit	Cortex
Medulla	Mesangial cells	Renal tubule
External sphincter	Creatinine	Visceral epithelial cells
Detrusor muscle	Blood urea nitrogen	Micturition
Afferent arteriole	Efferent arteriole	Renal pelvis
Ureterovesical junction	Urothelial epithelium	Trigone

1. The _____ consists of a series of spaces that carry urine from the kidney and hold it for urination.

2. The _____ is a broad, funnel-shaped space that gathers urine from the kidney.

3. The muscular tubes that convey urine from the kidney to the bladder are called the _____.

4. The _____ stores urine until elimination via the urethra.

5. With the exception of the terminal urethra, which is lined by squamous epithelium, the collecting system is lined by _____.

6. The _____ is sometimes called transitional epithelium because of its ability to transition between round and flat as the bladder fills and stretches.

7. The _____ is a one-way valve to prevent backflow of urine from the bladder into the ureter.

8. The opening to each ureter and the internal meatus of the urethra form an inverted triangle of bladder mucosa called the _____.

9. The muscular wall of the bladder is called the _____.

10. The _____ is the terminal conduit for urine and semen and extends from the neck of the bladder to the opening at the tip of the penis.

11. The process of expelling urine from the bladder by urination is termed _____.

12. The _____ is composed of smooth muscle, is involuntary, and is controlled by the autonomic nervous system.

13. The _____ circles the urethra immediately below the internal sphincter; it is composed of skeletal muscle that is under voluntary control.

14. The kidney is composed of two parts, the outer _____ and a central _____.

15. Supporting glomerular capillaries are _____, interstitial cells that fit between adjacent capillaries.

16. Each glomerulus is contiguous with the proximal end of a _____, which together with the glomerulus forms a _____.

17. Epithelial cells line the entire tubule including the outside of the glomerulus, called _____, the outer limit of Bowman space, called _____, and the remainder of the tubule, called _____.

18. The empty space in between the epithelial walls surrounding each glomerulus is called _____.

19. Blood is supplied to the glomerulus by a relatively large _____, and leaves through a smaller _____.

20. The _____ senses blood pressure and blood flow in the afferent arteriole and sodium concentration in the distal convoluted tubule, and secretes renin.

21. The so-called _____ is composed of the capillary endothelium, the glomerular basement membrane, and the glomerular visceral epithelium.

22. Part of the glomerular membrane has a fine mesh that allows only smaller particles through; this is called the _____.

23. The _____ is a clinically useful measure of renal function; it is defined as the amount of plasma cleared each minute.

24. _____ is a measure of renal function; it is derived from muscle metabolism and is elevated in renal disease.

25. _____ is a measure of renal function that refers to blood levels of nitrogen found in urea.

LEARNING OBJECTIVE 2: Explain the significance of some of the more important urine abnormalities such as glycosuria and others.

EXERCISE 15-3

Complete the paragraph below.

(1) _____ is an important body fluid that can be easily tested for clinically relevant abnormalities. For example, a urine (2) _____ made of paper containing bands of chemicals that test for various urine characteristics and substances can be used in the outpatient clinic. Urine glucose, blood (called [3] _____), and protein are commonly measured abnormalities.

EXERCISE 15-4   PATHOLOGY AS A SECOND LANGUAGE

Test your vocabulary by indicating if each statement below is true or false. If it is false, provide the correct word for the italicized term that will make the statement true.

_____ 1. *Bilirubinuria* indicates increased bilirubin in the urine and blood due to cholestasis or hemolysis of red blood cells.

_____

_____ 2. *Hematuria* is intact red blood cells in urine.

_____

_____ 3. *Occult hematuria* is blood in urine visible to the naked eye and can be due to trauma or malignancy.

_____

_____ 4. *Gross hematuria* is also called microscopic hematuria because it contains intact red blood cells despite appearing grossly normal.

_____

_____ 5. *Hemoglobinuria* is free hemoglobin in the urine, without necessarily having intact red blood cells.

_____

_____ 6. *Glycosuria* is urine with ketones as can be seen in diabetes.

_____

LEARNING OBJECTIVE 3: Explain the causes, manifestations, and consequences of urinary tract obstruction and reflux.

EXERCISE 15-5

Complete the paragraph below.

The urinary tract can be obstructed by cancer, stones, or fibrosis. In men, a common cause of obstructive symptoms is (1) _____; whereas, in women, a common cause is pregnancy. Regardless of the cause, urinary obstruction can lead to an obstructive uropathy, with dilation of the ureters, called (2) _____, and kidney damage. Stasis of urine can lead to various (3) _____ of the bladder and kidney.

> **Remember This!** Almost all of the glomerular filtrate is reabsorbed by renal tubules and returned to blood.

EXERCISE 15-6   PATHOLOGY AS A SECOND LANGUAGE

Test your vocabulary by indicating if each statement below is true or false. If it is false, provide the correct word for the italicized term that will make the statement true.

_____ 1. *Transurethral resection (TUR)* defines the surgical approach for resecting bladder tumors and for reducing the size of the prostate to alleviate obstructive symptoms.

_____

_____ 2. *Sclerosing retroperitoneal fibrosis* is an inflammatory condition associated with certain drugs, autoimmune disorders, and lymphomas.

_____

LEARNING OBJECTIVE 4: Compare and contrast the types of urinary stones capable of forming in the kidney.

EXERCISE 15-7

Complete the paragraphs below.

A variety of stones (also called [1] _____) can form in the urinary tract, in a process called (2) _____. Most stones form in the kidney, which is termed (3) _____.

When stones become large and conform to the shape of the renal pelvis and calyces, they are called (4) _____. Stones of this size cannot pass through the lower urinary tract. Some stones are readily identifiable on imaging studies. Virtually any stone that enters the lower urinary tract causes pain, bleeding, or obstruction. As a stone or fragment passes down the ureter, it causes a distinctive and extremely painful syndrome of cramping and flank pain known as (5) _____.

EXERCISE 15-8

Complete the table below.

Stone Type	Percentage	Cause	Characteristics/Imaging
(1) _____	75%	Some patients have hypercalcemia	Dark stones, opaque on X-ray imaging
(2) _____	20%	Infections/alkaline urine	Friable stones, less densely opaque on X-ray imaging
(3) _____	5%	Most patients do not have gout	Entirely invisible on X-ray imaging
(4) _____	1%	Metabolic disease	Faint on X-ray imaging

EXERCISE 15-9 PATHOLOGY AS A SECOND LANGUAGE

See Exercises 15-7 and 15-8 for key terms covered in this section.

LEARNING OBJECTIVE 5: Name the most important malignancies of the urinary tract, and describe the findings associated with each.

EXERCISE 15-10

Please review The Nature of Disease Figure 15.11 then complete the paragraph below.

The malignancies of the urinary tract include malignancies of the kidney, most of which are (1) _____, and malignancies of the lower urinary tract, most of which are (2) _____. Invasive urothelial carcinoma arises either from flat premalignant lesions called (3) _____ or from papillary urothelial carcinomas. Benign tumors also exist at these locations.

EXERCISE 15-11

Complete the table below.

Tumor Type	Derivation	Behavior
(1) _____ (*renal adenocarcinoma*)	Renal tubular epithelium	Malignant
(2) _____	Renal tubular epithelium (with abundant mitochondria)	Benign
Carcinoma of the renal pelvis	Urothelium	(3) _____
(4) _____	Urothelium	Initially noninvasive; unlikely to invade; low-grade atypical cells
(5) _____	Urothelium	Initially noninvasive; likely to invade; high-grade malignant appearing cells

EXERCISE 15-12 PATHOLOGY AS A SECOND LANGUAGE

Test your vocabulary by indicating if each statement below is true or false. If it is false, provide the correct word for the italicized term that will make the statement true.

_____ 1. *Papillary urothelial neoplasm of low malignant potential (PUNLMP)* is a benign papillary tumor that accounts for about 1% of urothelial neoplasms.

_____

_____ 2. *Urothelial papilloma* is a papillary neoplasm of urothelial cells with a limited degree of atypia.

_____

Remember This! Grossly visible painless hematuria should be considered a sign of urinary tract cancer until proven otherwise.

LEARNING OBJECTIVE 6: List the congenital abnormalities that may arise in the lower urinary tract.

EXERCISE 15-13

Complete the paragraph below.

Various congenital anatomic variations can occur in the lower urinary tract. Perhaps the most common is

(1) _____, which is defined as reverse movement of urine from the bladder to the ureters. This results from

incompetent valves where the ureters join the bladder or from blockage of urethral outflow that increases bladder

pressure. Vesicoureteral reflux predisposes to infections. In some cases, (2) _____ prevents urinary flow.

(3) _____ of the bladder is a rare but serious congenital anomaly in which the low anterior abdominal wall

and the anterior wall of the bladder fail to develop, leaving the bladder open to the environment.

EXERCISE 15-14 PATHOLOGY AS A SECOND LANGUAGE

See Exercise 15-13 for key terms covered in this section.

LEARNING OBJECTIVE 7: Describe the etiology, signs and symptoms, and treatment of lower urinary tract infections.

EXERCISE 15-15

Complete the paragraph below.

Infection and inflammation can impact the lower urinary tract and cause symptoms such as urgency, increased

frequency, and burning on urination. (1) _____ is the most common form of (2) _____, and is usually

attributable to infection by gram-negative fecal organisms. (3) _____ is bladder inflammation without infection.

(4) _____ is an especially painful chronic cystitis involving all layers of the bladder wall. (5) _____ is

inflammation of the urethra and can be due to a sexually transmitted infection (such as gonorrhea).

EXERCISE 15-16 PATHOLOGY AS A SECOND LANGUAGE

See Exercise 15-15 for key terms covered in this section.

LEARNING OBJECTIVE 8: List the possible causes of voiding disorders; be sure to distinguish between the various types of incontinence.

EXERCISE 15-17

Complete the paragraph below.

Voiding disorders include those that abnormally retain urine and those that fail to contain and store urine properly. (1) _____ is incomplete emptying of the bladder or cessation of urination. (2) _____ is involuntary loss of urine. (3) _____ is uncontrolled leakage of urine after a quickly developing uncontrollable urge to void. (4) _____ is urine leakage due to an abrupt increase of intra-abdominal pressure, as for example with sneezing, coughing, lifting, or laughing; it is common during pregnancy. (5) _____ is dribbling from an overly full bladder. (6) _____ is urine loss due to cognitive or physical impairment such as dementia or stroke. (7) _____ is temporary and treatable. (8) _____ is persistent and due to nerve or muscular problems.

EXERCISE 15-18   PATHOLOGY AS A SECOND LANGUAGE

See Exercise 15-17 for key terms covered in this section.

LEARNING OBJECTIVE 9: Distinguish between renal diseases and syndromes of renal disease.

EXERCISE 15-19

Complete the paragraph below.

Although renal diseases are specifically defined entities (see Learning Objective 11), many often lead to similar renal disease syndromes. The two primary syndromes of renal disease are the (1) _____ and the (2) _____. Irrespective of the cause, renal failure can be categorized as either (3) _____, which is uncommon and features rapid onset of azotemia and oliguria or anuria with urine output of about 400 ml/day or less, or (4) _____, which is characterized by long-standing, unremitting deterioration of renal function. In the United States, chronic renal failure is most commonly caused by (5) _____.

Mnemonic
*Causes of Acute Renal Failure = Patients can't **VOID RIGHT***
Vasculitis
Obstruction
Infection
Drugs
Renal artery stenosis
Interstitial nephritis
Glomerulonephritis
Hypovolaemia
Thromboembolism

EXERCISE 15-20   PATHOLOGY AS A SECOND LANGUAGE

Test your vocabulary by indicating if each statement below is true or false. If it is false, provide the correct word for the italicized term that will make the statement true.

_____ 1. *Azotemia* is renal failure that is manifested only by abnormal laboratory tests demonstrating excess nitrogen with no clinical signs of kidney dysfunction.

_____

_____ 2. *Hyperemia* is renal failure that is manifested not only with increased nitrogenous wastes in the blood, but also with clinical signs and symptoms.

_____

Mnemonic

Causes of Chronic Renal Failure = **DUG HIPPO**
Diabetes mellitus
Unknown
Glomerulonephritis
Hypertension
Interstitial nephritis
Pyelonephritis
Polycystic kidney disease
Obstruction

LEARNING OBJECTIVE 10: List the inherited, congenital, and developmental diseases that affect the kidney, and differentiate between the diseases capable of causing kidney cysts.

EXERCISE 15-21

Complete the paragraph below.

Congenital abnormalities may affect the kidney in addition to various cystic diseases. If one or both kidneys fail to develop, it is termed (1) _____. Alternatively, the kidneys can fuse, forming a single abnormal shape called a (2) _____. (3) _____ is a sporadic developmental disorder in which the fetal kidney develops as a small mass of cysts accompanied by islands of primitive cartilage and other immature tissue. (4) _____ are small incidental cysts usually just a few millimeters in diameter, filled with clear fluid, that are considered a normal variant. (5) _____ is generally divided into two forms, autosomal dominant polycystic kidney disease (ADPKD) and autosomal recessive polycystic kidney disease (ARPKD).

EXERCISE 15-22   PATHOLOGY AS A SECOND LANGUAGE

Test your vocabulary by writing the appropriate term in each blank from the list below.
Autosomal dominant polycystic kidney disease (ADPKD)
Autosomal recessive polycystic kidney disease (ARPKD)

1. _____, formerly called "juvenile" or "childhood" polycystic kidney disease, is caused by one of several genetic defects and usually appears at birth as massively enlarged kidneys and a variety of other defects. It is often associated with liver cysts and biliary duct abnormalities leading to cirrhosis, with death often occurring in the perinatal period.

2. _____, formerly called "adult" polycystic kidney disease, features renal cysts, berry aneurysms of the circle of Willis, and mitral valve prolapse; however, it is usually asymptomatic until adulthood. Patients come to medical attention because of hematuria, chronic urinary tract infection, or hypertension. The disease continues to renal failure requiring transplantation.

LEARNING OBJECTIVE 11: Explain the difference between nephritic syndrome and nephrotic syndrome, giving examples of each; pay special attention to those that are most common.

EXERCISE 15-23

Complete the paragraph below.

The two primary syndromes of renal disease are the (1) _____ and the

(2) _____. (3) _____ is marked by massive proteinuria and severe

generalized osmotic edema due to low plasma albumin secondary to protein loss. (4) _____

is caused by glomerular inflammation and leads to hematuria, azotemia, proteinuria, oliguria, edema, and

(5) _____. Most renal diseases fall nicely into one of those categories; however, some have

attributes of both, or progress from nephritic to nephrotic.

EXERCISE 15-24

Complete the table below.

Disease	Syndrome	Pathologic Characteristics	Clinical
(1) _____	Nephritic	Immune deposits in glomeruli, can progress to RPGN	Acute strep pharyngitis/ skin infection; check ASO titer
Rapidly progressive glomerulonephritis	Nephritic/Nephrotic	(2) _____	Common pathway toward chronic GN for many glomerular diseases, either primary or secondary renal failure
Membranous glomerulonephritis	(3) _____	Thick basement membrane	Most common nephrotic syndrome in adults
(4) _____	Nephritic/ Nephrotic	Thickening and splitting of the basement membrane, hypercellularity of glomerulus	Half develop renal failure in 10 years
(5) _____ **(aka lipoid nephrosis)**	Nephrotic	Effacement of podocytes (on EM)	Most common nephrotic in children; responds to steroids
(6) _____	Nephrotic	IgA deposits	Hematuria after respiratory/GI infections, often benign in children
(7) _____	Nephrotic	Immune deposits and mesangial sclerosis in portion of some but not all glomeruli	Primary or secondary to infection, drugs, or other glomerular diseases

Mnemonic

Features of Nephritic Syndrome = ***PHARAOH***

Proteinuria

Hematuria

Azotemia

RBC casts

Anti-streptolysin O (ASO)

Oliguria

Hypertension

Remember This! Almost all primary glomerular disease is autoimmune.

EXERCISE 15-25   PATHOLOGY AS A SECOND LANGUAGE

Test your vocabulary by writing the appropriate term in each blank from the list below.

Alport syndrome

Glomerulonephritis

Diabetic glomerulosclerosis

End-stage contracted kidney

Acute nephritic syndrome

Hereditary nephritis

Chronic glomerulonephritis (CGN)

Glomerulopathy

Diabetic nephropathy

Thin basement membrane disease (TBMD)

Renal ablation glomerulopathy

1. Inflammation of the glomerulus is called _____.

2. Glomerular conditions without an inflammatory component are called _____.

3. _____ can be caused by several genetic defects.

4. _____ is a hereditary nephritis caused by defect in the formation of type IV collagen.

5. _____ is usually due to *Streptococcal* infection and term acute post-*Streptococcal* glomeru-lonephritis.

6. _____ causes asymptomatic hematuria with possible mild proteinuria; however, renal function is normal.

7. _____ is the diagnosis applied to long-standing, end-stage, "burned out" chronic glomeru-lar disease.

8. _____ occurs when one-third to one-half of glomeruli is destroyed, thereby straining and damaging the remaining kidney and accelerating loss of kidney function.

9. _____ is due to end-stage chronic renal disease leading to a shrunken fibrotic kidney with cortical atrophy (nephrosclerosis).

10. _____ is a specific type of glomerulosclerosis due to uncontrolled diabetes with character-istic sclerotic nodules (Kimmelstiel-Wilson nodules).

11. _____ includes collective damage from glomerular disease that develops as an effect of hyperglycemia on the glomerular basement membrane, diabetic microangiopathy, hyaline arteriolar nephro-sclerosis, ischemic necrosis of the tips of the renal medullae, and even complicating bacterial pyelonephritis.

LEARNING OBJECTIVE 12: Describe the clinical presentation and course of acute kidney injury.

EXERCISE 15-26

Complete the paragraph below.

(1) _____ (also called acute tubular necrosis) is acute kidney injury characterized by sud-den decrease of renal function that is often, but not uniformly, accompanied by evidence of tubular injury or

tubular necrosis. This acute kidney injury is often due to (2) _____ or drugs/toxins, but also can be caused by (3) _____ from skeletal muscle breakdown. The etiology of this type of injury is thought to be due to the high energy expenditures and oxygen requirement of tubular cells and the resulting susceptibility to ischemia and toxins. Therefore, maintaining adequate (4) _____ is clinically important in preventing acute kidney injury. The three clinical phases are initiating phase, (5) _____, and the recovery phase.

EXERCISE 15-27   PATHOLOGY AS A SECOND LANGUAGE

See Exercise 15-26 for key terms covered in this section.

LEARNING OBJECTIVE 13: Discuss the etiologies, clinical features, diagnostic findings, and treatment of the various causes of tubulointerstitial nephritis.

EXERCISE 15-28

Complete the paragraph below.

There are a wide variety of causes of (1) _____, including drugs, (2) _____, infections, and chronic kidney diseases, including diabetes and cystic diseases. Tubulointerstitial nephritis is inflammation of the (3) _____ and tubules of the kidney. Tubulointerstitial nephritis can be primary, and due to drugs, or be (4) _____ to other causes, such as kidney infection (see pyelonephritis in Learning Objective 14).

EXERCISE 15-29   PATHOLOGY AS A SECOND LANGUAGE

Test your vocabulary by indicating if each statement below is true or false. If it is false, provide the correct word for the italicized term that will make the statement true.

_____ 1. *Chronic analgesic nephropathy* involves acute inflammation of the interstitium that evolves over a few days or months, usually due to an allergic reaction.

_____

_____ 2. *Acetate nephropathy* is a form of chronic tubulointerstitial nephritis caused by excessive and long-term use of analgesic that contain a mixture of aspirin or other NSAIDs, and either phenacetin or acetaminophen.

_____

_____ 3. *Acute drug-induced interstitial nephritis* is deposition of urate crystals (as in gout) in renal tubules causing tubulointerstitial inflammation and impaired renal function.

_____

LEARNING OBJECTIVE 14: Describe the signs, symptoms, and pathological features of pyelonephritis.

EXERCISE 15-30

Complete the paragraph below.

(1) _____ is an inflammatory disorder of renal tubules, interstitium, calyces, and pelvis caused by infection or some combination of infection, stasis, obstruction, or vesicoureteral reflux. Although infection is common, it is not always present. Infection is usually due to "ascending" infection from fecal source which infects the bladder, causing (2) _____ or urinary tract infection. The infection usually does not progress to the kidney; however, when there is stasis or reflux, the kidney can be involved causing acute pyelonephritis.

EXERCISE 15-31   PATHOLOGY AS A SECOND LANGUAGE

Test your vocabulary by writing the appropriate term in each blank from the list below.

Chronic obstructive pyelonephritis   Acute pyelonephritis
Reflux nephropath   Chronic pyelonephritis

1. _____ is acute pyogenic infection of the kidney.

2. _____ is chronic tubulointerstitial inflammation and scarring of the kidney that is associated with pathologic involvement of the renal calyces and pelvis.

3. _____ is the most frequent form of chronic pyelonephritis and usually occurs in children with congenital reflux due to failure of the one-way direction of downward urine flow.

4. _____ is a consequence of chronic urinary tract obstruction causing widespread calyceal dilatation, scarring, and cortical atrophy.

> **Remember This!** Chronic tubulointerstitial nephritis, urinary obstruction, stasis, infection, and stone formation are intimately related and may occur together.

LEARNING OBJECTIVE 15: Using examples from the text, discuss the primary mechanisms by which the kidney causes hypertension and the associated pathological changes in the kidney secondary to hypertension.

EXERCISE 15-32

Complete the paragraph below.

Not only does kidney damage cause (1) _____, but conversely, hypertension itself damages the arteries and arterioles of the kidney leading to further kidney damage. (2) _____ is a "wear and tear" pathologic change in the kidney that is related to advancing age and to blood pressure. It features sclerosis of small renal (3) _____ and (4) _____, which thickens the wall and narrows the lumen. In patients with hypertension, this damage occurs at an earlier age. (5) _____ is a much more severe form of nephrosclerosis seen in patients with advanced "malignant" hypertension. It is a medical emergency and must be treated with antihypertensives. Characteristic pathologic features include fibrinoid necrosis and "onion-skinning" of arterioles. (6) _____ reduces blood flow to the affected kidney and is usually due to atherosclerosis; however, in young women, it may be due to (7) _____ of the renal artery.

EXERCISE 15-33   PATHOLOGY AS A SECOND LANGUAGE

See Exercise 15-32 for key terms covered in this section.

Decisions Decisions

DECISION TREE 15.1: EVALUATION OF RENAL DISEASE

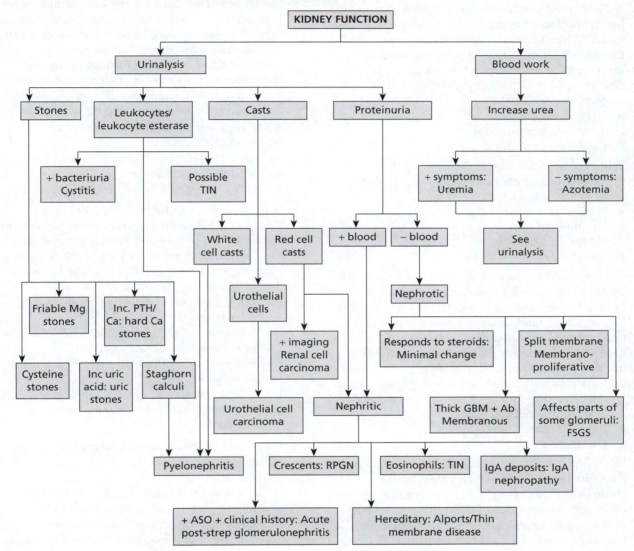

Test Yourself

I. MULTIPLE CHOICE

1. A 43-year-old Caucasian G4P4 female visits her gynecologist's office for her annual Pap smear. While there, she confides that when she lifts her children, laughs, or sneezes, she has urine leakage. What type of incontinence is she describing? [LEARNING OBJECTIVE 8]
   A. Stress incontinence
   B. Urge incontinence
   C. Transient incontinence
   D. Established incontinence

2. Which of the following is the most likely explanation of urinary obstruction in an older man? [LEARNING OBJECTIVE 3]
   A. Benign prostatic hyperplasia
   B. Urethral strictures
   C. Nephrolithiasis
   D. Prostate cancer

3. A 63-year-old Hispanic male is brought to the ER by his daughter, who is concerned by the presence of blood in her father's urine. His exam is notable for a palpable flank mass, while his labs reveal polycythemia. Imaging demonstrates a 10 cm mass in the left lower pole extending into the inferior vena cava as well as multiple pulmonary nodules bilaterally. What is your diagnosis? (Hint: Use the Decision Tree) [LEARNING OBJECTIVE 5]
   A. Transitional cell carcinoma
   B. Renal cell carcinoma
   C. Oncocytoma
   D. Any of the above

4. An eight-year-old female is brought to the clinic by her mother, who is concerned by her daughter's recent onset of bedwetting. A review of systems is notable for fever and nausea, and a recent history of sore throat (three weeks previous). The daughter's labs are notable for hematuria, elevated creatinine, and low complement, as well as a positive ASO titer. Which of the following etiologies explains her daughter's symptoms? (Hint: Use the Decision Tree) [LEARNING OBJECTIVE 11]
   A. Minimal change disease
   B. Rapidly progressive glomerulonephritis
   C. Acute streptococcal glomerulonephritis
   D. Focal segmental glomerulosclerosis

5. Red clear urine indicates the presence of what type of urinary abnormality? [LEARNING OBJECTIVE 2]
   A. Hemoglobinuria
   B. Occult hematuria
   C. Microscopic hematuria
   D. Aminoaciduria

6. Your 75-year-old grandfather calls you to give you the results of his surgery (the lung nodule was benign!) and to ask a very embarrassing question. Since undergoing surgery with anesthesia (with an anticholinergic drug), he has had a problem with urination, including feelings of urgency, incontinence (constant dribbling), and an inability to completely empty his bladder. A postvoid catheterization recovering 200 ml would confirm what diagnosis? [LEARNING OBJECTIVE 8]
   A. Stress incontinence
   B. Urinary retention
   C. Overflow incontinence
   D. More than one of the above

7. A renal biopsy conducted on a 25-year-old Caucasian male with recurrent bouts of hematuria following respiratory and gastrointestinal infections might demonstrate which of the following pathological findings? (Hint: Use the Decision Tree) [LEARNING OBJECTIVE 11]
   A. Arcs (crescents) of cells that proliferate in Bowman space
   B. Thickening of the glomerular basement membrane owing to antibody deposits
   C. Demonstration of IgA deposits in the mesangial cells
   D. Scattered mesangial sclerosis in portions of some, but not all glomeruli and immune deposits

8. Which of the following statements concerning reflux nephropathy is true? [LEARNING OBJECTIVE 14]
   A. Radiographic studies typically show small kidneys with irregular, broad renal scars.
   B. Reflux nephropathy without infection is especially silent and may be discovered in a workup for hypertension.
   C. Reflux backpressure causes chronic TIN and dilation of the renal pelvis and calyces.
   D. All of the above are true.

9. A 53-year-old African American male presents to the ER complaining of severe flank pain and cramping as well as recent onset of blood in his urine. His labs are notable for decreased PTH and increased calcium. An analysis of the passed stone might demonstrate which of the following features? (Hint: Use the Decision Tree) [LEARNING OBJECTIVE 4]
   A. Pleomorphic crystals, usually diamond-shaped
   B. Softer and more breakable (friable) stones
   C. large calyceal staghorn (antler-shaped) calculi
   D. Hard, dark stones secondary to blood accumulation in tiny crevasses of the stone

10. A 23-year-old Hispanic male is brought to the ER following a car accident. He appears to be in good shape, but your attending decides an MRI with contrast is necessary to rule out internal injuries. He is also admitted overnight for observation. Overnight, his catheter records less than 100 ml of urine, and his creatinine climbs rapidly. What is the most likely explanation of his renal failure? [LEARNING OBJECTIVE 12]
    A. Acute interstitial nephritis
    B. Acute tubular necrosis
    C. Membranoproliferative glomerulonephritis
    D. Renal ablation glomerulopathy

11. A 72-year-old Caucasian female with a five-year history of degenerative joint disease treated with over-the-counter medications is found to have hypertension on exam. A CT to assess joint damage also demonstrates blunting of her renal papillae. Which of the following drugs is responsible for her hypertension? [LEARNING OBJECTIVE 13]
    A. Acetaminophen
    B. Aspirin
    C. Caffeine
    D. All of the above

12. What type of proteinuria is caused by vigorous exercise? [LEARNING OBJECTIVE 2]
    A. Orthostatic proteinuria
    B. Persistent proteinuria
    C. Physiologic proteinuria
    D. Postural proteinuria

13. A 42-year-old African American male with a past medical history significant for substance abuse and HIV is found to have elevated urea levels during his monthly checkup. A renal biopsy demonstrates scattered mesangial sclerosis in portions of some, but not all glomeruli, as well as immune deposits. What is the most likely cause of his renal findings? (Hint: Use the Decision Tree) [LEARNING OBJECTIVE 11]
    A. Membranoproliferative glomerulonephritis
    B. Membranous glomerulonephritis
    C. Focal segmental glomerulosclerosis
    D. Rapidly progressive glomerulonephritis

14. Atrophic granular kidneys with thickened sclerotic renal arteries and arteriole walls, with narrowed lumen, seen as smooth glassy hyaline arteriolosclerosis on microscopy, are characteristic of which of the following diseases? [LEARNING OBJECTIVE 15]
    A. Benign nephrosclerosis
    B. Malignant nephrosclerosis
    C. Renal ablation nephropathy
    D. Chronic kidney disease

II. TRUE OR FALSE

15. _____ As urine accumulates, the bladder wall stretches, which sends signals to the micturition center within the lower spinal cord, which activates reflex contractions of the bladder wall and relaxation of the external, involuntary sphincter. [LEARNING OBJECTIVE 1]

16. _____ The majority of patients with kidney stones have repeat formation within five years. [LEARNING OBJECTIVE 4]

17. _____ Prerenal azotemia can be caused by shock, hemorrhage, or dehydration. [LEARNING OBJECTIVE 9]

18. _____ Despite surgical correction, patients with exstrophy are at increased risk for bladder carcinoma later in life. [LEARNING OBJECTIVE 6]

19. _____ Schistosomiasis is a parasitic disease that commonly causes cystitis in those living in Egypt and nearby nations. [LEARNING OBJECTIVE 7]

20. _____ The presence of glucose in urine is diagnostic of diabetes mellitus. [LEARNING OBJECTIVE 2]

21. _____ Cystitis is characterized by frequency, urgency, painful urination, and dull lower back pain. [LEARNING OBJECTIVE 7]

22. _____ Most aminoaciduria occurs in newborns and infants and is caused by inherited metabolic defects. [LEARNING OBJECTIVE 1]

23. _____ Acute drug-induced interstitial nephritis is a type I or type IV hypersensitivity reaction. [LEARNING OBJECTIVE 13]

24. _____ Renal ablation glomerulopathy begins to appear by the time one-third to one-half of glomeruli is destroyed by any renal disease. [LEARNING OBJECTIVE 11]

III. MATCHING

25. Match the following diseases to their description; answers may be used more than once: [LEARNING OBJECTIVE 10]
    i. Adult polycystic kidney disease
    ii. Simple cyst
    iii. Autosomal recessive polycystic kidney disease
    iv. Multicystic renal dysplasia
    A. Associated with liver cysts and biliary ductal hyperplasia, which lead to a cirrhosis-like scarring of the liver
    B. Sporadic developmental disorder characterized by small mass of cysts accompanied by primitive cartilage or other primitive tissues
    C. Range from a few millimeters to a few centimeters, characterized by a simple epithelial lining, and filled with clear fluid

D. Characterized by thousands of expanding renal cysts, berry aneurysms, and mitral valve prolapse

E. Comes to attention at birth as massively enlarged kidneys

26. Match the following characteristics with the appropriate phase of acute renal failure; answers may be used more than once: [LEARNING OBJECTIVE 12]
    i. Initiating phase
    ii. Maintenance phase
    iii. Recovery phase

A. Occurs within the first few days

B. Occurs in the first 24–48 hours

C. Characterized by dilute urine

D. Urine output returns to normal

E. Urine output falls dramatically and creatinine rises

F. Dialysis and supportive care are the treatment of choice for this phase

G. Characterized by increasing renal output

IV. SHORT ANSWER

27. What are the conditions that encourage nephrolithiasis? [LEARNING OBJECTIVE 4]

_____

_____

_____

28. A patient with chronic kidney disease has developed end-stage renal failure with anorexia, nausea, vomiting, oral inflammation (stomatitis), nocturia, fatigue, pruritus (itching), loss of mental acuity, muscle cramps, water retention, tissue wasting, gastrointestinal bleeding, peripheral neuropathy, and seizures. He asks in a moment of clarity whether a kidney biopsy might help you determine how to treat him. What is your response? [LEARNING OBJECTIVE 9]

_____

_____

_____

29. What are the factors that predispose women to bacterial bladder infections? [LEARNING OBJECTIVE 7]

_____

_____

_____

30. What effects does chronic obstructive uropathy have on the urinary tract? [LEARNING OBJECTIVE 3]

_____

_____

_____

31. What therapies are available for someone diagnosed with urothelial carcinoma? [LEARNING OBJECTIVE 5]

_____

_____

_____

32. Why is it important to make a diagnosis of renal artery stenosis early in the disease process? [LEARNING OBJECTIVE 15]

_____

_____

_____

33. What is your next step in the treatment of an adult diagnosed with minimal change disease? [LEARNING OBJECTIVE 11]

_____

_____

_____

Disorders of the Male Genitalia

CHAPTER 16

> ## The Big Picture
>
> Diseases of the male genitalia can disrupt male sexual development and function. Neoplasms can arise from various sites and include prostate adenocarcinoma and germ cell tumors of the testis.

Oh No! Not Another Learning Experience

LEARNING OBJECTIVE 1: Explain the function(s) of each part of the male genital system.

EXERCISE 16-1

Complete the paragraph below.

The (1) _____ is a copulatory organ that consists of two main parts, the shaft and the glans (head). The shaft is covered by skin, which folds over the head to form a retractable collar, the (2) _____ (foreskin). The penis contains three spongy cylindrical vascular compartments, two large dorsolateral ones and a single centerline ventral one. Each of the two dorsal cylinders is a (3) _____. The (4) _____ is a sac of skin that holds the testis, epididymis, and proximal vas deferens.

EXERCISE 16-2   PATHOLOGY AS A SECOND LANGUAGE

Please review The Nature of Disease Figures 16.1 and 16.2 then test your vocabulary by writing the appropriate term in each blank from the list below.

Seminal vesicles	Prostate gland	Spermatic cord
Erection	Leydig cells	Semen
Ejaculation	Epididymis	Vas deferens
Seminiferous tubules	Testosterone	Testis
Circumcision	Tunica vaginalis	Interstitial tissue
Prostate specific antigen		

1. _____ is the removal of the prepuce (preputial foreskin) of the penis.

2. The testis is contained within a smooth serosal sac called the _____.

3. The _____ is the male gonad.

4. _____ produce sperm and represent approximately 90% of the mass of the testis.

5. _____ fills the space between the tubules of the testis, and contains sex hormone-producing cells.

6. _____ is the primary male sex hormone and is produced by _____ of the testis.

7. The _____ is a long, coiled tube that forms an elongated, spongy mass that connects the testis to the vas deferens.

8. The _____ is a narrow, stiff, heavily muscled tube that travels upward over the pelvic brim and descends into the pelvis, where it merges with the duct from the seminal vesicle shortly before emptying into the urethra.

9. The _____ are small, elongated glands that are located near the prostate and produce components of the seminal fluid.

10. Blood vessels, nerves, and supporting tissue connecting to the testis are known collectively as the _____.

11. The _____ is a relatively large gland located at the base of the bladder, surrounding the urethra, and produces components of seminal fluid.

12. _____ is derived from an enzyme that dissolves clotted semen and allows sperm to migrate upward into the female genital tract; it is a serum marker for prostate cancer.

13. _____ is formed of mature sperm from the epididymis mixed with fluids from the seminal vesicles and prostate.

14. _____ is enlargement and stiffening of the penis in response to sensory signals that are mediated by the parasympathetic nervous system.

15. _____ is ejection of semen from the tip of the penis in response to sensory signals mediated by the sympathetic nervous system.

> **Remember This!** There is a "vas deferens" between boys and girls. The vas deferens is ligated (or cut) during a male sterilization procedure = vasectomy.

LEARNING OBJECTIVE 2: Briefly explain the causes of erectile dysfunction.

EXERCISE 16-3

Complete the paragraph below.

About half of men over age 50 may experience (1) _____, which is defined as an inability to attain or sustain an erection firm enough for satisfactory intercourse. Over 90% of cases are associated with physical factors such as decreased arterial inflow due to (2) _____, disease, or injury to nerves controlling penile blood flow (e.g., after [3] _____), hormone imbalances (e.g., low (4) _____), or therapeutic drugs (e.g., antihypertensives). Treatment is directed at the underlying cause. Oral (5) _____ drugs are now widely available and are preferred by most men over mechanical devices or direct injection of drugs.

EXERCISE 16-4   PATHOLOGY AS A SECOND LANGUAGE

See Exercise 16-3 for key terms covered in this section.

LEARNING OBJECTIVE 3: Discuss the various male factors taken into consideration when diagnosing the underlying etiology of infertility.

EXERCISE 16-5

Complete the paragraph below.

(1) _____ is the inability of a partner to contribute effectively to conception and affects approximately 20% of couples in the United States. Underlying etiologies include (2) _____ (about 35%), (3) _____ (20%), fallopian tube dysfunction (30%), abnormal cervical mucus (5%), and unknown (10%). Male sperm disorders include (4) _____ (low sperm count) due to endocrine disorders, infections, undescended testis, varicocele, or drugs, and (5) _____, which can be caused by diabetic neuropathy, prostatectomy, obstruction of the (6) _____, genetic conditions (e.g., most men with cystic fibrosis have bilateral agenesis of the vas deferens), or retrograde ejaculation into the bladder. Other problems include autoimmune antisperm antibodies and sperm with impaired motility. Diagnosis requires endocrine evaluation, semen analysis, including volume, liquefaction time, appearance, pH, sperm count, (7) _____, percent of sperm with normal morphology, and fructose concentration (the primary sugar in semen).

EXERCISE 16-6   PATHOLOGY AS A SECOND LANGUAGE

See Exercise 16-5 for key terms covered in this section.

LEARNING OBJECTIVE 4: Describe the etiology, signs and symptoms, pathological findings, treatment, and consequences of penile diseases, as applicable.

EXERCISE 16-7

Complete the paragraph below.

Penile diseases can be developmental, nonneoplastic, or neoplastic. The most common developmental abnormalities of the penis include (1) _____, which is an elongated slit on the distal ventral aspect of the penis; (2) _____, which is an elongated slit on the dorsum; and (3) _____, which is an inability to retract the foreskin over the glans. Neoplastic disorders include (4) _____, a generally benign sexually transmitted cauliflower-like growth caused by low-risk human papilloma virus; (5) _____, a squamous cell carcinoma in situ that forms a grayish or reddish plaque on the glans (it has not yet invaded past the basement membrane); and (6) _____, which generally arises in the squamous epithelium of the glans in uncircumcised males over age 40 or in the penile urethra.

EXERCISE 16-8   PATHOLOGY AS A SECOND LANGUAGE

Test your vocabulary by indicating if each statement below is true or false. If it is false, provide the correct word for the italicized term that will make the statement true.

_____ 1. A retracted foreskin (prepuce) that becomes trapped causing glans congestion, edema, pain, and acute urinary obstruction is termed *priapism*.

_____

_____ 2. Inflammation of the glans is *balanitis*.

_____

_____ 3. *Balanitis xerotica obliterans* is an inflammatory disease of unknown cause associated with a white, sclerotic patch of skin at the tip of the glans, which may constrict the urethral opening.

_____

_____ 4. *Peyronie disease* is a fibrosing condition of the tunica albuginea or corpus cavernosum.

_____

_____ 5. *Paraphimosis* is a painful, persistent erection in the absence of sexual desire.

_____

LEARNING OBJECTIVE 5: Name the diseases affecting the scrotum and groin.

EXERCISE 16-9

Complete the paragraph below.

Diseases of the scrotum and groin are often very worrisome because they can cause painless masses and therefore mimic (1) _____. (2) _____ is a protrusion of bowel into the inguinal canal or scrotum, which occurs as normal intra-abdominal pressure forces open a canal into the scrotum. (3) _____ are scrotal varicose veins, which may cause scrotal enlargement and infertility. (4) _____ is accumulation of fluid in the sac of the tunica vaginalis that surrounds the testis. Each of these can cause mass-forming lesions. In addition, (5) _____ ("jock itch") is an inflammation of the scrotum or inguinal skin caused by one of the varieties of *Tinea* fungal species.

Remember This! A testicular mass is considered malignant until proven otherwise.

Mnemonic
Causes of Scrotal Swelling = SHOVE IT
Spermatocele
Hydrocele
Orchitis
Varicocele
Epididymal cyst-**I**nguinal hernia
Testicular tumor (or torsion)

EXERCISE 16-10   PATHOLOGY AS A SECOND LANGUAGE

See Exercise 16-9 for key terms covered in this section.

LEARNING OBJECTIVE 6: Discuss the etiology, presentation, diagnosis, and treatment of the following disease of the testis and epididymis: epididymitis, orchitis, and torsion.

EXERCISE 16-11

Complete the paragraph below.

Inflammatory diseases can involve the testis (called [1] _____) or the epididymis (called [2] _____). Orchitis is often due to mumps virus in children, while epididymitis is most often caused by gonorrhea, *Chlamydia*, or *E. coli*. Twisting of the spermatic cord can cut off blood supply to the testis and is termed (3) _____. (4) _____ is a cyst of the epididymis that contains sperm and is formed by dilation of the epididymal tubule; much like a hydrocele or varicocele, it can form a mass lesion.

EXERCISE 16-12   PATHOLOGY AS A SECOND LANGUAGE

See Exercise 16-11 for key terms covered in this section.

LEARNING OBJECTIVE 7: Explain the role of cryptorchidism in malignancy, and differentiate between germ and nongerm cell tumors.

EXERCISE 16-13

Complete the paragraph below.

Failure of the testis to descend from the abdomen through the inguinal canal into the scrotum is called (1) _____ (or undescended testis). Usually this occurs on one side; rarely, both testes fail to descend. Early correction is desirable because an undescended testis that remains in the abdomen has a (2) _____ greater risk for testicular malignancy. Testicular neoplasms are generally (3) _____ and derived from germ cells. Often they have a mixture of various germ cell components (e.g., seminoma and yolk sac tumor, etc.) and are therefore called (4) _____.

EXERCISE 16-14

Please review The Nature of Disease Figures 16.5 and 16.6 then complete the table below.

Germ Cell Tumors			
Component	**Benign or Malignant**	**Pathologic Features**	**Clinical Features**
(1) _____	Usually benign	Composed of multiple mature (differentiated) tissues	Present in most mixed germ cell tumors
(2) _____	Malignant	Composed of primitive neoplastic spermatocytes with clear cytoplasm	Most common germ cell tumor
(3) _____	Malignant	Composed of very primitive cells	Elevated beta-HCG
(4) _____ **(endodermal sinus tumor)**	Malignant	Microcystic pattern and Schiller-Duval bodies	Pure tumor occurs almost exclusively in young boys, elevated serum AFP tumor marker
(5) _____	Malignant	Composed of placental chorionic-type cells (trophoblasts)	Very responsive to chemotherapy (methotrexate), elevated beta-HCG
Non-Germ Cell Tumors (Sex Cord-Stromal)			
(6) _____	Usually benign	Arise from Leydig progenitor cells and form sheets of eosinophilic cells	Produce steroids
(7) _____	Usually benign	Arise from progenitor Sertoli cells and form neoplastic tubules	Produce steroids

Mnemonic

Types of Testicular Germ Cell Tumors = TESTY

Teratoma

Embryonal carcinoma

Seminoma

Trophoblastic (choriocarcinoma)

Yolk-sac tumor

EXERCISE 16-15   PATHOLOGY AS A SECOND LANGUAGE

Please see Exercises 16-13 and 16-14 for additional vocabulary terms.

LEARNING OBJECTIVE 8: Characterize the types of prostatitis according to etiology, signs and symptoms, diagnostic findings, and treatment.

EXERCISE 16-16

Complete the paragraph below.

(1) _____ is inflammation of the prostate and is often caused by infection. *Bacterial prostatitis* is usually caused by *E. coli* or other bacteria that can cause urinary tract infections. (2) _____ is associated with fever, chills, dysuria, and pelvic discomfort or pain, with a swollen prostate, and positive urine cultures. Therapy is usually successful in the short term, but complete eradication of organisms is difficult and often the infection recurs, leading to (3) _____. (4) _____ is now the most common form of prostatitis and is of unclear etiology; pain management usually becomes the main goal.

EXERCISE 16-17 PATHOLOGY AS A SECOND LANGUAGE

See Exercise 16-16 for key terms covered in this section.

LEARNING OBJECTIVE 9: Compare and contrast the clinical and diagnostic features of benign prostatic hyperplasia and prostate cancer.

EXERCISE 16-18

Complete the paragraph below.

The prostate can be manually examined with a (1) _____ to determine if the prostate is enlarged or has a mass-forming lesion. (2) _____ is enlargement of the prostate caused by nodular hyperplasia of the prostate gland and the fibromuscular supporting tissue around the gland. This condition is very common in older men and can lead to (3) _____ with urine retention and subsequent complications. (4) _____ is the most common cancer overall, but is not nearly as lethal as other cancers, such as lung cancer. The incidence of this cancer increases greatly with age and is more common in African Americans. Most established prostate cancers are androgen dependent; therefore, (5) _____ is helpful clinically. Most prostate carcinomas remain confined to the gland and are not symptomatic. They are more often discovered by routine blood tests that reveal increased (6) _____ than by a digital rectal exam. Treatment also includes radiation therapy or surgical removal of the gland.

EXERCISE 16-19 PATHOLOGY AS A SECOND LANGUAGE

Test your vocabulary by indicating if each statement below is true or false. If it is false, provide the correct word for the italicized term that will make the statement true.

_____ 1. *Prostatic intraepithelial neoplasia (PIN)* is the precursor to prostatic adenocarcinoma.

_____

_____ 2. *Gleason score* is the grade of prostatic adenocarcinoma with a range of aggressiveness of tumors.

_____

Remember This! It is not necessary to treat all prostatic carcinomas.

Decisions Decisions

DECISION TREE 16.1: TESTICULAR DISEASE

Test Yourself

I. MULTIPLE CHOICE

1. A 28-year-old Caucasian male visits his primary care physician due to concerns over an enlarging scrotum. On exam, a nontender twisted mass with a texture similar to that of a bag of worms is palpated. An ultrasound confirms that the mass is composed of enlarged veins. What is your diagnosis? (Hint: Use the Decision Tree) [LEARNING OBJECTIVE 4]
   A. Cystocele
   B. Varicocele
   C. Hydrocele
   D. Spermatocele

2. Which of the following statements concerning phimosis is correct? [LEARNING OBJECTIVE 4]
   A. Phimosis is an acquired disorder resulting from infection.
   B. Phimosis is the result of poor hygiene and infection.

   C. Phimosis is associated with the development of squamous cell carcinoma.
   D. All of the above are correct.

3. A 10-year-old Hispanic male is brought to the children's hospital by his mother, who is concerned by a rapidly enlarging testicular mass. A serum AFP is elevated, but his labs are otherwise unremarkable. The patient is scheduled for surgery and the mass is removed. Histology demonstrates hair and thyroid tissue as well as cells that have features of primitive spermatocytes. What is your diagnosis? (Hint: Use the Decision Tree) [LEARNING OBJECTIVE 7]
   A. Benign teratoma
   B. Mixed tumor
   C. Seminoma
   D. Yolk sac tumor

4. Which of the following diseases is capable of distorting the penis and rendering erection painful and intercourse difficult? [LEARNING OBJECTIVE 4]
   A. Tinea cruris
   B. Paraphimosis
   C. Peyronie disease
   D. Balanitis xerotica obliterans

5. A 45-year-old African American male, with no significant past medical history, presents to the clinic complaining of waxing and waning pelvic pain of three months' duration. A urinalysis is notable for white blood cells; however, no bacteria are identified in the urine on cytology and cultures are negative. He denies previous urinary tract infections. What is the most likely etiology of his symptoms? [LEARNING OBJECTIVE 8]
   A. Urinary tract infection
   B. Acute bacterial prostatitis
   C. Chronic bacterial prostatitis
   D. Chronic nonbacterial prostatitis

6. What viral infection causes a cauliflower-like growth? [LEARNING OBJECTIVE 4]
   A. HPV
   B. HZV
   C. HSV
   D. RSV

7. A 63-year-old Caucasian male presents to the emergency room complaining of difficulty urinating. His past medical history is notable for urinary frequency, urgency, nocturia, and a weak intermittent stream. A urinalysis on a catheterized specimen is negative for bacteria, white blood cells, and leukocyte esterase, and a digital rectal exam demonstrates a tense rubbery prostatic gland. What is the most likely explanation for his constellation of symptoms? [LEARNING OBJECTIVE 9]
   A. Drug side effect
   B. Chronic prostatitis
   C. Prostatic carcinoma
   D. Benign prostatic hyperplasia

8. Which of the following statements concerning prostate cancer and its precursors is correct? [LEARNING OBJECTIVE 9]
   A. Prostatic intraepithelial neoplasia contains some of the molecular changes found in prostate cancer.
   B. T1 prostatic adenocarcinomas are usually discovered incidentally or by a PSA test and biopsy.
   C. T3 tumors extend minimally beyond the prostate.
   D. All of the above are true.

9. A 54-year-old African American male with a history of recurrent bladder infections status post multiple rounds of antibiotic therapy, presents to the clinic complaining of lower back and suprapubic pain. Prostatic secretions are positive for inflammatory cells and cultures demonstrate growth of

E. coli colonies. Why has treatment of his disease failed to alleviate the symptoms? (Hint: Use the Decision Tree) [LEARNING OBJECTIVE 7]
   A. His symptoms are the result of an acute infection.
   B. His symptoms are not the result of a bacterial infection.
   C. Antibiotics have a difficult time penetrating the prostate.
   D. None of the above are true.

II. TRUE OR FALSE

10. _____ Testosterone is produced only by cells within the testicular interstitium. [LEARNING OBJECTIVE 1]

11. _____ Hypospadias and epispadias are associated with incontinence infection, obstruction, and other congenital abnormalities. [LEARNING OBJECTIVE 4]

12. _____ Therapeutic drugs, especially antihypertensives, account for about 75% of erectile dysfunction. [LEARNING OBJECTIVE 2]

13. _____ The symptoms of pain experienced by patients with torsion owe to its interruption of arterial inflow as well as venous outflow. (Hint: Use the Decision Tree) [LEARNING OBJECTIVE 6]

14. _____ The etiology of infertility cannot be identified in approximately 10% of couples. [LEARNING OBJECTIVE 3]

15. _____ Orchitis is caused by the mumps virus. (Hint: Use the Decision Tree) [LEARNING OBJECTIVE 6]

16. _____ Enlargement and stiffening of the penis is mediated by parasympathetic-induced relaxation of arterial smooth muscle, while ejaculation is mediated by the sympathetic nervous system. [LEARNING OBJECTIVE 1]

III. MATCHING

17. Categorize the following causes of infertility; answers may be used more than once. [LEARNING OBJECTIVE 2 AND 3]
   i. Impaired sperm emission
   ii. Impaired spermatogenesis
   iii. Erectile dysfunction
   A. Nerve injury
   B. Hypothyroidism
   C. Infections of testis or epididymis
   D. Psychological factors
   E. Prostatectomy
   F. Vas deferens obstruction
   G. Cryptorchidism
   H. Genetic conditions
   I. Varicocele
   J. Retrograde ejaculation into the bladder
   K. Drugs
   L. Atherosclerosis

IV. SHORT ANSWER

18. A 22-year old female gives birth to a healthy baby boy, who has one undescended testicle. What topics need to be covered in your conversation regarding the necessary treatment? [LEARNING OBJECTIVE 5]

_____

_____

_____

19. What are the causes of priapism? [LEARNING OBJECTIVE 4]

_____

_____

_____

20. A 17-year-old male with a testicular mass refuses to undergo surgery to remove his testicle without a biopsy proving the presence of carcinoma. Why is such a biopsy ill advised? [LEARNING OBJECTIVE 7]

_____

_____

_____

21. What therapies are available in the treatment of BPH? [LEARNING OBJECTIVE 9]

_____

_____

_____

Disorders of the Female Genitalia and Breast

CHAPTER 177

The Big Picture

The female genital tract is necessary for sexual function, and in coordination with the breast, initiates and sustains new life. Directed by the hypothalamus and pituitary, the endometrium and ovary act in cycles to prepare for implantation of the developing embryo. Disease occurs when these processes are disrupted or when neoplasia arises from various sites. Cervical cancer was once the most common cause of cancer death in the United States and is still a major global problem. Breast cancer rates continue to be very high, and breast cancer represents the most common cancer in U.S. women other than skin cancer.

Oh No! Not Another Learning Experience

LEARNING OBJECTIVE 1: Name and describe the components of the female genitalia.

EXERCISE 17-1

Please review The Nature of Disease Figure 17.3 then complete the paragraph below.

The female (1) _____ (also called the vulva) consist of the mons pubis, labia majora, labia minora, clitoris, external urethral orifice, and the vaginal opening (introitus). The (2) _____ consist of the internal organs involved in reproduction, including the uterus and bilateral fallopian tubes and ovaries. The (3) _____ is composed of smooth muscle and consists of the uterine (4) _____ (or the uppermost portion called the [5] _____), which lies in the pelvis, and a lower (6) _____. The (7) _____ are bilateral thick folds of peritoneum that stabilize and support the adnexal structures including the fallopian tubes and ovaries.

EXERCISE 17-2   PATHOLOGY AS A SECOND LANGUAGE

Test your vocabulary by writing the appropriate term in each blank from the list below.

Oogenesis	Graafian follicles	Meiosis
Fallopian tubes	Cervical os	Endometrium
Ovaries	Oocytes	Primary follicle
Bartholin glands	Vagina	Ectocervix
Corpus luteum	Ovum	Ovulation

1. Lubricating mucous glands of the cervix are called _____.

2. The _____ is a mucosal canal that connects the uterine cervix with the vulva.

3. The portion of the cervix lined by squamous epithelium that protrudes into the upper vagina is the _____.

4. The central opening of the cervix is the _____.

5. The _____ lines the uterus and is composed of two types of tissue—supportive *stromal cells* and *glands* formed of columnar epithelium.

6. _____ lead from each corner of the uterus outward toward the ovaries.

7. _____ are the female gonads that lie within the broad ligament close to the fimbriated end of each fallopian tube.

8. _____ are the maternal germ cells.

9. The oocyte surrounded by a rim of granulosa cells is called the _____.

10. _____ is the production of ova from primary oocytes.

11. After puberty, primary follicles mature into small cysts called _____.

12. _____ is cell division occurring in gametogenesis that reduces the content of DNA (reduction division).

13. _____ is the mature female gamete or "egg cell."

14. _____ occurs when continued FSH stimulation causes the Graafian follicle to enlarge until it ruptures and releases its ovum into the peritoneal cavity.

15. _____ is a yellow endocrine body that forms after ovulation and secretes progesterone and small amounts of estrogen to prepare the endometrium for implantation of a fertilized ovum.

LEARNING OBJECTIVE 2: Discuss the hormonal and accompanying physiologic changes that occur during each stage of the menstrual cycle.

EXERCISE 17-3

Please review The Nature of Disease Figure 17.5 then complete the paragraph below.

During reproductive years, the hypothalamus secretes (1) _____, which stimulates the pituitary to release (2) _____, which causes ovulation, and *luteinizing hormone* (LH), which stimulates ovarian progesterone production. The (3) _____ (*or menstrual cycle*) proceeds in parallel with the ovarian cycle. The new menstrual cycle begins as pituitary FSH stimulates follicle growth and estrogen secretion. Estrogen in turn stimulates proliferation of endometrial stroma, a period of endometrial growth known as the (4) _____. After ovulation, LH stimulates conversion of the ruptured follicle into the corpus luteum, which secretes progesterone, causing glycogen production and a period of endometrial growth known as the (5) _____. If implantation does not occur, the corpus luteum degenerates into a *corpus albicans* (white body) and the endometrium sloughs, leading to menstrual bleeding. If implantation occurs, the conceptus begins secreting (6) _____, which acts like LH, thus maintaining the ovarian corpus luteum throughout pregnancy.

EXERCISE 17-4

Complete the table below.

(1) _____	Follicular Phase (follicles)	Ovulation	Luteal Phase (corpus luteum)
Uterus/Endometrium	Menstruation -> (2) _____		(3) _____ -> Menstruation
(4) _____	High then decreasing FSH, low LH	LH and FSH spike	Somewhat elevated LH, low FSH
Ovarian Hormones	(5) _____		(6) _____

EXERCISE 17-5 PATHOLOGY AS A SECOND LANGUAGE

See Exercises 17-3 and 17-4 for key terms covered in this section.

LEARNING OBJECTIVE 3: Discuss the advantages or disadvantages of hormone replacement therapy in women with menopause.

EXERCISE 17-6

Complete the paragraph below.

(1) _____ is the physiologic or iatrogenic cessation of menses due to decreasing ovarian function; it normally occurs at approximately 50 years of age. (2) _____ are episodes of vasomotor instability that affect most women going through menopause. The menopausal reduction of estrogen causes atrophy of the lower genital tract, predisposes to the development of thinning of bones called (3) _____, and leaves women susceptible to increased cardiovascular disease. Although it is on the decline, the common practice has been to treat symptomatic postmenopausal women with (4) _____, which generally includes estrogen. This practice is changing because of known increased risks for breast cancer, gallbladder disease, dementia, urinary incontinence, pulmonary embolism, thrombophlebitis, heart attack, and stroke.

EXERCISE 17-7 PATHOLOGY AS A SECOND LANGUAGE

See Exercise 17-6 for key terms covered in this section.

LEARNING OBJECTIVE 4: Describe the hormonal and resulting physiologic changes, including complications, that (may) occur with pregnancy.

EXERCISE 17-8

Complete the paragraphs below.

Pregnancy is a hormonal storm, including increased pituitary output of LH, FSH, ACTH, and TSH, and placental secretion of estrogen, progesterone, and pituitary-like hormones. The results are a rapidly growing uterus, skin changes, weight gain, increased blood volume, and increased metabolism. Pregnancy begins with (1) _____ and continues for nine calendar months (280 days, 40 weeks) as measured from the date of the onset of the last menstrual period (LMP). The nine months are divided into three three-month (2) _____, each of which encompasses certain fetal and maternal developments. The (3) _____ is used to track the development of the embryo and fetus until birth. The process of labor and birth is called (4) _____.

(5) _____ refers to the number of pregnancies a woman has had, while (6) _____ refers to the number of pregnancies in which the fetus was carried for at least 22 weeks. When a woman has her first pregnancy, she is called (7) _____; if she has had more than one child, she is called (8) _____. Although pregnancy itself is not necessarily a medical condition, many medical conditions are associated with pregnancy and some pregnancies are considered "high-risk" (e.g., when there are multiple fetuses).

EXERCISE 17-9   PATHOLOGY AS A SECOND LANGUAGE

Test your vocabulary by indicating if each statement below is true or false. If it is false, provide the correct word for the italicized term that will make the statement true.

_____   1. *Hypertensive disorders of pregnancy* (or gestational hypertension) refer to persistently increased blood pressure in pregnancy.

_____

_____   2. Hypertension, proteinuria (an indicator of renal damage) and fluid accumulation (edema) are a triad known as *preeclampsia* or toxemia of pregnancy.

_____

_____   3. When pre-eclampsia progresses to seizures it becomes *posteclampsia.*

_____

_____   4. *Abortion* is any interruption of pregnancy irrespective of the cause.

_____

_____   5. A pregnancy that ends with spontaneous death of the fetus after 22 weeks is called a *stillbirth.*

_____

_____   6. Implantation of the conceptus outside of the uterus produces a *placenta previa.*

_____

_____   7. If the placenta implants in the lower segment of the uterus, the condition is known as *ectopic pregnancy.*

_____

_____   8. If the placenta invades too deeply into the myometrium and does not separate spontaneously from the uterine wall after birth, the condition is known as *placenta accreta.*

_____

_____ 9. Deep invasions by the placenta into the uterine wall are called *placenta increta*.

_____

_____ 10. If the placenta perforates through the uterine wall into adjacent tissues, the condition is known as *placenta percreta*.

_____

_____ 11. *Molar pregnancy* is a pregnancy in which a nonviable fertilized egg implants in the uterus and grows into an abnormal mass with or without recognizable fetal parts.

_____

_____ 12. *Hydatidiform mole* is a benign tumor-like overgrowth of placental cells.

_____

_____ 13. A *partial mole* contains only paternal chromosomes and is formed when one or two normal sperm fertilize an ovum without a nucleus.

_____

_____ 14. A *complete mole* contains both maternal and paternal chromosomes.

_____

_____ 15. An *invasive mole* invades deeply into the myometrium, and may invade nearby pelvic structures.

_____

_____ 16. *Exaggerated placental implantation site* is a malignant proliferation of trophoblastic cells that invades and metastasizes, often to the lung.

_____

_____ 17. *Pelvic relaxation syndrome* refers to relaxed pelvic ligaments that predispose to organ prolapse.

_____

_____ 18. The uterus may slide downward into the vagina causing *uterine prolapse*.

_____

_____ 19. The rectum may bulge forward into the vagina, which is called a *rectocele*.

_____

_____ 20. The bladder also may bulge downward into the anterior aspect of the vagina, which is called a *hydrocele*.

_____

Remember This! Pregnancy is a stressful physiologic state that is vulnerable to complications.

Mnemonic

Triad of Pre-eclampsia = **PRE**-*eclampsia*
Proteinuria
Rising blood pressure (hypertension)
Edema

LEARNING OBJECTIVE 5: List the causes and treatment of female infertility.

EXERCISE 17-10

Complete the paragraph below.

Female infertility can have numerous possible causes, including uterine or fallopian tube scarring, endometriosis, leiomyomas (fibroids), abnormal cervical mucus, irregular ovulation, and endocrine or autoimmune disease. The most common preventable cause of infertility is (1) _____ , which is chronic infection of the fallopian tubes (and often the ovary and nearby peritoneum and ligaments) by sexually transmitted infections, such as *Chlamydia* and *Mycoplasma*. This condition can also lead to complications such as a (2) _____ (a collection of suppurative inflammation in the adnexa), or even (3) _____ . Treatment of infertility is directed at the cause, but may include assisted reproduction called (4) _____ which includes culturing and transferring an embryo to the endometrium for implantation.

EXERCISE 17-11   PATHOLOGY AS A SECOND LANGUAGE

See Exercise 17-10 for key terms covered in this section.

LEARNING OBJECTIVE 6: Compare and contrast the causes of leukoplakia.

EXERCISE 17-12

Complete the paragraph below.

There are multiple causes of the clinical finding of (1) _____ , a white, flat, scaly lesion or patch. A benign, hyperplastic overgrowth of surface squamous epithelium caused by chronic itching and scratching is called (2) _____ . (3) _____ is a nonneoplastic disease of unknown cause affecting the skin of the anogenital region and features chronic atrophy, scarring, and contractures. Squamous (4) _____ is a spectrum of mild dysplasia (condyloma) to carcinoma in situ of the vulva, due to HPV infection, that is analogous to the progression to cancer in the cervix.

EXERCISE 17-13   PATHOLOGY AS A SECOND LANGUAGE

See Exercise 17-12 for key terms covered in this section.

LEARNING OBJECTIVE 7: Differentiate between the various etiologies of vaginitis; include treatment where applicable.

EXERCISE 17-14

Complete the paragraph below.

There are various etiologies of (1) _____ , a common, transient, superficial mucosal inflammation of the vagina. It is generally due to atrophic changes of the vaginal mucosa as a result of (2) _____ (called [3] _____) or attributable to infections from bacteria, fungus (especially *Candida*), or (4) _____ .

EXERCISE 17-15 PATHOLOGY AS A SECOND LANGUAGE

Test your vocabulary by writing the appropriate term in each blank from the list below.

Candidiasis   Moniliasis   Leukorrhea
Trichomoniasis   Bacterial vaginosis

1. _____ is an inflammatory discharge of white cells.

2. _____ is a form of vaginitis due to alteration of normal flora in which lactobacilli decrease and anaerobic bacteria overgrow.

3. _____ is a sexually transmitted infection, caused by a parasite, which leads to vaginitis.

4. Infection with candida is called _____ or _____ .

LEARNING OBJECTIVE 8: Describe the conditions affecting the cervix; pay particular attention to the progression and prevention of HPV-induced carcinoma.

EXERCISE 17-16

Please review The Nature of Disease Figure 17.16 then complete the paragraph below.

The most important disease of the cervix is (1) _____, which is an STI that causes cervical dysplasia and cancer. After persistent infection with HPV, the squamous epithelium becomes dysplastic, progressing to the most severe form of dysplasia, (2) _____. After this stage, invasion occurs and the patient has invasive carcinoma. Another perhaps more accurate term for cervical dysplasia is (3) _____. The single, most important factor in the development of cervical dysplasia and carcinoma is the infectious spread of high-risk subtypes of HPV (these include [4] _____). Most viruses are cleared within two years, but persistent HPV infection can occur with constant reinfection or with immune dysregulation. Cervical dysplasia is detected by (5) _____, which guides further surveillance and treatment. Pap smear results are categorized according to the (6) _____. The vast majority of HPV infections can now be prevented by vaccination.

> **Remember This!** Carcinoma of the cervix is caused by long-term infection by high-risk human papilloma virus (HPV).

EXERCISE 17-17   PATHOLOGY AS A SECOND LANGUAGE

Test your vocabulary by indicating if each statement below is true or false. If it is false, provide the correct word for the italicized term that will make the statement true.

_____ 1. The area of temporarily transformed ectocervical epithelium is known as the *transformation zone*.

_____

_____ 2. *Ectropion* is the presence of endocervical glandular mucosa on the ectocervix.

_____

_____ 3. *Endocervical polyps* are benign proliferations made up of endocervical glands and fibrotic stroma with large vessels.

_____

_____ 4. *Acute cervicitis* is noninfectious cervicitis due to various causes in older women.

_____

_____ 5. *Chronic cervicitis* is generally infectious cervicitis often due to gonococci, *Chlamydia*, or herpes in younger women.

_____

_____ 6. *Low-grade squamous intraepithelial lesion (LSIL)* is Pap smear terminology that correlates to low-grade dysplasia in the cervix.

_____

_____ 7. *High-grade squamous epithelial lesion (HSIL)* is Pap smear terminology that correlates to high-grade dysplasia in the cervix.

_____

_____ 8. A device used to visually inspect the cervix with magnification is called a *colposcope*.

_____

_____ 9. A *LEEP* is the surgical "coring out" of a cone of cervix with a scalpel—also called conization.

_____

Classification Systems for Premalignant Changes in Cervical Squamous Epithelium			
Nomenclature for biopsy reports		**Nomenclature for Pap smear reports**	
Conventional microscopic terminology	World Health Organization classification	Bethesda system interpretation of Pap smear findings	Usual implications for treatment
Dysplasia/CIS	CIN	SIL	
Mild dysplasia	CIN I	LSIL	Watch-and-wait, resmear
Moderate dysplasia	CIN II		
Severe dysplasia CIS	CIN III	HSIL	Biopsy and treatment

LEARNING OBJECTIVE 9: Discuss the clinical presentation, diagnostic findings, and treatment as applicable for the etiologies responsible for pathologic and functional uterine bleeding and endometritis.

EXERCISE 17-18

Complete the paragraph below.

Various signs and symptoms are associated with uterine disease. These include the absence of menstruation, termed (1) _____; painful menstruation, termed (2) _____; or abnormal uterine bleeding. Several descriptive terms are used to categorize abnormal uterine bleeding. (3) _____ is excessive bleeding at the time of regular menstrual flow. (4) _____ is irregular bleeding between periods. (5) _____ is frequent, short cycles (less than three weeks). (6) _____ is few, long cycles (usually longer than six weeks). (7) _____ is bleeding due to identifiable anatomic abnormality (e.g., endometrial carcinoma). (8) _____ is any bleeding not due to identified anatomic abnormality. Treatment is often with progesterone; if intractable bleeding or bleeding due to malignancy, a surgical hysterectomy may be performed. Endometrial hyperplasia and carcinoma are discussed below, but often result from unopposed estrogen, which can occur in obesity.

EXERCISE 17-19 PATHOLOGY AS A SECOND LANGUAGE

Test your vocabulary by writing the appropriate term in each blank from the list below.

Leiomyomas   Simple hyperplasia   Chronic endometritis
Endometriosis   Adenomyosis   Leiomyosarcoma
Endometrial polyp   Endometrial hyperplasia   Clear cell carcinoma
Papillary serous carcinoma (type II carcinoma)   Complex hyperplasia
Endometrioid carcinoma (type I carcinoma)   Primary amenorrhea
Acute endometritis   Secondary amenorrhea

1. _____ is defined as failure of girls to begin menstruation at the appropriate age.

2. _____ is cessation of menses after they have begun at menarche.

3. _____ is due to bacterial infections that can arise after childbirth or abortion.

4. _____ can be due to retained products of conception, pelvic inflammatory disease, intrauterine contraceptive devices, or vaginitis.

5. _____ is deposits of endometrium outside of the uterine cavity.

6. Endometrium also may be found deep in the wall of the uterus, a condition called _____.

7. _____ is a benign proliferation having endometrial glands.

8. _____ is an overgrowth of endometrial glandular epithelium that can proceed to endometrial adenocarcinoma.

9. _____ features crowded glands that are simple tubes and often cystically dilated without atypia.

10. _____ features crowded irregular glands that are tightly packed and tortuous, and often has atypia.

11. _____ is a variably differentiated carcinoma that can somewhat resemble proliferative or secretory endometrial glands.

12. _____ is usually a poorly differentiated carcinoma; the glands have a papillary pattern and calcifications.

13. _____ is a rare high-grade carcinoma with clear cells and aggressive behavior.

14. _____ (also called fibroids) are common benign smooth muscle tumors of the uterus.

15. _____ is a rare malignant smooth muscle tumor that can arise from any site including the uterus.

Mnemonic

Causes of Secondary Amenorrhea = SOAP

Stress

Oral contraceptive pills (OCPs)

Anorexia

Pregnancy

LEARNING OBJECTIVE 10: Use imaging and pathologic findings to differentiate between the possible etiologies of an ovarian mass.

EXERCISE 17-20

Please review The Nature of Disease Figure 17.28 then complete the paragraph below.

Ovarian masses can be solid or cystic, benign or malignant; therefore, pathologic evaluation is critical to determining the category of disease and risk to the patient. Neoplastic cysts can be benign, borderline (low risk for bad behavior), or malignant, and can have different types of epithelial lining. (1) _____ tumors resemble the epithelium lining the fallopian tube, secrete a watery fluid, and are usually cystic. (2) _____ tumors resemble the epithelium lining the endocervix, secrete thick mucin, and are usually multicystic. (3) _____ tumors resemble endometrial epithelium and are less common. Any of these can progress to borderline tumors, then to invasive carcinoma, which can appear as solid areas on imaging. Please see Exercise 17-21 for additional information.

EXERCISE 17-21   PATHOLOGY AS A SECOND LANGUAGE

Test your vocabulary by indicating if each statement below is true or false. If it is false, provide the correct word for the italicized term that will make the statement true.

_____ 1. *Luteal cysts* are enlarged, unruptured Graafian follicles.

_____

_____ 2. *Follicle cysts* are formed of Graafian follicles that rupture and reseal in the luteal phase and accumulate fluid to become cystic.

_____

_____ 3. *Polycystic ovary syndrome* is a genetic disease with increased androgen, problems with ovulation, and cystic ovaries.

_____

_____ 4. *Teratoma* is a tumor composed of derivatives from all three germ layers.

_____

_____ 5. *Mature cystic teratoma* is a benign cystic lesion containing skin, hair, and other elements; it is sometimes called a dermoid cyst.

_____

_____ 6. Ovarian *fibromas* are benign solid neoplasms composed of fibrocyte-like, spindle cells.

_____

_____ 7. *Fibrothecoma* is a tumor of granulosa cells that secretes hormones and is usually benign.

_____

LEARNING OBJECTIVE 11: Describe the anatomy of the breast.

EXERCISE 17-22

Complete the paragraphs below.

The breast or mammary gland is composed of ducts and (1) _____ organized into lobules and housed within fibrous and fatty tissue. The network of ducts arising from the lobules gathers into large (2) _____ at the nipple. Ducts are lined by (3) _____ that produce milk and deeper (4) _____ that contract during lactation. (5) _____ refers to the production and delivery of milk.

During the first 10 days following delivery, breast secretions are called (6) _____ , which is high in protein and maternal antibodies that the infant can absorb. As progesterone levels fall after delivery, these secretions become (7) _____, which is higher in fat and calories.

Excessive breast tissue can form in men and is termed (8) _____, which means literally "female breast."

EXERCISE 17-23 PATHOLOGY AS A SECOND LANGUAGE

See Exercise 17-22 for key terms covered in this section.

LEARNING OBJECTIVE 12: Discuss the factors one should consider when evaluating a patient for breast cancer.

EXERCISE 17-24

Complete the paragraph below.

Breast symptoms are common; however, every breast complaint should be addressed to exclude or confirm breast cancer. The most common breast complaints are (1) _____, nipple discharge, lumpiness, and discrete mass. Clinical history including family history of (2) _____, and physical exam to assess for masses, symmetry, nipple inversion, discharge, dimpling, or bulging are necessary. (3) _____ is an uncommon event and never to be disregarded, and may point to cancer, especially if unilateral and bloody. (4) _____ is lactation in a nonpregnant female or male and points to endocrine disorders. If a mass is identified, (5) _____ is an especially useful tool in evaluating breast masses to see densities and calcifications. Additional imaging and biopsies can be used as needed for further evaluation.

EXERCISE 17-25 PATHOLOGY AS A SECOND LANGUAGE

See Exercise 17-24 for key terms covered in this section.

LEARNING OBJECTIVE 13: Compare and contrast the clinical findings of mastitis, subareolar abscess, and fat necrosis.

EXERCISE 17-26

Complete the paragraph below.

(1) _____ is a local inflammatory condition near the nipple that appears as a painful, inflamed mass.

(2) _____ is uncommon, and almost all cases are caused by infection in lactating women; it causes pain but not a mass. (3) _____ is a benign finding and a type of necrosis that occurs only in adipose tissue, but can cause a mass-forming lesion that may raise a concern for breast cancer. (4) _____ is an inflammatory disorder of the breast in diabetics that may also form a mass lesion.

EXERCISE 17-27 PATHOLOGY AS A SECOND LANGUAGE

See Exercise 17-26 for key terms covered in this section.

LEARNING OBJECTIVE 14: Name the key difference between nonproliferative and proliferative fibrocystic change of the breast, and explain why the difference is important.

EXERCISE 17-28

Complete the paragraph below.

(1) _____ is a common benign condition characterized by cystic dilation of terminal ducts, inflammation and increased fibrous stroma. This causes "lumpiness" of the breast and often leads to mammography. If these changes are accompanied by proliferation of the glandular elements, there is an increased risk for breast cancer. (2) _____ is characterized by proliferation of ductal epithelium and the absence of cellular atypia and confers a twofold increased risk for breast cancer. (3) _____ includes atypical ductal hyperplasia and atypical lobular hyperplasia and confers a fivefold increased risk for breast cancer.

EXERCISE 17-29 PATHOLOGY AS A SECOND LANGUAGE

See Exercise 17-28 for key terms covered in this section.

LEARNING OBJECTIVE 15: List the benign tumors of the breast, including fibroadenoma, phyllodes, and intraductal papilloma, and discuss their hallmark features.

EXERCISE 17-30

Complete the paragraph below.

Despite the alarm upon finding a breast mass, the majority of breast masses are benign. (1) _____ is a common benign tumor of breast stroma. (2) _____ is an uncommon, much larger, somewhat aggressive version of fibroadenoma, which has a "leaf-like" pattern of glands. Solitary (3) _____ is a benign neoplasm that most often occurs in the large milk ducts near the nipple. These can cause a bloody nipple discharge mimicking breast cancer. (4) _____, in which multiple papillomas arise in the ducts, are a variety of proliferative breast disease and as such carry an increased risk for breast carcinoma.

EXERCISE 17-31 PATHOLOGY AS A SECOND LANGUAGE

See Exercise 17-30 for key terms covered in this section.

LEARNING OBJECTIVE 16: Discuss the differential diagnosis of a malignant breast mass, and describe the signs, symptoms, and pathologic findings that aid in the diagnosis as well as the risk factors that affect patient prognosis.

EXERCISE 17-32

Complete the paragraphs below.

(1) _____ is the most common malignancy in women (other than skin cancer); 95% of the time, it is derived from the epithelium (i.e., carcinoma). All breast carcinomas arise from cells in the (2) _____; however, carcinomas are still divided into two main groups, (3) _____ and ductal carcinoma. Female gender and

(4) _____ are the most important risk factors for breast cancer. Most women with a family history of breast cancer do not have a known mutation. However, (5) _____ and (6) _____ are tumor-suppressor genes that have been identified as having harmful mutations that increase breast cancer risk. BRCA mutations are present in about 1 of every 300 people in the general population, with BRCA1 mutations conferring an approximate 70% lifetime risk and BRCA2 conferring an approximate 60% lifetime risk for breast cancer. About (7) _____ of all breast cancers are really carcinoma in situ (CIS) at time of diagnosis. This means that they have not yet invaded and therefore have an excellent prognosis. There are two microscopic types of breast CIS: ductal and lobular.

About 80% of CIS cases are (8) _____; they are often found by mammography because they are associated with calcifications or nodular density. Microscopically, ducts are filled with malignant cells and no stromal invasion is detectable. Surgery followed by radiation and/or chemotherapy is curative in 95% of cases.

The remaining 20% of CIS cases are (9) _____ and are usually an incidental finding. LCIS features atypical cells filling and expanding the lobules. In contrast to CIS, invasive carcinoma confers a worse prognosis. During surgery for breast cancer, (10) _____ are sampled to evaluate for metastatic disease.

> **Remember This!** All breast carcinomas arise from cells in the terminal duct-lobular unit.

> **Remember This!** The two most important of all pathologic distinctions in breast cancer are whether the tumor is in situ or invasive and whether or not lymph node metastasis has occurred.

EXERCISE 17-33   PATHOLOGY AS A SECOND LANGUAGE

Please review The Nature of Disease Figure 17.34 then test your vocabulary by writing the appropriate term in each blank from the list below.

Angiosarcoma	Invasive lobular carcinoma (ILC)
Paget disease	Invasive ductal carcinoma (IDC)
Inflammatory carcinoma	

1. _____ is a special variety of in situ carcinoma that occurs in the skin of the nipple in women who have a breast carcinoma immediately beneath the nipple.

2. Widespread lymphatic invasion may cause marked swelling and erythema of the entire breast, a condition referred to as _____.

3. _____ is the most common form of breast cancer composed of invasive malignant glands.

4. _____ is composed of malignant cells that infiltrate in rows or individual cells.

5. _____ is a malignant tumor of small blood vessels that can arise after chemoradiation treatment for breast carcinoma.

Mnemonic

Risk Factors for Breast Cancer = History ALONE

History of breast carcinoma in the family
Age
Late menopause, lack of breastfeeding
Obesity
Nulliparity
Early menarche

Decisions Decisions

DECISION TREE 17.1: GYNECOLOGIC DISEASE

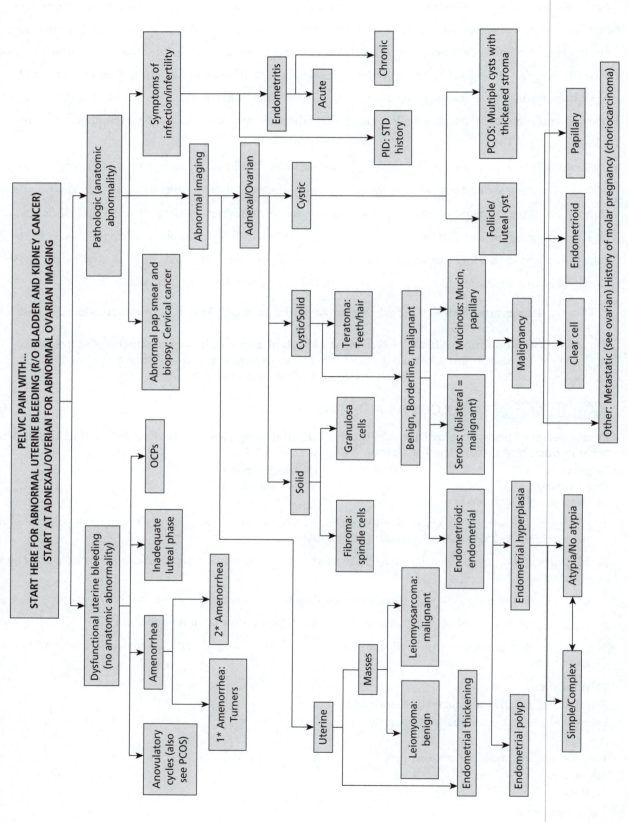

PELVIC PAIN WITH...

START HERE FOR ABNORMAL UTERINE BLEEDING (R/O BLADDER AND KIDNEY CANCER)
START AT ADNEXAL/OVARIAN FOR ABNORMAL OVARIAN IMAGING

Pathologic (anatomic abnormality)
- Symptoms of infection/infertility
  - Endometritis
    - Chronic
    - Acute
  - PID: STD history
- Abnormal imaging
  - Adnexal/Ovarian
    - Cystic
      - PCOS: Multiple cysts with thickened stroma
      - Follicle/luteal cyst
        - Papillary
        - Endometrioid
        - Clear cell
        - Other: Metastatic (see ovarian) History of molar pregnancy (choriocarcinoma)
      - Malignancy
      - Serous: (bilateral = malignant)
      - Mucinous: Mucin, papillary
      - Benign, Borderline, malignant
    - Cystic/Solid
      - Teratoma: Teeth/hair
    - Solid
      - Granulosa cells
      - Fibroma: spindle cells
- Abnormal pap smear and biopsy: Cervical cancer
- Uterine
  - Masses
    - Leiomyosarcoma: malignant
    - Leiomyoma: benign
  - Endometrial thickening
    - Endometrioid: endometrial
    - Endometrial hyperplasia
      - Atypia/No atypia
      - Simple/Complex
  - Endometrial polyp

Dysfunctional uterine bleeding (no anatomic abnormality)
- OCPs
- Inadequate luteal phase
- Amenorrhea
  - 2* Amenorrhea
  - 1* Amenorrhea: Turners
- Anovulatory cycles (also see PCOS)

232

DECISION TREE 17.2: BREAST LESIONS

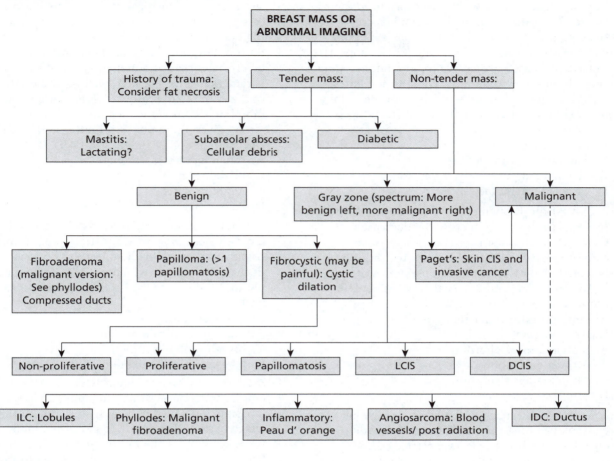

Test Yourself

I. MULTIPLE CHOICE

1. A 48-year-old Caucasian female visits her OB/GYN physician to address a very sensitive topic. She reports that her hot flashes, irritability, and headaches are manageable, but that she cannot tolerate the constant vaginal itching. A pelvic exam demonstrates a white discharge and thinning of the vaginal and vulvar epithelium. Biopsies taken at the time of exam to evaluate for possible dysplasia or malignancy are notable for vulvar atrophy. Which of the following treatments is clinically indicated? [LEARNING OBJECTIVE 3]
   A. Hormone replacement therapy
   B. Moisturizer
   C. Topical estrogen cream
   D. There is no treatment available

2. Postpartum cervicitis is most likely caused by which of the following infectious etiologies? [LEARNING OBJECTIVE 8]
   A. Chlamydia
   B. Herpes
   C. Gonococci
   D. Staphylococci

3. A 25-year-old G1P0 female at 36w5d visits her obstetrician for her 37-week checkup. She denies cramping and spotting, but notes that her feet are frequently swollen, especially at the end of the day. On exam, her blood pressure is elevated at 153/95. Concerned, you ask for a urine sample, which is positive for proteinuria on a dipstick test. What is your diagnosis? [LEARNING OBJECTIVE 4]
   A. Preeclampsia
   B. Eclampsia
   C. Gestational diabetes
   D. Gestational hypertension

4. A 53-year-old Hispanic female visits her gynecologist because she is concerned by the smooth white patches in her anogenital region. Her pelvic exam is notable for atrophic, whitish, parchment-like skin dotted with patches of leukoplakia as well as areas of atrophy and scarring. You prescribe a topical steroid for treatment of which of the following diseases? [LEARNING OBJECTIVE 6]
   A. Vulvar intraepithelial neoplasia
   B. Lichen sclerosus
   C. Lichen simplex chronicus
   D. Paget disease

5. A 55-year-old African American female, whose last menstrual period was four years ago, presents to the clinic complaining of vaginal bleeding. Imaging reveals multiple uterine masses; upon comparison to prior imaging, the masses appear to have decreased in size. A biopsy demonstrating smooth muscle without atypical mitotic figures would suggest a diagnosis of which of the following? (Hint: Use Decision Tree17.1) [LEARNING OBJECTIVE 9]
   A. Leiomyosarcoma
   B. Endometrial carcinoma
   C. Leiomyoma
   D. Cervical carcinoma

6. A 26-year-old Hispanic G2P1 female at 18 weeks presents to the ER concerned by decreased fetal movement. She is quickly taken to an exam room, where a fetal heartbeat cannot be detected. A pelvic exam demonstrates a uterus at 16 weeks size and a closed cervical os without evidence of bleeding. You console the patient and inform her that what has occurred? [LEARNING OBJECTIVE 4]
   A. A spontaneous abortion
   B. A threatened abortion
   C. An incomplete abortion
   D. A missed abortion

7. A 22-year-old Caucasian female is seen by her gynecologist for her annual exam. Her patient questionnaire lists her last menstrual period as over six weeks ago. She reports no concerns over the possibility of being pregnant, however, and states that her menstrual cycles have been irregular for the last several years. Her physical exam is notable for marked obesity and hirsutism. What ovarian ultrasonographic findings do you anticipate? (Hint: Use Decision Tree17.1) [LEARNING OBJECTIVE 10]
   A. Multiple smooth thin walled cysts (4–5 cm each)
   B. Multiple small (< 1 cm) follicle cysts beneath a thickened rind of ovarian stroma
   C. A large 6 cm multiseptated cyst with areas of echogenicity
   D. Solid bilateral 3.5 and 5 cm masses

8. Microscopic examination of the uterus of a 72-year-old woman reveals poorly differentiated malignant glands with a papillary epithelial growth pattern with lymphovascular invasion. What is your diagnosis based on the histology? (Hint: Use Decision Tree17.1) [LEARNING OBJECTIVE 9]
   A. Endometrioid carcinoma
   B. Papillary serous carcinoma
   C. Clear cell carcinoma
   D. Papillary cystadenocarcinoma

9. A 46-year-old African American woman, with no significant past medical history, visits her primary care physician for evaluation of a "rash" affecting her left breast. She denies a history of recent trauma, additional affected sites, and use of new detergents or fabric softener. Physical examination is remarkable for marked swelling and erythema of the entire left breast, which is also notable for dimpling. What is the most likely etiology of her "rash" given these physical findings? (Hint: Use Decision Tree17.1) [LEARNING OBJECTIVE 16]
   A. Inflammatory carcinoma
   B. Phyllodes tumor
   C. Acute mastitis
   D. Paget disease

10. A solitary round 2 cm mass in a 20-year-old female whose biopsy demonstrates dense fibrous tissue interspersed with compressed breast ducts is most likely which of the following neoplasms? (Hint: Use Decision Tree17.1) [LEARNING OBJECTIVE 15]
    A. Fibroadenoma
    B. Intraductal papilloma
    C. Invasive lobular carcinoma
    D. Invasive ductal carcinoma

11. A 33-year-old Hispanic female presents to the emergency room writhing in pain. You are unable to obtain a detailed clinical history due to the language barrier. You decide to perform a blood hCG while waiting for the interpreter, and it comes back positive. The subsequent uterine ultrasound demonstrates absence of a gestational sac. What is the most likely explanation of the patient's symptoms? [LEARNING OBJECTIVE 4]
    A. Ectopic pregnancy
    B. Appendicitis
    C. Missed abortion
    D. Pelvic inflammatory disease

12. A 32-year-old Caucasian woman, with a 20 pack-year smoking history, visits her primary care physician concerned by a painful inverted right nipple. A physical exam reveals a large, fluctuant mass beneath the nipple, and a biopsy of the area demonstrates cellular debris with inflammation. What is your diagnosis? (Hint: Use Decision Tree17.2) [LEARNING OBJECTIVE 13]
    A. Inflammatory carcinoma
    B. Phyllodes tumor
    C. Acute mastitis
    D. Subareolar abscess

13. A 45-year-old Caucasian female, with a past medical history of ductal carcinoma in situ, status/post radiation and tamoxifen therapy, is seen by her oncologist for her yearly mammography and checkup. Her physical exam is notable for an area of erythema near her previous incision

site. A biopsy of the area reveals a proliferation of small blood vessels. What is the most likely explanation for this constellation of symptoms? (Hint: Use Decision Tree17.2) [LEARNING OBJECTIVE 16]

A. Mastitis
B. Paget disease
C. Phyllodes tumor
D. Angiosarcoma

14. A 43-year-old Hispanic female presents to the ER following a car accident. She is complaining of severe abdominal pain. A sonogram reveals a large 8 cm right-adnexal mass. Surgical resection is performed and the mass is sent to pathology for evaluation. On gross exam, the mass is multiseptate and filled with mucin. Histology demonstrates endocervix-type epithelium with a papillary growth pattern. What is your diagnosis? (Hint: Use Decision Tree17.1) [LEARNING OBJECTIVE 10]

A. Papillary carcinoma
B. Serous carcinoma
C. Mucinous carcinoma
D. Endometrioid carcinoma

15. A 25-year-old African American female is seen at the free clinic for severe vaginal itching. Physical exam reveals copious, malodorous, greenish vaginal discharge, and a microscopic study of the discharge reveals motile organisms. Which of the following diseases is most likely to have caused her symptoms? [LEARNING OBJECTIVE 7]

A. Moniliasis
B. Bacterial vaginosis
C. Trichomoniasis
D. Chlamydia

16. Which of the following is a cause of primary amenorrhea? (Hint: Use Decision Tree17.1) [LEARNING OBJECTIVE 9]

A. Turner syndrome
B. Pregnancy
C. Stress
D. All of the above

17. A 33-year-old African American G2P2 female, with a past surgical history of C-section, undergoes an emergency hysterectomy after a manual extraction fails to remove the complete placental disc. Histologic evaluation reveals deep invasion of the placenta into the myometrial wall; however, surrounding tissue is unaffected. Which of the following conditions explains why manual extraction failed to remove the placenta? [LEARNING OBJECTIVE 4]

A. Placenta previa
B. Placenta accrete
C. Placenta increta
D. Placenta percreta

18. Chronic endometritis is usually associated with which of the following? [LEARNING OBJECTIVE 9]

A. Vaginitis
B. Retained products of conception
C. Intrauterine contraceptive devices
D. All of the above

19. An 18-year-old Hispanic female visits the free-care clinic for evaluation of vaginal bleeding. She reports her last menstrual period (LMP) as four months ago, and states that three months ago a urine pregnancy test was positive. The contents of the uterus are examined after dilation and curettage and demonstrate a watery mass of swollen, grape-like chorionic villi that microscopically are covered by hyperplastic chorionic epithelium. The karyotype of the villi is 69XYY. Based on these findings, what is your diagnosis? [LEARNING OBJECTIVE 4]

A. Invasive mole
B. Partial mole
C. Complete mole
D. Choriocarcinoma

II. TRUE OR FALSE

20. _____With the proper diet, a mother can avoid depletion of her own calcium and iron stores. [LEARNING OBJECTIVE 4]

21. _____Identification of endometrial glands within the walls of the uterus is diagnostic of malignancy. [LEARNING OBJECTIVE 9]

22. _____The gynecomastic breast is composed of an accumulation of orderly breast stroma and ducts with epithelial hyperplasia without atypia. [LEARNING OBJECTIVE 11]

23. _____Conception takes place near the site of implantation, within the uterine cavity. [LEARNING OBJECTIVE 1]

24. _____Even with as many as three consecutive abortions (miscarriages), there is a 70–80% chance the next pregnancy will go to term. [LEARNING OBJECTIVE 4]

25. _____A palpable breast mass is approximately 5 times more likely to be malignant in a postmenopausal woman compared to a premenopausal woman. [LEARNING OBJECTIVE 12]

26. _____Unlike invasive ductal carcinoma, invasive lobular carcinoma is more likely to metastasize to the bone and lungs. [LEARNING OBJECTIVE 16]

27. _____The most significant contributor to endometrial hyperplasia is obesity. [LEARNING OBJECTIVE 9]

28. _____The squamocolumnar junction, from where cervical cancer arises, is the meeting point

of squamous epithelium, which lines the ectocervix and vagina, and glandular epithelium, which lines the endocervix, endometrium, and fallopian tubes. [LEARNING OBJECTIVE 1]

29. _____The hormonal changes observed during pregnancy are the direct result of placental synthesis and secretion. [LEARNING OBJECTIVE 4]

III. MATCHING

30. Date the endometrium according to its microscopic findings (answers will be used only once): [LEARNING OBJECTIVE 2]
    i. Menstruation
    ii. Proliferative phase
    iii. Secretory phase
    A. Small glands composed of cuboidal cells with multiple mitotic figures
    B. Thin layer of endometrium present
    C. Richly vascular tissue with glycogen filled glands

31. Match the designations of cervical dysplasia/malignancy with the following pathologic findings, clinical behavior, and treatment (answers may be used more than once, and statements may have more than one answer): [LEARNING OBJECTIVE 8]
    i. ASCUS
    ii. LSIL
    iii. HSIL
    iv. CIN I
    v. CIN II
    vi. CIN III
    vii. CIS
    viii. Invasive carcinoma
    A. Usually regress
    B. Treated with conization
    C. Severe dysplasia
    D. Mild dysplasia
    E. Watch, wait, resmear
    F. Lesion which has penetrated the basement membrane
    G. Moderate dysplasia
    H. Treated with freezing, laser, vaporization, or electrocautery
    I. Biopsy and treatment
    J. More likely to progress
    K. Ambiguous dysplasia
    L. Treated with radical hysterectomy, radiation, and/or chemotherapy

IV. SHORT ANSWER

32. Your friend tells you about an amazing book she is reading that claims to reduce breast cancer risk through diet and lifestyle modifications, including maintaining an alkaline blood pH and the use of special dietary supplements (available for sale only through a website). What advice do you have to offer your friend regarding the risk factors of breast cancer? [LEARNING OBJECTIVE 16]

_____

_____

_____

33. What pathologic findings characterize fibrocystic breast disease with proliferative changes without atypia; how does it differ from proliferative changes with atypia? [LEARNING OBJECTIVE 14]

_____

_____

_____

34. Discuss the long-term consequences of pelvic inflammatory disease, and potential ways to reverse the damage. [LEARNING OBJECTIVE 5]

_____

_____

_____

35. Your best friend calls to tell you that she is expecting! Excited, you make plans to meet her at a local restaurant. Over lunch, she confides in you, as she pours eight sugars into her ice tea, that her doctor has put her on a strict diet as he is concerned about the fact that she has developed gestational diabetes. What tactful advice might you offer regarding her condition? [LEARNING OBJECTIVE 4]

_____

_____

_____

36. A 47-year-old physician calls for the results of her recent biopsy for a palpable breast mass confirmed on imaging. Histology of the biopsy was notable only for LCIS. What further actions should she take? [LEARNING OBJECTIVE 16]

    _____

    _____

    _____

CHAPTER 18

Disorders of Bones, Joints, and Skeletal Muscle

The Big Picture

Bone has mechanical, metabolic, and hematopoietic functions. Its mechanical properties are from its strength, which help it protect internal organs and act as a framework for the force of skeletal muscle contractions. Its metabolic properties are from its mineral content: bone is 65% mineral and 35% protein, and contains 99% of the body's calcium, 85% of the phosphorus, and 65% of the sodium, all of which are in constant flux. Its hematopoietic properties are derived from its central marrow cavity, where many bones also house the dynamic red marrow, production site for most blood cells. Joints allow for the movements of bones and their interconnections, while muscles move the bone! The body is truly a mechanic's dream; however, structural and functional diseases occur and neoplasia arises from these sites, the most dreaded being sarcoma.

Oh No! Not Another Learning Experience

LEARNING OBJECTIVE 1: Explain the functions of the skeletal system in relation to its organization.

EXERCISE 18-1

Complete the paragraph below.

The mechanical functions of bone require structural strength. Bone is composed of two types of bone tissue. (1) _____ is made slowly and is highly organized into parallel bundles of collagen that are mineralized into layers around a central vascular channel, called the (2) _____, to form a functional unit called the (3) _____. (4) _____ is formed from mineralization of an irregular lattice of crossing collagen fibers and numerous osteocytes. The (5) _____ of the (6) _____ is dense, solid lamellar bone tissue that forms the hard outer shell of bones, while the (7) _____ of the (8) _____ contains many small open spaces and a latticework of spicules. The central (9) _____ is surrounded by cortical and trabecular bone and houses blood cell progenitor cells responsible for hematopoiesis. Osteoclasts and osteoblasts help to regulate mineral balance in response to various stimuli.

EXERCISE 18-2 PATHOLOGY AS A SECOND LANGUAGE

Review Figure 18.1 in *The Nature of Disease*, then test your vocabulary by writing the appropriate term in each blank from the list below.

Short bones	Flat bones	Joint
Endosteum	Growth plate	Metaphysis
Long bones	Nutrient foramen	Osteoprogenitor cells
Osteoblasts	Osteoid	Osteocytes
Epiphysis	Diaphysis	Periosteum
Osteoclasts	Intramembranous ossification	
Appositional growth	Endochondral ossification	

1. The surface of spongy trabeculae is lined by a layer of cells called the _____.

2. The _____ or *physis* is a layer of cartilage where endochondral ossification allows the bone to grow until "closure."

3. The _____ is a cap of spongy bone, which extends from the growth plate to the distal (articular) end of the bone.

4. The _____ is a funnel-shaped area of spongy bone that extends from the growth plate toward the diaphysis.

5. The _____ is the long, slender, middle part of the length of the bone that joins the distal parts.

6. _____ refer to those in the extremities.

7. _____ and _____ constitute the feet, hands, skull, ribs, pelvis, scapula, and spine.

8. The place where bones meet is a _____, which may or may not pivot.

9. Bone is covered by a tough, collagenous membrane, the _____, which contains osteoblasts, nerves, and blood vessels.

10. The _____ is a passage within the Haversian system that allows entry of blood vessels.

11. _____ are pluripotent stem cells found in bone marrow and periosteum.

12. _____ are bone-forming cells.

13. Bone matrix protein fibers that are later mineralized are called _____.

14. Osteoblasts become trapped in tiny pores (*lacunae*) and become _____.

15. _____ are bone-dissolving cells derived from bone marrow stem cells.

16. Bone growth with direct accretion of layer upon layer of bone is a process called _____.

17. _____ is a manner of growth in which cartilage forms first, then is transformed into woven bone, and finally into lamellar bone.

18. _____ is bone growth that occurs on the surface of fibrous tissue, which becomes woven bone and then lamellar bone.

LEARNING OBJECTIVE 2: Categorize the types of joints and describe their components.

EXERCISE 18-3

Complete the paragraph below.

A (1) _____ is simply the place where two bones meet. There are a number of different types and categorizations. (2) _____ are synarthroses that join bones by a heavy weld of fibrous tissue so that no joint space is present and no movement occurs. (3) _____ are amphiarthroses that join bones by cartilage, have no space, and allow limited movement. (4) _____ are diarthroses that join bones by ligaments, have a joint space, and allow great range of motion.

EXERCISE 18-4   PATHOLOGY AS A SECOND LANGUAGE

Review Figure 18.2B in *The Nature of Disease*, then test your vocabulary by indicating if each statement below is true or false. If it is false, provide the correct word for the italicized term that will make the statement true.

_____ 1. The *synovium* is a special membrane that lines the fibrous tissue containing the outer edges of the bones together forming the joint space.

_____

_____ 2. The *synovial cells* secrete a lubricating fluid called *synovial fluid*.

_____

_____ 3. *Ligament* is the plate of cartilage at the end of the bone that cushions movement at the joint.

_____

_____ 4. The ends of the bones are usually bound together and kept in alignment by strong, fibrous straps called *articular cartilage*.

_____

_____ 5. *Abscesses* are small, closed, fibrous sacs lined by synovial cells, which secrete a lubricating fluid that partially fills the sac.

_____

LEARNING OBJECTIVE 3: Describe the anatomy of skeletal muscle and its connection to the nervous system.

EXERCISE 18-5

Complete the paragraphs below.

Skeletal muscles are composed of bundles of muscle cells, which are electrically active and respond to stimulation by lower motor neurons. These neurons relay a motor signal from the brain to muscle cells by attachment to them with a special nerve ending known as a (1) _____. The motor end plate and muscle cell join at the (2) _____. This is essentially a specialized (3) _____, a junction between two neurons or between a neuron and a muscle or gland cell. The fundamental functional element of the neuromuscular system is the (4) _____, which is composed of a lower motor neuron, a motor end plate, and a skeletal muscle cell (or cells).

The motor nerve action potential stimulates release of (5) _____ into the synaptic space. Acetylcholine quickly crosses the synaptic space and interacts with skeletal muscle to cause contraction of muscle fibers. In the process, acetylcholine is broken down by an enzyme, (6) _____, to reset the system for the next signal to cross the synapse. When electrically stimulated, the (7) _____ and (8) _____ filaments slide past each other and the muscle cell shortens (contracts). Some muscle stem cells persist into adulthood and are called (9) _____ because they are located in the interstitium near the edge of muscle fibers.

EXERCISE 18-6 PATHOLOGY AS A SECOND LANGUAGE

See Exercise 18-5 for key terms covered in this section.

EXERCISE 18-7

Complete the table below.

Muscle Fiber Types		
	(1) _____	(2) _____
Action	Sustained force or weight bearing	Sudden movement or purposeful motion
Color (due to fiber myoglobin content and vascular supply)	Red (dark)	Pale (white)
ATPase stain intensity	Dark	Light
Fat	Abundant	Scant
Glycogen	Scant	Abundant
Example of muscle with high fiber type content	Neck muscles	Eye muscles

LEARNING OBJECTIVE 4: Describe the clinical presentation of bone disorders affecting growth, maturation, modeling, and maintenance.

EXERCISE 18-8

Complete the paragraph below.

Myriad disorders affect the bone and can be reactive, genetic, or neoplastic. (1) _____ is the formation of new membranous bone in response to stress or injury to a bone or soft tissue, as in a fracture. (2) _____ is abnormal bone formation in a different tissue in response to injury; if this happens in muscle it is called "myositis ossificans." (3) _____ is the most common cause of genetic dwarfism and is due to failure of epiphyseal cartilage to form normally. (4) _____ is a non-neoplastic, tumor-like growth that features a short, bony stalk covered by a cap of cartilage. (5) _____ (or *Ollier disease*) is a bone-growth defect that features multiple deforming cartilaginous masses within bone.

EXERCISE 18-9

Complete the table below.

Disease	Alternate Name	Pathology	Clinical
(1) _____	Brittle bone disease	Disorder of bone maturation, collagen defect leading to easily fractured bones	Genetic; can be confused with child abuse; other features may include deafness, thin blue sclerae, etc.
(2) _____	Osteopetrosis; Albers-Schönberg disease	Disorder of bone remodeling with dense, sclerotic bone due to osteoclast defect	Genetic; may have hydrocephalus
(3) _____	None	Decreased density of bone (quantity)	May be primary or secondary
(4) _____	Rickets is one type	Soft quality of bone	One cause is lack of vitamin D; causes bowleg deformities
(5) _____	Osteitis deformans	Disorder of bone remodeling with irregular thickened characteristic bony trabeculae	Unknown cause; an uncommon disease; 1% may develop osteosarcoma

EXERCISE 18-10 PATHOLOGY AS A SECOND LANGUAGE

Test your vocabulary by writing the appropriate term in each blank from the list below.

Scoliosis   Kyphosis   Lordosis

1. _____ is abnormal lateral bending of the spine.

2. _____ is abnormal forward curvature.

3. _____ is abnormal backward curvature.

LEARNING OBJECTIVE 5: Distinguish between osteoporosis and osteomalacia, taking into consideration pathogenesis, clinical presentation, diagnosis, and treatment.

EXERCISE 18-11

Complete the paragraph below.

The key difference between osteoporosis and osteomalacia is quantity versus quality. (1) _____ is an acquired condition of decreased mineralization of bones, increased bone porousness, and decreased quantity of bone (decreased mass and density). (2) _____ means soft bones and is defective mineralization (calcification) of osteoid leading to a change in the quality of the hardness of bone. (3) _____ is a type of osteomalacia found in patients with failing kidneys similar to that found in patients with hyperparathyroidism. (4) _____ is a form of osteomalacia due to vitamin D deficiency in growing children.

See Exercise 18-9 for additional information.

Remember This! One-third of women over age 65 will suffer a fracture due to osteoporosis.

EXERCISE 18-12 PATHOLOGY AS A SECOND LANGUAGE

See Exercises18-9 and 18-11 for key terms covered in this section.

LEARNING OBJECTIVE 6: List fracture types, their potential risk factors, and their phases of healing.

EXERCISE 18-13

Review Figure 18.10 in *The Nature of Disease*, then complete the paragraphs below.

The most common lesion of bone is (1) _____ (a broken bone), of which there are several types. A (2) _____ is one in which bone has not broken through skin. If bone protrudes through skin, the fracture is an (3) _____. A single fracture line is a (4) _____. A simple fracture line extending all the way across the bone is a (5) _____; otherwise, the fracture is incomplete. Multiple fractures in a single site form a (6) _____. Children's bones are more flexible than adults and tend to bend or break partially (incompletely), in a manner known as a (7) _____. Twisting force can cause a (8) _____. Sudden end-to-end force that causes bone to collapse upon itself is an (9) _____, or a compression fracture. A (10) _____ is one that results from disease that has weakened bone locally, so that the fracture occurs with normal stress.

Fractures heal through phases as described below. This process is aided by realignment of the bone, called (11) _____, and stabilization with plates, pins, screws, called (12) _____.

EXERCISE 18-14 PATHOLOGY AS A SECOND LANGUAGE

Test your vocabulary by indicating if each statement below is true or false. If it is false, provide the correct word for the italicized term that will make the statement true.

_____ 1. The *blastic phase* of fracture repair is when fibroblasts, new blood vessels, and woven bone appear.

_____

_____ 2. The early *remodeling phase* involves formation of granulation tissue.

_____

_____ 3. The mixture of granulation tissue, fibrous tissue, and new islands of bone is called a *soft callus*.

_____

_____ 4. Dead bone is resorbed by osteoclasts and the lesion becomes a *bony callus*, which forms new spongy and compact bone and is capable of limited weight bearing.

_____

_____ 5. The *reparative phase* is when lamellar bone in the cortex aligns in the long axis.

_____

LEARNING OBJECTIVE 7: Name the types of bone infarctions and infections.

EXERCISE 18-15

Complete the paragraph below.

(1) _____ is bone death. In the absence of infection, it is often called (2) _____ or (3) _____.

Important causes include steroids and (4) _____. Bone infarction is also sometimes called "osteonecrosis" because

the bone becomes devitalized and the osteocytes die. Necrotic bone is also a part of infectious acute osteomyelitis.

EXERCISE 18-16   PATHOLOGY AS A SECOND LANGUAGE

See Exercise 18-15 for key terms covered in this section.

LEARNING OBJECTIVE 8: Discuss the most common etiologies of bone infection, noting the clinical and diagnostic features.

EXERCISE 18-17

Complete the paragraph below.

(1) _____ is most often a suppurative bacterial infection of bone and bone marrow due to staphylococci

and streptococci. It can occur after trauma or as a complication of vascular disease or (2) _____. Acute

bacterial infection of bone is accompanied by bone necrosis and inflammation. Acute bacterial osteomyelitis can

be difficult to treat, and requires vigorous and prolonged (3) _____; 5–10% of infections become a chronic

problem. Surgery may be necessary. (4) _____ affects the vertebral body and may be related to intravenous

drug abuse. Osteomyelitis caused by the tuberculosis bacterium (named [5] _____) remains a problem in

developing countries.

EXERCISE 18-18   PATHOLOGY AS A SECOND LANGUAGE

See Exercise 18-17 for key terms covered in this section.

LEARNING OBJECTIVE 9: Classify the tumors affecting the bone according to their composition, whether they are benign or malignant, their location, their pathological findings, and their prognosis.

EXERCISE 18-19

Complete the paragraphs below.

The most common tumor involving the bone is (1) _____, including carcinoma of the prostate, breast,

and lung. Primary bone tumors occur in specific sites with 80% occurring (2) _____ in the lower femur

or upper tibia and fibula. Forty percent of primary tumors are bone forming or cartilage forming, 40% are hema-

topoietic, and 20% are other. Benign tumors are much more common than malignant ones and occur mainly in

patients under age 30. Bone tumors in the elderly usually are (3) _____.

   Clinically, bone tumors present with pain, as a slow-growing mass, or as an unexpected pathologic fracture.

(4) _____ are an important part of the diagnostic assessment, but biopsy and pathologic assessment is

essential for diagnosis and prognosis. However, the rarity and diverse histologic appearance of primary bone

tumors often makes them difficult for pathologists and radiologists to diagnose correctly.

EXERCISE 18-20

Please review The Nature of Disease Figure 18.12 then complete the table below.

Tumors	Benign or malignant?	Tissue of origin	Pathology and Location	Prognosis
(1) _____	Benign	Bone	Usually a small, roundish, sessile benign tumor on the surface of a bone, often the head	Good; can be associated with colon cancer (Gardner)
(2) _____ (< 2 cm) **Osteoblastoma** (> 2 cm)	Benign	Bone (osteoblasts)	Lytic central nidus with sclerotic rim, osteoid and primitive woven bone are formed	More often in young males; osteoid osteomas are severely painful
(3) _____ (*osteogenic sarcoma*)	Malignant	Bone	Forms neoplastic bone, so-called "malignant osteoid"	Poor prognosis, no good treatments; usually in children or young adults
(4) _____ (*osteoclastoma*)	Benign	Osteoclast	Numerous osteoclast-like giant cells	Can be locally destructive
(5) _____	Malignant	Cartilage	Malignant chondrocytes making cartilage	Usually in older adults; good prognosis for low-grade lesions
(6) _____	Malignant	Fibrous connective tissue	Malignant fibrocytes invading soft tissues	Poor prognosis
(7) _____	Malignant, neuroectodermal differentiation		Malignant cells with primitive neuroectodermal differentiation, immature cells form rosettes	Usually in long bones of children; 75% 5-year survival

EXERCISE 18-21 PATHOLOGY AS A SECOND LANGUAGE

Test your vocabulary by writing the appropriate term in each blank from the list below.

Aneurysmal bone cyst   Fibrous compact defect (FCD)

Non-ossifying fibroma (NOF)   Multiple myeloma

Fibrous dysplasia   Malignant lymphoma

1. _____ and _____ are the same type of common fibrous bone lesion; however, one is small (< 2 cm) and one is larger.

2. _____ is a benign, nodular growth of fibrous and bone tissue that affects growing bones in children and teenagers.

3. _____ is not a tumor but forms tumor-like masses in the metaphysis of long bones of children and youth.

4. _____ and _____ are both hematopoietic neoplasms that can occur in bone, along with other disorders.

LEARNING OBJECTIVE 10: Characterize the kinds of arthritis according to etiology, signs and symptoms, diagnostic findings, and treatment.

EXERCISE 18-22

Review Figure 18.15, then complete the paragraph below.

(1) _____ is a painful joint condition associated with inflammation and joint abnormalities. The two most common forms are (2) _____ (also called "degenerative joint disease"), which features progressive, noninflammatory erosion of joint cartilage that is related to age and chronic trauma, and (3) _____, which is a chronic, systemic autoimmune disease that causes destructive inflammation of synovial joints, but can affect other tissues. One test for this condition is (4) _____ or circulating antibody complexes, which are sensitive, but not specific for the disease. In addition, (5) _____ is due to bacterial infection, and (6) _____ can cause excruciating joint pain and inflammation due to uric acid crystal deposition.

Remember This! Eighty percent of rheumatoid arthritis occurs in women.

EXERCISE 18-23   PATHOLOGY AS A SECOND LANGUAGE

Test your vocabulary by indicating if each statement below is true or false. If it is false, provide the correct word for the italicized term that will make the statement true.

_____ 1. *Pannus* is a highly vascular inflammatory membrane.

_____

_____ 2. Complete destruction of a joint with dense fibrous repair producing a welded immovable joint is called *ankylosing spondylitis*.

_____

_____ 3. Ulnar deviation in a rheumatoid arthritis patient is the classic *W deformity*.

_____

_____ 4. *Rheumatoid nodules* are painless 1–2 cm subcutaneous inflammatory nodules not found in other forms of arthritis.

_____

_____ 5. *Secondary amyloidosis* is due to deposition in various tissues of breakdown products of antibody immunoglobulin.

_____

_____ 6. *Juvenile idiopathic arthritis (JIA)* is any arthritis arising in someone less than 16 years old that persists for more than six weeks.

_____

_____ 7. *Still's disease* includes fever, skin rash, hepatosplenomegaly, and polyserositis.

_____

_____ 8. *Spondyloarthropathy* is an autoimmune, genetically influenced, vertebral arthritis that occurs in patients who do not have a specific antibody.

_____

_____ 9. *Reiter syndrome* is a chronic relapsing arthritis primarily affecting the joints of the vertebral processes of the spine and especially the sacroiliac joints.

_____

_____ 10. *Ankylosis* is defined as a syndrome of arthritis, nongonococcal urethritis or cervicitis, and conjunctivitis.

_____

_____ 11. *Enteritis-associated arthritis* is arthritis following GI infection but does not feature conjunctivitis or urethritis.

_____

_____ 12. *Ulcerative arthritis* affects small joints of the hands and feet and later the spine in 10% of patients with psoriasis.

_____

_____ 13. *Lyme disease* is a summer and fall bacterial infection caused by *Borrelia burgdorferi* harbored by ticks.

_____

_____ 14. *Polymyalgia rheumatica (PMR)* features stiffness and pain and may be related to giant cell arteritis.

_____

LEARNING OBJECTIVE 11: List the types of injuries to joints and periarticular tissues.

EXERCISE 18-24

Complete the paragraph below.

A (1) _____ is an injury to a *ligament* induced by stretching it too far; if the same injury occurs to a *tendon, it* is called a (2) _____. (3) _____ is displacement of one bone in a joint such that the articular surfaces no longer meet. (4) _____ is a lesser degree of separation within the joint.

Mnemonic
Treatment for Sprain/Strains = RICE
Rest
Ice
Compression
Elevation

EXERCISE 18-25   PATHOLOGY AS A SECOND LANGUAGE

See Exercise 18-24 for key terms covered in this section.

LEARNING OBJECTIVE 12: Name the distinguishing features that separate fibromyalgia from arthritis and other painful musculoskeletal syndromes.

EXERCISE 18-26

Complete the paragraph below.

(1) _____ is a clinical syndrome of fatigue, muscle and periarticular tendon and ligament pain, tenderness, and stiffness that is not associated with objective signs of disease. It is more common in (2) _____. Other painful musculoskeletal syndromes will have corresponding anatomic or pathological findings. For example, although sometimes (3) _____ cannot be explained by anatomic causes, most can be identified. (4) _____ occurs with age and can allow the nucleus pulposus to bulge or rupture outward impinging on spinal nerve roots; this is called a (5) _____. When vertebrae slide anteriorly or posteriorly out of alignment to a degree detectable by imaging studies, the condition is called (6) _____. These can cause spinal pain.

EXERCISE 18-27   PATHOLOGY AS A SECOND LANGUAGE

Test your vocabulary by writing the appropriate term in each blank from the list below.

Carpal tunnel syndrome	Tendinitis	Shin splints
Tennis elbow	Bursitis	Tenosynovitis

1. _____ is inflammation or pain in a tendon.

2. _____ is inflammation or pain of the synovial sheath through which tendons slide in their motion.

3. _____ is a painful condition of the ligaments that attach forearm extensor muscles to the lateral epicondyle of the humerus.

4. _____ is an affliction of runners that is characterized by pain and tenderness along the anterior aspect of the tibia where muscle attaches to bone.

5. _____ is a condition of the tendons and tendon sheaths of the ventral wrist in persons doing tasks that require repetitive finger and wrist motions.

6. _____ is inflammation of a bursa and is typically due to direct trauma or the stress of repetitive motion.

LEARNING OBJECTIVE 13: Differentiate between ganglion cysts and tenosynovial giant cell tumors using location, clinical presentation, and or diagnostic findings as applicable.

EXERCISE 18-28

Complete the paragraphs below.

(1) _____ refers to nonepithelial tissue that is not bone, cartilage, brain, nerve, meninges, bone marrow, or lymphoid tissue. Therefore, this includes (2) _____, ligaments and other fibrous tissue, skeletal and smooth muscle, and fat. Since, these tissue types are ubiquitous, neoplasms arising from them can occur anywhere.

The cause of most soft tissue tumors is unknown. Radiation-induced sarcoma, (3) _____ of AIDS, and the neurofibromas of neurofibromatosis are exceptions that have clear causes.

EXERCISE 18-29

Complete the table below.

Tumors	Benign or malignant?	Tissue of origin	Pathology	Prognosis
(1) _____	Malignant	Adipose tissue	Lipoblasts, fat, malignant appearing cells	Generally arises in deep tissues or retroperitoneum
(2) _____	Malignant	Fibrous connective tissue	Malignant fibrocytes invading soft tissues	Prognosis depends on grade
(3) _____	Malignant	Smooth muscle	Malignant cells arranged in a fascicular pattern	Any soft tissue location, also uterus; prognosis depends on grade
(4) _____	Malignant	Tumor of fibrocyte-like cells that arises near joint capsule	Densely cellular malignant neoplasm	Poor prognosis
(5) _____	Malignant	Skeletal muscle	Malignant cells with primitive muscle differentiation	Rare

EXERCISE 18-30   PATHOLOGY AS A SECOND LANGUAGE

Test your vocabulary by indicating if each statement below is true or false. If it is false, provide the correct word for the italicized term that will make the statement true.

____ 1. *Soft tissue* refers to any nonepithelial tissue that is not bone, cartilage, brain, nerve, meninges, bone marrow, or lymphoid tissue.

____ 2. *Mucous cyst* is a small (usually < 1.5 cm), smooth, fluctuant, fluid-filled, simple cyst that arises near a joint or tendon sheath.

____ 3. *Tenosynovial giant cell tumor* (formerly called "pigmented villonodular synovitis") is a benign neoplasm of synovial joints, bursae, and tendon sheaths.

____ 4. *Liposarcoma* is a benign tumor of fat cells and is by far the most common soft tissue tumor.

____ 5. *Desmoid tumor* is a benign mass of inflammatory, immature scar tissue that occurs most often on the forearm, back, or trunk.

____ 6. *Fibromatosis* is a confined proliferation of fibrous tissue that can be locally aggressive and may recur after excision, but does not metastasize.

____ 7. Fibromatosis in deep fascia is called *nodular fasciitis* and is somewhat more aggressive but does not metastasize.

____ 8. *Leiomyoma* is a benign tumor of smooth muscle.

LEARNING OBJECTIVE 14: Distinguish between neurogenic and disuse atrophy of skeletal muscle.

EXERCISE 18-31

Review Figure 18.3 in *The Nature of Disease*, then complete the paragraph below.

(1) _____ is caused by (2) _____ of the muscle and leads to muscle fiber atrophy of both type 1 and type 2. This type of atrophy can occur with many forms of nerve damage, including those associated with diabetes, called (3) _____. In contrast, (4) _____ occurs in muscles that are inactive due to some reason other than lower motor neuron denervation, as in immobilized patients, and selectively causes muscle fiber atrophy of type 2 fibers only.

EXERCISE 18-32   PATHOLOGY AS A SECOND LANGUAGE

Test your vocabulary by indicating if each statement below is true or false. If it is false, provide the correct word for the italicized term that will make the statement true.

_____ 1. *Parkinson disease* is an inherited autosomal recessive denervation atrophy disease that is associated with progressive degeneration of anterior horn cells.

_____

_____ 2. *Rhabdomyolysis* is a term used to describe sudden necrosis of skeletal muscle with release of large amounts of myoglobin into the circulation.

_____

LEARNING OBJECTIVE 15: Using examples from the text, characterize each of the dystrophies, congenital myopathies, inborn errors of metabolism, causes of myositis, and toxic myopathies according to the diagnostic and clinical findings.

EXERCISE 18-33

Complete the paragraphs below.

(1) _____ literally means disease of muscle and refers to muscle disease not related to its innervation. Sometimes included in this disease category are (2) _____, a group of hereditary, progressive, noninflammatory diseases of striated muscle—skeletal and cardiac—associated with defective contractility, which causes muscle weakness. The most well-known are (3) _____ and (4) _____. There are several rare forms, including (5) _____, which feature involuntary contractions of muscle.

(6) _____ refers to inflammation of the muscle (i.e., an inflammatory myopathy). (7) _____ are a diverse group of acquired disorders featuring weakness of proximal muscles, increased muscle enzymes in blood, and nonsuppurative inflammation of skeletal muscle. The most common forms are viral or parasitic infection with (8) _____ from eating infected, undercooked pork. Another category is the (9) _____, a large and diverse group of conditions, many genetic, that feature decreased muscle tone or (10) _____. This is sometimes referred to as (11) _____, irrespective of the cause.

EXERCISE 18-34

Complete the table below.

Category	Disease	Clinical	Pathology
Inflammatory/ autoimmune	(1) _____	Cell mediated, respond to corticosteroids	Endomysial infiltrate
	(2) _____	Antibody mediated, cutaneous symptoms (skin rash), associated with malignancy!	Perimysial, perifascicular, tubuloreticular inclusions
	Inclusion body myositis	No corticosteroid response. Quadriceps and finger flexors	Endomysial, rimmed vacuoles
Toxic	Statin-associated myopathy	Monitor CK levels	Nonspecific muscle fiber degeneration, necrosis, and regeneration
	(3) _____	Positive medication history	Type 2 fiber atrophy
Muscular	(4) _____	Early onset, wheelchair bound at age 12, death at age 30	No dystrophin, increased CK levels, muscle pseudohypertrophy
	(5) _____	Later onset, symptoms generally become noticeable at age 12	Some dystrophin present
Congenital	(6) _____	Autosomal dominant, ryanodine receptor mutations, malignant hyperthermia, nonprogressive muscle weakness	Central core pallor, decreased type 2 fibers
Metabolic	McArdle disease—a type of (7) _____	Can't break down glycogen; rhabdomyolysis; myoglobinuria; "second wind" syndrome	Absence of enzyme activity (on stain)

EXERCISE 18-35 PATHOLOGY AS A SECOND LANGUAGE

Test your vocabulary by writing the appropriate term in each blank from the list below.

Central nuclear myopathy   Thyrotoxic myopathy   Nemaline myopathy
Ethanol myopathy   Lipid myopathies   Glycogen storage diseases
Familial periodic paralysis

1. _____ features decreased type 2 fibers and rod-like intracytoplasmic inclusions.

2. _____ feature genetic defects that interfere with fatty acid metabolism and result in lipid droplet accumulation in muscle cells.

3. _____ are a diverse group of myopathies associated with an inability to degrade glycogen.

4. _____ is a family of autosomal dominant disorders that feature episodes of weakness or paralysis followed by quick recovery.

5. _____ is muscle weakness associated with hyperthyroidism and exophthalmic ophthalmoplegia.

6. Binge drinking can lead to rhabdomyolysis, myoglobinuria, and renal failure called _____.

7. _____ features nuclei in the center of the fiber rather than at the edge.

LEARNING OBJECTIVE 16: Explain the molecular pathogenesis of myasthenia gravis.

EXERCISE 18-36

Complete the paragraph below.

(1) _____ is an uncommon, acquired autoimmune disease of the neuromuscular junction, normally affecting young adult women. In this disease the patient produces antibodies against the (2) _____ present on muscle cells of the neuromuscular junction. These antibodies block acetylcholine binding, therefore making it very difficult to stimulate contraction in the muscle. Drooping eyelids and (3) _____ (double vision) from weak eye muscles may be the first complaint, but all muscles can be affected to varying degrees. Diagnosis is by measurement of blood AChR antibody levels and electromyography. Treatment involves circulating antibody by filtering plasma (plasmapheresis), steroids, anticholinesterase drugs, and surgical removal of (4) _____ if present.

EXERCISE 18-37   PATHOLOGY AS A SECOND LANGUAGE

See Exercise 18-35 for key terms covered in this section.

Decisions Decisions

DECISION TREE 18.1: BONE AND SOFT TISSUE MASSES/LESIONS

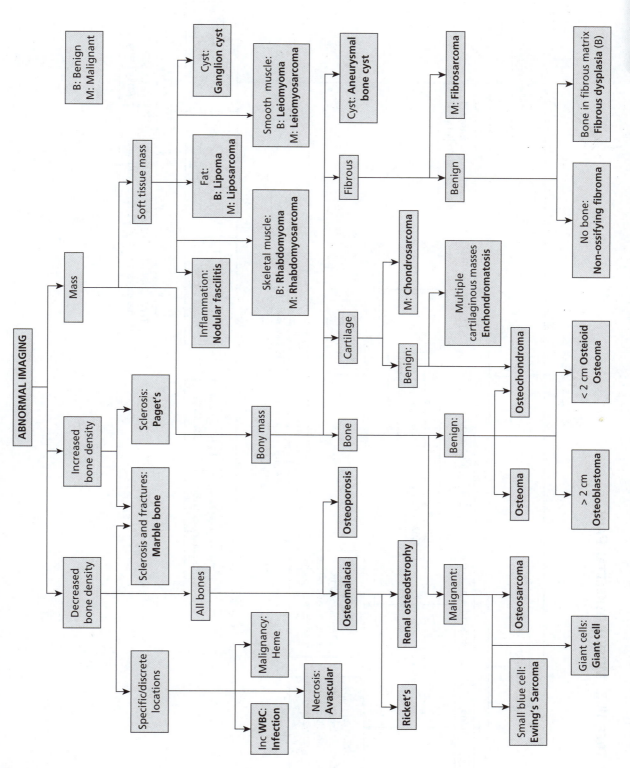

DECISION TREE 18.2: MUSKULOSKELETAL PAIN

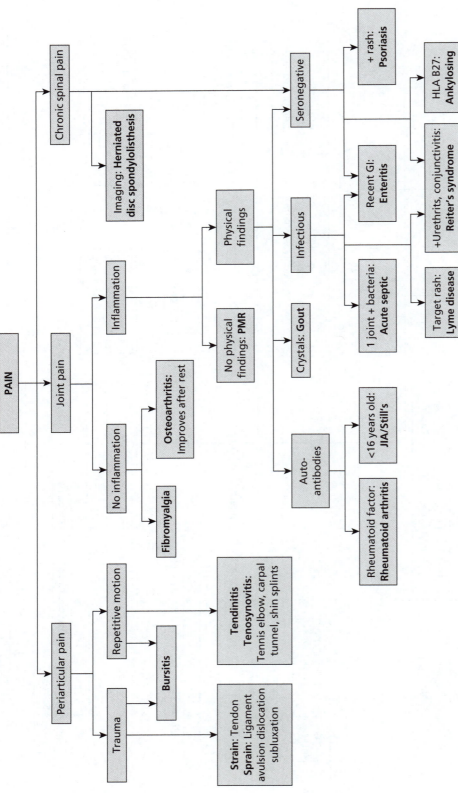

DECISION TREE 18.3: MUSCLE WEAKNESS

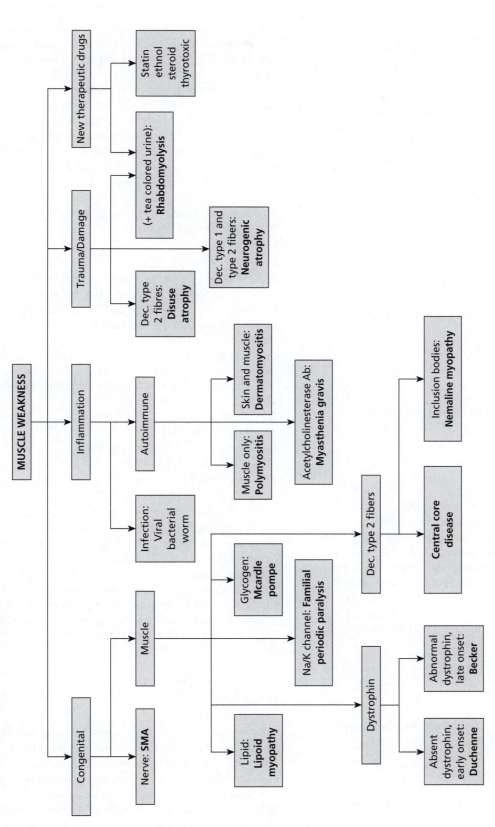

Test Yourself

I. MULTIPLE CHOICE

1. A 42-year-old martial arts black belt visits his doctor concerned by the nodule that has recently appeared on his right forearm. He reports a history of multiple traumas to this previous location secondary to competitions, the most recent a large 6 cm bruise that took over a month to heal. A biopsy of the mass reveals normal bone. What is the underlying etiology of this bony mass? [LEARNING OBJECTIVE 4]
   A. Reactive bone formation
   B. Heterotopic ossification
   C. Achondroplasia
   D. Osteochondroma

2. A high school wrestler visits his trainer complaining of terrible pain following a wrestling match in which his arm was twisted behind him. Based on this history, what type of fracture would you expect to identify on his radiographs? [LEARNING OBJECTIVE 6]
   A. Comminuted fracture
   B. Greenstick fracture
   C. Spiral fracture
   D. Impacted fracture

3. Which of the following produces abnormal bending of the spine? [LEARNING OBJECTIVE 4]
   A. Kyphosis
   B. Lordosis
   C. Scoliosis
   D. All of the above

4. A 55-year-old African American female suffers from pain in her hips, knees, and back that gets worse during the day, but improves after short rests. Her physical exam is notable for Heberden nodes and an absence of joint deformity. An X-ray demonstrates narrowing of the joint space with adjacent bony sclerosis and bone cysts. What is the most likely underlying etiology of her joint pain? (Hint: Use Decision Tree 18.2) [LEARNING OBJECTIVE 10]
   A. Osteoarthritis
   B. Gout
   C. Rheumatoid arthritis
   D. Psoriatic arthritis

5. What would you expect to see on histology during the early reparative phase of bone healing? [LEARNING OBJECTIVE 6]
   A. Fibroblasts, new blood vessels, and woven bone
   B. A mixture of granulation tissue, fibrous tissue, and new islands of bone
   C. New spongy and compact bone
   D. Newly formed lamellar bone in the cortex

6. A 64-year-old postmenopausal Caucasian female is seen at the clinic for evaluation of back pain. Given her age, and the fact that she underwent menopause over a decade ago, you decide to perform a bone density scan, which reveals only mildly diminished bone density. However, multiple radiographs of her back demonstrate a number of pseudofractures prompting an additional workup. Her labs were remarkable for an elevated phosphate and creatine kinase and decreased calcium. What is your diagnosis? (Hint: Use Decision Tree 18.1) [LEARNING OBJECTIVE 5]
   A. Primary osteoporosis
   B. Secondary osteoporosis
   C. Rickets
   D. Renal osteodystrophy

7. A 32 year-old Hispanic female is seen at the clinic for evaluation of a 1.5 cm painful mass on the lateral aspect of her wrist, which is impeding her job as a secretary. Gross examination of the excised mass reveals a fluid-filled cyst, which on histology appears to be connective tissue with myxoid degeneration without an internal lining cell layer. What is your diagnosis? (Hint: Use Decision Tree 18.1) [LEARNING OBJECTIVE 13]
   A. Ganglion cyst
   B. Nodular fasciitis
   C. Tenosynovial giant cell tumor
   D. Carpal tunnel syndrome

8. A 16-year-old male is brought to the clinic complaining of difficulty walking. He reports that he first noticed the symptoms approximately four weeks ago, and that it seems to have rapidly become much worse. A radiograph of his femur demonstrates multiple metaphyseal masses, which are diagnostic, and surgical excision is advised. Histology of the mass demonstrates large, richly vascular cysts containing pools of blood, which is consistent with a diagnosis of which of the following? (Hint: Use Decision Tree 18.1) [LEARNING OBJECTIVE 9]
   A. Giant cell tumor
   B. Aneurysmal bone cyst
   C. Fibrosarcoma
   D. Angiosarcoma

9. A 61-year-old female with a past medical history significant for hundreds of fractures died from complications of her disease, which included anemia, blindness, and deafness. At autopsy, her bones were remarkable for sclerosis and an absence of osteoclasts. Which of the following diseases explains her constellation of symptoms? (Hint: Use Decision Tree 18.1) [LEARNING OBJECTIVE 4]

A. Paget disease
B. Osteogenesis imperfecta
C. Achondroplasia
D. Marble bone disease

10. Which of the following is a complication of a herniated intervertebral disc? (Hint: Use Decision Tree 18.2) [LEARNING OBJECTIVE 12]
    A. Sciatica
    B. Foot drop
    C. Paralysis
    D. All of the above

11. A 64-year-old Hispanic male, with a past medical history of a left femoral neck fracture five years ago status post internal fixation with pins, is seen for his yearly checkup. He complains of pain in the left hip, which interferes with his daily activities and only partially responds to NSAIDs. His labs are unremarkable; his ESR and CRP are normal, as is his white count, and a hip aspiration is negative for crystals and neutrophils, while his cultures are negative to date. Radiology confirms your diagnosis, which is most likely which of the following? (Hint: Use Decision Tree 18.1) [LEARNING OBJECTIVE 7]
    A. Aseptic necrosis
    B. Acute osteomyelitis
    C. Chronic osteomyelitis
    D. Gout

12. What pathologic findings might you expect to find in a patient with a destructive tumor near the epiphysis of the tibia, radiology that demonstrates a "soap bubble" lesion, and metastatic tumor deposits containing osteoclast-like cells within the lung? (Hint: Use Decision Tree 18.1) [LEARNING OBJECTIVE 9]
    A. Tumor-like masses of bone within a fibrous matrix
    B. Small round blue cells
    C. A red–brown friable mass with multinucleate cells
    D. A benign mass of inflammatory, immature scar tissue

13. A 73-year-old African American female presents to her doctor with fatigue, pain, and joint stiffness that does not respond to NSAIDs. Her physical exam is notable for an absence of joint swelling, erythema, or deformity, but she complains of pain when you press on "trigger points" near joints in her neck, shoulders, lower back, and thighs. Her labs demonstrate no elevation in ESR or CRP and radiology is normal. A review of symptoms is also notable for insomnia and depression. Which of the following is the most likely explanation of her symptoms? (Hint: Use Decision Tree 18.2) [LEARNING OBJECTIVE 12]

A. Polymyalgia rheumatic
B. Osteoarthritis
C. Rheumatoid arthritis
D. Fibromyalgia

14. Which of the following is associated with primary osteoporosis? [LEARNING OBJECTIVE 5]
    A. Cigarette smoke
    B. Calcium deficiency
    C. Cortisone excess
    D. Immobilization

15. It is a beautiful day in late fall when a Maine farmer visits the clinic complaining of recurrent joint pain. He reports that today's pain is different than the pain he had two months ago, as this time he doesn't have the accompanying fever, fatigue, or rash. When prompted to describe the rash, he reports that it looked like little targets. A positive antibody test would confirm which diagnosis? (Hint: Use Decision Tree 18.2) [LEARNING OBJECTIVE 10]
    A. Osteoarthritis
    B. Rheumatoid arthritis
    C. Gout
    D. Lyme disease

16. A biopsy of a nodule mass in an area of trauma demonstrating benign inflammatory, immature scar tissue would prompt what treatment? (Hint: Use Decision Tree 18.2) [LEARNING OBJECTIVE 13]
    a. Excision
    b. Chemotherapy
    c. Radiation
    d. All of the above

17. A mother brings her six-year-old son to the clinic for evaluation of his poor motor skills. She reports that he was slow to walk and that now the progress he has made seems to be diminishing. She is concerned as one of her uncles had a similar disease and died at age 20 of respiratory failure. Based on this clinical history, which of the following familial diseases do you suspect? (Hint: Use Decision Tree 18.3) [LEARNING OBJECTIVE 14]
    A. Duchenne's muscular dystrophy
    B. Becker's muscular dystrophy
    C. Nemaline Myopathy
    D. McArdle disease

18. An injection of what drug would temporarily improve double vision due to periorbital and eye muscle weakness in a 33-year-old female with acetylcholine receptor (AChR) antibodies? (Hint: Use Decision Tree 18.3) [LEARNING OBJECTIVE 16]
    A. Edrophonium
    B. Acetylcholinesterase
    C. Infliximab
    D. Steroids

II. TRUE OR FALSE

19. _____ Unless prolonged antibiotic therapy is given, acute osteomyelitis can become chronic osteomyelitis requiring surgical drainage and wound debridement. [LEARNING OBJECTIVE 8]

20. _____ The majority of the body's calcium, phosphorus, and sodium are stored in bone. [LEARNING OBJECTIVE 1]

21. _____ Type 2 muscle fibers are responsible for sustained-force and weight-bearing activities. [LEARNING OBJECTIVE 3]

22. _____ The metaphysis is the most common site of osteomyelitis due to its vascularity. [LEARNING OBJECTIVE 8]

23. _____ Treatment for a tendon strain with avulsion requires rest, ice, compression, and elevation. [LEARNING OBJECTIVE 11].

24. _____ Signals are transmitted down nerve axons as action potentials in the cell membrane. [LEARNING OBJECTIVE 3]

25. _____ Aspirin is especially effective for pain relief caused by osteoblastoma. [LEARNING OBJECTIVE 9]

26. _____ Articular cartilage lacks blood supply, nerves, and lymphatics and is nourished with oxygen and nutrients from joint fluid. [LEARNING OBJECTIVE 2]

27. _____ Denervation, most commonly caused by diabetic peripheral neuropathy, affects type 1 fibers. [LEARNING OBJECTIVE 14]

III. MATCHING

28. Match the diagnostic findings with the test type of test conducted; answers may be used more than once. [LEARNING OBJECTIVE 9]
    i. Erythrocyte sedimentation rate
    ii. C-reactive protein
    iii. Alkaline phosphatase
    iv. Antinuclear antibody
    v. Rheumatoid factor
    A. Increased in Paget disease
    B. Increased in polymyalgia rheumatic
    C. Decreased in some diseases of red blood cells
    D. Increased in myositis
    E. Normal in fibromyalgia
    F. Increased in hepatic/biliary disease
    G. Increased in atherosclerosis
    H. Increased in osteomalacia
    I. Increased in infection
    J. Present in autoimmune arthritis
    K. Present secondary to therapeutic drugs
    L. Increased in autoimmune disease

29. Match the muscle disease to its description below. [LEARNING OBJECTIVE 15]
    i. Central core disease
    ii. Nemaline myopathy
    iii. Central nuclear myopathy
    iv. Lipid myopathy
    v. Pompé disease
    vi. McArdle disease
    vii. Familial periodic paralysis
    viii. Dermatomyositis
    ix. Polymyositis
    A. Decreased type 2 fibers
    B. Large amounts of intracellular glycogen that accumulate in muscle cells
    C. Type 1 fibers have a pale central core
    D. Features nuclei in the center of fibers
    E. Caused by deposition of circulating antigen-antibody complexes
    F. Patient's lack phosphorylase
    G. Defective transmembrane transport of sodium and potassium flux
    H. Due to direct muscle damage by autoimmune T cells
    I. Lipid droplets accumulate in muscle cells
    J. Contains rod-like intracytoplasmic inclusions

IV. SHORT ANSWER

30. What is the underlying etiology of carpal tunnel syndrome and how does it cause a patient's symptoms? [LEARNING OBJECTIVE 11]

_____

_____

_____

31. A 63-year-old Caucasian male is seen by his primary care doctor for evaluation of pain in his left big toe. The patient reports that he was in his normal state of good health until two weeks ago when his toe became swollen and red. He denies a history of trauma or additional symptoms. Needle aspiration of the joint demonstrates uric acid crystals. Additional labs demonstrate no evidence of renal disease or malignancy (leukemia/lymphoma). What is the next step in the treatment of this patient? (Hint: Use Decision Tree 18.2) [LEARNING OBJECTIVE 10]

    _____

    _____

    _____

32. The medical student on your rotation, after reviewing the patient's pathology, diagnoses the patient with a bony malignancy based on the abnormal histology that demonstrates in irregular lattice of crossing collagen fibers and numerous osteocytes. What mistake has he made? [LEARNING OBJECTIVE 1]

    _____

    _____

    _____

33. What is the importance of diagnosing rheumatoid arthritis early? How is it treated, and what are the complications of that treatment? [LEARNING OBJECTIVE 10]

    _____

    _____

    _____

34. A 48-year-old African American male, with a past medical history significant for hyperlipidemia treated with gemfibrozil (a fibrate) and newly supplemented with atorvastatin (a statin), is seen by his doctor for new onset muscle weakness and aches. Incidentally, he reports that his urine has been cola-brown in color since starting the statin. Labs demonstrate increased creatine kinase while a biopsy of the gastrocnemius demonstrates skeletal muscle with necrosis, regeneration, and minimal inflammation. What is your diagnosis? (Hint: Use Decision Tree 18.3) [LEARNING OBJECTIVE 14 AND 15]

    _____

    _____

    _____

CHAPTER 19

Disorders of the Nervous System

The Big Picture

The nervous system is fundamental to proper functioning of the body. It influences nearly every part of the body by acting as the primary communication system to sense and respond to changes in the internal and external environment. Improper functioning of this system leads to disease, and loss of function defines death ("brain death").

Oh No! Not Another Learning Experience

LEARNING OBJECTIVE 1: Name the parenchymal and ancillary cells of the central nervous system (CNS).

EXERCISE 19-1

Complete the paragraph below.

The nervous system is fundamentally divided into the (1) _____, consisting of the brain and spinal cord, and the (2) _____, consisting of a complex network of nerves connected to the CNS. The primary effector cells of the nervous system are (3) _____. Each neuron extends one or more short (4) _____ to connect with other brain cells, and a single long (5) _____ to connect with other neurons or with target tissue cells. Bundles of axons are gathered into (6) _____ (or "white matter") within the CNS and (7) _____ outside the CNS. Neurons collectively appear grossly grayish and are referred to as (8) _____. Nodular collections of neuron cell bodies in the brain are called (9) _____.

EXERCISE 19-2   PATHOLOGY AS A SECOND LANGUAGE

Test your vocabulary by writing the appropriate term in each blank from the list below.

Oligodendrocytes	Glia	Microglia
Synapse	Membrane potential	Neurotransmitter
Myelin	Astrocytes	

1. All of the non-neuronal cells in the brain form the _____.

2. _____ are star-shaped glial cells that support neurons and promote repair.

3. _____ are filled with _____ and wrap themselves around axons to insulate nerve signals passing down the axon.

4. _____ are the scavenger (phagocytic) cells of the CNS and are analogous to macrophages elsewhere.

5. A _____ is characterized by an exceedingly narrow space between the signaling nerve cell or its axon and the target cell.

6. _____ refers to differences in electrical potential, measured in millivolts.

7. _____ is a chemical signal that is released by a neuron into a synapse.

LEARNING OBJECTIVE 2: Discuss the architecture of the brain: the difference between gray matter and white matter; the production, circulation, and absorption of cerebrospinal fluid (CSF); and the arrangement and special properties of cerebral vasculature.

EXERCISE 19-3

Review Figure 19.3 in *The Nature of Disease*, then complete the paragraphs below.

The brain is an architecturally complex organ. The most superior and largest part of the brain is the

(1) _____, which is divided into left and right (2) _____. The midbrain, pons, and medulla

oblongata, are collectively called the (3) _____.

   The most superior part of the brainstem is the (4) _____, which contains nuclei important in eye and

head movements and mediates some hearing functions. The (5) _____, which is the middle and larg-

est part, contains nuclei important in regulating respiration. The lowest part of the brain (and brainstem), the

(6) _____, is where nerve tracts from one side of the body cross over to connect to the opposite cerebral

hemisphere. The other major portion of the brain is the (7) _____, which sits inferior to the cerebrum and

posterior to the brain stem. Connecting the brain to the peripheral nervous system is the (8) _____, which

passes out of the skull through a large opening in the base of the skull, the (9) _____. Bundles of axons are

gathered into nerve tracts within the CNS and are referred to as (10) _____; central nervous system neu-

rons collectively appear grossly grayish and are therefore referred to as (11) _____.

   The brain and spinal cord are filled with and surrounded by (12) _____, which is produced by small

papillary organs of specialized ependymal cells called (13) _____. CSF flows from the choroid plexuses

through the ventricles around the spinal cord and cerebellum, then around the cerebrum to be absorbed by

(14) _____, papillary projections of arachnoid matter extending into the superior sagittal sinus. Blood is

supplied to the brain via the carotid and vertebral arteries which supply the anterior and posterior portions of

the brain and interconnect through a loop of vessels called the (15) _____.

Mnemonic

Choroid = Creates **CSF**

Arachnoid granules = **A**bsorb **CSF**

> **EXERCISE 19-4** PATHOLOGY AS A SECOND LANGUAGE

Review Figure 19.5 in *The Nature of Disease*, then test your vocabulary by indicating if each statement below is true or false. If it is false, provide the correct word for the italicized term that will make the statement true.

_____ 1. *Ependymal cells* line the cerebral ventricles and the central canal of the spinal cord.

_____

_____ 2. *Pia mater* is a tough, thick sheet of fibrous tissue that is tightly stuck to the inside of the skull and surrounds the spinal cord inside the spinal canal.

_____

_____ 3. The *epidural space* lies between the dura and the bone of the calvarium.

_____

_____ 4. Immediately beneath the dura mater is a thin membrane called the *arachnoid mater*.

_____

_____ 5. Located beneath arachnoid matter is the *subarachnoid space*, which contains the cerebrospinal fluid (CSF).

_____

_____ 6. The *falx cerebri* is a vertical fold of dura mater that forms a thick membrane inside of the skull.

_____

_____ 7. *Dura mater* is a delicate membrane that closely surrounds the brain as the innermost layer.

_____

_____ 8. The *tentorial sinus* is an elongated lake of venous blood that runs front to rear under the center of the skull.

_____

_____ 9. The *tentorium cerebelli* is a horizontal fold of dura in the back of the skull, which separates the cerebral hemispheres above from the cerebellum, and contains the *superior sagittal sinus*.

_____

_____ 10. Hollow spaces in the center of each cerebral hemisphere filled with CSF are called the *right and left lateral (1st and 2nd) ventricles*.

_____

_____ 11. The tight junction of endothelial cells in brain capillaries forms the *blood–brain barrier*.

_____

LEARNING OBJECTIVE 3: Distinguish between the somatic and autonomic nervous systems.

> **EXERCISE 19-5**

Review Figure 19.11 in *The Nature of Disease*, then complete the paragraphs below.

The (1) _____ consists of a network of nerves, which exists mainly outside of the CNS but is connected to it. The (2) _____ is the voluntary portion of the PNS; it is composed of nerves that arise from the brain and spinal cord. These nerves carry incoming (3) _____ (afferent) signals from sensors for sight, smell, taste, hearing, touch, pain, heat, and others, and outgoing (4) _____ (efferent) signals to skeletal muscle.

In contrast, the (5) _____ is an involuntary system of nerves that carries motor and sensory signals to and from the hypothalamus. The (6) _____ (or thoracolumbar division) is a network of nerve fibers and ganglia that originates from neurons in the thoracic and lumbar spinal cord, and mediates the "fight or flight" response. The (7) _____ (or craniosacral division) is a network of fibers and ganglia that originates from neurons in the brain and lower (sacral) spinal cord, and mediates the "rest-and-digest" response.

EXERCISE 19-6

Review Figure 19.11 in *The Nature of Disease*, then complete the table below.

Organ	Effect of (1) _____ (Adrenergic effect)	Effect of (2) _____ (Cholinergic effect)
Iris	Dilation of pupil	Constriction of pupil
Lacrimal gland	—	Formation of tears
Sweat glands	Formation of sweat	—
Digestive glands	Inhibition of secretions	Stimulation of secretions
Intestinal motility	Decrease peristalsis	Increase peristalsis
Urinary bladder	Relaxation and expansion	Contraction and emptying
Heart	Increase in rate and power of contraction	Decrease in rate and power of contraction
Bronchioles	Dilation	Constriction
Penis	Ejaculation	Erection
Adrenal medulla	Secretion of epinephrine and norepinephrine	—
Liver	Release of glucose	—
Blood vessels	Dilation	Constriction
supplying:	Constriction	—
Skeletal muscle Skin	Dilation	Constriction
Lung	Constriction	Dilation
GI tract		

EXERCISE 19-7   PATHOLOGY AS A SECOND LANGUAGE

Test your vocabulary by writing the appropriate term in each blank from the list below.

Sympathetic chain   Adrenergic effect   Ventral root
Cranial nerves   Spinal nerves   Horn
White columns   Cholinergic effect   Dorsal root
Ganglion

1. _____ are nerves that arise from the brain.

2. Thirty-one pairs of _____ arise from both sides of the spinal cord.

3. Each wing of the spinal cord as seen in cross-section is called a _____.

4. A collection of neuron cell bodies outside the CNS is called a _____.

5. _____ are bundles of myelinated nerves within the spinal cord.

6. A _____ is the point where motor axons exit the cord, carrying outgoing signals.

7. A _____ is the point where sensory axons enter the cord, carrying incoming signals.

8. The _____ is a series of ganglia that runs vertically on either side of the thoracic and lumbar spinal column.

9. _____ refers to the action of the sympathetic nervous system.

10. _____ refers to the action of the parasympathetic nervous system.

LEARNING OBJECTIVE 4: Explain the causes and consequences of increased intracranial pressure.

EXERCISE 19-8

Complete the paragraph below.

Increased intracranial pressure can be due to intracranial masses, intracranial bleeds, (1) _____ due to increased fluid in or between brain cells, or (2) _____ (the accumulation of excess CSF). Any cause of increased intracranial pressure, especially if rapid, can cause herniation of brain tissue with resulting damage and correlated signs and symptoms. One sign of increased intracranial pressure is the bulging of the optic disc, where the optic nerve enters the eye, as seen on an ophthalmoscopic exam; this is called (3) _____. Treatment deals with the cause, (e.g., increased blood osmolality for edema or placing a shunt for hydrocephalus), but may also require a (4) _____ to relieve pressure. Although not associated with herniations, two other types of hydrocephalus should be recognized. (5) _____ is due to impaired absorption of CSF and may cause dementia, incontinence, and other symptoms. (6) _____ is increased CSF and enlarged ventricles due to atrophy of the brain, as in Alzheimer disease.

EXERCISE 19-9

Review Figure 19.13 in *The Nature of Disease*, then complete the table below.

Type	Brain Tissue	Structure	Symptoms
(1) _____	Medial aspect of the affected cerebral hemisphere	Herniates horizontally across the lower margin of the falx cerebri	Cerebral compression with motor and/or sensory defects
(2) _____	Medial temporal lobe ("uncus")	Herniates downward and medially past the tentorium cerebelli	Dilation of the pupils or impairment of eye motion; "blown pupil"
(3) _____	Lower cerebellum	Herniates downward through the foramen magnum	Compresses brainstem respiratory and cardiac centers

EXERCISE 19-10 PATHOLOGY AS A SECOND LANGUAGE

See Exercises 19-8 and 19-9 for key terms covered in this section.

LEARNING OBJECTIVE 5: List the congenital and perinatal diseases of CNS.

EXERCISE 19-11

Complete the paragraph below.

Most congenital brain defects result from interruptions of critical embryologic development or (1) _____, which causes syndromes affecting the entire body. For example, (2) _____ is one of the most common causes of mental retardation and is due to trisomy 21.

EXERCISE 19-12 PATHOLOGY AS A SECOND LANGUAGE

Test your vocabulary by indicating if each statement below is true or false. If it is false, provide the correct word for the italicized term that will make the statement true.

_____ 1. *Budd-Chiari malformation* is a defect in which the brainstem and cerebellum are compacted into a small posterior fossa.

_____

_____ 2. *Congenital hydrocephalus* is usually due to stenosis of the aqueduct of Sylvius.

_____

_____ 3. *Polymicrogyria* is an excessive number of narrow gyri.

_____

_____ 4. *Agyria* (also called "lissencephaly") is a smooth cerebral surface with an absence of gyri.

_____

_____ 5. *Macrocephaly* is an unusually small skull and brain.

_____

_____ 6. *Epilepsy* is a broad clinical term applied to permanent, nonprogressive motor problems (spasticity, paralysis) that arise owing to an insult to the brain before it reaches maturity.

_____

_____ 7. *Cerebral palsy* is a paroxysmal, transient disorder of brain function that is often associated with loss of consciousness, sensory or mental disturbance, and abnormal motor activity.

_____

LEARNING OBJECTIVE 6: Describe the clinical and pathologic findings (as applicable) of concussions, contusions, and diffuse axonal injury.

EXERCISE 19-13

Complete the paragraph below.

A (1) _____ is a clinical syndrome of temporary brain dysfunction following head injury. A (2) _____ is a superficial cortical bleed that is equivalent to a bruise in soft tissues. A (3) _____ occurs when blunt force to an immobile head causes injury to brain tissue immediately beneath the site of the blow. In contrast, a (4) _____ occurs if the brain is injured by being bounced into the skull opposite the site of the blow. (5) _____ refers to the stretching of brain nerve tracts (white matter) due to twisting. Objects such as bullets and knives that penetrate the brain produce a local disruption of the tissue called a (6) _____. (7) _____ refers to the spread of damage from a projectile due to its energy released into the tissue.

EXERCISE 19-14   PATHOLOGY AS A SECOND LANGUAGE

See Exercise 19-13 for key terms covered in this section.

LEARNING OBJECTIVE 7: Compare and contrast the anatomic location, the cause, and the consequences of subdural hematoma, epidural hematoma, and subarachnoid hemorrhage.

EXERCISE 19-15

Complete the paragraph below.

Intracranial hemorrhages can occur at various anatomic sites and are categorized according to the layers in which blood accumulates. (1) _____ occur when the skull is fractured, tearing the middle meningeal artery. These are usually fatal unless treated quickly with craniotomy. (2) _____ are due to venous bleeding of bridging veins that connect to the superior sagittal sinus and occur with or without a history of trauma to the head and a fracture need not be present. Patients are often on anticoagulants and the symptoms are nonspecific and include headache or dementia. (3) _____ are associated with vascular malformations and bleed when there is an increase in intracranial pressure, as during defecation. (4) _____ is nontraumatic bleeding directly into the substance of the brain and is usually due to hypertension.

EXERCISE 19-16

Review Figure 19.18 in *The Nature of Disease*, then complete the table below.

Type	Vasculature	Symptoms
(1) _____	Middle meningeal artery, blood accumulates between the skull and dura mater	Lucid interval; usually fatal, herniation occurs
(2) _____	Bridging veins, blood accumulates between the dura and arachnoid	None; headaches; dementia; rebleeding
(3) _____	Usually a ruptured saccular (berry) aneurysm, blood accumulates in the subarachnoid space	Sudden severe headache that rapidly proceeds to unconsciousness

Remember This! An epidural hematoma forms quickly, while a subdural hematoma forms slowly.

Mnemonic

Layers of the Meninges = **PAD**

Pia mater

Arachnoid

Dura mater

EXERCISE 19-17   PATHOLOGY AS A SECOND LANGUAGE

Test your vocabulary by writing the appropriate term in each blank from the list below.

Acute subdural hematoma   Chronic subdural hematoma   Shaken baby syndrome (SBS)

1. _____ is a form of subdural hematoma in infants under two years of age that is due to abrupt movement of the head.

2. _____ is usually due to anticoagulant drugs.

3. _____ is often asymptomatic, but can organize or enlarge over time and cause variable symptoms including seizures and dementia.

LEARNING OBJECTIVE 8: Distinguish between hemorrhagic and nonhemorrhagic infarct, noting the differences between the anatomic location, causative factors and/or precursors, and pathologic findings.

EXERCISE 19-18

Complete the paragraph below.

(1) _____ is the fourth-leading cause of death in the United States and can be due to ischemia, hypoxia and infarction from impairment of blood flow, or hemorrhage from rupture of a blood vessel. Any sudden, spontaneous vascular event in the brain is called a (2) _____ (or "stroke"). This may be caused by infarction (80% of cases) or hemorrhage into the brain. An (3) _____ in the brain is when the tissue dies secondary to (4) _____, usually a result of occluded arterial flow. Most infarcts are not associated with bleeding and are called (5) _____. In contrast, a (6) _____ is characterized by bleeding into the infarct.

EXERCISE 19-19   PATHOLOGY AS A SECOND LANGUAGE

Test your vocabulary by indicating if each statement below is true or false. If it is false, provide the correct word for the italicized term that will make the statement true.

_____ 1. *Ischemia* is the term pathologists use to refer to low oxygen partial pressure and often describes a global event (e.g., global ischemia).

_____

_____ 2. *Hypoxia* is low or absent blood flow, which deprives tissue of both oxygen and nutrients.

_____

_____ 3. Hypoxia may cause necrosis of a superficial layer of neurons in the cerebral cortex, a condition known as *laminar cortical necrosis*.

_____

_____ 4. Ischemia may produce infarction in the "watershed" areas of the cerebral cortex between two areas supplied by different cerebral arteries, called *watershed infarcts*.

_____

_____ 5. Dizziness, syncope (fainting), focal weakness, or other neurologic symptoms that last a few minutes or hours (always less than 24 hours), are termed *transient ischemic attacks (TIA)*.

_____

LEARNING OBJECTIVE 9: Classify the etiologies of CNS infections according to their site of infection and the population they infect.

EXERCISE 19-20

Complete the paragraph below.

CAS infections can occur at various sites. If the brain parenchyma is directly infected by a virus it is called (1) _____. Various viruses can cause encephalitis including HSV, CMV, arboviruses, measles and polio viruses. In contrast, (2) _____ is inflammation of the pia/arachnoid meninges and CSF. Meningitis can be viral or bacterial (the latter is more dangerous). (3) _____ causes a very dangerous variety of epidemic acute meningitis in barracks and dormitories by the bacteria *Neisseria meningitides*. (4) _____ can be caused by tuberculosis, syphilis, fungi, and amebae.

EXERCISE 19-21

Complete the table below.

Infection	Cells	Protein	Glucose	
Normal	0–5 Mononuclear cells	15–45	40–70	
(1) _____	Increased neutrophils	Increased	Decreased	
Aseptic/viral meningitis	(2) _____	Increased	Normal	
TB/fungal meningitis	Increased monocytes	Mild increase	(3) _____	

EXERCISE 19-22   PATHOLOGY AS A SECOND LANGUAGE

Test your vocabulary by writing the appropriate term in each blank from the list below.

Variant Creutzfeldt-Jakob disease (vCJD)   Brain abscess   Creutzfeldt-Jakob disease

1. As in other locations in the body, a _____ is a localized area of dead, liquefied tissue and acute inflammatory cell exudate caused by bacterial infection.

2. _____ is a spontaneous spongiform encephalopathy, with death ensuing approximately one year after diagnosis.

3. _____ is a spongiform encephalopathy that develops after eating contaminated meat; it is the human version of mad cow disease.

LEARNING OBJECTIVE 10: Discuss the probable cause, the signs and symptoms, and the pathologic findings of multiple sclerosis.

EXERCISE 19-23

Complete the paragraph below.

(1) _____ features widespread patches of demyelination in the brain and spinal cord. The pathological lesions are characterized by microscopic foci in white matter that show infiltrates of lymphocytes and macrophages, loss of myelin, and marked decrease of (2) _____. MS is caused by an autoimmune attack on components of the myelin sheath, with women more often affected. MS usually first appears in young adults with variable symptoms, including blurred vision or (3) _____ (spots), tingling, numbness, minor gait disturbances, stumbling speech, weakness, spasticity, bladder dysfunction, or mild mental impairment. Diagnosis

is by clinical suspicion, with fluctuating neural deficits and (4) _____ seen on neural imaging. Finding oligoclonal bands of (5) _____ in CSF is confirmatory. (6) _____ and other anti-immune therapy may be beneficial.

EXERCISE 19-24   PATHOLOGY AS A SECOND LANGUAGE

Test your vocabulary by indicating if each statement below is true or false. If it is false, provide the correct word for the italicized term that will make the statement true.

____ 1. *Central pontine myelinolysis* is a rare condition featuring patchy demyelination in the pons.

_____

____ 2. *Postinfectious or postvaccinal encephalomyelitis* primarily affects white matter and causes transient headaches and fever that may be mild or may progress to paraplegia, coma, and death.

_____

LEARNING OBJECTIVE 11: Catalogue the metabolic disorders of the CNS according to their cause.

EXERCISE 19-25

Complete the paragraph below.

Metabolic disorders of the CNS fall into several broad categories including lysosomal storage disorders, (1) _____, and toxic encephalopathies. (2) _____ are caused by inherited enzyme defects that cause the accumulation of upstream metabolic substrates within lysosomes normally involved in the synthesis of certain complex lipids and (3) _____. Metabolic disorders can be genetic or acquired, and innumerable drugs and toxins can negatively impact the brain, including illicit drugs.

EXERCISE 19-26

Complete the table below.

Lysosomal Storage Disease	Inheritance	Accumulated Substrate	Pathology/Clinical
(1) _____	Autosomal recessive	Glucocerebroside accumulation in tissue macrophages	Most common lysosomal storage disease; "Gaucher" cells that look filled with tissue paper
(2) _____	Autosomal recessive	Gangliosides accumulate in CNS neurons	Fatal in early childhood
(3) _____	Autosomal recessive	Mucopolysaccharides accumulate in neurons	Progressive mental decline in childhood
(4) _____	Autosomal recessive	Sphingolipid accumulates in macrophages and other tissues, including liver, spleen, and brain	Progressive ataxia and mental decline in childhood or failure to thrive in infancy
(5) _____	Autosomal recessive	Accumulation of cerebroside in CNS white matter (defects in synthesis of myelin)	Most common of the leukodystrophies; white matter lesions have pink change of blue dyes in affected tissues on pathologic evaluation

EXERCISE 19-27 PATHOLOGY AS A SECOND LANGUAGE

Test your vocabulary by writing the appropriate term in each blank from the list below.

Hypoglycemia	Ethanol	Methanol
Korsakoff psychosis	Hyperglycemia	Lead poisoning
Phenylketonuria (PKU)	Wilson's disease	Beriberi
Wernicke encephalopathy	Carbon monoxide intoxication	Cretinism
Hepatic encephalopathy	Vitamin B_{12} deficiency	Thiamine (vitamin B_1) deficiency

1. _____ is an autosomal recessive disorder that causes accumulation of phenylalanine in blood and tissue.

2. _____ is an autosomal recessive disorder that causes copper accumulation in tissues, including the brain.

3. _____ is severe hypothyroidism in infancy.

4. _____ is a common consequence of liver failure.

5. _____ can have severe and irreversible neurological defects from degeneration of the posterolateral white tracks in the spinal cord.

6. _____ (also called _____) is manifested by motor weakness because of peripheral neuropathy, and general weakness because of congestive heart failure.

7. _____ is a syndrome of chronic alcoholics and is associated with cerebellar features, ataxia, tremors, confusion, and paralysis of extraocular muscles.

8. _____ is a permanent defect affecting chronic alcoholics, impairing short- and long-term memory that leads patients to confabulate aimlessly.

9. _____ is high blood glucose that can lead to hyperosmolar coma.

10. _____ is low blood glucose that can cause laminar necrosis.

11. _____ is directly toxic to neurons.

12. _____ toxicity causes headache, weakness, seizure, retinal blindness, and other problems.

13. _____ can cause fatal global hypoxia by binding permanently to hemoglobin and displacing oxygen.

14. _____ may cause peripheral neuropathy with weakness, numbness, and tingling in the limbs, or seizures brought on by brain edema and increased intracranial pressure.

LEARNING OBJECTIVE 12: Explain the clinical and diagnostic features of the various causes of dementia, as well as their underlying biochemical dysfunction (where applicable).

EXERCISE 19-28

Complete the paragraph below.

The most common causes of dementia are (1) _____, vascular dementia, or a combination of the two.

(2) _____ is defined as a global, irreversible deterioration of cognition—mental capacities such as memory, attention span, and reasoning. This is normally preceded by (3) _____. Impairments include reduced ability to recognize people and things, called (4) _____; reduced ability to do previously learned motor skills, called (5) _____; and reduced comprehension and use of language, called (6) _____.

EXERCISE 19-29

Complete the table below.

Type	Morphology/Findings	Symptoms
(1) _____	Neurofibrillary plaques, tau protein	Memory, language, orientation, concentration
(2) _____	Absence of pigmented substantia nigra	Tremors, rigidity, bradykinesia, masked face, shuffling gait
(3) _____	Alpha-synuclein, Lewy bodies	Cognitive impairment
(4) _____	CAG expansion repeat	Dancelike movements
(5) _____	Frontal/temporal atrophy	Language, personality
(6) _____	Multiple infarcts	Memory, language, orientation, concentration

EXERCISE 19-30 PATHOLOGY AS A SECOND LANGUAGE

Test your vocabulary by writing the appropriate term in each blank from the list below.

Bulbospinal atrophy (BSA)   Spinal muscular atrophy   Amyotrophic lateral sclerosis

1. _____ is a degenerative condition of motor neurons in the gray matter of the cerebral cortex, brainstem, and spinal cord.

2. _____ is an X-linked Mendelian, adult-onset disorder featuring distal limb atrophy, fasciculations of the tongue, and dysphagia.

3. _____ is a group of disorders of lower motor neurons in children.

LEARNING OBJECTIVE 13: Classify the CNS neoplasms according to their cell/tissue type.

EXERCISE 19-31

Review Figure 19.34 in *The Nature of Disease*, then complete the paragraphs below.

CNS neoplasms are defined as any neoplasms that occur intracranially; they are divided into two main groups. (1) _____ neoplasms are tumors of glia, neurons, ependymal cells, choroid plexus, pineal gland, and embryonal cells. The (2) _____ neoplasms include tumors of meninges, the pituitary, and the cranial nerves, plus lymphomas, vascular tumors, and tumors of other tissue types. About two-thirds of intracranial tumors are not primary but (3) _____ from other body sites. Conversely, even highly malignant primary CNS tumors rarely spread to other parts of the body.

(4) _____ is a general term for neuroepithelial tumors of astrocytes, oligodendrocytes, or ependymal cells. (5) _____ are tumors of astrocytes and constitute the great majority of gliomas. The World Health Organization (WHO) grades them from I to IV according to aggressiveness.

EXERCISE 19-32

Complete the table below.

Tumor	Cell Type	Grade/Clinical Behavior
(1) _____	Astrocytes	Low-grade, WHO Grade I
(2) _____	Astrocytes	WHO Grade II
(3) _____	Astrocytes	WHO Grade III
(4) _____ (also glioblastoma multiforme)	Astrocytes	WHO Grade IV—very aggressive
(5) _____	Neurons and glial cells	Slow-growing tumor that usually appears in the temporal lobe and often presents with seizures
(6) _____	Oligodendrocytes	Intermediate grades
(7) _____	Ependymal cells that line the ventricles	Rare
(8) _____	Primitive embryological neuroectodermal cells	Aggressive, occurs in posterior fossa of children

EXERCISE 19-33   PATHOLOGY AS A SECOND LANGUAGE

Test your vocabulary by indicating if each statement below is true or false. If it is false, provide the correct word for the italicized term that will make the statement true.

_____ 1. *Microglioma* is a tumor of arachnoid epithelium that usually attaches to the dura.

_____

_____ 2. *Acoustic neuroma* is a misnomer as it is really a tumor of the Schwann cells (Schwannoma) of the eighth cranial nerve.

_____

_____ 3. *Meningioma* is a variety of lymphoma related to histiocytic lymphoma elsewhere in the body.

_____

_____ 4. *Primary CNS lymphoma* of the brain occurs in immunosuppressed patients and usually in the absence of lymphoma elsewhere in the body.

_____

_____ 5. *Pinealoma* is a tumor of the pineal gland.

_____

LEARNING OBJECTIVE 14: Review the diseases, both neoplastic and non-neoplastic, that affect peripheral nerves, giving their clinical and pathologic features.

EXERCISE 19-34

Complete the paragraph below.

(1) _____ is any non-neoplastic disease of peripheral nerve that is a malfunction of one or more nerves.

The most common type, (2) _____, is due to small vessel disease, followed by toxic neuropathies, including (3) _____. (4) _____ can occur from laceration, crush or stretch, or from prolonged pressure. (5) _____ is a life-threatening, T-cell–mediated immune neuropathy characterized by weakness and progressive ascending paralysis; it can occur after viral illness. (6) _____ is a paralysis of facial muscles resulting from impairment of the facial nerve (CN VII). (7) _____ is caused by nerve infection of Schwann cells by *Mycobacterium leprae* in cool areas of the body. (8) _____ is caused by an exotoxin from *Corynebacterium diphtheria,* and *varicella-zoster virus* causes painful, vesicular eruptions in the skin called (9) _____. Finally, peripheral neuropathies can also be hereditary. (10) _____ is the most well-known of this diverse group and presents in childhood with weakness and atrophy of the lower legs.

EXERCISE 19-35 PATHOLOGY AS A SECOND LANGUAGE

Test your vocabulary by writing the appropriate term in each blank from the list below.

Neurofibroma   **Malignant peripheral nerve sheath tumor (MPNST)**
Schwannoma   **Neurofibromatosis (NF)**

1. _____ is a slow-growing, benign, usually solitary tumor that arises from Schwann cells.

2. _____ is a tumor of Schwann cells, fibroblasts, and related perineural cells.

3. _____ is an autosomal dominant disorder associated with peripheral nerve tumors.

4. _____ is a malignant tumor of peripheral nerve with half arising in patients with neurofibromatosis type 1 (NF1).

Decisions Decisions

DECISION TREE 19.1: INTRACRANIAL LESIONS

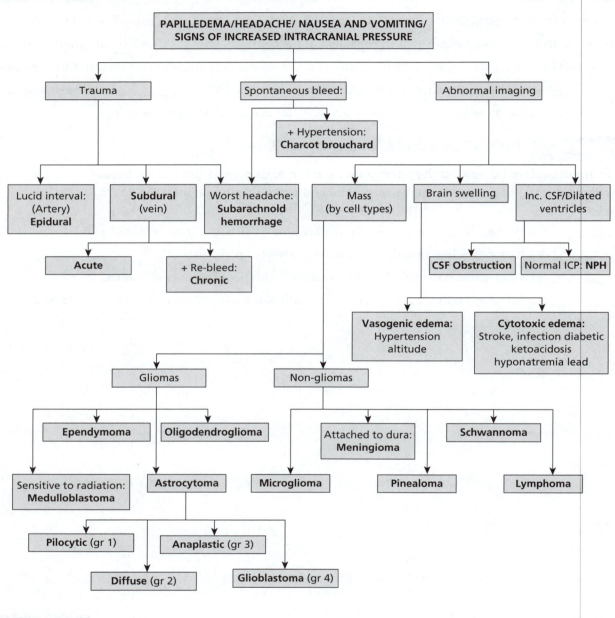

Test Yourself

I. MULTIPLE CHOICE

1. A 63-year-old male, with a past medical history of hypertension uncontrolled by medication, presents to the ER complaining of a severe headache and vomiting. While awaiting medical care, he loses consciousness. Over the next several days, he falls into a deep coma, with spasticity and fixed pupils. His autopsy demonstrates a hematoma in the basal ganglia. What is your preliminary cause of death? (Hint: Use Decision Tree 19.1) [LEARNING OBJECTIVE 8]

A. Epidural hematoma
B. Acute subdural hematoma
C. Chronic subdural hematoma
D. Charcot-Bouchard microaneurysms

2. Which of the following causes vasogenic edema? (Hint: Use Decision Tree 19.1) [LEARNING OBJECTIVE 4]

A. Brain tumors
B. Stroke
C. Diabetic ketoacidosis
D. All of the above

3. A five-month-old infant is seen at his pediatrician's office for a checkup. His mother notes that he has recently developed difficulty nursing. His physical exam is notable for a cherry red spot in the retina and weakness; hepatosplenomegaly is absent. The infant's symptoms are due to an accumulation of which of the following? [LEARNING OBJECTIVE 11]
   A. Glucocerebroside
   B. Mucopolysaccharide
   C. Ganglioside
   D. Sphingolipid

4. A 70-year-old African American male, with a past medical history of deep venous thrombosis treated with anticoagulants, is brought to the ER after being found unconscious at home by his son. His physical exam is notable for multiple bruises, and his son reports that his father fell a week ago, but a physician checked him over and sent him home. What vessel was damaged? (Hint: Use Decision Tree 19.1) [LEARNING OBJECTIVE 7]
   A. Middle meningeal artery
   B. A bridging vein
   C. Carotid artery
   D. Basilar artery

5. You are assigned to care for a 43-year-old female who has presented to the hospital in liver failure, despite her adamant denial of alcohol abuse. In performing a detailed physical exam, you decide to try out your new ophthalmoscope, and you identify a brown-green ring of color surrounding her corneas. What is the cause of liver failure in this patient? [LEARNING OBJECTIVE 11]
   A. Alcohol abuse
   B. Fatty liver disease
   C. Wilson disease
   D. Phenylketonuria

6. A young man is struck in the head with a flying hockey puck prior to falling backwards over the rink railing. After regaining consciousness, he is astonished to see the game is nearly over, as his last memory is the national anthem. What traumatic brain injury or injuries most likely occurred? [LEARNING OBJECTIVE 6]
   A. Coup contusion
   B. Contrecoup contusion
   C. Concussion
   D. All of the above

7. While visiting your uncle, who is in his 80s, you notice that he has a slow, coarse, resting tremor in his right hand. You continue to observe him over the course of your visit and perceive that in addition to the tremor, he walks with a slow shuffling gait and has a wooden facial expression. What pathologic findings accompany your uncle's illness? [LEARNING OBJECTIVE 12]

A. Neurofibrillary tangles
B. Expansion of the lateral ventricles
C. Demyelination of motor axons in the dorsolateral spinal cord
D. Absence of pigment in the substantia nigra

8. Which of the following causes a nonhemorrhagic infarct? [LEARNING OBJECTIVE 8]
   A. Thrombotic occlusion of the basilar arteries
   B. Cerebral vasculitis
   C. Embolic vegetations
   D. All of the above

9. A 23-year-old male is seen walking unsteadily down the clinic corridor before collapsing in an epileptic seizure. An MRI demonstrates a large mass in his cerebellum, which is surgically removed. The mass is determined to be a pilocytic astrocytoma on histology. What is the median survival for patients with this type of brain tumor? [LEARNING OBJECTIVE 13]
   A. ~ 10 years
   B. ~ 5 years
   C. ~ 18 months
   D. < 12 months

10. Untreated infection by which of the following organisms is capable of causing impaired proprioception, general paresis, psychotic behavior, and dementia? [LEARNING OBJECTIVE 9]
    A. Syphilis
    B. Rickettsia
    C. JC virus
    D. Herpes virus

11. A 21-year-old male is brought to the emergency room by his friends. While snowboarding earlier, he struck a tree and was knocked unconscious for a few minutes. When he woke up, he claimed he was fine, but after an hour, told his friends he wanted to go back to the hotel room to watch a movie. When they went to check on him after dinner, they found him unconscious in the bathroom with vomit in the toilet, which is when they brought him to the ER. His physical exam is notable for bradycardia, and his right pupil is dilated. The epidural hematoma has caused which of the following complications? [LEARNING OBJECTIVE 4]
    A. Tentorial herniation
    B. Cerebellar herniation
    C. Subfalcine herniation
    D. Diffuse axonal injury

12. The medulla contains nuclei that modulate which of the following? [LEARNING OBJECTIVE 2]
    A. Heart rate
    B. Peripheral vascular tone
    C. Coughing
    D. All of the above

13. A 65-year-old woman undergoes a brain MRI following a car accident. A solitary mass is identified on imaging. It appears to be attached to the dura of the parasagittal region. No other abnormalities are identified. Upon reviewing the films, the attending physician reports no treatment is required if the patient is without symptoms. What tumor has he diagnosed the patient has? (Hint: Use Decision Tree 19.1) [LEARNING OBJECTIVE 13]
    A. Medulloblastoma
    B. Glioblastoma
    C. Oligodendroglioma
    D. Meningioma

14. A 43-year-old male with a family history of neurodegenerative disease presents to the clinic concerned that he may have inherited the disease that affected his mother's uncles. He complains of dysphagia, and his physical exam is notable for distal limb atrophy and fasciculations of the tongue. This constellation of symptoms is diagnostic of which of the following neurological diseases? [LEARNING OBJECTIVE 12]
    A. Bulbospinal atrophy
    B. Amyotrophic lateral sclerosis
    C. Bell's palsy
    D. Multiple sclerosis

15. A 37-year-old female is admitted to the ICU for difficulty in breathing. She has no significant past medical history and reports that she was in her usual state of good health until a month ago when she contracted a mild respiratory infection. While recovering from the infection, she noticed that her lower legs felt weak and over the last several days the weakness has progressed to paralysis. Certain that you already know the diagnosis, a lumbar puncture revealing increased protein without inflammatory cells and a slow nerve conduction study are confirmative. From what disease does the patient suffer? [LEARNING OBJECTIVE 14]
    A. Amyotrophic lateral sclerosis
    B. Bell's palsy
    C. Guillain Barré
    D. Multiple sclerosis

16. Variant Creutzfeldt-Jakob disease can be caused by which of the following? [LEARNING OBJECTIVE 9]
    A. Consumption of contaminated meat
    B. Insertion of an internal appliance
    C. Corneal transplants
    D. All of the above

17. A 43-year-old female who originally presented with diplopia (double-vision) was found to have multiple CNS lesions on imaging and was diagnosed with multiple sclerosis. Which of the following statements concerning multiple sclerosis is correct? [LEARNING OBJECTIVE 10]
    A. It preferentially affects the motor neurons in the brain and spinal cord.

B. Unlike most autoimmune disorders, there is no familial tendency.
C. Men and women are equally affected.
D. Histology is notable for infiltrates of lymphocytes and macrophages, loss of myelin, and marked decrease of oligodendrocytes.

II. TRUE OR FALSE

18. _____ Mycobacterium leprae infects Schwann cells in the fingers, toes, tip of the nose, and external ear. [LEARNING OBJECTIVE 14]

19. _____ Specialized ependymal cells form the choroid plexuses are responsible for secretion of CSF. [LEARNING OBJECTIVE 1 AND 2]

20. _____ The somatic division is composed of *afferent* sensory signals and *efferent* motor signals. [LEARNING OBJECTIVE 3]

21. _____ Subarachnoid hemorrhages are the consequence of trauma, and typically occur in conjunction with traumatic bleeding in other parts of the body (Hint: Use Decision Tree 19.1) [LEARNING OBJECTIVE 7 AND 8]

22. _____ Because it takes several days for CSF to turn over, obstruction of CSF flow may take weeks to come to attention. [LEARNING OBJECTIVE 2]

23. _____ While two-thirds of adults experiencing an epileptic seizure will never have another, the large majority of seizures are attributable to an anatomic defect, which should prompt imaging for mass lesions. [LEARNING OBJECTIVE 5]

24. _____ Astrocytes are glial cells that support neurons and promote repair. [LEARNING OBJECTIVE 1]

25. _____ White matter is a collection of neurons, which form the inner layer of the brain, the cerebral cortex, and the central core of the spinal cord. [LEARNING OBJECTIVE 2]

26. _____ In contrast to parasympathetic ganglia, which are located along the vertebral column, sympathetic ganglia lie in or near the target tissue. [LEARNING OBJECTIVE 3]

27. _____ Cerebrovascular disease is the leading cause of death in the United States. [LEARNING OBJECTIVE 7]

28. _____ Acoustic neuroma is the most common peripheral nerve tumor to occur in the cranium. [LEARNING OBJECTIVE 13 AND 14]

III. MATCHING

29. Match the disease with its causative organism below. [LEARNING OBJECTIVE 9]
    i. Aerobic bacteria
    ii. Anaerobic bacteria
    iii. Poliovirus
    iv. Herpes virus
    v. Syphilis

vi. Rickettsia
vii. Escherichia coli
viii. Haemophilus influenza
ix. Streptococcus pneumoniae
x. Neisseria meningitides
xi. Tuberculosis
xii. Fungi
xiii. Amebae
xiv. Cryptococcus neoformans
A. Meningitis in people living in the military or in university dormitories

B. Encephalitis
C. Bacterial meningitis
D. Infects spinal motor neurons
E. Infects temporal lobes
F. Meningitis in newborns
G. Infect small blood vessels
H. Meningitis in children aged one to three years
I. Meningitis in mature adults
J. Brain abscess
K. Meningitis in people with basilar skull fracture
L. Chronic meningitis

IV. SHORT ANSWER

30. A 55-year-old female with a social history notable for alcoholism and homelessness is brought to the hospital for treatment of frostbite. She is notably dehydrated with a low blood sodium, glucose, and thiamine. The intern on the case orders treatment of her dehydration with a liter of normal saline. Why do you cancel these orders? [LEARNING OBJECTIVE 10]

31. The blood barrier is a protective mechanism. What are its parts and what is its function in the CNS? [LEARNING OBJECTIVE 2]

32. While at a football game, your cousin sees the quarterback make a big mistake! He ducks his head to ram his opponent out of his way. Play stops and the quarterback is seen lying on the field unable to move his legs. Concerned, your cousin asks whether this means the player is permanently paralyzed. What can you tell him about spinal injury? [LEARNING OBJECTIVE 6]

33. Using examples from Chapter 19 in *The Nature of Disease*, discuss important tests and procedures that should be completed on a newborn/infant. [LEARNING OBJECTIVE 9 AND 11]

34. What genetic or acquired conditions might raise the pretest probability of identifying a saccular aneurysm on imaging? [LEARNING OBJECTIVE 8]

35. A mother brings her infant to you for a second opinion. She has been told he has cerebral palsy, but she doesn't understand what has caused it. What can you tell her? [LEARNING OBJECTIVE 5]

CHAPTER 20

Disorders of the Senses

The Big Picture

Sensing is the detection of a stimulus by a sensory receptor, while **sensation** is the conscious perception of sensory signals by the cerebral cortex. Visceral senses are structures and mechanisms that detect changes in our internal environment. **Somatic senses** are simple structures with uncomplicated detection mechanisms, while **special senses** are complex systems with sophisticated detection apparatus. Special senses include vision, smell, taste, and hearing.

Oh No! Not Another Learning Experience

LEARNING OBJECTIVE 1: Describe the anterior segment (both the anterior and posterior chambers) and the posterior segment (including all layers) of the globe, and trace the flow of aqueous humor.

EXERCISE 20-1

Complete the paragraph below.

(1) _____ is the detection of light by the eye *and* integration into consciousness of the sensory signals produced. The (2) _____ is the organ of vision and connects to the visual cortex of the brain via the (3) _____. The (4) _____ and its accessory structures occupy a bony socket in the skull, called the (5) _____. The (6) _____ is divided into an anterior segment and a posterior segment, with the anterior segment having an anterior chamber and a posterior chamber. The (7) _____ of the globe consists of the cornea, iris, lens, and ciliary body, while the (8) _____ of the globe consists of the globe posterior to the lens. The (9) _____ is a fluid-filled space that lies behind the cornea and in front of the iris within the anterior segment. The (10) _____ lies behind the iris and in front of the lens. The (11) _____ is a highly vascular, doughnut-shaped organ that encircles and attaches to the iris and lens and secretes a clear, watery fluid, called (12) _____, into the posterior chamber. This is secreted from the ciliary body into the posterior chamber, then flows through the pupil to the anterior chamber where it is absorbed through the canal of Schlemm.

> **Remember This!** The anterior and posterior chambers are in the anterior segment of the globe.

EXERCISE 20-2 PATHOLOGY AS A SECOND LANGUAGE

Review Figures 20.1 and 20.3 in *The Nature of Disease*, then test your vocabulary by writing the appropriate term in each blank from the list below.

Cones	Cornea	Optic nerve
Iris	Lens	Pupil
Eyebrows	Eyelids	Conjunctiva
Tunics	Sclera	Choroid
Retina	Tarsal plate	External muscles
Schlemm's canal	Rods	Vitreous chamber
Macula	Fovea	Vitreous humor
Ciliary muscle	Suspensory ligaments	Uveal tract (uvea)
Nasolacrimal apparatus		

1. _____ shield the eye from particulate matter and glare.

2. The _____ (also called "palpebrae") are flaps of tissue covered externally by skin and lined internally by mucosa called the _____.

3. The _____ is a band of stiff, fibrous tissue that is especially dense along the lid edge and maintains the structure of the lid.

4. The _____ of the eye include six small skeletal muscles that move the globe.

5. The _____ consists of the lacrimal glands, one in the upper-outer edge of each orbit, which secrete tears, and the associated tear drainage ducts.

6. The wall of the globe is formed of three membranes or _____.

7. The outermost layer of the globe is the _____ (or fibrous tunic), a tough, fibrous, protective layer that forms the white of the eye and continues anteriorly to form the cornea.

8. The _____ (or vascular tunic) is a richly vascular, pigmented layer of the globe that also contains collagen fibers and melanocytes.

9. The choroid, ciliary body, and iris are collectively called the _____.

10. The innermost layer of the globe is the _____ (or neural tunic), a light-sensing layer of nervous tissue.

11. The _____ is a small and highly sensitive part of the retina responsible for detailed, central vision.

12. In the center of the macula is the _____, which is densely packed with cones and is responsible for the sharpest vision.

13. _____ discriminate only light and dark and are exquisitely sensitive to light.

14. _____ sense color but require bright light for peak performance.

15. The _____ connects the retina to the brain and can be visualized on an ophthalmic exam.

16. The _____ is the domed, clear anterior part of the eye, which has much more light-bending (focusing) power than the lens.

17. The _____ is a thin, pigmented membrane between the cornea and lens with a central opening called the _____.

18. The _____ is a flattened sphere that helps to focus light on the retina.

19. _____ attach to the outer edge of the lens to flatten it with tension.

20. The ring of circumferential smooth muscle that connects to the suspensory ligaments and controls flow into the canal of Schlemm is called the _____.

21. _____ is a tire-like duct in the ciliary body that encircles the anterior chamber and takes up aqueous humor.

22. _____ is the chamber of the posterior segment.

23. _____ fills the vitreous chamber and is composed of gelatinous material.

LEARNING OBJECTIVE 2: Discuss the causes and complications, where applicable, of strabismus and nystagmus.

EXERCISE 20-3 COMPLETE THE PARAGRAPH BELOW.

Normal vision requires that the eyes be precisely aligned and move together in strict coordination. (1) _____ (or "cross-eye") is an abnormal alignment of one eye that may be caused by neurologic disease or by weakness or shortening of an ocular muscle; it can lead to (2) _____ or permanent vision loss if uncorrected. (3) _____ is a rapid, involuntary, rhythmic, repetitive motion of one or both eyes caused by neurologic disease (especially of the cerebellum), disease of the inner ear, or drug toxicity. If the cause cannot be eliminated, oral or intraorbital drugs or surgery may be indicated.

EXERCISE 20-4 PATHOLOGY AS A SECOND LANGUAGE

See Exercise 20-3 for key terms covered in this section.

LEARNING OBJECTIVE 3: List the causes of ocular trauma.

EXERCISE 20-5

Complete the paragraph below.

(1) _____ is a superficial wound that does not penetrate much beyond the first few layers of corneal cells; however, it can become painful and infected. (2) _____ is hemorrhage into the anterior chamber due to more severe trauma and can lead to blindness. The most serious trauma is (3) _____, which always requires emergency intervention by a specialist. (4) _____ of the orbit, especially the floor, is fairly common with blunt facial injury. Chemical trauma from acids or caustics can cause severe scarring of the cornea and conjunctiva and may require corneal transplant.

EXERCISE 20-6 PATHOLOGY AS A SECOND LANGUAGE

See Exercise 20-5 for key terms covered in this section.

LEARNING OBJECTIVE 4: Name the causes of proptosis.

EXERCISE 20-7

Complete the paragraph below.

Forward displacement of the globe in the orbit, or bulging eyes, is called (1) _____; when both eyes are affected, it is called (2) _____. The usual cause is increased tissue and fluid in the orbit behind the globe caused by (3) _____. Proptosis also occurs with (4) _____, orbital inflammation, infection, or mass such as hemangioma, lymphoma, or lacrimal gland adenoma. Regardless of cause, displacement of the globe is associated with double vision and other visual symptoms, and should be treated surgically.

EXERCISE 20-8 | PATHOLOGY AS A SECOND LANGUAGE

See Exercise 20-7 for key terms covered in this section.

LEARNING OBJECTIVE 5: Compare and contrast myopia, hyperopia, presbyopia, and astigmatism.

EXERCISE 20-9

Review Figure 20.6 in *The Nature of Disease*, then complete the paragraphs below.

If the globe is elongated, rays converge in front of the retina, and the image is blurred, a condition called (1) _____. This is often referred to as "nearsighted" because the lens is usually able to overcome the defect for near objects. In contrast, if the globe is foreshortened, the retina is too close to the cornea, the focal point is behind the retina, and the image is blurred, a condition called (2) _____. This is often referred to as "farsighted" because the lens is often able to overcome the defect for distant objects.

Focusing power is gradually lost over the years and results in a slow decrease in the ability of the eye to focus on objects nearby, a condition called (3) _____. This is considered a natural part of the aging process and affects almost everyone. If the curvature of the cornea is not uniform, the image is properly focused in some areas and blurred in others and the condition is called (4) _____. This condition can be corrected surgically or with specialized contact lenses.

> **Remember This!** Almost everyone age 40 or older has some degree of presbyopia.

> **Remember This!** All refraction errors are caused by abnormal shape of the globe or cornea, or stiffness of the lens.

EXERCISE 20-10 | PATHOLOGY AS A SECOND LANGUAGE

See Exercise 20-9 for key terms covered in this section.

LEARNING OBJECTIVE 6: Catalog the disorders of the eyelid, conjunctiva, sclera, and lacrimal apparatus according to their underlying etiology (whether infectious, autoimmune, both, or other) and discuss their clinical presentation and treatment.

EXERCISE 20-11

Complete the paragraph below.

Most disorders of this area are not malignant, but inflammatory or benign. Inflammation of the conjunctiva is called (1) _____, and is usually bacterial, viral, or allergic. It causes "pink eye" and can be very contagious. *Chlamydia trachomatis* can cause a chronic conjunctival infection called (2) _____. Diffuse inflammation of the eyelids is called (3) _____. Inflammation of the lacrimal apparatus is called (4) _____. If there is chronic inflammation and destruction of lacrimal glands, a clinical syndrome of chronic dry occurs due to insufficient tear formation and is called (5) _____.

EXERCISE 20-12   PATHOLOGY AS A SECOND LANGUAGE

Test your vocabulary by indicating if each statement below is true or false. If it is false, provide the correct word for the italicized term that will make the statement true.

_____ 1. *Chalazion* (also called "hordeolum") is localized inflammation (sometimes a small abscess) of the eyelid resulting from bacterial infection of the sebaceous glands in the lid.

_____

_____ 2. *Sty* is a local inflammatory reaction of sebaceous glands of the eyelid except that it is a long-lasting condition characterized by chronic granulomatous inflammation.

_____

_____ 3. *Subconjunctival hemorrhage* is bleeding under the conjunctiva.

_____

_____ 4. *Pterygium* is the most common lesion and is usually seen as a small lump on the nasal side of the cornea in an elderly person.

_____

_____ 5. *Pinguecula* is a larger, less common, growth of tissue of the cornea and sclera and is shaped like an insect wing.

_____

LEARNING OBJECTIVE 7: Distinguish between infectious and noninfectious disorders of the cornea, and discuss the accompanying signs and symptoms.

EXERCISE 20-13

Complete the paragraph below.

Inflammation of the cornea is called (1) _____, and can be caused by bacteria, viruses, and parasites; it can also be associated with a corneal ulcer. In contrast, (2) _____ is a noninflammatory disease of the cornea, of which there are several.

EXERCISE 20-14   PATHOLOGY AS A SECOND LANGUAGE

Test your vocabulary by writing the appropriate term in each blank from the list below.

| Corneal dystrophy | Keratoconus | Band keratopathy |
| Arcus senilis | Fuchs endothelial dystrophy | |

1. _____ is a white arc of lipid deposited around the edge of the cornea.

2. _____ is an opaque, horizontal band of calcium deposits across the cornea that usually affects only one eye.

3. _____ is a bilateral, noninflammatory clouding of the cornea, usually as a result of a genetic defect.

4. _____ is a leading cause for corneal transplant in which endothelial cells degenerate and allow aqueous humor from the anterior chamber to diffuse into the cornea causing it to turn cloudy.

5. _____ is a misshaped cornea that is conical instead of spherical.

LEARNING OBJECTIVE 8: Explain the pathophysiology of cataracts.

EXERCISE 20-15

Complete the paragraph below.

A (1) _____ is a clouded lens that is a common cause of poor vision and blindness around the world. It can be due to age-related degeneration of lens fibers, which allows water to enter the lens, or a variety of other conditions, most importantly (2) _____, in which excessive blood sugar seeps into the lens and is converted into (3) _____, a molecule with high osmotic power that attracts water. Other causes of cataracts include hereditary disease, glaucoma, chronic steroid therapy, and congenital (4) _____ infection.

EXERCISE 20-16 PATHOLOGY AS A SECOND LANGUAGE

See Exercise 20-15 for key terms covered in this section.

LEARNING OBJECTIVE 9: List the components of the uveal tract and discuss the types, etiologies, and complications of uveitis.

EXERCISE 20-17

Complete the paragraph below.

The uveal tract (or uvea) is composed of the choroid, ciliary body, and iris. Inflammation of the uvea is called (1) _____, and can be due to trauma, infections, and autoimmune disease. It is dangerous as it can lead to scarring and blindness. (2) _____ is inflammation of only the iris, (3) _____ is inflammation of the iris and ciliary body, and (4) _____ is inflammation of the choroid. (5) _____ is an autoimmune uveitis involving the entire uveal tract that occurs after a latent period following injury. This is due to the unmasking of retinal antigens to the immune system.

EXERCISE 20-18 PATHOLOGY AS A SECOND LANGUAGE

See Exercise 20-17 for key terms covered in this section.

LEARNING OBJECTIVE 10: Discuss the differential diagnosis for someone experiencing vision loss, noting key signs and symptoms that can be used to discriminate amongst the etiologies.

EXERCISE 20-19

Complete the paragraph below.

The differential diagnosis for vision loss includes retinal detachment, retinal ischemia (arterial occlusion), macular degeneration, and glaucoma. (1) _____ is a peeling away of the retina from the retinal pigmented epithelium and usually becomes evident due to loss of part of the field of vision or due to painless visual disturbances such as large numbers of floaters or flashes of light. (2) _____ is not a problem and does not interfere with vision, but can precede retinal detachment. (3) _____ is a consequence of some other condition, most often diabetic retinopathy, but also trauma and retinal detachment. Blood in the posterior segment blocks light and is toxic to the retina. The most common and serious retinal vascular disease is (4) _____, with one-third of diabetic patients having disease on presentation and virtually all having retinal disease after 10 to 15 years. Early diabetic retinopathy progresses to (5) _____ in which new vessels form and can lead to blindness. Blockage of either the central retinal artery or vein is called (6) _____, and can be due to temporal arteritis or atherosclerosis. (7) _____ is due to arteriolosclerosis and causes "A-V nicking" on ophthalmic exam. (8) _____ is deterioration of the macula, the central part most needed for detailed central vision, and is the most common cause of blindness in the elderly in the United States. About 90% of patients have "dry" ARMD, which features retinal atrophy, with the remaining 10% developing "wet" ARMD, with neovascularization. (9) _____ is an inherited disease that leads to degeneration of the retinal pigmented epithelium and blindness. (10) _____ is an iatrogenic condition induced in premature infants by high oxygen treatment after birth, which damages developing retinal blood vessels.

Remember This! The eye is profoundly affected by diabetes.

EXERCISE 20-20   PATHOLOGY AS A SECOND LANGUAGE

See Exercise 20-19 for key terms covered in this section.

LEARNING OBJECTIVE 11: Distinguish between primary open-angle glaucoma, primary closed-angle glaucoma, and secondary glaucoma, and discuss the relationship of intraocular pressure to glaucoma.

EXERCISE 20-21

Review Figure 20.16 in *The Nature of Disease*, then complete the paragraph below.

(1) _____ is generally a disease of increased intraocular pressure or (2) _____ that damages the optic nerve and causes progressive vision loss. (3) _____ is caused by developmental abnormalities that interfere with aqueous drainage. (4) _____ develops in patients without underlying eye disease. (5) _____ features normal anatomy, but flow out of the anterior chamber is impeded and intraocular pressure rises. (6) _____ features a narrow lateral angle.

Remember This! Glaucoma and increased intraocular pressure are not synonymous.

EXERCISE 20-22   PATHOLOGY AS A SECOND LANGUAGE

Test your vocabulary by indicating if each statement below is true or false. If it is false, provide the correct word for the italicized term that will make the statement true.

____ 1. *Papilledema* can be due to plugging of outflow tract by red cells, white cells, or scarring.

_____

____ 2. *Secondary glaucoma* is edema of the head of the optic nerve where it enters the globe at the optic disc.

_____

____ 3. *Optic neuritis* is caused by diminished blood flow (ischemia) in the optic artery and leads to necrosis of all or part of the nerve.

_____

____ 4. *Ischemic optic neuropathy* describes loss of vision owing to demyelination of optic nerve fibers, preventing transmission of nerve signals from the retina to the brain.

_____

LEARNING OBJECTIVE 12: Compare and contrast ocular malignant melanoma and retinoblastoma.

EXERCISE 20-23

Complete the paragraph below.

Although very rare, (1) _____ is the most common malignant neoplasm of the eye. Benign melanocytic (2) _____ can occur as well. Late metastases (as long as 25 years later) can occur with this form of melanoma, at which point the disease is universally fatal. Treatment is usually surgical removal of the globe (called [3] _____). In contrast, (4) _____ is the most common primary ocular malignancy in children. It is a tumor of primitive neuronal cells in the retina and may be identified as something white inside the pupil instead of blackness (white reflex on eye exam). It may be a spontaneous or an inherited mutation in the (5) _____. Treatment is surgery or radiotherapy.

EXERCISE 20-24   PATHOLOGY AS A SECOND LANGUAGE

See Exercise 20-23 for key terms covered in this section.

LEARNING OBJECTIVE 13: Name the three anatomic divisions of the ear, and describe the anatomy responsible for hearing and equilibrium.

EXERCISE 20-25

Review Figure 20.17 in *The Nature of Disease*, then complete the paragraph below.

(1) _____ is the detection of sound waves by the ear and their integration into consciousness. The ear is constructed of three anatomic divisions. The (2) _____ consists of the (3) _____ (also called the "pinna"), a flap attached to the side of the head, and the (4) _____. The (5) _____ begins with the (6) _____ (also called the "eardrum"), which stretches across the canal like the head of a drum. Deepest in the temporal bone is a cavity that contains the (7) _____, which consists of the (8) _____ (for hearing) and the (9) _____.

EXERCISE 20-26 PATHOLOGY AS A SECOND LANGUAGE

Test your vocabulary by writing the appropriate term in each blank from the list below.

Round window	Vestibular apparatus	Otolith organs
Semicircular canals	Equilibrium	Tympanic cavity
Oval window	Vestibulocochlear nerve	Cochlea
Ossicles		

1. _____ is the sense of balance.

2. The _____ is an air-filled space in the temporal bone that is lined by simple cuboidal epithelium.

3. The _____ are the bones of the middle ear. They include the malleus, incus, and stapes.

4. The _____ is also called the "auditory nerve" or "cranial nerve VIII."

5. The _____ is a hollow tube coiled upon itself like a snail shell.

6. The cochlea interfaces with the tympanic cavity of the middle ear via the _____ and the _____.

7. The _____ is composed of the otolith organs and semicircular canals.

8. The _____ are a sac that senses the orientation of the head relative to gravity and senses linear acceleration.

9. The _____ are tubular arcs that arise from the otolith organ sac and sense rotational acceleration.

LEARNING OBJECTIVE 14: Discuss the risk factors, etiology, and signs and symptoms of otitis externa.

EXERCISE 20-27

Complete the paragraph below.

(1) _____, also known as "ear wax," can occlude the external auditory canal and impede hearing.

(2) _____ (sometimes called "swimmer's ear") is inflammation of the external ear and usually comes to medical attention because of pain and inflammation in the ear canal; it is usually due to bacteria.

EXERCISE 20-28 PATHOLOGY AS A SECOND LANGUAGE

See Exercise 20-27 for key terms covered in this section.

LEARNING OBJECTIVE 15: Distinguish between the types of otitis media.

EXERCISE 20-29

Complete the paragraph below.

(1) _____ is acute inflammation of the middle ear, and requires antibiotics in children under the age of two.

(2) _____ is an effusion in the middle ear that results from incomplete resolution of AOM or from obstructed drainage (without infection) through the Eustachian tube. If it is persistent, the patient may undergo myringotomy and have "tubes" put in the tympanic membrane for drainage. (3) _____ is persistent (> six weeks) suppurative drainage into the auditory canal through a perforated tympanic membrane.

EXERCISE 20-30 PATHOLOGY AS A SECOND LANGUAGE

Test your vocabulary by indicating if each statement below is true or false. If it is false, provide the correct word for the italicized term that will make the statement true.

____ 1. A *granulation tissue polyp* is a vascular growth that prolapses through the perforation into the auditory canal.

_____

____ 2. *Otosclerosis* is an accumulation of keratin debris in the middle ear caused by ingrowth of keratinizing squamous epithelium from the ear canal through the perforation.

_____

____ 3. *Cholesteatoma* occurs when bone deposits in the oval window limiting the ability of the ossicles to transfer sound vibrations to the inner ear from the eardrum.

_____

LEARNING OBJECTIVE 16: Explain the differential diagnosis of a patient suffering with vertigo.

EXERCISE 20-31

Test your vocabulary by writing the appropriate term in each blank from the list below.

Vestibular neuritis   Meniere's syndrome   Meniere's disease
Vertigo

1. _____ is a false sensation of movement of self or the environment and may be different than "dizziness."

2. _____ is a clinical triad of *vertigo*, *fluctuating hearing loss*, and *tinnitus*.

3. *Vertigo*, *fluctuating hearing loss*, and *tinnitus* of unknown etiology is called _____.

4. Viral infection of the CN VIII is believed to be responsible for a clinical condition known as _____.

EXERCISE 20-32   PATHOLOGY AS A SECOND LANGUAGE

See Exercise 20-31 for key terms covered in this section.

LEARNING OBJECTIVE 17: Name the three general categories of hearing loss.

EXERCISE 20-33

Complete the paragraph below.

(1) _____ is hearing loss that interferes with speech perception. (2) _____ is a slowly progressive, age-related decline of hearing acuity caused by otosclerosis. There are three basic categories of deafness; these include (3) _____, which is interference with transmission of sound to the tympanic membrane or of sound vibrations beyond the footplate of the stapes; (4) _____, which is interference with cochlear conversion of vibrations into sensory nerve signals and is often due to drugs/toxins or excessive noise; and (5) _____, which is interference with sensory nerve signals in the vestibulocochlear nerve or from lack of cortical integration of sensory signals into consciousness. Sensory and neural losses are often lumped together as (6) _____ hearing loss. Most hearing loss is permanent and cannot be reversed; however, hearing aids can be very helpful, but must be carefully tailored to the cause of the loss.

Mnemonic
Causes of Conductive Hearing Loss = **ChOP Wax**
Chronic otitis media
Otosclerosis
Perforation of tympanic membrane
Wax

Mnemonic

Causes of Sensorineural Hearing Loss = A MIND

Age

Meniere's syndrome/disease

Infection

Neuroma ("acoustic neuroma" of CN VIII)

Drugs

EXERCISE 20-34 PATHOLOGY AS A SECOND LANGUAGE

See Exercise 20-33 for key terms covered in this section.

LEARNING OBJECTIVE 18: Explain the mechanisms responsible for taste and smell, and their relationship to one another.

EXERCISE 20-35

Complete the paragraph below.

(1) _____ is sensed by chemoreceptors on the tongue and throat that respond to chemicals in food and drink. All tastes are a combination of five tastes: sour, salty, sweet, bitter, and (2) _____ ("savory," "meaty," or glutamate). The signal is relayed by cranial nerves VII, IX, and X to the gustatory cortex in the temporal lobe. Perception of taste is also greatly influenced by smell. (3) _____ (also called "olfaction") is sensed by chemoreceptors high in the nasal cavity immediately beneath the cranium that respond to volatile chemicals; these chemoreceptors can distinguish about 10,000 different odors based on the peculiar molecular mix of each. Odorant signals travel through the (4) _____ to multiple areas of the brain, including the cortex and (5) _____.

EXERCISE 20-36 PATHOLOGY AS A SECOND LANGUAGE

See Exercise 20-35 for key terms covered in this section.

LEARNING OBJECTIVE 19: List the disorders that affect taste and smell.

EXERCISE 20-37

Complete the paragraph below.

(1) _____ is the inability to taste, hypogeusia is a decreased ability to taste, and dysgeusia is distorted taste. Many conditions are capable of impairing taste, including (2) _____ (dry mouth), poor oral hygiene, malnutrition, zinc deficiency, and use of zinc lozenges. (3) _____ is an inability to detect odors, hyposmia is a diminished ability, and dysosmia is distorted detection of odors, which is sometimes cognitive, as in the inability to identify odor called (4) _____. Dysfunction of taste and smell may be due to peripheral (conductive) interference with signal transport or with cortical interpretation of the signal. CNS disease such as Alzheimer disease or (5) _____ may also interfere with smell, and can be a prodrome.

EXERCISE 20-38 PATHOLOGY AS A SECOND LANGUAGE

There are no vocabulary terms in this section.

LEARNING OBJECTIVE 20: Name the receptors of sensation and their corresponding somatic sense.

EXERCISE 20-39

Complete the paragraph below.

Somatic senses are detected by receptors in virtually every millimeter of skin, muscle, bones, joints, tendons, and other tissues. (1) _____ detect touch and pressure; temperature is sensed by (2) _____; and pain is sensed by free sensory nerve endings called (3) _____. (4) _____ is perceived within a fraction of a second and rises almost instantly to peak intensity. (5) _____ begins more than one second after the stimulus, and rises to a peak over several seconds or minutes. (6) _____ is the sensing and perception of the position of body parts relative to one another by receptors called (7) _____.

EXERCISE 20-40 PATHOLOGY AS A SECOND LANGUAGE

See Exercise 20-39 for key terms covered in this section.

LEARNING OBJECTIVE 21: Using examples from the text, discuss the etiology and clinical findings of patients with somatosensory disorders.

EXERCISE 20-41

Complete the paragraph below.

Primary (1) _____ consist of an inability to discriminate basic sensing information, and can be inherited or acquired. They can also include impaired cognition, including an inability to recognize the tactile features of an object, called (2) _____. (3) _____ is a related sensory disorder not due to brain damage but to cortical interpretation of sensory signals and can occur after limb loss. (4) _____ consists of pain severe enough to warrant medical attention and to cause disruption of the patient's normal social or occupational function, and includes fibromyalgia.

EXERCISE 20-42 PATHOLOGY AS A SECOND LANGUAGE

See Exercise 20-41 for key terms covered in this section.

DECISION TREE 20.1: VISION CHANGES

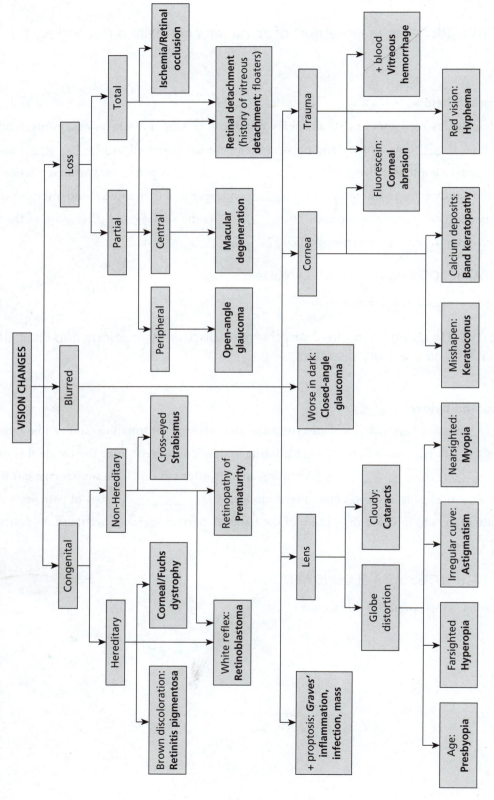

Test Yourself

I. MULTIPLE CHOICE

1. A five-year-old male is brought to the clinic by his adoptive mother, who is concerned by the fact that her son has been bumping into objects when walking. An optic exam, which is notable for deviation of his left eye, is otherwise normal without evidence of pathologic abnormality. You tell his mother that his problem is attributable to previously uncorrected strabismus. What complication has occurred? [LEARNING OBJECTIVE 2]
   A. Nystagmus
   B. Amblyopia
   C. Diplopia
   D. Retinoblastoma

2. Cataracts can be caused by which of the following? [LEARNING OBJECTIVE 8]
   A. Hereditary disease
   B. Glaucoma
   C. Chronic steroid therapy
   D. All of the above

3. A 55-year-old male, with a past medical history significant for hyperlipidemia, is seen in the eye care clinic for an exam and a new prescription. The optometrist notes a white arc of lipid deposited around the edge of the cornea. What is the cause of this finding? [LEARNING OBJECTIVE 7]
   A. Keratopathy
   B. Wilson disease
   C. Keratoconus
   D. Arcus senilis

4. A 63-year-old male with a past medical history of hypertension visits his optometrist because of concern for flashing lights in his right eye. An eye exam demonstrates a normal cornea and retina but a marked increase in floaters since his last exam. You caution him that the condition can result in retinal detachment. From which of the following diseases does he suffer? (Hint: Use the Decision Tree) [LEARNING OBJECTIVE 10]
   A. Vitreous detachment
   B. Vitreous hemorrhage
   C. Hyphema
   D. Keratopathy

5. A small growth on the nasal side of the conjunctiva is observed to grow over the outside edge of the cornea. What is your diagnosis? [LEARNING OBJECTIVE 6]
   A. Pinguecula
   B. Trachoma
   C. Pterygium
   D. Hordeolum

6. Looking through her recent photos, a woman is startled to see her son's pupils are different colors, one is red and the other is white. She takes her son to the pediatrician who diagnoses him with which of the following? (Hint: Use the Decision Tree) [LEARNING OBJECTIVE 12]
   A. Retinoblastoma
   B. Ocular malignant melanoma
   C. Fuchs Dystrophy
   D. Retinitis pigmentosa

7. Which of the following is an inability to taste? [LEARNING OBJECTIVE 19]
   A. Hypogeusia
   B. Dysgeusia
   C. Ageusia
   D. Anosmia

8. A 22-year-old Hispanic female comes to the clinic complaining of episodes of dizziness, nausea, and vomiting for the last several weeks. She reports she has had several similar episodes over the last year. She denies hearing loss and ringing of the ears. Which of the following is the most likely explanation of her symptoms? [LEARNING OBJECTIVE 16]
   A. Ménière's syndrome
   B. Meniere's disease
   C. Aspirin overdose
   D. Vestibular neuronitis

9. Which of the following is associated with hypercalcemia and inflammatory diseases? (Hint: Use the Decision Tree) [LEARNING OBJECTIVE 7]
   A. Band keratopathy
   B. Keratoconus
   C. Arcus senilis
   D. Keratitis

10. A 32-year-old ranch hand visits the ER complaining of pain and the feeling that something is stuck in his left eye. He jerks away from the ophthalmoscope light when you attempt to examine his eye. Conjunctival instillation of a drop of fluorescein dye confirms the diagnosis. What has caused the pain in his eye? (Hint: Use the Decision Tree) [LEARNING OBJECTIVE 3]
    A. Corneal abrasion
    B. Hyphema
    C. Conjunctivitis
    D. Blepharitis

11. Obstruction of the lacrimal duct due to allergic rhinitis can cause which of the following? [LEARNING OBJECTIVE 6]
    A. Keratoconjunctivitis sicca
    B. Blepharitis
    C. Chalazion
    D. Dacryocystitis

12. A 45-year-old African American female presents to the ER complaining of severe eye pain that started while she was watching a movie. An eye exam is remarkable for tearing, redness, blurred vision, puffy eyelids, and increased intraocular pressure (though according to her electronic medical record it was normal last week). What is the most likely cause of her symptoms? (Hint: Use the Decision Tree) [LEARNING OBJECTIVE 11]
    A. Primary open-angle glaucoma
    B. Congenital glaucoma
    C. Secondary glaucoma
    D. Primary closed-angle glaucoma

13. Which of the following findings is characteristic of hypertensive retinopathy? [LEARNING OBJECTIVE 10]
    A. A film of reactive gliosis and delicate new blood vessels, which bleed easily and obscure vision
    B. A growth of a neovascular membrane from the choroid onto the surface of the retina in addition to retinal atrophy
    C. A scarred detached fibrous tissue behind the lens
    D. Stiff, hard, shiny, narrow vessels with AV nicking, flame-shaped hemorrhage, and white cotton wool patches

14. A 32-year-old female is in the hospital for a severe infection treated with vancomycin. Periodic hearing tests are conducted to evaluate for what type of hearing loss? [LEARNING OBJECTIVE 17]
    A. Presbycusis
    B. Conductive
    C. Sensory
    D. Neural

15. Which of the following requires treatment with cleaning of the auditory canal several times daily with installation of steroids and antibiotics to prevent deafness? [LEARNING OBJECTIVE 15]
    A. Secretory otitis media
    B. Acute otitis media
    C. Chronic otitis media
    D. Cholesteatoma

II. TRUE OR FALSE

16. _____Proptosis is diagnostic of Graves disease. [LEARNING OBJECTIVE 4]

17. _____Glaucoma is the leading cause of preventable blindness. [LEARNING OBJECTIVE 11]

18. _____The most common cause of otitis externa is bacterial infection, often associated with swimming and water in the ear canal. [LEARNING OBJECTIVE 14]

19. _____Parosmia is the perception of odor without an odor present. [LEARNING OBJECTIVE 19]

20. _____ The three anatomic parts of the ear (external, middle, and inner ear) are involved in both hearing and balance. [LEARNING OBJECTIVE 1]

21. _____Ocular malignant melanoma metastasizes via the vasculature, most commonly to the liver. [LEARNING OBJECTIVE 12]

22. _____Otitis media occurs almost exclusively in young children, secondary to a narrow Eustachian tube and an immature immune system. [LEARNING OBJECTIVE 15]

23. _____The three types of cones, which sense blue, green, and red, each connect through the optic nerve to a single cortical neuron. [LEARNING OBJECTIVE 1]

24. _____Orthostatic hypotension is the leading cause of vertigo. [LEARNING OBJECTIVE 16]

25. _____Emotional factors play an important role in pain disorders. [LEARNING OBJECTIVE 21]

III. MATCHING

26. Match the following descriptors with the appropriate globe defect: (Hint: Use the Decision Tree) [LEARNING OBJECTIVE 5]
    i. Myopia
    ii. Hyperopia
    iii. Presbyopia
    iv. Astigmatism
    A. Rays converge in front of the retina
    B. Foreshortened globe
    C. Nearsighted
    D. Farsighted
    E. Irregularities in the curvature of the cornea
    F. A natural part of the aging process
    G. Results in partially blurred and partially focused images
    H. Elongated globe
    I. Rays converge behind the retina

IV. SHORT ANSWER

27. Which cranial nerves are important in the tasting process? [LEARNING OBJECTIVE 18]

_____

_____

_____

28. Why is it that every time a person cries, his or her nose runs? [LEARNING OBJECTIVE 1]

_____

_____

_____

29. Compare and contrast fast and slow pain. [LEARNING OBJECTIVE 20]

_____

_____

_____

30. Why is it important that cataracts be treated? [LEARNING OBJECTIVE 8 AND 9]

_____

_____

_____

CHAPTER 21

Disorders of the Skin

The Big Picture

Skin is the largest human organ and is supremely important as it protects us from the environment. In addition to this barrier function, skin is critical in body temperature control and immunity. Skin diseases are common. They can be primary, such as psoriasis, or skin can be secondarily affected by systemic disease, such as the rashes typical of many infectious diseases, Kaposi sarcoma in AIDS, rheumatoid nodules in rheumatoid arthritis, and others. Pathologic evaluation of skin overlaps with clinical dermatologic terms, because for skin disease, gross pathology and clinical description are one and the same.

Oh No! Not Another Learning Experience

LEARNING OBJECTIVE 1: Differentiate between dermis, epidermis, and subcutis using architecture, function, and the elements contained within each.

EXERCISE 21-1

Review Figures 21.1 and 21.2 in *The Nature of Disease*, then complete the paragraph below.

Skin is a complex organ that is divided into the epidermis, dermis, and subcutis (or subcutaneous tissue). The (1) _____ is the surface layer and is composed of stacked pancake-like cells called (2) _____. These form the primary barrier, with layers of keratin and cells that are welded together. The deepest layer of the epidermis is composed of (3) _____, which rest on the basement membrane and from which new squamous cells mature, flatten, and accumulate keratin to form the (4) _____, the layer of dry, dead cells at the surface. Within the epidermis are (5) _____, which produce pigment, and (6) _____, which are specialized immune system cells that trap microbes and other antigens. The middle layer of skin is the (7) _____, a framework of fibrous and elastic tissue that lies below the basement membrane. It is divided into the superficial (8) _____, which interdigitates with folds of the epidermis, and the deeper (9) _____. Below this is a pelt of fatty tissue called the (10) _____. The hair shafts and follicles arise in the dermis, then extend through the epidermis to the surface.

EXERCISE 21-2   PATHOLOGY AS A SECOND LANGUAGE

See Exercise 21-1 for key terms covered in this section.

LEARNING OBJECTIVE 2: Using examples from the text, classify the general conditions of skin according to their underlying etiology and provide their accompanying signs and symptoms.

EXERCISE 21-3

Review Figure 21.3 in *The Nature of Disease*, then complete the paragraph below.

There are many general skin conditions. Skin color is an important clue to disease. (1) _____ is blue skin color due to poorly oxygenated blood and can be due to heart or lung disease. Reddened skin is due to (2) _____, as can occur in inflammatory conditions or (3) _____. Yellow skin is called (4) _____ and can be seen in liver or hemolytic disease. Pale skin may point to anemia. Pregnancy can cause (5) _____ (also called "stretch marks"), temporary darkening of facial skin caused by increased melanin pigment called (6) _____, and small vascular lesions on the face or upper body that have a small, central arteriole and tiny radiating capillary spokes called (7) _____. Diabetes, thyroid disease, HIV, lipid diseases, blood diseases, and autoimmune conditions all can have various skin manifestations. (8) _____, a genetic syndrome of peripheral nerve cell tumors, is associated with café-au-lait spots, or brown macules, on the skin. (9) _____ (also called "phototoxicity") is an exaggerated reaction to sunlight and can occur in certain disease or as a side effect to drugs.

EXERCISE 21-4   PATHOLOGY AS A SECOND LANGUAGE

See Exercise 21-3 for key terms covered in this section.

LEARNING OBJECTIVE 3: Discuss the infections and infestations that affect the skin.

EXERCISE 21-5

Complete the paragraph below.

Infections and infestations commonly affect the skin. (1) _____ can take up residence and cause itching, swelling, and redness. These include (2) _____, which are exceedingly small insects, almost invisible to the unaided eye, that cause pruritic rashes. A (3) _____ is a type of mite that can cause a purulent reaction. (4) _____ is an obligate human parasite that is easily contagious, very itchy, and can become disseminated throughout the body surface in immunocompromised individuals. Infestation by wingless, blood sucking insects that cling to hair or fabric threads or (5) _____ is called "pediculosis." (6) _____ are insects that live in bedding and cloth-covered furniture and feed on blood.

EXERCISE 21-6

Complete the table below.

Disease	Agent	Findings	Treatment
(1) _____	Staphylococcus or Streptococcus	Common, highly contagious, superficial skin infection	Topical antibiotics
(2) _____	Staphylococcus or certain types of streptococci	Densely red skin infection	Systemic antibiotics
(3) _____	Group of fungi that metabolize keratin	Common superficial skin, hair, and nail infections	Topical antifungals
(4) _____	HSV	Causes common cold sores and genital infections	Antivirals including acyclovir
(5) _____	Certain types of HPV	Common papillary growths of epidermis	Liquid nitrogen, salicylates, excision
(6) _____	One variety of the poxvirus	Papules with central "umbilication"	Self-limited (goes away in several months)
(7) _____	Candida fungus "yeast"	Common fungus that causes redness, more likely in immunocompromised states and diabetes	Topical antifungals

EXERCISE 21-7   PATHOLOGY AS A SECOND LANGUAGE

See Exercises 21-5 and 21-6 for key terms covered in this section.

LEARNING OBJECTIVE 4: Describe the differences between acne and rosacea.

EXERCISE 21-8

Complete the paragraph below.

(1) _____ is an infectious disease associated with the bacterium *Propionibacterium acnes* and generally occurs in adolescents and young adults. In contrast, (2) _____ is an inflammatory disorder of hair follicles and sebaceous glands that mimics acne in older individuals. This disease is not thought to be related to hormonal status.

EXERCISE 21-9   PATHOLOGY AS A SECOND LANGUAGE

See Exercise 21-8 for key terms covered in this section.

LEARNING OBJECTIVE 5: List and classify the types of dermatitis as acute or chronic, noting the clinical characteristics, underlying etiology, and treatment options where applicable.

EXERCISE 21-10

Complete the paragraphs below.

(1) _____ is an inflammatory skin disease that is usually superficial and associated with inflammatory cell infiltrates. (2) _____ usually lasts a few days or weeks with red and itchy or moist and crusted skin due to an inflammatory cell infiltrate generally composed of lymphocytes and macrophages and accompanied by vasodilation and edema. (3) _____ is a general term (not a specific diagnosis) for any acute inflammatory reaction in skin characterized by itchy, weepy, crusted, red lesions.

(4) _____ tends to last for years and is usually dry, scaly, and rough. The epidermis is thickened due to epidermal hyperplasia caused by the underlying disease or by chronic rubbing or scratching. Specific diseases are outlined below.

EXERCISE 21-11

Complete the table below.

Type	Acute/chronic	Findings	Treatment
(1) _____ (also called "hives")	Acute	Localized allergic reaction	Antihistamines, steroids
(2) _____	Acute	Red, itchy skin in patients with other "atopic" diseases like asthma, type I hypersensitivity rxn	Antihistamines, steroids
(3) _____	Acute	Delayed-type immune hypersensitivity reaction caused by contact with a sensitizing agent, such as poison ivy or latex gloves	Remove offending agent, treat with antihistamines and/or steroids
(4) _____	Acute	Direct toxicity to skin by environmental toxins such as soaps, solvents, acids, and alkalis	Washing, removal
(5) _____	Acute	Symmetric eczema that begins days or weeks after drug exposure	Removal of drug
(6) _____	Acute	Develops on sun exposure of skin with a previously applied chemical	Avoidance
(7) _____	Acute	Self-limited, allergic (type II hypersensitivity) reaction, targetoid skin lesions	Caused by drugs, vaccines, or autoimmune reaction to HSV, remove or treat
(8) _____	Acute	Skin necrosis, blistering, and sloughing, SJS if < 10% of skin surface is involved (otherwise same as TEN)	Remove offending agent, supportive care
(9) _____	Acute	TEN if involvement is > 30% (otherwise same as SJS)	Remove offending drug, supportive care, may need to go to burn unit

(continued)

Type	Acute/chronic	Findings	Treatment
(10) _____	Chronic	Epidermal hyperplasia that forms salmon-colored, dry, scaly, sharply delineated plaques	Anti-immune agents, chemotherapies, steroids
(11) _____	Chronic	Accompanies varicose veins and venous stasis in the legs, brown "woody" discoloration	Treatment aimed at improving blood flow
(12) _____	Chronic	Dandruff (white flakes of dead skin) plus dermatitis	Topical treatments
(13) _____	Chronic	"the six Ps:" pruritic, purple, polygonal, planar papules and plaques	Generally no treatment

EXERCISE 21-12   PATHOLOGY AS A SECOND LANGUAGE

See Exercises 21-10 and 21-11 for key terms covered in this section.

Remember This! Eczema is a descriptive term, not a specific diagnosis.

LEARNING OBJECTIVE 6: Compare and contrast scleroderma with panniculitis.

EXERCISE 21-13

Complete the paragraph below.

(1) _____ (also called "systemic sclerosis") is a chronic systemic autoimmune disease most often of young women. It is characterized by dense fibrosis of the dermis that destroys hair follicles and other structures. It can also affect other organ systems. In contrast, (2) _____ is a subacute to chronic inflammatory and fibrotic disease of the deeper subcutaneous tissues (the "panniculus"). (3) _____ is a more acute form of this disease; it is self-limited and probably due to autoimmunity. It is characterized by red, extremely tender nodules of chronic inflammation and fibrosis in the subcuticular tissue on the anterior aspect of the lower legs, most often associated with infections, drugs, or systemic diseases like (4) _____. (5) _____ is a rare condition of widespread panniculitis.

EXERCISE 21-14   PATHOLOGY AS A SECOND LANGUAGE

See Exercise 21-13 for key terms covered in this section.

LEARNING OBJECTIVE 7: Categorize the blistering diseases according to the skin layer in which they are formed, and discuss their clinical and pathologic features.

EXERCISE 21-15

Complete the paragraph below.

(1) _____ of skin are mainly characterized by blisters, which can be small, called (2) _____, or large, called (3) _____. These blistering diseases are best categorized by the (4) _____ in which they are formed. (5) _____ form beneath the surface-cornified layer of the epidermis. (6) _____ form immediately above the layer of basal cells. (7) _____ form at the basement membrane, beneath the epidermis and dermis.

EXERCISE 21-16   PATHOLOGY AS A SECOND LANGUAGE

Test your vocabulary by writing the appropriate term in each blank from the list below.

Epidermolysis bullosa	Porphyria	Pemphigus
Dermatitis herpetiformis	Bullous pemphigoid	

1. _____ is a serious blistering disease that features intraepidermal and suprabasilar blisters with autoimmune attack on desmosomes, the connections between squamous cells of the epidermis.

2. _____ is a chronic blistering disease resulting from an autoimmune autoantibody attack against the basement membrane. It causes large subepidermal blisters (bullae).

3. _____ is an autoimmune disease that is associated with celiac sprue. IgA deposits in dermis and epidermis, causing Herpes-like vesicles.

4. _____ is a group of rare blistering diseases caused by genetically defective binding of epidermis to dermis at the basement membrane.

5. _____ is a group of inherited disorders of porphyrin metabolism (necessary for hemoglobin and myoglobin) that leads to skin manifestations.

LEARNING OBJECTIVE 8: Describe the etiology, clinical features, and treatment (as applicable) of vitiligo, albinism, freckles, and lentigos.

EXERCISE 21-17

Complete the paragraph below.

(1) _____ is a dark brown pigment made by (2) _____ located in the lower epidermis.

(3) _____ is a common acquired disorder, likely autoimmune, characterized by white macules that may

coalesce into large patches of bone-white, utterly depigmented skin. (4) _____ is a very rare, genetic lack

of melanin pigment owing to an inability of melanocytes to produce melanin pigment. A (5) _____

(also called an "ephelis") is a small macule of increased pigment in basal cells of the epidermis. (6) _____

are patches of dark skin, but differ from freckles and melasma. Lentigo is caused by a localized hyperplasia of

melanocytes in skin. These are all non-neoplastic disorders of skin pigmentation.

EXERCISE 21-18   PATHOLOGY AS A SECOND LANGUAGE

See Exercise 21-17 for key terms covered in this section.

LEARNING OBJECTIVE 9: Discuss the spectrum of melanocytic lesions; pay particular attention to the diagnostic and prognostic features of melanoma.

EXERCISE 21-19

Review Figures 21.38 and 21.39 in *The Nature of Disease*, then complete the paragraph below.

A (1) _____ is an acquired benign tumor of melanocytes, sometimes called a "mole". A (2) _____ is a distinctive clinical lesion worthy of note because of its relationship to malignant melanoma as a potential precursor to malignancy. It is known that patients with multiple dysplastic nevi and a family history of malignant melanoma may have a genetic condition called (3) _____. (4) _____ is a malignant neoplasm of melanocytes that is aggressive and can occur in younger people with fair skin with excessive sun exposure. Most do not arise from a pre-existing mole. This malignancy may begin as only intraepidermal, called (5) _____. It progresses to superficial spreading melanoma, which doesn't normally metastasize, then grows deep (vertical) to become (6) _____, which can easily metastasize. Melanoma is treated by surgical excision, chemotherapy, and immunotherapies.

Mnemonic
Causes of Concern for Melanoma in a "Mole" = ABCs of Melanoma = ABCDE
Asymmetry
Borders (irregular)
Color (variation)
Diameter (> 6mm)
Elevation

Remember This! Melanoma is the most common malignancy in women ages 25 to 29.

EXERCISE 21-20   PATHOLOGY AS A SECOND LANGUAGE

See Exercise 21-19 for key terms covered in this section.

LEARNING OBJECTIVE 10: List several neoplasms or neoplasm-like lesions of the dermis, catalog them as hyperplastic, premalignant, or malignant, and explain their pathogenesis.

EXERCISE 21-21

Complete the paragraph below.

Non-melanoma skin neoplasms are classified according to the tissue or cells from which they arise. Tumors of the (1) _____ include keratoses, (2) _____, and basal and squamous carcinoma; tumors of the (3) _____ include tumors of sebaceous and sweat glands and other adnexal structures; and tumors of the dermis and (4) _____ include lipoma, (5) _____, hemangioma, and neurofibroma. Tumors can also form from immune system cells.

EXERCISE 21-22

Complete the table below.

Disease	Malignancy potential	Findings
(1) _____	None	Innocent polypoid growths
(2) _____	Non-neoplastic	Inclusion of squamous debris and keratin
(3) _____	Benign	Pigmented, superficial, velvety, dry over-growth of epidermal cells with a thick, loose layer of surface keratin
(4) _____ (also called "solar keratosis")	Precancerous	Atypical squamous epithelium, forerunner of squamous cell carcinoma of skin
(5) _____	Malignant	Tumor of epidermal cells that mature toward keratinizing squamous cells
(6) _____	Low-grade malignancy	Squamous tumor of sun-exposed skin that can be alarming because of rapid growth
(7) _____	Malignant, but only very rarely metastasizes	Tumor of primitive basal cells located deep in the dermis along the basement membrane
(8) _____	Benign	Mature fat cells
(9) _____	Benign	Innocuous fibrous tumors that appear as small, brownish, sharply outlined, hard dermal nodules
(10) _____	Benign, recur locally	Nodular masses of exaggerated scar tissue that far exceed the degree of injury and the expected repair response
(11) _____	Benign	Abnormal collections of blood vessels
(12) _____	Malignant	A primary T-cell lymphoma of the skin
(13) _____	Malignant	Tumor of cutaneous dendritic cells mostly occurring in children
(14) _____	Malignant	Tumor of vascular endothelial cells caused by a herpesvirus in AIDS patients
(15) _____	Benign	Growths of specialized glandular epithelium
(16) _____	Benign	Tumors of peripheral nerves usually seen in the dermis of patients with von Recklinghausen neurofibromatosis

EXERCISE 21-23 PATHOLOGY AS A SECOND LANGUAGE

See Exercises 21-21 and 21-22 for key terms covered in this section.

LEARNING OBJECTIVE 11: Provide a differential diagnosis for hair loss.

EXERCISE 21-24

Complete the paragraph below.

Most hair diseases feature abnormal hair loss called (1) _____. (2) _____ is characterized by well-circumscribed areas of total hair loss, usually on the scalp. (3) _____ is loss of all scalp hair. (4) _____ is loss of all body hair, including eyebrows. (5) _____ is a natural consequence of aging attributable to male hormones, which act to shorten the growth (or anagen) phase of hairs until, ultimately, no hair grows. (6) _____ is a sudden, diffuse shedding of resting (or telogen) hairs (about 10% of all hairs) that occurs several weeks after severe illness, trauma, or emotional upset. (7) _____ is the growth of dark, thick hair in women in locations where hair is normally minimal or absent.

EXERCISE 21-25   PATHOLOGY AS A SECOND LANGUAGE

See Exercise 21-4 for key terms covered in this section.

LEARNING OBJECTIVE 12: Compare and contrast onychogryphosis, onycholysis, paronychia, and onychomycosis.

EXERCISE 21-26

Complete the paragraph below.

Nail diseases are usually innocuous but cosmetically displeasing. (1) _____ is nail dystrophy, and refers to thickened, deformed nails. (2) _____ is loss of the nail at the bed. Bacterial infection of the cuticle is called (3) _____, while fungal infection of the nail is called (4) _____. Fungal infections of the nail can be difficult to treat and may require months of antifungal therapy.

EXERCISE 21-27   PATHOLOGY AS A SECOND LANGUAGE

See Exercise 21-26 for key terms covered in this section.

Decisions Decisions

DECISION TREE 21.1: SKIN DISEASE

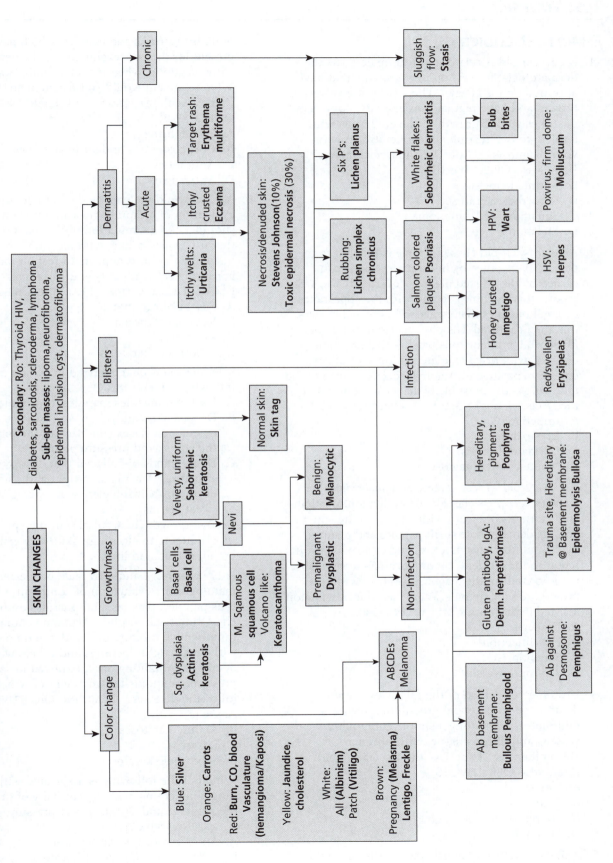

SKIN CHANGES

Secondary: R/o: Thyroid, HIV, diabetes, sarcoidosis, scleroderma, lymphoma
Sub-epi masses: lipoma, neurofibroma, epidermal inclusion cyst, dermatofibroma

Color change

Blue: **Silver**

Orange: **Carrots**

Red: Burn, CO, blood
Vasculature
(hemangioma/**Kaposi**)

Yellow: Jaundice,
cholesterol

White:
All (**Albinism**)
Patch (**Vitiligo**)

Brown:
Pregnancy (**Melasma**)
Lentigo, Freckle

Growth/mass

Sq. dysplasia
Actinic keratosis

Basal cells
Basal cell

Velvety, uniform
Seborrheic keratosis

M. Sqamous
squamous cell
Volcano like:
Keratoacanthoma

Nevi

Normal skin:
Skin tag

Premalignant
Dysplastic

Benign:
Melanocytic

ABCDEs
Melanoma

Dermatitis

Acute

Itchy welts:
Urticaria

Itchy/
crusted
Eczema

Target rash:
Erythema multiforme

Necrosis/denuded skin:
Stevens Johnson(10%)
Toxic epidermal necrosis (30%)

Rubbing:
Lichen simplex chronicus

Six P's:
Lichen planus

Chronic

Sluggish
flow:
Stasis

White flakes:
Seborrheic dermatitis

Salmon colored
plaque: **Psoriasis**

Blisters

Infection

Honey crusted
Impetigo

Red/swellen
Erysipelas

HSV:
Herpes

HPV:
Wart

**Bub
bites**

Poxvirus, firm dome:
Molluscum

Non-Infection

Ab basement
membrane:
Bullous Pemphigold

Gluten antibody, IgA:
Derm. herpetiformes

Ab against
Desmosome:
Pemphigus

Hereditary, pigment:
Porphyria

Trauma site, Hereditary
@ Basement membrane:
Epidermolysis Bullosa

Test Yourself

I. MULTIPLE CHOICE

1. A 63-year-old African American male visits the dermatologist for several new growths that have appeared on his cheeks. The lesions are velvety, brown, and have regular borders. Histology demonstrates an overgrowth of the epidermis with a thick, loose layer of surface keratin. What is your diagnosis? (Hint: Use the Decision Tree) [LEARNING OBJECTIVE 10]
   A. Actinic keratosis
   B. Seborrheic keratosis
   C. Squamous cell carcinoma
   D. Melanoma

2. An eight-year-old Hispanic male is brought to the pediatrician's office by his mother, who is concerned by the crusted plaques covering his legs. She reports that the illness began with the appearance of small pustules that escalated into small blisters that then ruptured. His physical exam is notable for several erythematous patches that are "honey-crusted" with dried exudate. Cultures of the exudate were positive for staphylococcus. Which of the following is the most likely diagnosis? (Hint: Use the Decision Tree) [LEARNING OBJECTIVE 3]
   A. Impetigo
   B. Erysipelas
   C. Dermatophytosis
   D. Molluscum contagiosum

3. A 43-year-old African-American female visits her primary care physician for the evaluation of fatigue and shortness of breath with a dry hacking cough. You incidentally note small papules and plaques, mainly around her nose, lips, and eyes, which you report to the resident. He orders an X-ray and lab work to confirm the diagnosis prior to writing a prescription for steroids. What has your observation assisted in diagnosing? [LEARNING OBJECTIVE 2]
   A. Diabetes
   B. HIV infection
   C. Sarcoidosis
   D. Thyroid disease

4. Pathology on which of the following would demonstrate a polypoid growth of a few millimeters containing a simple core, blood vessels, and fibrous tissue, with unremarkable epidermis. (Hint: Use the Decision Tree) [LEARNING OBJECTIVE 10]
   A. Nevus
   B. Skin tags
   C. Dysplastic nevus
   D. Melanoma

5. A 35-year-old Asian female presents to the clinic complaining of itchy red welts over her arms, torso, and legs. Her physical exam is notable for pale pink, firm streaks and papules, which have been present for the last several hours. She denies difficulty breathing, wheezing, and trouble swallowing. What treatment would you recommend? (Hint: Use the Decision Tree) [LEARNING OBJECTIVE 5]
   A. Epinephrine
   B. Corticosteroids and antihistamines
   C. Antibiotics
   D. Antifungals

6. A 56-year-old male visits the dermatologist for evaluation of a rapidly growing mass on his shoulder. An examination of the mass reveals that it is volcano-like, with a central crater; on histology the mass appears to rest on malignant-appearing cells. What is your diagnosis? (Hint: Use the Decision Tree) [LEARNING OBJECTIVE 10]
   A. Basal cell carcinoma
   B. Keratoacanthoma
   C. Psoriasis
   D. Seborrheic keratosis

7. Scleroderma is characterized by which of the following? [LEARNING OBJECTIVE 6]
   A. Dark red macules, papules, or nodules
   B. Dozens of small, yellow–red papules on extensor surfaces (the back of the forearms or the shins) and pressure points
   C. Dense bands of collagen that destroy dermal structures, leaving skin tight and smooth and devoid of hair follicles, sebaceous glands, or sweat glands
   D. Overgrowth (hyperplasia) of the epidermis, producing thick, rough skin with exaggeration of normal skin lines

8. A 17-year-old Caucasian male is referred to a dermatologist for evaluation of confluent, erythematous papules, patches, and pustules on his face, chest, and back. A physical exam is notable for an innumerable mixture of papules and pores, some with small, tight openings and others with large openings containing dark, oxidized melanin. You prescribe retinoids for treatment of which of the following diseases? [LEARNING OBJECTIVE 4]
   A. Acne
   B. Actinic keratoses
   C. Rosacea
   D. Seborrheic keratoses

9. Which of the following is associated with *Candida* fungal infections of skin, especially of or near the genitals, and skin ulcers at pressure points? [LEARNING OBJECTIVE 2]
   A. An excess of thyroid hormone
   B. A deficiency of thyroid hormone
   C. Diabetes
   D. Blood lipid abnormalities

10. An 11-year-old Caucasian female with severe hay fever is brought to the pediatrician's office for treatment of a worsening rash, which she reports is itchy. A physical exam demonstrates weepy, crusted eruptions on her cheeks, chest, and extensor surfaces. What is your diagnosis? (Hint: Use the Decision Tree) [LEARNING OBJECTIVE 5]
    A. Psoriasis
    B. Seborrheic dermatitis
    C. Lichen planus
    D. Atopic eczema

11. White macules coalescing into large patches of depigmented skin are associated with which of the following autoimmune diseases? (Hint: Use the Decision Tree) [LEARNING OBJECTIVE 8]
    A. Diabetes
    B. Addison disease
    C. Pernicious anemia
    D. All of the above

12. A 43-year-old Asian woman presents for her initial patient visit at a dermatology clinic through which you are rotating. Her physical exam is remarkable for clusters of vesicles, papules, and urticarial wheals. She reports that these itchy lesions gradually appeared on her elbows, knees, buttocks, and sacrum. A punch biopsy of the edge of a blister is notable for IgA deposits in the superficial dermis. What is the most likely cause of her symptoms? (Hint: Use the Decision Tree) [LEARNING OBJECTIVE 7]
    A. Epidermolysis bullosa
    B. Pemphigus
    C. Bullous pemphigoid
    D. Dermatitis herpetiformis

13. Small, firm, dome-shaped, white–pink nodules containing a semisolid cheesy white material are observed to have large inclusion bodies on histology. Infection by which of the following organisms is responsible for these lesions? (Hint: Use the Decision Tree) [LEARNING OBJECTIVE 3]
    A. HPV
    B. Poxvirus
    C. Herpesvirus
    D. Fungus

14. A 40-year-old African American female, with a past medical history significant for systemic lupus erythematosus, is seen at the clinic for evaluation of an itchy red rash on her wrists and ankles. Her physical exam demonstrates pruritic, purple, polygonal, planar papules and plaques on her wrists and ankles, as well as white capped oral plaques. What is the most likely explanation for this constellation of symptoms? (Hint: Use the Decision Tree) [LEARNING OBJECTIVE 5]
    A. Simplex chronicus
    B. Seborrheic dermatitis
    C. Psoriasis
    D. Lichen planus

15. Infected thick, yellow, and unsightly nails with ridges would prompt which of the following diagnoses? [LEARNING OBJECTIVE 12]
    A. Onychogryphosis
    B. Onycholysis
    C. Paronychia
    D. Onychomycosis

II. TRUE OR FALSE

16. _____ Although the epidermis contains nerves and glands, it does not contain blood vessels and gets its nourishment by diffusion across the basement membrane. [LEARNING OBJECTIVE 1]

17. _____ Epidermolysis bullosa, which is characterized by blisters at sites of pressure or minor trauma on hands and feet, is caused by genetically defective binding of epidermis to dermis at the basement membrane. (Hint: Use the Decision Tree) [LEARNING OBJECTIVE 7]

18. _____ Kaposi sarcoma is the result of herpes infection in a patient with HIV. [LEARNING OBJECTIVE 10]

19. _____ Diagnosis of Weber-Christian disease should prompt a search for underlying conditions, including pancreatitis, pancreatic carcinoma, infections, autoimmune disorders, or occult neoplasms. [LEARNING OBJECTIVE 6]

20. _____ Melanocytes are derived from the embryonic nervous system. [LEARNING OBJECTIVE 1]

III. MATCHING

21. Match the following bugs with the sentences that describe them: [LEARNING OBJECTIVE 3]
    i. Chigger
    ii. Scabies
    iii. Head lice
    iv. Body lice
    v. Pubic lice
    vi. Bedbugs

    A. Most common variety of mite bite
    B. Found in outdoor warm, dry climates
    C. It occurs opportunistically in AIDS and other immunocompromised patients
    D. Infect webs of the fingers or toes, wrists, waistline, and genitals
    E. Live on the scalp
    F. Live on bedding and clothing, not on people
    G. Transmitted sexually

IV. SHORT ANSWER

22. What are the most important clinical alarm signals for melanoma? [LEARNING OBJECTIVE 9]

_____

_____

_____

23. A dermatology specimen is processed for a rush read the following morning, with a requisition form questioning drug hypersensitivity. A review of the patient's electronic medical record is notable for a recent history of a urinary tract infection treated with sulfa antibiotics followed by a fever and blisters, which ruptured to leave ulcerations covering 35% of her body. The histology demonstrates necrosis and a missing epidermis, which is consistent with what diagnosis? How should she be treated? (Hint: Use the Decision Tree) [LEARNING OBJECTIVE 5]

_____

_____

_____

24. How does androgenic alopecia (hair loss caused by androgens) differ in men versus women? [LEARNING OBJECTIVE 11]

_____

_____

_____

25. An African American graduate student, who recently moved from Texas to Massachusetts, complains to you that since moving to Massachusetts she has had difficulty sleeping and has felt depressed, especially as the days have gotten shorter. Can you think of an explanation for this? [LEARNING OBJECTIVE 2]

_____

_____

_____

Disorders of the Stages and States of Life

CHAPTER

22

Congenital and Childhood Disorders

The Big Picture

Pediatric disease including congenital and childhood disorders represents an entirely different spectrum of disease than that of adults. Children are especially susceptible to genetic disorders, developmental disorders, specific infections, and differing types of cancers.

Oh No! Not Another Learning Experience

LEARNING OBJECTIVE 1: Describe the timeline of embryonic and fetal development throughout a normal pregnancy.

EXERCISE 22-1

Review Figure 22.1 in *The Nature of Disease*, then complete the paragraph below.

(1) _____ (gravidity) begins with fertilization (conception) and ends with birth. It is divided into three

(2) _____, each about 13 weeks long. In the first two weeks after fertilization, the blastocyst forms and

(3) _____ occurs. During the first eight weeks, organogenesis occurs, allowing the brain and spinal cord,

the heart, the eyes, the limbs, and the genitals to develop; the developing human is called the (4) _____

during this period. After eight weeks and until parturition (birth), the developing human is termed

a (5) _____.

EXERCISE 22-2 PATHOLOGY AS A SECOND LANGUAGE

Test your vocabulary by writing the appropriate term in each blank from the list below.

Decidua   Chorionic villi   Parity
Embryonic plate   Placenta   Umbilical cord
Chorionic gonadotropin   Gravidity

1. _____ is a term designating the number of times a woman has been pregnant.

2. _____ is a term designating the number of pregnancies that have reached 24 weeks.

3. _____ is a hormone secreted by the developing placenta as soon as the fertilized ovum implants in the endometrium.

4. The three germ layers, including the endoderm, mesoderm, and ectoderm, are collectively referred to as the _____.

5. The _____ is a temporary organ of pregnancy that supplies oxygen and nutrients to the developing embryo/fetus.

6. Blood travels between the embryo/fetus and the placenta via the _____.

7. The _____ is the maternal portion of the placenta. It is really the uterine endometrium, is thickened and modified by the effect of progesterone.

8. _____ are fingerlike projections of the placenta containing fetal blood vessels that extend into lakes of maternal blood in the decidua.

LEARNING OBJECTIVE 2: Compare and contrast malformations and deformations.

EXERCISE 22-3

Complete the paragraph below.

A (1) _____ or congenital anomaly refers to an abnormality present at birth. These may be caused by mechanical factors (e.g., clubfoot), genetic factors (e.g., Trisomy 21 [Down syndrome]), or (2) _____ (maternal) factors (e.g., maternal alcohol abuse), or they may be multifactorial (due to a mix of influences). (3) _____ are caused by maternal mechanical factors that distort the fetus. In contrast, (4) _____ are fetal defects that are due to either environmental or genetic factors.

EXERCISE 22-4 PATHOLOGY AS A SECOND LANGUAGE

See Exercise 22-3 for key terms covered in this section.

Remember This! All disease owes to the interplay of genetic and environmental forces.

LEARNING OBJECTIVE 3: Describe the environmental factors responsible for causing congenital malformations including: nutrient deficiencies, radiation, teratogens/drugs, and infections.

EXERCISE 22-5

Complete the paragraphs below.

(1) _____ are fetal defects due to either environmental or genetic factors. Most birth defects originate in the first trimester, especially the first eight weeks (the [2] _____) because of the complexities of organ formation occurring during that period. Environmental factors include but are not limited to nutrient deficiencies, (3) _____, teratogens/drugs, and infections. Congenital defects typically arise from the failure of an embryologic space to close properly. For example, because adequate levels of folate are essential for proper

closure of the embryonic neural tube, deficiency of folate may cause the neural tube to fail to close, causing (4) _____, or fail to form, causing (5) _____. In addition, congenital defects can be due to failure of embryologic tissue to divide (e.g., syndactyly), failure of an embryologic structure to disappear normally (e.g., thyroglossal duct cyst), or failure of tissue or organ to differentiate or grow (e.g., limb agenesis). The opposite of a deficiency is the presence of a toxin or a (6) _____, which is an environmental force that causes a congenital malformation; it can be physical, chemical, or microbial. For example, excessive (7) _____ supplementation is teratogenic, increasing the risk of craniofacial malformations, including cleft lip and palate, as well as heart defects and central nervous system abnormalities. (8) _____ (e.g., X-rays) can pass through the mother's tissue to harm ovarian germ cells or the developing fetus by damaging DNA, leading to birth defects. (9) _____, either illicit or therapeutic, that enter the mother's body can easily cross the placenta and make their way from maternal into fetal blood.

There are many chemical teratogens, but the most important is alcohol (ethanol). Alcohol abuse in pregnancy accounts for a variety of impairments collectively known as (10) _____. Smoking, all classes of illicit drugs, and the use of certain prescription and over-the-counter medications can be harmful. For example, (11) _____, a sleeping pill introduced in the 1950s, resulted in the birth of thousands of children with short, deformed limbs. (12) _____ of the mother also can cross the placenta to infect the developing embryo/fetus. Infection by cytomegalovirus or herpesvirus may produce severe fetal damage even as late as the third trimester. (13) _____ is a highly distinctive clinical syndrome characterized by severe brain, bone, dental, and ophthalmic problems. On the other hand, (14) _____ develops in children in much the same way it does in adults and is characterized by opportunistic infections and malignancies; it does not usually cause congenital defects.

EXERCISE 22-6   PATHOLOGY AS A SECOND LANGUAGE

See Exercise 22-5 for key terms covered in this section.

Remember This! Most birth defects originate in the first eight weeks of pregnancy.

Mnemonic
Congenital (Teratogenic) Infections = **TORCH**
Toxoplasmosis
Other (syphilis, hepatitis B, HIV, many others)
Rubella
Cytomegalovirus
Herpesvirus

LEARNING OBJECTIVE 4: Describe different types of mutations and how they affect the genetic code.

> **EXERCISE 22-7**

Complete the paragraph below.

(1) _____ is a long molecule packed into the *nucleus* of every body cell; it contains the instructions for the cells. A (2) _____ is any permanent change in DNA. When a DNA "spelling" error involves the replacement (substitution) of one base by another it is called a (3) _____. (4) _____ are those in which one or more bases are inserted. Conversely, (5) _____ are those in which one or more bases are missing. Insertion or deletion errors that shift sets of bases right or left are called (6) _____. Generally, these mutations occur in genes or affect the expression of genes. (7) _____ are relatively short segments, each of which instruct the cell in how to make a particular protein.

> **EXERCISE 22-8**   PATHOLOGY AS A SECOND LANGUAGE

Test your vocabulary by indicating if each statement below is true or false. If it is false, provide the correct word for the italicized term that will make the statement true.

_____ 1. The sequence of nucleotide bases in coding DNA is the *genetic code*.

_____

_____ 2. *Base pairs* are large units of DNA each of which is a packet containing a unique set of genes not present in the other pairs.

_____

_____ 3. A *karyotype* is a photographic or drawn display of chromosomes.

_____

_____ 4. Specialized *somatic cells* in the ovary and testis produce ova and sperm.

_____

_____ 5. *Germ cells* form all other tissues and organs.

_____

_____ 6. *Chromosomal notation* for a normal male is 46,XY; a normal female is designated 46,XX.

_____

_____ 7. *Phenotype* is the genetic make-up of a person.

_____

_____ 8. *Genotype* is the physical traits of a person.

_____

Remember This! Only germ cells (ova or sperm) can transmit defective DNA code from one generation to the next. Defective DNA in somatic cells, as in cancers, cannot be transmitted.

LEARNING OBJECTIVE 5: Using examples from the text, describe the different modes of inheritance, and the different types of genes that may be mutated.

EXERCISE 22-9

Review Figures 22.8, 22.9, and 22.10 in *The Nature of Disease*, then complete the paragraphs below.

Genetic diseases that involve only a single gene are called (1) _____; they are passed down by strict rules of inheritance from parent to child (see below). In contrast, (2) _____ develop under the influence of many genes as they interact with environmental factors, and (3) _____ are caused by extra or absent whole chromosomes. The three basic inheritance mechanisms for single-gene characteristics are called (4) _____. These rules involve (5) _____, which are genes that influence a trait. Alleles are said to be (6) _____ if they are identical; alleles that are not identical are said to be (7) _____.

The first type of inheritance is (8) _____ in which the trait or disease is expressed phenotypically (physically) even if the matching allele is normal. The second type of inheritance is (9) _____ in which the trait or disease is expressed phenotypically (physically) only if both alleles are defective. The third type of inheritance is when a recessive allele on one of the mother's two X chromosomes is transmitted in Mendelian fashion to half of her offspring (either male or female) and the disease occurs only in sons; it is called (10) _____.

EXERCISE 22-10 PATHOLOGY AS A SECOND LANGUAGE

Test your vocabulary by writing the appropriate term in each blank from the list below.

Receptor   Proto-oncogenes   Expressivity
Enzymes   Penetrance   Transport protein
Cystic fibrosis (CF)   Expression   Carrier
Tumor suppressor genes

1. Dominant genes have a greater effect or greater power of _____ than do recessive genes.

2. A person who is healthy but carries a recessive disease trait is called a _____.

3. _____ is the percentage of individuals with the disease allele that actually have the disease.

4. _____ is the manner of manifestation of the disease.

5. _____ are proteins that accelerate chemical reactions and mutations; they can cause monogenic diseases with accumulation of substrate or deficiency of product (e.g., glucocerebroside accumulation in Gaucher disease).

6. When a protein attaches to and carries a molecule from one place to another, it is called a _____ and when mutated, can cause disease (e.g., copper transporter in Wilson disease).

7. _____ proteins attach to chemical messenger molecules and relay messenger instructions (e.g., mutated LDL receptor in familial hypercholesterolemia).

8. _____ are normal genes that promote cell growth in a normal physiologic setting; they can be permanently turned "on" by mutation.

9. _____ normally inhibit cell growth (e.g., mutated NF1 in neurofibromatosis).

10. _____ is an autosomal recessive genetic disease of exocrine glands that primarily affects the lungs and gastrointestinal tract.

LEARNING OBJECTIVE 6: Name the categories of single gene defects that are transmitted in a non-Mendelian fashion.

EXERCISE 22-11

Complete the paragraph below.

The categories of single gene defects that are transmitted in a non-Mendelian fashion include the following: (1) _____ is characterized by several hundreds or thousands of abnormal repeating DNA bases, which get worse each generation (called "anticipation"). For example, excess repeats of the CGG triplet result in the most common form of familial mental retardation, (2) _____. (3) _____ occurs when a single gene defect behaves differently according to whether it was inherited from mother or father and causes disease. (4) _____ are transmissible to the next generation only by the mother. For example, (5) _____ causes abnormal conduction in the heart and episodes of tachycardia.

EXERCISE 22-12 PATHOLOGY AS A SECOND LANGUAGE

See Exercise 22-11 for key terms covered in this section.

LEARNING OBJECTIVE 7: Using examples from the text, define the pathogenesis of multifactorial diseases.

EXERCISE 22-13

Complete the paragraph below.

The (1) _____ is the sum of all of our genes, but typically requires (2) _____ such as alcohol abuse, smoking, radiation, or overeating to cause disease. This type of disease is called (3) _____ and represents the majority of disease. For example, southwestern tribes of American Indians have very high rates of obesity and diabetes when compared to other populations eating a similar diet. Diabetes is controlled by environment, but also by at least 40 or more genes involved in (4) _____ and regulation of body weight. In addition to obesity and type 2 diabetes mentioned above, other notable examples of multifactorial disorders are cleft lip, congenital heart disease, gallstones, gout, and mental retardation. (5) _____, arthritis, osteoporosis, many forms of cancer, and an array of other common, chronic diseases are also known to be multifactorial.

Remember This! Most diseases are multifactorial: they are a product of genetic influence and environmental factors.

EXERCISE 22-14 PATHOLOGY AS A SECOND LANGUAGE

No key terms are covered in this section.

LEARNING OBJECTIVE 8: Describe the signs, symptoms, and cytogenetic changes found in Turner, Klinefelter, and Down syndromes.

EXERCISE 22-15

Review Figures 22.14 and 22.15 in *The Nature of Disease*, then complete the paragraph below.

(1) _____ results from abnormalities involving large parts of chromosomes or entire chromosomes and may affect any chromosome. The three most common defects are: one or more extra chromosomes,

(2) _____, or a structural abnormality of chromosomes, such as missing parts (deletion), parts that have been moved from one chromosome to another ([3] _____), or parts that detach and reattach upside down (inversion). (4) _____ is the most common cytogenetic disorder in the United States and the single most common cause of mental retardation; it is caused by having three copies of autosome 21 or (5) _____. Sex chromosome cytogenetic disease most commonly produces ova or sperm with an extra sex chromosome or none. For example, if an ovum contains an extra X chromosome (24,XX instead of 23,X) and is fertilized by a normal sperm (23,Y) the result is 47,XXY, which is recognized clinically as (6) _____. The patient is tall and effeminate, with long arms and legs, a small penis and atrophic testicles, scant pubic hair, no beard, and female-like hip shape. In contrast, if an abnormal sperm with no sex chromosome fertilizes a normal (23,X) ovum, the genotype is 45,X0, which is recognized clinically as (7) _____. The patient presents as a sexually immature female, with infertile ("streak" ovaries), short stature, a wide, webbed neck, a low hairline on the back of the neck, a broad, flat chest with widely separated nipples, scant pubic hair, and multiple pigmented skin lesions.

EXERCISE 22-16 PATHOLOGY AS A SECOND LANGUAGE

See Exercise 22-15 for key terms covered in this section.

LEARNING OBJECTIVE 9: Understand the indications for genetic screening, and the tests available.

EXERCISE 22-17

Complete the paragraph below.

Indications for genetic testing include the following: (1) mother _____ or older, parents who already have a child with a known genetic disease, other family history of genetic problems, or parents from ethnic group with increased incidence of a particular genetic disorder. Prenatal testing includes the noninvasive maternal (2) _____ which has low sensitivity and a 5% false positive rate. Needle aspiration of amniotic fluid, called (3) _____, can be performed to obtain fetal cells for analysis. A placental biopsy called (4) _____ can be taken earlier in pregnancy to obtain material for analysis of the DNA, and so on. (5) _____ is a faster, more targeted way to look for chromosomal abnormalities than traditional karyotyping.

EXERCISE 22-18 PATHOLOGY AS A SECOND LANGUAGE

See Exercise 22-17 for key terms covered in this section.

LEARNING OBJECTIVE 10: Describe the changes that take place after an infant's birth, including pulmonary, cardiovascular, hemoglobin production, immune system, renal function, and liver function (glucose metabolism and metabolism of bilirubin).

EXERCISE 22-19

Complete the paragraphs below.

The (1) _____ is the time from the 28th week of pregnancy to the seventh day after birth. The (2) _____ is the first month after birth. (3) _____ is the length of time the fetus has been in the womb. A (4) _____ pregnancy is a pregnancy that passes beyond the last day of the 37th week.

When an infant is born, it is a sudden and uniquely stressful change from intrauterine dependence on the mother to independent life. With its first breath, a newborn's lungs switch from being filled with (5) _____ to being filled with air. This process requires (6) _____, a slick, soapy fluid that decreases surface tension of intra-alveolar fluid and helps keep the alveoli open. (7) _____ begin secreting surfactant as the fetal lungs mature rapidly between 28 and 32 weeks. Cardiovascular changes are perhaps the most dramatic. In the fetus, intrapulmonary pressure is high and blood is shunted around the lungs. With the first breath, the lungs fill with air, intrapulmonary pressure falls and blood immediately surges into the lungs. (8) _____ can occur in premature infants and is a severe inflammatory condition of the gastrointestinal tract. Newborns lose passive transfer of maternal (9) _____ across the placenta, but don't have a fully developed immune system; therefore, they are prone to infections. Kidneys do not fully develop until age two and have limited capacity to excrete metabolic acids and water. The neonate must generate its own glucose, and derives it initially from glycogen storage in the neonatal liver although this process is slow. Failure to adequately convert hepatic glycogen stores to glucose can cause severe (10) _____. All neonates develop high blood bilirubin, but prematurity or illness may exaggerate the phenomenon and cause (11) _____. If left untreated, a syndrome of severe brain damage due to accumulation of unconjugated bilirubin in the brain can occur called (12) _____. (13) _____ is an abnormal or difficult childbirth and occurs more often in larger infants. (14) _____ is a broad clinical term for a nonprogressive syndrome of motor impairment due to brain damage.

Remember This! The placenta functions as the fetus's lungs, digestive system, and kidneys.

EXERCISE 22-20   PATHOLOGY AS A SECOND LANGUAGE

Test your vocabulary by indicating if each statement below is true or false. If it is false, provide the correct word for the italicized term that will make the statement true.

_____ 1. *Post-term* infants are those born before the end of the 37th week and are also called "preterm."

_____

_____ 2. *Premature* infants are those born after 42 weeks.

_____

_____ 3. *Normal birth weight* is approximately 3,500 grams.

_____

_____ 4. *Low birth weight* is less than 2,500 grams.

_____

_____ 5. *Virginia score* is a numerical assessment of an infant's condition immediately after birth.

_____

LEARNING OBJECTIVE 11: Discuss the problems that arise in premature infants.

EXERCISE 22-21

Complete the paragraph below.

Although the exact cause of prematurity is unknown, premature infants are at increased risk for disease and mortality. (1) _____ is defined as birth before the first day of the 37th week of gestation. If severely premature, the newborn may develop (2) _____, which is a condition that occurs almost solely in premature infants stemming from a lack of surfactant in immature infant lungs of the newborn. This is also called (3) _____. Patients are often treated with (4) _____; however, if the oxygen level is too high, it may damage the developing neonatal retina, leading to (5) _____.

EXERCISE 22-22 PATHOLOGY AS A SECOND LANGUAGE

Test your vocabulary by writing the appropriate term in each blank from the list below.
Appropriate for gestational age (AGA)
Large for gestational age (LGA)
Small for gestational age (SGA)

1. _____ infants are those whose birth weight is below the 10th percentile for gestational age.

2. _____ infants are those weighing as much as expected at any given gestational age.

3. _____ infants are those whose birth weight is above the 90th percentile for gestational age.

LEARNING OBJECTIVE 12: Know the infectious processes that present in the perinatal/neonatal period.

EXERCISE 22-23

Complete the paragraph below.

Infections in the (1) _____ and neonatal period differ from infections in infants and children because the newborn immune system is less mature, and there is a different source of infection (placental, vaginal) with different infecting microbes and behavior of the disease. (2) _____ may be a serious fetal threat if a pregnant woman suffers an outbreak of genital herpes at the time of delivery and may require a Caesarean section. Neonatal herpes infection may be confined to skin, eyes, or mouth, but may disseminate to cause fatal encephalitis, hepatitis, and pneumonia. (3) _____ is a purulent inflammatory reaction of the conjunctiva most often caused by *Chlamydia trachomatis*, gonorrhea, or another sexually transmitted infection acquired from the mother. (4) _____ is systemic infection spread by the bloodstream. Symptoms are varied and include lethargy, jaundice, failure to suckle, apnea, bradycardia, temperature instability, respiratory distress, vomiting, and diarrhea, with positive blood culture. Severe or prolonged hyperbilirubinemia associated with other causes is often termed (5) _____ until a definitive cause can be identified. Actual obstruction of bile flow usually results from bile duct obstruction due to failed development or inflammatory scarring as in (6) _____ and requires surgical intervention. Neonatal hepatitis is often found to be caused by (7) _____, which is vertically transmitted from mother to infants during vaginal birth by their infected mothers. This can be prevented by vaccination programs in adults.

EXERCISE 22-24 PATHOLOGY AS A SECOND LANGUAGE

See Exercise 22-23 for key terms covered in this section.

LEARNING OBJECTIVE 13: Be able to recognize the presentation of the following diseases:

a. *RSV, bronchiolitis, whooping cough, croup, diphtheria, epiglottitis, mono*
b. *Acute otitis media*
c. *Chickenpox*
d. *Measles, mumps, rubella*
e. *HIV/AIDS*

EXERCISE 22-25

Complete the paragraph below.

Childhood infections are the most common causes of childhood illness. Most infections are (1) _____ with many of them causing acute upper respiratory illnesses featuring fever, cough, and rhinorrhea. Viral illnesses can be mild or (2) _____. Diagnosis is usually by clinical observation and does not require use of laboratory tests or imaging. In most of these diseases, the illness is short, the prognosis is good, and treatment is symptomatic and supportive. Commonly, after viral upper respiratory infection, one of the most common bacterial diseases of children that can develop is (3) _____. It is usually due to *Streptococcus pneumoniae* and *Haemophilus influenzae*. Some bacterial infections can be fatal. (4) _____ is a contagious bacterial disease caused by *Bordetella pertussis* and consists of intense inflammation in the larynx, trachea, and bronchi that can cause fatal asphyxia in infants; it causes severe spasms of coughing and the sharp, inspiratory barking sound (stridor, or whoop). (5) _____ is caused by a gram-positive bacillus, *Corynebacterium diphtheriae*, which produces a pharyngitis and laryngitis associated with a thick, obstructive gray inflammatory membrane. Acute bacterial (6) _____ is a disease of school-aged children caused by *H. influenzae* and marked by hoarseness, painful swallowing, and drooling.

Mnemonic
Symptoms of Croup = 3 Ss
Stridor
Subglottic swelling
Seal-bark cough

EXERCISE 22-26 PATHOLOGY AS A SECOND LANGUAGE

Test your vocabulary by indicating if each statement below is true or false. If it is false, provide the correct word for the italicized term that will make the statement true.

_____ 1. *Ebola virus* is a common virus that causes a syndrome of acute bronchitis, bronchiolitis, and bronchopneumonia in children.

_____

_____ 2. *Bronchiolitis* is a winter epidemic syndrome of low-grade fever, wheezing respiration, and shortness of breath.

_____

_____ 3. *Croup* is an acute inflammatory viral disease of the upper airway of children.

_____

_____ 4. *Measles*, also called *rubeola*, is a highly contagious respiratory virus best known for the skin rash it produces and similar lesions of the oral mucosa.

_____

_____ 5. *Mumps* is caused by the rubella virus and presents as sore throat, skin rash, and enlarged lymph nodes.

_____

_____ 6. The *rubella* virus causes acute inflammation of the parotid salivary gland, and occasionally causes inflammation of the testes (orchitis), pancreatitis, or encephalitis.

_____

_____ 7. *Infectious mononucleosis* is caused by the *varicella-zoster* virus, which causes an acute febrile illness characterized by vesicular skin eruptions.

_____

_____ 8. *Chickenpox* is a self-limited, mild syndrome of fever, sore throat, listlessness, lymphocytosis, and splenomegaly, caused by the Epstein-Barr virus.

_____

_____ 9. *HIV/AIDS* in infants is generally transmitted from the mother and follows a similar clinical course, although the treatment regime differs slightly.

_____

LEARNING OBJECTIVE 14: Be able to name the risk factors associated with SIDS.

EXERCISE 22-27

Complete the paragraph below.

(1) _____ is the abrupt and unexpected death of an infant between two weeks and one year of age in which an autopsy fails to reveal the cause of death. The risk factors include: age generally under six months, sleep in the prone position, prematurity or low birth weight, male sex, maternal age < 20 years, (2) _____, maternal drug abuse, African American and American Indian ethnicity, overly hot or cold sleeping conditions, bulky and soft bedding and blankets, and sibling of SIDS victims. Pathologic findings at autopsy are minimal. The American Academy of Pediatrics recommends infants be placed in a (3) _____ for sleep (on the back), that care be taken to avoid overheating, and that infants not sleep in the same bed as their parents.

EXERCISE 22-28 PATHOLOGY AS A SECOND LANGUAGE

See Exercise 22-27 for key terms covered in this section.

LEARNING OBJECTIVE 15: Answer the following questions: What are the differences between choristoma, hamartoma, and teratoma? What are the most common tumors, by tissue, in children?

EXERCISE 22-29

Complete the paragraph below.

A (1) _____ is a common benign nodule of normal tissue in an abnormal location; it is also called an

(2) _____. A (3) _____ is a benign growth composed of tissue elements normally found at that site that are growing in a disorganized mass. A (4) _____ is a neoplastic growth of tissue not normally found at the site.

EXERCISE 22-30   PATHOLOGY AS A SECOND LANGUAGE

Test your vocabulary by writing the appropriate term in each blank from the list below.

Neuroblastoma   Wilms' tumor

Retinoblastoma   Sacrococcygeal teratoma

1. _____ is a benign teratomatous mass found at the base of the spine in newborns.

2. _____ is a malignancy of primitive neural cells that is unique to children.

3. _____ is a malignancy of the kidney that arises from primitive embryologic renal cells.

4. _____ is a rare ophthalmic malignant tumor of primitive retinal neurons due to a defect in the Rb gene.

Decisions Decisions

DECISION TREE 22.1: GENETIC DISEASE

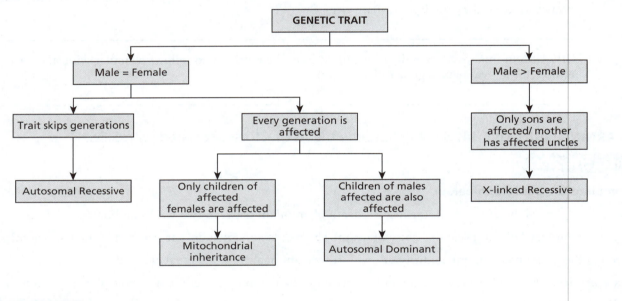

Test Yourself

I. MULTIPLE CHOICE

1. A seven-year-old Caucasian female is brought to the pediatrician's office by her father for evaluation of an itchy blister-like rash, fatigue, and fever. A physical exam demonstrates multiple vesicles, but is otherwise unremarkable. A positive Tzanck smear would support a diagnosis of which of the following? [LEARNING OBJECTIVE 13]
   A. Varicella zoster
   B. Epstein Barr
   C. Herpes virus
   D. Rubeola virus

2. Which of the following is a complication of dystocia? [LEARNING OBJECTIVE 10]
   A. Fetal death
   B. Paralysis of an upper extremity
   C. Cerebral palsy
   D. All of the above

3. A 42-year-old G3P2 presents at the maternal fetal medicine clinic for establishment of care. Her last menstrual period was eight weeks ago, and a home pregnancy test was positive. She is concerned about the possibility of Down syndrome given her age, and asks when she can undergo an amniocentesis. When is the earliest possible date she can undergo this procedure? [LEARNING OBJECTIVE 9]
   A. In 2 weeks (10 weeks from her LMP)
   B. In 7 weeks (15 weeks from her LMP)
   C. Now (at 8 weeks)
   D. In 4 weeks (12 weeks from her LMP)

4. Spina bifida is the result of which of the following defects in embryogenesis? [LEARNING OBJECTIVE 2]
   A. Failure of an embryologic space to close properly
   B. Failure of embryologic tissue to divide

C. Failure of an embryologic structure to disappear normally

D. Failure of tissue or organ to differentiate or grow (agenesis)

5. An 18-year-old African American male is seen at the clinic for failure to undergo puberty. He is tall, with long arms and legs, a femalelike hip shape, and gynecomastia. His condition is the result of fertilization by normal sperm bearing a Y chromosome of which of the following female gametes? [LEARNING OBJECTIVE 8]

A. 22, O
B. 23, XX
C. 24, XX
D. 23, XO

6. A six-year-old boy is brought to the emergency room by his mother. She is concerned by his difficulty in breathing and swallowing. She denies significant past medical history and sick contacts, and reports that he has not received any vaccinations, as she and her husband believe they cause autism. On exam, the child appears acutely ill; his head is held forward, and he breathes in rapid shallow breaths. He is also notably drooling. Concerned, you prepare an intubation kit prior to examining his airway. What infectious etiology is the most likely explanation for the patient's symptoms? [LEARNING OBJECTIVE 13]

A. Respiratory syncytial virus
B. Parainfluenza
C. Haemophilus influenza
D. Bordetella pertussis

7. While shadowing at a genetic counseling clinic, you have the opportunity to sit in on a family-planning session. The 33-year-old nulligravida female is concerned that she might pass on a heart arrhythmia that affects both her and her two siblings (a sister and a brother) to her future children. She mentions that both of her sister's children are affected, but none of her brother's children have symptoms. What is the inheritance pattern of this arrhythmia, and the likelihood that she will pass it on to future children? (Hint: Use the Decision Tree) [LEARNING OBJECTIVE 6]

A. Autosomal recessive inheritance, 25%
B. Mitochondrial inheritance, 100%
C. Autosomal dominant, 50%
D. X-linked recessive, 100% for male and 50% for female

8. The mother of an infant born with severe brain, bone, dental, and ophthalmic problems likely has which of the following stages of syphilis? [LEARNING OBJECTIVE 3]

A. Primary syphilis
B. Latent syphilis
C. Tertiary syphilis
D. All of the above

9. A 23-year-old G1P0 female is rushed to the operating room for a stat C-section. After the incision through the uterus is completed, the umbilical cord is clamped and the infant is handed to the waiting pediatrician. The infant is actively moving, and completely pink. He grimaces with insertion of the nasal catheter. His vital signs are also concerning: his heart rate is low (< 100) and his respiratory effort is slow. Based on these physical findings, what is his Apgar score? [LEARNING OBJECTIVE 10]

A. 5
B. 9
C. 6
D. 7

10. A three-year-old boy is brought to the pediatrician's office by his mother, who is concerned by a cough he has developed over the last several days. As if on cue, the boy emits a hoarse, brassy, barking cough, which he quickly follows with a crowing sound on inspiration. She reports he has received all his vaccinations. You prescribe steroids and careful monitoring of his breathing. A negative throat culture would confirm your diagnosis of which of the following infectious etiologies? [LEARNING OBJECTIVE 13]

A. Haemophilus influenza
B. Respiratory syncytial virus
C. Parainfluenza
D. Bordetella pertussis

11. Which of the following is an X-linked recessive disease? [LEARNING OBJECTIVE 5]

A. Classic hemophilia
B. Duchenne muscular dystrophy
C. Red–green colorblindness
D. All of the above

12. A female germ cell in the resting state has which of the following karyotypes? [LEARNING OBJECTIVE 4]

A. 23X
B. 23Y
C. 46XX
D. 46XY

II. TRUE OR FALSE

13. _____ Cytogenetic disorders are not inheritable. [LEARNING OBJECTIVE 4]

14. _____ Although ionizing radiation can damage a fetus in utero, it poses no threat to a woman's future offspring. [LEARNING OBJECTIVE 3]

15. _____ Genetic susceptibility equates to only an approximate 5–10% increase in risk for multifactorial diseases. [LEARNING OBJECTIVE 7]

16. _____ A fetal heart rate can be detected as early as week 4, after the heart forms. [LEARNING OBJECTIVE 1]

17. _____ Approximately 50% of spontaneous first trimester abortions have chromosome abnormalities. [LEARNING OBJECTIVE 8]

18. _____ There is no such thing as too much vitamin A during pregnancy, as it is necessary for the proper formation of the heart, limbs, eyes, and ears, and deficiency can lead to congenital malformations and premature birth. [LEARNING OBJECTIVE 3]

19. _____ The origin (whether from the mother or father) of a gene makes no difference in its expression. [LEARNING OBJECTIVE 6]

20. _____ Insertion errors cause more than a single amino acid change; they are a chain reaction changing everything that comes after the insertion site. [LEARNING OBJECTIVE 4]

21. _____ Trophoblast cells develop into the fetus and amniotic sac. [LEARNING OBJECTIVE 1]

22. _____ Most humans carry about six to eight defective genes. [LEARNING OBJECTIVE 5]

III. MATCHING

23. Match the following examples with their proper classification; answers may be used more than once, and each may have more than one answer. [LEARNING OBJECTIVE 15]

    i. Choristoma
    ii. Teratoma
    iii. Hamartoma
    iv. Benign neoplasia
    v. Malignant neoplasia

A. Hemangiomas
B. Pancreas found in the stomach wall
C. Nonossifying fibroma
D. Salivary gland found within (inside) the mandible (jaw bone)
E. Disorganized bile ducts in the liver
F. Neuroblastoma
G. Disorganized bronchial cartilage, epithelium, blood vessels, and lymphoid tissue in the lung
H. Ovarian mass with teeth, hair, and skin

IV. SHORT ANSWER

24. What precautions can be taken to minimize the risk of SIDS? [LEARNING OBJECTIVE 14]

_____

_____

_____

25. At birth, an infant is noted to have an internally rotated left foot (also known as a clubfoot). What pregnancy factors might have contributed to the development of this deformation? [LEARNING OBJECTIVE 2]

_____

_____

_____

26. A 17-year-old G1P0 female with a past medical history significant for HSV1 infection is brought to the ER in labor. A quick physical exam reveals multiple genital vesicles. You ask for an OR to be readied. What concerns prompted this request? [LEARNING OBJECTIVE 12]

_____

_____

_____

27. What changes are responsible for the alteration in blood circulation at birth? [LEARNING OBJECTIVE 10]

_____

_____

_____

28. What long-term complications are associated with Down syndrome? [LEARNING OBJECTIVE 8]

_____

_____

_____

29. Cystic fibrosis is a disease with a wide spectrum of deficiencies that can all be traced back to a single genetic defect. What is this defect and how does it cause the disease's manifestations? [LEARNING OBJECTIVE 5]

   _____

   _____

   _____

30. What are the contributing factors/causes of premature birth? [LEARNING OBJECTIVE 11]

   _____

   _____

   _____

CHAPTER

23

Disorders of Daily Life

The Big Picture

The body can be exposed to physical trauma, thermal changes, and chemical exposures including drugs and toxins, and nutrient deficiencies. Although these cause a great number of injuries and death, the most important public health problem may indeed be overnutrition with macronutrients, especially fats, which lead to the metabolic syndrome and all of its consequences.

Oh No! Not Another Learning Experience

LEARNING OBJECTIVE 1: Name several of the most common causes of death in the United States, and discuss the environmental aspects.

EXERCISE 23-1

Review Figure 23.1 in *The Nature of Disease*, then complete the paragraphs below.

The major causes of death in the United States are (1) _____ and (2) _____. These are followed by (3) _____, chronic lung disease, and accidents.

In addition to accidents, physical trauma is often due to (4) _____ or homicide (included in "Other"). (5) _____ is defined as any injury to the body caused by sudden violence or accident. (6) _____ occurs when there is not an open wound.

A (7) _____ is a blunt force injury that results in local hemorrhage in any tissue. In contrast, sharp objects or other types of force may cause open wounds called (8) _____.

EXERCISE 23-2   PATHOLOGY AS A SECOND LANGUAGE

See Exercise 23-1 for key terms contained in this section.

LEARNING OBJECTIVE 2: Distinguish between the grades and types of injury that occur with burns (including electrical) and cold and heat exposure; describe the potential complications of each.

EXERCISE 23-3

Review Figures 23.3 in *The Nature of Disease*, then complete the paragraph below.

Injury can occur with too much or too little heat. First-degree frostbite involves freezing of the superficial skin and is also called (1) _____, which acts like a burn. In contrast, (2) _____ is cold injury to dermis or deeper tissues that can lead to swelling, blistering, and gangrene. (3) _____ is exceptionally low body temperature that slows body functions, causes confusion, and can lead to loss of consciousness and death. (4) _____ are spasms of voluntary muscle caused by electrolyte loss. (5) _____ is a more serious condition and is characterized by profuse sweating, sudden weakness, and disorientation or fainting owing to the inability of the cardiovascular system to compensate for water loss. This leads to (6) _____, which is hyperthermia (> 104°F) that causes multiple organ dysfunction, including mental dysfunction. (7) _____ is a rare autosomal dominant genetic condition in which certain anesthetics and anesthesia-related drugs induce hyperthermia by causing skeletal muscles to burn energy at an extraordinarily high rate; it is treated with dantrolene. (8) _____ are caused not only by production of heat, but also by disruption of electrical signals in the body (heart, nerves, muscles, etc.). Types of burns are discussed next.

EXERCISE 23-4

Complete the tables below.

Types of Burns		
(1) _____	Dermal hyperemia, absence of necrosis.	Ex. Sunburn
Second Degree	Blisters, epidermal and superficial dermal necrosis. Heals without (2) _____.	Ex. Iron/ curling iron burn
Third Degree	Full thickness necrosis of epidermis and (3) _____, with sparing of deep skin appendages. Scars with healing.	Ex. Burns sustained in house fire
Cold Exposure		
(4) _____: occurs in cold conditions.	Firm white patches on face, ears, fingers, or toes with peeling and blistering on rewarming.	
(5) _____: occurs in subfreezing conditions.	Swollen, red, painful blisters on rewarming. Ice crystals in cells cause necrosis. Deep blisters may result in gangrene.	
(6) _____: body temp < 90°F.	Lethargy, clumsiness, confusion, hallucinations, loss of consciousness, cardiac arrhythmia.	
Heat Exposure		
(7) _____	Voluntary muscle spasms. May occur after exercise.	Treatment: • Fluid replacement • Rest • Relief from environment
(8) _____: Temp near 102°F.	Profuse sweating, sudden weakness, disorientation, or fainting.	
(9) _____: > 104°F.	Thermoregulation fails, sweating stops, flushed skin. **Complications:** hypotension, shock, cardiac arrhythmias/ arrest, seizures, coma, DIC, rhabdomyolysis-> renal failure due to released myoglobin.	
Death	Possible with temp > 106°F.	

EXERCISE 23-5   PATHOLOGY AS A SECOND LANGUAGE

See Exercises 23-3 and 23-4 for key terms contained in this section.

LEARNING OBJECTIVE 3: Discuss the manifestation of, and the variables that influence, radiation injury.

EXERCISE 23-6

Complete the paragraph below.

The effect of radiation injury is determined by (1) _____, or area of the body exposed; (2) _____, as DNA is vulnerable to ionization during cell division; and (3) _____, because radiation creates reactive oxygen species (ROS) which further damage DNA. In addition, the type of radiation and the cumulative dose of radiation are critical. (4) _____ includes visible light, radio waves, and radar, none of which packs enough punch to cause ionization of tissue molecules. (5) _____ includes ultraviolet light, X-rays, and gamma rays. (6) _____ follows intense exposure and is characterized by severe infections, owing to bone marrow and immune system failure, and by severe diarrhea and intestinal infections due to damage to the intestinal mucosa. Chronic exposure leads to (7) _____ and other damage, including excess wrinkling of the skin.

EXERCISE 23-7 PATHOLOGY AS A SECOND LANGUAGE

See Exercise 23-6 for key terms contained in this section.

LEARNING OBJECTIVE 4: Using examples from the text, briefly discuss the clinical presentations and findings of occupational pollutant, toxin, and drug exposure; include asbestos, silica, ozone, second hand smoke, carbon monoxide, organophosphate, lead, mercury, arsenic, cadmium, and iron.

EXERCISE 23-8

Review Table 23.1 in *The Nature of Disease*, then complete the paragraphs below.

A (1) _____ is any substance that is injurious to health or dangerous to life. (2) _____ is mostly physical trauma (90%) but also develops because of long-term exposure to toxins in the job. A (3) _____ is a substance in air or water that can injure those exposed to it.

Smoking is arguably the most important factor that decreases health. (4) _____ is a mixture of two forms of smoke from burning tobacco products, sidestream smoke and (5) _____, which includes carbon monoxide and many other chemical toxins.

EXERCISE 23-9

Complete the table below.

Toxin	Presentation	Findings	
Asbestos	Postobstructive pneumonia, lung mass	Lung cancer, occupational exposure	
Silica	Shortness of breath	Chronic pulmonary disease, lung cancer, occupational exposure	
Ozone	Pollutants converted to ground level ozone, aggravates pre-existing asthma or emphysema	None	
Carbon monoxide (CO)	(1) _____ skin, loss of consciousness, death	CO exposure history, carboxyhemoglobin	
(2) _____	Sweating, blurred vision, constricted pupils, salivation, bronchospasm, muscle twitching (fasciculation), paralysis, and respiratory arrest	Insecticide exposure	
(3) _____	Anemia, kidney disease, abdominal cramps, headache, memory loss, numbness and pain in the arms or legs, and distinctive bone deposits visible by X-ray imaging, or if long term, neurologic symptoms	Paint exposure	
(4) _____	Coma, renal failure, tremors, bizarre behavior, or death, if chronic then can be neurotoxic to developing fetus	Ingestion of fish (swordfish, shark, or other large carnivorous species), occupational (e.g., mad hatter)	
(5) _____	Headaches, confusion, and diarrhea, if chronic, increases risk of cancer	Intentional poisoning, chronic contamination of groundwater (SE Asia)	
(6) _____	Lung and kidney disease	Batteries, landfill contamination of groundwater	
(7) _____	Hemorrhagic gastroenteritis, metabolic acidosis, cardiovascular collapse or coma, death	Overdose of vitamins or supplements containing this metal	

EXERCISE 23-10   PATHOLOGY AS A SECOND LANGUAGE

See Exercises 23-8 and 23-9 for key terms contained in this section.

LEARNING OBJECTIVE 5: Discuss the risks associated with the following therapeutic agents: hormone replacement therapy, oral contraceptives, anabolic steroids, aspirin, and acetaminophen.

EXERCISE 23-11

Complete the paragraph below.

Utilization of therapeutic agents should not be taken lightly, as there are usually significant side effects and toxicities. (1) _____ consists of long-term estrogen and progesterone administration and can increase risk of breast cancer, thromboembolism, and stroke. (2) _____ are safe and effective overall, but increase risk of heart disease, venous thrombosis, and pulmonary thromboembolism, and lead to development of hepatic adenomas, which can cause life-threatening bleeds. (3) _____ are synthetic versions of testosterone used to improve athletic performance, but cause testicular atrophy, gynecomastia, acne, stunted growth in adolescents, hirsutism, abnormal menstruation, and psychological problems. (4) _____ (an antipyretic) is the most widely used medicine in the world and increases bleeding tendency. Acute toxicity stimulates respiration and causes respiratory alkalosis, which is followed by (5) _____, tinnitus, and death. Furthermore, aspirin use in children for treatment of fever associated with a viral syndrome can sometimes cause (6) _____. Chronic aspirin toxicity is called (7) _____ and leads to gastrointestinal problems (including irritation and ulceration of the stomach), dizziness, tinnitus, deafness, and mental problems. (8) _____ is one of the most widely used drugs and is directly toxic to the liver, accounting for fully half of all cases of acute liver failure. Overdose must be quickly treated.

EXERCISE 23-12 PATHOLOGY AS A SECOND LANGUAGE

See Exercise 23-11 for key terms contained in this section.

LEARNING OBJECTIVE 6: Name several diseases other than lung cancer that are related to cigarette smoking.

EXERCISE 23-13

Review Figures 23.7 in *The Nature of Disease*, then complete the paragraph below.

Smoking is arguably the most deleterious single behavior for one's health. Therefore, when taking a patient history, one of the most important facts to obtain is whether or not a patient has smoked, and if so, how much for how long. A useful standard is (1) _____, or the number of packs per day multiplied by the number of years smoking. Smoking is an addictive behavior largely due to (2) _____, the stimulant that is present in tobacco. Smoking causes a wide range of negative health consequences in addition to (3) _____. These include other cancers of the head and neck (lips, tongue, oral cavity, larynx), esophagus, kidney, pancreas, bladder, and (4) _____. Smoking causes chronic obstructive pulmonary disease, including chronic bronchitis and (5) _____. Smoking accelerates atherosclerotic disease of the coronary arteries and increases risk for (6) _____. It causes premature aging of the skin. In fetuses, it causes decreased birth weight, prematurity, and increased (7) _____.

EXERCISE 23-14 PATHOLOGY AS A SECOND LANGUAGE

See Exercise 23-13 for key terms contained in this section.

> **Remember This!** Stopping smoking is the single, most important action the average person can take to improve health and prolong life.

LEARNING OBJECTIVE 7: Name several conditions associated with alcohol abuse.

EXERCISE 23-15

Review Figure 23.9 in *The Nature of Disease*, then complete the paragraphs below.

(1) _____ is the active ingredient in alcoholic drinks and has sedating properties. In the United States, the legal definition of drunkenness is blood alcohol content of 80 mg/dL (0.08%) or higher. (2) _____ causes 75,000 deaths per year in the United States. (3) _____ is a chronic disease in which people fail to stop drinking even though their drinking causes neglect of important family and work obligations. (4) _____ can be assessed using a short questionnaire (see below). Alcohol affects every organ system, with the (5) _____ being most severely affected (fatty liver, cirrhosis, liver cancer).

   Alcohol abuse causes acute and chronic (6) _____, gastrointestinal (GI) bleeds, and increases risk of GI cancers. It causes dilated cardiomyopathy and increased risk of cardiovascular disease. Abuse affects the brain and the peripheral nervous system, and can result in cerebellar ataxia (stumbling gait), peripheral neuropathy, (7) _____ (severe neurologic dysfunction that may proceed to coma and death), or (8) _____ (impaired recent memory, confusion, and rambling speech). Unfortunately, alcohol abuse during pregnancy also causes (9) _____, which is the most common preventable cause of mental retardation.

EXERCISE 23-16 PATHOLOGY AS A SECOND LANGUAGE

See Exercise 23-15 for key terms contained in this section.

Mnemonic

Are you an alcoholic? = **CAGE** *questionnaire*
Have you ever felt a need to **C**ut down on drinking?
Have people **A**nnoyed you by complaining about your drinking?
Have you ever felt **G**uilty about drinking?
Have you ever felt the need to have a drink first think in the morning (an **E**ye opener) to steady your nerves or to get rid of a hangover?

LEARNING OBJECTIVE 8: List the complications of drug abuse, and explain why intravenous use is especially risky.

EXERCISE 23-17

Complete the paragraph below.

(1) _____ refers to abuse of any substance other than alcohol and nicotine. Drug abuse is associated with suicide, homicide, assaults, motor vehicle injury, HIV infection, pneumonia, mental illness, hepatitis, and sudden death from cardiac disease or coma. (2) _____ have a sedative or calming effect and include *ethanol*, *barbiturates*, and *benzodiazepines*. (3) _____ enhance the sense of awareness and produce euphoria. The other major drug categories include (4) _____, which are opioids that are derived from the opium poppy plant or similar synthetic drugs that bind opioid receptors, and (5) _____, which are drugs that distort reality or produce altered

sensory experiences. Intravenous (IV) drug use is especially dangerous because it is associated with the constant threat of (6) _____, HIV/AIDS, staphylococcal abscesses, bacterial endocarditis, and other infections.

EXERCISE 23-18

Complete the table below.

Category	Effect	Example
(1) _____	Sedative or calming effect, decreases inhibitions or, in sufficient doses, causes coma or death	*Ethanol*: most abused *Barbiturates*: relieve anxiety; abrupt withdrawal may cause seizures *Benzodiazepines*
(2) _____	Enhances sense of awareness and awakeness, euphoria	*Cocaine*: Increases peripheral catecholamines -> hypertension, cardiac arrhythmia, sudden cardiac death. May cause septal perforation, atherosclerosis, placental hypoperfusion (miscarriage, fetal growth retardation, hypoxia leading to brain damage) or congenital anomalies *Amphetamines*: overdose produces delirium, convulsions, cardiac arrhythmias, coma, and death
(3) _____	Derived from opium poppy plant or synthetic substances with similar properties	*Morphine* *Heroin*: sedative effect; painful, possibly fatal withdrawal (respiratory depression or cardiac arrhythmia) *Demerol*
(4) _____	Distorts reality or produces altered sensory experiences	*Marijuana*: gynecomastia and testicular atrophy; can relieve intraocular pressure associated with glaucoma and nausea associated with chemo *LSD, PCP* *Mescaline*

Remember This! Personal habits are the most important factor in the majority of U.S. deaths.

EXERCISE 23-19   PATHOLOGY AS A SECOND LANGUAGE

Test your vocabulary by writing the appropriate term in each blank from the list below.

Marijuana   Heroin   Cocaine   Amphetamine

1. _____ is a highly addictive stimulant drug that produces euphoria. It can cause hypertension, cardiac arrhythmias, seizures, and sudden cardiac death.

2. _____ is a stimulant that is sometimes abused by students for studying. It can cause convulsions, cardiac arrhythmias, coma, and death.

3. _____ is a highly addictive opioid that produces euphoria then sedation. It causes potentially fatal withdrawal symptoms.

4. _____ rarely causes hallucinations, but is classified as a hallucinogen. It is the most widely abused of all illegal drugs.

LEARNING OBJECTIVE 9: Explain the potential consequences of diets containing a calorie deficiency or excess, and be able to calculate body mass index.

EXERCISE 23-20

Review Figure 23.15 in *The Nature of Disease*, then complete the paragraph below.

The major health problem in the United States is not (1) _____, or insufficient dietary intake or intestinal absorption of protein or calories, but rather overnutrition. Ingesting too many calories increases body fat. One widely used way to estimate body fat is the (2) _____, a measure of the ratio of body weight to height as expressed by body weight in kilograms divided by the square of the height in meters. (3) _____ is excess body fat such that the BMI > 30. (4) _____ is defined as a constellation of findings, including abdominal obesity, abnormal glucose metabolism, abnormal plasma lipids (dyslipidemia), and hypertension. (5) _____ is a risk factor for type 2 diabetes, hypertension, coronary artery disease, gallstones, stroke, cancer (especially of the endometrium and breast), and pulmonary disease. Morbidly obese patients are even more vulnerable to health problems, including (6) _____, pulmonary hypertension, esophageal reflux, urinary incontinence, infertility, and osteoarthritis.

EXERCISE 23-21 PATHOLOGY AS A SECOND LANGUAGE

Test your vocabulary by indicating if each statement below is true or false. If it is false, provide the correct word for the italicized term that will make the statement true.

_____ 1. Undernutrition is clinically referred to as *protein-energy malnutrition (PEM)*.

_____

_____ 2. Deprivation of *both* protein and calories leads to *kwashiorkor*.

_____

_____ 3. If the diet contains some calories from carbohydrate but is very low in protein, the child develops *marasmus*.

_____

_____ 4. *Cachexia* is a variety of malnutrition that occurs as a complication of patients with certain types of advanced cancer or AIDS and may be due to cytokines.

_____

_____ 5. *Bulimia* is self-induced starvation and weight loss.

_____

_____ 6. *Anorexia nervosa* is binge overeating followed by purging using induced vomiting.

_____

_____ 7. *Fatty heart syndrome* is a condition in which heart muscle accumulates fat and loses contractile power.

_____

Remember This! One in every eight deaths in the United States is caused by an illness directly related to being overweight or obese.

LEARNING OBJECTIVE 10: Using examples from the text, discuss how the differences between fat-soluble and water-soluble vitamins are reflected in vitamin deficiency and toxicity.

EXERCISE 23-22

Complete the paragraph below.

(1) _____ are organic substances essential in minute amounts for every aspect of human physiology. Four vitamins are (2) _____; they are *vitamins* A, D, E, and K. The rest are (3) _____; they include vitamin C, the B vitamins, niacin and folate. With the exception of (4) _____, which is stored in the liver, deficiencies of water-soluble vitamins can develop after a few months of poor nutrition, whereas deficiencies of fat-soluble vitamins take more than a year to develop because of body fat stores. Fat-soluble vitamins are more likely to accumulate to excess and cause (5) _____, because of the lipophilic nature of tissues. By contrast, excess amounts of the water-soluble vitamins are quickly excreted in stool or urine, so toxicity is not typically a concern, but (6) _____ is more common. (7) _____ are elements such as chromium, copper, fluoride, iodine, iron, manganese, selenium, and zinc. They account for a tiny fraction of body weight but have an important role in metabolism.

EXERCISE 23-23   PATHOLOGY AS A SECOND LANGUAGE

See Exercise 23-22 for key terms contained in this section.

Decisions Decisions

DECISION TREE 23.1: TOXIC AGENTS/DRUGS

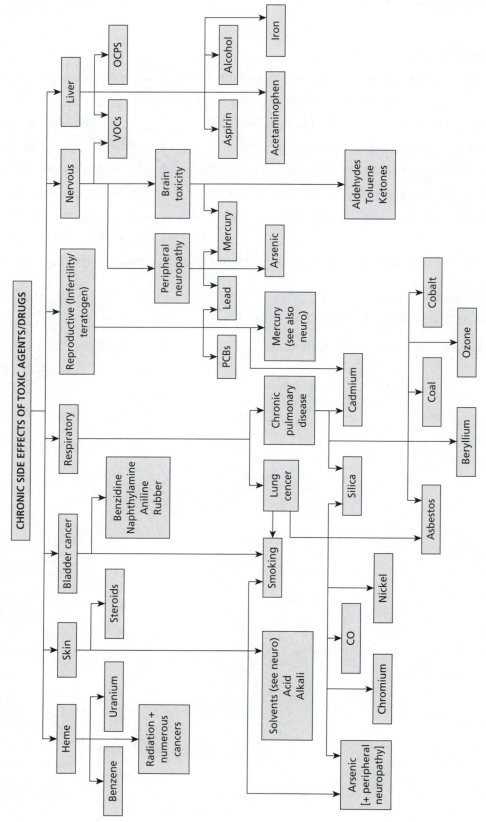

DECISION TREE 23.2: ACUTE TOXICITIES/DRUG EFFECTS

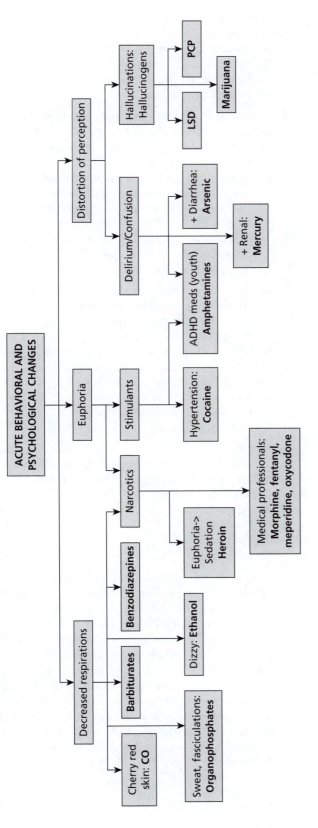

333

Test Yourself

I. MULTIPLE CHOICE

1. A 28-year-old Korean runner completes her marathon and promptly faints at the finish line after running a personal best. She is carried to the medic tent where a quick exam reveals profuse sweating and a body temperature of 101.5°F degrees. Fluids are given, and she is kept in the tent until her weakness and disorientation subside. What caused her symptoms? [LEARNING OBJECTIVE 2]
   A. Heat exhaustion
   B. Heat stroke
   C. Heat cramps
   D. Malignant hyperthermia

2. Acute radiation sickness is characterized by which of the following? [LEARNING OBJECTIVE 3]
   A. Severe infections
   B. Bone marrow fibrosis
   C. Thyroid cancer
   D. All of the above

3. A 31-year-old Hispanic male, post-op day 3 for appendicitis complicated by obstipation, complains of nausea, vomiting, and feeling flushed during your morning rounds. Concerned about the possibility of infection, you examine the patient, who is afebrile, and note that he is sweating profusely and his hands are shaking. He is also extremely anxious. Which of the following is the most likely explanation for his symptoms? [LEARNING OBJECTIVE 7]
   A. Alcohol withdrawal
   B. Cocaine intoxication
   C. Aspirin overdose
   D. Organophosphate poisoning

4. Which of the following statements concerning cocaine is correct? [LEARNING OBJECTIVE 8]
   A. Despite the severe consequences of long-term use, recreational use is considered harmless.
   B. Cocaine use can result in cardiac arrhythmias and sudden cardiac death.
   C. Cocaine use causes depletion of peripheral catecholamines.
   D. Cocaine use can result in hypotension, premature atherosclerosis, and stroke.

5. You pick your friend up at the airport following her cruise to the Caribbean. She warily maneuvers into your car, careful to keep her legs off the hot leather seat. You notice that her legs are red and swollen, without blisters, and that the skin appears dry. She ruefully tells you she forgot to pack sunscreen and didn't want to buy it from the ship's gift shop. What type of burn does she have? [LEARNING OBJECTIVE 1]
   A. Superficial burn
   B. Partial thickness burn
   C. Deep partial thickness burn
   D. Full thickness burn

6. Which of the following statements concerning anorexia nervosa is true? [LEARNING OBJECTIVE 9]
   A. Unlike bulimia, anorexia nervosa is not an obsessive-compulsive disorder.
   B. It results in decreased thyroid hormone, resulting in dry skin, diarrhea, and slowed heart rate.
   C. Endocrine effects are the most severe, and amenorrhea is nearly universal.
   D. It is defined by eating only a limited amount of certain foods and the absence of binging and purging behavior.

7. A four-year-old boy is featured on a documentary about children going hungry in a third-world country. His features are pathognomonic; he has sandy red hair, thin arms and legs, swollen feet, a potbelly, and splotches of white skin depigmentation. From which of the following diseases does he suffer? [LEARNING OBJECTIVE 9]
   A. Marasmus
   B. Lysosomal storage disorder
   C. Metabolic disease
   D. Kwashiorkor

8. Which of the following is a water-soluble vitamin for which deficiency is less of a concern? [LEARNING OBJECTIVE 10]
   A. Vitamin A
   B. Vitamin E
   C. Vitamin C
   D. Vitamin B_{12}

9. A 35-year-old Hispanic male suffering from erythromelalgia, a disease causing burning pain in the hands and feet, fell asleep with his feet in ice water, which he was using to numb the pain. When he woke up his toes were numb with patches of hard white tissue. He was taken to the ER where he was given pain relief, and his feet were gradually rewarmed, resulting in blister formation over the previously white lesions. His left big toe, however, remained devitalized and amputation was recommended. What did the immersion in ice water cause? [LEARNING OBJECTIVE 2]
   A. Frostbite
   B. Frostnip
   C. Hypothermia
   D. Freezer burn

II. TRUE OR FALSE

10. _____ Though cocaine is derived from a narcotic, it is a stimulant. [LEARNING OBJECTIVE 8]

11. _____ Nicotine, which is the most addictive of all substances present in cigarettes, is responsible for many of the pathologic effects. [LEARNING OBJECTIVE 6]

12. _____ Unlike toxins, which usually can be cleared from the body, radiation damage is cumulative over a lifetime, and each new dose adds to the burden. [LEARNING OBJECTIVE 3]

13. _____ Bladder cancer is associated with occupational exposure to aniline, a toxic chemical used in the manufacture of dyes, rubbers, and other products. [LEARNING OBJECTIVE 4]

14. _____ While smokers have a life filled with more disability and disease, their life expectancy is comparable to that of nonsmokers. [LEARNING OBJECTIVE 6]

15. _____ Most blunt injuries are caused by motor vehicle accidents. [LEARNING OBJECTIVE 1]

16. _____ Prescription narcotics are a particularly common problem among healthcare workers. [LEARNING OBJECTIVE 8]

III. MATCHING

17. Match the following symptoms/items with their associated toxic agent (Hint: Use Decision Trees 23-1 and 23-2) [LEARNING OBJECTIVE 4]

    i. Carbon monoxide
    ii. Iron
    iii. Volatile organic compounds
    iv. Petroleum products
    v. Organophosphates
    vi. Lead
    vii. Mercury
    viii. Arsenic
    ix. Cadmium

A. Found in batteries.
B. Acute symptoms include headaches, confusion, and diarrhea.
C. Especially harmful to patients suffering from respiratory disease.
D. Causes death due to hemorrhagic gastroenteritis, metabolic acidosis, cardiovascular collapse, or coma.
E. Can cause neurologic and behavioral problems and lower intelligence in children.
F. A component of secondhand smoke.
G. Important ingredient in solvents, glues, paint remover, and charcoal lighter fluid.
H. Increased intestinal absorption of this compound occurs in alcoholics.
I. By-product of gas space heaters, furnaces, stoves, and internal combustion engines.
J. Chronic exposure includes risk for liver toxicity, neuropathies, bone marrow suppression, and leukemia.
K. Absorbed through skin or lungs and have their effect by blocking nerve signal transmission at synapses.
L. Acute exposure can be associated with dizziness, unsteady gait, confusion, and nausea.
M. Acute toxicity causes sweating, blurred vision, constricted pupils, salivation, bronchospasm, fasciculation, paralysis, and respiratory arrest.
N. Found in pain and earthen cookware.
O. Can be caused by repeated blood transfusions.
P. Acute toxicity produces anemia, kidney disease, abdominal cramps, headache, memory loss, numbness and pain in the arms or legs, and distinctive bone deposits.
Q. Found in thermometers.
R. Acute exposure can cause tremors, coma, renal failure, and death.
S. Chronic exposure leads to lung and kidney disease.

IV. SHORT ANSWER

18. A 24-year-old body-builder visits his primary care physician for treatment of his acne. A complete physical demonstrates excess facial hair and gynecomastia. You caution him that use of anabolic steroids in building muscle can have a number of side effects. What are these side effects? [LEARNING OBJECTIVE 5]

_____

_____

_____

19. Central obesity is a risk factor for what diseases? [LEARNING OBJECTIVE 9]

_____

_____

_____

20. What is the prognosis of a gentleman who has burned the front of his torso and the front of one arm, and what complications is he at risk for? [LEARNING OBJECTIVE 2]

_____

_____

_____

21. What risks do oral contraceptives pose? [LEARNING OBJECTIVE 5]

_____

_____

_____

Aging, Stress, Exercise, and Pain

The Big Picture

Stress, aging, pain, and exercise are not specific to an organ system, but impact all systems. Although stress is an intimate part of the human experience, it is the chronicity of stress and the response to it that encourages or discourages disease. Stress can be helpful ("eustress"; e.g., exercise) or harmful ("distress"; e.g., death of a loved one). Therefore, stress is also closely related to pain and disease ("dis-ease").

Oh No! Not Another Learning Experience

LEARNING OBJECTIVE 1: Explain the role of telomere length, reactive oxygen species (free radicals), environmental toxins, and apoptosis in cellular aging.

EXERCISE 24-1

Complete the paragraph below.

Age-related deteriorations, known as (1) _____, are associated with reduced physiologic capacity, diminished adaptability to environmental changes, and increased disease (2) _____. These changes occur throughout life, but are most apparent in (3) _____, defined as anyone 65 years of age or older. The cellular basis of senescence is complex and involves changes in DNA.

EXERCISE 24-2   PATHOLOGY AS A SECOND LANGUAGE

Test your vocabulary by writing the appropriate term in each blank from the list below.

Antioxidants	Apoptosis	Telomere
Free radical	Reactive oxygen species (ROS)	

1. _____ are molecules containing an oxygen atom with an unpaired electron and can cause cumulative damage to DNA.

2. A _____ is any molecule or atom with an unpaired electron.

3. Cells control ROS production and action by the use of natural _____ (also called "scavengers").

4. A _____ is a region of DNA structure at the end of each chromosome that loses a few nitrogenous bases with every cell division and limits the number of times a cell can divide.

5. _____ is an orderly process of "natural suicide" of the cell.

LEARNING OBJECTIVE 2: Compare the form and function of different body systems between young and older adults.

EXERCISE 24-3

Review Figure 24.2 in *The Nature of Disease*, then complete the paragraph below.

The age-related decrease in quality of life and increase in death rate reflects changes in every body system. These changes are due to cellular (1) _____, decreased capacity to repair tissues, and increased (2) _____ to disease. Therefore, certain conditions are found much more commonly or exclusively in the elderly as compared to young adults.

EXERCISE 24-4

Complete the table below.

System	Effects of Aging	
Skin	Wrinkling, solar damage, skin cancer	
Musculoskeletal	Osteoarthritis, (1) _____, kyphosis, decreased muscle mass	
(2) _____	Decreased cardiac output, hypertension, atherosclerosis	
(3) _____	Decreased vital capacity, COPD	
(4) _____	Decreased appetite, decreased liver capacity, constipation, dry mouth, dehydration	
Kidneys/Urinary Tract	Decreased renal function due to nephro/glomerulosclerosis, urinary incontinence or obstruction	
(5) _____	Decreased libido, dyspareunia, erectile dysfunction	
Neurological	(6) _____, stroke	
Special Senses	Decreased taste, presbyopia, cataracts, glaucoma, macular degeneration, high pitch deafness, poor balance	

EXERCISE 24-5   PATHOLOGY AS A SECOND LANGUAGE

No key terms are covered in this section.

Remember This! DNA plays a critical role in senescence.

LEARNING OBJECTIVE 3: Describe the three phases of the stress response.

EXERCISE 24-6

Review Table 24.1 and Figure 24.3 in *The Nature of Disease*, then complete the paragraph below.

(1) _____ means "drawn tight" and refers to psychological, emotional, or physical strain or tension. Stress occurs in response to a (2) _____, which is anything that causes stress. Stressors can be (3) _____, such as exercise or being deprived of food or water, or emotional and psychological, such as beginning or ending a relationship or watching a scary movie. The stress response includes three phases that may not occur sequentially. The first response to a stressor is called the (4) _____, due to sympathetic nerves and hormones (epinephrine, ACTH) that increase heart rate, respiratory rate, and blood pressure to support the "fight or flight" reaction. The second phase of the stress response is called (5) _____, in which the stressor elicits less of an

alarm response, as often occurs in repeated exposure. If adaptation fails, or if the threat is ongoing and real, then the third phase occurs; it is called (6) _____. In this phase, cortisol secretion stays high for a period of time to help cope with the situation.

Remember This! Stress can be beneficial or detrimental.

EXERCISE 24-7   PATHOLOGY AS A SECOND LANGUAGE

See Exercise 24-6 for key terms covered in this section.

LEARNING OBJECTIVE 4: Compare and contrast the effects of cortisol and the sympathetic nervous system during the stress response.

EXERCISE 24-8

Complete the paragraph below.

The (1) _____ responds quickly to stress, while the endocrine reaction is slower but longer lasting. The sympathetic nerves stimulate (2) _____ release from the adrenal medulla, which causes the "fight or flight" reaction. In addition, (3) _____ is secreted by the brain and circulated to the adrenal cortex (endocrine mechanism), increasing blood levels of cortisol. This second, endocrine arm of the alarm phase is slower and devoted to a longer, sustainable reaction to (4) _____.

EXERCISE 24-9   PATHOLOGY AS A SECOND LANGUAGE

No key terms are covered in this section.

LEARNING OBJECTIVE 5: Describe the deleterious effects that occur with stress exhaustion.

EXERCISE 24-10

Complete the paragraph below.

The (1) _____ is beneficial for short-term physical stressors, such as food deprivation and predators; however, it can be deleterious for long-term (chronic) and/or psychological stressors. (2) _____ ensues, which is linked to deleterious changes including *chronic inflammation, accelerated cellular aging, increased oxidative stress,* (3) _____ (leading to infections), insulin resistance, and high blood sugar. In addition to physical effects, mental effects of chronic stress play a major role in interpersonal discord, (4) _____, child abuse, drug abuse, and other social ills. (5) _____ follows an acute psychological trauma and features a few days of terrifying recollection and avoidance of related stimuli. In contrast, (6) _____ is a longer-term syndrome occurring for > one month with symptoms of nightmares, flashbacks, and feelings of helplessness.

EXERCISE 24-11   PATHOLOGY AS A SECOND LANGUAGE

No key terms are covered in this section.

LEARNING OBJECTIVE 6: List some stress-related diseases and disorders affecting different body systems.

EXERCISE 24-12

Complete the table below.

Body System	Disease or Condition
(1) _____	Decreased mass of lymphoid tissue Infections Cancers
(2) _____	Ulcers (oral, gastric, etc.) Irritable bowel syndrome Diarrhea or constipation
(3) _____	Eczema Acne
(4) _____	Heart rhythm disturbances (arrhythmias) Coronary artery disease Hypertension Stroke
(5) _____	Asthma Hay fever, other allergies Frequent respiratory infections
(6) _____	Diabetes mellitus
(7) _____	Erectile dysfunction Infertility Amenorrhea (absence of menstrual periods)
(8) _____	Migraines Fibromyalgia, other pain disorders Multiple sclerosis Depression Insomnia or sleepiness Posttraumatic stress disorder Appetite changes Learning difficulties
(9) _____	Backache, muscle spasms Rheumatoid arthritis

EXERCISE 24-13   PATHOLOGY AS A SECOND LANGUAGE

No key terms are covered in this section.

LEARNING OBJECTIVE 7: Explain how exercise training improves the functioning of different body systems.

EXERCISE 24-14

Review Figure 24.4 in *The Nature of Disease*, then complete the paragraph below.

If you don't "use it," you will "lose it". Exercise is a form of beneficial stress or (1) _____. According to the U.S. Surgeon General, only 30 minutes per day of exercise on most days can greatly improve health. Regular exercise has many benefits including: (2) _____, with increased maximal cardiac output, oxygenation, endurance, decreased atherosclerosis, and decreased resting blood pressure; (3) _____, (4) _____, and (5) _____. These changes in body composition greatly reduce the risk of metabolic syndrome (including insulin resistance) and all of its complications. In addition, exercise provides (6) _____ and improved ability to cope with stress and help prevent stress exhaustion from psychological stressors.

EXERCISE 24-15 PATHOLOGY AS A SECOND LANGUAGE

No key terms are covered in this section.

Remember This! Exercise is good for health.

LEARNING OBJECTIVE 8: Identify the three main types of sports injuries, and be able to give examples of each.

EXERCISE 24-16

Complete the paragraph below.

For those who exercise regularly, especially those in (1) _____, injury is common and usually due to overuse, (2) _____, and acute soft tissue strains and sprains. (3) _____ is one of the most common and can involve bones, ligaments, tendons, cartilage, fascia, and bursae in any combination. Many of these are (4) _____ and (5) _____ including ligament tears, meniscal damage, and strains or sprains. The treatment of most athletic injuries is RICE (see below) and (6) _____.

Mnemonic
Treatment for Sprain/Strains = **RICE**
Rest
Ice
Compression
Elevation

EXERCISE 24-17   PATHOLOGY AS A SECOND LANGUAGE

Test your vocabulary by indicating if each statement below is true or false. If it is false, provide the correct word for the italicized term that will make the statement true.

_____ 1. *Rotator cuff injury* occurs at the shoulder joint with repeated overhead motion of throwing, swimming, weightlifting, and racket sports.

_____

_____ 2. *Golfer's elbow* is pain due to inflammation and microtears in the tendons of the extensor muscles of the forearm where they attach to the lateral epicondyle of the humerus.

_____

_____ 3. *Tennis elbow* is pain due to inflammation and microtears in the tendons of the flexor muscles of the forearm where they attach to the medial epicondyle of the humerus.

_____

_____ 4. *Piriformis syndrome* is compression of the sciatic nerve as it travels from the sacrum to the greater trochanter of the femur causing chronic ache, pain, or tingling of the buttock.

_____

_____ 5. *Metatarsal stress fractures* are also called shin splints and cause pain along or posterior to the tibia.

_____

_____ 6. *Achilles tendon injuries* are common in runners and include inflammation, tears, or complete rupture of this attachment of the calf muscles.

_____

_____ 7. *Medial tibial stress syndrome* are small fractures of the foot caused by repeated weight-bearing stress as in excessive running.

_____

LEARNING OBJECTIVE 9: Describe the effects of immobility of different body systems.

EXERCISE 24-18

Complete the paragraph below.

(1) _____ occurs as a result of other diseases, but it causes additional problems. Because flexor muscles are usually stronger than extensors, an unused and atrophied limb may flex and scar into an irreversible deformity called a (2) _____. (3) _____ are pressure sores that result from immobility and are made worse by other diseases and malnutrition. These can become infected and lead to sepsis and death. (4) _____ is thrombus formation in the venous circulatory system that can arise quickly, especially after surgery. To prevent this, patients are routinely treated with heparin (or another anticoagulant) and serial leg compression devices. When a person is immobile, (5) _____ increases, aggravating the shortness of breath associated with congestive heart failure; this is called (6) _____. Pulmonary secretions are retained, which in turn favors (7) _____ and atelectasis. Urinary stasis and retention in the bladder promote kidney stone formation and (8) _____. The main gastrointestinal problem is (9) _____ and is due to a number of factors including dehydration, lack of fiber, and use of opioid analgesics.

Remember This! Immobility is bad for health.

EXERCISE 24-19   PATHOLOGY AS A SECOND LANGUAGE

See Exercise 24-18 for key terms covered in this section.

LEARNING OBJECTIVE 10: Understand the subjective nature of pain and be able to describe types of pain.

EXERCISE 24-20

Complete the paragraph below.

Pain is an unpleasant subjective sensation. (1) _____ is the most common reason patients seek medical care; it has both sensory and emotional components. (2) _____ is pain accompanying acute tissue injury and disappears with healing and lasts for less than one month. It is usually associated with anxiety and hyperactivity of the (3) _____ including increased heart rate, blood pressure, and rapid breathing. (4) _____ is longer lasting and is usually associated with fatigue, depressed mood, loss of appetite, and other vegetative signs. When pain from tissue damage at a particular anatomic area appears to be coming from somewhere else, the pain is called (5) _____. Pain relief is called (6) _____. (7) _____ is loss of all sensation, either locally or generally, not just the sensation of pain.

EXERCISE 24-21   PATHOLOGY AS A SECOND LANGUAGE

Test your vocabulary by writing the appropriate term in each blank from the list below.

Non-steroidal anti-inflammatory drugs (NSAIDs)   Local anesthesia   Nociceptive pain
Complex regional pain syndrome   General anesthesia
Chronic pain   Neuropathic pain

1. _____ arises from injury and activation of tissue pain receptors.

2. _____ results from injury to or dysfunction of the nervous system.

3. _____ is pain that persists for > three months, or for more than one month after resolution of an acute injury, or pain that accompanies a chronic disease or unhealed injury.

4. _____ is a special variety of chronic neuropathic pain with two types.

5. _____ is a drug-induced, coma-like state in which there is a loss of all sensation owing to the effect of drugs on the brain.

6. _____ is drug-induced loss of all sensation in the distribution of a peripheral nerve or nerves.

7. The most widely used nonopioid analgesics are the _____.

Decisions Decisions

DECISION TREE 24.1: IMPACT OF STRESS

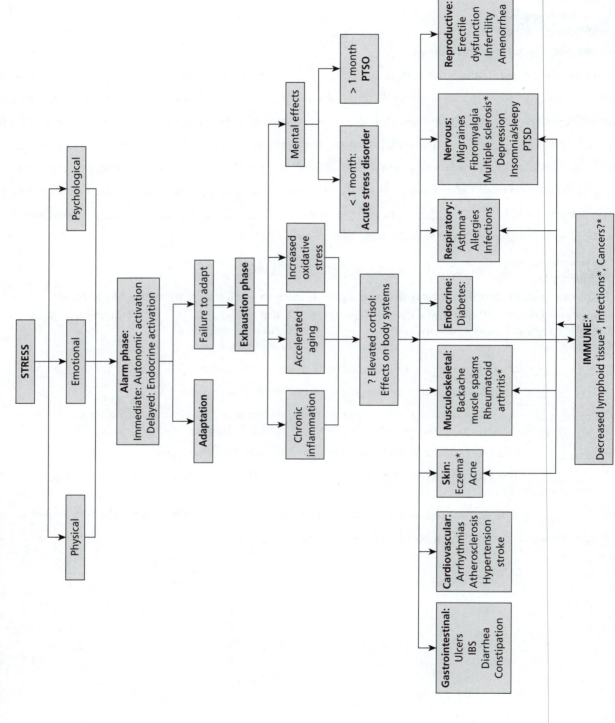

* denotes an immune component.

Test Yourself

I. MULTIPLE CHOICE

1. A 35-year-old Caucasian male visits his primary care physician complaining of pain in his left elbow. He is an avid athlete, playing tennis, golf, and baseball at least once per week with his colleagues. His physical exam is normal, except for pain centered over the medial epicondyle of his humerus. You prescribe NSAIDs for treatment of his pain, and recommend that he abstain from sports for the next month. What injury does he suffer from? [LEARNING OBJECTIVE 5]
   A. Rotator cuff injury
   B. Tennis elbow
   C. Golfer's elbow
   D. Piriformis syndrome

2. Which of the following are consequences of decreased estrogen? [LEARNING OBJECTIVE 2]
   A. Osteoporosis
   B. Hot flashes
   C. Incontinence
   D. All of the above

3. As seen in question 2, central to many age-related deteriorations is the decline of the endocrine system. Decline in which of the following endocrine hormones is responsible for causing increasing abdominal girth and loss of muscle mass and strength? [LEARNING OBJECTIVE 1]
   A. Insulin
   B. Estrogen
   C. Growth hormone
   D. Testosterone

4. A 32-year-old Caucasian female visits her family doctor requesting Ambien. She was recently mugged and since the occurrence a few days ago has had difficulty going to sleep and staying asleep. She notes that she has also begun to suffer from terrifying recollections of the events and has started avoiding the place where it occurred. What is your diagnosis? (Hint: Use the Decision Tree) [LEARNING OBJECTIVE 6]
   A. Post-traumatic stress disorder
   B. Acute stress disorder
   C. Bipolar disorder
   D. Depression

5. Which of the following is true regarding the benefits of exercise? [LEARNING OBJECTIVE 7]
   A. Exercise improves vascular function with decreased atherosclerosis due to decreased HDL "bad" lipoprotein and increased LDL "good" lipoprotein.
   B. Resistance exercises are important in the reduction of body fat while endurance exercises increase muscle mass.

   C. Exercise enhances physiologic well-being and improves one's ability to cope with stress.
   D. All of the above are true.

6. A 28-year-old female whose medical history includes multiple surgeries for a crush injury sustained to her left foot a year ago (following a car accident) complains of burning and aching pain in her left foot. She also complains that the foot alternates between periods of pallor and redness (during which time it is also swollen). Which of the following is the most likely explanation of her symptoms? [LEARNING OBJECTIVE 10]
   A. Complex regional pain syndrome
   B. Fibromyalgia
   C. Polymyalgia rheumatic
   D. Drug-seeking behavior

7. A 19-year-old newly enlisted army recruit visits the base doctor complaining of cramplike pain in his left forefoot. He reports that the pain started shortly after he began physical training, and while it was originally relieved with rest, the pain is now constant. He confirms his training is carried out in his combat boots. His physical exam is notable for high arches and pain to palpation over the medial dorsal aspect of his foot. Which of the following injuries has occurred? [LEARNING OBJECTIVE 8]
   A. Metatarsal stress fracture
   B. Achilles tendon injury
   C. Compartment syndrome
   D. Piriformis syndrome

8. Which of the following statements concerning reactive oxygen species is correct? [LEARNING OBJECTIVE 1]
   A. Free radicals cause DNA, protein, and lipid damage via oxidation.
   B. Reactive oxygen species are a natural part of body chemistry and play a role in enzymatic reactions.
   C. Vitamins C and E are antioxidants, which can neutralize free radicals.
   D. All of the above are true.

II. TRUE OR FALSE

9. _____ The best way to relieve pain is to remove the offending stimulus. [LEARNING OBJECTIVE 10]

10. _____ Although cardiac function declines with age, respiratory capacity remains intact with less than a 5% decrease in vital capacity between a person's physical peak and age 70. [LEARNING OBJECTIVE 2]

11. _____ The autonomic (parasympathetic) nervous response is quick, while the endocrine reaction is a slower but longer-lasting phase devoted to a longer sustainable reaction to stress. [LEARNING OBJECTIVE 4]

12. _____ The pain felt in the left jaw, neck, or arm during a heart attack is called "referred pain." [LEARNING OBJECTIVE 10]

13. _____ Bony prominences such as the sacrum, elbows, heels, ischial tuberosities, and greater trochanters are especially at risk of decubitus ulcers. [LEARNING OBJECTIVE 9]

14. _____ The 30 minutes of physical activity needed to optimize health need not be performed all at once, but can be accumulated over the course of a day. [LEARNING OBJECTIVE 7]

15. _____ Stressors can be physical, emotional, or psychological. (Hint: Use the Decision Tree) [LEARNING OBJECTIVE 3]

16. _____ Neuropathic pain is the result of stimulation of nociceptors, somatic or visceral. [LEARNING OBJECTIVE 10]

III. MATCHING

17. Match the following injuries with the items that describe them: [LEARNING OBJECTIVE 8]
    i. Overuse injury
    ii. Rotator cuff injury
    iii. Tennis elbow
    iv. Golfer's elbow
    v. Piriformis syndrome
    vi. Medial tibial stress syndrome
    vii. Sprain
    A. Caused by compartment syndrome
    B. Involves bone
    C. Involves ligaments
    D. Involves nerves
    E. Involves tendons
    F. Involves bursae
    G. Involves muscle
    H. Treated with rest and strengthening exercises
    I. Best treatment is RICE: rest, ice, compression, and elevation . . . and a few NSAIDs

IV. SHORT ANSWER

18. What types of considerations must be considered in the day-to-day care of a patient recovering from surgery who has limited mobility? [LEARNING OBJECTIVE 9]

_____

_____

_____

19. Stress affects a number of body systems, but some of these may be a function, at least in part, of the effects of stress on the immune system. What are some examples? (HINT: See Decision Tree 24.1) [LEARNING OBJECTIVE 6]

_____

_____

_____

20. How does pain become chronic? [LEARNING OBJECTIVE 10]

_____

_____

_____